Theatrical Companion to Coward

Mr. Noël Coward

Noël Coward, by Max Beerbohm, from *Heroes and Heroines of Bitter Sweet*, 1929

Theatrical Companion to Coward

A Pictorial Record of the Theatrical Works of Noël Coward

Raymond Mander
Joe Mitchenson

With an appreciation of Coward's work in the theatre by Terence Rattigan

Updated by
Barry Day
Sheridan Morley

Second Edition

OBERON BOOKS, LONDON

First published in Great Britain in 1957 by Rockliff Publishing Corporation

Second edition, revised and with additional material, published in 2000 by Oberon Books Ltd (incorporating Absolute Classics), 521 Caledonian Road, London N7 9RH
Tel: 020 7607 3637 / Fax: 020 7607 3629 / Email: oberon.books@btinternet.com

A catalogue record for this book is available from the British Library

ISBN: 1 84002 054 7

Front cover photograph of Noël Coward: Horst Tappe
Back cover photograph: Vandamm

All photographs reproduced courtesy of the Raymond Mander and Joe Mitchenson Theatre Collection (copyright photographs © the copyright holders), except for jacket photographs of Sheridan Morley and Barry Day, and production photographs of *Semi-Monde* at Glasgow Citizens Theatre, copyright © John Vere Brown 1977

Jacket and book design: Richard Doust

Printed in Great Britain by Antony Rowe Ltd, Reading

10 9 8 7 6 5 4 3 2 1

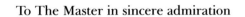
To The Master in sincere admiration

Blue Harbour
Port Maria
Jamaica, B.W.I.

4 May 1957

Dear Ray and Joe

Having just finished the proofs of the *Theatrical Companion to Coward*,
I must say I am filled with gratitude to you both for the loving care
with which you have ferreted out of the past not only everything
I can remember having written and composed, but a great deal that
I had completely forgotten. It was indeed an immense labour and it
seems to me that you have accomplished it with consummate skill
and accuracy.

The Human Ego, at some time or another, is prone to fly for
balm and solace to the Confessional, the Fortune Teller or the
Psychiatrist. This book has placed me beyond such needs by setting
me comfortably in the centre of the stage for approximately 400
pages. What more could any entertainer ask?

I naturally cannot expect that others will derive so much nostalgic
pleasure from reading it as I have done, but I hope and believe that
there are still enough people sufficiently interested in my work who,
when they "are old and grey and full of sleep", will take down this
book and not put it back too hurriedly.

I am obviously enchanted with Terry Rattigan's witty and generous
preface and most touched by your own charming dedication.

With all my grateful best wishes to you both.

Master

CONTENTS

PART I

PART II

FILM, RADIO AND TELEVISION

PART III

MISCELLANEOUS SONGS AND SKETCHES CONTRIBUTED TO REVUES
IN LONDON AND NEW YORK OF WHICH COWARD WAS NOT THE
SOLE AUTHOR

PART IV

APPENDICES

ALPHABETICAL INDEX TO THE PLAYS, ETC. (IN PART I)

(The numbers refer to the order of plays in the text)

PREFACE

Raymond Mander and Joe Mitchenson were the leading theatrical historians of the postwar years: archivists, researchers and creators of what remains under Richard Mangan's management the best independent theatre collection in Europe.

Their *Theatrical Companion to Coward* was first published in 1957, and has never until now been reprinted or updated. Noël was to live on for more than fifteen years, and his considerable output of late plays and musicals has thus never been chronicled; in completing the marathon task they started, we have essentially followed their original style, updating and correcting their entries where necessary but trying wherever possible to keep the focus of their painstaking and loving *Companion* intact. The original edition does not always cover American productions and we have attempted to rectify this. We have also left out the original Discography which, if updated, would be weighty enough to fill a book in its own right.

What follows are Mander and Mitchenson's original acknowledgements, to which we have, of course, added ours; but our greatest acknowledgement must be to them, both sadly now deceased, for the pioneering work they undertook more than forty years ago.

Barry Day and Sheridan Morley, 2000

Noël Coward, 1925

PREFACE TO THE FIRST EDITION

It was at Coward's suggestion that we invited Terence Rattigan to write the foreword to this book – a task which he most willingly undertook.

Once again we have followed the lines we laid down for ourselves in the previous volumes. Our quotations, unless otherwise stated, are from Noël Coward's first autobiography, *Present Indicative*. For permission to reprint from this, and his second autobiography, *Future Indefinite*, and for the prefaces to his collected plays, under the title, *Play Parade*, we have to thank his English publisher, Messrs William Heinemann Ltd, and his American publisher, Messrs Doubleday & Co Inc.

For the use of his cartoon of Noël Coward, we have to thank the late Sir Max Beerbohm, who in reply to our request, last October wrote in his courtliest manner: "Gentlemen, yes certainly, reproduce that drawing of Noël Coward, with good wishes."

Throughout our work we have had the utmost co-operation from Mr Coward himself, who has unflinchingly answered our third-degree questioning; but without the help of Mrs Lorn Loraine, his right hand for over thirty years, we could not have hoped to have filled in so many missing pieces of the jigsaw; to her and her secretary, Joan Sparks [Hirst], and to Mr Cole Lesley, Mr Coward's secretary, we offer our sincere thanks. For the synopses, transcribing our notes, and many other invaluable services, we have again to thank Miss Frances Fleetwood, who is always so ready at our beck and call.

We would like to thank the newspapers and magazines for permission to reprint criticisms from their columns. The under-mentioned libraries and museums have also been most helpful to us:

BBC Libraries (both Research and Music); Birmingham Public Library; British Film Institute; Harvard Theatre Collection (Miss Mary Rearden); Manchester Central Library; New York Public Library (Mr George Freedley and Mr Paul Myers have been of invaluable assistance in checking American productions); Victoria and Albert Museum (Mr George Nash and his staff).

Our thanks also to Mr Coward's publishers, both of books and music, whose representatives on both sides of the Atlantic have given us the utmost assistance. These include: Messrs William Heinemann, Messrs Doubleday, Messrs William Chappell, Messrs Ascherberg, Hopwood, and Crew, Messrs Keith Prowse, Messrs Francis Day and Hunter, the Herman Darewski Music Publishing Company, Messrs William Paxton, Messrs Samuel French.

Our grateful thanks also to all who have so willingly answered our questions: Miss Vivienne Byerley of the H. M. Tennent Office; Mrs Bent of the John C. Wilson Office; Messrs Roy Plomley, Ian MacBey, Maynard Morris, and Brian Rust; Miss Phyllis Mathews; Miss Beatrice Lillie; Mrs Edward Stirling; Mr John Walsh of the Columbia Broadcasting System, New York; Mr Edgar Martelew; Mr Wilson Barrett; Mr David Robinson; the Information Department of the *Stage*, who have answered many of our persistent inquiries with extreme courtesy; Mr Gerard Fay, the London Editor of the *Manchester Guardian*, for enabling us to obtain some Manchester programmes from Miss Rhoda Dessard and Mr Ernest Ashby; Miss Carrington of Picture Show; Mrs Joan Saunders of *Writers' and Speakers' Research*; Miss Maidie Andrews, Mr Glen Farmer.

We are indebted to the following photographers who have allowed us to reproduce their pictures: Anthony, Cecil Beaton, Evening News, Illustrated, McBean, Sasha, Vandamm, Vickers.

We wish to thank the Management of the Theatre Royal, Drury Lane, for their permission to use the photographs of Pacific 1860 taken by Baron, and Theatre World for the loan of photographs from their files.

Raymond Mander and Joe Mitchenson, 1957

Thanks must go for this new edition to Orion publishers and to Da Capo in the US, for permission to quote from the *Noël Coward Diaries* (1982), to Methuen for permission to quote from the *Noël Coward Autobiography,* which incorporates *Present* and *Future Indicative,* (1999); to Stephen Cole, whose book, *Noël Coward: A Bio-Bibliography of Coward*, published by Greenwood Press in the US (1993), proved an invaluable resource; to Richard Mangan at the Raymond Mander and Joe Mitchenson Theatre Collection for trawling through the archives; to Lyn Pullen and the Citizens Theatre Glasgow for their help and to Rosalind Fayne and the late Martin Tickner. All the song lyrics referred to in the text are now available in *Noël Coward: The Complete Lyrics* (Methuen/Overlook, 1998).

Barry Day and Sheridan Morley, 2000

Noël Coward
An Appreciation of His Work in the Theatre
Terence Rattigan

All playwrights of experience suffer, in varying degree, from persecution mania, coupled with amnesia, on the subject of their past treatment at the hands of dramatic critics. Noël Coward is no exception. I have heard him state, with apparently firm conviction, that his greatest successes had always had uniformly bad notices, and though the occasion for this remark was the characteristically generous urge to minister comfort after a first night to a sorely wounded colleague, nevertheless one has only to read the prefaces to his collected plays to realise that it would have needed no great degree of duplicity on his part to have induced him to utter so barefaced a mis-statement.

For mis-statement it certainly is. Let him confound himself out of this volume by re-reading, for instance, St John Ervine's panegyric on *This Year of Grace!* – I suppose the best notice ever written anywhere by anyone about anything – or Agate's paean about *Bitter Sweet* – it's not bad to be compared to Wagner – or Parsons' rhapsody about *Cavalcade*, with its closing words – which could not surely have been entirely displeasing at the time: "Drury Lane has come into its own again – our national theatre has a theme worthy of itself."

It is in fact very pleasant to read now these tributes to Coward from major and responsible critics – and there are many others in the ensuing pages beside those I have cited – not merely because, in removing a libel it does belated justice to the press – and who wants to do justice to the press? – but mainly because it relieves my conscience of a certain burden of guilt regarding a past misdeed and opens the way to a frank confession. Probably the most irritating, unimaginative, pompous, patronising and misguided notice Coward could ever have received was written by myself.

Received, fortunately, does not mean read, or our friendship would certainly have perished before it was begun. The article, all traces of which have happily now disappeared, was published in 1931 in an Oxford undergraduate magazine for which I acted as dramatic critic, and which on this occasion had commissioned me to write a notice of *Cavalcade*. My fee was a matinée upper-circle seat at Drury Lane and my third-class return fare to London – I did not consider myself underpaid – and before going I received a fairly strong hint from my editor that I was not expected to be over-effusive. It appeared that the rival undergraduate magazine had published, the week before, an article entitled 'Noël Coward: Genius and Prophet'. My own notice, therefore, when composed, bore the heading: 'No, No, Noël'. Our journalistic standards were racier than our rivals'.

The notice, on the other hand, was not racy at all. With immense portentousness it asked itself the question: Whither Noël Coward? and more in sorrow than in anger answered itself: No whither at all. His early plays had led serious students of the drama to believe that a young, revolutionary dramatist of immense promise had emerged. Alas, he had succumbed to the lures of mere commercial success, and sold his soul to the devils of Shaftesbury Avenue. *Cavalcade* was only an ephemeral triumph, made possible by the political climate of 1931. At the first change in that climate, which must come in a few years, it would be forgotten, while its author's reputation would hardly outlast the thirties. If only he had continued in the path set by *The Vortex* (which I had not been allowed to see, my parents not considering it suitable but which I knew to be serious) or *Post-Mortem* (which I had at least read) then his fame would have been secure. Alas, he had chosen the easy road, the road that can only lead to oblivion. Ah well. *Requiescat Noël Coward in pace*. He was quite good while he lasted.

I am emboldened to remind myself of this act of juvenile delinquency by the interesting discovery, among the ensuing pages, of a judgement delivered, a whole year earlier than mine, by a brilliant and world-famous critic who, having the excuse neither of extreme youth nor of editorial instruction, should now be blushing far more rosily than I. Mr Ivor Brown, writing of *Private Lives* in October 1930, asked himself the question: "...what the younger critics of 1950 will say of Mr Noël Coward..." and answered himself thus: "Within a few years the student of drama will be sitting in complete bewilderment before the text of *Private Lives*, wondering what on earth those fellows of 1930 saw in so flimsy a trifle."

I am sure that Mr Ivor Brown, the best and most generous of critics, would hasten to agree with me that the above-quoted judgement is not just a floater but a real old-fashioned clangeroo; while he would certainly and categorically answer his question about "the younger critics of 1950" did I not now have the happy chance of expiating my own offence by answering it for him.

The younger critics of 1950 say of Noël Coward exactly what they have always said of him, that he is a brilliant man of the theatre, a fine craftsman and a superb entertainer. They admit, as ever, his wit, and doubt, as ever, his wisdom. They grant, as ever, his skill, and deplore, as ever, its shallowness. They worry, as they have worried for the last thirty years or more, about his future, and are gravely perturbed about his apparent inability to develop as a dramatist. In the meantime they admit that the play – whatever Coward play of the fifties they happen to be writing about – *Relative Values*, say, or *South Sea Bubble* – they admit freely that it is brilliantly and hilariously entertaining and a good deal better than other plays of its kind to be seen in London at the same moment.

They may, on occasions, say worse things, and on others, perhaps, better, but I believe that the foregoing is a fair resumé of modern critical opinion regarding Coward, which has varied by hardly an iota from that current in the early twenties.

If that is so, a curious fact emerges. A playwright who, from his earliest days, has been assured that his vogue cannot possibly last, founded as it is upon a superficial method, a highly personal idiom and a complete lack of characterisation, that he is no more than a brilliant flash in the pan, fated, because of his inability to develop, to fade quickly into limbo – this same playwright, after 35 years of not particularly arduous toil, finds himself with his vogue not only undiminished but surely more firmly established than ever. Are his first nights less brilliant now than in the twenties? Is his name less widely known? Are his sayings and doings less widely reported in the press? Is it so easy to get a table at the Café de Paris when he is performing there? Incidentally, and in parenthesis, what an incredible thing it is that Coward, who when still in his twenties had already seemed to have done everything that a man could do in the field of entertainment, should, in his fifties, have found yet one more world to conquer, and have conquered it, as he has conquered all others, with such masterful Alexandrine ease.

In 1956, then, the star of Noël Coward, that has never at any period burnt very dim, is blazing over our heads more dazzlingly than ever before. In the history of the theatre no other fashionable playwright has held sway for quite so long. Maugham's reign was shorter, though admittedly its end was self-determined. Pinero and Henry Arthur Jones both saw their popularity wane in the early 1900s. Shaw hardly counts as a 'fashionable' playwright and both Barrie's and Galsworthy's decline was spectacular.

How, then, do we explain Coward's longevity? Not, plainly, by mere luck. Luck certainly plays a large part in the theatre, but no man's luck lasts for 35 years.

Logic seems to provide us with a choice between two answers. The secret of Coward's continuing popularity lies either in the fact that he writes the sort of play that is as entertaining to an audience of the fifties as to one of the twenties – i.e. the sort of play that does not 'date' – or the critics are wrong and he has in fact developed as a playwright.

I believe the truth to be a combination of the two. His plays, in general, do not 'date'. Admittedly the idiom is personal and he often writes much as, in real life, he speaks; but that is merely to say that he writes with wit; and wit is a quality that does not date. The things that do date, in the theatre, are attitudes of mind inspired by purely contemporary factors – political opinions, for instance, or moral judgements, or messages on How to Save the World. All such paraphernalia are happily mainly absent from Coward's work. He is interested only in humanity, its quirks and foibles, its vanities and idiocies, its prejudices and pomposities, and these things, as Congreve and Sheridan have taught us, are changeless. What is more, he expresses that interest with a verbal dexterity unmatched in our time. It is not a difficult idiom to imitate – and many have done so – but it is impossible to reproduce. In fact, it is the imitators who now sound dated, not Coward.

I will return later to this question of Coward's use of the spoken word, an all-important factor in any assessment of his work, but for the moment I must attempt to make good my other claim – that he has, contrary to most critics' opinion, developed as a dramatist since the twenties.

Now the word 'develop' is probably the most fearsome weapon in the whole critical armoury. It is continually being brandished over our heads, making us all morbidly self-conscious – the worst failing any creative writer can have – miserably sure that we are all pathological cases of acute arrested development, and inducing us all to try to write the sort of plays of which we are not only incapable at the moment, but will probably never be capable, even if we live to the age of Bernard Shaw.

Now Coward, very wisely, has never fallen for this trap. He knows, as we all know in our hearts but possibly recognise with less clarity than he, that 'development' in the critics' sense is pure bunk. A playwright writes the best play of which he is capable at any given time, and he writes it in the style and the method which best fit his own particular talent. To do anything else is not only self-betrayal, but arrant folly. If, for instance, Christopher Fry were to allow himself to be goaded by those critics who are continually begging him to find a good plot into writing a whodunit on the lines of *Dial M for Murder*, I hardly feel I am guilty of libel when I say with absolute conviction that, however hard he tried, I am sure he would do it very, very badly. Equally fatal would it surely be if Noël

Coward tried to write like Strindberg; although it might, I suppose, be claimed that he once did. But I suspect that *Point Valaine* was composed far more because he wanted to give the Lunts two whoppingly effective parts than because of the critics' urgings that he should write a play of serious moment. The truth still remains. Throughout his career Noël Coward has most wisely continued to write like Noël Coward, and like nobody else.

How then has he developed? I would say, in the way we all develop – not only all creative writers, but indeed all members of the human race, whatever their craft or occupation – by the simple process of growing older and gathering experience. Is it said that Coward still writes as if he were a boy? If it is it can only be because the critic has confused exuberance with vitality. Exuberance Coward put aside after the very early plays. Vitality he has never lost, and, let us hope, never will. Take three comedies of the later period, *Present Laughter, Blithe Spirit* and *Relative Values*, and compare them to *The Young Idea, Fallen Angels* and *Hay Fever*. Which are the more carefully constructed, gracefully composed and stylishly expressed? I'll leave it to you – to name, incidentally, another comedy of the exuberant era. To me the answer is obvious.

I suppose that the kernel of the critics' argument regarding Coward's development is that he has not developed from a writer of comedy to a writer of serious drama. Pinero is cited as an example. The progression from *Dandy Dick* to *The Second Mrs Tanqueray* is a 'development' spectacularly apparent to all, and which critics lustily applaud. But surely the point about such a 'development' – I leave on one side the question whether *Dandy Dick* was all that inferior a work to *Mrs Tanqueray* – is that no man becomes a serious dramatist who has not the firm ambition of becoming so. I hardly believe that Coward has. True, he has written serious plays, and some of them, notably *Still Life* and *The Astonished Heart,* are among the best things he has given us. But it is difficult, one feels, for him to sustain a serious mood for long – the two plays cited above are one-acters – unless gripped by some such violent passion as the anger that must have inspired *Peace in Our Time* and *Post-Mortem*, and the patriotic fervour that must have inspired *This Happy Breed* and *Cavalcade*. The more turbulent emotions are not always conducive to the best work. Despite the recent prevalence of 'angry' plays by 'angry' young men, I have always held the, perhaps, prejudiced view that it is really the gentler emotions – pity, compassion, nostalgia, love, regret – that are likely to inspire the most worthwhile and durable drama. Anger rarely breeds understanding, and without understanding a play becomes too subjective to make good drama. Exciting, perhaps, at its immediate impact; but forgotten soon afterwards.

This view, I repeat, is a personal one, as indeed is my firm belief that the four plays mentioned above will not last in the memory of posterity a tenth as long as *Private Lives*, *Present Laughter* and *Hands Across the Sea*. It is with a brief study of these three masterpieces that I would like to end this foreword. I have said masterpieces and I will not lightly retract, for these three happen to be my favourite 'Coward' comedies, and that fact, in itself, is sufficient justification to me for my choice of word.

Authors usually write shockingly badly about their own work, and the author of *Private Lives* is no exception. In his preface to the play he has the barefaced effrontery "to dismiss it as...a reasonably well-constructed duologue for two experienced performers, with a couple of extra puppets thrown in to assist the plot and to provide contrast...as a complete play it leaves a lot to be desired...."

Exactly what, I would like to know, does it leave to be desired? Does its poor, bemused creator not realise that *Private Lives* deals with a theme of timeless and universal significance – the equation of love and hatred – and that it deals with it not only with grace and wisdom and hilarity, but with an objective truth that endows it with that touching quality that is so often the concomitant of great comedy? What if it is just "a duologue for two experienced performers"? So, if I may express myself thus cursorily, what? The duologue reveals two characters alive and fresh and glowing, and, withal, high-spirited enough to make their duel over the three acts an evening of intoxicating delight. What, then, I repeat, are we left desiring? One day I really must have this out with him in person.

Present Laughter deals with no theme of more universal significance than that most theatre people are mad, and that those about them usually have a pretty hectic time looking after them. But for sheer virtuosity it probably beats anything else that Coward has done. It also firmly nails the lie that Coward cannot create minor characters. Roland Maule is a superb creation, and so, in their lesser ways, are Monica Reed, Miss Erikson and Fred.

It is in this play, that would have been burdened in lesser hands by a trite plot and a conventional theme, that Coward's verbal dexterity, to which I have already alluded, seems me to reach its fullest fruition. I cite as example a speech of the actor, Garry Essendine, in the third act. It is a long speech, as speeches go these days, but it bears the virtue, as do all good pieces of prose writing, of being quite 'uncuttable'. And so I quote it in full:

GARRY: I'm sick to death of being stuffed with everybody's confidences. I'm bulging with them. You all of you come to me over and over again and pour your damned tears and emotions and sentiment over me until I'm wet through. You're all just as badly behaved as I am really, in many ways a great deal worse. You believe in your lachrymose, amorous hangovers, whereas I at least have the grace to take mine lightly. You wallow and I laugh because I believe now and I always have believed that there's far too much nonsense talked about sex. You, Morris, happen to like taking your paltry attachments seriously. You like suffering and plunging into orgies of jealousy and torturing yourself and everyone else. That's your way of enjoying yourself. Henry's technique is a little different; he plumps for the domestic blend. That's why he got tired of Joanna so quickly. Anyhow, he's beautifully suited with poor Elvira. She's been knee-deep in pasture ever since she left Roedean. Joanna's different again. She devotes a great deal of time to sex, but not for any of the intrinsic pleasures of it, merely as a means to an end. She's a collector, a go-getter, an attractive, unscrupulous pirate. I personally am none of these things. To me the whole business is vastly overrated. I enjoy it for what it's worth and fully intend to go on doing so for as long as anybody's interested, and when the time comes that they're not I shall be perfectly content to settle down with an apple and a good book!

The aspiring playwright would do well to read this speech to himself aloud and to use his reaction to it as a touchstone of his own sense of theatre. If at the end of it he feels no more than that it is a reasonably well-phrased prose passage, and is blind to its *theatrical* brilliance, its use of words as stage music – "lachrymose, amorous hang-overs"– the exact spacing and the timing of the laughs, and the superbly skilful comic climax of "apple and a good book", if he be blind to all this, then let him throw away his pen for ever, or just become a novelist.

Hands Across the Sea is, I think, just about the best short comedy ever written. In form it is little more than an elongated revue sketch, embracing a single situation, and a not particularly promising one at that, but to it Coward brought to bear his full armoury of comic invention. Unencumbered by the exigencies of plot or characterisation, the author's flight of fancy transports us into a world of hilarious lunacy in which, by some magic, he persuades us that the only unreal elements are the sad, dreadfully sane couple from Malaya, crouching timidly in a corner, and watching the goings-on with wide, wondering eyes. Them we instantly reject, as "things from another world". Everything else – the duck that quacks "Land of Hope and Glory" when its behind is pinched, the Maharajah who may or may not have a religious objection to Douglas Byng, the son of a lunatic mother who did something unspeakable in Hong Kong because, apparently, of the climate – all this we accept as substantial, tangible, true and of this world.

It is an intensely funny play both in performance – and who that was lucky enough to see her will ever forget Gertrude Lawrence in the part – and in reading. But I think it is a good deal more than just an intensely funny play. The Aldwych farces were intensely funny. *Hands Across the Sea* has qualities of imagination – albeit an outrageous imagination – that raise it to the level of a work of art.

There are many other Coward plays I could and indeed would like to write about. I have chosen these three because they are my favourites, and my space is running short. I could have written about his music, although I am not qualified to do so, save to say that I have found it almost invariably delightful. I could also, I suppose, have touched on his lyrics, which would have brought me to the inevitable judgement that they are the best of their kind since W. S. Gilbert. I could have praised his skill as an actor, and as director, I could have mentioned his talent as a film-maker, and I could have noted that he has written at least two short stories that deserve posterity's attention. Let us face the fact frankly that the man's talent is too extraordinary and too diffuse to be covered in a few brief pages. He is simply a phenomenon, and one that is unlikely to occur ever again in theatre history. Let us at least be grateful that it is our own epoch that the phenomenon has so signally adorned.

Terence Rattigan, 28 September 1956

PART I

THE PLAYS, REVUES AND OPERETTAS

Early Collaborations

Coward's earliest attempts at playwriting were undertaken with his childhood friend and fellow actor, Esmé Wynne, under the pen name 'Esnomel' (a clumsy combination of their Christian names).

Two of these collaborations were produced:

The Last Chapter (Ida Collaborates)
A Comedy in One Act

FIRST PRESENTED by Charles Steuart at the Theatre Royal, Aldershot, 20 August 1917.

Characters	**Aldershot, 1917**
ARTHUR PEMBROKE	William Vaughan
CECILIA WYECROFT	Aishie Pharall
IDA WALDER	Esmé Wynne
Director	*Charles Steuart*

SCENE: Arthur Pembroke's study.

Esmé Wynne was in the touring company of Cyril Harcourt's comedy *A Pair of Silk Stockings* (originally produced at the Comedy Theatre, 23 February 1914). The tour was under the management of Charles Steuart. Esmé joined for the spring tour of 1917, and was with the autumn tour when, as a curtain-raiser, *The Last Chapter* was performed at Woolwich, the opening date.

The Last Chapter does not seem to have been reviewed in either the *Stage* or the *Era* until it was retitled *Ida Collaborates*. The change of title took place at the New Theatre, Cambridge, on 17 September 1917. Although the play was performed at Hastings, Eastbourne and Southend before reaching Cambridge, it was not submitted to the Lord Chamberlain until 13 September 1917, under the title *Ida Collaborates*.

The *Stage*, 13 September 1917:

"The scene is laid in the study of Arthur Pembroke, an author, and the fact is soon revealed that Ida Walker secretly idolises him, although he, Pembroke, is quite oblivious of the fact, and his inclinations lie in another direction concerning Cecilia Wyecroft, a cold and unemotional lady with whom he collaborates.

"Occasion arising, Ida betakes herself to Pembroke's flat as temporary substitute for her mother, who is the charwoman, and we are introduced to her in the study, in the act of tidying up. She takes up a book of Pembroke's and the author himself appears and wants to know who she is and why she is there. He then asks her what she was doing with the book, whereupon Ida tells him how, in her opinion, the finish of the story might have been improved upon, and made 'more lovable'. Not above taking a hint, Pembroke humours the maid, and asks her how she herself would propose to end the story. Thereupon Ida throws her whole heart into the business of making love to Pembroke, and Cecilia appears... Ida then leaves the study. After some commonplaces, Arthur proposes to Cecilia and is accepted, and the betrothed pair shortly afterwards retire. Ida, who has been listening outside the door, made herself acquainted with what has transpired, then returns to the study, takes up a portrait of Cecilia from the table, glances at it and bursts into tears.

"The piece gives Miss Esmé Wynne full opportunities of showing her talents, and she does not fail to take advantage of them. Mr William Vaughan plays well as the author, and Miss Aishie Pharall is satisfactory as Cecilia."

NOTES

The Last Chapter continued to be used as the curtain-raiser until the tour reached Wimbledon Theatre, by which time Esmé had left the company. On 21 January 1918, *Woman and Whisky*, another one-act play by the same authors (though not using the pseudonym) was produced.

Woman and Whisky
A One-Act Play

Characters	Kings, 1918
MAJOR CURTIS	Cyril Melton
MR LONER	Kenneth Black
MRS VANDELEUR	Aishie Pharall
NORAH CHAMBERS	Nancy Bevill

Woman and Whisky was used until the tour finished on 6 April 1918.

The *Stage*, 24 January 1918:

> "*Woman and Whisky*, which forms the curtain-raiser to Mr Cyril Harcourt's comedy *A Pair of Silk Stockings*, at Mr Mulholland's Wimbledon house this week, is quite interesting and entertaining up to a point, but its central idea is somewhat weak. It is rather difficult in fact to discover any ingenuity of purpose in the story, and no one is inclined to suggest the adoption of a more applicable title than the rather melodramatic appellation used at present. There is no apparent reason why Major Curtis, who has become fatigued with the exertion of a lengthy dance, should have refrained from taking some much-needed refreshment, or to have appeared non-plussed because of Mrs Vandeleur's sudden entrance. Even presuming the desirable bottle of whisky was not intended for the Major's delectation, and one is not quite certain on this point, his particularly obvious uneasiness and awkwardness would certainly have given him away to a woman scarcely as broad-minded and intelligent as Mrs Vandeleur appears to be. Any reasonable man of the world would find a more reasonable way out of the difficulty than by relating to his unwelcome visitor and Norah Chambers who joins them later, a supposedly terrifying experience he encountered at Poona. The Major's frequently interrupted story is certainly entertaining rather than frightful, and he finally resorts to referring to his imaginary wife as a means to hasten the departure of his unwelcome company.
>
> "The most convincing character is Mrs Vandeleur, and this is due to the excellent handling of the part by Miss Aishie Pharall. Mr Cyril Melton makes the most of this opportunities as the irritable Major Curtis, and Miss Nancy Bevill does notably well as the philandering and giddy-headed Norah Chambers. The cast is completed by Mr Kenneth Black in a small but effective part."

PUBLICATIONS

Woman and Whisky is published in *Collected Revue Sketches and Parodies* (Methuen, 1999).

NOTES

Before her death in January 1972, Esmé Wynne confirmed that these were the only two of their joint efforts to be produced; but there was a three-act comedy called *Little Lovers*, of which she said: "As the idea, plot, characterisation and serious dialogue were mine, Noël, when he began to write on his own, decided it was fairer to remove his part of the dialogue and the play was eventually produced under my name (Esmé Wynne-Tyson) by the Repertory Players at the Aldwych Theatre on 22 October 1922."

1
THE RAT TRAP
A PLAY

Written in 1918

FIRST PRESENTED by George Carr, Raymond Massey, and Allan Wade at the Everyman Theatre, Hampstead, London, 18 October 1926 (12 performances).

CHARACTERS	Everyman, 1926
OLIVE LLOYD-KENNEDY	Mary Robson
SHEILA BRANDRETH	Joyce Kennedy
KELD MAXWELL	Robert Harris
NAOMI FRITH-BASSINGTON	Elizabeth Pollock
EDMUND CROWE	Raymond Massey
BURRAGE	Clare Greet
RUBY RAYMOND	Adrianne Allen
Director	*George Carr*
Designer	*Peggy Fremantle*

ACT I:	Dining-room of Olive Lloyd-Kennedy's flat.
ACT II:	Study in Keld Maxwell's house.
ACT III:	The same as Act II.
ACT IV:	Living-room of a cottage in Cornwall.
	(When produced, Acts III and IV became Act III, Scenes 1 and 2.)

❖

SYNOPSIS

ACT I: On his wedding eve, Keld Maxwell, an aspiring young playwright, is dining with his fiancée Sheila Brandreth at the flat which she shares with a friend, Olive Lloyd-Kennedy. After toasting the future happiness of the pair, Olive goes to fetch a literary couple, Naomi Frith-Bassington and Edmund Crowe, who are living in "mild, unassuming sin" on the first floor. ("They'd much rather be married, really, but someone once told them that free love was bohemian.")

Meanwhile, Sheila – who has already written a successful first novel – and Keld look forward to a life together in which their love and careers shall be perfectly balanced and harmonious. Keld is quite confident that this is possible, but Sheila sounds a trifle nervous. So as not to disappoint their friends, they arrange to be discovered embracing when Olive returns with the couple from downstairs.

The topic of marriage leads Naomi to launch into a panegyric on free love, but Sheila points out that this comes rather hard upon any children of the union: for the time being, she says, the world has put convention firmly under its thumb, but one day convention may again assert itself.

When the visitors have left, Olive and Sheila settle down to an intimate talk. The older woman warns that when two brilliant egotists marry there is bound to be trouble; she may have to sacrifice her personality to Keld, or even give up writing altogether. This would be a tragedy, thinks Olive, for Sheila has the potential to become really great, whereas Keld will never be more than popular. Sheila declares that she is quite capable of standing out against Keld, but that, whatever happens, she will go on loving him to the end of her life.

ACT II: Six months later the Maxwells are settled in a comfortable house in Belgravia. Keld is in his study, typing busily, when the cook-housekeeper, Burrage, comes to question him about the arrangements for dinner, excusing herself on the grounds that "the mistress said she was going to be busy all the morning". He becomes sarcastic, and his temper is not improved when he is further disturbed by a visitor. This is Ruby Raymond, a common but very pretty musical comedy actress who is playing the cocotte in his play – his first to be produced, and her first venture into straight acting. She is a trifle uneasy about her relations with the leading lady, Irene Harrison; but Keld, his ill-temper melted by her ingenuous manner, promises to write an extra scene specially for her.

Hardly has she gone when Sheila enters in quest of a pencil, only to be greeted irritably as a fresh interruption. A quarrel quickly works up, centred round Burrage and the dinner. Then they make it up, kiss, and start polite inquiries about each other's work. Sheila confesses that her new novel, *The Shadow Show*, has got stuck after the first two chapters. When Keld tries to discuss the scene he proposes writing for Ruby Raymond, his wife declares that it is all wrong psychologically and that he knows nothing about women. This starts a new quarrel, which really alarms Sheila. She feels that their continual bickering must have an underlying cause; but when she tries to talk it out with Keld he is exasperatingly flippant. The crisis comes when Burrage asks what they want for lunch. Keld, heavily sarcastic, gives orders which are quietly countermanded by Sheila. As soon as the housekeeper has gone, Keld furiously insists that he will not be made to look ridiculous in front of servants. He has put up with slovenly meals, eternal disturbances, lack of enthusiasm for his work, but now he has had enough – one or other of them will have to surrender. Equally angry, Sheila flings at him that Olive's warning has come true – they are like two rats in a trap, fighting, fighting, fighting. When he tries to master her, she slaps his face and tells him to go away. As Burrage comes to announce that lunch is ready, Sheila hears the front door slam behind him.

ACT III: A year has passed, and Sheila is entertaining Naomi and Edmund to tea. They congratulate her on the successful first night of Keld's second play and inquire about her own writing. Evasively, she says that she has got no further with her novel... she is merely basking in the reflected glory of Keld, whose third play is due in a month's time.

Ruby Raymond calls and is introduced to the other visitors: she is angling for the lead in Keld's forthcoming historical play. The others discuss her after she has left, and Naomi is visibly annoyed by Edmund's interest in her. They are just leaving when Keld appears, tired from all the excitement. He settles down to read his press notices to Sheila, but is distracted by Burrage who engages her in a long discussion about the laundry. He slams out of the room in a temper.

Suddenly there is an unexpected visitor – Olive, who has dropped in on her way through town. She is now a travelling journalist, with a strenuous and exciting career which makes Sheila envious. At once Olive notices her depressed air and makes her confess that she is regretting her vow, taken after the big row the previous year, not to write any more.

During her travels Olive has heard a rumour that Keld is having an affair with Ruby Raymond, and she attributes Sheila's depression to her knowledge of this. The idea is a great shock to Sheila, and when, after Olive's departure, a note comes from Ruby for Keld, she opens and reads it; then she breaks open his desk and finds a packet of letters from Ruby. Catching her with these in her hand, Keld is furious. He maintains that he was merely "flirting around" with Ruby because her vivacity amused him, and eventually asks Sheila to forgive him. She, however, declares that she is sick of the drudgery of married life, that she is finished with him and never wants to see him again.

ACT IV: Four months later, Olive brings Keld down to the cottage in Cornwall where Sheila has been living since she left him. Sheila, who is not expecting Olive until next day and has no idea that Keld has come too, has gone for a walk.

Burrage brings in tea, over which Keld confides his nervousness at the prospect of Sheila's reactions to him. He is now quite prepared, if she will return, to let her live her own life and go on with her writing. He goes out to wait on the cliffs until Olive has told Sheila of his arrival. The housekeeper, whose sympathies are with her mistress, remarks that Olive has been writing hard and is happier than she has been for years.

Sheila, in oilskins and a souwester, returns from a long walk in the rain. She tells Olive that she has finished *The Shadow Show* and that her publishers are delighted with it. When Olive breaks the news that Keld is outside, Sheila says she knows – she saw him as she passed. They call him in and she says calmly that, although she does not love him any more, she is coming back to him, because she is going to have a baby and feels "so alone and so dreadfully frightened".

James Agate in the *Sunday Times*, 24 October 1926:

"What a pity it is that Mr Noël Coward ever published *The Rat Trap*, thereby making impossible any juggling with dates! What should we have said, I wonder, if this play had followed the Ruritanian excursion with the usual West End fanfare and implication that this was Noël's very latest thing in Nolly Dialogues! To produce the piece on the fringe of town, half apologetically and as a work of youth and curiosity, was to damage it in advance.

"The play's theme is the old one – that at a dinner party it is poor diplomacy to put together two clergymen of slightly different shades of belief, whereas a bishop and a jockey will get on famously. Only for the dinner party we are to substitute married life, and consider a couple of literary geniuses interested in each other's work only in so far as they are jealous of it. Even before the marriage, an outsider predicts that one of them will have to go under, and that Sheila, being the cleverer of the two, will be the one to make the sacrifice. The second act shows us the ménage at high literary pressure, like rival blast-furnaces. Sheila wants to read her husband her latest chapter, while Keld is equally anxious that Sheila should hear his new last act. The cook can get no orders from anybody, tempers rise, and the whole thing works up into a blazing row. Sheila sees suddenly that what her husband needs is a commonplace, dull, domesticated wife to hang on his words and tell him of their unbelievable brilliance. The objection may be made here that people who are geniuses don't go on like this, and that whereas the really clever man would be annoyed with a stupid helpmeet, the man who thinks himself clever will not be satisfied with any other kind.

"In the third act, Sheila, resigned, settles matters in the way Jane Carlyle settled them, by renouncing her own aspirations and sinking herself in her husband's fame. For Keld has achieved fame and is now a popular playwright, with two plays running at the same time. The cases are not quite on all fours, since Mr Coward asks us to assume that in his play the wife has the better mind and the greater talent. But this only gives the situation an additional touch of irony. Sheila says there is no need for her to write any more since her husband does it all. Whereupon Keld purrs complacently that he supposes he does turn out a good bit. Now that his wife is in subjection, he feels that he can afford to be kind. He would like to hear if anything in the household goes wrong: Sheila must let his shoulders bear something of the domestic burden. He wishes his wife were the famous one instead of him. Isn't it rather a pity for Sheila to waste the whole of her talent? Couldn't she start work again – some little thing to occupy her spare time? And so on and so forth. Sheila takes all this at its proper value, and I am not sure that Mr Coward's later work has shown anything more receptive than this little scene. And then the explosion comes which has nothing to do with letters. Sheila becomes jealous, not as in Jane's case of a highly cultivated woman, but of an entirely commonplace little hussy. Keld proffers the usual excuses – that the frivolity and vulgarity of the creature satisfy a side of him about which Sheila knows nothing, that it is absurd to talk about love, that essentially he is not unfaithful. To this the wife makes reply that she has made every possible sacrifice to Keld – ambition, working-power, intelligence. She has slaved and drudged for him, and all that she said about being content with slaving and drudging was a lie. She loathed it all the time. Now she loathes Keld and is going to leave him. This is really the end.

"Sheila was very brilliantly played by Miss Joyce Kennedy, who was best in the quiet passages. The storm scenes were not quite as successful, but it is possible that the writing was not good enough to bear all that the actress tried to do. Was Mr Robert Harris, looking not more than nineteen, a trifle too young for Keld? Sheila dominated him too much, and one felt that the pair would have settled down into an entirely happy Mrs and Mr Humphrey Ward. Miss Adrianne Allen gave a really witty impersonation of the fluffy, feather-brained baggage, not overdoing the commonness and keeping well within the bounds of credibility. Miss Elizabeth Pollock was amusing as a literary vessel of exceeding emptiness, Mr Raymond Massey contributed a sketch of Chelsea at its lankiest, which must have wrung many withers, and Miss Clare Greet was so perfect in the small part of the cook that I very nearly forgot to mention her."

PUBLICATIONS

The Rat Trap was first published in the *Contemporary British Dramatists* series (Volume 13), Ernest Benn (London, 1924). It is undedicated.

NOTES

Noël Coward was born in Teddington, Middlesex, on 16 December 1899. He made his first appearance before an audience at an end-of-term concert by the pupils of St Margaret's, Sutton, on 23 July 1907, at the Public Hall, Sutton. He sang "Coo" from *A Country Girl*, followed by a song at the piano, "Time Flies", for which he received an encore. Holidays at Broadstairs introduced him to concert party and the children's competitions, at one of which he received the prize of a large box of chocolates. From the age of five he was always taken to a theatre on his birthday.

The family's move to Battersea Park in 1907 brought him nearer to his destiny. After training for the Chapel Royal Choir, he failed to gain admittance but continued to sing in choirs on Sundays and at concerts on weekdays. As a natural sequel, he took dancing lessons. In 1911, through answering an advertisement in the *Daily Mirror*, he made his professional début in a children's play, *The Goldfish*, at the Little Theatre. He received a notice in the *Stage* for his singing of, "My Queen". June Tripp – later one of Pavlova's Snowflakes and the musical comedy star – was also in the cast.

From then on, Coward's time was divided between school and stage engagements of an ever-increasing importance. The scope of this work can be judged by reference to the list of his personal appearances in the appendix (page 590). He also made an excursion into production as early as 1911. While playing William in *Where the Rainbow Ends* at the Savoy Theatre, he produced a one-act play by the 11-year-old Dot Temple (who was playing Betty with him in *The Rainbow*). The play was called *The Daisy Chain*, and was put on at a special matinée with another short play, *The Prince's Bride*, at the Savoy Theatre on 2 February 1912. Before and during his army service (spent mostly in hospitals) he wrote a number of songs, of which "Forbidden Fruit" ("Every Little Peach") in 1915 was the first. After his discharge from the army he sang these songs to his own accompaniment at many musical comedy and revue auditions. By 1918, he says, he had ambitions to be a playwright, composer, lyric-writer and novelist. He comments in his autobiography, *Present Indicative*: "My actual achievements up to date amounted to very little. I had written quite a lot, in spare moments, during the last few years: plays singly and in collaboration with Stoj (Esmé Wynne), short stories, verses and one meretricious full-length novel. I had also composed a good many songs, and written lyrics for some tunes of Max Darewski and Doris Joel." These include "When You Come Home On Leave" with Darewski, "The Baseball Rag" with Doris Joel, and "The Story Of Peter Pan", sung in *Tails Up!* He wrote a second novel in the autumn of 1918 called *Cherry Pan* (unfinished). He had also sold several short stories to magazines and obtained a contract to provide lyrics to Herman Darewski's songs.

At the end of 1918, he wrote: "I conceived a passably good plot for a play, and as, in those days, conception was only removed from achievement by the actual time required for putting the words on paper, it was completed inside a week. It was entitled *The Last Trick* and was a melodrama in four acts. The first and second acts were quite amusing, the third act good, and the last act weak and amateurish. The plot hinged on the 'revenge' motif and wasn't particularly original, but the dialogue was effective, and showed a marked improvement on my other work. I took the play to Gilbert Miller, and he seemed to be impressed with it. He said that he was leaving for New York in a few weeks' time and would like to take it with him, and that he might possibly be able to arrange for it to be produced. I lunched with him a few days later, and he told me the plots of several plays that he had seen in Vienna, Berlin, Paris and Budapest. He also gave me some useful pieces of advice on the art of playwriting. He said, among other things, that although my dialogue was nearly always good, my construction was 'lousy'. He said that someone had told his father, who in turn had told him, that the construction of a play was as important as the foundations of a house, whereas dialogue, however good, could only at best be considered as interior decoration. This I recognised immediately as being authentic wisdom. He said, on parting, that he was quite convinced that before long I would write a first-rate play, and when I did he would be only too delighted to produce it.

"Buoyed up by Gilbert Miller's encouragement, I wrote two bad plays and one better one. The first two are not worthy of discussion, but the third, *The Rat Trap*, was my first really serious attempt at psychological conflict. Even in the light of later experience, I can still see in it two well-written scenes. As a whole, of course, it was immature, but it was much steadier than anything I had done hitherto. The last act, as usual, went to pieces, but when I had finished it, I felt, for the first time with genuine conviction, that I could really write plays."

The "two bad plays" mentioned were *The Impossible Wife* and *The Unattainable.*

Before *The Rat Trap* was eventually produced, eight eventful years were to pass. Coward never saw it, as it was produced at the Everyman Theatre, Hampstead, while he was away in America. His mature verdict upon it, given in the introduction to *Play Parade, Volume III,* was: "It is not without merit. There is some excruciatingly sophisticated dialogue in the first act of which, at the time, I was inordinately proud. From the point of view of construction, it is not very good, except for the two principal quarrel scenes. The last act is an inconclusive shambles and is based on the sentimental and inaccurate assumption that the warring egos of the man and wife will simmer down in to domestic bliss merely because the wife is about to have a dear little baby. I suppose I was sincere about this at the time, but I find it very hard to believe. I think it will only be interesting as a play to ardent students of my work, of which I hope there are several. I do not believe that it has ever been done since its original production, even by amateurs, which is a pity, as I would love to see it."

In August 1919, while playing at the Birmingham Repertory Theatre in *The Knight of the Burning Pestle*, Coward received a cablegram from Gilbert Miller in New York saying that Al Woods was taking up a year's option on *The Last Inch* for $500, which later developed into an offer for the outright sale of the play for a further $1,500. Al Woods thought it necessary for it to be rewritten by a more technically expert playwright. The offer was accepted. When Coward was in New York in 1921, he met Al Woods, who told him that the play had been rewritten several times, by several different people, but he feared nothing could ever be done with it.

At the time of writing, *The Rat Trap* has never been revived in a professional production in the UK or America.

2
I'LL LEAVE IT TO YOU
A LIGHT COMEDY IN THREE ACTS
Written in 1919

FIRST PRESENTED by Gilbert Miller at the Gaiety Theatre, Manchester, 3 May 1920 (24 performances).

FIRST PRESENTED IN LONDON by Mary Moore at the New Theatre, 21 July 1920 (37 performances).

CHARACTERS	Manchester and New, 1920
MRS DERMOTT	Kate Cutler
OLIVER (her son)	Douglas Jefferies
EVANGELINE (her daughter)	Muriel Pope
SYLVIA (her daughter)	Stella Jesse
BOBBIE (her son)	Noël Coward
JOYCE	Moya Nugent
DANIEL DAVIS (her brother)	Farren Soutar (Manchester)
	E. Holman Clark (New)
MRS CROMBIE	Lois Stuart
FAITH CROMBIE	Esmé Wynne
GRIGGE (butler)	David Clarkson
Director	*Stanley Bell*
Designer	*Chiswick Scenic Studios*

SCENE: The action of the play takes place at Mulberry Manor, Mrs Dermott's house a few miles outside London. Eighteen months elapse between Acts I and II, and one night between Acts II and III.

Music for the song "Faith" in Act II by Noël Coward; lyrics by Esmé Wynne.

SYNOPSIS

ACT I: Round a log-fire in the comfortable hall of Mrs Dermott's country house Mulberry Manor, on a snowy December afternoon, the family are discussing the future – Joyce, the schoolgirl sister, pretty Sylvia, musical Bobbie, and Evangeline, who has literary aspirations. Since their father's recent death they have been living on a substantial cheque sent by their Uncle Daniel from South America, but this cannot last indefinitely, and they know that their mother is anxious about money. When they fetch Mrs Dermott and question her, she admits that they are ruined – when everything is settled she will only have £1,500 a year. The rent is paid for two years ahead, but after that they will have to give up the house. Her only hope lies in her brother Daniel, who is a bachelor and has "a ranch and a mine and things". She has cabled to him for help. When she begins to cry, the young people suggest without enthusiasm that they could work, but soon start to squabble among themselves.

A telegram from Uncle Daniel, "Arriving this afternoon", throws everyone into a flutter. Mrs Dermott sends them all to make preparations, in the midst of which the eldest brother Oliver returns from a "keep fit" walk and is told the news. Sylvia is alone in the hall when her uncle unexpectedly arrives. They take an instant liking to each other. Mrs Dermott welcomes her brother affectionately and tells him her troubles. When he asks what the young people intend to do, she is vague: Oliver, she says, is uncertain whether to be a barrister or an engineer, Bobbie composes a little, Evangeline writes the words for his songs, Sylvia helps in the house and Joyce is still at school. "They sound a pretty hopeless lot," comments Daniel.

One by one they come down, smartened up, and are introduced. He tells them to prepare for a shock – just before sailing he was told that he had only three years to live. He proposes to leave his fortune to whichever one of them has carved out a career and made good. They accept the challenge, but it takes them aback. "How on earth are we to start?" asks Sylvia. "I'll leave it to you!" is Daniel's benign reply.

ACT II: It is a summer day 18 months later. Evangeline sits typewriting, while Joyce is laboriously copying out Bobbie's music. On the piano stands a model engine made by Oliver. Mrs Dermott asks them to tidy up as she is expecting visitors – a Mrs Crombie and her daughter Faith, invited by Bobbie rather inopportunely, as Uncle Daniel is due back from America at any moment.

Bobbie comes in and plays over the music copied by his sister, until the visitors are announced. Mrs Crombie is a somewhat flashy woman, while Faith, although very pretty, is a trifle too self-assured and not over-intelligent.

Tactfully, Mrs Dermott takes the others into the garden, leaving Faith with Bobbie. The young man plays a hackneyed tune, which Faith accepts unquestioningly as something he has composed especially for her. Undeterred by this, he proposes to her, but is temporarily interrupted by his mother who brings in a telegram for Evangeline from her publisher inviting her to lunch with him to discuss royalties. ("It sounds so snobbish," comments Mrs Dermott, who cannot grasp technical terms.) When Faith demurs that her mother might not think him a good enough match, Bobbie tells her the story of his Uncle Daniel's challenge, which has resulted in all the family making good:

Evangeline has already had her first novel published; Sylvia is on the way to becoming a film star; Oliver is assistant manager of the motor works which he joined as a mechanic; Joyce has won prizes at school and is training to be an artist; while he himself is making money with his songs. He adds, under the seal of secrecy, that Uncle Daniel has promised to leave the money to him personally, provided he proves his worth. As his songs are a real success, he thinks the inheritance is a certainty. Upon this, Faith agrees to marry him and then sends him into the garden while she tells her mother the news. Mrs Crombie, unimpressed, points out that Uncle Daniel may live on indefinitely and that, in any case, they do not know whether he really has any fortune to leave.

Shortly afterwards Daniel himself arrives with Sylvia, who has driven him from the station. After the first introductions and polite inquiries after his health – to which he replies incautiously that he has "never had a day's illness" – Daniel gives several rather unconvincing descriptions of life in South America. When he is left alone with Sylvia, she declares that she is making plenty of money on the films and would really rather he did not leave everything to her, as it would be unfair to the others. Later, Oliver tells his uncle that he is thoroughly enjoying the sensation of financial independence, so he had better make Evangeline his heir instead. But she too, sending her brother away, is beginning to say the same thing when she is interrupted by Mrs Crombie, who subjects Daniel to an intense cross-examination about his gold-mine and his prospects. He promises to give everyone full information by the end of the day; meanwhile, he says only that he is proud of his nephews, and that Faith will be lucky if she marries Bobbie. Evangeline makes a second attempt to talk to him, but he goes upstairs, pretending that he feels ill.

Then Joyce rushes in, dragging Faith after her. She calls the others and when they are all assembled, repeats Bobbie's story about his uncle's intentions, which she has heard from Faith. They realise that Daniel has made the same promise to each one of them. Bobbie rushes up to fetch him, and they all furiously demand an explanation. Unruffled, Daniel says that they were a set of idle young bounders who had never done a stroke of work in their lives. So he determined to make them help themselves and their mother out of their predicament – and he has done it. He has not a penny in the world to leave them: his mine is worthless, the cheque he sent them came from a win on horses, and the money for his trips to England was borrowed. In any case, his health is excellent and he intends to live to be at least 82.

They all leave him, thoroughly disgusted, except Sylvia, who kisses him and says, laughing, that she knew all along that he was a fraud, because "no one with a smile like yours could ever have a bob".

ACT III: Before breakfast next morning Bobbie talks things out with Faith, who has thrown him over. Faith blames her mother for the decision and suggests that, if he really becomes rich through his songs, he might ask for her again in a few years' time. In utter disillusionment, Bobbie comments savagely upon her inappropriate name, says she is incapable of real love and that he is through with women. She bursts into tears, says she hates him, and runs upstairs again. Bobbie stamps out in a rage, colliding with Sylvia as she enters.

Sylvia catches Daniel stealing downstairs, suitcase in hand, on his way to the village inn. His unpopularity is too much for him, and he had hoped to escape before anyone was stirring. He is particularly hurt that Bobbie, whom he likes best of all, shows no sense of humour about the matter. Sylvia explains that he is upset about Faith, adding that he is very lucky to be rid of her, as she would have been a millstone round his neck. She is sure she can talk the family round, and she makes her uncle promise to wait at the inn till she sends for him.

Gentle Mrs Dermott is really angry when she learns at breakfast-time that her brother has gone. Sending the car to fetch him back, she reproaches her family with ingratitude and with being unable to take a joke, and then retires in tears. Sylvia's language is even stronger: she calls them ghouls "waiting for a man to die and then getting disagreeable because he says he doesn't want to", and she reminds them that they owe their recent successes entirely to their uncle. However, they are still sulky, and when Daniel reappears only Sylvia is there to greet him.

In due course the others relent and, one by one, come to offer him an apology, which after some demur he accepts. At the moment of reconciliation Daniel receives a telegram announcing the discovery of gold in his mine. All are wild with excitement, except Sylvia, who asks him quietly:

"Uncle, did you send that telegram to yourself?" "Yes!!!" admits Daniel as the curtain falls.

Neville Cardus in the *Manchester Guardian*, 4 May 1920 on the first production: "Mr Noël Coward's new play is perhaps the neatest thing of its sort we have lately had in Manchester – and a vast amount of that sort have we had. The author calls it light comedy, but, as Mr Curdle would say, the term is much too strong. Let us call it (for labels are important in the theatre) an essay in facetiousness. A few years ago the characters would have led wild and disarranged lives in unashamed farce until ten o'clock precisely, at which hour the uncle who had been mistaken for the plumber and unaccountably locked in the bathroom would come out and scatter his fortune on the rest of the family. With Willie Edouin as the uncle, Mr Noël Coward's play – granted one or two painless extractions from the dialogue – might easily have followed in the tracks of *Charley's Aunt* and performed the rather incredible feat of making all London laugh. The broad grin, however, is no longer so fashionable in our theatre as it was. Mr Coward therefore gives us a rich uncle who performs a moral and social duty. Finding a family of ne'er-do-wells (children of a slightly harassed widow), the uncle stirs them into activity by announcing that he will leave his fortune to whichever of them most successfully turns over a new leaf and makes good. At this the ne'er-do-wells develop severally into composer, cinema actress, novelist, engineer, and artist. Then Uncle lets it be known that he has no money at all – he has been cruel simply to be kind; without the incentive of his offer, the ne'er-do-wells would have continued in idleness. Naturally, everybody rounds on Uncle peevishly – except Sylvia and his widowed sister, Mrs Dermott, who are left to put the uncle's case, point the moral, and make the reconciliation easy in the last act. The final curtain is so cleverly brought down that one must be silent as to the means. It is, however, in the traditional vein of farce – the old Adam comes out at last through all the thin veneer of social satire and sentimental moralising. It is difficult to understand why we are expected so often nowadays to take our laughter in the theatre in this apologetic way. Last night's audience certainly enjoyed themselves best when they took the bull of farce by the horns and regarded the allegory much as Hazlitt told us to regard the allegory in Spenser's *Faerie Queene* – that is, not to bother about it, as it wouldn't bite. It was not so easy, unfortunately, to avoid the facetiousness of the dialogue. Why do all the characters in modern comedy talk for all the world as the Charivari in *Punch* has talked since somebody other than Walter Emmanuel took it up?

"One would not begrudge Mr Coward's play the success it will almost certainly achieve in London when it goes there. It is deftly done on the whole. But, in common with a host of similar productions that we have had in Manchester this season, it simply puts anything in the way of honest comedy out of court. Theme is restricted to that of the idle bourgeoisie, as M. Romain Rolland has said, and whenever ideas are about they are used sentimentally. Our authors will go a certain way with them, but not all the way. Instance Mr Maugham's play that we had here only last week. The astonishing thing is that in all these rather nerveless plays – things compact of the sheerest tricks of the trade – the acting is invariably vital. It was so last night at the Gaiety. Miss Kate Cutler and Mr J. Farren Soutar gave us a dexterous play of witty light and shade which, operating on the material in hand, reminded one of a Kreisler playing Ernst – sheer mastery of technique giving animation and strength whenever the pulse was in a low state. The play was most warmly received."

G.M. in the *Daily Mail*, 22 July 1920 on the London production:

"*I'll Leave It to You*, which caused much amusement at the New Theatre last night, is not the tacit invitation to a heart declaration, but rather to a call of spades, as it is the answer given to some youthful slackers who want to know how to make good. The new farce, in fact, contains one of the oldest jokes in the world – that of the fabled buried treasure.

"A mysterious but familiar uncle, played with innocent artfulness by Mr Holman Clark, prescribes the work cure for sleeping sickness when he promises to leave all he has to the nephew or niece who makes most money. He is not, of course, going to live long, so that one of them will soon have the great possessions they take on trust.

"The joke is well sustained and points the moral that if the uncle had really been rich instead of being almost a pauper, one of the youngsters would have had no further need to work, which, like Eccles, is a thing he likes to see them do. Moreover, work agrees with them, though it does not entirely put an end to the family jars that provoke such hearty laughter.

"Freshly written and brightly acted, the piece betrays a certain striving after ultra-comic effect. Mr Noël Coward, the author, who is not yet 21, is almost too successful in making the younger nephew a most objectionable boy. But Miss Kate Cutler is perfect as the children's absurdly young mother. Inconsequent, tender-hearted, and altogether charming, she converts a conventional figure of fun into a vivid, comical character.

"Her ineffectual struggle to read *The Times*, which slowly becomes a rag-baby in her fair hands, fairly brought down the house, and she did nothing, however small, that she did not adorn.

"Miss Muriel Pope and Miss Stella Jesse were equally admirable in their clever contrast to two dissimilar sisters. And Miss Esmé Wynne cruelly took off the airs and graces of the modern maiden who is not such a fool as she looks.

"There is, indeed, plenty of promise in this pleasing performance."

PUBLICATIONS

I'll Leave It to You was first published in an acting edition by Samuel French (London, 1920). It is dedicated to "My Mother". The song "Faith" (music by Coward and lyrics by Esmé Wynne) is printed with the play.

NOTES

Gilbert Miller continued to take an interest in Coward's work, and on his return to London late in 1919, after selling the rights of *The Last Trick* in New York, he again lectured the young writer on play construction and suggested that he should write a play for Charles Hawtrey on an idea which he had himself.

Coward recalls in *Present Indicative*: "I was then, as I am now, extremely chary of the thought of writing anything based upon somebody else's idea, but I persevered, and within the next few weeks manufactured an amiable little play entitled (by Gilbert Miller) *I'll Leave It to You*. The dialogue, on the whole, was amusing and unpretentious, and the construction was not bad, but it was too mild and unassuming to be able to awake any really resounding echoes in the hearts of the great public, and although I was naturally entranced with it, Gilbert was not quite as enthusiastic as I had hoped he would be.

"He suggested several alterations, some of which I agreed to, and all of which I made, and after a series of discussions, he departed for America again, having promised me that on his return he would arrange for a try-out production at the Gaiety Theatre, Manchester, in April. I had to content myself with this, and the reflection that although six months was a long time to wait, I had at least had the sense to write a part in the play for myself, in which I should undoubtedly, when the moment came, score an overwhelming personal triumph."

The play eventually opened successfully in Manchester on 3 May but it was not thought strong enough for Hawtrey, and it seemed as if London would not see it; but Coward was determined that this should not be the fate of the first play of his to be produced. He gained the interest of Lady Wyndham (Mary Moore), who presented it at the New Theatre, London, two and a half months after its Manchester try-out. After the run he sold the amateur rights to Samuel French and set to work on a play called *Barriers Down*, which, he says, "was awful". Nothing more is recorded of this play. At this period he was also working on the lyrics for an opera, *Crissa*, the book of which was by Doris Joel and the music by Max Darewski. In September it was announced that Darewski was going to America to make arrangements for its production there, but the work was never finished, and passed into oblivion.

I'll Leave It to You was the first Coward play to be seen in the US, produced in Boston in 1923. It has never been seen in New York, but was revived by the Noël Coward Company which toured the UK from September to November 1932. While in America in 1921 Coward turned it into a short story for *Metropolitan Magazine*.

3
THE YOUNG IDEA
A COMEDY OF YOUTH IN THREE ACTS
Written in 1921

FIRST PRESENTED by Robert Courtneidge at the Prince's Theatre, Bristol, 25 September 1922 (6 weeks' tour).

SUBSEQUENTLY PRESENTED at the Savoy Theatre, London, 1 February 1923 (60 performances).

REVIVED by Alec L. Rea at the Embassy Theatre, Swiss Cottage, London, 14 July 1931 (16 performances), and revived at the St Martin's Theatre, London, 31 August 1931 (63 performances).

CHARACTERS	Bristol, 1922 and Savoy, 1923
GEORGE BRENT	Herbert Marshall
GERDA (his daughter)	Ann Trevor
SHOLTO (his son)	Noël Coward
JENNIFER (his first wife, divorced)	Kate Cutler
CICELY (his second wife)	Muriel Pope

RODNEY MASTERS	Martin Lewis (tour), Leslie Banks (Savoy)
PRISCILLA HARTLEBERRY	Phyllis Black
CLAUD ECCLES	Ronald Ward
JULIA CRAGWORTHY	Naomi Jacob
EUSTACE DABBIT	Clive Currie
SYBIL BLAITH	Mollie Maitland
HIRAM J. WALKIN	Ambrose Manning
HUDDLE (the butler)	Walter Thompson
MARIA (Italian servant at villa)	Irene Rathbone
Director	*Robert Courtneidge*
Designer	*George F. Wiggins*

CHARACTERS	**Embassy, 1931**
GEORGE BRENT	Cecil Parker
GERDA	May Collie
SHOLTO	Arthur Macrae
JENNIFER	Sybil Arundale
CICELY	Leonora Corbett
RODNEY MASTERS	Lawrence Hardman
PRISCILLA HARTLEBERRY	Celia Clement
CLAUD ECCLES	Hugh Dempster
JULIA CRAGWORTHY	Patience Grandison
EUSTACE DABBIT	Roy Findlay
SYBIL BLAITH	Mary Roberts
HIRAM J. WALKIN	Clifford Heatherley
HUDDLE	George F. Wiggins
MARIA	Barbara Basil
Director	*A. R. Whatmore*
Designer	*George F. Wiggins*

CHARACTERS	**St Martin's, 1931**
GEORGE BRENT	Cecil Parker
GERDA	Ann Trevor
SHOLTO	Arthur Macrae
JENNIFER	Iris Hoey
CICELY	Jane Millican
RODNEY MASTERS	Cecil Ramage
PRISCILLA HARTLEBERRY	Celia Clement
CLAUD ECCLES	John Boxer
JULIA CRAGWORTHY	Margaret Halstan

EUSTACE DABBIT	A. R. Whatmore
SYBIL BLAITH	Doris Ramsay
HIRAM J. WALKIN	Bobbie Comber
HUDDLE	E. Vivian Reynolds
MARIA	Barbara Basil
Director	*A. R. Whatmore*
Designer	*George F. Wiggins*

ACT I: The hall of George Brent's country house.
ACT II: The same.
ACT III: Jennifer Brent's villa at Alassio, Italy.

❖

SYNOPSIS

ACT 1: Roddy Masters calls at the Brents' house in the hunting country to see George Brent's wife, Cicely, with whom he is in love. They are kissing passionately when George comes in, but he pretends not to have noticed. However, when Roddy has gone to start up his car, prior to taking Cicely for a drive, George tackles her firmly: he no longer loves her, but he does not intend to have a scandal – if she gets herself talked about there will be trouble. Cicely sends a message out to Roddy that she has decided not to come.

She is already angry because George has invited Sholto and Gerda, his son and daughter by his previous wife Jennifer, to stay with them, and she emphatically turns down his request to be nice to them. When she hears their car, she goes upstairs.

The young people, who have lived all their lives on the continent, are full of high spirits. They greet their father in the style of a Victorian novel and are delighted when he takes their measure and answers in the same vein. After a rattle of talk, they produce two large photographs of their mother in her garden at Alassio, which Sholto, unnoticed by his father, puts on the mantelpiece before they go up to their rooms.

A group of guests enters in hunting kit – Priscilla Hartleberry, Sybil Blaith and Claude Eccles, followed later by Julia Cragworthy and Eustace Dabbit. They comment on the photographs, but only Eustace recognises Jennifer. This brings up the subject of George's domestic affairs, and they have just started to couple the name of his second wife with Roddy when Cicely herself comes down. She is obviously annoyed when she sees the

45

photographs; but when George has introduced his children he, too, catches sight of them, bursts out laughing, and tells Gerda and Sholto to take them down.

The conversation has reverted to hunting when Roddy's entrance causes a diversion. He has had bad news – his only brother has died in Jamaica, so he himself will have to go out there and take over his plantation. The brother and sister notice Cicely's perturbation at this, and decide that they are going to get some fun out of their visit.

ACT II, Scene 1: The house-party guests are gathered in the hall after dinner, dressed for a hunt ball. While the others go to practise dance-steps in another room, Sholto and Gerda try to clear things up with Cicely, asking her why she hates them so much; but she merely makes a withering reply and leaves them. Certain now that she really is an unpleasant woman, they decide to make use of their suspicions about her affair with Rodney. Their first move is to enlist the sympathies of Priscilla Hartleberry by representing them-selves as objects of compassion: their mother, they invent glibly, eloped with an Italian count and now drinks like a fish – they want to stop Cicely from making the same fatal mistake. The guileless Priscilla is beginning to tell them all she knows about Cicely and Roddy when they are interrupted.

Getting their father alone, the young people decide to work on his memories of Jennifer, saying that every year she revisits the scenes of their honeymoon. George tells them frankly that he is no longer in love with Jennifer and has no interest in themselves beyond a certain sense of responsibility: he is quite content with his life as an English country gentleman and has not the slightest desire to uproot himself and go abroad. But they are not so easily beaten. They describe to him the delights of a journey to Italy and beg him to come back with them. Though obviously shaken, he replies that he must stick to Cicely as long as she sticks to him. Gerda replies cryptically that in this case they will have to manage things in their own way. The sight of their stepmother drives them out of the room.

Cicely complains to George of their rudeness to her, and his spirited defence of them leads to a quarrel. He leaves her in such a state of fury that, when Roddy asks her to go away with him, she is quite willing. They arrange to drive up to London overnight, see about her passport next morning, and sail from Liverpool in the afternoon. The curtain falls as they embrace.

Scene 2: It is half-past two in the morning. Sholto and Gerda have returned from the ball ahead of the other guests, bored by the bad dancing and dull conversation. They are just going upstairs when they hear a car and see Cicely and Roddy get out. Hiding behind the curtains, they hear their stepmother say that she has left a note for her husband and is going to fetch her suitcases.

Their delight is short-lived, for another car brings their father with Priscilla, who has warned him of the elopement. Still hiding, the young people watch the scene that develops as the lovers, coming downstairs, are confronted. Cutting into Priscilla's agitated expostulations, George quietly points out to his wife that life in colonial society with a man to whom she is not married will be most unpleasant – adding that she does not really love Roddy, but is merely bored with himself and "in a general bad temper over everything", which are very bad reasons for eloping.

Cicely is wavering when Sholto and Gerda rush in and tip the balance by imploring her not to go, because "we're going to stay here always". She repulses them violently and goes out with Roddy. "Great Scott!" exclaims Sholto. "They've forgotten their bags!" He and Gerda each take up a suitcase and rush after the eloping couple.

ACT III: In her villa at Alassio, Jennifer Brent is roused from her siesta by her maid Maria announcing a visitor – Hiram J. Walkin. He has come with a large bunch of flowers to propose to her, expecting her usual refusal, and has quite a shock when she accepts him. She admits that she does not love him, but she thinks her children need a man's influence, and it will be nice for them to live in his house by the sea "and be able to run straight out with mackintoshes over their bathing dresses". Mr Walkin (she firmly refuses to call him Hiram) is taken aback by these reasons, but Jennifer assures him brightly that she can never take anything seriously after eleven o'clock in the morning.

Maria excitedly announces that the carriage bringing the children home is in sight, and Jennifer asks her suitor to wait in another room until she has broken the news to them. After a rapturous reunion, the young people say they have a "surprise" for her; so has she, replies Jennifer, and tells them about her American suitor. They contrive not to show their dismay and, while she is fetching him, hurriedly discuss a plan of action.

Mr Walkin is startled to find that the "children", whom he had imagined to be about twelve, are practically grown-up, and he is even more aghast at Gerda's story that their father is not divorced at all, but is a raving lunatic, and that their mother's sanity is doubtful. At the end of this tale George himself enters, and is introduced by the resourceful Sholto as "Mr Peasemarsh". Gerda then starts another preposterous story, but Mr Walkin cuts it short, remarking dryly that he is no half-wit and has had enough of their "joshing" him: "If you didn't want me to marry your mother, why couldn't you say so?"

At this George explodes, but his protest is drowned when Maria, recognising him from his photograph, greets him ecstatically in floods of Italian. All are shouting at the top of their voices when Jennifer, attracted by the noise, enters and sees her husband. The American, imagining that the scene is a put-up job between them all, makes an offended exit, declaring that he is going straight back to Chicago.

Then Jennifer, thoroughly upset by the shock, starts to have a row with George, while the young people, finding this quite in order, slip away. Gradually, George wears down his wife's defences, though she holds out to the last. Realising that she still loves him, he exclaims: "The only thing in the world that matters is youth. And I've got it back again... Come and kiss me!"

James Agate in the *Saturday Review*, 17 February 1923:

"One remembers Mr Noël Coward's first play as a very light and entirely admirable comedy. His second, *The Young Idea*, at the Savoy Theatre, if you examine it closely, reaches after more than it can grasp – a good fault in a young writer. Superficially it is exhilarating and great fun. The two plays together suggest original talent, a feeling for the theatre, and a quite extraordinary belief in the existence of an audience capable of intellectual delight. It is unusual to find an actor sufficiently interested in plays to undertake the writing of them, and perhaps I may suggest that Mr Coward is not, primarily, a player. He always seems to me to stand beside his impersonations, to turn them inside out for curious inspection, to quiz them. Whatever character he essays at once becomes unoriginal, and the original fellow is always the actor's own self. The onlooker is stimulated by a piece of vivisection rather than illuded by a creation, is conscious of an intelligence rather than a temperament.

"When it comes to playwriting, Mr Coward follows the old painter's recipe, and mixes his characters with his brains. One would call his play a farcical comedy if that term had not been debased to mean unreal people behaving as it is impossible that even unreal people should behave. Broadly speaking, all but two of Mr Coward's characters are real; the comedy consists in the way in which these are led to act by two deliberately unreal people of the genus *enfant terrible*, horrific as humanity would be if it were put together with synthetic malice, in the laboratory. The play is styled a 'comedy of youth'; it is really a comedy of impingement. Sholto and Gerda are George Brent's children by a wife whom he has allowed to divorce him. They and their mother live in Italy. Brent has now married Cicely, who is continually unfaithful to him and at the moment is 'carrying on' with Rodney Masters. The boy and girl arrive on a visit, sentimentally agog to reunite their father and mother, cynically prepared to foster any scheme whereby this may be accomplished. Their first entrance strikes the note of wilful improbability, beginning with parodies of the conventional return to paternal arms, of the conventional attitude towards 'second' mothers. At once we ask ourselves whether these people are real, and are perfectly satisfied with the answer that they are not meant to be real. Mr Coward uses them as his slaves of the ring, to tilt at absurd notions and preposterous people, the hunting-folk who talk of 'hands' and 'seat' to the exclusion of philosophy and art, the young bloods who, when they slide down banisters on a tea-tray, hide drunken folly under the cloak of an 'amusing rag'. Brother and sister engineer Cicely's elopement, and return to Italy to complete the reconciliation on their mother's side.

"Let me reiterate that throughout the play the young folk did not utter a single word which, in the circumstance, could normally have been uttered. They made dialectical Puckish rings round their elders, always on the theme of: 'Lord, what fools these mortals be!' Numberless situations were saved by the concoction of an impossible story. You didn't believe, and, to pretend that you did, shot your mind to some upper storey of ironic meaning, for all the world as if you were at an Ibsen play. The grown-up reply would be on the matter-of-fact or downstairs plane, then up to the attic again, then down once more, and so on, so that full comprehension became a feat of intellectual gymnastics. To judge by the comfortable laughter round about me, other people seemed to find the play easier of apprehension; perhaps they just took the excellent jokes as they came. But there is something in the make-up of this young playwright beyond the mere farceur. And therefore I would suggest to him that the habit – to change the metaphor – of driving tandem with Comedy at the wheel and Intellectual Farce frisking in the lead, is one of which even more practised whips have fought shy. Wilde knew better than to attempt it; to swop single horses in the middle of a play was risk enough for him. Three of his comedies he wrote in relays, always happy to relinquish the reins of Sentiment to snatch at those of Paradox. His one perfect comedy, *The Importance of Being Earnest*, was accomplished in a single stage. *The Young Idea* has something of the quality of Wilde's best play, with this difference, that more than half the characters are supposed to be perfectly real creatures. I suggest that at the end of the second act the play is moving on no less than four planes at once. Cicely – who is very carefully drawn – and her lover are going off together, as very reasonably they may be expected to do; Puck and his sister are peering upon the mischief which it is not reasonably probable that they could have brought about; their father stands halting between the world of the rational and of the irrational; while there is some irrelevant fun at the expense of a minor personage. The situation is not new, it is serious, impish, and satirical all at once. Now, the best and most single-hearted laughter occurs when something happens which is 'irresistibly' comic. You laugh 'without knowing why', and without wanting to know why. But if you were to analyse that something you would probably discover a unity of drollery. You laugh wholeheartedly when Grock toboggans down the lid of the piano; you would laugh less freely if his partner were at the same time doing something funny with his fiddle. At the climax of Mr Coward's play there is thrust and pull, stress both shear and tangential. Whence the effect is not irresistibly, but resistingly, comic.

"Mr Coward is not only witty, but is also clever at covering up his wit. 'I did not drive you into your lover's arms,' says Brent. 'Why should I? You were trotting there quite comfortably on your own accord.' 'You use banter to conceal your lack of courage,' retorts Cicely. Now, this is very neat cover. Brent's remark, we had felt, did not proceed out of the situation, but purely out of the author's inability to resist a, for the nonce, rather poor joke. Banter being conceded, our objection fades away and we are floated over to the next consideration, that of George's courage. There are some excellent flashes, like 'I lent that woman the top of my thermos flask, and she never returned it. She's shallow, that's what she is. Shallow!' Mr Coward has spun this play out of his own wit and entrails, but hardly out of human nature. If he will only be content to observe a little more, and give observation back in his own way, he bids fair to become admirable successor to Hubert Henry Davies and Harold Chapin. I look to him not for 'heart interest', but for the gentle castigation of manners. Let Mr Coward go on giving us closely-observed people babbling of matters of general interest and not, sempiternally, of their green passions. It was an immense relief to realise that Sholto and Gerda could not be lovers.

"Miss Muriel Pope plays the odious Cicely with the nicest discrimination, Mr Herbert Marshall the difficult, noncommittal husband in an engaging, noncommittal way. As Gerda, Miss Ann Trevor shows as certain a touch in glittering comedy as she did recently in the lachrymose. As Sholto, Mr Coward gives an admirable performance of – Mr Coward. I am tired of praising Miss Kate Cutler. 'Darling,' she says to her husband returning after 15 years, 'you should have given me notice, and I would have *put a lamp in the window*!" Miss Cutler handles lines like this with extraordinary deftness and precision. She has the finest feeling for the parodying of sentimental enormity. As Penelope, however, she is quite unthinkable; and she knows it."

PUBLICATIONS

The Young Idea was first published in an acting edition by Samuel French (London, 1920). It is undedicated.

❖

NOTES

While appearing at the St James's Theatre in *Polly with a Past*, which opened in March 1921, Coward was not idle as a writer. He says in *Present Indicative*: "*Polly with a Past* bored me early in its run, but I was working hard outside the theatre. Songs, sketches and plays were bursting out of me far too quickly, and without nearly enough critical discrimination. My best effort during that period was a comedy in three acts, *The Young Idea*, which was primarily inspired by Shaw's *You Never Can Tell*, Dolly and Philip being my original prototypes for Sholto and Gerda. I felt rather guilty of plagiarism, however inept, and when the play was finished, J. E. Vedrenne kindly sent it to Shaw to find out whether or not he had any objections. A short while afterwards, I received my script back from Shaw, scribbled all over with alterations and suggestions, and accompanied by a long letter, which, to my lasting regret, I was idiotic enough to lose. However, the gist of it was that I showed every indication of becoming a good playwright, providing that I never again in my life read another word that he, Shaw, had ever written. It was, as might be expected, a brilliant letter, and I took its advice only half-heartedly. But there was more than brilliance in the trouble that that great man had taken in going minutely over the work of a comparatively unknown young writer."

(Since he wrote this in 1937, Coward was lucky enough to regain the lost letter.)

In May 1921, Coward visited America for the first time. During his stay he turned *The Young Idea* into a short story for the *Metropolitan Magazine*. He arrived back in London in the November. Between then and the production of *The Young Idea*, other plays were to be written.

In June 1922, Robert Courtneidge took up an option on *The Young Idea*, to be toured in the autumn. It was eventually produced in London in February 1923. There have been very occasional amateur-stage revivals of *The Young Idea* since this time, and two professional, one in Guildford 19 July to 5 August 1989, with Honor Blackman and William Lucas, and the other in Chester 15 October to 6 November 1999, with Benjamin Whitrow and Jane How.

4
SIROCCO
A PLAY IN THREE ACTS

Written in 1921. Revised in 1927

FIRST PRESENTED by Basil Dean at Daly's Theatre, London, 24 November 1927 (28 performances).

CHARACTERS	Daly's, 1927
MISS JOHNSON	Ada King
MRS BREEZE	Margaret Watson
MRS GRIFFIN	Helen Ferrers
FRANCINE TROTT	Blyth Daly
LUCY GRIFFIN	Frances Doble
SIRIO MARSON	Ivor Novello
THE REV. SAMPSON CRUTCH	Aubrey Mather
STEPHEN GRIFFIN	David Hawthorne
PIETRO	Tony de Lungo
GIULIA	Margery Gabain
GIANETTA	Doris Garrick
ANTONIO PIOCCHI	Arturo Gomez
GIUSEPPE	George Coulouris
WAITER	Mario Mariani
MARIA	Elizabeth Vaughan
Director	*Basil Dean*
Designer	*G. E. Calthrop*

SCENE:	The action of the play takes place in Northern Italy.
ACT I:	The smoking lounge of the Palace Hotel, Bellagualia.
ACT II:	Scene I: The Combattente club, Bellagualia.
	Scene 2: The same. An hour or so later.
ACT III:	Sirio Marson's studio in Florence. A week later.

❖

SYNOPSIS

ACT I: In the Palace Hotel at Bellagualia in Northern Italy, two elderly English ladies, Mrs Breeze and Miss Johnson, sit chatting. They discuss a fellow-guest, Stephen Griffin, who is going to Tunis on business and leaving his young wife Lucy behind. When his mother, Mrs Griffin, enters, they sympathise with her. She agrees that Lucy will miss her husband very much, as they have never been parted for longer than a week. Lucy herself is obviously on edge and brusquely repulses their well meant efforts at consolation.

An American guest, Francine Trott, suggests that she should join the party which the English parson, Mr Crutch, is making up to attend the local *festa* that evening. Lucy says sharply that she hates Mr Crutch – he is pompous and stupid. She works up a quarrel with Francine, who walks out in a huff.

Then Sirio Marson enters – a slim, dark young man with a black spaniel called "Mrs Robinson" (after its donor), through which he gets into conversation with Lucy. She compliments him on his good English, and he explains that his father was an Englishman, further confiding that he is a painter who is convalescing after trying to poison himself over an unhappy love-affair. These confidences somewhat embarrass Lucy, who snubs him when he asks her to call him by his Christian name and begins to pay her compliments. She walks out, leaving him to discuss the *festa* with Francine and Mr Crutch. He sells tickets for it to Mrs Breeze and Miss Johnson.

Lucy comes back with her husband. The other English people say goodbye to him and tactfully leave them alone. She urges him to go by the next train and take her with him, but he firmly refuses, saying that North Africa is an unsuitable place for her. She tells him she is bored to death in Italy and is just "waiting for something to happen" – if he leaves her behind, she is afraid that something will get hold of her.

Stephen, quite bewildered, thinks she merely wants him to make a fuss of her. While he is saying goodbye to his mother, Lucy has a few words with Sirio, who tries unavailingly to sell her a ticket for the *festa*; then she goes to the station with her husband.

ACT II, Scene 1: The English people, attending the *festa* at the Combattente Club, sit drinking lemonade and making patronising comments. When an Italian, "dared" by his companions, asks Miss Johnson to dance, she refuses indignantly; but Lucy somewhat scandalises her friends by dancing with

Sirio Marson. He flatters her and makes her promise to come back later, when the others have gone. In due course Mr Crutch makes a speech in halting Italian (to which the local people listen with polite applause and impolite "asides"), and takes his party home.

Scene 2: With the departure of the English guests the proceedings have brightened up. People are dancing, drinking, laughing, and quarrelling. The noise and confusion startle Lucy, but Sirio looks after her, finds her a table and offers her cakes and wine. He soon begins to make love to her, but breaks off when a fight begins between two Italians. Separating them, Sirio receives a slight stab wound in the hand, which Lucy bandages with some concern. An old man with an accordion begins to play and Sirio sings, addressing his song to Lucy. The bystanders, scenting a romance, drift out and leave them together.

Sirio again begins to make love to Lucy so ardently that he forces her to admit that she loves him. They are interrupted by a drunken quarrel between two Italian women, but Sirio continues to urge Lucy to come away with him until, swept off her feet by passion, she consents.

ACT III: A week later Lucy is with Sirio in his studio-flat in Florence. The daily woman has not come, so the place is in a rather squalid disorder. Starting to tidy up, Lucy calls Sirio to come and help, but he is comfortable in bed and does not want to move. Eventually she persuades him to take the dog for a walk and bring back some milk.

While Lucy is laying breakfast, her husband and mother-in-law appear and demand explanations. Stephen insists on seeing "that blackguard" and vows: "I'll make him answer for this!" His wife retorts calmly that Sirio is "not the sort of person you could make answer for anything". She makes no attempt to justify herself: "It just happened – I don't think I could really help myself," is all she can say.

The postman knocks, and while Lucy fetches the letter, Mrs Griffin urges her son to come away and leave her. For her part, Lucy is quite determined not to go back. Stephen has come prepared to be magnanimous, to take her back and give her "a chance to atone". That Lucy should reject this magnificent offer is beyond Mrs Griffin's comprehension: she calls her a wicked, ungrateful woman. Rather wearily, Lucy says that if Stephen had really loved her the situation could never have arisen: they were both heartily bored with each other, so it is far better that they should part. Asked what she proposes to do when the affair is over, she replies that she has an allowance and can work. She begs them both to go away.

No sooner have they gone than Sirio, who has been listening on the landing, comes in. He declares that Lucy was wonderful, "Like Joan of Arc", but she detects in his voice a shade almost of regret at her refusal to return to her husband.

While Lucy gets the coffee Sirio reads his letter, showing signs of intense irritation. Over breakfast she tries to talk seriously to him, though he complains he cannot face things so early in the morning. She makes him admit that his letter is from his mother, who is in difficulties and wants him to come home, and she insists that he must do it. She herself will go to Paris alone, and think things out.

A long wrangle ensues, which Sirio tries to stop by taking her in his arms and kissing her. She breaks away, but he pursues her. There is a fight, during which he hits her in the face, she throws the coffee-pot at his head, the table is upset and they fall on the floor. Finally, Sirio rushes off into the bedroom, fetches his hat and overcoat and goes out, throwing some money on to the table.

Lucy, left alone, exclaims exultantly: "I'm free – free for the first time in my life!" Then she adds, "God help me!" and drops her head on her arms.

St John Ervine in the *Observer*, 27 November 1927:

"Mr Coward's gaiety and spirit are immense. With him, it is a case of one down, t'other up. If misfortune, a rare visitor to him, darkens his doorstep, he cheerfully waves his hand to her and accepts her rebuffs with so much grace that the lady retreats abashed. All of us are ready with our good advice to Mr Coward. Heaven knows that I have wrestled with his soul for long enough. But his gaiety defeats us. We knock him down, but he is nimbly on his feet again before we have quite recovered our balance. There are times when I itch to smack Mr Coward's head, but at the end of my itching I am compelled to acknowledge that there is a very vivacious mind in his head. Just what he is going to do with it is a puzzle. We must not allow ourselves to be dazzled by his youth. After all, Marlowe wrote *Tamburlaine the Great* before he had left Cambridge. Shakespeare was doing decent stuff before he was the age Mr Coward now is, Mr Somerset Maugham was a terrific chap as a writer before he was 24, and I am bound to say that I was a bit of a prodigy myself at that age. What Mr Coward now has to do is not to make us realise how young he is, but that he is growing up. Is he? This play, in my opinion, proves that he is. It proves, too, that the process is painful.

"What we have to consider is the important fact that there is more 'theme', more 'idea', in *Sirocco* than there has been in any play by Mr Coward since he wrote *The Vortex*. Young Mrs Griffin, married to a beefy oaf and obliged to spend too much time in Italy in the society of elderly, frowsty and mentally bankrupt persons, finds herself in that state of danger to which young, beautiful and romantic women are prone when they discover themselves to be unsuitably married. She seeks relief from her boring life in the tempestuous, but tawdry, passion of Sirio Marson, son of an English father and an Italian mother, and allows herself to be seduced by him in a low-class dancing-saloon. Thereafter she lives with him in his slovenly studio for a week. At the end of that time she has no illusions left about the glory of romantic passion. The whole business has become unutterably disgusting to her, and Sirio, with his Elinor Glyn emotions, is discovered to be a nasty little dago with the spiritual and mental outlook of an enlarged newt. Mr Coward has, in short, written a tract. 'This', he says in effect, 'is what all this cinema romance amounts to, something foul and sluttish and finally impossible. Routine affection may be, and no doubt is, devastatingly dull, but vamp-love, movie-passion – these are duller still, and those who mistake Hollywood for heaven are likely to land in hell. I protest against the assumption, now too commonly made, that Mr Coward is a flippant youth who delights in the pretence that vice is virtue. The faults in this play are numerous, and Mr Coward is frequently jejune when he intends to be impressive, but *Sirocco* is not a piece of pornography, nor is its author a man without serious intention. I am very certain that Mr Coward has quality, although I am bound to acknowledge that he too often attempts to conceal it from us. He does not respect himself as highly as he should, nor does he permit his mind to brood sufficiently over its ideas. There are great gaps in his knowledge of people. He has a young man's cruelty. He permits himself to sneer at the old and at the impoverished. He attaches too much importance to trivial matters. But all these faults are the faults of a young mind, made excessively indignant by what it conceives to be wrongs and injustices. His sincerity is transparent, and his motives, though they may be badly expressed, are generous. When Mr Coward took the stage at the end of this play in face of a hostile audience, I thought that he displayed a courage which was wholly admirable.

"His indignation, as indignation in excess nearly always does, robs him of his sense of humour. There are situations and lines in this play of a banality which is unbelievable. The flippant Mr Coward would not have invented them, but the deadly earnest Mr Coward naturally does because his earnestness is greater than his experience. His dialogue is poor, not because he cannot write good dialogue, but because he seems to have enslaved himself to some theory of realism which compels him to repeat too faithfully the conversation of daily life. The talk we hear about us is dull talk, and the job of the dramatist is to illuminate it so that, even when he is suggesting its dullness, he makes it interesting. Mr Coward must free himself from this slavery. He is gravely damaging his work by his submission to it. And he must get over the juvenile habit of imagining that anything foreign is superior to anything English. Stephen Griffin was undoubtedly a dull dog, although this may be said for him, that Mr Coward gave him no opportunity to prove himself anything else. But was Sirio Marson a model to him or to any other person? I dare say whist drives in Runcorn are dreary affairs, but that *festa* in Italy seemed to me to be about as cheerful as a conference of undertakers on the subject of premature burial. And is it terribly funny to think of people spending a honeymoon at Ilfracombe? Is Ilfracombe more comic than its Italian equivalent? That sort of fun, Mr Coward must permit us to say, is not quite up to his standard.

"The play was moderately well acted. Miss Frances Doble has great beauty, but she is still amateurish. Her voice lacks variety; she has very little sense of the value of words and she ruins lines by misplacing emphasis; her movements are clumsy, and her gestures are meaningless and impotent; and she allows herself to be overpowered by her own performance. But occasionally she shows signs of ability that may some day make a considerable actress of her. She had good moments in the last act. What she needs is about five years of incessant drudgery in a provincial repertory theatre. She had, it is true, to act against a singularly ill-behaved audience, and she did so with much grit. Mr Ivor Novello gave the best performance that I have yet seen him give in any play. He has grown remarkably. The best performance was that of Miss Ada King, a gem of observation. Mr Aubrey Mather in an entirely farcical part was excellent. The evening seemed to be a sad one, but it will probably prove to be the turning-point in Mr Coward's career. I regard *Sirocco* as the most significant and hopeful play he has yet produced."

PUBLICATIONS

Sirocco was first published by Martin Secker (London, 1927). It is dedicated to Mrs Astley Cooper.

NOTES

The idea for the *festa* scene in *Sirocco* came to Coward while in Italy in 1920, and the play was written in America in the spring of 1921. He originally had Eva Le Gallienne and Joseph Schildkraut in mind for the leading parts. He says in *Present Indicative*: "I finished it quickly and had no particular cause to regret it until several years later." In 1927, when *Home Chat* was written and ready for production, he says:

"Basil had for a long while been anxious to produce *Sirocco*, the play I had written in New York in 1921, and after we had had a series of discussions about it, I rewrote a great deal of it and we decided to put it into rehearsal directly after we had launched *Home Chat*."

After the latter had been produced and had been badly received by the gallery on the first night, the production of *Sirocco* followed. The happenings at Daly's Theatre have passed into stage history. They are best told in Coward's own words:

"Probably nobody not connected with the theatre could appreciate fully the tension and strain of that dreadful evening. The first night of any play is uncomfortable enough for those who are intimately concerned with it. And in the case of *Sirocco* it was a losing battle from the word 'Go!' The first act was received dully. Ivor got a big reception from the gallery when he came on; apart from that there was nothing but oppressive stillness, broken, only very occasionally, by two or three half-hearted titters on certain comedy lines.

"The curtain fell to scattered applause, and in the orchestra pit a quintet, with almost shocking vivacity, struck up the Henry VIII dances. G. B. Stern came to my box and said that she was sitting at the back of the stalls close to the pit, and that there was going to be trouble...

"The storm broke during Ivor's love scene with Bunny Doble. The gallery shrieked with mirth and made sucking sounds when he kissed her, and from then onwards proceeded to punctuate every line with catcalls and various other animal noises.

"The last act was chaos from beginning to end. The gallery, upper circle, and pit hooted and yelled, while the stalls, boxes and dress circle whispered and shushed. Most of the lines weren't heard at all. Ivor and Bunny and the rest of the cast struggled on doggedly, trying to shut their ears to the noise and get the torture done with as quickly as possible. The curtain finally fell amid a bedlam of sound...

"Whether or not the demonstration was organised by personal enemies I neither knew nor cared; I was conscious only of an overwhelming desire to come to grips in some way or other with the vulgar, ill-mannered rabble.

When I reached the side of the stage, Basil, who never attended first nights of his own productions, and had been quietly dining somewhere, was standing in the prompt corner smiling and ringing the curtain up and down. From where we stood, the tumult in the front of the house might conceivably be mistaken for cheering and he, having no idea of the horrors of the evening, was happily convinced that it was.

"I quickly disillusioned him and walked on to the stage. Without once looking at the audience, I went along the frightened line of the company to the centre, shook hands with Ivor, kissed Bunny Doble's hand, presenting my behind to the public as I did so, and walked off again.

"This, as I expected, increased the booing ten thousandfold. I whispered hurriedly to Basil that I was going on again and that he was to take the curtain up and keep it up until I gave him the signal. If we were to have a failure, I was determined that it should be a full-blooded one.

"I went on again and stood in the centre, a little in front of Bunny and Ivor, bowing and smiling my grateful thanks to the angriest uproar I have ever heard in a theatre. They yelled abuse at me, booed, made what is known in theatrical terms as 'raspberries', hissed, and shrieked. People stood up in the stalls and shouted protests, and altogether the din was indescribable.

"It was definitely one of the most interesting experiences of my life and, my anger and contempt having reduced me to a cold numbness, I was able almost to enjoy it.

"I stood there actually for about seven minutes until their larynxes became raw and their breath failed and the row abated a little. Then someone started yelling, 'Frances Doble'; it was taken up, and she stepped forward, the tears from her recent emotional scene still drying on her face and, in the sudden silence following what had been the first friendly applause throughout the whole evening, said in a voice tremulous with nerves: 'Ladies and gentlemen, this is the happiest moment of my life.'

"I heard Ivor give a giggle behind me and I broke into laughter, which started a fresh outburst of booing and catcalls. Bunny stepped back, scarlet in the face, and I signalled to Basil to bring the curtain down."

After reading the notices the next morning, he says:

"My first instinct was to leave England immediately, but this seemed too craven a move and also too gratifying to my enemies, whose numbers by then had swollen in our minds to practically the entire population of the British Isles...

"It seemed absurd to embark on further theatrical enterprise in London with the press and the public so obviously against me. An absence of a year or so would give them time to forget and enable me to make a come-back with a more reasonable chance of success.

"Having decided upon this, we strapped on our armour, let down our visors, and went to the Ivy for lunch...

"Doubtless the reader will wonder why, in the circumstances, we went to the Ivy at all. Why, in addition to the strain and anxiety of the night before, and in the face of such thoroughgoing disaster, we elected to make ourselves the target for possibly still further slings and arrows. The reader will also probably say to himself or herself: 'How foolish, how unnecessary, and, above all, how conceited to imagine that the mere failure of a play was of such importance. To believe, for an instant, that the press and the public were really interested enough in so small an event as to feel exultant.'

"In this the reader would be completely justified. Even at the time we realised in our hearts that the bulk of the public knew nothing about *Sirocco* and cared less. The theatre world, however, was different, and it was with the theatre world that we had to deal. We went to the Ivy that day as a gesture – not to our friends, nor our acquaintances, nor our enemies, but to ourselves. Nor was it entirely a gesture of defiance. To hang our heads in private and not be seen about anywhere would only make our ultimate emergence more embarrassing, and it seemed much more sensible to take the bull, however fetid its breath, by the horns at the outset.

"Ivor, we were delighted to see, had decided upon the same course, and was sitting, surrounded by his coterie, at a large table just opposite to us. His gaiety seemed, even to me, to be genuine, and we all joined up for coffee and discussed the miseries of the night before with growing hilarity, and it wasn't until we had separated and gone our different ways that I realised that, on the whole, I had enjoyed myself."

Sirocco is the only time that the careers of Noël Coward and Ivor Novello crossed professionally in the theatre. (Novello also made the film version of *The Vortex*, playing Coward's part.)

After Novello died in 1951 a Charity Memorial Performance was presented at the London Coliseum on 7 October, *Salute to Ivor Novello*; for this Coward wrote and spoke as an epilogue the following tribute:

> Dear Ivor. Here we are, your world of friends
> The theatre world, the world you so adored,
> Each of us in our hearts remembering
> Some aspect of you, something we can hold

Untarnished and inviolate until
For us as well the final curtain falls.
For some of us your talent, charm and fame
The outward trappings of your brilliant life,
Were all we knew of you and all we'll miss.
But others, like myself, who loved you well
And knew you intimately, here we stand
Strangely bewildered, lost, incredulous,
That you, so suddenly, should go away.
Those of us here tonight who have performed
And sung your melodies and said your words
Professionally, carefully rehearsed,
Have felt, I know, behind their actor's pride
In acting, a deep, personal dismay –
A heartache underlying every phrase.
The heartache will eventually fade,
The passing years will be considerate,
But one thing Time will never quite erase
Is memory. None of us will forget,
However long we live, your quality;
Your warm and loving heart; your prodigal,
Unfailing generosity, and all
Your numberless, uncounted kindnesses.
I hope, my dear, that after a short while
There'll be no further sorrow, no more tears.
We must remember only all the years
Of fun and laughter that we owe to you.
Mournfulness would be sorry recompense
For all the joy you gave us, all the jokes
Your lovely sense of humour let us share.
Gay is the word for all our memories,
Gay they shall be for ever and a day,
And there's no greater tribute we can pay.

Novello also starred in the film version of *The Constant Nymph* (1927) playing the role that Noël had created on stage; *Sirocco* itself has never had a West End or American revival but was presented at the Citizen's Theatre, Glasgow, 17-26 March 1983.

5
THE BETTER HALF
A COMEDY IN ONE ACT
Written in 1921

FIRST PRESENTED by José G. Levy in the Eighth Series of London's Grand Guignol at the Little Theatre, London, 31 May 1922 (29 performances).

CHARACTERS	Little, 1922
ALICE	Auriol Lee
MARION	Ivy Williams
THE HUSBAND	Ian Fleming
Director	*Lewis Casson*
Designer	*Francis H. Bull*

SCENE: No scene specified in the programme.

SYNOPSIS

In her luxurious Mayfair bedroom, Alice is chatting to her friend Marion as she makes up before dressing for a ball. Discussing marriage and divorce, she wonders what her husband David would do if she were unfaithful. "He'd be wonderful – he'd forgive you," replies Marion, and she defends David so warmly against his wife's rather disparaging remarks that Alice realises she is in love with him. Denying it hotly, Marion asks why she is dissatisfied with him.

"Because he's so 'big' about everything," replies Alice, explaining that she finds his continual pose of broadminded sympathy extremely irritating and would like to shatter his smug complacency. Marion then confesses that she does love David and has told him so, and he has been "splendid" about it. She leaves the room in a huff after Alice has declared that David is in love with neither of them, only with himself.

Immediately afterwards David enters in full evening dress, surprised that Alice is not yet ready. They talk of a divorce case, in which a certain Mrs Harrison has left her husband after he has thrashed her for misconduct.

Alice takes the husband's part, but David thinks he would have done better to talk things over calmly.

After letting him know that she has heard all about Marion's advances, Alice tests him by asserting that she herself has been unfaithful with a mutual friend. David laughs, assuming that she is paying him out because she is jealous of Marion. Then Alice adds details, but, as she expects, David remains magnanimous and "understanding". Finally, she declares that she has had lovers for years past. Her husband merely says that he will leave her to think things over, and will be ready to forgive and forget.

"How dare you go on like that?" exclaims Alice in exasperation. She avers passionately that he is beneath contempt: if he had loved her the least little bit he would have behaved like Irene Harrison's husband, instead of preserving his noble pose in face of her revelations – which were completely untrue. With a forced laugh, David says he knew this all along, but Alice is not placated. She says that he has been less than nothing to her ever since she saw through him. His high aspirations are nothing but silly, cheap shams, to make women like Marion believe that he is intellectual and advanced. Roused at last, David grabs at her and twists her arm, vowing that he is going to kill her. He dares not, retorts Alice, for this would take him off his self-made pedestal: "No really noble husband would murder his wife just because she was not unfaithful."

Their altercation is stopped by Marion's return. Alice then declares that since David and Marion both read Kipling and have a similar outlook they are obviously made for each other, and she is quite ready to relinquish him. To satisfy the divorce laws, she will take a lover and "live in flaming sin – possibly at Claridges".

She goes out, leaving the other two at a loss. Both are convinced that she did not mean a word of it and will come back in due course, and the curtain falls on David's lofty statement: "To my mind, we should all try to make ourselves see things from every point of view."

The *Clarion*, 22 June 1922:
"The last of the five little plays is a comedy by Noël Coward called *The Better Half*. Alice is sick of her husband's everlasting nobility and tries to provoke him to a little human brutality. The moment she succeeds she calls him a bully. At last, leaving her husband with a woman as aspiring as himself, she departs in search of a less noble mate.

"I admit that this bald account is not quite just. There is more in the play than this. There is form, though loose. There is sense of character, though lax. And there is irony, though smartish. Withal there is the assurance that Mr Coward is one of our most promising young playwrights. I only trust that his little play will not breed a little tribe of Rochesters.

"The wife-thrasher is not the sole alternative to the nobility-stunter – though a wife with a dressing-table so wallowing in mauve and perfumery was simply asking for it. And surely the typical nobility-stunt husband is the nervous dreamer. Mr Ian Fleming made him up as an elderly city man who never was nervous even of his dentist, and who never dreamed of anything but percentages. Miss Auriol Lee's wife, however, certainly deserved a thrashing.

"Miss Lee is the best stage adventuress in England. She has all that kind of footlights lure at her finger-tips, all the subtly-simple theatricality, all the witching glances, the loose-wristed graces, the sinuous movements and resplendent mannerisms. On the stage she is verily the fascinating feminine that can twist mere males round her beautiful little finger. Indeed, she might inspire a little shelf of Melvillian Sardoudledum for the exercise of her broad Cheverleyesque art, for she is mistress of all its forms, moods, and shows, all its trappings and suites, from the cooing menace in a caressing voice to the seductive langour in half-closed eyes with the inviting poise of a tilted head. Miss Lee is excruciatingly clever on the stage, but the sense of her own cleverness confines her work to a supremacy in one role.

"I wonder if Mr Coward meant the wife in his little play to be just that type of woman. If he did, I could tell her the novel in which she would meet the strong and masterful man she has gone to seek."

PUBLICATIONS
The Better Half is unpublished.

NOTES

The play was the last in the Eighth Programme of the Grand Guignol Season. The other plays were:

A Happy New Year, adapted by Seymour Hicks from the French of Gustave du Clos.

The Sisters' Tragedy, by Richard Hughes.
To be Continued, by M. Jean Bastia (adapted by Sewell Collins).
The Hand of Death, by André de Lorde and Alfred Binet.

The play was also acted, with the original cast, at a matinée in aid of the Deptford Babies Home at the Prince of Wales Theatre, London, 12 December 1922.

Of this play Coward says: "In May a one-act comedy that I had written a year before was produced by the London Grand Guignol at the Little Theatre. It was called *The Better Half* and was wittily played by Auriol Lee. In spite of this, it was received with apathy; I think, possibly, because it was a satire and too flippant in atmosphere after the full-blooded horrors that had gone before it. Nevertheless, it was quite well written and served the purpose, if only for a little, of keeping my name before the public."

Just before the production of *The Better Half*, Coward wrote a sketch for the Newpaper Press Fund Matinée at Drury Lane on 16 May 1922. It is described on the programme as "*Bottles and Bones*, a Brief Duologue". It was performed by Nelson Keys and George Grossmith. The sketch was not submitted to the Lord Chamberlain and no longer exists.

The Better Half has never been revived.

6
THE QUEEN WAS IN THE PARLOUR

(Originally called *Nadya*, then *Souvenir*.)

A PLAY IN THREE ACTS

Written in 1922

FIRST PRESENTED by Basil Dean at the St Martin's Theatre, London, 14 August 1926. Transferred to the Duke of York's Theatre, London, 4 October 1926 (136 performances).

CHARACTERS	St Martin's, 1926
NADYA	Madge Titheradge
SABIEN PASTAL	Francis Lister
ZANA	Freda Godfrey
GENERAL KRISH	C. M. Hallard
MISS PHIPPS	Ada King
COURT USHER	C. Disney-Roebuck

PRINCE KERI OF ZALGAR	Herbert Marshall
THE GRAND DUCHESS EMILIE OF ZALGAR	Lady Tree
Director	*Basil Dean*
Designers	*Set: George W. Harris*
	Décor: Gladys Calthrop

❖

ACT I: Scene 1: Nadya's flat in Paris. 5 a.m.
              Scene 2: The same. A few hours later.

ACT II: The private apartments of the Queen. One year later in the afternoon.

ACT III: Scene 1: The same as Act II. In the evening.
              Scene 2: The same. A few hours later.

The various songs and national airs are composed by the author.

❖

SYNOPSIS

ACT I, Scene 1: It is dawn when Nadya, the charming young widow of Archduke Alexander of Krayia, enters her Paris flat with her fiancé, Sabien Pastal. They have been dancing all night and are slightly tipsy and in high spirits as they discuss their fellow-guests at the party. While Nadya goes to prepare coffee, Sabien meditates impersonally upon suicide. Over the coffee Nadya describes her unhappy life with her late husband; but when Sabien wants to know whether she has entirely broken with her country she confesses that she would like to go back there some day.

Both of them are tired of parties, so Sabien suggests that they may as well get married at once, instead of waiting till the date originally fixed. In gales of laughter they ring up a friend, Suzanne, asking her to come and be their witness later in the morning. Standing in the early sunlight, they drink champagne to their future happiness, but as they do so the sun goes behind a cloud.

Scene 2: Sabien has gone home and Nadya's maid, Zana, is tidying up the room when an unexpected visitor calls – General Krish, who has come straight from Krayia with momentous news: the King has been assassinated and Nadya, being the next in succession, must return to Krayia as its Queen.

She protests frantically that she cannot renounce the freedom and happiness that she has found for the first time in her life. In any case, she says, she is not fit to be Queen – she has racketed around in Paris and is now on the point of marrying a commoner. But the General is adamant. No one can control destiny, he declares – to be royal is to be born in a cage: "Your country comes first... You cannot help yourself."

At last Nadya gives way. She tells Zana to pack, as they are leaving Paris by the next train; then she sits at her desk to write a farewell letter to Sabien.

ACT II: A year has passed. From the balcony of the Queen's private apartments in the palace at Rodella, the capital of Krayia, Zana and Miss Phipps, the Queen's English secretary, are watching the scene in the street below as Nadya receives Prince Keri of Zalgar, whom she is to marry next day, and his aunt, the Grand Duchess Emilie. They hear a shot, followed by a commotion – an assassin has fired at the Queen, but his aim has been deflected by a man in the crowd.

Wearing her State robes, Nadya enters with General Krish. She sinks down, exhausted, hands Zana her coronet and asks for an apple, which she starts to eat. Krish congratulates her on her calmness during the attack and suggests that she should grant her preserver a private audience to thank him.

They discuss the unrest in the country – partly due to rumours about Nadya's disorderly life in Paris – and the danger of revolution, which Krish thinks the coming marriage will avert; then Nadya calls in Miss Phipps and makes a telephone appointment with her fiancé. She goes to divest herself of her official robes, while General Krish tells Miss Phipps the real seriousness of the situation, advising her to go back to England – a suggestion which she firmly rejects.

Prince Keri – a diffident young man – is received by the General; then Nadya returns in a tea-gown and the two – meeting each other in private for the first time – have a tête-à-tête. At first they are nervous and constrained, but when Nadya finds out that the Prince has a sense of humour, and that he too has sacrificed the real love of his life for the political necessity of this marriage, she begins to like him. They mutually decide to fortify themselves with aspirin against the ceremony, and to start their married life on a basis of friendship.

When the shrewd old Grand Duchess – who has herself had three husbands – arrives for tea, accompanied by General Krish, she quickly sizes up the situation. After they have left, Nadya confides to her maid that Keri is "an absolute dear" and she now feels much happier at the prospect of marrying him.

The hero of the shooting incident (who has given his name as "Monsieur Florent") is now shown in, and Nadya receives him alone. It is Sabien, pale and agitated. "Oh, how could you be so cruel!" exclaims Nadya, beseeching him to go away. In face of his passionate pleading, she begins to laugh hysterically. Then she pulls herself together, declaring that she is now quite indifferent to him; but when he takes her in his arms the pretence breaks down. Half-fainting, she returns his kisses and admits her love. He begs her to let him spend this one night with her, and next day he will kill himself – for in any case he will not live to see her married to another man. After a show of resistance, she consents.

ACT III, Scene 1: Sabien, in full evening dress and cloak, is ushered in by Zana, who warns him not to make a noise. Hearing footsteps, Zana gives him a box of cigarettes and pushes him quickly into her own room, just as Miss Phipps enters. This highly respectable Englishwoman has been dining at the notorious Blue Rose, in an attempt to find out about the revolution. "But," gasps Zana, trying to stifle her mirth, "the Blue Rose isn't in the least revolutionary, only thoroughly immoral." Miss Phipps goes upstairs, announcing that she intends to remain dressed all night, in case of trouble.

Escorted by Prince Keri, Nadya returns from a State dinner. There is a moment's awkwardness when, offering him a cigarette, she realises that the box is missing and Zana confesses that she has taken it into her own room, but the incident is smoothed over and Keri takes his leave, promising to be her friend, "come weal, come woe".

Zana wheels in a supper trolley and Nadya calls Sabien. They sit down and begin to exchange light-hearted reminiscences of their Paris friends. Then their laughter dies away. They talk about their unhappiness at the moment when they were parted, and then sit staring at each other in silence.

Scene 2: It is four in the morning. In the Queen's ante-room, Krish and Prince Keri are keeping watch, expecting any minute the telephone call which will tell them that the revolution has begun. Finding them there, and knowing that Sabien is in Nadya's room, Zana is terrified, and she insists on remaining to keep them company. Suddenly the lights flicker and fail, the telephone rings and then goes dead – the rebels have evidently seized the power station and cut the telephone wires. Krish orders Zana to wake the Queen. He is astonished when, instead of going in, the girl bangs on the door and then tries to prevent him from entering. After a while Nadya comes out, with a light wrap thrown over her nightgown.

Told of their plans for her escape, she flatly refuses to go. She sends Miss Phipps away and tries to do the same to Zana, but the girl will not leave her.

Outside, the murmur of the crowd is growing louder. A stone crashes through the window. Nadya picks it up, rushes to the balcony and hurls it back. Then she harangues the crowd, telling them to shoot her – if they have the courage. Keri, still smoking, strolls to her side and suggests quietly: "Why don't you all go home to bed?" The crowd laugh at this and disperse, singing their national anthem.

Nadya turns to Prince Keri and begs his forgiveness. He is puzzled, but at that moment there comes a shot from the bedroom and General Krish enters, saying: "Your Majesty, a man has been shot trying to get in at your window." Keri, now understanding everything, sinks on one knee and kisses Nadya's hand.

Alan Parsons in the *Daily Mail*, 25 August 1926:

"A romantic costume melodrama by Mr Noël Coward – that was the surprise sprung upon the audience at the St Martin's Theatre last night when *The Queen Was in the Parlour* was produced.

"The dramatist who has been accused of 'defiling' the stage, of picturing only degenerates, had actually presented a play which did not include London, which departed from Paris after the first act, and which for the rest of the action concerned itself with a sort of Ruritanian country, where a revolution was in full swing, and where the young queen, clad in her nightdress – there are no pyjamas this time! – won the loyalty of her rebellious subjects by means of a few well-spoken words spoken from her balcony.

"It is all strong stuff, some of it witty stuff, some of it hot stuff, but Mr Coward shows that he can construct what is called a 'well-made' play with the best of the Victorians.

"Indeed, it is strange but true that one of the leaders of 'the new school' has given us a piece which in its technique dates back to the eighties.

"It is impossible not to feel that Mr Coward wrote the play with his tongue in his cheek. It is as if he remembered that he had been accused of depicting only unsavoury people and had made up his mind to present only people sound of heart. For even those characters in *The Queen Was in the Parlour* whose morals are decidedly 'rocky' are good and true and noble really.

"The Queen may have had a lurid past, but one leaves her convinced that she will prove herself in the future a loyal wife and a devoted mother. The Prince is the ideal of manhood from the first, and the young man who made the Queen forget for one passionate night that she was about to marry another man on the next day nobly shoots himself in the morning.

"When those who had expected something typical of Mr Coward had recovered from the shock of being given something different, they set themselves to enjoy scenes of violence and romance – 'big scenes', as the Victorians called them. And at the end the applause was as loud and as long as anything ever given to the same author's alleged 'nasty' plays.

"The acting was brilliant, with Miss Madge Titheradge, Mr Herbert Marshall, Mr Francis Lister, Mr C. M. Hallard, Miss Ada King, and Lady Tree all at their splendid best."

PUBLICATIONS

The Queen Was in the Parlour was first published in the *Contemporary British Dramatists* series (Volume 26), Ernest Benn (London, 1926). It is dedicated to G. B. Stern.

NOTES

After writing *The Young Idea* and his visit to America (see previous note), Coward returned to London in November, 1921. It was for him a period of acute financial embarrassment. He says in *Present Indicative*:

"Nobody seemed to be interested in my plays, nobody seemed anxious to offer me parts at even reasonable salaries. Every now and then I managed to sell a short story or a song; and once I got a hundred pounds for grinding out an adaptation of a French play for Dennis Eadie. Altogether it was a gloomy and depressing period."

This play was an adaptation of Louis Verneuil's *Pour Avoir Adrienne*, under the title of *A Young Man's Fancy*, and was written in early 1922. The original play had been performed in London at the Garrick Theatre on 8 July 1921, during a season of French plays, and the English rights were purchased by Dennis Eadie. Coward's adaptation was not produced; but eventually the play, with the title *The Love Habit*, in an adaptation by Seymour Hicks, was presented by Dennis Eadie at the Royalty Theatre, 7 February 1923 (46 performances).

In Louis Verneuil's autobiography, *Rideau à Neuf Heures*, of which only the first volume (1911-20) was published (New York, 1944, in French), he says of this play:

"The same comedy also played a part in the debut of a very celebrated theatrical personage. It was only recently that I heard about it. Reassured by the names of the English cast, I had never bothered to find out the name of the translator, and I never knew who it was. In March 1940, I was lunching at Bougival with Gaby Morlay, and a fellow guest was Noël Coward, who spent the whole of the winter of 1939-40 in Paris, working for the British Government.

"'Do you know,' he said, 'that my first job in the theatre was to adapt one of your plays into English?'

"'Really?' I said. 'Which one?'

"'*Pour Avoir Adrienne*. Dennis Eadie paid me fifty pounds flat, with no royalties. And very glad I was to take it, too. Just think! It was the first time a manuscript brought me in any money.'"

It would seem that Verneuil was under the impression that Coward's version was the one produced. This anecdote shows how 'table talk' can be misreported and make history all wrong, unless refuted by other proofs!

The original typescript of Coward's play came into the hands of a London dealer at the disposal of the effects of L. E. Berman (an associate of Dennis Eadie in his management of the Royalty Theatre) when he died. The manuscript was repurchased by Noël Coward. The translation is unpublished.

The Queen Was in the Parlour was originally titled *Nadya*, and at the time of its production it was announced in *Theatre World*, August 1926, as *Souvenir*.

It was written in the spring of 1922 at St Mary-in-the-Marsh, near Dymchurch in Kent, propped up against a family tombstone in the churchyard. Coward says in *Present Indicative*:

"Nothing could be further removed from that play than the surroundings in which I wrote it. Its passionate love-scenes and Ruritanian splendours emerged from my mind to the gentle cawing of rooks and the bleating of new-born lambs."

He adds in his introduction to *Play Parade, Volume III*:

"It was my one and only expedition into Ruritania and I enjoyed it very much. Ruritania is a dangerous country where romantic clichés lurk in every throne-room, but at that time I was young and eager and valiantly oblivious of them. Anthony Hope had blazed the trail, and what was good enough for Anthony Hope was good enough for me. I thought, with an arrogant *naïveté* at which I can now smile tolerantly, that my brisk, modern mind could fill old bottles with heady new wine, that the dated glamour of Rassendyls and Flavias and crusty, lovable old generals could, by the application of some sophisticated 1922 spit and polish, be brought up to a nice shine. Here I was wrong. *The Queen Was in the Parlour* will be old-fashioned long before *The Prisoner of Zenda* and *Rupert of Hentzau*. However, on the whole, I didn't make a bad job of it. The first act in Paris is a little forced and over-hectic, but the second and third acts contain some good moments, notably the scene between Keri and Nadya and the characterisations of the Queen Mother and the English governess. General Krish is, of course, a cliché from the top of his grizzled head to his jingling spurs, but the other characters are redeemed by occasional flashes of originality and, taking into consideration the intrinsic Ruritanianism of the situation, they behave reasonably and sensibly. The whole play was illuminated by the magic of Madge Titheradge's acting. Her restrained emotion in the farewell supper scene with Sabien and her stillness and dignity at the very end of the play I shall always remember with loving gratitude. As a matter of fact, the entire cast, which included Herbert Marshall, Francis Lister, Ada King, and Lady Tree, was excellent and had the advantage of being impeccably directed by Basil Dean."

FILM VERSIONS

A silent version of *The Queen Was in the Parlour* was made in the UK by Gainsborough Pictures in 1927. It was directed and adapted for the screen by Graham Cutts.

CHARACTERS	Gainsborough Pictures, 1927
NADYA	Lili Damita
SABIERI PASTAL (SABIEN)	Paul Richter
ZANA	Rosa Richards
GENERAL KRISH	Klein Rogge
PRINCE KERI OF ZALGAR	Harry Leichke
GRAND DUCHESS EMILIE OF ZALGAR	Trude Hesterberg

The film was first shown in London at the Avenue Pavilion, February 1928.

It was remade with sound as *Tonight is Ours* in America by Paramount, 1932. It was directed by Stuart Walker and adapted for the screen by Edwin Justus Mayer.

CHARACTERS	Paramount, 1927
NADYA	Claudette Colbert
SABIEN PASTAL	Fredric March
ZANA	Ethel Griffies
GENERAL KRISH	Arthur Byron

PRINCE KERI OF ZALGAR	Paul Cavanagh
GRAND DUCHESS EMILIE OF ZALGAR	Alison Skipworth
SEMINOFF	Clay Clement
ALEX	Warburton Gamble
DELEGATE	Edwin Maxwell

The film was first shown in London at the Plaza, March 1933.

On stage, *The Queen Was in the Parlour* was first revived by the Noël Coward Company, a touring company led by Kate Cutler and the young James Mason at the Festival Theatre Malvern in September 1932; since then, despite many amateur and repertory productions, it has never enjoyed a major London or New York revival.

7
MILD OATS
A PLAY IN ONE ACT
Written in 1922

Unproduced.

CHARACTERS

HE (HUGH LOMBARD)
SHE (MARY JEVON)

❖

SCENE: A study.

❖

SYNOPSIS

A young man brings a girl into his flat at half-past midnight. After some awkward attempts at conversation, he offers her a whisky and soda, which she pretends to like.

Abruptly he tells her she had better go. She faints on to his shoulder and, on recovering, bursts into tears, declaring she is utterly ashamed. Then she confesses that she is a perfectly respectable girl who, having advanced views on sexual freedom, is taking advantage of her aunt's absence to experiment in London night life. He in turn admits that the flat is not his – it has been lent to him by a friend, and he has come up from the country to have a "gay time" before going out as a soldier to India.

They both agree that they would much prefer a cup of tea to whisky and soda, and have a friendly talk. He then offers to see her to a taxi, and, saying goodbye, impulsively asks her to marry him. He takes her in his arms and kisses her, and "they go out together, his arm protectively round her".

PUBLICATIONS

Mild Oats was first published in *Collected Sketches and Lyrics* (Hutchinson, 1931) and was published more recently in *Collected Revue Sketches and Parodies* (Methuen, 1999).

NOTES

Mild Oats has never been produced, and Coward makes no comment on it in *Present Indicative*.

8
LONDON CALLING!
REVUE

Written in 1922 and 1923, in collaboration with Ronald Jeans

FIRST PRESENTED by André Charlot at the Duke of York's Theatre, London, 4 September 1923 (316 performances).

Book by Ronald Jeans and Noël Coward. Lyrics and music by Noël Coward. Staged by Herbert Mason. Additional numbers by Philip Braham and Sissel and Blake. Dresses and costumes by Molyneux. Scenery by Marc Henri and Laverdet. Orchestra under the direction of Philip Braham.

PART I

1st Call, Breaking It Gently (Ronald Jeans and Noël Coward)

PARKER	Eileen Molyneux
HORTON	Arthur Lowrie
RONALD	Noël Coward
EVELYN	Gertrude Lawrence
SIR HUBERT	Tubby Edlin
LADY FRUGLE	Maisie Gay

2nd Call, Great Expectations (Ronald Jeans)

MONTAGUE	Noël Coward
BERYL	Eileen Molyneux
BRACE	Billy Fry
MISS GRIPPS	Jill Williams
MR DUNN	Tony Williams

3rd Call, Tamarisk Town
Gertrude Lawrence and Chorus

4th Call, Devon
Tubby Edlin

5th Call, The Ministering Angel (Ronald Jeans)

HERBERT (the patient)	Billy Fry
MILDRED (his wife)	Eileen Molyneux
DR. STUBBS	Tony Williams
NURSE DOODAH	Maisie Gay

6th Call, Other Girls
Noël Coward and Chorus

7th Call, The Finish (Ronald Jeans and Tubby Edlin)

LORD SUMMERCRUISE	Arthur Lowrie
SIMPSON	Tubby Edlin

8th Call, Rain Before Seven

TOM	Noël Coward
MARY	Gertrude Lawrence

9th Call, When My Ship Comes Home

THE GIRL	Winifred Satchell

10th Call, The Old Lady Shows Her Muddles (Ronald Jeans)

MRS PARISH	Maisie Gay
FREDDIE	Arthur Lowrie
REV. PAUL PARISH	Tubby Edlin
JOYCE	Sybil Wise

11th Call, Carrie Was A Careful Girl
Gertrude Lawrence

12th Call, Little Baggy Maggy

PART II

14th Call, There's Life In The Old Girl Yet
Maisie Gay and Chorus

15th Call, Early Mourning

POPPY BAKER	Gertrude Lawrence
HER MAID	April Harmon

16th Call, London Calling (Ronald Jeans)

17th Call, Russian Blues
Noël Coward, Eileen Molyneux, Childs Brothers, Dolores Sisters,
Betty Nicholas and Chorus

18th Call, Love's Labour (Ronald Jeans)

JIM	Tubby Edlin
BERT	Tony Williams
EFFIE	Gertrude Lawrence
GWEN	April Harmon

19th Call, Prenez Garde, Lisette
Maisie Gay and Chorus

20th Call, You Were Meant For Me (called *I Was Meant For You* in the first
night programme) (Sissel and Blake; choreography by Fred Astaire)
Gertrude Lawrence and Noël Coward

21st Call, The Swiss Family Whittlebot

THE INTRODUCER	Tubby Edlin
GOB	Leonard Childs
SAGO	William Childs
HERNIA WHITTLEBOT	Maisie Gay

22nd Call, Sentiment (Lyrics by Noël Coward; music by Philip Braham; choreography by Fred Astaire)
Noël Coward

23rd Call, Parisian Pierrot
Gertrude Lawrence, Eileen Molyneux, Jill Williams and Chorus

24th Call, An Atmospheric Drama (Ronald Jeans)

COMPERE	Tubby Edlin
VIVIAN	Arthur Lowrie
VERONICA	Wyn Clare
FATHER	Billy Fry
MOTHER	Betty Nicholas

25th Call, What Love Means
Maisie Gay

26th Call, Follow A Star
Gertrude Lawrence and Company

A second edition of the revue was produced on 1 December 1923. Dorothy Clarke and Joyce Barbour replaced Gertrude Lawrence and Eileen Molyneux.

New material by Noël Coward included:
"Temperamental Honeymoon" Noël Coward and Chorus
"I Prefer To Be On The Safe Side" Joyce Barbour

A third edition was produced on 20 February 1924. Of the four original stars (Maisie Gay, Gertrude Lawrence, Tubby Edlin and Noël Coward) only Maisie Gay remained. The new cast included Teddie Gerard, A. W. Baskomb, and Lance Lister.

New material by Noël Coward included:
"When We Were Girls" Maisie Gay and A. W. Baskomb
"A Spanish Grandee" Teddie Gerard and Chorus

The Times, 5 September 1923:
> "Those cynics who aver that the modern revue is only a conglomeration of ill-assorted music-hall 'turns' should pay a visit to the Duke of York's Theatre to see Mr Charlot's new production, *London Calling!* In so far as this, like its

fellows, is made up of a series of incidents entirely unrelated to each other, the definition may be said to be correct, but there are two great differences – one common to all revues and the other peculiar to this one and a very few others. The first is that, whereas in a music-hall the 'stars' have their allotted time and then make way for the smaller fry, in revue they disappear only to appear again; the second that in *London Calling!* they all bear the same stamp, either of wit or of beauty. The production has more real humour – and more subtle humour – in it than many much more pretentious productions, and some of the spectacles are beautiful in the extreme.

"At present it is just a little too long, but of the 25 items that go to make it up some can be easily eliminated, not because they are bad, but because they are not up to the very high level of the rest. These include one sketch called 'The Finish' another called 'Rain Before Seven', of which the undoubted cleverness does not quite redeem it from being rather 'unpleasant', 'An Atmospheric Drama', and a couple of songs. With some such condensation, *London Calling!* would emerge the best revue that even Mr Charlot has given us. It is impossible to single out all the items which deserve praise, but of the sketches 'The Old Lady Shows Her Muddles' introduces us to a very amusing Mrs Malaprop, who perpetrates all her malapropisms in trying to humour her son by using modern slang, 'Early Mourning', practically a monologue giving Miss Gertrude Lawrence an opportunity of distinguishing herself, and 'Love's Labour'. 'The Swiss Family Whittlebot' is a broad and amusing satire on very modern poetry.

"Then there are the beautiful spectacular scenes. 'Parisian Pierrot' is the most striking of them, but several others are much above the average, and the costumes are not only striking, but tasteful in the extreme. It is worthy of remark, too, that stockings have once more come into fashion in this kind of piece. Miss Gertrude Lawrence takes an amazing variety of parts, and plays them all well. Mr Tubby Edlin is humorous when he relapses into his characteristic vein, and will be very funny indeed when he settles down into his many parts. Miss Maisie Gay, as always, turns to humour nearly everything she touches, and Miss Eileen Molyneux and Mr Arthur Lowrie do what they have to do easily and capably. Mr Noël Coward is the Pooh-Bah of the production. He takes a leading part in it, and acts, dances, and sings with credit; he helped Mr Ronald Jeans to write the 'book' and also wrote the lyrics and music. To him, therefore, the greatest praise is due, for it was his handiwork that gave the others many of their opportunities of shining. The piece received a very enthusiastic reception after its first performance yesterday afternoon."

NOTE. Items from this revue were used again in various Charlot revues (see Part III, page 563).

"What Love Means" was used again in *This Year of Grace!*

"Rain Before Seven" was revived by the Noël Coward Company on tour in 1932.

NOTES

After the tour of *The Young Idea* had finished, Coward went to Davos to stay with Ned Lathom and his sister for the Christmas of 1922. He says in *Present Indicative*:

"Ned, who had always been badly stage-struck, had financed Charlot's last revue, *A to Z*, and still appeared to be avid for punishment. He made me play to him all the songs I had written, and when he realised that there were enough comparatively good ones to make up a score, he wired to Charlot commanding him to come out immediately. I was thrilled at the thought of doing a whole revue, but scared that Charlot, when he arrived, might not be quite as eager and appreciative as Ned. However, when he *did* arrive in due course he was expansive and benign, and a series of cigar-laden conferences ensued, during which *London Calling!* was born."

Before this revue was produced, Coward was to play in *The Young Idea* and have his one-act play, *The Better Half* produced at the Little Theatre. Eventually it was decided that Ronald Jeans should collaborate in the book and Philip Braham in the music. Coward did not originally intend to appear in the revue, but in the end allowed himself to be persuaded.

It was at the preliminary rehearsals that Coward met Elsie April, who was from then on to be of inestimable help to him in the music. He says of her:

"Amid the hurly-burly of countless Charlot productions there had lived and breathed and strummed, for many years, a small, sharp-eyed woman named Elsie April, whose mastery of musical technique was miraculous. She could transfer melody and harmony on to paper with the swiftness of an expert shorthand stenographer. Her physical endurance, too, was staggering. She could sit at the piano through the longest rehearsals, the most tedious auditions, seldom, if ever, playing a wrong note and only demanding for sustenance an occasional cup of tea.

"When I had been working with her for some time, I asked her why it was that she continued to lavish her musical talent and experience on the work of others and never composed anything herself. Her reply was evasive, 'Well, dear, I never seem to have any time.'"

After the usual hectic rehearsals, says Coward: "At last we actually opened, oddly enough, with a matinée, according to an eccentric whim of Charlot's which, nevertheless, had a certain amount of common sense to it. He figured that as we were all tired, a matinée, which didn't matter very much, would tire us just so much more and ensure us playing the first night entirely on our nerves. In this he was perfectly right. We did. We flagellated ourselves into giving a remarkably slick and good performance.

"The hits of the show were primarily Maisie's singing of 'What Love Means To Girls Like Me', and her performance of Hernia Whittlebot, my little burlesque on the Sitwells. Next in order of applause came Gertie singing 'Carrie' and the duet 'You Were Meant For Me' which she and I did together, with a dance arranged by Fred Astaire.

"Gertie sang 'Parisian Pierrot' exquisitely, and Edward Molyneux had made it one of the loveliest stage pictures I have ever seen. Then there was Maisie as a tired soubrette singing 'There's Life In The Old Girl Yet'.

"The only complete and glorious failure of the whole show was my performance of a single number, 'Sentiment' which had gone so well at the dress rehearsal and been so enthusiastically applauded by the friendly company in the stalls that I bounded on at the opening performance fully confident that I was going to bring the house down. It certainly wasn't from want of trying that I didn't. I was immaculately dressed in tails, with a silk hat and a cane. I sang every witty couplet with perfect diction and a wealth of implication which sent them winging out into the dark auditorium, where they fell wetly, like pennies into mud. After this, discouraged but not quite despairing, I executed an intricate dance, painstakingly sweated over by Fred Astaire, tapping, after-beating, whacking my cane on the stage, and finally exiting to a spatter of applause led, I suspected, by Mother and Gladys (Calthrop). "Unfortunately, the number could not be taken out, owing to the running order of the revue, and so nightly the audience and I were forced to endure it."

Of the Sitwell burlesque he goes on to say:

"During the first two weeks of the run, I received, to my intense surprise, a cross letter from Osbert Sitwell – in fact, so angry was it, that I first of all imagined it to be a joke. However, it was far from being a joke, and shortly afterwards another letter arrived, even crosser than the first. To this day I am still a little puzzled as to why that light-hearted burlesque should have aroused him, his brother and his sister to such paroxysms of fury. But the fact remains that it did, and I believe still does."

The revue ran into several editions with changes of cast, owing to Charlot's taking Gertrude Lawrence and a number of the small-part actors and dancers to New York for his revue there (*André Charlot's London Revue of 1924*, see Part III, page 563) By the end of the run it had become an almost entirely reconstructed show. After six months Coward himself left the cast to pay his second visit to America.

Some of the songs in *London Calling!*, most notably "Parisian Pierrot" have been used in stage anthologies of Coward's songs, in recordings, and in *Star!* (1969), the film of Gertrude Lawrence's life. The 'Hernia Whittlebot' parodies were published in *A Withered Nosegay* (Methuen, 1984), and at the Coward 70th birthday tribute in 1969, *A Talent to Amuse* (Phoenix Theatre), Irene Worth performed *Sorry You've Been Troubled*.

9
WEATHERWISE
A COMEDY IN TWO SCENES
Written in 1923

FIRST PRESENTED by the Noël Coward Company at the Festival Theatre, Malvern, 8 September 1932 (3 performances, followed by tour).

CHARACTERS	Malvern, 1932
LADY WARPLE	Marjorie Harwood
MONICA (her daughter)	Agatha Carroll
CYNTHIA (her daughter)	Joyce Wodeman
VIOLET (her daughter)	Marjorie Taylor
THE REV. HAROLD BASSET (Monica's husband)	Keith Shepherd
REGGIE WHISTLER	James Mason
A BUTLER (a maid)	Janet Burnell
DR. TWICKENHAM (a psychoanalyst)	Farries Moss
Director	*Noël Coward*
Designer	*Arthur Hambling*

SCENE: The action takes place in the library of Warple Manor,
           in the county of Leicestershire. One week elapses between
           Scenes 1 and 2.

SYNOPSIS

Scene 1: Lady Warple, a dignified and austere-looking old lady, sits knitting
by the fire. Her daughters, Cynthia and Violet, and their cynical young
friend, Reggie Whistler, are discussing spiritualism – her latest enthusiasm.
She tells them the story of a woman who refused to believe and, falling into
a trance at a séance, became possessed by an evil spirit.

Cynthia suggests trying the ouija board, and they sit down to it in the dark
– the others all accusing Reggie of pushing it. A spirit announces itself as
"Queen Victoria" and spells out the message: "What dreadful weather. Oh,
dear. Bow, bow." (Which Reggie interprets as meaning "bow-wow".)

Lady Warple's married daughter, Monica, then enters with her husband,
the Rev. Harold Basset. They turn up the lights and find her Ladyship in a
trance. She is revived with brandy and the smell of burnt feathers (for which
Reggie sets light to one of the best brocade cushions).

All goes well until the Rev. Basset mentions that it is pouring with rain,
whereupon Lady Warple begins to growl like a dog and careers round the
room on all fours. They humour her and suddenly she sits up straight,
opens her eyes and asks for her knitting.

Scene 2: A week has passed, during which every mention of the weather
has caused Lady Warple to perform canine pranks – the results of which
have been blamed on the dog Rover.

The family have called in a psychoanalyst, Dr. Everard Twickenham, who
diagnoses her condition as the consequence of having been hit on the head
with a toy dog at the age of four. His recipe for a cure is that, during tea, at a
signal from him, the rest of the family should pretend to be dogs.

Lady Warple behaves quite normally, and when the others begin to run
about on all fours, barking, she merely laughs and goes on with her knitting.
The doctor then declares her cured, but unfortunately remarks that the
weather has turned mild. Immediately, Lady Warple makes a spring at his
throat, knocks him down and worries him like a rat, snarling ferociously.
Monica pulls her away, while Reggie feels the doctor's heart: "He's quite,
quite dead" is his verdict. "Now we shall have to destroy Rover."

PUBLICATIONS

Weatherwise was first published in *Collected Sketches and Lyrics* (Hutchinson, 1931) and is also published in *Collected Revue Sketches and Parodies* (Methuen, 1999).

NOTES

Weatherwise was produced at Malvern as an after-piece to *Home Chat* by the Noël Coward Company in September 1932. Coward makes no reference to this play in *Present Indicative* and it has had no subsequent revival.

10
FALLEN ANGELS
A COMEDY IN THREE ACTS
Written in 1923

FIRST PRESENTED by Anthony Prinsep at the Globe Theatre, London, 21 April 1925 (158 performances).

REVIVED by Lance Hamilton and Charles Russell and Peter Daubeny Productions at the Shakespeare Memorial Theatre, Stratford-upon-Avon, 14 November 1949 (also at Plymouth, 21 November).

SUBSEQUENTLY PRESENTED at the Ambassadors Theatre, London, 29 November 1949 (299 performances).

REVIVED by Clement Scott Gilbert and Michael Ecobank at the Vaudeville Theatre, London, 4 April 1967 (79 performances). This production first opened at the Ashcroft Theatre, Croydon, 6 March, followed by Wimbledon Theatre and the Theatre Royal, Brighton.

CHARACTERS	Globe, 1925
JULIA STERROLL	Tallulah Bankhead
FREDERICK STERROLL	Arthur Wellesley
SAUNDERS	Mona Harrison
WILLIAM BANBURY	Gerald Ames
JANE BANBURY	Edna Best
MAURICE DUCLOS	Austin Trevor

| Director | *Stanley Bell* |
| Designer | *Joseph and Phil Harker* |

CHARACTERS	**Tour and Ambassadors, 1949**
JULIA STERROLL	Hermione Baddeley
FREDERICK STERROLL	Gerald Case
SAUNDERS	Diana Lincoln
WILLIAM BANBURY	Maurice Denham
JANE BANBURY	Hermione Gingold
MAURICE DUCLOS	Paul Dupuis

| Director | *Willard Stoker* |
| Designer | *Anthony Holland* |

CHARACTERS	**Tour and Vaudeville, 1967**
JULIA STERROLL	Joan Greenwood
FREDERICK STERROLL	Nicholas Phipps
SAUNDERS	Ann Lancaster
WILLIAM BANBURY	Peter Myers
JANE BANBURY	Constance Cummings
MAURICE DUCLOS	Bernard Brown

Director	*Philip Wiseman*
Designers	*Set: Carl Toms*
	Costumes: Worth

❖

ACT I: Dining-room of the Sterrolls' flat.
ACT II: The same. The evening of the same day.
ACT III: The same. The next morning.
(The 1949 revival was presented in two Acts, Acts II and III becoming Act II, Scenes I and 2. The Vaudeville revival was played in three acts, and was set in 1934 using the revised version of the play – see Notes.)

❖

SYNOPSIS

ACT I: Over breakfast in their flat, served by the new parlourmaid Saunders, Fred and Julia Sterroll are discussing their plans for the day: Fred is going out golfing with his friend Willy Banbury, and may possibly stay away overnight; Julia and Willy's wife, Jane, will lunch together and see a matinée.

Julia has a presentiment that "something damnable" is going to happen. She has been married for five years and is no longer really in love with her husband, who is rather upset to hear that she has talked over her feelings for him with Jane.

Willy calls to fetch Fred. When they have gone, Julia sits at the piano and sings a French song, of which the first line and theme (which gives its title to the play) is: "*Même les Anges succombent à l'amour.*" She is still singing when Jane arrives in travelling clothes with a suitcase, declaring agitatedly: "We must go away at once!"

A postcard has come from Maurice Duclos – who had been (in succession) the lover of both women before they were married – announcing his arrival in London. In panic, Jane suggests staying at Brighton until they can get visas for America. Julia, however, prefers to face the situation. They are still arguing about it when Saunders brings in a similar postcard addressed to her.

Their bosom friendship is soon in peril. Jane insinuates that Julia's refusal to leave London is merely a desire to have Maurice to herself. Neither will go away without the other – and if they both stay they will fight like tigers when they meet Maurice again. They vow that, however badly they behave during the crisis, they will make it up afterwards: "Perfect friendship again and no apologies."

Julia rings for Saunders, asking her to pack a suitcase, and they laboriously compose a note in French, telling Maurice that they have been called away. They are on the point of leaving, suitcases in hand, when the doorbell rings. Nonplussed, they look at each other and put their bags down. "Anyhow," says Julia with determination, "it will be good for our French."

ACT II: It is nine in the evening, and Julia and Jane, elaborately gowned, are awaiting Maurice's arrival. The room is decked with flowers and the supper-table elegantly laid for two. Their idea is that he should find them "quietly dining together in charming domestic surroundings"; but his lateness has disconcerted them and they are very hungry.

At last Julia rings for cocktails and orders dinner. Every time they hear a taxi they rush to the window, but always they are disappointed. A telephone call from a relative and someone ringing the door-bell by mistake, raise their hopes in vain.

Saunders brings in a bottle of champagne, which they drink liberally during the meal, while they exchange reminiscences of Maurice. Jane is the first to show signs of intoxication, but by the dessert both are giggling hysterically. A "wrong number" completes their discomfiture, and the strong liqueur with which they round off their dinner leaves them definitely drunk. Soon they have a violent quarrel, which ends by Jane triumphantly telling Julia that she has known all the time where Maurice is, and that she is going straight to him. She flounces out, and Julia flings herself on the sofa in violent hysterics.

ACT III: At breakfast next morning Julia is venting her ill-humour upon Saunders when Willy calls in a state of agitation: having quarrelled with Fred, he has returned home by the first train and has discovered Jane's absence.

He is bewildered when Julia explains that she and Jane have quarrelled after getting violently drunk; and still more so when she says that Jane has gone off with a Frenchman. At first he merely thinks that Julia is hysterical; but when he learns that both woman have been the mistress of Maurice Duclos he shows signs of distress, blaming Julia for her conduct but making excuses for Jane. He insists that Julia help him look for his wife.

They have just gone out together when a telephone message comes from Maurice. Saunders has just taken it when Fred returns. Surprised not to find his wife, he sends Saunders round to Jane's flat to look for her, and he is idly playing the piano when Jane herself enters – still in bedraggled evening dress. He asks in astonishment what she has been doing.

At first Jane refuses explanations, but when Saunders returns, saying that Julia has gone out with a "dark man", she assumes it was Maurice and, in her rage, tells Fred everything. Describing the quarrel, she explains that she walked straight out and went to an hotel, not really having any idea of Maurice's whereabouts.

Fred indignantly accuses her of having "led Julia into that blackguard's clutches", and insists that she shall come with him to look for her. When she objects he tries to drag her by main force, and she is struggling and screaming when Julia and Willy return together.

Mutual explanations follow and the two wives, seeing that their husbands intend to be unpleasant, forget their quarrel and decide to stand together.

An impending scene is side-tracked by the arrival of Maurice, who now speaks excellent English. He gracefully kisses the hands of both women, who, in some embarrassment, introduce their husbands. When he realises that the discourtesy of Fred and Willy is due to jealousy, he bursts out laughing and declares that the whole business has been a "put-up job", engineered by Jane and Julia because they felt that their husbands were not paying them enough attention. He adds that he has just taken the flat upstairs for a year. Jane and Julia go up there with him, on the pretext of helping him choose cretonne for curtains.

Meanwhile, Fred and Willy have a drink together; but it suddenly strikes them that they have been unwise to let their wives go upstairs alone; and they are still more disturbed when, through the ceiling, they hear Maurice singing "*Même les Anges...*"

Joseph Thorp in *Punch*, 29 April 1925:

"Julia and Jane are two very, very modern young women who discuss anything and everything, if not with greater knowledge (as they think) than their Victorian sisters, at least with indefinitely greater candour. They are the closest friends, and they have one unique link in their friendship. Each has had a serious temporary love affair with a conquering French gentleman, the one in Pisa and the other in Venice.

"Each has married meanwhile one of those immense, pleasant, unreflective golfers who go to swell the volume of our unemployed. Julia has her Fred; Jane her Will. They are happy, they agree, and they love their husbands; but they are no longer in love. There is no devastating excitement about it.

"Julia has waked that morning with a presentiment. She has distractedly sent off her own Frederick and Jane's Will – the two are inseparable – to their golf. Jane bursts in obviously agitated. She also had waked with a presentiment, and the post brought her a picture-postcard from Venice (or Pisa). Maurice is coming to London 'this week'. And this is Saturday. What shall they do? And while they are debating it, Saunders, the new maid, brings in a picture-postcard from Pisa (or Venice). Maurice hopes to do himself the honour of calling upon Julia.

"They must both take flight – to Brighton. Jane has come with her suitcase; Saunders is to pack Julia's. Saunders, knowing her Brighton (not the Brighton of A.P.H., but the other Brighton of popular legend), packs with a selective emphasis – for which she is duly reproved. Here are two honest wives flying from an adventure they would love, and do in fact fear for the sake of their faithful Fred and Willy. ('Wouldn't it be awful if Fred and Willy were killed by a tree falling on the golf-course?')

"And just as the two irresolutely virtuous dears are passing out to the taxi a ring is heard. Maurice? As a matter of fact, it is the plumber. But the pause is enough to check the expedition. They will meet their man with courage, each fortified by the other's resolution, and each watching the other as cat watches cat.

"And so a hectic day passes with many false alarms from telephone and door-bell, till, practically starved owing to anxiety mingled with suspicion of each other's good faith, two overwrought young women sit down to a dinner preceded by a particularly potent cocktail; to peck at excellent food and to split with unwise enthusiasm a large bottle of champagne followed by a generous liqueur.

"This is no diet for 'angels'. They reach, via friendly stages of excessive wisdom, dignity, and careful inaccuracy of speech – "Bring the Saunders right away, coffee" – a mood of mutual recrimination. Charges and counter-charges are made: "Julia, you're unhinged"; "I'm perfectly hinged" – which strikes me as an entirely pleasant retort. Still no Maurice.

"Jane, asserting (falsely as it happens) that she knows where that Lothario is and is forthwith going to him, falters out of her friend's house, declaring herself unable any longer to put up with Julia's insults. In fact, she spends the night in an hotel in Bayswater, 'because that was where the taxi-man took her' and arrives next morning in evening dress to find a tangle of trouble. The infuriated Julia has betrayed her to the disturbed golfer, William, whose brain does not work quickly enough to make him very difficult. Jane, however, retorts by telling tales of Pisa and the Grand Lagoon. *Contretemps de quatre!* A bell. The bland and debonair Maurice is announced. Grasping intuitively the essence of the situation, he declares the whole thing a diverting and ingenious jest, and his unconquerable politeness effectively stymies the hardly-convinced husbands. Will they all come up and help him to choose his curtains? He has taken the flat just above. The men, sulking but baulked, will not. The two angels will. And in a few moments is heard that fruity and infectious *Liebeslied* which the wives have been humming all day and the husbands trying to play with one finger on the piano -Maurice's seductive tenor mingling with the quavering sopranos of the angels.

"An unpleasant subject, you may say? Well, not edifying or elevating, certainly, but Mr Noël Coward has written it so gaily and wittily and they play it so lightly and briskly that it is relieved of all offensiveness. Many a play that draws carefully to a sunny and happy ending can be and has been furtively offensive all through. We ought really to rid our minds of cant in these matters. I don't remember a better piece of stage-craft in this type of play since Mr Maugham's *Home and Beauty*, with the ever-to-be-lamented Hawtrey.

"The dialogue goes like a fencing bout. Nice, silly jokes and flashes of audacious wit, candour and gaiety and an appropriate air of fantastic unreality, with the absence of false and hedging sentiment, to save it from any real unwholesomeness. Perhaps I am too simple a soul, or, on the other hand, too depraved, but that is my impression. A brilliant performance, not for *vieilles filles* perhaps, but certainly harmless to the inoculated.

"This was emphatically a play for the two women. They will be the envy of their sister artists. The men are mere foils. Even Maurice, who dominates the situation, is withheld till the last few moments by a very judicious artistry.

"Miss Edna Best, whose escape from fatuous parts has made an actress of her, or, rather, allowed her talent to appear, made a delicious thing of her Jane. Miss Tallulah Bankhead, who played, at four days' notice, the part allotted to Miss Margaret Bannerman, was as effective in her very different mood. There was no sign of hesitation in a long and exacting part. A *tour de force* indeed.

"Miss Mona Harrison's Saunders, who was 'rather grand', deserves commendation. Mr Arthur Wellesley and Mr Gerald Ames were very plausible husbands in this queer world; and Mr Austin Trevor, who always brings intelligence to his parts, made an engaging thing of the reprehensible and absolutely imperturbable Maurice.

"The production was admirable. Speed is of the essence of this genre. The smartest ping-pong rally would be slow compared with it."

PUBLICATIONS

Fallen Angels was first published in the *Contemporary British Dramatists* series (Volume 25), Ernest Benn (London, 1924). It is dedicated to Edward Molyneux. Also published in *Noël Coward Collected Plays: One*, Methuen World Classics (London, 1999).

NOTES

During the run of *London Calling!*, Coward wrote *Fallen Angels* and *The Vortex*. For the next two years these plays went round the London managers, and before *Fallen Angels* was eventually staged both *Hay Fever* and *Easy Virtue* had been written and *The Vortex* produced, followed by his first revue with Cochran, *On with the Dance*.

At one time Gladys Cooper was to play *Fallen Angels* with Madge Titheradge. No sooner had *The Vortex* been successfully launched in the West End of London, after its Hampstead try-out, and *On with the Dance* produced at Manchester for its preliminary run before opening at the Pavilion, than rehearsals commenced for *Fallen Angels*, which had been bought by Anthony Prinsep as a vehicle for Margaret Bannerman at the Globe. During these rehearsals she had a nervous breakdown and was replaced by Tallulah Bankhead. Coward says:

"The press notices for *Fallen Angels* were vituperative to the point of incoherence. No epithet was spared. It was described as vulgar, disgusting, shocking, nauseating, vile, obscene, degenerate, etc., etc. The idea of two gently nurtured young women playing a drinking scene together was apparently too degrading a spectacle for even the most hardened and worldly critics. The *Daily Express* even went so far as to allude to these two wayward creatures as 'suburban sluts'.

"All this was capital for the box-office and the play ran for several months. It had one disagreeable effect, however, which was to unleash upon me a mass of insulting letters from all parts of the country. This was the first time I had ever experienced such a strange pathological avalanche, and I was quite startled. In the years that followed, of course, I became completely accustomed to anonymous letters dropping into the letter-box."

There were even protests in the theatre, as the following newspaper reports shows:

"The last performance at the Globe Theatre, on Saturday night of Mr Noël Coward's much-discussed play *Fallen Angels* was made the occasion of a protest by a Mrs Hornibrook, who had resigned her membership of the London Council for the Promotion of Public Morality in view of her fellow-members' dislike of public protests.

"At the end of the second act she stood up in a box and began to speak against the play, but her words were drowned by the orchestra, which began to play 'I Want To Be Happy'.

"This incident followed a protest made by Mrs Hornibrook last Monday at a lecture at the Ambassadors Theatre, on the plays of Eugene O'Neill, the American dramatist.

"On that occasion Mrs Hornibrook spoke of the undesirability of Mr O'Neill's plays being introduced to this country, and observed that London playgoers did not go to the theatre to see plays with sordidness, immorality and sexuality as their theme.

"To Mrs Hornibrook's protest, a woman retorted by asking whether sordidness did not exist in the minds of people who went to see a play with the object of finding something immoral in it."

Coward also says: "With *Fallen Angels*, *On with the Dance*, and *The Vortex* all running at once, I was in an enviable position. Everyone but Somerset Maugham said that I was a second Somerset Maugham, with the exception of a few who preferred to describe me as a second Sacha Guitry."

The play was revived, on tour, during 1948 and 1949. It was this production, reproduced and recast, which eventually came to the Ambassadors Theatre in November 1949. On the opening night, and for part of the run, it was preceded by a revival of *Fumed Oak* (see *Tonight at 8.30*).

Since its production at the Vaudeville Theatre in 1967, major revivals of *Fallen Angels* have included New York, 1980 (with Jo Henderson and Carol Teitel, 104 performances), BBC Television, October 1963 (with Moira Redmond and Ann Morrish) and ITV, 1975 (with Joan Collins, Susannah York and Sacha Distel). There have also been BBC Radio revivals, and a French version called *Le Printemps de Saint Martin* (1928).

US PRODUCTIONS

PRESENTED by the Actor's Theatre Inc. at the 49th Street Theatre, New York, 1 December 1927 (36 performances).

CHARACTERS	49th Street, 1927
JULIA STERROLL	Fay Bainter
FREDERICK STERROLL	Gordon Ash
SAUNDERS	Eileen Beldon
WILLIAM BANBURY	Gerald Haner
JANE BANBURY	Estelle Winwood
MAURICE DUCLOS	Luis Alberni
Director	*Guthrie McClintic*

The *New York Times*: "As his previous plays have revealed him, Mr Coward has a pretty talent, but a slight one. *Fallen Angels* is no exception to the rule that if prettiness does not win, the slightness will."

PRESENTED by Charles Bowden and Richard Barr in association with H. Ridgely Bullock Jr. at the Playhouse, New York, 17 January 1956 (239 performances).

CHARACTERS	Playhouse, 1956
JULIA STERROLL	Nancy Walker
FREDERICK STERROLL	William Windon
JASMINE	Alice Pearce
WILLIAM BANBURY	William LeMessena
JANE BANBURY	Margaret Phillips
MAURICE DUCLOS	Efrem Zimbalist Jr.
Director	*Charles Bowden*

The *New York Post*: "Since *Fallen Angels* always was distinctly minor Coward, those of us who are among his veteran admirers certainly can't say he is being betrayed in this rather free revival. As a latecomer to the ranks of Miss Walker's enthusiasts, I think her humour justifies everything."

The *New York Journal-American*: "Nancy Walker is certainly one of our funniest ladies."

11
THE VORTEX
A PLAY IN THREE ACTS
Written in 1923

FIRST PRESENTED by Norman Macdermott at the Everyman Theatre, Hampstead, London, 25 November 1924 (12 performances). Transferred to the Royalty Theatre, London, 16 December 1924 (224 performances), then to the Comedy Theatre, London, 9 March 1925, and to the Little Theatre, London, 4 May 1925.

REVIVED by Tennent Productions at the Theatre Royal, Brighton, 18 February 1952 (and at Cambridge, 25 February). Subsequently at the Lyric Theatre, Hammersmith, London, 4 March 1952 (31 performances). Transferred to the Criterion Theatre, London, 9 April 1952 (44 performances).

CHARACTERS	Everyman and Royalty, 1924–5
PRESTON	Claire Keep
HELEN SAVILLE	Mary Robson
PAUNCEFORT QUENTIN	F. Kinsey Peile
CLARA HIBBERT	Millie Sim

FLORENCE LANCASTER	Lilian Braithwaite
TOM VERYAN	Alan Hollis
NICKY LANCASTER	Noël Coward
DAVID LANCASTER	Bromley Davenport
BUNTY MAINWARING	Molly Kerr
BRUCE FAIRLIGHT	Ivor Barnard
Director	*Noël Coward*
Designers	*Set: G. E. Calthrop*
	Costumes: William Chappell

CHARACTERS	**Brighton, Lyric and Criterion, 1952**
PRESTON	Neville Prescott
HELEN SAVILLE	Adrianne Allen
PAUNCEFORT QUENTIN	Robert Andrews
CLARA HIBBERT	Sylvia Coleridge
FLORENCE LANCASTER	Isabel Jeans
TOM VESYAN	Anthony Forwood
NICKY LANCASTER	Dirk Bogarde (Brighton and Lyric)
	Michael Gough (Criterion)
DAVID LANCASTER	Nicholas Hannen
BUNTY MAINWARING	Janet Butler
BRUCE FAIRLIGHT	Peter Jones
Director	*Michael MacOwan*

❖

ACT I: The Lancasters' flat in London. Wednesday.
ACT II: The hall of the Lancasters' country house. Sunday.
ACT III: Florence Lancaster's bedroom. The same night. (Two hours
            have elapsed.)
TIME: The 1952 revival was set in the original period: the 1920s.

❖

SYNOPSIS

ACT I: Two of Florence Lancaster's smart friends, Helen Saville and Pauncefort
       Quentin (an elderly batchelor, generally called "Pawnie"), are shown into
       the drawing-room of her London flat. In Florence's absence they discuss

her latest affair with the handsome but rather stupid Tom Vetyan, who is 24 – the same age as her son Nicky.

Another friend, the singer Clara Hibbert, comes in to borrow a green fan for her recital. Complaining of a headache, she asks the maid Preston to fetch her a cachet and lies down on the sofa.

Florence, a brilliantly dressed, young-looking woman, comes in with Tom. She lends the fan to Clara, who goes out, while the others indulge in cocktails and gossip before drifting off for their evening's engagements. Helen warns Florence that Tom is much less in love with her than she with him, and that, by trying to keep young indefinitely, she is storing up trouble for herself.

She is just leaving when Nicky Lancaster arrives unexpectedly from Paris, where he has been studying music. He is extremely well dressed, but looks thin and overstrung. It is a disappointment to him when his mother will not put off her date with Tom Veryan; however, she tells him consolingly that he can join them afterwards at the Embassy Club.

David Lancaster, a pleasant, elderly man, greets his son and asks him to come and have a chat with him later in his study. Florence is upset when Nicky tells her that he is engaged; but he mollifies her by saying that the girl, Bunty Mainwaring, has raved over Florence's photographs and commented that she looked like "a heroic little boy". He adds that he has asked Bunty to come round that evening.

When the girl arrives, Florence is very amiable and gives her a pressing invitation to her weekend country house-party. Then she goes off to dress. The two young people, left together, feel a slight sense of anti-climax at having met with so little opposition.

Tom Veryan arrives and recognises Bunty as a childhood friend. Instantly jealous, Nicky goes to talk to his father, leaving them to their reminiscences.

ACT II: Florence's house-party is in full swing. While she sits talking to the dramatist Bruce Fairlight, Clara Hibbert dances with Tom Veryan, Helen with Pawnie, and Nicky with Bunty. Snatches of conversation are heard as each couple in turn passes near the footlights. The dancers complain that the gramophone music is too fast, and change partners as Nicky sits at the piano to play for them. Florence now dances with Tom, and Bunty with Bruce. Helen comes to ask Nicky for a match. While he plays on, she takes a box out of his pocket, but he starts up and snatches it from her. Then from another pocket he takes his matchbox and lights her cigarette. She looks at him queerly for a moment while he re-starts the gramophone.

Florence and Tom are squabbling as they dance, and soon they break off. Everyone is tired by this time, and most of the guests drift off to play mah-jong in another room, while Florence and Tom continue their discussion by the fire. The quarrel is patched up, but when Florence tries to arrange an evening together he puts her off, on the evidently invented excuse that he is going out with his mother. He goes into the next room and Florence works off her annoyance upon her husband.

Nicky finds her obviously upset, and is angry when she starts criticising Bunty. Walking out in a huff, she collides with Helen, who knows that Nicky has already had a row with his fiancée. Helen talks seriously to him, telling him that he must give up drugs: she has suspected it for some time, and has realised the significance of the box she took from his pocket.

His father then comes in and Helen leaves them together. David is worried by Nicky's run-down appearance, and gladly accepts the young man's offer to come down and stay quietly at the farm for a few days.

Bunty then has a talk with Nicky, in which she uses their tiff and Florence's obvious dislike of her as pretexts to break off their engagement. The mah-jong party come back and there is one final dance, at the end of which Nicky slams off in a rage. Everyone is surprised at his bad temper, until Bunty explains that she is the cause.

When the others have gone to bed, Bunty and Tom are left together. They agree that they are both "reverting to type" and are out of tune with the house-party. Suddenly Bunty bursts into tears. Tom takes her in his arms and kisses her. At this moment Florence comes in, followed by Nicky. There is a violent scene, during which Florence orders Bunty out of the house and tells Tom (who confesses that he loves the girl) to get out of her sight. When he takes her at her word, she runs up the stairs after him, imploring him to come back. All the while Nicky plays stormily on the piano.

ACT III: Florence is lying on her bed in hysterics, while Helen administers comfort and sensible advice. She points out that Tom and Bunty are obviously the right type for each other – so Florence had better give up her struggle against middle age and be a graceful loser.

Nicky then bursts in, clad in dressing-gown and pyjamas, asking Helen to leave him alone with his mother. He insists upon knowing the truth: Has Tom Veryan been her lover? Florence at first denies it, but he breaks down her resistance and makes her confess that she has been involved with not only Tom, but other men as well. He accuses her of having drained his father of personality and ambition, and of having ruined his own life by her selfishness and vanity. She is not even happy, he says – she is fighting all the time to keep her youth and her looks, which really matter so little. When he admits that he is taking drugs, Florence at last realises the harm that has been done. She makes him swear to give it up, and promises to help him.

Nicky replies that, if she is to be of any use, she must give up her lovers: "You're not going to he beautiful and successful ever again – you're going to be my mother for once." She gives the required promise and the curtain falls as, with tears streaming down her cheeks, she strokes Nicky's hair in an effort to calm him.

James Agate in the *Sunday Times*, 30 November 1924:

"Like the lady of fashion, your theatre manager is always declaring that he has nothing to put on. Well, here is a piece which is the *dernier cri* in the theatrical mode, *un peu schoking* perhaps, but no less popular on that account. It has a cast of moderate size, and as for setting, its demands are exorbitant only in the way of good taste. The reception of the piece was as extravagant and sincere as any author would desire, and I should not be surprised to learn that on the following morning Mr Coward had to engage a secretary to help him to turn down the offers. But could no West End manager foresee that the piece could not fail? And will some of those now so sorely disappointed ones commission this very clever young playwright to prepare a new piece specially for him? Must the risks accepted by these gentry always be the absurd ones? Brains must ultimately come by their own, even in the theatre; and Mr Coward has brains to spare.

"The first act is a-shimmer with wit of the best theatrical kind – the non-literary sort that has to be spoken in the situation. The milieu is that of *Our Betters*, without the Americans. Into this viciously silly and crazily-perverted minority, which makes a noise entirely disproportionate to its numbers, importance, or influence, comes one Nicky Lancaster, who has been finishing his schooling in Paris. He finds his mother languishing on the breast of Tom Veryan, a sturdy young Guards officer – a 'tame cat', in Sir Arthur Pinero's old phrase. Nicky is himself tarred with the degenerate brush. He dopes, his tongue takes the convenient path of the superlative, and is familiar with the 'too adorable', 'too divine', 'too perfectly marvellous', which have taken the place of the 'too utterly utter' of the nineties.

"But Nicky is not 'too foul'. He has some notion of decency, and is in love with a comparatively 'nice' girl, one Bunty Mainwaring. There is this to be said for Bunty – that she is a frank little savage, who likes to be amoral, but does not believe in giving vice a halo. And now it appears that Bunty and Veryan are, again to use Sir Arthur's phraseology, not strangers to one another.

Act I. Sheila Brandreth (Joyce Kennedy), Edmund Crowe (Raymond Massey),
Naomi Frith-Bassington (Elizabeth Pollock), Keld Maxwell (Robert Harris)
and Olive Lloyd-Kennedy (Mary Robson)

Act III. Sheila Brandreth (Joyce Kennedy) and Keld Maxwell (Robert Harris)

I'LL LEAVE IT TO YOU, New Theatre, 1920

Act II. Bobbie (Noël Coward)
and Faith Crombie (Esmé Wynne)

THE YOUNG IDEA, Savoy Theatre, 1923

Jennifer Brent (Kate Cutler), George Brent (Herbert Marshall), Sholto (Noël Coward)
and Gerda (Ann Trevor)

Act II, Scene 2. Sirio Marson (Ivor Novello) on the bar, and Lucy Griffin (Frances Doble) seated in the foreground

Act III. Sirio Marson (Ivor Novello) and Lucy Griffin (Frances Doble)

Act I, Scene 1. Nadya (Madge Titheradge) and Sabien (Francis Lister)

Act II. General Krish (C. M. Hallard), Nadya (Madge Titheradge), The Grand Duchess (Lady Tree) and Prince Keri (Herbert Marshall)

Act III, Scene 1. Nadya (Madge Titheradge)
and Sabien (Francis Lister)

Act III, Scene 2. Nadya (Madge Titheradge), General Krish (C. M. Hallard), Miss Phipps (Ada King),
Prince Keri (Herbert Marshall) and Zana (Freda Godfrey)

"Other Girls" Noël Coward and Chorus

"Parisian Pierrot" Gertrude Lawrence, Eileen Molyneux, Jill Williams and Chorus

"Early Mourning" Poppy Baker (Gertrude Lawrence)

"Rain Before Seven" Tom (Noël Coward) and Mary (Gertrude Lawrence)

"The Swiss Family Whittlebot" The Introducer (Tubby Edlin), Gob (Leonard Childs), Sago (William Childs) and Hernia Whittlebot (Maisie Gay)

"Russian Blues" Noël Coward

Act I. Jane Banbury (Edna Best) and Julia Sterroll (Tallulah Bankhead)

Act II. Julia Sterroll (Tallulah Bankhead) and Jane Banbury (Edna Best)

Act III. Jane Banbury (Edna Best), Maurice Duclos (Austin Trevor) and Julia Sterroll (Tallulah Bankhead)

Act I. Helen Saville (Mary Robson), Nicky Lancaster (Noël Coward) and Florence Lancaster (Lilian Braithwaite)

Act II. Florence Lancaster (Lilian Braithwaite), Nicky Lancaster (Noël Coward)
and David Lancaster (Bromley Davenport)

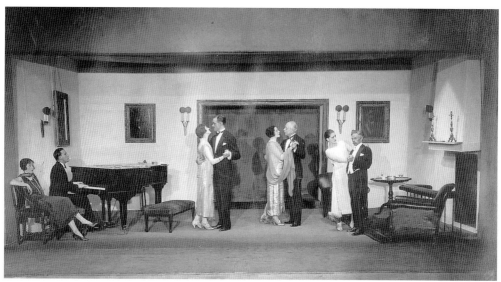

Act II. Clara Hibbert (Millie Sim), Nicky Lancaster (Noël Coward), Florence Lancaster (Lilian Braithwaite),
Tom Veryan (Alan Hollis), Helen Saville (Mary Robson), Pauncefort Quentin (F. Kinsey Peile), Bunty Mainwaring
(Molly Kerr) and Bruce Fairlight (Ivor Barnard)

Act III. Nicky Lancaster (Noël Coward) and Florence Lancaster (Lilian Braithwaite)

Act I. Sorel Bliss (Helen Spencer), Richard Greatham (Athole Stewart), Jackie Coryton (Ann Trevor), Sandy Tyrell (Patrick Susands), David Bliss (W. Graham Browne), Myra Arundel (Hilda Moore), Simon Bliss (Robert Andrews) and Judith Bliss (Marie Tempest)

Act II. Judith Bliss (Marie Tempest) and David Bliss (W. Graham Browne)

HAY FEVER, Ambassadors Theatre, 1925

Act III. Myra Arundel (Hilda Moore), David Bliss (W. Graham Browne), Jackie Coryton (Ann Trevor), Simon Bliss (Robert Andrews), Sandy Tyrell (Patrick Susands), Judith Bliss (Marie Tempest), Sorel Bliss (Helen Spencer) and Richard Greatham (Athole Stewart)

EASY VIRTUE, Empire Theatre, New York, 1925

Act III. Larita (Jane Cowl), centre, and Company

Act I. Colonel Whittaker (Marcus Barron), Hilda (Joan Clement Scott), Larita (Jane Cowl),
John (James Raglan), Mrs Whittaker (Mabel Terry-Lewis) and Marion (Marda Vanne)

Act II. Colonel Whittaker (Marcus Barron), Larita (Jane Cowl), Marion (Marda Vanne), Mrs Whittaker
(Mabel Terry-Lewis) and Hilda (Joan Clement Scott)

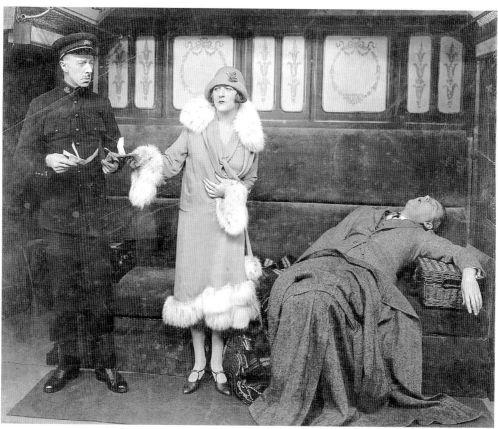

"Travelling Light" An Attendant (Ernest Thesiger), a Young Woman (Alice Delysia)
and a Young Man (Nigel Bruce)

"First Love" Rupert (Lance Lister)
and Mlle (Alice Delysia)

"Oranges and Lemons" Violet Banks (Ernest
Thesiger) and Grace Hubbard (Douglas Byng)

Inez Zulietta (Ann Mitchell) and Cyril Hardacre (Rory Edwards)

Jerome Kennedy (Mark Lewis), Owen Marshall (Paul Bentall), Tanis Marshal (Pauline Moran),
Elise Trent (Alison Mullin)

Act I and Act III. Setting for the Studio

Act II. Setting for the Flat

Act 1, Scene 2. Edward Churt (A. E. Matthews) and
Carol Churt (Francine Larrimore)

Act II. Evelyn Bathurst (Bernard Merefield)
and Carol Churt (Margaret Vaughan)

This is a pretty kettle of fish, even for a young man of 1924, to come home and find that his sweetheart's former lover is the *amant en titre* of his own mother. The scene of the discovery is as good a bit of theatre as I have seen for a long time. It might be just disagreeable, but Mr Coward, by a stroke of pure genius, lifts it into the region of philosophic comment. Nicky is by way of being a pianist, and he covers up his mother's outburst of jealousy with a crescendo of discordant jazz. You feel that he will go to his mother by-and-by.

"And so he does. The third act is a very fine piece of work. Florence has offended not only the boy's father, but the boy himself. Yet Nicky is not all denunciation; the century has altered. He tells his mother how he has watched her jig, amble and lisp, and forces her to a confession. But he is no severe judge, and would understand wantonness. Has his mother a case? She has, but it is a wretched one, and the boy tears it to pieces. It will be all different in the morning, he knows, but let them look truth in the face for one night. He loves her, and if she be but the least bit desirous to be blessed he'll blessing beg of her. And as he lays his sobbing head upon his mother's knees the curtain comes down.

"There is the imprint of truth upon this play. These creatures are nauseating as animalculae in a pond, but they interest. The craftsmanship is beyond reproach, and the dialogue is taut and spare, and of an admirable *vraisemblance*. The piece was magnificently acted. First by Mr Coward, who lived the part with his nerves, and was so lifelike that you seemed to be in the same room with him. Next by Miss Lilian Braithwaite, who gave a display of comic artifice and emotional power far in excess of anything she has been allowed to do for a very long time. Why should this clever actress be so often condemned merely to simper and pour out tea? Miss Molly Kerr, with her vanity, and her sleek aristocratic head prepared for the mob's guillotine, was admirable; while Mr Kinsey Peile and Mr Bromley Davenport, each in his so different way, was perfect. Only Miss Millie Sim was not quite right in her suggestion of the chorus.

"I have four criticisms to offer. The caricature of the well-known novelist is offensive, and should be deleted. The third act is too long, there is too much piano-playing in the second, and ladies do not exhale cigarette smoke through the nose."

PUBLICATIONS

The Vortex was first published in the *Contemporary British Dramatists* series (Volume 19), Ernest Benn (London, 1925). It is undedicated. Also published in *Noël Coward Collected Plays: One*, Methuen World Classics (London, 1999).

NOTES

On his return from America in the autumn of 1924, Coward added *Hay Fever* and *Easy Virtue* to the pile of plays awaiting production. Among the many managers who had been reading these plays was Norman Macdermott who in 1920 had turned an old drill hall in Hampstead into what was, by 1924, the flourishing try-out and repertory theatre, the Everyman. In *Present Indicative* Coward comments:

"Norman Macdermott was a short, affable man with nice eyes and a faintly unreliable expression. He invited me to go to see him after he had read *Hay Fever* and *The Vortex*, and announced, to my joy, that he would produce one of them, but that he had not quite decided which would stand the greater chance of success. He had a slight bias towards *Hay Fever*, but as there was no good part for me in that, I managed to steer him over to *The Vortex*."

After casting difficulties, rehearsals were all set to commence when a financial crisis developed which was only averted by the timely assistance of Michael Arlen; then, when all seemed well, Coward says:

"Our next obstacle appeared to be insurmountable and reared itself up in the most unexpected quarter. Kate Cutler, for whom I had written the part of Florence, suddenly refused flatly to go on rehearsing. I have never quite known to this day what strange devil got into her."

Suffice to say that in the ensuing dispute Coward was faced with finding a new leading lady at a week's notice, or reverting to the last act as originally written, omitting the revisions he had made to strengthen the big scene. He says:

"I decided, quite firmly and without passion, that neither then nor at any time in my life would I allow myself to be dictated to in the age-old battle between actor and author: a resolution, I am proud to say, that I have kept more or less shining and unsullied to this day."

It was Lilian Braithwaite who stepped into the breach – but troubles were even then not at an end. Coward goes on:

"Meanwhile, I was having a spirited duel with the Lord Chamberlain (Lord Cromer) in his office at St James's. He had at first refused point-blank to grant a licence for the play because of the unpleasantness of its theme, and it was only after a long-drawn-out argument, during which, I must say, he was charming and sympathetic, that I persuaded him that the play was little more than a moral tract. With a whimsical and rather weary smile, he finally granted the licence."

The play was produced at last, and Coward says in his introduction to *Play Parade, Volume I*: "It was an immediate success and established me both as a playwright and as an actor, which was very fortunate, because until then I had not proved myself to be so hot in either capacity. With this success came many pleasurable trappings. A car. New suits. Silk shirts. An extravagant amount of pyjamas and dressing-gowns, and a still more extravagant amount of publicity. I was photographed, and interviewed, and photographed again. In the street. In the park. In my dressing-room. At my piano. With my dear old mother, without my dear old mother – and, on one occasion, sitting up in an over-elaborate bed looking like a heavily-doped Chinese illusionist. This last photograph, I believe, did me a good deal of harm. People glancing at it concluded at once, and with a certain justification, that I was undoubtedly a weedy sensualist in the last stages of physical and moral degeneration, and that they had better hurry off to see me in my play before my inevitable demise placed that faintly macabre pleasure beyond their reach. This attitude, while temporarily very good for business, became irritating after a time, and for many years I was seldom mentioned in the press without allusions to 'cocktails', 'post-war hysteria', and 'decadence'.

"My original motive in *The Vortex* was to write a good play with a whacking good part in it for myself, and I am thankful to say, with a few modest reservations, that I succeeded. It is a good play, and although I am fully aware that it could be a good deal better, I am quite reasonably satisfied with it. At the time, I need hardly add, I considered it a masterpiece. At all events, the first night of its production at the Henry Miller Theatre, New York, was a very great moment in my life, and for this I shall never cease to be grateful."

After its two weeks at the Everyman, the play transferred to the Royalty Theatre, and during its run moved to both the Comedy and Little Theatres. While at the Comedy, Coward was required to go to Manchester for the dress rehearsal and opening of his revue, *On with the Dance* (16 and 17 March 1925). He arranged for his understudy to play for him at these two performances. He says:

"I would never behave so casually to the public nowadays, but then I was new to stardom and unencumbered by any particular sense of responsibility. Incidentally, my understudy happened to be a keen young actor named John Gielgud, so in the light of later events the public were not really being cheated at all."

John Gielgud also played the part on 21 April 1925, to allow Coward to attend the first night of *Fallen Angels*, and finished the run after Coward had left for America for the production there of *The Vortex*. This was the first Coward play to be seen in New York, and his first appearance there as an actor.

An interesting note appeared in the programme of *The Vortex* at the Royalty: "The audience are asked not to demand the raising of the curtain at the ends of Acts I and II, but should they desire it it will be raised at the conclusion of the play."

At that date it was still the custom for the company to take calls at the end of each act. It was a habit that Coward was anxious to abolish for the sake of the continuity of the production; but theatrical traditions die hard, and we find recorded that, as late as the first night of *Sirocco* in November 1927, the convention still existed, though it was soon to disappear entirely.

Major UK revivals since 1952 have included productions at Greenwich Theatre, 20 October – 1 November 1975, directed by James Roose Evans, with Vivien Merchent and Timothy Dalton; the Citizens Theatre, Glasgow, 22 January – 13 February 1988, with Maria Aitken and Rupert Everett, directed and designed by Philip Prowse, which transferred to the Garrick Theatre 26 January 1989; and BBC Television 1969, with Margaret Leighton and Richard Warwick. It has also been revived on BBC Radio and was one of the original productions of the Noël Coward Company (Malvern 1932).

US PRODUCTIONS

PRESENTED by Sam Harris and Irving Berlin, J. P. Bickerton Jr and Basil Dean at the National Theatre, Washington, 7 September 1925 and subsequently at the Henry Miller Theatre, New York, 16 September 1925 (157 performances).

CHARACTERS	Washington and Henry Miller, 1925
PRESTON	George Harcourt
HELEN SAVILLE	Auriol Lee
PAUNCEFORT QUENTIN	Leo G. Carroll
CLARA HIBBERT	Jeanette Sherwin
FLORENCE LANCASTER	Lilian Braithwaite
TOM VERYAN	Alan Hollis
NICKY LANCASTER	Noël Coward
DAVID LANCASTER	David Glassford
BUNTY MAINWARING	Molly Kerr
BRUCE FAIRLIGHT	Thomas Braidon
Director	*Basil Dean (with the help of Coward)*

The Broadway production was followed by a short road tour in which Rose Hobart replaced Molly Kerr.

The *New York World*: "The walls of Henry Miller's pretty theatre shook last evening with the first cheers of the new season, honest, hearty, well earned cheers. I suspect the young Noël Coward will have to live on and on for an almost intolerably long time before he will be able to forget a night that was a true triumph for himself – a triumph for his work both as a playwright and an actor."

The *New York Post*: "*The Vortex* is only within two or three feet of being the sort of play to burn the town down about. But Mr Coward, who can do many things, is no preacher, and his last act is preaching. *The Vortex* is laughable, deft and sophisticated entertainment."

The *New York Telegram*: "Mr Coward showed some of the qualities that have made him the toast of the younger English intellectuals. The strain of being both author and actor seemed to check his histrionic activity in the early stages, but the quality of his performance grew with the enthusiasm of the audience."

The New York production was to have been staged jointly by impresarios Charles Dillingham and Abe Erlanger in conjunction with Basil Dean. Soon after Noël and the key members of the London cast arrived in town, a conference was called in the Erlanger offices. As Noël recounts in *Present Indicative*:

"This was my first meeting with Mr Erlanger, and I had not been in the room five minutes before he informed me that the play could not open in New York until I had rewritten the last act. Although he never removed his feet from his desk throughout the entire interview, he was patient and fatherly with me, explaining that mother-love in America was a real and universally recognised ideal, and that the public would assuredly arise as one man and leave the theatre at the spectacle of a son so vilely abusing the woman who gave him birth. He added, gently, that the little question of reconstruction would not be difficult as he would come to rehearsals and tell me what to do."

Listening to the impresario, Noël recalled all the difficulties he had had to surmount to stage the original production: "I remembered also the impact of that last act upon the first-night audience. And here was this theatrical magnate, soggy with commercial enterprise, prattling to me about the ideal of mother-love and imagining that I would agree to rewrite my play at his dictation... I must say, to my credit, that I controlled any outward display of temper and waited, politely, until he had finished. Then, ignoring Dillingham's frantic grimaces, I said quite calmly that I intended to play the play exactly as it was, and that, far from listening to any of his suggestions for the altering of the script, I would not even allow him inside the theatre while I was rehearsing. With which I made a swift exit."

On opening night Coward received an immediate personal ovation. "There was no false modesty in my astonishment at such an ovation. I had never appeared in New York before. They had no reason to make the smallest demonstration until the end of the evening when they could decide whether or not I merited it. As it was, they made me feel as though I were one of their most beloved and established stars, and I tried with everything I had in me to deserve it. I do know, to my lasting satisfaction, that I gave the best performance that night that I have ever given in my life."

His first experience of touring America was less to his taste. When explaining years later to a reporter why Chicago was not on the itinerary for *Design for Living* he replied:

"I went there once with *The Vortex*, a sobbing tragedy. The more I cried, the more the Chicagoans laughed. They greeted the most pathetic parts with shouts and screams and roared and rolled in the aisles among the ermine and opera hats. After the first night the house was empty except for Pauline Lord, who was playing next door and used to come nipping in in make-up to applaud at the curtains. Chicago may come to New York if it wants to. I hear the train service is great."

FILM VERSION

A silent film version of *The Vortex* was made in the UK for Gainsborough Pictures in 1927. It was directed and adapted for the screen by Adrian Brunel.

CHARACTERS	Gainsborough Pictures, 1927
HELEN SAVILLE	Dorothy Fane
PAUNCEFORT QUENTIN	Kinsey Peile
FLORENCE LANCASTER	Willette Kershaw
TOM VERYAN	Alan Hollis
NICKY LANCASTER	Ivor Novello
DAVID LANCASTER	Sir Simeon Stuart
BUNTY MAINWARING	Frances Doble
THE DANCER	Julie Suedo

The film was first shown in London at the Marble Arch Pavilion, March 1928.

12
HAY FEVER
A NEW COMEDY
Written in 1924

FIRST PRESENTED by Alban B. Limpus at the Ambassadors Theatre, London, 8 June 1925. Transferred to the Criterion Theatre, London, 7 September 1925 (337 performances).

REVIVED by Charles B. Cochran at the Shaftesbury Theatre, London, 17 November 1933 (26 performances).

REVIVED by Wilson Barrett at the Vaudeville Theatre, London, 1 April 1941 (8 performances).

CHARACTERS	Ambassadors, 1925
JUDITH BLISS	Marie Tempest
DAVID BLISS	W. Graham Browne
SOREL BLISS	Helen Spencer
SIMON BLISS	Robert Andrews
MYRA ARUNDEL	Hilda Moore
RICHARD GREATHAM	Athole Stewart
JACKIE CORYTON	Ann Trevor
SANDY TYRELL	Patrick Susands
CLARA	Minnie Rayner
Director	*Noël Coward*
Designer	*G. E. Calthrop*

CHARACTERS	Shaftesbury, 1933
JUDITH BLISS	Constance Collier
DAVID BLISS	Eric Cowley
SOREL BLISS	Helen Spencer
SIMON BLISS	Louis Hayward
MYRA ARUNDEL	Joyce Barbour
RICHARD GREATHAM	Alan Napier
JACKIE CORYTON	Ann Trevor
SANDY TYRELL	Hargrave Pawson
CLARA	Gladys Henson

Director	*Noël Coward*
Designer	*G. E. Calthrop*

CHARACTERS	**Vaudeville, 1941**
JUDITH BLISS	Enid Sass
DAVID BLISS	George Larchet
SOREL BLISS	Joan Benham
SIMON BLISS	John Marquand
MYRA ARUNDEL	Phyllis Barker
RICHARD GREATHAM	Owen Reynolds
JACKIE CORYTON	Joan Lang
SANDY TYRELL	Neil Crawford
CLARA	Kitty de Legh
Director	*Charles Hickman*

❖

SCENE: The hall of the Blisses' house at Cookham.
ACT I: Saturday afternoon.
ACT II: Saturday evening.
ACT III: Sunday morning.

❖

SYNOPSIS

ACT I: The beautiful retired actress Judith Bliss is spending the weekend at her country house near Cookham with her husband, the author David Bliss, their hobbledehoy artist son, Simon, and their pretty daughter, Sorel. Unknown to the others, each of them has invited someone to stay: Sorel's choice is a suave diplomatist, Richard Greatham; Simon has an "awfully amusing" friend, Myra Arundel (whom Judith considers "a self-conscious vampire" and far too old for him); Judith's own guest is a young sportsman named Sandy Tyrell; while David has invited "a perfectly sweet flapper", who is an abject fool, he admits, but a useful type for him to study. Each wants the "Japanese room" reserved, and Clara – the ex-dresser housekeeper – is thoroughly out of temper, especially as the housemaid is ill with toothache.

   In the family scene that follows these revelations, Sorel bursts into tears and Judith announces her intention of returning to the stage. They are in the midst of acting a dramatic moment from one of her successes, *Love's Whirlwind*, when the door-bell rings. The first guest – Judith's hearty young admirer, Sandy Tyrell – has arrived. Sorel and Simon give him a chilling reception and go off upstairs.

Sandy is surprised that Judith has grown-up children, and even more so to learn that she is living with her husband (whom he thought dead). However, his admiration withstands these shocks and he is soon settled comfortably on the sofa with Judith, deciding that they must have been friends in a previous reincarnation, when they are interrupted by the arrival of Myra. She greets Judith effusively, explaining (untruthfully) that she has been invited by Sorel.

Judith takes Sandy upstairs and sends Simon down. He has spruced himself up for Myra's benefit and makes love to her with an engaging youthful awkwardness.

The remaining guests – Richard Greatharn and David's "sweet flapper", Jackie Coryton – arrive together, having waited for the return of the only station taxi, engaged by Myra. Unceremoniously, Simon takes Myra off into the garden, leaving the visitors alone. They are making polite conversation when Judith comes downstairs, followed by Sandy, his arms full of cushions. Without paying any attention to the others, they go out into the garden.

Richard goes on trying to entertain Jackie until at last Sorel appears, full of apologies, sends the girl off to find David in his study, and settles down to talk to him. Clara then begins to set the tea; the rest of the party gather and are mutually introduced. The curtain falls on their disjointed attempts to get a conversation started.

ACT II: Parlour games after dinner on Saturday evening are not a success. The family choose 'adverbs', which none of the guests knows how to play, but which Judith enjoys as she is the one person who knows how to act "in the manner of the word". Sorel is sent outside while, after protracted argument, the others decide upon "winsomely". Jackie, who is (or pretends to be) very shy, says it is a hateful game and she doesn't want to play; but she apologises so "winsomely" to Sorel for her stupidity that the word is guessed at once.

There is a general family quarrel, which ends in Simon taking Jackie into the garden and Sorel retreating into the library with Sandy. David pairs off with Myra, leaving Judith and Richard alone.

This is Judith's opportunity to make a dead set at him. After she has sung him a French song, told him she is "wistful and weary", and established themselves on a Christian-name footing, she asks for a cigarette. Bending forward to light it, he kisses her on the neck. Judith then dramatically declares that her husband must be "told everything"... Her life had been only a hollow shell, but now once more she is under the magic spell of romance. She pushes her highly embarrassed and alarmed victim out into the garden, telling him to "wait for her".

Opening the library door in search of her husband, she is shocked to find Sorel and Sandy embracing. They come out, looking rather sheepish. Judith plays a grand "renunciation" scene, giving Sandy up to Sorel, and goes upstairs, leaving her daughter to explain that, in their family, no one ever means what they say. She knows perfectly well that Sandy doesn't love her, and insists that he is under no obligation to her.

They go back into the library just as David comes in with Myra, who tells him that she only accepted the invitation because she admired his work so much and wanted to meet him. On the contrary, admits David, his novels are very bad, and she, being an intelligent person, must know it. After a sparring flirtation, when he exasperates her into slapping his face, he takes her in his arms and kisses her.

From the top of the stairs Judith sees this and, with tremendous enjoyment, stages another renunciation scene, sweeping aside Myra's attempts to protest. She has barely finished when Simon rushes in from the garden announcing his engagement to a bewildered and somewhat reluctant Jackie.

Myra at last makes herself heard, declaring that: "This house is a complete feather-bed of false emotions – you're posing, self-centred egotists, and I'm sick to death of you." This precipitates a scene in which they all try to shout one another down. In the midst of it Richard enters, somewhat apprehensive that this may be a result of Judith having confessed that she loves him.

"What's happened?" he asks. "Is this a game?"

"Yes!" replies Judith. "And a game that must be played to the finish." It is a cue for the melodramatic finale of *Love's Whirlwind*, and the family, who know it by heart, play up to her. They go through it with gusto, up to the point where Judith falls in a swoon, while the guests look on, "dazed and aghast".

ACT III: It is about ten o'clock on Sunday morning. Sandy is making a hasty breakfast when Jackie comes downstairs looking very miserable. She bursts into tears and opines that the Blisses are all mad and that she doesn't want to be engaged to Simon. Sandy agrees that Judith's forcing tactics are very upsetting, and that he was relieved when Sorel released him from their engagement. Having bolted his breakfast, he gets hiccups, and Jackie, picking up the sugar-bowl, takes him into the library to try a cure that consists of drinking coffee from the wrong side of the cup, "sort of upside-down".

Myra and Richard then appear and discuss the situation. After a night in the suffocating boiler-room (known to the family as "Little Hell"), he feels unwell, but Myra is very bright. As there is no sugar, they ring for Clara, who is mystified at its disappearance; but at a shriek from Jackie she rushes into the library: the hiccups experiment has led them to break the cup and spill coffee all over the carpet... However, the shock has effected a cure.

All four guests then agree that they cannot stand another day in the house. There is no train for some hours, so Sandy offers to take them all back to London in his car. Richard, on behalf of the party, tips Clara, and they go upstairs to pack.

Judith then comes down, followed by Sorel, and they look at the theatre news in the Sunday papers. Simon brings in one of his sketches, while David, in great glee, announces that he has just finished his novel. He starts to read the final pages, with interruptions from the family.

A violent argument ensues when he makes his heroine, in her scarlet Hispano, sweep "out of the Rue St Honoré into the Place de la Concorde". They have no map of Paris, but Judith declares categorically that this street does not run into the Place de la Concorde; David demonstrates with the breakfast crockery; Simon starts to draw a map, and they work themselves up to such a pitch of fury that they do not even notice when the visitors, suitcases in hand, creep downstairs. They are, however, roused by the slam of the front door, and when Sorel sees the car drive away they realise that everyone has gone. Beyond a casual comment that "people really do behave in a most extraordinary manner these days", they take no notice, but, the dispute forgotten, let David go on reading out the end of his novel.

The Times, 9 June 1925:

"Everybody will remember the queer Bohemian household in *The Constant Nymph*. The Bliss family in *Hay Fever* is just such another, only a little more so. Father is a romantic novelist, Mother an ex-actress, while the youngsters, Sorel and Simon, are just a pair of those precocious, quarrelsome, impudent children that Mr Coward is so fond of portraying. Each of the four invites a weekend guest, independently of the others, and then leaves the guest to arrive unwelcomed, abashed and bewildered. They all pair off, however, and begin flirting furiously, until Mother, the chief offender – for she ogles not one swain, but two – discovers Father embracing one of the guests, to whom she promptly and magnanimously 'gives' him. And did she not catch Sorel being kissed by another visitor in the billiard-room, and as promptly 'give' her to that visitor? Simon, too, got 'engaged' to someone else in the shrubbery, and duly received the maternal blessing. And, to crown all, Mother was so emotionally stirred that she dashed into a recital of one of her old parts, with the 'support' of Sorel and Simon.

"Next morning the four guests, supposing the family (not without reason) to be mad, silently stole away with their luggage behind the backs of the family, all quarrelling furiously about a mistake in Parisian topography in Father's new novel (does the Rue St Honoré run into the Place de la Concorde, or do you have to go down the Rue Boissy d'Anglas"), and Mother said: 'How rude!' Curtain.

"It will be seen that it is all, as usual, Mr Coward's fun. All the better fun, be it added, for being punctuated, as usual, with Mr Coward's wit. Its main purpose, however, is to serve as a vehicle for Miss Marie Tempest's brilliantly comic acting. She takes it gaily as an opportunity for displaying her virtuosity (including her old musicianship in the warbling of a French ballad), and is altogether at her brightest and best. Miss Helen Spencer's Sorel is a dainty piece of girlish impudence, and the rest of the cast all enter with gusto into the madcap humour of the evening. The audience were delighted, and insisted on a speech of thanks from Mr Coward, who claimed that his play, whether it pleased or wearied, was, at any rate, 'as clean as a whistle'. Be that as it may, it certainly did not weary."

PUBLICATIONS

Hay Fever was first published in the *Contemporary British Dramatists* series (Volume 27), Ernest Benn (London, 1925). It is undedicated. Also published in *Noël Coward Collected Plays: One*, Methuen World Classics (London, 1999).

NOTES

Written on his return from America in the autumn of 1924, Coward says in *Present Indicative*:

"The idea came to me suddenly in the garden, and I finished it in about three days, a feat which later on, when I had become news value, seemed to excite gossip-writers inordinately, although why the public should care whether a play takes three days or three years to write I shall never understand. Perhaps they don't. However, when I had finished it and had it neatly typed and bound up, I read it through and was rather unimpressed with it. This was an odd sensation for me, as in those days I was almost always enchanted with everything I wrote. I knew certain scenes were good, especially the breakfast scene in the last act, and the dialogue between the giggling flapper and the diplomat in the first act, but apart from these it seemed to me a little tedious. I think that the reason for this was that I was passing through a transition stage as a writer; my dialogue was becoming more natural and less elaborate, and I was beginning to concentrate more on the comedy values of situation rather than the comedy values of actual lines. I expect that, when I read through *Hay Fever* that first time, I was subconsciously bemoaning its lack of snappy epigrams. At any rate, I thought well enough of it to consider it a good vehicle for Marie Tempest, and so I took it up to London to read it to her. Both she and Willie Graham-Browne were kind and courteous as usual, and listened with careful attention, but when I had finished they both agreed with me that it was too light and plotless and generally lacking in action, and so back I went to the country again and wrote *Easy Virtue*."

Hay Fever nearly achieved production in place of *The Vortex* at the Everyman. The success of *The Vortex* soon set managers looking for other plays by Coward. While this play was running, *Fallen Angels* was produced in April 1925, and *Hay Fever* in the following June. The revue, *On with the Dance* had been written and produced in the meantime.

"*Hay Fever*," Coward says, "was suddenly taken out, dusted off and put into rehearsal at the Ambassadors Theatre." He continues:

"This all came about because Alban Limpus and Charles Kenyon wanted a play for Marie Tempest, who was no longer under her own management, but under theirs. I told them that I didn't think she would do it, as she had already turned it down once. They insisted, however, that it would be a good idea for her to read it again. This she did, and, much to my surprise, said that she was delighted with it and that I must produce it. This scared me somewhat because, although my opinion of my own talents was reasonably high, I hardly, even in my most bumptious moments, visualised myself showing Marie Tempest how to act. Nevertheless, I agreed and arrived at the first rehearsal probably more nervous than I have ever been in my life.

"Actually I needn't have worried. Moreover, I should have known that an artist as fine and experienced as Marie Tempest automatically takes direction with more graciousness and docility than a dozen small-part actresses rolled into one. She stamped her foot at me early in rehearsals and said sharply with the utmost decision: 'Come up here, Noël, and play this scene for me. You wrote it and you know it. I didn't write it, and don't!' I clambered obediently on to the stage and played the scene as well as I could, whereupon she kissed me and said: 'Excellent, my dear. You've shown me exactly where I was wrong. Let's go back.'"

Its production, after the trouble which *Fallen Angels* had incurred, ran smoothly.

Looking back upon it, Coward says, in his introduction to *Play Parade, Volume I*: "*Hay Fever* is considered by many to be my best comedy. Whether or not this assertion is true, posterity, if it gives it a glance, will be able to judge with more detachment than I. At any rate it has certainly proved to be a great joy to amateurs, owing, I suppose, to the smallness of its cast, and the fact that it has only one set, which must lead them, poor dears, to imagine that it is easy to act. This species of delusion being common to amateurs all over the world, no word of mine shall be spoken, no warning finger of experience raised, to discourage them, beyond the timorous suggestion that from the professional standpoint *Hay Fever* is far and away one of the most difficult plays to perform that I have ever encountered.

"To begin with, it has no plot at all, and remarkably little action. Its general effectiveness therefore depends upon expert technique from each and every member of the cast.

"The level of acting in the original London production, led brilliantly by Miss Marie Tempest, was extremely high; consequently, the play was a tremendous success. The press naturally and inevitably described it as "thin" "tenuous" and "trivial" because those are their stock phrases for anything later in date and lighter in texture than *The Way of the World*, and it ran, tenuously and triumphantly, for a year...

"I am very much attached to *Hay Fever*. I enjoyed writing it and producing it, and I have frequently enjoyed watching it."

The revival at the Vaudeville Theatre in 1941 was in a repertory season of English comedies, each of which was put on for one week only.

Since then, major UK productions of *Hay Fever* have included the National Theatre revival (the first prodution there to be written and directed by a living playwright) at the Old Vic, 27 October 1964 (72 performances). The production was first seen at the Opera House, Manchester, 8 October. Coward himself directed "a cast that could have played the Albanian telephone directory". This production was largely responsible for the start of the 'Noël Coward Renaissance'.

Also revived by Peter Bridge at the Duke of York's Theatre, London, 14 February 1968 (71 performances). The production was first seen at the O'Keefe Centre, Toronto, Canada in January 1968 for two weeks.

CHARACTERS	**Old Vic, 1964**
JUDITH BLISS	Edith Evans (succeeded by Celia Johnson for eight performances)
DAVID BLISS	Anthony Nichols
SOREL BLISS	Louise Purnell
SIMON BLISS	Derek Jacobi
MYRA ARUNDEL	Maggie Smith
RICHARD GREATHAM	Robert Lang
JACKIE CORYTON	Lynn Redgrave
SANDY TYRELL	Robert Stephens
CLARA	Barbara Hicks
Director	*Noël Coward*
Designer	*Motley (assisted by Peter Key)*

CHARACTERS	**Duke of York's, 1968**
JUDITH BLISS	Celia Johnson
DAVID BLISS	Roland Culver
SOREL BLISS	Lucy Fleming
SIMON BLISS	Simon Williams
MYRA ARUNDEL	Diana Fairfax
RICHARD GREATHAM	Richard Vernon
JACKIE CORYTON	Prunella Scales
SANDY TYRELL	Michael Graham Cox
CLARA	Betty Baskcomb

The play's many revivals include a tour by Phyllis Calvert in 1975, and a production by Michael Blakemore starring Constance Cummings at the Lyric Hammersmith on 23 April 1980. On 25 October 1983, a production at the Queen's Theatre starred Penelope Keith and Moray Watson. On 4 May 1988 Googie Withers starred in a Chichester revival and in August 1989 Dora Bryan commenced a UK tour at the Redgrave Theatre, Farnham. At Theatre Clwyd in October 1992, Alan Stachan directed Maria Aitken and John Standing in a revival which transferred to the Albery Theatre on 24 November 1992, and on 9 June 1999 Geraldine McEwan starred in a production at the Savoy Theatre by Declan Donnellan. On BBC Radio in July 1937, Dame Marie Tempest played her original stage role (CBS Radio first broadcast the play in America in June 1937); it was also the first of Coward's plays ever to be televised, by NBC in New York in August 1939 with Isobel Elsom in the lead. Subsequent television broadcasts of the play have included BBC, 1960 (Dame Edith Evans, Richard Wattis, George Devine, Maggie Smith, Pamela Brown); and BBC, 1968 (Celia Johnson, Denis Price, Ian McKellen, Anna Massey, Richard Briers). There have been several other radio revivals on both sides of the Atlantic, and at the time of writing (1999), plans for the first film version are being made.

US PRODUCTIONS

PRESENTED by Messrs Schubert at the Maxine Elliott Theatre, New York, 5 October 1925 (49 performances).

CHARACTERS	**Maxine Elliott, 1925**
JUDITH BLISS	Laura Hope Crews
DAVID BLISS	Harry Davenport
SOREL BLISS	Frieda Prescourt
SIMON BLISS	Gavin Muir
MYRA ARUNDEL	Phyllis Joyce
RICHARD GREATHAM	George Thorpe
JACKIE CORYTON	Margot Lester
SANDY TYRELL	Reginald Sheffield
CLARA	Alice Belmore Ceiffe

The *New York Times*: "If Mr Coward had packed his play with half the humour the actors bring to their parts, *Hay Fever* might be steadily amusing; at present, it has many colourless moments."

PRESENTED by Patterson McNuff at the Avon Theatre, New York, 29 December 1931 (95 performances).

CHARACTERS	**Avon, 1931**
JUDITH BLISS	Constance Collier
DAVID BLISS	Eric Cowley
SIMON BLISS	Betty Linley
SIMON BLISS	Anthony Kemble-Cooper
MYRA ARUNDEL	Julia Hoyt
RICHARD GREATHAM	Edward Cooper
JACKIE CORYTON	Valerie Cossart
SANDY TYRELL	Terence Neill
CLARA	Alice Belmore Cliffe
Director	*Constance Collier*

The New York Times: "It is theatrical satire, and infernally delicate and accomplished. It is dry, subtle, mettlesome comedy, and it is enormously entertaining."

PRESENTED by Leonard Sillman at the Helen Hayes Theatre, New York, 9 November 1970 (24 performances).

CHARACTERS	**Helen Hayes, 1970**
JUDITH BLISS	Shirley Booth
DAVID BLISS	John Williams
SOREL BLISS	Roberta Maxwell
MYRA ARUNDEL	Sam Waterston
RICHARD GREATHAM	Michael McGuire
JACKIE CORYTON	Carole Shelley
SANDY TYRELL	John Tillinger
CLARA	Susie Bond
Director	*Arvin Brown*

The *New York Times*: "Noël Coward's *Hay Fever* is almost a classic – which is about as good as being almost a virgin. Coward's play is brilliantly written but poorly crafted. The writing is nothing but a delight, but the play itself is too thin. It contains an idea rather than tells a story. *Hay Fever* must be high comedy if it is anything at all, and here high comedy it isn't."

PRESENTED by Roger Peters in association with MBS Co. at the Music Box Theatre, New York, 12 December 1985 (124 performances).

CHARACTERS	**Music Box, 1985**
JUDITH BLISS	Rosemary Harris
DAVID BLISS	Roy Dotrice
SOREL BLISS	Mia Dillon
SIMON BLISS	Robert Joy
MYRA ARUNDEL	Carolyn Seymour
RICHARD GREATHAM	Charles Kimbrough
JACKIE CORYTON	Deborah Rush
SANDY TYRELL	Campbell Scott
CLARA	Barbara Bryne
Director	*Brian Murray*

The *New York Times*: "In the unlikely event that you stop laughing and start thinking at the sparkling new Broadway revival of *Hay Fever*, you may notice that Noël Coward's comedy has skin-deep characters, little plot, no emotional weight or redeeming social value and very few lines that sound funny out of context. All of which goes to show that some plays defy the laws of theatrical gravity. In this now 60-year-old jape, Coward demonstrates that pure fluff also rises..."

The revival also included a new Cowardesque song ("No, My Heart") affectionately contributed by Kander & Ebb.

13
EASY VIRTUE
A PLAY IN THREE ACTS
Written in 1924

FIRST PRESENTED by Charles Frohman Inc. at the Broad Theatre, Newark, USA, 23 November 1925, and subsequently at the Empire Theatre, New York, 7 December 1925 (147 performances).

FIRST PRESENTED IN THE UK by Basil Dean as *A New Play in Three Acts* at the Opera House, Manchester, 31 May 1926, and subsequently at the Duke of York's Theatre, London, as *Easy Virtue*, 9 June 1926 (124 performances).

CHARACTERS	Broad, US, 1925
MRS WHITTAKER	Mabel Terry-Lewis
MARION	Marda Vanne
COLONEL WHITTAKER	Halliwell Hobbes
HILDA	Joan Clement Scott
FURBER	Lionel Hogarth
JOHN	Robert Harris
LARITA	Jane Cowl
SARAH HURST	Joyce Carey
CHARLES BURLEIGH	Vernon Kelso
PHILIP BORDON	Peter Carpenter
MR HARRIS	William Podmore
NINA VANSITTART	Gipsy O'Brien
HON. HUGH PETWORTH	Peter Macfarlane
BOBBY COLEMAN	C. Bailey Hick
LUCY COLEMAN	Constance Best
REV. HENRY FURLEY	Wallace Wood
MRS HURST	Grace Hampton

MRS PHILLIPS	Nancy B. Marsland
MARY BANFIELD	Marlon Evensen
ADDITIONAL GUESTS AT PARTY	Madge Whiteman, Grizelda Hervey, Marjorie Heatherington, Prudence Russell, Dene Morel, George Sloane, Joan Hill, Laurier Lister

Director	*Basil Dean*
Designer	*George W. Harris*

CHARACTERS	**Manchester and Duke of York's, 1926**
MRS WHITTAKER	Mabel Terry-Lewis
MARION	Marda Vanne
COLONEL WHITTAKER	Marcus Barron
HILDA	Clement Scott
FURBER	Claud Graham
JOHN	James Raglan
LARITA	Jane Cowl
SARAH HURST	Joyce Carey
CHARLES BURLEIGH	Vernon Kelso
PHILIP BORDON	Deering Wells
MR HARRIS	Philip Wade
NINA VANSITTART	Adrianne Allen
HON. HUGH PETWORTH	Peter Macfarlane
BOBBY COLEMAN	Humphrey Morton
LUCY COLEMAN	Diana Beaumont
REV. HENRY FURLEY	Wallace Wood
MRS HURST	Gertrude Sterroll
MRS PHILLIPS	Edith Barker-Bennet
MARY BANFIELD	Anne Hyton
ADDITIONAL GUESTS AT PARTY	Madge Whiteman, Grizelda Hervey, Marjorie Heatherington, Prudence Russell, Dene Morel, George Sloane, Joan Hill, Laurier Lister

Director	*Basil Dean*
Designer	*George W. Harris*

❖

SCENE: The action of the play takes place in the hall of Colonel Whittaker's country house in England.

ACT I: A spring morning. Before lunch.
ACT II: A summer afternoon. Three months later.
ACT III: Evening of the same day.

❖

SYNOPSIS

ACT I: Colonel and Mrs Whittaker and their elder daughter, Marion – who, after a disappointment in love, has sought consolation in exaggerated religious views – are in the hall of their country house, talking about Rose Jenkins, a servant dismissed for immorality. Mrs Whittaker has written to the girl's prospective employer, Mrs Phillips, saying that Rose ought to be sent up to London. Marion's view is that a "straight-from-the-shoulder talk" might make the girl see the error of her ways. The Colonel suggests mildly that Rose is in her own village, and that it is for her parents to decide her future – a standpoint that strikes his wife and daughter as irritating and irresponsible.

Hilda, the Whittakers' schoolgirlish younger daughter, brings in a wire from their son, John, saying that he is arriving that morning with his new wife Larita. Mrs Whittaker is exceedingly put out, but gives orders to have a bedroom and sitting-room prepared for the couple, and sends Hilda to arrange the flowers. To Marion she confides her shock and distress at the marriage of her only son to a woman they do not know. Her daughter advises her to put her trust in Divine Providence and "have a straight talk to John".

The Colonel is keeping an open mind, prepared to welcome his daughter-in-law. Hilda is frankly excited. Suddenly Marion remembers that Sarah Hurst, whom they had expected John to marry, is coming to lunch. She telephones to warn her, but Sarah only laughs and asks if she can bring a friend, Charles Burleigh, with her.

They hear a car approaching and wait in silence to receive the couple. But John comes in alone, explaining that Larita is waiting for him "to get the first joys of reunion over". Then Larita follows. She is a tall, beautiful woman, exquisitely made-up and perfectly gowned.

Mrs Whittaker greets her with cold politeness, the Colonel kindly, and Hilda with gushing enthusiasm. As they sit making conversation, it transpires that this is her second marriage, and that she has been divorced by her first husband. (He was a brute, comments John.) This confirms Mrs Whittaker's fears. When Hilda has taken Larita up to her room, the Colonel remarks to his son that she is considerably older than he had expected, but he hopes they will he happy.

Everyone has gone to get ready for lunch when Sarah and Charles appear. She is a boyish, attractive girl with a sense of humour, and he a pleasant-looking man in his thirties. They are looking forward to watching the reactions of Mrs Whittaker and Marion to their new relative.

Hilda takes Sarah off into the garden, so that Charles is alone when Larita reappears. After introducing themselves, they find that they have various mutual friends in France. By the time the others come in they are chatting happily together. Sarah is introduced to Larita and they all go in to lunch.

ACT II: It is a fine but cool summer day three months later, and most people are playing tennis; but Larita is lying on the sofa, smoking as she reads Proust's *Sodom and Gomorrah*, and throwing her cigarette-ends on the veranda. Mrs Whittaker complains of this and asks why she does not go out and watch the tennis. She herself is busy making arrangements for a dance they are giving that evening; so is Marion, who also asks why Larita is not watching the game.

When John repeats the same question, Larita is exasperated. She says the tennis court is exposed to the wind and she is already cold, and she asks John for her fur coat, which he fetches with some annoyance.

Finding her on the verge of tears, the Colonel cheers her up by playing bezique with her. She confesses that she is terribly bored with the country and feels that John is tired of her – nobody else likes her, except Sarah (Hilda's original schoolgirl passion has turned to hatred, out of jealousy). She goes upstairs with the vehement comment: "You know and I know – it's all a rotten failure."

Marion, preoccupied with Japanese lanterns for the dance, sees Larita's book, which she describes as "silly muck". This brings a reproof from her father, who advises her not to be truculent just because she has affiliated herself with the Almighty. Her mother also sees the book and tells her to take it up to Larita's room: "I don't like that kind of literature left in the hall." It is her secret hope that, once John's infatuation has cooled, it may be possible to arrange a divorce.

The tennis players come in, hot and thirsty. Hilda, slightly ahead of the others, is furious because she thinks Larita is vamping Philip Bordon – a callow youth about whom she herself feels proprietary.

Over lemonade and cigarettes the young people discuss with Mrs Whittaker the arrangements for the dance. When the others have drifted off, John and Sarah have a serious talk: she says he is neglecting Larita and suggests that he should study her wishes and give her more of his time.

John feels that he has behaved badly towards Sarah, but she assures him that she quite understands – she will certainly marry some day (not Charles

Burleigh, who is "too old"), when she finds someone to give her "thrills and glamour and passionate love-letters". Had she married John, it would only have been for friendship and convenience. John then blurts out that he still loves her; at which she flares up, calling him a cad and saying he is not fit to black Larita's boots.

This last remark is overheard by Larita; but Sarah turns it off lightly, saying that she and John have been squabbling about tennis.

When Hilda and Philip come in, John wants to return with them to the tennis court, but, at a hint from Sarah, he stays behind with his wife.

He apologises for neglecting her, and she quickly realises that Sarah has put the idea into his head. She asks him to go back abroad, and when he refuses she loses her temper and explains how miserable and out of place she feels in this country-house environment. They have a lengthy quarrel, but finally they make it up and she sends him back to his tennis with a kiss.

Then Marion comes in, wanting a talk with her. This resolves itself into the advice not to encourage Colonel Whittaker, who has been "a bit of a dog in his day". It ends with Larita calling Marion a disloyal hypocrite and sending her off in a rage.

Philip comes in, eager to book a couple of dances with Larita. Starting to pay her compliments, he is disconcerted by her ironical attitude. She turns to go, but he catches hold of her hand to retain her, and Hilda enters just in time to see this. An unpleasant scene is temporarily averted by the appearance of Mrs Whittaker; then the tennis players come in, and finally Marion and the Colonel. But when the visitors, Sarah and Philip, have gone home, Hilda, beside herself with fury, triumphantly produces a newspaper cutting as proof of Larita's moral turpitude. It is the report of a suicide case, 15 years before, in which she was involved as a witness and held responsible for the tragedy. "Does John know about this?" asks Marion.

At this point the local handyman, Mr Harris, comes to ask for instructions about hanging the Japanese lanterns and fairy lights for the ball. Marion and her mother are too much upset to deal with the matter, but Larita and the Colonel quite calmly give the necessary orders.

Then the discussion is resumed. The Colonel, who has torn the cutting up after reading it, apologises to Larita for the scene and suggests that she should be allowed to explain. She says quietly that the newspaper reports were exaggerated, and that the man's own weakness and cowardice, not her behaviour, brought about his death. It all happened so long ago that she did not think it necessary to tell John about it.

Defending herself with spirit, she says that the Colonel is the only one of them all who has kept a true sense of values, uncluttered by hysterical moral codes and false sentiments. When Marion sneers, Larita reveals, in front of Mrs Whittaker, the tenor of their previous quarrel and Marion's insinuations against her father. Marion's mind, she says, is a morass of inhibitions, because she has placed physical purity too high and mental purity not high enough.

After Marion has stalked out, slamming the door, Mrs Whittaker requests that Larita go up to her room and remain there during the dance. She and the Colonel go out, and Hilda hysterically begs Larita's pardon, saying she "didn't mean it". Larita tells her not to be a little toad, but to have the courage of her convictions, and Hilda runs out in tears.

Left alone, Larita settles on the sofa and tries to read her book; then she relieves her feelings by hurling it at a statuette of the Venus de Milo. "I've always hated that damned thing!" she remarks as it smashes. The curtain falls, and rises momentarily to show her lying with her face buried in the sofa cushions. Her shoulders are heaving, "whether with laughter or tears it is difficult to say".

ACT III: The dance is in full swing, and the hall has been adapted as a sitting-out place, with the buffet on the veranda, just out of sight. Clustered round it is a group of young people; others are scattered about the hall. Two of them, Nina Vansittart and the Hon. Hugh Petworth, are chatting on the sofa. Another, Bobby Coleman, takes Nina off to dance; then Hilda exchanges a few words with Hugh. He goes to look for his next partner and Hilda sees Philip, who is looking unhappily for Larita. She tells him that her sister-in-law is upstairs with a bad headache, and they go off to dance together.

Then Charles and Sarah come out: Sarah also has been told the "headache" story and disbelieves it. She is worried, because she has tried to slip upstairs and talk to Larita, but has been headed off by Mrs Whittaker. John, she feels, is making his wife very unhappy by his obtuseness, and he has shrunk considerably in her own estimation.

Charles takes his cue to propose to her, half seriously, but she good-naturedly turns him down, and they go off together to the buffet.

Marion enters with her partner, Henry Furley, who goes to fetch her a drink. Then Mrs Whittaker comes out with Sarah's mother, Mrs Hurst, who wants to slip off early, leaving her daughter and friends to follow. Mrs Phillips (to whom Mrs Whittaker has written about the errant servant, Rose Jenkins), inquires after Larita and is told about the headache.

The group is joined by Charles and Sarah, Marion and Henry Furley and John with his partner, Mary Banfield. Just as Mrs Whittaker is explaining that her daughter-in-law is too ill to see anyone, Larita herself appears at the top of the stairs – strikingly dressed in a low-cut white gown, glittering with jewellery, and carrying a scarlet ostrich-feather fan.

Her entrance is sensational. She demolishes Mrs Whittaker's polite fiction about her headache; sends her bewildered husband (who has not been told about the family row) to fetch her a drink and a sandwich, and pointedly insults Mrs Phillips by hoping that Rose Jenkins has done well "in the profession you've sent her to".

When John reproves her for wearing too much jewellery, she is so flippant that he slams off in a rage. Philip Bordon claims his belated dance with her, leaving Sarah and Charles to discuss her strange behaviour. Opining that it is a "swan-song", Charles takes Sarah off to dance.

Mrs Whittaker and her two daughters have an agitated conference, but cannot decide what to do. It is a relief to them all when supper is announced. John tries to find out from Sarah what is the matter with Larita, but she tactfully evades the question and asks him to escort her to supper.

Returning from the dance-room, Larita sends her partner to have supper with Hilda; then she has a chat with Charles – the only person who "talks her language". She confesses that marrying John was the most cowardly thing she ever did: "He falls short of every ideal I ever had."

When Charles asks what she intends to do, she says she hasn't yet decided, and asks him to send Sarah to her. Meanwhile, she refuses young Hugh Petworth's invitation to dance, suggesting shrewdly that he has only asked her in order to win a bet.

To Sarah she says that she is going away that very night – and for good, hinting at the scene that has taken place. (Sarah had already been shown the newspaper cutting, and had emphatically told Hilda not to make use of it.) Larita then asks her to look after John, implying her hope that they will one day marry.

John himself then comes to apologise for making a fuss about her jewellery (which she says she put on "as a gay gesture"). She kisses him good night and watches as Sarah takes him back to the dance-room.

Then the manservant Furber comes to tell her that the car is ready. She sends him to fetch her cloak, and for a while stands looking out into the garden "with an expression of hopeless sadness". Then she says goodbye to Furber and walks out, amid the laughter and music from the dance.

The *New York Times*, 8 December 1925, on the American production:
"At the close of the second act of Mr Coward's third play for the season, *Easy Virtue*, put on last evening at the Empire, Larita, the lady so impertinently

described in the title, knocked a little statue of Venus from the table, across the stage to the footlights, where it rolled around in fragments. Coming at the close of a bitter scene of metaphorical hair-pulling, with Jane Cowl retaining what dignity the occasion afforded, it made an effective curtain, and at length proved to be the climax of the play. For the curtain of the close of the first act had dropped tamely on a domestic scene, and the final curtain represented merely the conclusion of a spotty play.

"In many respects that second-act gesture represented also the technique of Mr Coward's plays, as *The Vortex* and *Hay Fever* have previously suggested: a group of modernistic English folk in the midst of the trivialities of their life; smart talk and piercing retorts; tedious debates; and a quick, theatrical gesture or two for condiment. And although the result may provide the 'thrills' of which the ecstatic flapper speaks in the current play, it leaves many bare spots in the evening. On Sunday evening, Sir Benjamin Backbite, in an older piece, described the result more adroitly as 'a rivulet of text meandering through a meadow of margin' – or in words to that effect.

"Mr Coward knows the people of whom he is writing, and with unerring precision goes to the source of their various weaknesses. *Easy Virtue*, a sort of *Second Mrs Tanqueray* brought down to date, collects a fair assortment of these folk. On the one hand, he represents the strict, moralistic, tight-lipped English society immersed in its own round of conventionalities, and suspicious of anything else. Mrs Whittaker, with her genius for organisation, and her mannish daughter, Marion, who regards sex as 'tosh' with broadminded smugness, represent the Puritanical decline, somehow 'affiliated with God' as Colonel Whittaker describes them. On the other hand, the brilliant Larita, from several French watering-places, who takes pride in never having an affair with a man she does not love, represents in her fashion the decline of the cavalier tradition, devoted to love. When young John Whittaker takes her for his wedded wife, forever more to hold his peace, Mr Coward brings these two forces together. And there comes a flash.

"In fact, it seems to be a flash rather than a play. In spite of the numerous flickers of light that decorate the text frequently throughout three acts, and in spite of Miss Cowl's beauty and deep-bitten playing. In spite of the fact, moreover, that Mr Coward's piece frequently makes conventionality, prejudice and complacence look as ridiculous as they do in the more penetrating plays of George Bernard Shaw. For this purpose, Mrs Whittaker serves admirably, with her strong sense of responsibility, the simplicity of her code of ethics, and the negative quality of her sense of humour. Miss Lewis articulates these characteristics in an angular composition of acting, as admirable for what it has sifted out as for what it has retained.

"Perhaps Marion Whittaker serves the purpose of ridicule even better. For in that part Miss Vanne does a capital bit of acting just this side of caricature. Thus represented, Marion emerges as mannish and efficient with a preoccupation with health and sanitation that seems almost frantic beneath the impassivity of its exterior. Here is a modern young woman whose ostentatious strength of character, with its pride in cosmic understandings, is merely a leering mask for the timidity hidden beneath. During the bravura moment in the second act, already described, Larita in a passion sums up Marion's entire stock in the world's trade as with a case from the text of Freud. It is a telling scene, exposing Marion's inhibitions, whilst Larita is releasing several of her own more obvious repressions.

"The fireworks, the sympathy, the truth, such as it is, are confined to the part of Larita, who follows the convention of modern women by marrying her inferior. And under the spell of Miss Cowl's acting this young person with a broad and generous past commands more than her share of admiration. If Miss Cowl appears to truckle to her audience once or twice, with a confidence intended for those who are not in the play, the part is written in that vein and presupposes a dramatic virtue 'easy' in its own peculiar way. At her first entrance, Miss Cowl is radiant. Her last entrance in the third act is based entirely upon histrionic and personal radiance; and Miss Cowl carries it off magnificently. For this moment is another gesture of defiance, when the painted lady, defeated by the hostility of her husband's family, invades the Whittakers' astringent supper-dance for the neighbours, dressed in a resplendent evening gown and all the jewellery she ever owned. There is a surface lustre about this entrance. But there is a suggestion of humility and compassion about Miss Cowl's acting that rounds out her conception of the part.

"As Colonel Whittaker, Mr Hobbes seems more benevolent than the sting of his lines warrants. Miss Clement Scott makes an ecstatic or sullen flapper, according to the direction of the part. Miss Carey makes a womanly Sarah Hurst of spirit and understanding. Mr Kelso puts warmth into the rather casual part of Charles Burleigh. The play is equipped with the usual bric-a-brac of tennis flannels, pastel sweaters, lemon squash, ginger beer, evening clothes, white gloves, and guests at the evening party."

James Agate in the *Sunday Times*, 13 June 1926, on the UK production:
"The higher the brow the narrower the mind. That is if one is a fashionable young playwright familiar with the tawdry round of the Riviera and unable to conceive a world elsewhere. Give your aesthete a horse he can't ride –

and farewell, Leicestershire! We all remember the playwright's definition of the hunting squire as 'the unspeakable in pursuit of the uneatable'. But might not the modern vixen be described with equal justice as the uneatable in pursuit of the unspeakable? Is not the exotic young woman who on a fine summer morning mews herself up with Proust's novel of the unmentionable title just as ridiculous as the cross-country gentleman who should talk horse at the Russian Ballet? At the most the *plage* at Deauville and the Casino at 'Monte' do not exceed half the world. The Cotswolds and the Mendips exist, and not to know what to make of them is to be as unsmart as to turn up at Ascot in knickerbockers.

"Mr Noël Coward gets younger with every play, and in *Easy Virtue* has attained to that pure idealism which prompts the schoolboy who has been taken to see *La Dame aux Camélias* to believe for the next ten years that a cocotte is the noblest work of man if not of God. Larita, his heroine, 'lives emotionally' which means that for such hours as the sun shines she is a bore to herself and a nuisance to everybody else. John Whittaker, his hero, is, to borrow from another of this author's plays, 'a hearty young thing in flannels'. To play cricket for your school or university is to earn the contempt of Mr Coward's modish world; that folly goes unchastened which marries an adventuress out of hand without inquiring as to the number of previous husbands or means of existence between marriages. Sir Arthur Pinero made you feel that Aubrey Tanqueray's mistake was not so much in marrying Paula as in condemning her to live 40 miles out of London. It was the woman who was 'wrong' – and not the country, whereas Mr Coward would have it the other way about.

"At first it looked as though he was going to write his best play. John's family was well drawn. The mother was a little narrow-minded, perhaps, a little intolerant of lapses from virtue on the part of servant-girls, and not unnaturally prejudiced against daughters-in-law arriving without credentials from nowhere in particular. Yet Mrs Whittaker was recognisably a woman of breeding, bred in this country and no other. The father was English also – English as Mr Bennett, tolerant to the point of laxity, yet, unlike Jane Austen's paterfamilias, something inclined to be put upon. The sisters, too, were well done – the strong-minded elder keen upon social service with opinions cropped as her hair, and the boisterous younger a healthy pickle. The stir antecedent to the arrival of the unhappy pair, the embarrassed welcome, the lady's corona of unsuitability, the ease with which she cottoned to some stray detrimental – all these things suggested that Mr Coward was going to see both sides of his case.

"Unfortunately, as soon as the play began to move it went to pieces. Larita remained true to type. She was as bored as a town mouse who goes to stay with a country cousin, and behaved after the normal fashion of little ladies who are not amused. It was the family which became improbable. The elder sister accused Larita of trying to seduce her father; the younger hunted up old newspaper files till she found the record of Larita's past, which she promptly produced at the tea-table; the mother ordered her daughter-in-law to her bedroom. One didn't believe that these things could happen. But the theatre is the theatre, and Larita's natural indignation and the means she took to pay off these new and unheard – of scores aroused the natural Adam in every spectator. The offended lady, bedizened to outvie the Queen of Sheba, descending from her imprisonment first to stagger a county with a greater show of jewels than comports with married life and then to rout it with a courtesan's insolence, aroused sympathy and the fighting instinct in every member of the audience. The two scenes of gathering exasperation and subsequent explosion had been very well contrived, and in Larita we recognised a first-class disciple of that school which enjoins that at least half a dozen perfectly explicit Rolands shall be returned for every half-hinted Oliver. The piece excited even to the point of making us believe that by taking her hook for Paris and the sunnier and more expensive continental spas Larita showed herself a more admirable creature than the average young Englishwoman who on a wet day puts on thick boots and a mackintosh and tramps the country lanes. It was not till we got home that we reflected that a light and wandering lady is, God help us, a thing of naught.

"Miss Jane Cowl received a tremendous ovation after the second act and again at the end of the play. It is a foolish thing to declare any actress first-class on the strength of a single part or performance. But if Miss Cowl can play anything else – and her Juliet has won renown – then she is a very fine artist indeed. She has no devastating prettiness; her features are a battleground for the emotions rather than a lawn for garden-party simpering. She has, as Byron puts it, 'a velvet brow, with two pitch-balls stuck in her face for eyes', and her countenance not only betrays past storms, but foretells those to come. This actress has poise, and pace, and she delivers the second-act tirade as such things ought to be delivered, while her sullens at the end are magnificent. Miss Cowl acts with her whole body, and her gestures are expressive enough to convey meaning to anybody who should know no English. She has that style which is almost a physical quality, understanding, and temperament. Finally, she possesses what the French call *le 'la' du rôle*. Miss Mabel Terry-Lewis played the English châtelaine with as much delicacy and discrimination as her author would let her, and perhaps only those who remembered Miss Marda Vanne as the ineffectual wife of the missionary in *Rain* realised how much acting was contained in her firm portrait of the cropped zealot. As to this character, I must be permitted another word. 'There are moments, are there not, when one doesn't think of girls?' Mr Beerbohm made Mr George Moore say in his pastiche. But there are no moments, apparently, in which Mr Coward, the playwright, refrains from thinking in terms of sex, and to attribute Marion's proselytism to repressed desire seems to me to be just nonsense. Larita's taunts about concealed pruriency should be deleted, the implication being that they are true and not charges made by a woman in a temper. Mr Marcus Barron's Whittaker *père* was particularly good. And now, please, may we see Miss Cowl in something else?"

PUBLICATIONS

Easy Virtue was first published in America by Harper Brothers (New York, 1926) and in Britain in the *Contemporary British Dramatists* series, Volume 26, Ernest Benn (London, May 1926). It was undedicated, though when it was included in *Play Parade II*, Heinemann (London, 1950), it was dedicated to Basil Dean. Also published in *Noël Coward Collected Plays: One*, Methuen World Classics (London, 1999).

NOTES

Easy Virtue was written immediately after *Hay Fever* in the autumn of 1924. Coward, in his introduction to *Play Parade, Volume II*, says:

"From the eighties onwards until the outbreak of the 1914-18 War, the London theatre was enriched by a series of plays, notably by Somerset Maugham or Arthur Pinero, which were described as 'drawing-room dramas'. I suppose that the apotheosis of these was *The Second Mrs Tanqueray*, but there were many others; *Mid-Channel*, *Lady Frederick*, *The Notorious Mrs Ebbsmith*, *His House in Order*, *Jack Straw*, *The Tenth Man*, *Smith*, etc., etc. There were also the more specialised Oscar Wilde comedy-dramas and the too infrequent, beautifully constructed plays of Haddon Chambers.

"All of these 'drawing-room dramas' dealt with the psychological and social problems of the upper-middle classes. The characters in them were, as a general rule, wealthy, well-bred, articulate and motivated by the exigencies of the world to which they belonged. This world was snobbish, conventional, polite and limited by its own codes and rules of behaviour, and it was the contravention of these codes and rules – to our eyes so foolish and old-fashioned – that supplied the dramatic content of most of the plays that I have mentioned. The heroine of *His House in Order* rebelled against the narrow pomposities of the family into which she had married. Lady Frederick, by gallantly and daringly exposing the secrets of her dressing-table, deflected the attentions of a young man who was infatuated by her into a more suitable alliance. In a recent revival of the play, this scene still proved to be dramatically impeccable. The unhappy Paula Tanqueray tried valiantly to live down her earlier moral turpitude, but ultimately gave up the struggle and perished off-stage in an aura of righteous atonement just before the final curtain. It is easy nowadays to laugh at these vanished moral attitudes, but they were poignant enough in their time because they were true. Those high-toned drawing-room histrionics are over and done with. Women with pasts today receive far more enthusiastic social recognition than women without pasts. The narrow-mindedness, the moral righteousness, and the over-rigid social codes have disappeared, but with them has gone much that was graceful, well-behaved and endearing. It was in a mood of nostalgic regret at the decline of such conventions that I wrote *Easy Virtue*. When it was produced, several critics triumphantly pounced on the fact that the play was similar in form and tone and plot to the plays of Pinero. I myself was unimpressed by their perception, for the form and tone and plot of a Pinero play was exactly what I had tried to achieve. *Easy Virtue* was played by Jane Cowl both in New York and London, and, being an expert actress with great personality and charm, she swept the play into success in both countries."

This was the first play of Coward to receive its world premiere in America. With the success of *The Vortex*, several offers were made for the production of this play in New York. It was finally settled that Basil Dean should take over the play for presentation in New York, together with *Easy Virtue* and *The Queen Was in the Parlour*. Coward left the London cast of *The Vortex* and sailed for New York in August 1925. After the successful production of that play there in September, he produced *Hay Fever* in October, and rehearsals commenced for *Easy Virtue*, which, after a preliminary out-of-town try-out, arrived on Broadway in the December.

After the New York run of *The Vortex*, Coward toured America with the play. The tour finished at Cleveland, and he says:

"I don't ever remember feeling so relieved and happy as I felt on that last night. I had played the part over four hundred and fifty times, and although during the tour I had forced myself to write a play (*Semi-Monde*, see page 140), it had been a tremendous strain, and I felt that many months of creative impulse had been frustrated."

After *Easy Virtue* finished its run in New York, it came to England with practically the same company. The play opened in Manchester. Coward says: "The Manchester Watch Committee, for some strange reason known only to itself, refused to allow us to use the title *Easy Virtue*, and so it was announced merely as *A New Play in Three Acts*. At the cinema next door to the theatre a film entitled *Flames of Passion* was complacently advertised for the whole week: perhaps, however, the vigilance of the Watch Committee did not extend to mere celluloid." On its production in London the original title was restored.

Since 1926, there have been several professional revivals. The play was produced at Richmond Theatre 14 September 1953 with Vanda Godsell, and on 13 January 1988 at The King's Head Theatre in Islington with a cast headed by Jane How and Avril Angers under the direction of Tim Luscombe. This transferred to the Garrick Theatre on 21 April 1988 when Zena Walker replaced Avril Angers.

The *Daily Mail*: "A deadly and radical assault on all the deep-seated prejudices and smug moral certainties with which the middle-class have defended themselves against anything they fail to understand."

In July 1999, Maria Aitken directed a second major revival for the Festival Theatre, Chichester. It starred Greta Scacchi, Wendy Craig, Michael Jayston and Jenny Quayle.

FILM VERSION

A silent film version of *Easy Virtue* was made in the UK by Michael Balcon for Gainsborough Pictures in 1927. It was directed by Alfred Hitchcock, and adapted for the screen by Eliot Stannard.

CHARACTERS	**Gainsborough Pictures, 1927**
MRS WHITTAKER	Violet Farebrother
MARION	Dacia Deane
COLONEL WHITTAKER	Frank Elliot
HILDA	Dorothy Boyd
JOHN	Robert Irvine
LARITA FITTON	Isabel Jeans
HER HUSBAND	Franklyn Dyall
SARAH HURST	Enid Stamp-Taylor
THE CO-RESPONDENT	Eric Bransby-Williams
PLAINTIFF'S COUNSEL	Ian Hunter

The film was first shown in London at the Stoll, March 1928.

14
ON WITH THE DANCE
REVUE
Written in 1924 and 1925

FIRST PRESENTED by Charles B. Cochran at the Palace, Manchester, 17 March 1925 (ran till 11 April).

SUBSEQUENTLY PRESENTED at the London Pavilion, 30 April 1925 (229 performances).

Book and lyrics by Noël Coward. Music by Philip Braham and Noël Coward. Staged by Frank Collins. 'The Rake' and 'Crescendo' ballets and 'Hungarian Wedding' produced by Leonide Massine. Other dances and ensembles by Max Rivers. Orchestra under the direction of J. B. Hastings.

PART I

Scene 1, Café de la Paix, Paris

Scene design	*Gustavo Bacarisas*
GUIDE	Ernest Thesiger
FIRST ENGLISHMAN	Richard Dolman
SECOND ENGLISHMAN	Nigel Bruce
FIRST ENGLISH GIRL	Greta Fayne
SECOND ENGLISH GIRL	Jessie Taylor
FRENCHWOMAN	Violet Gould
FRENCHMAN	Ernest Lindsay
MR HAMMAKER	Harry Baker
MRS HAMMAKER	Betty Shale
HARRY	Emmott Baker
IRMA	Joan Nurick
A FLOWER-GIRL	Hermione Baddeley
MRS HUBBARD	Douglas Byng
ADA	Dolly Nepean
VIOLET	Helen Gardom
REGGIE	Richard Dolman
FREDA	Dorothea Varda
JAMES	Nigel Bruce
A WOULD-BE SUICIDE	Lance Lister

A COMMISSIONAIRE	Fred Winn
A COSMOPOLITAN LADY	Alice Delysia
THE PUPILS	Greta Beronius, Nora Lorri More, Decilia Mobray, Vera Bryer, Terri Storri, Rita Robinson, Hettie Steer, Florence Desmond, Thalia Barberova, Nancy Barnett, Averil Haley, Peggy Heather
HER ADMIRER	Ernest Thesiger
VISITORS, WAITERS, STREET-HAWKERS, ETC.	

Song: "Cosmopolitan Lady"   Alice Delysia

Scene 2, So In Love
Pat and Terry Kendall

Scene 3, The Club (Marc Henri)

Scenes and costume design   *Doris Zinkeisen, after Toulouse-Lautrec.*

Empire Theatre, 1890

CECIL	Lance Lister
WAITER	Douglas Byng
SIR HENRY PENNYFACE	Nigel Bruce

Gaiety Theatre, 1888

Song: "Georgie"	Chateau and Albertino
VANONI	Alice Delysia

Dances:

Pas de Quatre, Meyer Lutz	Greta Beronius, Vera Bryer, Thalia Barberova, Terri Storri

Moulin Rouge, 1888-90
Quadrille (Offenbach)

LA GOULUE	Amelia Allen
GRILLE D'EGOUT	Joesphine Head
CASQUE D'OR	Pat Kendall
LA MÉLINITE	Lauri Devine
VALENTIN LE DÉSOSSÉ	Terry Kendall

Scene 4, Oranges And Lemons

Scene design   *G. E. Calthrop*

GRACE HUBBARD	Douglas Byng
VIOLET BANKS	Ernest Thesiger

STEPHEN HARRI	Nigel Bruce
CHARLIE FRENCH	Lance Lister

Scene 5, On With The Dance

Costume design	*Doris Zinkeisen*
THE HUSSARS	Decilia Mobray, Nancy Barnett, Peggy Heather, Thalia Barberova
DANSE ECCENTRIQUE	Florence Desmond
THE FAUN	Terri Storri
VALSE MODERNE	Greta Beronius
OLD MOSCOW	Vera Bryer
THE CHARLESTON	Hettie Steer, Florence Desmond, Peggy Heather, Rita Robinson, Terri Storri, Decilia Mobray, Nora Lorrimore, Greta Beronius, Averil Haley, Thalia Barberova, Vera Bryer, Nancy Barnett

Scene 6, Poor Little Rich Girl

FAY (the poor little rich girl)	Hermione Baddeley
LOUISE (her maid)	Alice Delysia
CLARE (her friend)	Helen Gardom
FRED (her friend)	Lance Lister
FREDA (her friend)	Joan Nurick
HARRY (her friend)	Nigel Bruce
GEORGIE (her friend)	Donald Neville

Scene 7, 3 a.m.
Percy Val

Scene 8, The Rake (A Hogarth impression)

Choreography	*Léonide Massine*
Music	*Roger Quilter*
Costume design and stage scenery	*William Nicholson*
Masks	*Betty Muntz*

Massine has taken a number of Hogarth's characters – symbolic and realistic. William Nicholson has given them a characteristic environment for a Hogarthian orgy.

The Rake lolls drunkenly in a chair while his wanton companions disport around him. The black Cupid is busy with bow and arrows, plumbing the hearts of his victims; and the worship of women and wine whips itself up into a passionate whirl. And while the revellers seek their pleasure, the sages are rapt in contemplation of their globe, and a window frames the faces of a curious crowd, who see, and are silent.

FIRST DANCER	Greta Fayne
SECOND DANCER	Greta Beronius
THIRD DANCER	Florence Desmond
POSTURE WOMAN	Betty Oliver
CORSET WOMAN	Eleanora Marra
FIRST FAT WOMAN	Betty Shale
SECOND FAT WOMAN	Violet Gould
THE RAKE	Terry Kendall
MUSICIANS:	
THE DOG	Jessie Taylor
THE BULL	Joan Nurick
THE CAT	Ernest Lindsay
THE COCK	Billy Reynolds
THE WOMAN WITH THE BOUND HAIR	Amelia Allen
THE THIN MAN	Richard Dolman
THE BEAU	Leonide Massine
MAN DANCER	Jean Perrie
BOOT MAN	Donald Neville
GIANT	Kenneth Henry
GLOBE MAN	Fred Wallace
MAN WITH COMPASS	Fred Winn
CUPID	Arthur Howe
BLACK WOMAN	Emma Williams

Dances:

Trio	Greta Fayne, Greta Beronius and Leonide Massine
Solo	Eleanora Marra
Duo	Eleanora Marra and Leonide Massine
Entrance of Grotesques	Donald Neville, Kenneth Henry and Amelia Allen

Scene 9, An Episode

THE MAN	Albert Zapp
THE GIRLS	Josephine Head and Lauri Devine
THE VIOLINIST	Enid Hudson

Scene 10, First Love

Scene design	*G.E. Calthrop*
EFFIE	Hermione Baddeley
RUPERT	Lance Lister
MADEMOISELLE	Alice Delysia

Scene 11, Couldn't We Keep On Dancing? (Braham)

Dolly Nepean, Richard Dolman and Greta Beronius, Vera Bryer, Hettie Steer, Nancy Barnett, Nora Lorrimore, Terri Storri, Florence Desmond, Averil Haley, Decilia Mobray, Rita Robinson, Thalia Barberova, Peggy Heather

Scene 12, On With The Dance (Marc Henri)

Costume design for Amelia Allen, Greta Fayne and Laurie Devine	*Doris Zinkeisen*

Dances:

One	Greta Fayne
Two	Vera Bryer, Florence Desmond, Terri Storri, Decilia Mobray, Nancy Barnett, Thalia Barberova, Douglas Byng, Billy Reynolds, Kenneth Henry, Fred Wallace, Donald Neville, Jean Perrie
Three	Pat and Terry Kendall
Four	Lauri Devine
Five	Josephine Head and Albert Zapp
Six	Amelia Allen
Seven	Alice Delysia and the Sterling Saxophone Four
Finale	Entire Company

PART II

Scene 13, Soldier Boys

Max Rivers and the Trocadero Four

Scene 14, Fête Galante, A Vicarage Garden Party (Marc Henri)

Introduction	Nigel Bruce
THE SCOUTMASTER	Ernest Lindsay
THE SPINSTERS	Helen Gardom, Jessie Taylor, Florence

	Desmond, Violet Gould
FIRST GIRL	Vera Bryer
SECOND GIRL	Dolly Nepean
THIRD GIRL	Kate Strudwick
NELLIE	Hermione Baddeley
CHOIRBOYS	Louie Bermon, Victor Tunwell, Herbert Richards, Walter Gore, Jimmy Gilbert, Tom Hilary
THE VICAR	Douglas Byng
THE CURATE	Ernest Thesiger
THE VICAR'S WIFE	Betty Shale

Musical Numbers (Coward and Braham)

Opening chorus	The Scoutmaster and Company
Quartette	The Spinsters
Song, "The Vicarage Dance"	Nellie and Company
Sextet	The Choirboys
Duet, "Even Clergymen Are Naughty Now And Then"	Vicar and Curate
Finale, "Church Parade"	The Vicar's Wife and Entire Company

Scene 15, Come A Little Closer (Braham)

Greta Fayne and Richard Dolman

Scene 16, Class

| *Scene design* | *G. E. Calthrop* |
| Introduction | Ernest Thesiger |

(a) ALF HIGGINS	Lance Lister
ADA (his wife)	Helen Gardom
MR HIGGINS	Nigel Bruce
MRS HIGGINS	Violet Gould
MAUDE	Hermione Baddeley

(b) ALFRED HIGGINS	Lance Lister
ADA HIGGINS (his wife)	Helen Gardom
SIR HERBERT HIGGINS, BART.	Nigel Bruce
LADY HIGGINS	Violet Gould
A BUTLER	Ernest Lindsay
A FOOTMAN	Jean Perrie

MAUDE	Hermione Baddeley

Scene 17, That Means Nothing To Me (Worton David and Godfrey)

Alice Delysia

Scene 18, Crescendo (A modern ballet)

Choreography	*Léonide Massine*
Scene and costume design	*G.E. Calthrop*

In an age when the romance of machinery is superseding the lilies and languors of Victorianism, art must of necessity reflect the angular tendencies of the time. Man becomes a puppet, and beauty a slave to the new forms of the relentless progress of civilisation. *Crescendo* is an attempt to portray the transition from the ethereal to the material: the gentle tranquillity of Les Sylphides is rudely shattered by the insistent clamour of modernity, contemporary types push aside the dim memories of yesterday, Massine as the spirit of the age dominates the scene, and his puppets jig to the tune of cocktails and jazz, until, willy-nilly, they are swept up to a frenzied climax of impressionistic movement.

SYLPHIDES	Noranna, Greta Beronius, Betty Oliver
ROMANTIC BOY	Jean Perrie
THE FILM STAR	Alice Delysia
MANNEQUIN	Pat Kendall
PERFUME GIRL	Amelia Allen
STENOGRAPHER	Josephine Head
MANICURE GIRL	Eleanora Marra
THE BOYISH GIRL	Lauri Devine
THE DUKE	Nigel Bruce
THE DUCHESS	Violet Gould
THE PINK SHIRT BOY	Dorothea Varda
THE GOLF BOY	Donald Neville
NIFTY NUTS	Richard Dolman, Terry Kendall, Kenneth Henry
BOBO	Léonide Massine
CHAUFFEURS	Jean Perrie, Fred Wallace

Dances:

Quartette	Greta Beronius, Noranna, Betty Oliver, Jean Perrie
Solo	Leonide Massine

"Three Nifty Nuts"	Richard Dolman, Terry Kendall and Kenneth Henry
Sextet	Pat Kendall, Amelia Allen, Léonide Massine, Josephine Head, Lauri Devine, Eleanora Marra
Sextet	Pat Kendall, Josephine Head, Eleanora Marra, Richard Dolman, Terry Kendall, Kenneth Henry
The Automobile Age	Léonide Massine and Ensemble

Scene 19

The Sterling Saxophone Four

Scene 20, Travelling Light (John Bull)

A YOUNG WOMAN	Alice Delysia
A YOUNG MAN	Nigel Bruce
AN ATTENDANT	Ernest Thesiger

Scene 21, The Serpent

| *Costume design* | *Doris Zinkeisen* |

Amelia Allen

Scene 22, A Hungarian Wedding

| *Scene and costume design* | *Geza Farago* |

Imre Magyari and Tzigane Orchestra

THE BRIDE	Greta Fayne
THE BRIDEGROOM	Terry Kendall
THE BEST MAN	Jean Perrie
THE CHIEF BRIDESMAID	Pat Kendall
THE GROOM'S MAN	Kenneth Henry
THE SECOND BRIDESMAID	Helen Gardom
THE MAID OF HONOUR	Jessie Taylor
SERVING MEN	Fred Wallace, Billy Reynolds
THE HOST	Nigel Bruce
THE HOSTESS	Alice Delysia
THE "CONGRATULATING" BOYS	Douglas Byng, Ernest Lindsay
LITTLE GIRLS	Joan Nurick, Averil Haley

LITTLE BOYS	Louie Bernon, Walter Gore
HORSE BOYS	Betty Oliver, Greta Beronius, Hettie Steer, Terri Storri, Peggy Heather, Nancy Barnett
PEASANT GIRLS	Vera Bryer, Nora Lorrimore, Florence Desmond, Decilia Mobray, Rita Robinson, Thalia Barberova
THE HIGHWAYMAN	Léonide Massine
GIPSY GIRL	Eleanora Marra
Finale	Entire Company
Song: "Hungarian Song" (Anderson and Bela)	Alice Delysia

In Manchester the running order was slightly different from that finally presented in London. Scene 7 was 'More Dancing – Max Rivers', for which '3 a.m. – Percy Val' was substituted in London; and Scene 13 was a ballet, 'A Porcelain Idyll', conceived and designed by Stowitts and staged from his directions.

A PORCELAIN MAIDEN	Toshiko
A PORCELAIN KNIGHT	Ashida

In London a dance, 'Soldier Boys' – Max Rivers and the Trocadero Four – was substituted for this.

Also before London there were minor alterations to some of the items and rearrangements of casting. Joan Clarkson also left the cast.

The song, "Poor Little Rich Girl", was given a new presentation in London. In Manchester it was performed by:

A POLICEMAN	Fred Wallace
JIM	Fred Winn
A WOMAN	Betty Shale
DAISY	Alice Delysia
THE MAN	Nigel Bruce
THE POOR LITTLE RICH GIRL	Hermione Baddeley

❖

The *Morning Post*, 1 May 1925:

"Mr Charles Cochran's new revue is at once the most decadent and most brilliant thing he has ever done. The whole thing is more than modern, bizarre, grotesque, fantastic, unnatural. The speed of the change from scene to scene, of the performance of each number, is feverish, burlesquing the speed of our overheated life. At times the players seemed mad, intoxicated with the desire to force their bodies to do something faster, faster.

"As befits Mr Coward's genius, many of the incidents are as nature seen through a glass crookedly, and when we see some normal little typical revue duet-dance face to face, it seems positively dull – an effort to restore the company to a state of mental balance. Those arid, futile people that Mr Coward puts into his plays dash about the stage, worked into a frenzy by the syncopated music.

"M. Massine, who produced the two amazing ballets, 'The Rake', suggested by engravings of Hogarth, and 'Crescendo', an attempt to 'shatter the gentle tranquillity of Les Sylphides by the insistent clamour of modernity' – both left one gasping – danced brilliantly. His resource is magnificent, his multiplicity of movement astonishing, his accuracy marvellous. But all, of course, bizarre, preposterous, in so much that the beautiful stately 'Hungarian Wedding' with which the revue ended almost perished because the contrast was too great. The number at the end of the first part, 'Couldn't We Keep On Dancing?' should be taken as the finale.

"One was astonished to find oneself laughing at the sight of Mr Ernest Thesiger and Mr Douglas Byng, dressed as middle-aged women, disrobing in a bedroom. Or that fragment in the railway compartment, wherein Mlle Alice Delysia obtains from Mr Nigel Bruce the wherewithal to purchase a sleeper!

"After such fare, the whirlwind dancing, much of it sensational, of Miss Amelida Allen, Miss Josephine Head, Mr Terry and Miss Pat Kendall, Miss Laurie Devine, Miss Greta Fayne, Miss Eleanora Marra – the endless dancing – the extraordinarily clever skits on old London music-halls, and the drolleries of Miss Hermione Baddeley, were as welcome as they were remarkable.

"Mlle Delysia and Mr Cochran both acknowledged the enthusiastic reception."

PUBLICATIONS

The following items from this revue are included in:

(a) *Collected Sketches and Lyrics* (Hutchinson, 1931) and *Collected Revue Sketches and Parodies* (Methuen, 1999)

"Fête Galante" (written 1923)
"Travelling Light" (written 1924)
"First Love"(written 1924)
"Poor Little Rich Girl" (written 1925)
"Café De La Paix" (written 1925)
"Cosmopolitan Lady "(written 1925)
"Class" (written 1924)

(b) *The Noël Coward Song Book* (Michael Joseph, 1953)
"Poor Little Rich Girl."

Separate sheet music of the following numbers was published by
Ascherberg, Hopwood, and Crew:
"Ladybird"
"Cosmopolitan Lady"
"Poor Little Rich Girl"
"First Love"
"I'm So In Love"

NOTES

In *Present Indicative*, Coward says: "Soon after the opening of *The Vortex* (November 1924), I started work on a revue for Cochran. This had been tentatively discussed before. There had been an interview with C.B. in his office in Old Bond Street, in course of which we bickered for about two hours because he wanted me only to write the book of the revue, and I wished to compose the entire score as well. Finally, his armour of evasive politeness cracked, and he was forced to say that he was very sorry, but he frankly did not consider my music good enough to carry a whole show, and that he intended to engage Philip Braham as composer. That settled it for the time being, and I retired, vanquished, to concentrate on ideas for sketches and burlesques."

He continues: "*On with the Dance*, which was the title finally selected for the revue, was lavish to a degree and very good in spots. There were two ballets created and danced by Léonide Massine, and an excellent cast, including Douglas Byng, Nigel Bruce, Hermione Baddeley, Ernest Thesiger and several others. The star, of course, was Delysia. Everything she did she did well, with a satisfying authority and assurance. She was occasionally temperamental and flew into a few continental rages, but to me she was always easy to work with and extremely agreeable."

The revue was a big success and set London singing Coward melodies. With *Fallen Angels* and *The Vortex*, it made up a trio of Coward successes.

A second edition of the revue, called *Still Dancing*, was produced on 19 November 1925. Though the ballets were retained from the original production, none of the Coward material remained.

The sketch 'Oranges And Lemons' was revived in *Non-stop Revels*, a variety programme at the Leicester Square Theatre, 1 August 1936, with Freddie Forbes (Grace), Garry Lynch (Violet), Al and Betty Gold (Stephen and Charlie). This revival was later the subject of a court case, when Coward was granted an injunction to prevent the performance of the sketch in a form other than that in which it was written. It was alleged that the script had been amended and unpleasant suggestions and some unsavoury words had been included, such as to damage the author's reputation.

At the Theatrical Garden Party, in aid of the Actors' Orphanage, 17 June 1934, 'Oranges And Lemons', was performed in the Theatre Royal with David Hutchinson (Grace), Reginald Purdell (Violet), Jack Hobbs (Charlie), and Jerry Verno (Stephen). Noël Coward was President of the Actors' Orphanage from April 1934 to 1956.

It was also revived for *The Night of 100 Stars* at the London Palladium on 21 July 1960, with Laurence Olivier, Kenneth More, Jack Hawkins and Rex Harrison.

In October or November 1924 Coward wrote and appeared in *A Special Sketch*, at 11 Carlton House Terrace, an afternoon performance in aid of the Working Boys Red Triangle Clubs. We can find no trace of what this sketch was or a programme of the performance.

A touring version of the revue *Twice Nightly*, called *Keep Dancing*, opened at the Empire Theatre, Stratford East on 18 October 1926.

Though, like virtually all revues, *On with the Dance* has never been revived, and its sketches have disappeared from view, many of its songs have turned up throughout the 1970s, 80s and 90s in such anthologies as *Cowardy Custard* (page 530), *Oh, Coward!* (page 534) and *Noël and Gertie* (page 537).

15
SEMI-MONDE

(Originally called *Ritz Bar*)

A PLAY IN THREE ACTS

Written in 1926

FIRST PRESENTED at the Citizens Theatre, Glasgow, 11 September 1977
(21 performances).

CHARACTERS	Citizens, 1977
PIERROT	John Doyle
YOUNG GIRL	Madalyn Morgan
YOUNG MAN	Richard Ommanney
A WAITER	Dafydd Burne-Jones
TANIS MARSHALL	Pauline Moran
DOROTHY PRICE	Katherine Kitovitz
SUZANNE FELLINI	Sian Thomas
MIKE CRAVEN	Patrick Hannaway
BERYL FLETCHER	Robin Pappas
BEVERLEY FORD	Robin Hooper
CYRIL HARDACRE	Rory Edwards
ALBERT HENNICK	Paul Geoffrey
OWEN MARSHALL	Paul Bentall
INEZ ZULIETTA	Ann Mitchell
CYNTHIA GABLE	Angela Chadfield
MARION FAWCETT	Jean Gilpin
JEROME KENNEDY	Mark Lewis
NORMA KENNEDY	Corinna Seddon
JULIUS LEVONOVITCH	Brian Jennings
ELISE TRENT	Alison Mullin
HARRY LEFTWICH	Pierce Brosnan
GEORGE HUDD	Christopher Jagger
LUKE BELLOWS	Garry Cooper
JOSHUA DRAKE	Richard Rees
FREDDY PALMER	Ciaran Hinds
MRS HANCOX	Linda Spurrier
PHYLLIS HANCOX	Suzan Crowley
A GERMAN GENTLEMAN	Giles Havergal

A BELL BOY	Alun Wright
Piano player	Robert David Macdonald
Director and designer	*Philip Prowse*

❖

SCENE: The action of the play passes in a hotel in Paris.

ACT 1:   1924
Scene 1: The lounge (Place du Coeur) January. Late afternoon.
Scene 2: Communicating passage between Place du Coeur and
Rue Gilon. A few days later, before lunch.
Scene 3: The bar. Lunchtime. March.

ACT II: 1925
Scene 1: The lounge (Rue Gilon). January.
Scene 2: The bar again. February. Before lunch.
Scene 3: Corner of the terrace outside the grill room. June.
Lunchtime.

ACT III: 1926
Scene 1: The men's bar. Before dinner. January
Scene 2: The lounge (Rue Gilon side). The same night. 3 a.m.
Scene 3: The lounge (Place du Coeur) June. Late afternoon.

❖

SYNOPSIS

NOTE: It is impossible to synopsise *Semi-Monde* in detail without risk of
boring the reader with copious descriptions of passing incidental action as
the many characters enter from outside and take the lift to their room, or
emerge from the lift either to go out, pair off with somebody else's partner
or make a furtive rendezvous in the lounge. The characters order drinks,
gossip, greet each other, tip porters, read newspapers – everything that
comes naturally when staying in a hotel.

ACT I: The world the play describes is one of shrieking, bitchy, self-conscious
intrigue and is probably the most accurate stage representation of the twenties
milieu Coward inhabited that we have. In Act 1, Coward clearly intends us to
enjoy his satirical take on the comings and goings and occasional collisions
of this large number of elegant guests staying in an expensive hotel in Paris.

He weaves an ambitious number of storylines which merge in the foyer, lounge and bar area. Clandestine affairs and betrayal feature prominently in a decadent atmosphere.

ACT II: Coward turns the tables on his frivolous creations: "We're all silly animals, gratifying our own beastly desires, covering them with a veneer of decency and behaviour." The many tensions that run beneath the surface in Act 1, come to the surface in Act 2, literally exploding when one of the guests, Mike Cavan, shoots his Russian rival in love in the cocktail bar. The climax of the play is an exposé of sexual and emotional indulgence within one group of characters that would do justice to a Tennessee Williams plot. Nemesis makes a grand appearance in the form of biting self-discovery; and while the subtext may not be new, it is universal – we are the cause of our own suffering and cursed by our own natures. The characters have no one to blame but their own superficial selves.

Michael Coveney in the *Financial Times*, September 1977:

"In Philip Prowse's breathtaking production, history is closing more rapidly than perhaps Coward knew or intended. A page boy previously in search of Mrs Simpson walks through the final scene calling for 'Madame la Duchesse de Windsor', while Cyril, now in an RAF uniform, confers anxiously with his married lover. Sirens mingle with Debussy and the hotel vacuum cleaner. The stage picture is austerely transformed with white streamers and balloons. The lilacs have been replaced with tiger lilies.

"Every now and then there is a moment of vintage Coward. Jerome Kennedy, an ageing novelist, says goodbye to Tania Marshall, who is stunningly attired in transparent mauve lace and fighting back the tears with banal comments about the new hit revue. And when someone yelps 'Oh God!' as the tension escalates, he is chided with 'That remark no longer has any dramatic significance. One uses it when one can't find a taxi.' The characters talk about returning to London, being homesick for the South of France, living for the moment... The young cast, all thirty of them, project an idea of world-weary insouciance rather than its embodiment. This is consistent with the company style and allows for both affection and mockery in the production."

Michael Billington in the *Guardian*, September 1977:

"As so often with Coward, it is not so much the people themselves that grip you as his own equivocal attitude towards them. He was, by instinct, a puritan dandy with a martini in one hand and a moral sampler in the other. And in *Semi-Monde* you can see clearly that, while he envies the rich their style, he also has the true lower middle-class boy's belief that a life without work cannot be pure. Even his attitude to homosexuality is not exactly encouraging; he seems to suggest it should be practised but not preached…

"Significantly, the one homosexual who earn's Coward's approval is a student-singer who is encouraged to devote himself to his career. This fits in with Coward's own code of constant work and sexual discretion… Mr Prowse has pushed the later scenes forward in time so that we get Hitler on the radio, and the break up of the glittering tribe. This strikes me as over-literal. The whole point of Coward in the mid-twenties was that he was uneasy without being prophetic."

Donald Campbell for BBC Radio Scotland (transcript):
"The first thing is that in itself this isn't a very exciting play; it doesn't analyse, interpret, or even satirise its subject – it merely depicts it. It's like an animated wall painting of a particularly privileged section of society during the last decade of its existence, circa 1930 to circa 1940. Set in the plush lounge of a Paris hotel where the members of the smart set pause in their journeys to and from places like St Moritz, Biarritz and Monte Carlo, we're shown in a series of lightning sketches the decay and ultimate destruction of this parasitical but extremely stylish way of life. It doesn't make any sort of comment, but the interesting thing is this – when Coward wrote the play it would have been a comedy of contemporary manners, now it's a period piece, and the Citizens have quite rightly treated it as such, concentrating on evoking the period and shifting the focus, I would imagine, from the numerous and rather trivial plot-lines to the overall effect. They do this magnificently.

"It's superbly designed and directed by Philip Prowse and the cast play their parts with an exceptional awareness of genre. They're not playing real people, you see, but pampered children who are acting out roles. They capture this effect exactly.

"I've no real complaints about it, but I was a little bit disappointed by how few genuine Cowardisms there were in the script. I only actually spotted one when a girl said, 'Mike won't fly; he's afraid he'll be caught in an air pocket.' But really that's a quibble. If this play had to rely on its dialogue it really wouldn't be that much. It's a visual experience which I enjoyed tremendously. In fact, it was quite simply – and I can't resist saying it – divine!"

❖

PUBLICATIONS

Semi-Monde was first published in 1999 in *Noël Coward Collected Plays: Six*, Methuen World Classics (London).

NOTES

Semi-Monde was never professionally staged in Coward's lifetime. He comments in *Present Indicative*: "It was well-constructed and, on the whole, well written; its production in London or New York seemed unlikely as some of the characters, owing to lightly suggested abnormalities, would certainly be deleted by the censor; Max Reinhardt, however, was enthusiastic about it, and it was translated into German by Rudolf Kommer and taken in due course to Berlin, where for years it escaped production by a hair's breadth until eventually Vicky Baum wrote *Grand Hotel*, and *Semi-Monde*, being too closely similar in theme, faded gently into oblivion."

Semi-Monde was written in 1926. Coward had already challenged audiences with *The Vortex*, but the fact that *Semi-Monde* introduces openly homosexual characters to the stage, albeit discreetly, at a time when homosexuality was illegal, must have been particularly shocking; indeed too shocking to risk angering the Lord Chamberlain. Legal speculation aside, the homosexual content plus the expense of employing a cast of twenty-nine actors, may well have contributed to the play's virtual disappearance without a single performance until its world premiere in 1977.

16
THIS WAS A MAN
A COMEDY IN THREE ACTS
Written in 1926

FIRST PRESENTED by Basil Dean at the Klaw Theatre, New York, 23 November 1926 (31 performances).

FIRST PRESENTED IN EUROPE by Max Reinhardt at Die Komödie Theatre, Berlin, 25 November 1927, in a German translation by Rudolf Kommer as *Die Ehe von Welt* (*Society Wedding*) (70 performances).

FIRST PRESENTED IN EUROPE IN ENGLISH by the English Players at Le Théâtre Albert 1er, Paris, 11 January 1928 (over 150 performances in repertory).

CHARACTERS	Klaw, US, 1926
CAROL CHURT	Francine Larrimore
HARRY CHALLONER	Terence Neill
EDWARD CHURT	A. E. Matthews
LADY MARGOT BUTLER	Violet Campbell
BERRY	Leonard Loan
LORD ROMFORD	Mackenzie Ward
ZOE ST MERVIN[*1]	Auriol Lee
MAJOR EVELYN BATHURST	Nigel Bruce
BLACKWELL	Horace Pollock
Director	*Basil Dean*
Designer	*George W. Harris and G. E. Calthrop*

CHARACTERS	Berlin, 1927
CAROL CHURT	Greta Mosheim
HARRY CHALLONER	Hans Ulrich Chapius
EDWARD CHURT	Paul Otto
LADY MARGOT BUTLER	Blandine Ebinger
BERRY	Friedrich Jolowicz
LORD ROMFORD	Fritz Eckert
ZOE ST MERRYN	Ludmilla Hell
MAJOR EVELYN BATHURST	Johannes Riemann
BLACKWELL	Eduard Rothauser
THE DUCHESS OF RUTHERFORD[*2]	Reneé Kohler
KENNETH EATON[*2]	Hans Von Ecke
Director	*Forster-Larrinaga*
Designer	*Ernest Schütte*

CHARACTERS	Paris, 1928
CAROL CHURT	Margaret Vaughan
HARRY CHALLONER	Wilfred Bentley
EDWARD CHURT	Edward Stirling
LADY MARGOT BUTLER	Cynthia Elton
BERRY	Gilson McCormack
LORD ROMFORD	Victor Garland
ZOE ST MERRYN	Violet Bruce
MAJOR EVELYN BATHURST	Bernard Merefield
BLACKWELL	Alfred Dent

Director	*Edward Stirling*
Designer	*Pierre Evrard*

*[1] Spelt Merryn in the published play and in the German version, also in Paris.

*[2] There were two extra characters in the German version.

❖

ACT I: Scene 1: Edward Churt's studio in Knightsbridge. 2.30 a.m.
            Scene 2: The same. A few weeks later.
ACT II: Evelyn Bathurst's flat. The same night.
ACT III: The same as Act I. The following morning.

❖

SYNOPSIS

ACT I, Scene 1: Carol, wife of the successful portrait painter, Edward Churt, enters her husband's studio clandestinely at 2.30 a.m., escorted by Harry Challoner. Both are in evening dress. They take drinks and cigarettes and then, after listening at Edward's bedroom door and hearing nothing, proceed to kiss each other passionately. Harry leaves and Carol goes to bed, upon which Edward Churt rises from the armchair where he has been sitting throughout this scene, takes up a plate of sandwiches, and retires to his own room.

    Scene 2: A few weeks later Edward is in his studio painting a portrait of Lady Margot Butler. When the sitting ends he offers her some tea. She is expecting to be fetched by her lover, Bobbie (Lord Romford), and is slightly hurt by Edward's disapproving attitude towards her affair. The conversation turns to the recent divorce of a mutual friend, Zoe St Merryn. In due course Bobbie Romford appears, followed soon afterwards by Zoe, who is just back after a year abroad. Margot inquires after her own husband, whom Zoe has met in Barcelona, explaining that they are living apart, "except for religious festivals, like Easter and Christmas", but do not want the attendant troubles of a divorce. "What a sham Margot is, isn't she?" comments Zoe after the other two have left. She herself is thankful to have made a definite break, but slightly depressed at seeing all her friends in the same old groove. Edward strikes her as "dim" and drained of vitality. He confesses that his marriage has gone wrong. Zoe sympathises with him and he confides to her that he does not want either to go away or to divorce Carol: being the product of a civilised age, he has lost his "red-blooded honest-to-God emotions", and merely feels nauseated and bored by her behaviour.

At any rate, says Zoe, Edward is better equipped for dealing with life than his friend, "Evie" Bathurst – one of those strong, silent men who crumple up when faced with a situation beyond their limited range... She understands the type, having been married to one of them. To Edward's implied comment that her husband has behaved like a cad in divorcing her instead of letting her divorce him, Zoe rejoins that she insisted upon this, as the reverse process would have harmed his military career, and as they were thoroughly bored with each other a break was inevitable.

A tall, soldierly figure is ushered in – Major Evelyn Bathurst ("Evie"), just back from Morocco. He agrees with Zoe that Edward is looking off-colour and advises him to take more exercise. Zoe soon leaves and Evelyn comes to the real point of his visit, which is to warn Edward that people are talking about Carol. Rather wearily, Edward says that his wife is a human being, not a piece of property over which he can assert legal rights. Urged to "show a little spirit", he maintains that nothing will change Carol – things will have to take their course. His friend, however, has a cut-and-dried plan: Carol must be "taught a lesson" and he himself proposes to do it. Edward politely tells him not to interfere.

At this point Carol enters. On hearing of Zoe's visit, she turns slightly catty. She announces her intention of dining with "the Challoners" at the Embassy; but, when Edward has gone to dress, Evelyn, who has always treated her with considerable reserve, begins to pay her compliments and suggests that she should cancel her previous engagement and dine with him in his flat. After some mock hesitation, she agrees and telephones to put off Harry Challoner.

ACT II: As Evelyn enters his flat with Carol, his man Blackwell is putting the finishing touches to the dinner table – roses and champagne. The flat strikes Carol as being like its owner – "solid and rather austere". Blackwell brings cocktails and then serves the dinner.

Over caviare they make exploratory conversation; with the soup Carol offers to teach Evelyn to dance and invites him to a first night. While Blackwell serves them with partridge they discuss Edward, and Carol forces her host to admit that he has been talking about her to her husband. Evelyn says he was lecturing Edward for paying too much attention to his work and not enough to her – a statement which the astute Carol does not believe.

She subtly implies that Edward's affection for her is cooling off and this is making her unhappy.

By the time Blackwell returns with Pêche Melba, Carol is hinting that Zoe St Merryn has set her cap at Edward. Between the sweet and the coffee she enlists Evelyn's sympathy by a nicely-timed burst of tears.

Having at last dismissed Blackwell for the night, they put on the gramophone and dance. With the excuse of giving Evelyn a dancing lesson, Carol incites him to kiss her; but this startles him into remembering the object of his invitation. Striding up and down, he reads her a lecture upon her behaviour, which ends by Carol calling him a fatuous prig and Evelyn declaring that she has the soul of a harlot. This sends her into fits of laughter. When she has recovered a little, she calls him a cad and slaps his face. Then she stages a faint, has to be revived with brandy and, between sobs, professes herself repentant.

Evelyn, distressed at having upset her so much, is completely conquered when she asserts that she has only flirted with other men because she was heartbroken at Edward having an affair with Zoe. He believes all this and apologises profusely. Then Carol declares that she loves him and insists on going home alone, after making a pact of friendship with him. She kisses him good night and apparently leaves. On hearing the front door slam, he collapses with his head in his hands. Carol softly returns with her cloak over her arm, slips into his bedroom and closes the door behind her.

ACT III: Next morning Evelyn, very white and strained, is ushered into the studio. He asks to see Edward and is taken aback when Carol comes in instead. She is aghast when he says he will tell Edward everything, and tries to stop this by vowing that she really loves him.

While they are arguing there is a ring at the front door and Zoe enters. To her surprise, Evelyn greets her very coldly and immediately leaves. The two women have a rather frigid exchange of polite remarks, till Carol excuses herself on the plea of a headache and goes upstairs. Soon afterwards Edward enters, delighted to see Zoe, and asks her to go out to lunch with him.

Again she broaches the subject of his relations with Carol, calls him "a lazy idealist" and says he really must take some action. He rejoins that Evelyn has already been telling him this, and has even offered to teach Carol a lesson. ("Poor Evie!" comments Zoe.) Suddenly Edward asks whether she would marry him if he were free. It transpires that he has already proposed to her once, before their respective marriages, and that both of them are regretful that he took her initial refusal as final. Zoe says firmly that she will have to go back abroad: they are in danger of falling in love again, and she, having a pre-war conscience, does not want to come between man and wife. She kisses him lightly and leaves, arranging to meet him for lunch at the Berkeley.

The telephone rings – it is Harry Challoner for Carol, who answers him rather curtly and rings off. Edward tells her to sit down and proceeds to "have it out" with her, stating as a fact that she has been unfaithful to him and asking what she intends to do about it. He mentions the names of three men – all of them married – with whom she has misconducted herself, threatening that next time she does it he will divorce her. Carol, pretending to be repentant, bursts into tears and begs for his forgiveness. Kind, but unimpressed, he advises her to lie down and take some aspirin.

Hardly has she gone when Evelyn returns, looking still more harassed. Edward is bewildered by his statement that he has come to say goodbye because he is going to Australia, and still more so when he says that he tried to shoot himself that morning. At last Evelyn blurts out that their friendship is over for ever. In some annoyance Edward exclaims: "Stop all this melodrama and tell me what's the matter."

Evelyn stammers out something about himself and Carol… In a flash, Edward understands and bursts out laughing. Warning Evelyn that men of his sort should stick to athletics and not attempt psychology, he sends for Carol and demands an explanation. She refuses, but Edward, quietly reconstructing the situation, tells Evelyn that he has behaved like a pitiful fool, and that his interest in Carol's morals probably arose because she had snubbed him several times and he was very much attracted to her.

Edward ends with an ultimatum: Carol must leave him and go abroad, and he will make it easy for her to divorce him; otherwise he will divorce her, naming Evelyn as co-respondent. The other two ask for time to think this over, and Edward goes to his rendezvous at the Berkeley, leaving them together. Carol comes to sit beside Evelyn. "There is still time for you to shoot yourself," she says sweetly.

J. Brooks Atkinson in the *New York Times*, 24 November 1926, on the American production:
"Acting of good drawing-room quality and two attractive settings give a pleasant exterior to Noël Coward's meretricious drama, *This Was a Man*, unveiled at the Klaw last evening. As the blatantly unfaithful wife of a

society painter, Miss Larrimore speaks glibly and moves gracefully about the stage and over chairs and couches. Mr Matthews's deportment as the offended husband (cuckold, they used to say in Fielding's robust time) is impeccable beyond reproach. Miss Lee makes an intelligent confidante and childhood friend who has just endured the horrors of the divorce court; and when she is not set to talking into the scenery she speaks Mr Coward's facile lines intelligently. Mr Bruce contrives a stiff and amusingly dull-witted man of war, fatuous and opaque. And the minor parts, of which there are several, are expertly cast, and played with a *savoir faire* worthy of Pinero in his glory. The settings provide a delightful background. One, of a modish studio in Knightsbridge, London, has the charm and flavour of conspicuously good taste. The second, of a bachelor's flat in Half Moon Street, conveys skilfully the phlegmatic conventionality of the tenant. All the equipment of a good drama of manners has been lavished upon this thinly-spun conversation about – what? – why, about infidelity. The director, Mr Dean, has done well.

"But by the time the first act is half over, one begins to suspect that Mr Coward has contributed very meagrely to the occasion. Last year, as the author of three plays, of *The Vortex* in particular, he brought smart worldly life within the reach of common theatregoers. Now he is at it again, with an enervating exposition of sinful life among Londoners of high breeding. An impulsive little wretch, Carol Churt, carries on boldly with almost anyone save her husband. Quite aware of these scandalous proceedings, Edward Churt, the famous portrait painter, is too bored to defend his tedious respectability. His closest friend, however, Major Evelyn Bathurst ('The British Army does not specialise in wit,' he confesses), proceeds to give Carol a much-needed lesson. Alone with her in his flat, he leads her to think that he is enamoured, and then suddenly berates her for her loose morals. More pliable than he is, she tricks him into betraying her husband's confidence. Being ostentatiously a man of honour, he confesses to Edward Churt, who, in a jaded voice, delivers an unemotional ultimatum.

"Mr Coward's tendency to express his dramas in prolonged conversations between two characters has been carried to an extreme in *This Was a Man*. Occasionally the people speak brightly. 'Marriage is an overrated amusement,' says Carol. 'Let's go to a decent play,' Zoe remarks. 'There ought to be no trouble in buying tickets,' replies Harry, who is quick on the uptake. 'I like love stories in which there is no mention of sex,' she goes on. 'You ought to have been a critic,' he responds. For the most part, however, the talk runs on without distinction, and in the easiest possible method of playwriting. Whenever a new character comes on the stage, making the number of those present actually three, one of them rushes away in high fettle lest the duologues be interrupted. For characters left stranded, with no one to talk to at all, there is always the telephone. Common as these devices may be, they are not unserviceable. But Mr Coward's insistence upon them becomes an exhibition of weakness. He has made his task much too simple.

"Last spring the Lord Chamberlain, solicitous for the morals of his countrymen, forbade the production of *This Was a Man* in London. Perhaps because the talk is frequently as loose as the characters; or perhaps because Carol Churt slips into the Major's bedchamber for a showy second-act curtain. In a fit of temperament, Mr Coward is reported to have said: 'I shall in future concentrate on New York, where I am taken seriously as a serious writer, whereas in England people think I am out for salacious sensations. I shall from time to time write a pleasant little trifle for London.' The tone of *This Was a Man* is obviously serious. But the drama is trifling. Possibly Mr Coward has confused his audiences."

Alfred Kerr in the *Berliner Tageblatt*, 26 November 1927, on the German production:
"The break-up of marriage. The breakdown of marriage. Not only all over the world, but (Mr Coward seems to say) more particularly in England. It is, he considers, a consequence of our times. That is not impossible.

"They have had unfortunate consequences (the Treaty of Versailles, for instance), and if the painter Churt is apparently betrayed by Mrs Churt four times in the course of the play – with three married men and a bachelor Major (she can hardly do it often enough!), this would never have happened before the World War.

"Or would it? Perhaps, but it would not have been done so lightheartedly, but more secretly, more carefully, with much more fear of being found out.

"And, secondly, before the World War the painter would not have forgiven his better half so quickly, so casually, so spinelessly. He would have stood up for himself and got excited.

"In any case, the portrait painter Churt, who has a good social standing and an income to correspond, wants a quiet life... Perhaps also his little affairs... For the latter, of course, he has Miss Ebinger. And he even puts up with her occasional inaudibility – what does it matter when one is in love? Miss Ebinger is his model. Surely this final scene, when the model creeps in to him at night, is not in Coward's original play, but has been added by the producer, Forster-Larrinaga, although I cannot prove it. Did Forster-Larrinaga want only to underline the lack of morals in London? ... But don't let us stir up international discord.

"There are three European playwrights who are also actors; or three actors who write plays and act in them themselves. In France, Sacha Guitry; in Germany, Curt Götz in collaboration with Paul Rosenhayn; in England, that man Coward.

"Coward's *Weekend* (*Hay Fever*) was breathtaking. At the end of the performance I laughed over it for half an hour on the Schiffbauerdamm – to such an extent that I was nearly arrested. Now, however, no astonished policeman came up to me. (At times he might have reproachfully pointed out that it is forbidden to sleep in public places.)

"The painter Churt (to come back to him) does not know whether it is lack of time that makes him so weak and indulgent to his erring wife; or whether it is that no human being has the right to oppose the liberation of the senses and the 'development of the individuality'. (This is quite well observed.)

"He seems to want to marry a third person, Ludmilla Hell – who evidently came to London from Munich. How close the relations of the two nations have become is shown by the most honourable person in the play, the Major (played attractively and with charm by Johannes Riemann), who unquestionably has come straight from Berlin to become a member of the English Army.

"Whenever are we going to get on with describing the plot? Well, the Major is horrified to find that his cuckolded friend (I'm still talking about the painter) has so little spirit. He wants to unmask the faithless wife. He wants to reduce her; she wants to seduce him. She succeeds better than he does. He first succeeds; then she. Next morning, the Major confesses: there is something left of honour. (This was a man.) But the milksop painter-husband (pleasantly played by Paul Otto) will have none of it. Yes, indeed, the World War!

"All ethics have to be revised today. I tried to do this recently with the relationship between Shylock and the Venetians (and Herr Schmal, a person disadvantaged by Nature, took their part in the Kreuzzeitung). The ethics of the new England says, 'Have we come to this?', adding: 'Where are they who, standing firm, have never faltered or compromised?' ... Nowhere – they have all compromised; but without any good reason.

"There remains Greta Mosheim. She remains – in the memory. At the end she was inadequate. But up till then...

"The flapper, the eternal schoolgirl turned wife. With all kinds of mock-innocent intonations of a carefree, impudent youthfulness –

a delightful portrayal. (Even the naughty wife of the painter, judging from her accent, comes from Berlin. But stop! I really must not stir up international discord.)"

❖

PUBLICATIONS

This Was a Man was first published in America by Harper Brothers (New York, 1926), and in the UK in *Three Plays and a Preface*, Martin Secker (London, 1928). It is dedicated to John C. Wilson.

❖

NOTES

On his return in 1926 from playing in *The Vortex* in America, Coward, while waiting for the London production of *Easy Virtue* in May, took a holiday. He says:

"While in Palermo I wrote a new comedy called *This Was a Man*. It was primarily satirical and on the whole rather dull; the bulk of its dullness lay in the second act, which was an attenuated dialogue between two excessively irritating characters. The fact that the characters were intended to be irritating in no way mitigated the general boredom, and this vital error in construction ultimately cost the play its life.

"On my return to London I showed it to Basil (Dean), who thought it excellent, and so we sent it to Lord Cromer for a licence with the intention of producing it immediately after *Easy Virtue*. The licence, however, was refused, principally, I think, because of a scene in the last act when the husband, on being told that his annoying wife had committed adultery with his still more annoying best friend, burst out laughing. The fact that the circumstances of the story made this behaviour more than permissible weighed not a jot with the Board of Censors, who like the commandments are broken solemnly or not at all, and so, after a little gleeful publicity in the press, the play was shelved for later production in America."

The production did not take place till November. Meantime, *The Queen Was in the Parlour* was produced and Coward was to play in *The Constant Nymph* in London. His first play, *The Rat Trap*, was eventually produced while he was on his way to New York for the production of *This Was a Man*.

The play was moderately successful. It had its European premiere in Germany in 1927. Coward's plays were very popular in Germany. *Hay Fever* and *Fallen Angels* were both produced in Berlin in 1926.

Coward says in his preface to *Play Parade, Volume III*, that in New York "many first-nighters complained that the dinner scene in the second act was the longest meal they had ever sat through. The play failed in spite of some patches of expert acting and also, I hasten to add, some patches of expert writing. But these, alas, were not enough to relieve the general tedium. It was not at that time produced in England because the Lord Chamberlain took exception to the fact that when, in the last act, the husband learns that his wife, who is unscrupulous, has seduced his best friend, who is unintelligent, he goes off into gales of laughter. Some years later the official ban on facetious adultery was lifted and the play was produced by a repertory company – I think at Malvern – with distinguished lack of success. The fundamental error in the play is the second act, which is a long drawn-out duologue between the wife and the ultimately seduced friend, both of whom are tiresome characters. If it had been written with less meticulous veracity and more wit, it might have succeeded, but even so I doubt it. Bores on the stage, however ironically treated, inevitably bore the audience. Perhaps it will be more interesting to read than to see."

The production in England to which Coward refers cannot be traced. The Noël Coward Company which opened at Malvern in 1932 did not include the play in its repertoire; and the Lord Chamberlain's office assures us that *This Was a Man* has not been submitted to them for their reconsideration since they refused to license it in 1926. It is still officially a banned play, and no public performance can take place in this country. It is extremely unlikely that any repertory company would produce an unlicensed play, and even if they had done so in ignorance, proceedings would have immediately followed. It would seem that Coward is mistaken in his information, or is thinking of the Paris production, which was performed in English.

The Paris production by Edward Stirling was revived by him at Monte Carlo during his season there in December 1929. Of his Paris production he says in his autobiography, *Something to Declare*, published by Frederick Muller (London, 1942):

"At the opening of the Christmas season (1927) I received a visit from Lord D'Abernon, who had been our Ambassador in Berlin. He came to see one of our plays, and asked me afterwards if I had read Noël Coward's *This Was a Man*, which had been given in German in Berlin. It apparently had a big success there, and he suggested that it might be worth while to do it in Paris in English. Lord D'Abernon seemed much interested, not only in the theatre, but in all the arts, and I valued his advice, sent for the play, read it, liked it very much, and then discovered it was banned in England on account of its tolerant attitude towards collusion.

"The play opens with a very well-written little scene between the wife and her lover. It is late and the studio is in darkness but for a small table lamp. After the lovers leave the stage empty, the husband emerges from his armchair, where he has been hidden from sight. There was always a gasp of surprise when he was revealed to the audience, and it set the stage for what was to follow. But apparently, in the Berlin production, the director (I believe it was Reinhardt) had the idea of improving the play. For the end of it an epilogue was written in which the wife, having been allowed by her husband to divorce him, and having married again (not the lover of the Prologue, but another who appeared in Act II), reproduces the situation of the Prologue almost line for line. She enters with her latest lover, they play the same scene, and the second husband emerges from the same hiding place as his predecessor. I much preferred to give the version as Coward wrote it.

"We produced it on January 11, 1928, and it broke all records. Extra police were called up to regulate the crowds waiting outside in the rue du Rocher. With a new play, banned in England, by Noël Coward, this wasn't surprising. *The London Evening News* wrote: 'The English Players are again championing the freedom of the stage by putting on a London-banned play in Paris... A crowded audience, which included many prominent members of the British and American colonies, applauded some brilliant acting by Edward Stirling as the deceived husband, and by Bernard Merefield as one of the deceivers, and Miss Margaret Vaughan exploited to its utmost an unsympathetic part. Why *This Was a Man* should have been banned in London puzzled the many French critics present.' We gave the play over a hundred and fifty times (in the following 12 months) and had we not retained our system of repertory, I think we could have run it much longer."

The play was revived during the Company's seasons in Zurich, Monte Carlo, Belgium, Holland, Hamburg, Egypt and South America until 1934.

At the time of writing (1999) there have been no other professional revivals of *This Was a Man*.

17
THE MARQUISE
A NEW COMEDY
Written in 1926

FIRST PRESENTED by Alban B. Limpus at the Criterion Theatre, London, 16 February 1927 (129 performances).

CHARACTERS	Criterion, 1927
THE COMTE RAOUL DE VRIAAC	W. Graham Browne
ADRIENNE (his daughter)	Eileen Sharp
JACQUES RIJAR (his secretary)	Robert Harris
ESTEBAN, EL DUCO DESANTAGUANO	Frank Cellier
MIGUEL (his son)	Godfrey Winn
FATHER CLEMENT	Colin Johnston
HUBERT (servant in the Château de Vriaac)	Rupert Lister
THE MARQUISE ELOISE DE KESTOURNEL	Marie Tempest
ALICE (her maid)	Lilian Cavanagh
Director	*W. Graham Browne*
Designer	*William Nicholson*

SCENE: The action of the play takes place in the main living-room of the Château de Vriaac, not far from Paris, in 1735.

ACT I: Ten o'clock on a September evening.

ACT II: The following morning.

ACT III: The same evening.

The songs were arranged by Alfred Reynolds.

SYNOPSIS

ACT I: In his château on a September evening in 1735 Count Raoul de Vriaac is giving a dinner to celebrate the betrothal of his daughter Adrienne to Miguel, son of his old friend Esteban, Duke of Santaguano. Also present are his young secretary, Jacques Rijar, and his confessor, Father Clement.

Rather pompously, Raoul toasts the young couple, urging them to live with "clarity of purpose and humility of spirit", but Esteban's advice to them is: "Enjoy yourselves as much as possible; it will pass the time pleasantly and lead you into old age with a few gay memories to cheer you." During this speech Jacques Rijar abruptly leaves the room.

The young people go out on the terrace and Father Clement says good night, leaving the two old friends together. Under the influence of his late wife and her confessor, Raoul has settled down into dull respectability, and he is quite annoyed when Esteban recalls the gay times they had together in their youth. Under pressure, he admits that he did have one real love-affair, about which Esteban never heard, as they were parted at the time; but before he can say more Miguel and Adrienne return. The older men go into the library.

Adrienne seems depressed: she insists that Miguel does not really love her "with passion"; but, once she has made him admit it, she cheers up and confesses that she is in love with her father's secretary. Miguel, who really loves a dancer in Paris, promises to help her, and when Jacques comes in he makes an excuse to leave them together. They fly into each other's arms, and have only just time to stop kissing before Esteban comes back with Raoul, to fetch his son away. Watching them leave from the terrace, Raoul and Adrienne see the lights of a stationary coach on the high road.

When Adrienne has gone to bed, Raoul reproves his secretary for leaving the table during the Duke's speech. The young man, delirious with happiness, answers his employer recklessly, accusing him of being afraid – of youth, of life, of suffering. He is sent to bed in disgrace.

The Count remains gazing at his late wife's portrait, until he is startled by a tapping at the terrace window. He opens it, and the Marquise de Kestournel steps in, exquisitely dressed for travelling.

"Eloise!" gasps Raoul, who had thought her dead. After a few comments on the changes in the room since she last saw it, she asks: "Where is my child?" "Your child is dead!" says Raoul, and then softens the blow by adding: "As far as you are concerned." At this Eloise is indignant. Adrienne, he says, believes that his wife was her mother. He asks Eloise why she has sprung this surprise on him. She says she has come back for good, and produces a letter written by him at the time of their parting, in which he declared that, if ever she felt weary and alone, he would always be waiting for her.

Repudiating these sentiments, he affirms that his wife has changed him: he has repented of his loose living and now has faith and peace and nobility of purpose. Eloise walks out. He calls after her, but she has gone.

Raoul takes out a box containing a packet of Eloise's letters, smashes it open and flings the letters into the fire, with a number of trinkets and other mementoes.

Roused by the noise, Adrienne comes down. Her father sharply orders her to go back to bed, and when she refuses asks her to fetch Father Clement. The girl says firmly that she wants to talk to him, and proceeds to confess that she does not want to marry Miguel because she loves Jacques Rijar. ("He shall leave my service immediately!", threatens the Count.)

When Raoul appeals to here in the name of her "dear dead mother", Adrienne says violently that her mother cared nothing for either of them. "She only loved herself and God and Father Clement." She adds that his whole life is a pretence – he does not love her, or he would not force her to marry against her will. He may send her to a convent if he likes, but she will not marry Miguel.

As she sobs hysterically there is a peal at the front door bell, and the servant Hubert ushers in "Madame la Marquise de Kestournel". Eloise, followed by her maid Alice, stands in the doorway. She greets Raoul ceremoniously as a total stranger, explaining that her coach has broken down and she is obliged to ask hospitality for the night. Raoul refuses it, on the ground that there is no room, but his daughter (abetted by Hubert, who has recognised the Marequise) insists that she shall stay.

ACT II: Next morning Miguel calls, in response to a note from Adrienne, who is upset because her father is dismissing Jacques. The young man consoles her, promising to ask for his father's help, and goes to find Esteban. Jacques is disconsolate, feeling it his duty to renounce Adrienne; but she begs him not to go away immediately. They slip out to the terrace as Eloise comes down to breakfast. She exchanges a few words with Hubert, who, delighted to see here back, opines that both M. le Comte and his daughter need cheering up.

Father Clement brings a message from Raoul, regretting that a headache will prevent him from saying goodbye to her before she leaves, but she does not take the hint.

Then Adrienne comes back and, with very little coaxing from Eloise (to whom she has taken an instant liking), confides the story of her troubles. She runs off as her father appears.

Raoul is in a very bad temper. He tells Eloise to go at once, reiterating that she is sinful and shall not enter his life again... she can go back to St Cloud. No, replies Eloise; her house is sold, so certain was she that he would welcome her with open arms. She hands him his letter, which he throws into the fire, and she then exclaims that she had given him a dressmaker's bill by mistake; whereupon he stamps out in a rage.

As Jacques creeps downstairs with a travelling bag in his hand Eloise intercepts him, tells him to stay, and promises to find him work and help him win Adrienne. He goes back upstairs just as Esteban is announced.

At the sight of each other, Esteban and Eloise are astonished. They fall into each other's arms, and she asks him for news of her child, François. "Miguel," rectifies Esteban, explaining that the boy had been re-named at his family's request. Realising that this is Adrienne's fiancé, Eloise goes into peals of hysterical laughter. Esteban does not know that she has met the Count before, and she begs him not to reveal that they are old friends, as it might lead to complications. He too has written, promising her his help and protection at need, but they mutually feel that their love is over, though it will be the basis of friendship.

Having recovered his temper, Raoul comes to say that he is taking Adrienne away to Paris; meanwhile, his house is at the service of Madame la Marquise. Surprised at this sudden decision, Esteban, before he leaves, politely invites Eloise to have supper with him. After a last appeal to Raoul not to let Adrienne marry Miguel, Eloise takes matters into her own hands, sends for Father Clement and insists, at the pistol point, on his marrying Adrienne to Jacques, while Raoul thunders helplessly on the locked door.

ACT III: About eight o'clock that evening Raoul is seated alone at supper. He sends for Hubert, demands wine, and proceeds to get drunk, in company with his servant. When Esteban comes to fetch Eloise, he is astonished to find Raoul still at the château, and still more so when his respectable friend declares his longing for Paris, the city of sin: "Vivid, scarlet sin – it warms one up, you know." Hubert explains that the Marquise and Father Clement have both left, and that Adrienne has been married to Jacques and has gone to Paris with him.

Still in an exalted mood, Raoul apostrophises his wife's portrait, declaring that he forgives her for being a determined and unmitigated bore; he climbs on a chair and, with Esteban's help, lifts the picture down.

A drink of black coffee clears his brain, and he confirms Hubert's account of the morning's proceedings. When he refers to the Marquise as "Eloise",

Esteban is taken aback. He then learns for the first time that she has been Raoul's mistress and is the mother of Adrienne. It is lucky that the girl has married Jacques, comments Esteban: Miguel would hardly have been a suitable match – he is her brother! The two men compare notes as to when and where they met Eloise, and drink to her damnation.

As they do so, Eloise herself quietly enters from the terrace, where she has been listening. Both men accuse her of having betrayed them and lied to them. Unruffled, she replies that she expects one or the other to marry her. Again Raoul loses his temper, accuses Esteban of being a traitor and a hypocrite, and slaps his face. They decide to fight a duel on the spot. The Count sends Hubert to fetch a rapier, the furniture is pushed aside, and Esteban draws his sword. Eloise, thoroughly enjoying the situation, sits perched on a spinet, eating an orange and encouraging the combatants. When she decides that they have had enough, she throws a cloth over their blades and orders them to stop.

Esteban is still angry, but she tells him brightly that if he slaps Raoul's face they will be quits. He does so, recovers his sense of humour, and bursts out laughing. Having reconciled them, Eloise reveals that she has never been married at all – they were the only two men in her life, and for the past 16 years she has lived an entirely virtuous existence, earning her living as an actress. The reason she left Esteban was to prevent his family from disinheriting him and ruining his career: as for Raoul, he never once suggested marriage to her.

The Count is still sulky, but Esteban courteously offers her his hand. Eloise makes no immediate reply, until abruptly Raoul says that he loves her and goes out on the terrace. Esteban is obviously relieved when he realises that her choice will fall on Raoul. She kisses him good night and he leaves them. Eloise sits down at the spinet and begins to play, while Raoul comes in again and rests his head on her shoulder as the curtain falls.

The *Morning Post*, 17 February 1927:

"Last night, at the Criterion, an eighteenth-century comedy by Mr Noël Coward, entitled *The Marquise*, was performed for the first time, and a very amusing and well-constructed piece it proved to be.

"This is the first of Mr Coward's plays to have a good first act. The quality of the craftsmanship was kept up in the second and third acts, with a bad lapse, not in craft, but in feeling, when the young lovers, Rijar and Adrienne, told their love for each other.

"Mr Coward still cannot write an effective love scene; his imagination is defeated when he cannot be flippant about the mating of true lovers. In time, no doubt, his innate sincerity will enable him to conquer such scenes, but that time is not yet, and I am obliged frankly to say that what should have been a fragrant interlude was tiresomely banal.

"But the rest of the play is delicious and done with dexterity and delicacy. If some of the wit was too facile, more of it was brilliant, and the surprise at the beginning of the second act was as good a surprise as any dramatist has ever invented. The French dramatist, Henry Becque, was lately held up to us as a master of surprise in the opening of *La Parisienne*; Mr Coward need not fear to be compared with the Frenchman.

"This is the story. The Comte Raoul de Vriaac – observe the punctiliousness with which the title is spelt – a reformed sinner, is about to marry his daughter to Miguel, the son of his former boon companion, El Duco de Santaguano. The young couple have grown up together and are fond of each other, but Adrienne adores Jacques Rijar, her father's secretary, while Miguel has lost his heart to a dancer in Paris.

"A feast is held to celebrate the betrothal, after which the guests depart. Then a tap is heard on the window and the Marquise Eloise de Kestournel enters. She is the former mistress of the Comte and the mother of Adrienne, but, as Comte Raoul had never asked her to marry him, she had left him, and the abandoned gentleman consoled himself in marriage with a pious lady, now deceased, whose daughter Adrienne imagined herself to be.

"The Marquise has come to see her child, and by a pretty trick contrives to be invited to spend the night in the Château de Vriaac, much against the Comte's wish. On the following day, El Duco de Santaguano calls and discovers in the Marquise his former mistress and the mother of Miguel!

"Thereafter, there are stratagems by which Rijar is married by a terrorised priest to Adrienne, and Comte Raoul, after a duel with El Duco, consents to be married to the Marquise.

"The story is an excellent one, and it is excellently well told. Mr Coward makes no attempt to put archaic speech into the mouths of his people. They say 'Splendid!' as easily as if they were alive today, but he quite admirably suggests the gracious manners of a more elegant age than that which he customarily puts upon the stage.

"The play was charmingly acted. Miss Tempest, looking radiant and dainty and delicate, has a part such as she must often have dreamt about, and Mr Frank Cellier as a gallant gentleman was a fine figure of a man. Mr Graham Browne's repentant sinner, who recovers humanity when he abandons piety, was a well-composed performance, and there was a charming Adrienne in

Miss Eileen Sharp, and a jolly Miguel in Mr Godfrey Winn. The Father Clement of Mr Colin Johnston was a fatly unctuous one, a gargoyle of a holy man.

"The audience seemed to be delighted with the play, and Miss Tempest seemed to be delighted with the audience."

PUBLICATIONS

The Marquise was first published in the *Contemporary British Dramatists* series (Volume 55), Ernest Benn (London, 1927). It is dedicated to Marie Tempest. Also published in *Noël Coward Collected Plays: Two*, Methuen World Classics (London, 1999).

NOTES

While in America for the production of *This Was a Man* (November, 1926), Coward was not in the best of health, and while supposed to be resting at White Sulphur Springs he wrote *The Marquise*. He says:

"I really should have rested completely, but I had promised Marie Tempest that I would write a comedy for her, and as an idea had been kicking about inside me for some time, I huffed and puffed and poured out nervous energy which I should have been conserving, and finally completed a pleasant little eighteenth-century joke called *The Marquise*. The last act was a bit weak, but I thought on the whole it would make a good evening's entertainment."

He sent the play to London and went on a long holiday to the East. He returned to New York and then to England. Meantime, *The Marquise* had opened in February, and he went to see it directly he got back to London.

Coward says in his preface to *Play Parade, Volume III*: "I remember sitting in the stage box of the Criterion Theatre just before the rise of the curtain and wondering how much the actual performance I was about to see would differ from the idealised, imagined performance she [Marie Tempest] had given for me in my room at White Sulphur Springs. It was a curious experience. The curtain rose, the play started and presently in she walked through the French windows, accurate and complete. There was everything I had envisaged; the 'tricorne' hat, the twinkle in the eye, the swift precision of movement. Every remembered intonation was there too, every sharply delivered line, every little gurgle. It was for me obviously an enchanting evening, and it has made me forever incapable of judging the play on its merits. If, with intense concentration, I could detach myself for a moment from Marie Tempest's personality and performance, I might perhaps see what a tenuous, frivolous little piece *The Marquise* is. I might, if only I could forget her in the last act eating an orange and watching Raoul and Esteban fighting a duel, realise how weak and meretricious the last act is. I might, bereft of her memory, read with disdain the whole play; sneer at its flippancy; laugh at its trivial love scenes and shudder at the impertinence of an author who, for no apparent reason except perhaps that pictorially the period is attractive, elects to place a brittle modern comedy in an eighteenth-century setting. But I am not and never shall be bereft of the memory of Marie Tempest, and any reader who shares this privilege will, I am sure, agree that *The Marquise* is gay, brilliant, witty, charming, and altogether delightful."

In *William Nicholson* by Marguerite Steen (Collins, 1943) we are told: "For *The Marquise*, William [Nicholson] designed and painted a grand set in what he describes as a "rather wonderful red" of an octagonal room with the floor painted to represent black and white marble. His association with the management was not a wholly peaceful one: there was trouble over a chandelier and, with Marie Tempest, over a superb costume of sulphur yellow and black which he had designed for one of the actors, and which she declared was going to 'kill' her own appearance. Strange that so supreme a mistrell of her art could not realise its value as a challenge; stranger still that she should have so little confidence in her own powers as to fear the rivalry of a dress. William stubbornly refused to alter his design in any way, and she had to accept it; long acquaintance had probably shown her the imprudence of arguing with William on his own subject!

"One of the backers 'treated' the production to a beastly brownish chandelier [William's description], heavy and graceless, which, without William's permission, was hung in the middle of his scene. He immediately had it taken down – to the disapproval of the management, who thought that his unusual set would be disliked by the audience. "But it cost so much! – and so-and-so (the donor) would be so offended!" William did not give a damn for so-and-so's offence, but he was so infuriated by the attitude of Marie Tempest and Graham Browne that he would not go near the theatre on the first night. When Graham Browne rang him up, after the show, to tell him what a success it had been, and how much his décor had been admired, William was very frigid, and actually did not return to see the effect of his set for some time.

"When he did – or at any rate, shortly after – he came near to causing a personal furore: as, like many people who are not used to the wings of a theatre (which William was), he managed to fall foul of one of the flats, and discovered himself on the stage in full view of the audience. (As it was a 'Box set' he must have crossed between the French window at its 'backing'). The sudden appearance, in period set, of a character in gents' evening suitings must have been sensational: mercifully, Mary (at the height of one of her important scenes) had her back turned. The only person who appeared to notice was the stage manager, who, from the prompt corner, made hideous faces and gestures at William, who proceeded to do the only thing possibly: which was to stroll calmly across to the opposite exit, where he was met by the stage-manager in a state of approaching apoplexy. William took the words out of his mouth. "Don't you ever say one word about this!" he threatened him: and left the theatre – this time for good. So far as he knows, Mary was never told, and as for the audience – they probably thought they dreamt it."

Since 1927 there have been a few revivals. Both Margaret Lockwood and Evelyn Laye toured in the UK after the war but neither production reached the West End. Evelyn Laye once asked Noël to prepare a musical version of it for her but this idea was firmly rejected, since he felt she no longer had the vocal range. Moira Lister toured the play in 1981 directed by Ted Craig.

Celia Johnson appeared in a BBC Television production in 1969 and Diana Rigg for Yorkshire TV in 1993 with Richard Johnson and James Villiers.

US PRODUCTIONS

PRESENTED by Kenneth MacOwen and Sidney Ross at the Biltmore Theatre, New York on 14 November 1927 (80 performances).

CHARACTERS	Biltmore, 1927
THE COMTE RAOUL DE VRIAAC	Arthur Byron
ADRIENNE	Madge Evans
JACQUES RIJAR	Theodore St John
ESTEBAN, EL DUCO DE SANTAGUANO	Reginald Owen
MIGUEL	Rex O'Malley
FATHER CLEMENT	Harry Lillford
HUBERT	William Kershaw
THE MARQUISE ELOISE	Billie Burke
ALICE	Dorothy Tree

Director	*David Burton*
Designer	*Jo Mielziner*

The *New York Times*: "It is a play written with all of Mr Coward's impudence and about half of his accustomed skill at dialogue, the result being a pleasant and forgettable evening at the theatre."

ADDITIONAL NOTE

On his return to England in March 1927, Coward wrote a special sketch for the *Then and Now* matinée in aid of the Sadlers Wells Fund (This was the appeal by Lilian Baylis for money to rebuild the theatre).

The first part of the programme, given at the New Theatre, 26 April 1927, consisted of contributions by the old and new members of the Old Vic Company, etc., under the title *The Good Old Days*. The second part, titled the *Hectic Present*, concluded with a night club scene and cabaret: *Pretty Prattle* by Mr Noël Coward.

CHARACTERS	**New Theatre, 1927**
LADY GWENDOLEN VERNEY	Miss Lilian Braithwaite
ZUSHIE WINKETT	Miss Cathleen Nesbitt
MARIAN PHEDAS	Miss Hilda Moore
THE HON. MILLICENT BLOODWORTHY	Miss Heather Thatcher
ROGER BRAMPTON	Mr George Grossmith
MEMBERS AND GUESTS OF THE NIGHT CLUB	Miss Marie Ault, Miss Minnie Rayner, Miss Marjorie Gabain, Miss Marie Ney, Miss Winifred Oughton, Miss Viola Lyel, Miss Pollie Emery, Mr John Gielgud, Mr Keneth Kent, Mr Edwin Underhill, Mr Hilton Edwards, Mr Eric Portman, Mr Harry Knox, Mr Claude Whinney, Mr Lionel Millard, Mr Michael Watts, Mr Kenneth Barnes, Mr Esmond Knight, Mr Gerald Bonnin, Mr Charles Marford, Mr Maurice Farquharson

The manuscript of this sketch is now lost. It also does not appear to have been submitted to the Lord Chamberlain, as there is no copy in their files.

18
HOME CHAT
A PLAY IN THREE ACTS

Written in 1927

FIRST PRESENTED by Basil Dean at the Duke of York's Theatre, London, 25 October 1927 (38 performances).

CHARACTERS	Duke of York's, 1927
PALLETT	Pauline Newton
MAVIS WITTERSHAM	Marda Vanne
PAUL EBONY	George Relph
MRS CHILHAM	Nina Boucicault
MRS EBONY	Henrietta Watson
LAVINIA HARDY	Helen Spencer
JANET EBONY	Madge Titheradge
PETER CHELSWORTH	Arthur Margetson
TURNER	Tom Woods
ALEC STONE	George Curzon
Director	*Basil Dean*
Designer	*G. E. Calthrop*

ACT I: Janet Ebony's house in Chelsea.
ACT II: Peter Chelsworth's flat in St James's. The following day.
ACT III: Same as Act I. Two weeks later.

SYNOPSIS

ACT I: The parlourmaid, Pallett, ushers Mavis Wittersham into the Ebonys' drawing room in Chelsea. Ostensibly, Mavis has called to see Janet Ebony, who is expected back from Paris; but it is evident that her real interest is in Janet's husband Paul – a fashionable novelist whom Mavis regards as her 'soul-mate'. They are joined by Janet's mother, Mrs Chilham, looking slightly harassed. Under pressure from Paul, she reveals that Janet has been involved in a train smash, which she had not mentioned to Paul in the telegram announcing her arrival. Mavis also knows about the accident and has purposely avoided telling Paul about it. It transpires that Janet was sharing a sleeping compartment with her old friend Peter Chelsworth, and, as they were the only people uninjured in the carriage, their escape has been widely publicised. Paul stands up for his wife, purporting to find the incident quite normal. He continues to champion her when his own mother, Mrs Ebony, arrives, full of suspicion and indignation.

Pallett then announces an unexpected visitor, Lavinia Hardy. She is engaged to Peter Chelsworth and has come to "have it out" with Janet. Paul offers her tea and they have started the meal when Janet appears, very gay and self-possessed. Peter, she says, is downstairs, paying the taxi, and will be with them in a minute. At this, Lavinia bursts into tears. When Peter comes in she tells him she never wants to see him again and rushes out, slamming the door. Peter and Janet demand tea – the others demand explanations. Janet says simply that, as the train was crowded and Peter had chivalrously given up his seat to an old lady, she naturally asked him to take the vacant berth in her sleeper. She adds caustically that, though they have been in a very serious accident, no one has expressed the slightest concern for the shock they have suffered, or relief at their escape – everyone is obsessed by the idea that two persons of opposite sexes cannot spent a night together innocently. Aggressively, she asserts that Peter is her lover, and he, though obviously taken aback, gallantly supports the statement, which drives the two older women away. Mavis leaves with them and, while Paul escorts them to the door, Janet snatches a few words with Peter. They both apologise for having compromised each other and Peter hurriedly takes his leave as Paul returns.

Husband and wife are now at last alone. Janet explains that her assertion about Peter was only made to shock her mother-in-law, but Paul evidently does not believe her. When she finds that he, though believing her guilty, is ready to "forgive" her, she flares up, calls him a prig and walks out, with the warning: "When I come back – if I ever do come back – you're going to have a good deal more to forgive than you ever bargained for."

ACT II: Next morning in Peter Chelsworth's flat his servant Turner is setting the breakfast-table when Peter, who has spent the night in an hotel, telephones to say that he will be back for breakfast. Janet, entering in a négligée, chats to Turner about the newspaper accounts of the railway accident. She has just started breakfast when Peter appears. They discuss their curious situation, which worries Peter only because of its probable effect upon Lavinia. Janet confesses herself quite indifferent to her husband and says she is longing to find someone to love her.

The doorbell rings and they just have time to disappear into the bedroom before Turner ushers in Mrs Chilham and Mrs Ebony, who have met on the doorstep. The former tries to stand up for her daughter against Mrs Ebony's moral indignation, but both are taken aback when they hear through the door what is apparently a passionate love-scene between Janet and Peter.

Then Janet enters with a fine show of surprise, assuring them that Peter has lent her his flat and gone off to Scotland. Upon this, Peter rushes into the room and out again. The two older women are dumbfounded, but when Mrs Ebony rallies sufficiently to call Janet shameless and vile, her mother comes gallantly to her defence. Mrs Ebony marches out in dudgeon, leaving mother and daughter together. But Janet is disappointed when her mother, obviously believing her guilty, merely advises her to conduct her liaison with Peter more discreetly. Janet sends her away and has just settled down to a quiet cigarette with Peter when the doorbell rings again. She climbs on to Peter's knee and is sitting there affectionately when Turner shows in Major Alec Stone – an attractive man of about thirty-five. He is apologetic and embarrassed, but they explain that their position was assumed because they thought he was Janet's husband. Dryly, he comments that guilty lovers seldom remain clasped in each other's arms in broad daylight with the front doorbell ringing.

Alec has come to ask Peter to lunch, and he now includes Janet in the invitation. Asked for his advice, he admits that it shocks him to see an obviously charming woman deliberately compromising herself. Then he leaves them.

Janet has just gone to dress when Lavinia rushes in, full of remorse and ready to make up her quarrel with Peter. But when she hears Janet's voice from the bedroom she is again furious. However, Janet comes out and succeeds in convincing her that Peter is quite blameless. She sends them off together and remains alone, looking rather miserable. When Alec Stone returns he finds her in tears, because she has decided to go back to her husband and is depressed at the anti-climax. He cheers her up and takes her off to lunch.

ACT III: Once again Pallett shows Mavis Wittersham into Paul's drawing-room. A fortnight has elapsed, and Mavis has now come to an understanding with him that he will marry her after divorcing Janet, who is in Paris – they assume with Peter Chelsworth.

When Mrs Chilham calls, however, she assures them that Peter is in London – she has seen him the previous day in Hyde Park and he has told her "a secret", The next caller is Mrs Ebony, who startles Janet's mother by mentioning the impending divorce. At that moment Peter and Lavinia are announced as "Mr and Mrs Chelsworth" – their marriage was the "secret" told to Mrs Chilham. Lavinia explains that the "love-scene" overheard by Janet's mother and mother-in-law was a put-up job, merely intended to shock them. She adds that Janet's companion in Paris is a woman friend, Valerie Marshall. At this Mavis bursts into tears, explaining her agitation as remorse for the way everyone has treated "poor Janet". But she is obviously very much upset, and when the Chelsworths have gone she asserts that Janet is a liar and that she herself does not intend to apologise to her. She is on the point of leaving when Janet appears in a defiant mood – to be greeted with a warmth that evidently surprises her.

They all apologise for having doubted her original story, and will not believe her now when she declares that she has been staying in Paris with Alec Stone and is in love with him. The two mothers go out, leaving Paul, Mavis and Janet together. Paul then confesses that he loves Mavis and wants a collusive divorce. He begs for, and receives, Janet's forgiveness and her agreement to his plans, which she freely accords – on condition that they both go away at once. When she is alone the telephone starts to ring. She takes the receiver, rapturously hailing the caller as "darling".

E. W. B., in the *Westminster Gazette*, 26 October 1927:

" 'We expected better.'

" 'So did I.'

"This 'conversation piece' between a 'voice' in the gallery and Noël Coward when he came forward to take a call at the end of his new play, *Home Chat*, last night, is a succinct criticism of the piece. As it is endorsed by the author, it can confidently be put on record.

"It is also easy to accept Mr Coward's subsequent eulogies of the producer and the actors. Basil Dean and the company have worked wonders with a play which is slender in plot and not particularly scintillating in dialogue.

"All it amounts to, if considered apart from its epigrammatic trimmings and its characterisation, is that a woman's husband and his and her relatives will not believe her to be innocent when she is, and are equally set on believing her not to be guilty when she really has an affair.

"Mr Coward has treated this theme flippantly and a little cynically. It was obvious last night that the gallery did not take to the cynical ending – the husband pairing off with a woman who had aspired to be his soul-mate, and the wife beginning, as the final curtain descended, a tender conversation over the telephone with the Guards officer with whom she had spent a week in Paris.

"Although the first act is slow, there is an element of comedy in the idea of everybody putting a horrid construction on the fact that the wife and a man friend were returning to Europe in the same *wagon-lit* – a fact which emerged because the train was wrecked and most of the passengers killed or injured.

"But Mr Coward seems to feel it to be his mission to be flippant at all costs, and unfortunately many of the lines are less Cowardian than usual.

"Where Mr Coward has scored is in his amusing character portraits. Madge Titheradge as the wife, George Relph as the husband, Nina Boucicault and Henrietta Watson as the mothers, Arthur Margetson as the man in the sleeper, and George Curzon as the officer in the Guards act in the proper spirit of comedy, but, good as are their performances, one must not forget the author's share in making these amusing people.

"But the gallery was right. We expected better."

PUBLICATIONS

Home Chat was first published by Martin Secker (London, 1927). It is dedicated to Mary Borden.

NOTES

Coward spent the spring and summer of 1927 at his country house, Goldenhurst, in Kent. He says:

"During the summer I wrote a comedy called *Home Chat*. It had some excellent lines and a reasonably funny situation, but I was not entirely pleased with it. However, I read it to Madge Titheradge, for whom I had visualised the leading part, and she liked it, and, as Basil also thought it good, we settled to do it in the early autumn."

Coward says in his preface to *Play Parade, Volume III*: "The opening performance was rendered agonising by one of the more elderly actresses in the company forgetting her lines continually, with the result that the pauses she made while trying to remember them, coupled with the intentional pauses that Basil Dean had carefully rehearsed, frequently brought the play to a standstill. There were boos at the end, and I bounded on to the stage with my usual misguided valour and had a brisk interchange of unpleasantness with the gallery. However, no good came of any of it, and the play closed after a few weeks. I do not think it would have lasted that long had it not been for the acting of Madge Titheradge. When I wrote it, I naturally considered it good; so did she and everybody concerned, but we were wrong. It was a little better than bad, but not quite good enough, and that was that."

Home Chat was revived by the Noël Coward Company at Malvern and on tour in 1932, but there have been no other major revivals.

19
THIS YEAR OF GRACE!
REVUE
Written in 1927 and 1928

FIRST PRESENTED by Charles B. Cochran at the Palace, Manchester, 28 February 1928 (ran to March 17), as *Charles B. Cochran's 1928 Revue.*

SUBSEQUENTLY PRESENTED at the London Pavilion, 22 March 1928, as *This Year of Grace!* (316 performances).

Book, lyrics and music by Noël Coward. Polka and Waltz Finale (Part I), 'Gothic' and 'Arabesque' by Tilly Losch. Other dances and ensembles by Max Rivers.

Staged by Frank Collins. Orchestra under the direction of Ernest Irving. Pianist, Leslie Hutchinson.

Cast of the London production:

PART I

1. A Tube Station (Marc Henri and Laverdet)

FRED (a bookstall attendant)	Fred Groves
FEMALE PASSENGERS	Madeline Gibson, Florita Fey, Greta Taylor, Marjorie Robertson, Betty Davis, Gladys Godby, Peter May, Marjorie Browne, Peggy Wynne, Marie Masters, Dinka Starace, Nancy Barnett, Decilia Mobray, Doreen Austin,

	Nancy Fielder, Isla Bevan, Nora Olive, Kathleen Coram
AN OFFICE BOY	Tommy Hayes
MALE PASSENGERS	Arthur Warren, Syd Shields, Eddie Grant, Edward Coventry, Charles Farey, Frank Fox, Richard Haydon, Fred Le Roy, Fred Herries
A BANK CLERK	Sonnie Hale
A LIFT MAN	Billy Shaw
LADY GWENDOLYN VERNEY	Joan Clarkson
THE HON. MILLICENT BLOODWORTHY	Ann Codrington
HARRY (a booking clerk)	Lance Lister
CECIL	William Cavanagh
LAWRENCE	Cecil Stafford
CHARLES	Douglas Byng
MARY	Jessie Matthews
FIRST GIRL	Sheilah Graham
SECOND GIRL	Moya Nugent

| Song, "Waiting In A Queue" | Sonnie Hale |

2. Mary Make Believe

Jessie Matthews and Mr Cochran's Young Ladies

3. The Theatre Guide

| ANNOUNCER | Lance Lister |
| PAGE | Nora Olive |

(a) The Wrecker

THE LOVERS	William Cavanagh, Moya Nugent
A PORTER	Syd Shields
A SIGNALMAN	Charles Farey
A DETECTIVE	Eddie Grant

(b) The Silver Cord

| A YOUNG MAN | Robert Algar |
| A WOMAN | Betty Shale |

(c) Young Woodley

| TWO SCHOOLBOYS | Lance Lister, Douglas Byng |

(d) *Any Noël Coward Play*

THE LEADING LADY	Joan Clarkson
HER SUPPORT	Ann Codrington, Dinka Starace, Arthur Warren, Edward Coventry

4. *Mad About You*

Dress design — Ada Peacock

Sheilah Graham, William Cavanagh, and Mr Cochran's Young Ladies

Speciality Dance — Jean Barry and Jack Holland

5. *The Bus Rush*

THE PEOPLE	Maisie Gay, Madge Aubrey, Betty Shale, Moya Nugent, Betty Davis, Ann Codrington, Dinka Starace, Arthur Warren, Cecil Stafford

6. *Lorelei*

Adrienne Brune's dress — *Kitty Shannon*
*Lauri Devine's and
    William Cavanagh's dress* — *Oliver Messel*
Scene design — *Oliver Messel*

SINGERS	Sonnie Hale, Adrienne Brune
LORELEI	Lauri Devine
SAILOR	William Cavanagh

7. *Snowball*

Speciality by a child dancer

8. *Ignorance Is Bliss*

Dress design in '1890' — *G. E. Calthrop*
Scene designs — *G. E. Calthrop*

(a) *1890*

MRS BLAKE (proprietress of private hotel)	Maisie Gay
HUSBAND	Sonnie Hale
WIFE	Jessie Matthews
ANNIE (a servant)	Moya Nugent

(b) *1928*

RECEPTION CLERK	Douglas Byng
HUSBAND	Lance Lister
WIFE	Joan Clarkson
PAGE	Tommy Hayes

9. Arabesque (Dance Of The Hands)

Tilly Losch

10. A Room With A View (Marc Henri and Laverdet)

Jessie Matthews, Sonnie Hale, Adrienne Brune

11. It Doesn't Matter How Old You Are

Maisie Gay

12. Teach Me To Dance Like Grandma

Jessie Matthews and Mr Cochran's Young Ladies

Dances:

Polka	Tilly Losch
Mazurka	Tilly Losch, Sonnie Hale

POLKA CHILDREN	Gladys Godby, Marie Masters, Betty Davis, Decilia Mobray, Isla Bevan, Nora Olive, Kathleen Coram, Doreen Austin
YOUNG LADIES	Peter May, Florita Fey, Greta Taylor, Marjorie Browne, Peggy Wynne, Madeline Gibson, Nancy Barnett, Marjorie Robertson
YOUNG GENTLEMEN	Arthur Warren, Edward Coventry, Billy Shaw, Frank Fox, Richard Haydon, Charles Farey, Fred Herries, Fred Le Roy

THE THREE GRACES:

TAGLIONI	Jessie Matthews
GRISI	Sheilah Graham
ELLSLER	Moya Nugent

Waltz	Jean Barry, Jack Holland
Finale	Entire Company
The Polka, Mazurka and Waltz dress design	*Doris Zinkeisen*

13. *The Lido Beach*

THE CONTESSA	Betty Shale
LADY FENCHURCH	Joan Clarkson
LADY SALTWOOD	Ann Codrington
LADY VERLAP	Lauri Devine
SIR JOHN VERLAP	Robert Algar
SIR FREDERICK SALTWOOD	Sonnie Hale
THE COMTE	Fred Groves
SIR CHARLES FENCHURCH	Lance Lister
YOUNG MAN	William Cavanagh
BARONESS KURDLE	Douglas Byng
MR CLARK	Cecil Stafford
VIOLET	Jessie Matthews
RUTH	Sheilah Graham
JANE	Madge Aubrey
IVY	Moya Nugent

Opening Chorus,
   "Little Women"

Jessie Matthews, Sheilah Graham,
Madge Aubrey, Moya Nugent

14. *The English Lido Beach*

Scene design	*G. E. Calthrop*
ANNOUNCER	Lance Lister
MR FREEMAN	Fred Groves
MRS FREEMAN	Ann Codringtoon
ALICE	Moya Nugent
FRANKIE	Tommy Hayes
OFFICIAL	Melville Cooper
MADGE	Sheilah Graham
DORIS	Marjorie Browne
MR HARRIS	Sonnie Hale
MRS HARRIS	Joan Clarkson
VI	Kitty Jacobs
GEORGE	Jack Kosky
MRS CLARK	Madge Aubrey
PHYLLIS	Lolita Hudson
MRS JONES	Betty Shale
DAISY KIPSHAW	Maisie Gay

Opening Chorus,
   "Mother's Complaint"

Ann Codrington, Joan Clarkson,
Madge Aubrey, Betty Shale

"Britannia Rules The Waves"   Maisie Gay and Company

15. Ballet: The Legend Of The Lily Of The Valley

Dress and scene design   *C. E. Calthrop*

ANNOUNCER   Sonnie Hale
FLANNELETTE   Tilly Losch
BERGAMOT   Lauri Devine
FAIRIES   Florita Fey, Marjorie Robertson, Gladys
                       Godby, Marjorie Browne, Nora Olive,
                       Madeline Gibson
FEMALE COURTIERS   Betty Davis, Marie Masters, Nancy
                       Barnett, Nancy Fielder, Isla Bevan,
                       Kathleen Coram
MALE COURTIERS   Arthur Warren, Charles Farey, Edward
                       Coventry, Richard Haydon, Fred Le
                       Roy, Fred Jeffries
MARQUIS DE POOPINAC   Douglas Byng

16. Rules Of Three (Marc Henri and Laverdet)

Joan Clarkson's dress design   *Doris Zinkeisen*

ANNOUNCER   Joan Clarkson

(a) (Barrie)
   THE WIFE   Moya Nugent
   THE LOVER   Melville Cooper
   THE HUSBAND   Fred Groves

(b) (Lonsdale)
   THE WIFE   Jessie Matthews
   THE LOVER   Sonnie Hale
   THE BUTLER   William Cavanagh
   THE HUSBAND   Lance Lister

(c) (Wallace)
   THE WIFE   Ann Codrington
   THE LOVER   Douglas Byng
   THE HUSBAND   Robert Algar

17. Dance, Little Lady   Sonnie Hale

Mask and dress design   *Oliver Messel*

THE LITTLE LADY   Lauri Devine

DANCERS	Betty Davis, Gladys Godby, Peter May, Marjorie Browne, Nora Olive, Kathleen Coram, Billy Shaw, Arthur Warren, Syd Shields, Eddie Grant, Edward Coventry, Frank Fox

18. Chauve Souris

Dress design	*Doris Zinkeisen*
THE GREAT MAN	Lance Lister
SINGERS	Maisie Gay, Fred Groves, Sonnie Hale, Douglas Byng, Robert Algar

19. Gothic

Scene and dress design	*Doris Zinkeisen*

Tilly Losch, Lauri Devine

20. Try To Learn To Love

Jessie Matthews, Sonnie Hale and Mr Cochran's Young Ladies

21. Law And Order (Marc Henri and Laverdet)

POLICE WOMAN PELLET	Douglas Byng
MATCH-SELLER	Betty Shale
YOUNG GIRL	Moya Nugent
YOUNG MAN	Edward Coventry
POLICEWOMAN WENDLE	Maisie Gay

22. A Spanish Fantasy

Jean Barry's costume design	*Doris Zinkeisen*

Jean Barry, Jack Holland

23. Castleton And Mack

Speciality by two American comedians

24. Finale

Scene design	*Marc Henri and Laverdet*

Entire Company

In Manchester, where the production was titled *Charles B. Cochran's 1928 Revue*, two numbers were included which were later cut for the London production (26 items in Manchester and 24 in London). A song was also cut from one of the other numbers for the London revue. The three omitted items were:

Dress and scene designs	G. E. Calthrop

(a) *After Dinner*

PAGE	Nora Olive

(b) *1908*

YOUNG ENGLISHMEN	Fred Groves, Douglas Byng, Lance Lister, Melville Cooper

1928

YOUNG ENGLISHWOMEN	Joan Clarkson, Moya Nugent, Betty Shale, Madge Aubrey

Grand Production Number: *Jewels And Perfumes*

Maisie Gay and Mr Cochran's Young Ladies

ANNOUNCER	Lance Lister

(This item was first performed in Lou Nadle's *Daggles* at the Theatre Royal, Puddleton.)

(c) *Caballero*

Dress design	*Doris Zinkeisen*
SINGER	Adrienne Brune
SPANISH GIRLS	Marjorie Robertson, Betty Davis, Greta Taylor, Peggy Wynne, Marie Masters, Nancy Barnett, Nancy Fielder, Nora Olive
SPANISH RIDING GIRLS	Florita Fey, Gladys Godby, Marjorie Browne, Isla Bevan
A SPANISH IMPRESSION	Tilly Losch
Dance: Tango	Jean Barry, Jack Holland

In London on the first night "Caballero" became "A Spanish Fantasy", and was danced by Jean Barry and Jack Holland.

Later in the run the song was restored and sung by Paula Ruby, with the solos and dancers as originally, but retaining the title, "A Spanish Fantasy".

During the London run the plays burlesqued in *Theatre Guide* were changed. *The Trial Of Mary Dugan, Show Boat, The Squeaker*, and "Any Sunday Night Show" were included at various times.

In September Maisie Gay substituted "What Love Means To Girls Like Me" (from *London Calling!*) for "It Doesn't Matter How Old You Are", and a new item, 'Lilac Time', the Beggar Maid: Maisie Gay and the Gardener: Sonnie Hale, replaced 'Law And Order'.

In October a sketch from *Charlot's Revue* (Prince of Wales Theatre, 1924) was introduced:

Love, Life, And Laughter (Paris, 1890)

Scene and dress design	*G. E. Calthrop*
HERBERT	Fred Groves
ROBERT	Douglas Byng
A WOMAN	Moya Nugent
MADAME CRAPOTTE	Betty Shale
CUSTOMERS of "La Chatte Vierge"	Ann Codrington, Madge Aubrey, Sheilah Graham, William Cavanagh, Robert Algar, Cecil Stafford
A WAITER	Melville Cooper
LA FLAMME	Maisie Gay

The revue was produced in New York at the Selwyn Theatre, 7 November 1928, with Noël Coward and Beatrice Lillie in the cast. For this production Coward wrote several new items (as well as a new Finale for the Company):

"World Weary", sung by Beatrice Lillie
"Velasquez"

Arrangement	*Tilly Losch*
Scene and dress design	*Doris Zinkeisen*
SINGER	Rita Mackay
TWO PAGES	Robinson Powell, Timothy Dobson
DANCERS	Marjorie Moss, Georges Fontanne

The sketches, 'Love, Life, And Laughter' (Paris, 1890), and 'Lilac Time' were also introduced. These replaced "Mad About You", "It Doesn't Matter How Old You Are", "Spanish Fantasy", the two Tilly Losch items – 'Gothic' and 'Arabesque', and the specialities of Castleton and Mack and Snowball.

The third potted play (Edgar Wallace) in 'Rules of Three', was replaced by 'Any Civic Repertory Play'. (This was published as 'The Order of the Day', burlesquing Elmer Rice's Street Scene in *Collected Sketches and Lyrics*.)

The plays burlesqued in *Theatre Guide* on the first night in New York were *The Trial of Mary Dugan*, *The Silver Cord*, and 'Any Civic Repertory Play'.

After the New York production had been launched, three of the numbers used there were introduced into the London production in December. These were "World Weary", sung by Jessie Matthews, and the "American Finale".

The numbers "I Can't Think" and "Velasquez" were not performed in London.

St John Ervine in the *Observer*, 25 March 1928:

"I must be careful with my superlatives, so I will say only this, that *This Year of Grace!* is the most amusing, the most brilliant, the cleverest, the daintiest, the most exquisite, the most fanciful, the most graceful, the happiest, the most ironical, the jolliest, the most kaleidoscopic, the loveliest, the most magnificent, the neatest and nicest, the most opulent, the pithiest, the quickest, the richest, the most superb and tasteful, the most uberous, the most versatile, the wittiest – blow, 'x' has stopped me! After that marvellous exhibition of self-restraint, I will now let myself go, and say that if any person comes to me and says that there has ever, anywhere in the world, been a better revue than this, I shall publicly tweak his nose.

"Mr Coward has many and various gifts; nearly all of them are displayed in this entertainment, which is produced with a celerity which makes me imagine that Mr Cochran must have learned by heart Henley's poem which begins, 'Speed, in the name of the Lord, speed!' We are given liberally, but not excessively, all sorts of scenes, including one, entitled 'Dance, Little Lady' which is full of Hogarthian humour. In this scene a clever dancer, Miss Lauri Devine, mimes the part of a modern girl dancing in that lifeless, exhausted, unsmiling fashion that is common among the young who were reared on food-tickets and were bombed into neurosis. Mr Oliver Messel has designed masks for this scene which faithfully reproduce the mirthless, vacuous expression one may see for oneself any night in smart restaurants and clubs, where empty-looking youths dance with empty-looking maidens in an empty shuffle. The scene is almost cruel in its veracity, but it is a genuine satire on our time, and it confirms me in my belief that Mr Coward's talents are growing. The skits on contemporary plays are very funny, and there are two gorgeously comic scenes, 'The Bus Rush' and 'The English Lido Beach', and many amazing dances. Miss Maisie Gay is richly humorous in every scene in which she appears, and Miss Jessie Matthews, who grows in grace, is charming and dainty in all that she does.

"The entire company is brilliant, and if I do not mention all of its members, it is not because all of them do not deserve to be mentioned, but simply that sustained adulation is tiring, and I can find no excuse for adding some acid to this cloyingly sweet criticism. Miss Jean Barry, a lady with lovely long legs, and Mr Jack Holland dance so superbly that they must overthrow the most restrained audience, but their ability is no greater than that of Miss Tilly Losch and Miss Lauri Devine, who, in a scene called 'Gothic', excite our admiration with a performance that is beautiful. Mr Cochran's Young Ladies maintain the high reputation which the English chorus-girl enjoys through out Europe. He has given us his finest revue."

PUBLICATIONS

The book of *This Year of Grace!* was included in *Play Parade, Volume II* (Heinemann, 1939), and the musical score was published by William Chappell, 1928.

The following items from the revue are included in:

(a) *Collected Sketches and Lyrics* (Hutchinson, 1931; all written in 1928).
Those marked (*) are included in *Collected Revue Sketches and Parodies* (Methuen, 1999).
*"Rules Of Three" (Barrie, Lonsdale, and French Farce)
*"Lido Beach"
*"The English Lido"
"Ignorance Is Bliss"
"It Doesn't Matter How Old You Are"
*"Law And Order"
"Try To Learn To Love"
"Chauve Souris"
*"The Legend Of The Lily Of The Valley"
*"The Tube"
*"The Order Of The Day" (American version of the revue)

(b) *The Noël Coward Song Book* (Michael Joseph, 1953):

"Dance, Little Lady"
"A Room With A View"
"World Weary"

The vocal score of the revue was published by William Chappell (London, 1928). They also published a book of the lyrics and separate sheet music for the following numbers:

"Dance, Little Lady"
"I'm Mad About You"
"It Doesn't Matter How Old You Are"
"Little Women"
"Lorelei"
"Mary Make Believe"
"A Room With A View"
"Teach Me How To Dance Like Grandma"
"Try To Learn To Love"
"World Weary"
"Caballero"

NOTES

After the fiasco of *Sirocco* (see page 52), Coward, who had a contract to appear in *The Second Man* and to write a revue for Cochran, felt it unfair to proceed with either of these projects. When he suggested that he should be released from the play, the management gallantly refused and, as he says:

"Cochran had almost laughed at me for wanting to postpone doing his revue. He said, with a kindly wisdom born of many years of battling with success and failure, that in a few weeks' time any hubbub over *Sirocco* would be entirely forgotten and that he was quite sure that the revue would turn out to be a triumphant one in the eye for the lot of them."

After a holiday in France, Coward returned to London, and appeared at the Playhouse in January 1928, in *The Second Man*, by S. N. Behrman. Meantime, the revue was in course of writing, and it went into rehearsal as soon as the play had opened.

Coward says:

"The finding of a title for the revue caused us all many racked hours of the day and many sleepless nights. We sat round with pencils and papers flogging our brains and shooting forth anything we thought of, however inappropriate, in the hope that the very fatuity of our suggestion might inspire somebody else with an idea. All the ideal revue titles seemed to have been done: *Vanity Fair, Bric-à-Brac, London, Paris, and New York, Odds and Ends*, etc., etc. Finally, Lorn said *This Year of Grace!*, and we instantly knew that we were all right. *This Year of Grace!* it was, and I still think it one of the best revue titles I have ever heard."

Coward says in his introduction to *Play Parade, Volume II:* "*This Year of Grace!* is always dominated for me by the rich, comic personality of Maisie Gay. I can see her so clearly in my memory standing, flurried and helpless, waiting for that imaginary bus, clutching all those parcels and the balloons for the children while her hat got pushed farther and farther on to one side and her hair began to come down from sheer exertion.

"I can remember Beatrice Lillie in the New York production sitting at a high desk, dressed as a grubby little office-boy and singing, with infinite pathos, 'World Weary' while she munched an apple."

The revue has never been revived; Sheilah Graham, from its original London cast, subsequently married F. Scott Fitzgerald.

20
BITTER SWEET

(Originally called *Sari Linden*)

AN OPERETTA

Written in 1928 and 1929

FIRST PRESENTED by Charles B. Cochran at the Palace Theatre, Manchester, 2 July 1929 (2 weeks).

SUBSEQUENTLY PRESENTED at His Majesty's Theatre, London, 12 July 1929 (697 performances). Transferred to the Palace Theatre, 2 March 1931. The run ended 21 March. The company then played Streatham Hill (1 week), and Golders Green (2 weeks), and returned to the West End to continue the run at the Lyceum Theatre, 13 April 1931 (32 performances).

ACT I, *Scene 1: Lady Shayne's house in Grosvenor Square, 1929.*

PARKER (a butler)	Claude Farrow
DOLLY CHAMBERLAIN	Dorothy Boyd
LORD HENRY	William Harn
VINCENT HOWARD	Billy Milton
THE MARCHIONESS OF SHAYNE	Peggy Wood

NITA	Isla Bevan
HELEN	Nancy Bevill
JACKIE	Maureen Moore
FRANK	Arthur Alexander
GUESTS	Dodo Jay, Joan Panter, Nora Chapman, Mary Tudor, Victoria Yates, Gladys Godwin, Nina Carleton, Mabel Couper, Joan Brooke, Alfred O'Farrell, Billy Skyrme, Kenneth Ware, Ray Rivington, Hugh French, Eric Lauriston, Sydney Grammer, John Allen, Frank Linden, Penryn Bannerman
MUSICIANS	Leonard Pemell, Harry Young, Leonard Bryant, Tom Johnson

Scene 2: The Millicks' house in Belgrave Square, 1875.

SARAH MILLICK	Peggy Wood
CARL LINDEN	George Metaxa
MRS MILLICK	Elaine Inescort
MR HUGH DEVON	Robert Newton

Scene 3: The ballroom of the Millicks' house in Belgrave Square, 1875.

CARL LINDEN	George Metaxa
LADY DEVON	Winifred Davis
MRS MILLICK	Elaine Inescort
MR HUGH DEVON	Robert Newton
SIR ARTHUR FENCHURCH	Clifford Heatherley
SARAH MILLICK	Peggy Wood
THE MARQUIS OF STEERE	Robert Algar
LORD EDGAR JAMES	Victor Robson
LORD SORREL	Gerald Nodin
MR VALE	Roy Russell
MR BETHEL	John Gatrell
MR PROUTIE	Richard Cornish
VICTORIA	José Fearon
HARRIET	Maie Drage
GLORIA	Rose Hignell

HONOR	Eva Sternroyd (Manchester)
	Isla Bevan (His Majesty's)
JANE	Eileen Carey
EFFIE	Mary Pounds
FOOTMEN	Robert Sturtivant, Kenneth Ware, R. J. Thurgood, Cyril Whittle
GUESTS	Gladys Godwin, Joan Panter, Mabel Couper, Margery Lancaster, Kitty Gordon, Keira Tuson, Betty Huntley-Wright, Dodo Jay, Joan Brooke, Olive Darby, Freda Marcus, Fedora Roselli, Norah Chapman, Vera Bertie, Nancy Bevill, Mary Tudor, Victoria Yates, Nina Carlton, Marcelle Turner, Maureen Moore, Betty Bucknell, Doris Treverne, Marjorie Heal, Millie Sim, Alfred O'Farrell, Penryn Bannerman, Arthur Alexander, Tom Paxford, Anthony Brian, Billy Skyrme, Ray Rivington, Hugh French, Eric Lauriston, Sydney Grammar, John Allen, Frank Linden, Claude Farrow, Hugh Cuenod
MUSICIANS	Leonard Pemell, Frank Freeman, Leonard Pearce, Leonard Bryant, Harry Young

ACT II, *Scene 1: Herr Schlick's café in Vienna, 1880; Twelve o'clock noon.*

WAITERS	Cyril Whittle, R. J. Thurgood, Robert Sturtivant, Kenneth Ware, Hugh French, Penryn Bannerman, Tommy Hayes
CLEANERS	Vera Hertie, Fedora Roselli, Joan Panter, Margery Lancaster, Gladys Godwin, Marjorie Heal
LOTTE	Millie Sim
FREDA	Betty Huntley-Wright
HANSI	Marjorie Rogers

FRITZ (a waiter)	Kenneth Ware (Manchester) (the part was cut in London)
GUSSI	Norah Howard
CARL LINDEN	George Metaxa
MANON (la crevette)	Ivy St Helier
CAPTAIN AUGUST LUTTE	Austin Trevor
HERR SCHLICK	Clifford Heatherley
SARI LINDEN	Peggy Wood
MUSICIANS	William Reid, Leonard Pemell, Frank Freeman, Harry Young, Leonard Pearce

Scene 2: Herr Schlick's Café in Vienna, 1880; About 2 a.m.

Prater Girls' Dance arrangement	*Tilly Losch*
CARL LINDEN	George Metaxa
CAPTIAN SCHENZI	Gerald Nodin
SARI LINDEN	Peggy Wood
LOTTE	Millie Sim
CAPTAIN LUTTE	Austin Trevor
GUSSI	Norah Howard
LIEUTENANT TRANISCH	Arthur Alexander
HANSI	Marjorie Rogers
FREDA	Betty Huntley-Wright
HERR SCHLICK	Clifford Heatherley
THE PRATER GIRLS:	
GIRLS	Audrey Pointing, Sheila Rawle, Ena Wood Sims
BOYS	Verena Shaxon, Mai Orton, Yvonne Bose
MANON (la crevette)	Ivy St Helier
OFFICERS, GUESTS, WAITERS and MUSICIANS	Robert Algar, Victor Robson, Richard Cornish, John Gatrell, Roy Russell, Alfred O'Farrell, Eric Lauriston, Tom Paxford, Billy Skyrme, Anthony Brian, Ray Rivington, Cyril Whittle, R. J. Thurgood, Robert Sturtivant, Kenneth Ware, Hugh French, Penryn Bannerman, Tommy Hayes, William Reid, Leonard Pemell, Frank Freeman, Harry Young, Leonard

Pearce, Maureen Moore, Nina
Carleton, Joan Panter, Freda Marcus,
Fedora Roselli, Isla Bevan, Mabel
Couper, Margery Lancaster, Doris
Treverne, Dodo Jay, Joan Brooke, Betty
Bucknell, Nancy Bevill, Norah
Chapman, Mary Tudor, Olive Darby,
Gladys Godwin, Marjorie Heal, Kitty
Gordon, Victoria Yates, Marcelle
Turner, Keira Tuson, Vera Bertie,
Sydney Grammar, John Allen, Frank
Linden, Claude Farrow, Lionel
Stamford, Arthur Wilson, Jack Ricketts,
Frank Worth, G. Martin, Charles Apsey,
Jack Rose, Charles S. Cartwright, Allan
Thorp, Kingston Trollope

ACT III, *Scene 1: Lord Shayne's house in London, 1895.*

BURLEY (a butler)	Anthony Brian
THE MARQUIS OF SHAYNE	Alan Napier
MRS BETHEL (Effie)	Mary Pounds
MR BETHEL	John Gatrell
MRS VALE (Jane)	Eileen Carey
MR VALE	Roy Russell
MRS PROUTIE (Gloria)	Rose Hignell
MR PROUTIE	Richard Cornish
THE DUCHESS OF TENDERTON* (Victoria)	José Fearon
THE DUKE OF TENDERTON	Robert Algar
LADY SORREL (Honor)	Eva Sternroyd (Manchester)
	Isla Bevan (His Majesty's)
LORD SORREL	Gerald Nodin
LADY EDGAR JAMES (Harriet)	Maie Drage
LORD EDGAR JAMES	Victor Robson
SIR HUGH DEVON	Robert Newton
LADY DEVON	Keira Tuson
MADAME SARI LINDEN	Peggy Wood
VERNON CRAFT	Eric Lauriston (Manchester)
	Arthur Alexander (His Majesty's)
CEDRIC BALLANTYNE	William Harn

*Tenterden in the published play

BERTRAM SELLICK	Hugh Cuenod (Manchester)
	Eric Lauriston (His Majesty's)
LORD HENRY JADE	Penryn Bannerman
ACCOMPANIST (to Madame Linden)	Leonard Pearce
GUESTS	Gladys Godwin, Joan Panter, Mabel Couper, Margery Lancaster, Kitty Gordon, Dodo Jay, Betty Huntley-Wright, Joan Brook, Olive Darby, Freda Marcus, Fedora Roselli, Norah Chapman, Vera Bertie, Nancy Bevill, Mary Tudor, Marcelle Turner, Nina Carleton, Maureen Moore, Victoria Yates, Betty Bucknell, Doris Treverne, Marjorie Heal, Alfred O'Farrell, Tom Paxford, Billy Skyrme, Ray Rivington, Cyril Whittle, John Allen, Sydney Grammer, Frank Linden, Jack Rose, Claude Farrow, Robert Sturtivant

Scene 2: The same as Act I, Scene 1

Director	*Noël Coward*
Designer, Act I, sets and costumes for Scenes 2 and 3, Act III, sets and costumes	*G. E. Calthrop*
Act II, sets and costumes	*Ernst Stern*
Orchestral director	*Reginald Burston*
Orchestrations	*Orellana*

MUSICAL NUMBERS

(The titles and numbers in brackets are in the score only, not noted on the programme)

ACT I, *Scene 1*

("That Wonderful Melody"	Dance Band Singer)
"The Call Of Life"	Lady Shayne and Chorus

Scene 2

"If You Could Only Come With Me"	Carl
"I'll See You Again"	Sarah and Carl

Scene 3

"Tell Me, What Is Love?"	Sarah and Chorus
"The Last Dance"	Marquis of Steere, Lord James, Lord Sorrel, Mr Vale, Mr Bethel, Mr Proutie, Victoria, Harriet, Gloris, Honor, Jane, Effie
Finale	Sarah, Carl, Victoria, Effie, Harriet, Honor, Jane, Gloria and Footmen

ACT II, *Scene 1*

Opening Chorus ("Life In The Morning")	Waiters and Cleaners
"Ladies Of The Town"	Lotti, Freda, Hansi and Gussi
"If Love Were All"	Manon
"Evermore And A Day"	Sari and Carl
"Little Café"	Sari and Carl

Scene 2

Officers' Chorus	Officers and Chorus
"Tokay"	Captain Schenzi, Officers and Chorus
"Bonne Nuit, Merci"	Manon
"Kiss Me"	Manon and Chorus

ACT III, *Scene 1*

"Ta Ra Ra Boom De Ay"	Mr Bethel, Mr Vale, Mr Proutie, Duke of Tenderton, Lord Sorrel, Lord James, Victoria, Harriet, Gloria, Honor, Jane, Effie
"Alas, The Time Is Past"	Victoria, Harriet, Gloria, Honor, Jane, Effie
"Green Carnations"	Vernon Craft, Cedric Ballantyne, Bertram Sellick, Lord Henry Jade
"Zigeuner"	Sari

Scene 2

Finale, "I'll See You Again"	Lady Shayne and Chorus

The duet for Sari and Carl, "Evermore And A Day" in Act II, is included in the score and the published play, but was cut in the UK production. It was sung in the American production.

The waiter Fritz has a short scene with Manon, leading up to her song, "If Love Were All". This dialogue was omitted in London.

In the 1934 revival in Washington a short scene was inserted into Act II in which Herr Schlick and his wife tease the waiter, Fritz. The dialogue leads into a trio "It's Always The Man Who's Pursued". There is no evidence that the number survived the out of town performance.

Gerald Nodin, who originally played Lord Sorrel and Captain Schenzi, and understudied the part of Carl Linden (which he played on occasions), left the London company to play the same parts in the American production; but at the last moment he took over the part of Carl Linden (Boston, October 1929; New York, November 1929).

Evelyn Laye, who played Sarah Millick in America, replaced Peggy Wood in London at His Majesty's Theatre from November, 1930, to January, 1931. After the London run and the short tour, Evelyn Laye again played the part during the final farewell four weeks at the Lyceum Theatre.

SYNOPSIS

ACT I, Scene 1: In the year 1929 the Marchioness of Shayne is giving a small dance at her house in Grosvenor Square. The stage is crowded with dancers, but when supper is announced they pass through double doors at the back, and the members of the band go on to the balcony for a breath of fresh air. Only the pianist, Vincent Howard, remains, softly playing improvisations.

An engaged couple, Dolly Chamberlain and Henry Jekyll, come in from the library. Dolly is pretty and lively, but her fiancé is inclined to be pompous. Evidently she is slightly dubious about their future happiness. They discuss Lady Shayne, who at 70 is still (according to Henry) "a gay old bird". She must have had a thrilling life, thinks Dolly; but Henry opines that she was thoroughly immoral, consorted with "awful second-rate people", and was very lucky to get back into society by marrying Lord Shayne.

This attitude annoys Dolly, who tells him to "shut up and go away". He walks off into the supper-room in a huff, leaving his fiancée with Vincent, who confesses his hopeless love for her. She is clasped in his arms when Lady Shayne surprises them.

Vincent apologises, taking the blame upon himself, and assuring her that his intentions are "quite honourable, if presumptuous". Lady Shayne asks Dolly what she intends to do, and, getting the reply, "I don't know," tells her sharply that she detests indecision.

Some of the guests return from the supper-room and Vincent plays a jazz tune for them and they start to dance; but Lady Shayne, stamping her foot, orders them to stop. "You none of you know anything or want anything beyond noise and speed," she declares. "Come with me a little – I'll show you – listen – listen –" And she sings them "The Call Of Life".

The lights slowly go out and through the darkness her voice grows younger and younger, until presently the lights come up again, revealing her as a girl in a Victorian gown.

Scene 2: The year is 1875 and Sarah Millick, a girl of 16, is singing for her music-master, Carl Linden. At the end of the song he tells her that he wrote it for her when he was 16. That cannot be true, protests Sarah, for they have only known each other for a year. Carl explains that it was written for his ideal woman, someone just like her, and he goes on to tell her of the colourful festivals in his native Austria. He sings of his beautiful land and his longing that she might be able to see it with him. He tells her that he will not be able to play at her wedding, as he is going abroad.

Under the guise of a singing exercise they launch into a duet, "I'll See You Again", at the end of which Sarah's fiancé, Hugh Devon, enters with her mother, Mrs Millick. The latter puts an end to the lesson, declaring that Sarah has an appointment with her dressmaker.

Carl says goodbye, bows deeply and goes out. While the orchestra strikes up "The Call Of Life", the girl repulses her fiancé and falls weeping into her mother's arms.

Scene 3: Mrs Millick is giving a ball, to which Sarah's friends and their titled admirers (forming a double sextet of young men and girls) have been invited. The orchestra is being conducted by Carl Linden.

Mrs Millick and Hugh's mother, Lady Devon, comment rather anxiously upon Sarah's air of flushed excitement. The girl has – semi-intentionally – spilled a glass of claret over the shirt-front of one of the more important guests, Sir Matthew Fenchurch, who takes his leave politely, but with obvious annoyance. Sarah, unrepentant, explains that he was pompous and had annoyed her by patting her hand. Her fiancé, baffled and disturbed by her changing moods, reproves her when she calls to Carl to "play something gay". The band strikes up the number, "What Is Love?", during which Sarah begins to waltz round the stage. She is gradually joined by the other young people, all whirling round, laughing and chattering. Then the band plays "God Save The Queen" and the party breaks up. Sarah stands with her mother to say goodbye to the guests. She tries to make up her quarrel with Hugh, but he is still on his dignity.

Then the chaperones go to find the girls – Harriet, Gloria, Effie, Jane, Honor and Victoria – who are sitting out with their escorts. When they have gone the young people steal in and sing a number, "The Last Dance", at the end of which the men (all except Mr Proutie, Gloria's beau, who hides behind the sofa) creep out, leaving the girls demurely seated.

Mrs Millick discovers Mr Proutie and sends him away, sharply scolding Gloria. The girls plead to stay up a little longer. They chatter for a while and then start playing Blind Man's Buff, with Sarah as "he", Carl Linden has collected his music and is on his way out when Sarah, blindfolded, throws her arms round his neck. Losing all restraint, he kisses her passionately on the mouth. She snatches the bandage from her eyes and they gaze at each other while the girls watch, aghast. "It's you I love – now and always," says Sarah softly. And they sing a duet, confessing their mutual devotion.

Gloria and Harriet are remonstrating with them when four footmen come to clear the room. Everyone hides behind sofas and chairs while the footmen sing a quartet and then extinguish the lights. As they go out, the girls come from their hiding places and Harriet lights two candles.

Sarah says she has made up her mind – she is going with Carl. One of the girls brings her a hat and a cape, and the young lovers go out through the open window into the darkness, singing "The Call Of Life".

ACT II, Scene 1: It is morning in Schlick's café in Vienna, in the year 1880. Carl Linden, in his shirt-sleeves, is rehearsing with the orchestra at the back, and a chorus of waiters and cleaners are singing as they tidy the tables, polish up brasses and scrub the floor. Seated at a table, three customers – Lotte, Hansi, and Freda sing "Ladies Of The Town", after which they go off.

Then the singer, Manon La Crevette, rehearses with Carl, arguing about the tempo of her song. She had loved him before his marriage to Sarah (or Sari as she is now called), and admits that she is being "difficult" because she is jealous. Ordering herself a drink, she runs through her song, "If Love Were All", at the end of which she goes off and Carl dismisses his orchestra. He comes down from the dais and chats with a good-natured tart, Gussi, who, realising that he and Sari are hard up, gives them a pressing invitation to lunch with her.

The debonair, imposing Captain August Lutte then enters, and Gussi makes a dead set at him; but he has come to talk to the proprietor, Herr Schlick. He complains that the new dancer, Sari, is "an iceberg", and insists that she must sup with him in a private room that night. As he turns to go, Sari comes in. To Schlick's annoyance, she refuses the Captain's invitation

Act I. Miguel (Godfrey Winn) and
Adrienne (Eileen Sharp)

Act II. Esteban (Frank Cellier) and
The Marquise (Marie Tempest)

Act III. Esteban (Frank Cellier), The Marquise (Marie Tempest) and Raoul (W. Graham Browne)

Act I. Janet Ebony (Madge Titheradge), Mrs Chilham (Nina Boucicault), Mavis Wittersham (Marda Vanne), Mrs Ebony (Henrietta Watson), Paul Ebony (George Relph), Lavinia Hardy (Helen Spencer) and Peter Chelsworth (Arthur Margetson)

Act II. Alec Stone (George Curzon), Peter Chelsworth (Arthur Margetson) and Janet Ebony (Madge Titheradge)

Act III. Mrs Ebony (Henrietta Watson), Mavis Wittersham (Marda Vanne), Mrs Chilham (Nina Boucicault), Peter Chelsworth (Arthur Margetson), Paul Ebony (George Relph) and Janet Ebony (Madge Titheradge)

"Teach Me To Dance Like Grandma" Jessie Matthews and Chorus. (Left to right: Nancy Barnett, Madeline Gibson, Marjorie Browne, Peter May, Florita Fey, Marjorie Robertson (Anna Neagle), Peggy Wynne and Greta Taylor)

"Law And Order" Policewoman Pellet (Douglas Byng), Policewoman Wendle (Maisie Gay) and Company

"The English Lido Beach" Opening Chorus

"Dance, Little Lady" The Little Lady (Lauri Devine), with Sonnie Hale and Dancers

"A Room With A View" Jessie Matthews and Sonnie Hale

"The Bus Rush" Maisie Gay

Finale: Entire Company

Selwyn Theatre, New York, 1928

"Lilac Time" The Gardener – Noël Coward   "Dance, Little Lady" Noël Coward

Act I, Scene 1. Vincent Howard (Billy Milton) at the piano; Dolly Chamberlain (Dorothy Boyd) and
The Marchioness of Shayne (Peggy Wood), centre

Act I, Scene 2. Sarah Millick (Peggy Wood) and
Carl Linden (George Metaxa)

Act I, Scene 3. Sarah Millick (Peggy Wood), Carl Linden (George Metaxa) and the Bridesmaids

Act II, Scene 1. "Ladies Of The Town". Freda (Betty Huntley-Wright), Hansi (Marjorie Rogers), Lotte (Millie Sim) and Gussi (Norah Howard)

Act II, Scene 1. Sari Linden (Peggy Wood) and Manon (Ivy St Helier)

Act II, Scene 2. Manon (Ivy St Helier)

Act II, Scene 2. Captain Lutte (Austin Trevor), Sari Linden (Peggy Wood) and Carl Linden (George Metaxa), centre

Act III, Scene 1. "Green Carnations" Vernon Craft (Arthur Alexander), Cedric Ballantyne (William Harn), Bertram Sellick (Eric Lauriston) and Lord Henry Jade (Penryn Bannerman)

Act III, Scene 1. The Marquis of Shayne (Alan Napier) and Sari Linden (Peggy Wood), centre

Act III, Scene 2. Vincent Howard (Billy Milton) at piano; Dolly Chamberlain (Dorothy Boyd) and The Marchioness of Shayne (Peggy Wood), centre

Ziegfeld Theatre, New York, 1928

Evelyn Laye as Sarah and as The Marchioness of Shayne

Act I. Amanda Prynne (Gertrude Lawrence) and
Elyot Chase (Noël Coward)

Act I. Victor Prynne (Laurence Olivier) and
Sybil Chase (Adrianne Allen)

Act II. Elyot Chase (Noël Coward) and Amanda Prynne (Gertrude Lawrence)

Act II. Victor Prynne (Laurence Olivier), Sybil Chase (Adrianne Allen), Amanda Prynne (Gertrude Lawrence) and Elyot Chase (Noël Coward)

Act III. Amanda Prynne (Gertrude Lawrence), Elyot Chase (Noël Coward), Victor Prynne (Laurence Olivier) and Sybil Chase (Adrianne Allen)

PRIVATE LIVES, Phoenix Theatre, 1930

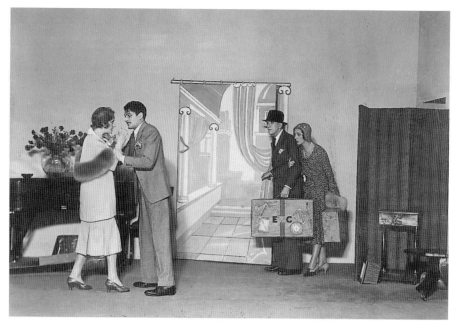

Act III. Sybil Chase (Adrianne Allen), Victor Prynne (Laurence Olivier), Elyot Chase (Noël Coward) and Amanda Prynne (Gertrude Lawrence)

CAVALCADE, Theatre Royal, Drury Lane, 1931

Part 1, Scene 1. The Drawing-Room. Robert Marryot (Edward Sinclair), Jane Marryot (Mary Clare), Alfred Bridges (Fred Groves), and Ellen Bridges (Una O'Connor)

Part 1, Scene 4. Mafeking Night at a Theatre. *Mirabelle*.

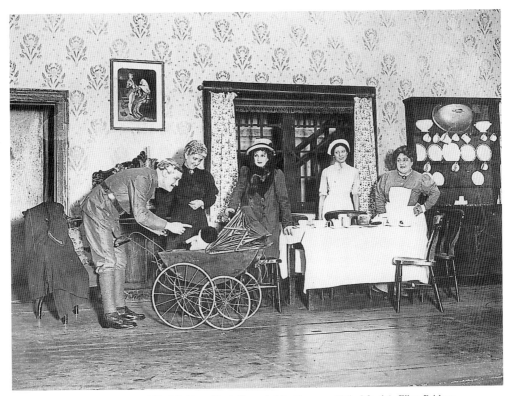

Part 1, Scene 5. The Kitchen. Alfred Bridges (Fred Groves), Mrs Snapper (Edie Martin), Ellen Bridges (Una O'Connor), Annie (Merle Tottenham) and Cook (Laura Smithson)

Part 1, Scene 6. Kensington Gardens. In Mourning for Queen Victoria

Part 1, Scene 8. The Grand Staircase of a London House. Robert Marryot (Edward Sinclair) and Jane Marryot (Mary Clare), centre

to lunch. The proprietor hurries off to pacify his client, while Manon (who has overheard the previous conversation) warns Sari what has been arranged.

Carl then comes in and Sari clings to him, begging him to leave Schlick and go back to street-singing: she has a presentiment that something terrible will happen. He soothes her, saying that if they can only hold on a few weeks longer they will have saved enough money to open a little café of their own. They sing the duet, "Little Café", and the curtain falls as they embrace.

Scene 2: It is about 2 a.m. and the café is crowded with dancers. A dozen smart officers come marching on and sing a concerted introductory number with the girls. After this, Captain August enters with Lieutenant Tranisch and sings "Tokay", accompanied by the officers. Then they all settle down and order wine.

Sari is left alone when Tranisch carries off Manon, with whom she has been sitting; but before Captain August can claim her, Carl descends from the dais and adroitly heads him off. He quietly promises his wife that this shall be their last night at that café. Tranisch comes back with Gussi (to whom Manon, at his request, has introduced him), and the other two "ladies of the town" chat to Sari until Captain August invites her to dance. Angry at her refusal, he complains to the proprietor, who reprimands Sari, reminding her that she is engaged as a dancing partner for his guests. When she says that she and Carl are leaving next day, Schlick threatens to retain their salaries unless she dances "willingly and agreeably" with the Captain and anyone else who may ask her.

He then announces the evening's entertainment, which begins with a number by six dancing-girls. Manon la Crevette sings a saucy French song, "Bonne Nuit, Merci", and, as encore, a waltz song, in which everyone joins.

General dancing is resumed and the Captain claims his waltz with Sari, while Carl watches anxiously from the dais. August becomes progressively more amorous, until at last he stops dead in the centre of the floor and kisses Sari on the mouth. At this Carl stops the music with a crash, leaps down, drags his wife away, and strikes the Captain in the face.

August draws his sword, Tranisch hands a weapon to Carl, and the two men fight a duel. Soon Carl is disarmed and mortally wounded. He dies in Sari's arms.

ACT III, Scene 1: Fifteen years have passed. Lord Shayne, a distinguished old man, is giving a party, at which the young girls of Act I, now smart society matrons, are present. Lady James (Harriet) and Mrs Proutie (Gloria) are announced with their husbands; likewise Mrs Bethel (Effie), Lady Sorrel

(Honor), Mrs Vale (Jane), and the Duchess of Tenterden (Victoria). Their entrance and Lord Shayne's reception of them constitute the opening chorus; then the ladies sing a sextet, "Alas, The Time Is Past".

After chattering about their husbands, they speculate upon the famous European singer, Madame Sari Linden, whom Lord Shayne has invited them to meet. Overhearing them, their host declares that she is "one of the few really beautiful people in the world".

Hugh Devon, now a pompous diplomat, enters with his fat, vague wife, just before Madame Sari Linden is announced. She is greeted with astonished cries of "Sarah!" – for she had let all her friends think that she was dead. With gracious tact, she bridges the embarrassing meeting with her ex-fiancé and his wife.

Lord Shayne takes her in to supper and the others follow, leaving four exquisitely dressed young men – Vernon Craft, a poet, Cedric Ballantyne, a painter, Lord Henry Jade, a dilettante, and Bertram Sellick, a playwright, to sing a quartet, satirising the aesthetes of the 'nineties', "We All Wore A Green Carnation"

They go off, and Lord Shayne re-enters with Sari. He proposes to her, as he has done often before, and this time she does not definitely refuse him, but promises to "think it over".

The others come back and Sari sings for them; first "Zigeuner", a song by Carl Linden about a princess who loved a gipsy, then the refrain of "I'll See You Again", during which the lights fade out...

When they come up again, the stage is set as it was in the first scene, and Sari is an old woman, singing to a group of young people sprawling on the floor. Dolly Chamberlain springs up and flings her arms round Vincent, vowing that she loves him. He gently disengages himself, goes to the piano and begins to play "I'll See You Again" as a fox-trot. Everyone goes off dancing, and Lady Shayne, left alone, begins to laugh "a strange, cracked, contemptuous laugh". Then, holding her arms wide, she sings:

> Though my world has gone awry,
> Though the end is drawing nigh,
> I shall love you till I die,
> Goodbye!

James Agate in the *Sunday Times*, 21 July 1929:

"The programme bears the notification 'The Entire Production by Noël Coward', and perhaps a good way of attacking, in the friendly sense, the stupendous opus which is this 'operette' would be to consider how much Mr Coward has really put into it. I suggest that to arrive at this estimate we must subtract from 'the entire production' the delightful scenes and dresses designed by Professor Ernst Stern, the dance arranged by Miss Tilly Losch, and, of course, the brilliant orchestration of the play's tunes by Mr Orellana. This leaves the plot, the dialogue, the lyrics, the melodies as originally executed on a baby grand, the stagecraft, the evening's sparkle, irresponsibility, wit, and fun, the power to conceive its visual delight, and the general notion of what makes a thoroughly good light entertainment. Not even Mr Coward's warmest admirers can claim for him that he created the seventies and the nineties; but they are surely entitled to credit him with re-creating them. Night life in Vienna was never the outcome of Mr Coward's genius; on the other hand, its reproduction is one of his happiest inspirations.

"On the whole, I suggest that readers who have done the sum with me will agree that what is left after subtracting other people's efforts is a thundering job. If anybody can do the same sum and make more of it, let him come forward! He won't have any difficulty in getting a theatre; all the theatres will be tumbling over each other to get him. Of course, the country may be teeming with people who are capable of doing what Mr Coward has done. Only nobody else has done it yet. Nobody else has ever done it, except Wagner. And *Meistersinger* is not strictly an operette.

"Consider what Mr Coward's achievement means. Mozart had need of Beaumarchais, Richard Strauss of Hoffmansthal, Johann Strauss of lots of people, and ditto Oscar Strauss. Offenbach, Lecocq, Planquette, Hervé, Audran, Messager – all the Frenchmen had their librettists, and it might be conveniently remembered here that in the days when Meilhac and Halévy were writing for the French vaudeville and comic opera stage, the librettist was a more important person than the provider of the music. Gilbert and Sullivan were the perfect marriage, after which comic opera rapidly degenerated into musical comedy and the licentious state, whereby the composer took at least 16 lyric-writers to his bosom. I have no doubt that somebody will write to tell me that at some obscure theatre, near the Oval, some gentleman did in the seventies, for one performance only, produce an opera which was the fruit of single cogitation. I shall not deny it. Doubtless somebody else discovered America before Columbus. But Columbus did achieve something. Let the same be said of Mr Coward.

"Since the entire country, so recently as Friday morning last, was ringing with the plot of *Bitter Sweet*, it is unnecessary to recapitulate it. Besides, it would not be a fair description of the entertainment any more than it would be a fair description of the Venus de Milo to enumerate her bones. This plot is only the skeleton to enchantment. Sufficient to say that in order to persuade a modern young woman to run away with her jazz-band lover a great lady recounts how, as a girl, she ran away with a pianoforte teacher, became a dancing partner in a Viennese café, was duly insulted, was present at the death in a duel of her avenging but inexpert husband, became a prima donna, and sang 'Tosti' in overheated drawing-rooms for the edification of Lady Midas, Mrs Ponsonby de Tomkyns, and others of George du Maurier's delicious circle, and finally married the Marquis of Shayne. I think we believed all this, except possibly the bit about the prima donna; voices, unlike piano scores, cannot be orchestrated.

"Is the libretto of this opera as good as the author's plays? No. For if it were we should not need the music. On the other hand, how good is the music? Let me say that, to uninstructed ears, it is what you might call travelled music. It is stuff which musicians all the world over, before the era of saxophones muted with bowler hats, would have recognised as light music. It is cultivated, deft, witty, and, above all, tuneful. If butcher-boys do not whistle snatches of it, it will not be the fault of the snatches. To argue that a sextet of good-night-bidding young ladies would have been done better by Sullivan is about as helpful as to say that no new essay on old china can be as good as Charles Lamb's. Much better to suggest that the quartet entitled 'Ladies Of The Town' could go into any comic opera that was ever written and not be shamed. Because of *Rosenkavalier*, must there be no more Viennese waltzes? Go to! Mr Coward's gingerbread is pleasantly hot in the mouth, though we may know where the gilt comes from. Some exception has been taken to the 'Green Carnations' quartet. But one would retain it, if only to prove once more that in this country, while your serious writer may not look over the hedge, your stage jester may steal every horse in the field. Finally, the piece would be worthwhile if only for the second act, in which Mr Coward shows himself to be possessed of the triple gift of your true man of the theatre – the faculty for entertaining both the eye, the ear, and the mind. The Viennese rout is delicious, and the episode of the faithful cocotte is moving.

"Let it be said without hesitation that Miss Ivy St Helier ran off with all the acting in the play, and that if this were the nineties and she were to wear long black gloves, all the highbrow essayists would be writing volumes about her. It would be a moderate statement to say that on Thursday night one deemed this artist to be as good as Yvette Guilbert and Louie Freear put together. Miss St Helier succeeded in resembling both perfectly and at the same moment. Except for Mr Austin Trevor, who contributed a good little sketch, and Mr Metaxa, who looked convincingly un-English, the rest of the acting did not seem to me to be worthy of the piece or of the occasion. Miss Peggy Wood invited one to believe that mid-Victorian staidness is the quality looked for by Viennese officers in Viennese cafés at two o'clock in the morning, and though Miss Wood sang agreeably enough I am not convinced that she was well cast. The dancing was excellent, though too many members of the company suggested by their accents that recruiting for this production had taken place in and about Blackpool. There were scenes of great excitement at the finish, and Mr Coward put the coping-stone on his triumph by steadfastly declining to appear."

PUBLICATIONS

Bitter Sweet was published by Martin Secker (London, 1929) and the vocal score by William Chappell (1929). The book is undedicated, but the score is dedicated to Elsie April, who worked with Coward from 1923 to 1946:

"My dear Elsie, I am dedicating this score to you in gratitude for all the unfailing help and encouragement you have given me in music."

The following songs, as separate sheet music, were also published by William Chappell:

"Dear Little Café"
"If Love Were All"
"Green Carnations"
"I'll See You Again"
"Kiss Me"
"Ladies Of The Town"
"Tokay"
"Zigeuner"

The following songs are included in *The Noël Coward Song Book* (Michael Joseph, 1953):

"If Love Were All"
"I'll See You Again"
"Zigeuner"
"If You Could Only Come With Me"

Bitter Sweet is also published in *Noël Coward Collected Plays: Two*, Methuen World Classics (London, 1999).

NOTES

With the success of the new revue and his return to acting (in *The Second Man*), Coward rehabilitated his lost prestige. He says:

"The idea of *Bitter Sweet* was born in the early summer of that year, 1928. It appeared quite unexpectedly and with no other motivation beyond the fact that I had vaguely discussed with Gladys the possibilities of writing a romantic operette. She and I were staying with Ronald Peake, her family solicitor, in Surrey, and an hour or so before we were due to leave, Mrs Peake happened to play to us on the gramophone a new German orchestral record of *Die Fledermaus*. Immediately a confused picture of uniforms, bustles, chandeliers, and gas-lit cafés formed in my mind, and later, when we were driving over Wimbledon Common, we drew the car to a standstill by the roadside, and in the shade of a giant horse-chestnut tree mapped out roughly the story of Sari Linden.

"The uniforms, bustles, chandeliers and gas-lit cafés all fell into place eagerly, as though they has been waiting in the limbo for just this cue to enter."

He goes on:

" It seemed high time for a little romantic renaissance, and very soon a few of the preliminary melodies began to form in my head. However, the whole idea had to be shelved for a while owing to the urgency of other plans."

The other plans were the production of *This Year of Grace!* in New York, in which Cochran had persuaded Coward himself to appear. He went to America to arrange for the production, and he tells us that:

"During that voyage I wrote, roughly, the first act of *Bitter Sweet*, and when I read it to Cockie and explained to him the story of the rest of it, he became at once enthusiastic. One of his greatest qualities is his amazing flair for visualising a play completely from the barest outline, and he decided then and there that he would do it, providing that I could finish it in the time, in the spring of the following year, 1929."

During the run of *This Year of Grace!* in New York, which opened in November 1928, work continued on *Bitter Sweet*. Coward says:

"During that winter, January and February 1929, I finished *Bitter Sweet*, on which I had been working intermittently for the last few months. The book had been completed long since, but the score had been causing me trouble, until one day, when I was in a taxi on my way back to the apartment after a matinée, the 'I'll See You Again' waltz dropped into my mind, whole and complete, during a 20 minutes' traffic block. After that everything went smoothly, and J. cabled to Cockie in London suggesting that he start making preliminary arrangements regarding theatre, opening date, etc."

On Coward's return to London the operette went into rehearsal at the end of May. The whole production was a great success, and an American version soon followed, for which he again went to New York.

Coward says in his introduction to *Play Parade, Volume I*:

"*Bitter Sweet* has given me more complete satisfaction than anything else I have ever written up till now. Not especially on account of its dialogue, or its lyrics, or its music, or its production, but as a whole. In the first place, it achieved and sustained the original mood of its conception more satisfactorily than a great deal of my other work. And, in the second place, that particular mood of semi-nostalgic sentiment, when well done, invariably affects me very pleasantly. In *Bitter Sweet* it did seem to me to be well done, and I felt accordingly very happy about it.

"The late William Bolitho, in an article on *Bitter Sweet* published in the *New York World* (one of the very few journalistic excursions relating to myself that I have ever wished, proudly, to keep), finished his essay with a discussion of the quality of the play. He said of this: 'You find it faintly when you look over old letters the rats have nibbled at, one evening you don't go out; there is a little of it, impure and odorous, in the very sound of barrel-organs, in quiet squares in the evenings, puffing out in gusts that intoxicate your heart. It is all right for beasts to have no memories; but we poor humans have to be compensated.'"

When *Bitter Sweet* was published in America in a volume with *Easy Virtue* and *Hay Fever* (*Bitter Sweet and Other Plays*, Doubleday, Doran, New York, 1929), W. Somerset Maugham contributed the following introduction:

"The day is no longer approaching; the day has come. Henrik Ibsen put his own forebodings into the mouth of his master builder. He foresaw that the younger generation would come knocking at his door and shaking their fists, shout: 'Make room, make room, make room.' 'Then there's an end of Halvard Solness.' For us English dramatists the younger generation has assumed the brisk but determined form of Mr Noël Coward. He knocked at the door with impatient knuckles, and then he rattled the handle, and then he burst in. After a moment's stupor, the older playwrights welcomed him affably enough and retired with what dignity they could muster to the shelf which with a sprightly gesture he indicated to them as their proper place. For my part, I have made myself quite comfortable there. The knowing Lucretius in a passage that has given the world a little shiver ever since it was written remarked that it was sweet, when on the great sea the winds troubled the waters, to behold from land another's deep distress; 'not that it is a pleasure and delight that any should be afflicted, but because it is sweet to see from what evils you are yourself exempt. It is sweet also to look upon the mighty struggles of war arrayed along the plains without sharing yourself in the danger.' But I look upon it as a very graceful attention on Mr Coward's part to reach up to my shelf with a volume of his plays and flatter me with the request that I should write a preface to them. I sit up and let my legs dangle in the air. I let myself down cautiously to the floor and give it a stamp to feel that it is really solid under my feet. And now as with a palsied hand I take up my pen I have just the sort of sensation I can imagine a man having who goes to lunch with his former wife and her second husband. It must be curious and entertaining for him to see from another angle circumstances with which he is so familiar, and I suspect that he allows himself an inward chuckle when he considers that in a few minutes after he has drunk his coffee he will find himself once more in the open street. But his successor remains behind.

"*Suave, mari magno turbantibus aequora ventis....*

"It would be foolish of me to write a criticism of the three plays in this volume. The reader will read them, and unless he is very silly he will not let my opinion of them in the least influence him. The critic whose judgement you trust may render you the service of putting you on to a book you would otherwise have neglected, but when he has done that the only thing that matters is what the book means to you. It may be a masterpiece, but if it gives you nothing you have only wasted your time in reading it.

"I should like, however, to say a little on a matter that has of late exercised the critics and the dramatists, since I venture to think that it is one upon which the future of the English drama depends. And since there is no one now writing who has more obviously a gift for the theatre than Mr Noël Coward, nor more influence with young writers, it is probably his inclination and practice that will be responsible for the manner in which plays will be written during the next 20 years.

"Mr St John Ervine published a few months ago a little book called *How to Write a Play*. Mr Ervine is a dramatist as well as a critic and his book is pithy and sensible. It is a work that any writer for the theatre can study with profit. He has exploded the fallacy that there is something mysterious in dramatic technique. Ponderous tomes have been written on the subject by persons who did not know what they were talking about. It is evident that people who have no feeling for the theatre will find it very difficult to write a play, just as people who have no ear will never understand music, and I think it may be admitted that to write a play requires a peculiar gift. It is not a very exalted one, for it can exist without intelligence or originality (one of the most distinguished dramatists of the last generation had the mind and the education of a bartender and wrote notwithstanding clever and charming plays); I think it would be better to call it a peculiar knack. I suspect that the whole secret of dramatic technique can be told in a sentence: stick to the point like grim death. But I mention this book of Mr Ervine's now because he has some interesting things to say about dialogue, and especially about Mr Noël Coward's. It is in his dialogue that Mr Coward has shown something of an innovator, for in his construction he has been content to use the current method of his day; he has deliberately avoided the epigram that was the fashion 30 years ago (when an early play of mine, Lady Frederick, was bought by Mr George Tyler, he told me that it was not epigrammatic enough, so I went away and in two hours wrote in 24) and has written dialogue that is strictly faithful to fact. It does not only represent everyday language, but reproduces it. No one has carried naturalistic dialogue further than he. Mr St John Ervine attacks it. He finds it common-place and dull. He gives a passage from *Home Chat* and another from *This Was a Man* to make his point, and similar passages could certainly be found in any of the three plays in this volume. He contends that the dramatist should 'heighten and lengthen and deepen the common speech, and yet leave it seeming to be the common speech'.

"Dialogue has gradually been growing more natural. It was inevitable that some dramatist should eventually write dialogue that exactly copied the average talk, with its hesitations, mumblings and repetitions, and broken sentences, of average people. I do not suppose anyone can ever do this with more brilliant accuracy than Mr Coward. My only objection to it is that it adds greatly to the difficulty of the author's task. It is evident that when he represents dull and stupid people they will be as stupid and dull on the stage as in real life and they will bore us in the same way. When he exposes his theme or joins together the various parts of his story (and I should think it was impossible to write a play in which certain explanations, of no interest in themselves, can be avoided) he will only with difficulty hold the attention of his audience. The author limits himself to characters who are in themselves exciting or amusing and to a theme which is from the beginning of the first act to the end of the last naturally absorbing. It is asking a great deal. I may point out in passing that as Ibsen's dialogue grew more naturalistic he was led to deal with singularly abnormal characters. On the other hand, I do not think it can be denied that when a scene is dramatic, naturalistic dialogue vastly enhances its effectiveness. You have a very good example in the last scene of the second act of *Easy Virtue*. Its dramatic value is greatly heightened by the perfect naturalness of the dialogue. In the same play the value of the beautifully drawn character of Marion Whittaker is increased by the absolute fidelity with which her conversation is reproduced. I do not know that Mr

Coward has ever created a personage more vivid, pathetic, abominable, and true than this. When the characters and the theme allow, as in *Hay Fever*, the naturalistic dialogue can produce a masterpiece in miniature. But I have an impression that Mr Coward has gone as far as anyone can go in this direction. A blank wall faces him. There is less difference between Mr Ervine and Mr Coward than Mr Ervine seems to think. One seeks to reproduce dialogue; the other to represent it. I wonder if here too you do not come upon a blank wall. I wonder if the current fashion to be slangy and brief and incoherent has not blinded the dramatists to the fact that a great many people do talk grammatically, do choose their words, and do make use of expressions that on the stage would be thought 'bookish'. It has seemed to me that during the last twenty years or so the increase of reading has affected current speech. If Mr Ervine read a shorthand report of his own conversation over the luncheon table he would be surprised to find how 'bookish' it was. If he spent an evening in a public house in Lambeth he would be surprised to discover how unusual were the words and complicated the phrases, learnt from the Sunday papers and the films, he would hear from the people standing around him. The present mode in dialogue debars the writer from introducing into his play educated people who express themselves in an educated way. It may be true that the English are a tongue-tied people, but are they so tongue-tied as all that? Listen to the conversation of barristers, doctors, politicians, parsons, and you will find that they express themselves quite naturally in a way that on the stage would be called absurdly literary. Stage dialogue has been simplified out of relation with all life but that of the cocktail bar. It seems to me a great loss.

"It is evident that the cinema has had a great effect on the drama. In the first place, it has quickened the apprehensions of the public so that they take a point very rapidly, and what a generation ago would have needed a long scene to explain can now be made plain in a couple of sentences. Further, it has done so many things better than the spoken drama can do them that it has made it futile for the spoken drama to attempt them. I suggest that the spoken drama must from now on look for its material only in places where the pictures cannot compete with it. They have made physical action more than a trifle tame, but the drama depends on action, and so it looks as though the drama must henceforward deal with action that is purely spiritual. Wit and emotion are demesnes that can never be taken away from it. Now, wit is artificial. It has been my good fortune to know most of the celebrated wits of my day, but they sparkle very intermittently. No one in private life shines so continuously as a witty character should in a play, he is seldom so pointed, finished and apt. A play of wit demands an elaborate and polished dialogue which has little relation to the conversation of real life. When you come to the play of emotion, the situation is more complicated. Mr O'Neill in *Strange Interlude* dealt with it by making his characters say what he thought they would have said under the circumstances and then adding in an aside what they thought. It was an ingenious and interesting experiment, but I do not think that he or anyone else can repeat it. It seems to me plain that if he is seeking to represent states of mind and affections of the soul, the dramatist is handicapping himself unnecessarily if he confines himself to the baldness of contemporary speech. I am not convinced that it is true to life, for my impression is that persons under stress of emotion express themselves with more fluency, elaboration and often with more eloquence than is generally suspected. I do not see why the dramatist should not put into the mouth of his characters what they feel rather than what they say. It is true that for a moment an audience used to naturalistic dialogue would think the words they heard strange, but an audience can be coaxed or driven to accept any formula. After all, copying life, representation, is merely an aesthetic procedure like another: naturalism is no more to be preferred to formalism than a leg of mutton is to be preferred to a sirloin of beef. Now that naturalistic dialogue has been carried as far as it can go, I cannot but think it might be worth trying a dialogue that does not reproduce the conversation of the day and only very vaguely represents it, but is deliberately and significantly formal. And since the future of the English drama is in the hands of Mr Noël Coward this, as I climb back laboriously on to my shelf, with my blessing, is the suggestion I offer him."

Excerpts from Act II were revived with Evelyn Laye and Company at the "... Merely Players" performance, Drury Lane, 4 February 1951.

Bitter Sweet was revived on tour in 1949 with Eve Lister and in 1970 with June Bronhill. In recent years the most significant revival was at Sadler's Wells in February 1988 (subsequently on a national tour) with Valerie Masterson alternating with Ann Mackay (Sara), Martin Smith (Carl) and Rosemary Ashe (Manon). The cast recording was the first to include the complete score.

In 1997 a major BBC Radio 2 production was directed by John Langridge.

US PRODUCTIONS

PRESENTED by Florenz Ziegfeld & Arch Selwyn at the Ziegfeld Theatre, New York on 5 November 1929 (159 performances) after a tryout at the Tremont Theatre, Boston on 22 October 1929.

CHARACTERS	Ziegfeld, 1929
SARI	Evelyn Laye
CARL	Gerald Nodin
MANON	Mireille
VINCENT HOWARD	Max Kirby
HUGH DEVON	Tracy Holmes
GUSSI	Sylvia Leslie
MARQUIS OF SHAYNE	John Evelyn
MRS MILLICK	Isabel Ohmead
MARQUIS OF STEERE	Donald Gordon
LOTTE	Zoe Gordon
FREDA	Nancy Barnett
HANSI	Dorothy Debenham
CAPTAIN AUGUST LUTTE	Desmond Jeans
HERR SCHLICK and SIR ARTHUR	Charles Mortimer
LT. TRANSICH	Louis Miller
EFFIE	Vesta Sylva
VICTORIA	Marjorie Raymond
HARRIET	Audrey Pointing
GLORIA	Nancy Brown
JANE	Winifred Talbot
HONOR	Isla Bevan
DOLLY	Audrey Pointing
PARKER	Trevor Glyn
LORD HENRY	Patrick Ludlow
LADY DEVON	Kathleen Lambelet
LORD EDGAR JAMES	Richard Thorpe
LORD SORREL	Hopper Russell
MR VALE	Leslie Bannister
MR BETHEL	Anthony Neville
MR PROUTIE	Douglas Graeme-Brooke

The *New York Times*: "Mr Coward is the master of little things, and the virtuosity of his talents amounts to genius. Although considerable showmanship has gone into the staging and the organisation of the story, it is not a musical show in the rapid, flamboyant style to which we have become accustomed. But it is sheerly delightful by reason of the delicate perfection of the workmanship and radiant splendour of Evelyn Laye, who has the principal role. It is charming; it is subtle and witty. By his mastery of little things Mr

Coward has mastered the artistry of musical entertainment in a refreshingly civilised style."

It was clear to Broadway that the leading lady Noël had always had in mind, Gertrude Lawrence – for whom he had originally conceived the show – did not possess the vocal range for the songs. Laye turned down the role out of pique as a snub to Cochran and, to some degree, Noël. In *This Year of Grace!* Cochran had been the means of introducing Jessie Matthews to Laye's then husband, Sonnie Hale, who subsequently left her for Matthews. Having realised her mistake when she saw the London production, Laye fought hard to get the Broadway assignment and it was the turning point of her career.

PRESENTED by the Shuberts at the 44th Street Theatre, New York on 7 May 1934.

CHARACTERS	44th Street, 1934
SARI	Evelyn Herbert
CARL	Alan Jones
MANON	Hannah Toback
VINCENT HOWARD	Cameron York
HUGH DEVON	Henry Rabke
GUSSI	Kay Simmons
MARQUIS OF SHAYNE	Clyde Kelly
MRS MILLICK	Elizabeth Crandall
MARQUIS OF STEERE	Jay Conley
LOTTE	Carol Boyer
FREDA	Beatrice Berenson
HANSI	Marion Carlisle
CAPTAIN AUGUST LUTTE	Leonard Ceeley
HERR SCHLICK and SIR ARTHUR	Victor Casmore
EFFIE	Beulah Blake
VICTORIA	Martha Boyer
HARRIET	Marion Carlisle
GLORIA	Beatrice Berenson
JANE	Anna Werth
HONOR	Ruth Adams
DOLLY	Mary Wrick
LORD HENRY	Jack Richards
LADY DEVON	Frances Marion Comstock
LORD EDGAR JAMES	Samuel Thomas

LORD SORRELL	Brian Davis
MR VALE	Jack Richards
MR BETHEL	Harold Abbey
MR PROUTIE	Truman Gaige
Director	*Pierre Dereeder*

FILM VERSIONS

A film version of *Bitter Sweet* was made in the UK by British and Dominion Films, 1933. It was directed by Herbert Wilcox. Adapted for the screen by Herbert Wilcox and Moncton Hoffe.

CHARACTERS	**Dominion Films, 1933**
SARAH MILLICK	Anna Neagle
CARL LINDEN	Ferdinand Graavey
CAPTAIN AUGUSTE	Miles Mander
THE FOOTMAN	Gibb McLaughlin
HERR SCHLICK	Clifford Heatherley
HUGH DEVON	Esmé Percy
LIEUTENANT TRANISCH	Stuart Robertson
VINCENT	Hugh Williams
DOLLY	Pat Paterson
HENRY	Patrick Ludlow
GUSSI	Kay Hammond
MRS MILLICK	Norma Walley
MANON LE CREVETTE	Ivy St Helier

This film omitted Act III of the stage version completely. It was first shown in London at the Carlton, Haymarket, in September 1933.

It was re-made in America by Metro-Goldwyn-Mayer in technicolour, 1941, directed by W. S. Van Dyke II. Adapted for the screen by Lesser Samuels.

CHARACTERS	**Metro-Goldwyn-Mayer, 1941**
SARAH MILLICK	Jeanette MacDonald
CARL LINDEN	Nelson Eddy
BARON VON TRANISCH	George Sanders
LORD SHAYNE	Ian Hunter
MAX	Felix Bressart

HARRY DAVENTRY	Edward Ashley
DOLLY	Lynne Carver
JANE	Diana Lewis
ERNST	Curt Bois
MRS MILLICK	Fay Holden
HERR SCHLICK	Sig Rumann
LADY DAVENTRY	Janet Beecher
HERR WYLER	Charles Judels
MANON	Veda Ann Borg
MARKET-KEEPER	Herman Bing
MAMA LUDEN	Greta Meyer

The film was first shown in London at the Empire, Leicester Square, 1941.

The plot was considerably altered in this version; and the songs allotted to other characters in the stage version were divided between Jeanette MacDonald and Nelson Eddy, who, besides the original songs in their parts, sang "If Love Were All" as a duet; "Tokay" (Nelson Eddy); "Ladies Of The Town" (Jeanette MacDonald with Muriel Goodspeed and Pamela Randall). Additional lyrics were by Gus Kahn to rearrangements of Coward's music. This included:

"What Is Love?" (Jeanette MacDonald and Nelson Eddy)
"Serenade In Vienna" (Jeanette MacDonald and Nelson Eddy), with
    a reprise of the "Barcarolla" section by Jeanette MacDonald
"Love In Any Language" (Jeanette MacDonald)

A synopsis issued in conjunction with this film may be of interest:
    "On the eve of her marriage to Harry Daventry, a pompous young Englishman, Victorian belle Sarah Millick scandalises her family and friends with her unnaturally excited conduct at a ball in London, and then elopes to Vienna with her singing teacher, Carl Linden. There they live in poverty – but happily – among Carl's friends, including Max and Ernst, penniless musicians, who pawn Carl's furniture when all else fails. After an unlucky experience, in which they attempt to give music lessons to the child of a market-keeper in exchange for food, Sarah and Carl become street-singers with Max and Ernst at Baden. Carl's hope of selling an operetta he had written to Herr Wyler, the impresario, meets with no response, but fortunes change when Sarah wins the attention of young Lord Shayne and his gambling opponent, Baron von Tranisch, of the Imperial Cavalry. Shayne believes that Sarah's singing brings him luck.

Von Tranisch has a more personal, romantic interest. He instructs Herr Schlick to hire Sarah as entertainer in his Vienna café, where Carl is to lead the orchestra. When von Tranisch pays unwelcome attentions to Sarah, she resists. But Daventry, appointed to the Viennese Embassy by now, and Jane, the fluttery but calculating belle who had finally married him, are witnesses to von Tranisch's advances, and report the matter to Carl. He takes no interest in their smug gossip, but Sarah refuses to return to the café. There comes a night, however, when Herr Wyler is believed to be a guest at the café and is willing to hear Carl's operetta. Max and Ernst go to bring Sarah, that she may sing it. But again von Tranisch makes himself offensive. Carl finds himself forced into a duel which he has no hope of winning, and von Tranisch runs him through. He dies in the agonised Sarah's arms. She finds new hope, however, in the fact that her friend and benefactor, Lord Shayne, has persuaded Wyler to produce the operetta with her as star. Thus Carl's music will live on through her singing, and every time she sings his music she will feel that he is with her."

21
PRIVATE LIVES
AN INTIMATE COMEDY IN THREE ACTS
Written in 1929

FIRST PRESENTED by Charles B. Cochran at the King's Theatre, Edinburgh, 18 August 1930 (5 weeks' tour, Liverpool, Birmingham, Manchester and Southsea); and subsequently at the Phoenix Theatre, London, 24 September 1930 (101 performances).

REVIVED by Martin Sabine at the Victoria Palace, London, 25 May 1936, in a season by The London Repertory Company (12 performances).

REVIVED by H. M. Tennent Ltd. and John C. Wilson at the Theatre Royal, Newcastle, 10 July 1944 (14 weeks' tour), and subsequently presented at the Apollo Theatre, London, 1 November 1944 (716 performances). Transferred, with changes of cast, to the Fortune Theatre, 10 June 1946.

CHARACTERS	**Edinburgh and Phoenix, 1930**
SYBIL CHASE	Adrianne Allen
ELYOT CHASE	Noël Coward
VICTOR PRYNNE	Laurence Olivier
AMANDA PRYNNE	Gertrude Lawrence
LOUISE (a maid)	Everley Gregg
Director	*Noël Coward*
Designer	*G. E. Calthrop*

CHARACTERS	**Victoria Palace, 1936**
SYBIL CHASE	Valerie Lang
ELYOT CHASE	Basil Langton
VICTOR PRYNNE	Peter Scott
AMANDA PRYNNE	Beryl de Quenton
LOUISE (a maid)	Daphne Martyn
Director	*Martin Satire*

CHARACTERS	**Newcastle and Apollo, 1944**
SYBIL CHASE	Peggy Simpson, Leslie Brook (tour)
ELYOT CHASE	John Clements (succeeded by Hugh Sinclair, 10 December 1945)
VICTOR PRYNNE	Raymond Huntley
AMANDA PRYNNE	Kay Hammond (succeeded by Googie Withers, 10 December 1945)
LOUISE (a maid)	Yvonne Andre
Director	*John Clements*
Designer	*G. E. Calthrop*

❖

ACT I: The terrace of a hotel in France. Summer evening.
ACT II: Amanda's flat in Paris. A few days later – evening.
ACT III: The same. Next morning.

The song, "Some Day I'll Find You" in Act I by Noël Coward.

The 1944 revival was set in the period "A few years ago".

SYNOPSIS

ACT I: Two honeymoon couples have just arrived at a French hotel. They are in adjacent suites, both opening on to the terrace on which the action is played. We first see Elyot Chase and his young bride, Sybil, whom he describes as "a little sharp-eyed blonde kitten". In her anxiety to find out how much he loves her, she cannot help harping on his first wife, Amanda, though the topic obviously annoys him. She makes him admit that Amanda was prettier than herself and danced far better, and that their divorce was collusive.

As they go in to dress for dinner, Amanda comes out of the other room with her new husband, Victor Prynne. He, too, keeps talking about her previous marriage and elicits from her that she spent her honeymoon at St Moritz and started quarrelling straight away. "Honeymooning is a very overrated experience," she opines. Victor is a conventional person who seems rather uneasy at Amanda's independent views – he likes "womanly" women. She remarks that very few people are completely normal really deep down in their private lives: she and Elyot were like "two violent acids bubbling about in a nasty little matrimonial bottle".

When they in turn have gone to dress, Elyot comes out with cocktails. So, after a while, does Amanda, but they are sitting with their backs to each other. Suddenly the band strikes up a tune that they recognise. Elyot begins to hum it, and Amanda, leaping up, looks over the plants that separate the two balconies and sees him. She sits down again and takes up the tune, till Elyot in turn gets up and looks at her. "Thoughtful of them to play that, wasn't it?" says Amanda calmly. They tell each other that they are honeymooning, and she goes indoors, politely bidding him "*Au revoir*".

Sybil finds Elyot very much upset. When he insists on leaving the hotel at once she thinks he must be mad or drunk. The only reason he can give is that he has "a presentiment of disaster". After a violent quarrel they go in, while Victor and Amanda come out. She too wants to leave without delay, but her husband sees through her pretexts and makes her confess that she has caught a glimpse of Elyot. Victor flatly refuses to have his honeymoon upset and, after she has called him a pompous ass, stalks back to his bedroom in dudgeon.

By this time Sybil is hysterical, and Elyot comes out to soothe his nerves with a cigarette. Amanda asks him for one, and then joins him to share his untouched cocktails. They discuss the situation, and Elyot promises to leave next day.

Once more the band plays the tune that they remember from their honeymoon. Talking over the wonderful moments they had together, they suddenly find themselves in each other's arms. The only thing to do, they decide, is to escape together at once. Amanda suggests going to her flat in Paris, but soon they start to bicker over the arrangements. Realising the danger, they make a compact that, if they are about to quarrel, one of them will say "Solomon Isaacs" and both will keep silence for two minutes. Having arranged this, they rush off together through Elyot's suite.

Soon afterwards Victor and Sybil come out, looking for them, meet each other and exchange polite conversation. Victor offers her one of his cocktails and they toast "absent friends".

ACT II: It is a few days later in Amanda's charming Paris flat, tastefully furnished and provided with a Steinway grand piano and a gramophone. After several evenings at home, Amanda and Elyot are still happy in each other's company, and are not much concerned about the reactions of their ex-partners. As soon as their respective divorces are through they plan to remarry, though Amanda doubts whether it will be a success.

Unfortunately, they begin to probe into each other's private lives since their parting, and jealousy soon brings them to the verge of a quarrel; but instead they dance to the gramophone. Amanda then begins to wonder how Sybil and Victor are getting on, and a fresh dispute breaks out, which has to be settled with their neighbours. When she tries to start it again the dispute quickly turns into a struggle. "Sollocks!" warns Elyot. "Sollocks yourself!" is Amanda's reply as she breaks the record over his head. Soon they are fighting like wild cats on the floor. At this moment Victor and Sybil enter quietly and stand staring at them in horror, while Amanda screams abuse at Elyot.

ACT III: It is about 8.30 next morning. The room is still in chaos after the fight, and Sybil and Victor are sleeping on two sofas – his dragged in front of Amanda's door and hers in front of Elyot's. The maid Louise rouses Sybil. Neither of the visitors can speak much French, but they gather that Louise dare not wake the others until they ring.

Soon, however, Amanda comes out, dressed in travelling clothes and carrying a suitcase. When Victor protests that she cannot leave until they have talked matters out, she goes into the kitchen to order coffee for them all. Meanwhile, Sybil is in tears.

Then Elyot – also in outdoor clothes and carrying his bag – appears. He flippantly counters Victor's efforts to force an explanation. Amanda returns in a high-handed mood, determined to carry the situation off lightly, but before long the two men are threatening to fight each other. Highly enjoying this, Amanda hustles Sybil into the bedroom and leaves them to it.

Elyot is determined not to give her the satisfaction of being fought over. He talks Victor into a reasonable state of mind, and they discuss what is to be done. The solution, in Victor's opinion, is for Elyot to remarry Amanda after a double divorce. This he declines, saying that she is a vile-tempered woman and he doesn't want to marry her. He goes back to his room, leaving Victor – whom he has called "a rampaging gas-bag" – speechless with fury.

When the two women come back they are disappointed that there has been no fight. Sybil goes into Elyot's room to talk to him, while Amanda has an explanation with her husband. He generously proposes that they should live apart until Sybil has got her divorce, and that then he will let her divorce him. At this point the other two return, Sybil declaring triumphantly that she is not going to divorce Elyot for a year.

They all settle down amicably to breakfast, making general conversation, until gradually Victor and Sybil, in defence of their respective wife and husband, work up to a violent quarrel. Once more in harmony, Amanda and Elyot, unnoticed, go smilingly out of the door with their suitcases.

Ivor Brown in the *Weekend Review*, 4 October 1930:

"A few days ago I was reading a dramatic notice written by a journalist of tough mind and tender years. He has learning and his observations have a particular interest for me because he speaks for years and opinions not my own. He had been to see one of the more famous comedies by Henry Arthur Jones, and I gathered that, as far as he was concerned, this fossil might originally has been 'featured' at a court entertainment to be enacted at Stonehenge or commissioned for a mead-party given by Hengist to Horsa. It bewildered him that the cultivated playgoers of any time should have paid respectful attention to this curiously renowned Jones. Naturally enough, with this in mind, I fell a-wondering, after a visit to the Phoenix's baptism of fireworks, what the younger critics of 1950 will say of Mr Noël Coward and Mr Frederick Lonsdale.

"The fashionable plays of 30 years ago had form and workmanship and a show of big assemblance. They were 'jobs of work'. You cannot imagine Sir Arthur Pinero boasting that he had polished off a *Tanqueray* or two in a weekend, though similar announcements are the common stuff of up-to-date theatrical publicity. The larger works of that period do seem stilted because they are unslangy, but they usually contained seven or eight parts which had been carefully prepared and were assembled with some sense of design.

You never feel that Jones and Pinero dictated from their baths bits and pieces of dialogue which a secretary took down in the intervals of turning on the gramophone and mixing a drink. But that is the sensation I frequently receive at a contemporary success.

"I am not grumbling. The grave and grandfatherly censure will not come from me. I am merely examining in a cursory way the history of vogue in entertainment. The difference between the theatre of Coward-Lonsdale and the theatre of Jones-Pinero is that in the former the 'job of work' comes later in the process. *Private Lives*, as put before you at the Phoenix, is a piece of immensely skilled labour, but the writing is the least part of it. The brilliance of the business lies in Mr Coward's capacity, as producer and as actor, to persuade us that his lines are witty and that his thin little projections of humanity are the real and triumphant clowns of eternal comedy. He does persuade us. He enormously entertains. That is all the critic has to record. But the historian of the theatre knows that vogue alters readily, and that the reaction to the solid, well-made and carefully reasoned comedy will soon be upon us. Within a few years the student of drama will be sitting in complete bewilderment before the text of *Private Lives*, wondering what on earth those fellows in 1930 saw in so flimsy a trifle.

"Well, they saw Mr Coward as actor and producer and they saw Miss Gertrude Lawrence; in short, they saw a species of magic. The first attribute of a successful magician is cheek; nerves, shame, hesitation are unknown to him. He must trust implicitly in his wrist and his rabbit. Mr Coward has exactly the right effrontery for a first-rate conjuror, and a first-rate conjuror, be it added, is a first-rate artist of the theatre. He has sometimes observed life and recorded it (witness the Anglo-Italians in *Sirocco*), but on the whole he prefers to trust in wrist and rabbit and to the virtuosity which elicits a comedy from a sheet of blank paper. The smart audience of today is quite uninterested in the architecture of a play: it prefers the art of improvisation. The successful teams of the time (e.g. the Walls-Lynn combination) toil extremely hard to create that happy-go-lucky atmosphere. In the same way, when Mr Coward and Miss Lawrence battle and squabble through a whole act together you do not feel you are watching a play, but rather that you have been admitted to a charade. The seeming spontaneity of the chatter has only been attained by the most industrious stage-craft and a remarkable sense of timing and of tones. The success lies in giving the charade illusion. There is little enough in Mr Coward's text; there is everything up his sleeve. He snaps his fingers at all the old rules of the play-maker and the gesture acts more potently than all the 'Walk up' roaring of any showman in town.

"Four characters and a maid suffice for *Private Lives*. Miss Adrianne Allen and Mr Laurence Olivier impersonate the two dull folk who have rashly married two of the dithering, delightful, mutable, all-of-a-sudden people whose odiousness in actuality has never prevented them from being the eternal hero and heroine of the playhouse. Mr Coward, as the wayward Elyot, is Harlequin Noël. Miss Gertrude Lawrence, as his Amanda, is no Columbine, but another Harlequin who goes to a dressmaker instead of to a tailor. These two have been married and divorced and, when they meet on their new honeymoons, each with a dullard attached, they naturally renew old acquaintance and old strife. Here is the foursome, and of their entanglements renewed the charade is fashioned. The combination of the characters is perfect and Miss Lawrence has an absolute command of the comedy whose essence is caprice. She says 'Hey, presto' with a tilt of the nose, and the illusion is supreme. The result is all shimmer and spangles with a little slapstick – in short, Harlequinade *à la mode*."

PUBLICATIONS

Private Lives was first published in America by Doubleday, Doran (New York, January 1930) and in the UK by Heinemann (London, September 1930). It is dedicated to "Jeffery" (Amherst). Also published in *Noël Coward Collected Plays: Two*, Methuen World Classics (London, 1999).

NOTES

After seeing *Bitter Sweet* launched successfully in New York, Coward went for a long holiday to the East, leaving America in November 1929. He was in Tokyo the following month. During a sleepless night at the Imperial Hotel, he says:

"The moment I switched out the lights, Gertie appeared in a white Molyneux dress on a terrace in the South of France and refused to go again until 4 a.m., by which time *Private Lives*, title and all, had constructed itself.

"In 1925 the play would have been written and typed within a few days of my thinking of it, but in 1929 I had learned the wisdom of not welcoming a new idea too ardently, so I forced it into the back of my mind, trusting to its own integrity to emerge again later on, when it has become sufficiently set and matured."

The revision was done in Hong Kong. During the rest of the trip arrangements were made for its production on his return to London, which took place in the autumn of 1930.

Coward says in his introduction to *Play Parade, Volume I*: "It was described in the papers variously as being 'tenuous' 'thin' 'brittle' 'gossamer' 'iridescent' and 'delightfully daring'. All of which connoted, to the public mind, 'cocktails' 'evening dress' 'repartee' and irreverent allusions to copulation, thereby causing a gratifying number of respectable people to queue up at the box office.

"There is actually more to the play than this, however, but on the whole not very much. It is a reasonably well-constructed duologue for two experienced performers, with a couple of extra puppets thrown in to assist the plot and to provide contrast. There is a well-written love scene in Act I, and a certain amount of sound sex psychology underlying the quarrel scenes in Act II.

"As a complete play, it leaves a lot to be desired, principally owing to my dastardly and conscienceless behaviour towards Sybil and Victor, the secondary characters. These, poor things, are little better than ninepins, lightly wooden, and only there at all in order to be repeatedly knocked down and stood up again. Apart from this, *Private Lives*, from the playwright's point of view, may or may not be considered interesting, but at any rate, from the point of view of technical acting, it is very interesting indeed.

"To begin with, there is no further plot and no further action after Act I, with the exception of the rough-and-tumble fight at the curtain of Act II. Before this, there is exactly 40 minutes of dialogue between the leading protagonists, Amanda and Elyot, which naturally demands from them the maximum of resource and comedy experience, as every night, according to the degree of responsiveness from the audience, the attack and tempo of the performance must inevitably vary. This means a constant ear cocked in the direction of the stalls, listening for the first sinister cough of boredom, and, when it comes, a swiftly exchanged glance of warning and an immediate, and, it is to be hoped, imperceptible speeding up of the scene until the next sure-fire laugh breaks and it is permissible to relax and breathe more easily for a moment.

"This strenuous watchfulness is, of course, necessary in the playing of any high comedy scene, but as a general rule the considerate author provides life-lines for his actors in the shape of sharply-etched cameos for the subsidiary members of the cast, who can make bustling little entrances and exits in order to break the monotony. He may even, on occasion, actually provide a sustained plot for them to hang on to when all else fails.

"In the second act of *Private Lives*, however, there was no help from the author over and above a few carefully placed laugh lines, and, taken all in all, it was more tricky and full of pitfalls than anything I have ever attempted as an actor. But, fortunately for me, I had the inestimable advantage of playing it with Gertrude Lawrence, and so three-quarters of the battle was won before the curtain went up."

Private Lives was the first production at the newly built Phoenix Theatre in Charing Cross Road.

The balcony scene (Part of Act I) was performed by Kay Hammond and John Clements at the "... Merely Players" performance, London Coliseum, 20 November 1949, and at the "Stars at Midnight" performance, London Palladium, 28 May 1953.

Major UK revivals of *Private Lives* since the Second World War include:

Hampstead, London, 24 April 1963, with Rosemary Martin and Edward de Souza, directed by James Roose Evans. Transferred under the management of Michael Codron to the Duke of York's Theatre, 3 July 1963 (212 performances). Set in the contemporary period.

Queen's Theatre, London, 21 September 1972 (517 performances). Transferred to the Globe Theatre, 2 July 1973, with Maggie Smith (succeeded by Jill Bennett) and Robert Stephens (succeeded by John Standing). Set in 1929.

Dutchess Theatre, 16 April 1980, with Maria Aitken and Michael Jayston, directed by Alan Strachan.

Aldwych, London, 19 September 1990, with Joan Collins, Keith Baxter and Sarah Crowe, directed by Tim Luscombe.

Royal National Theatre, 13 May 1999, directed by Philip Franks, with Juliet Stevenson and Anton Lesser.

A scene from *Private Lives* is played by Julie Andrews in the 1968 film *Star!*

Television productions have included:

1959: BBC: Maxine Audley and Peter Gray

1976: BBC: Penelope Keith and Alec McCowen

The play has also been produced for radio, notably:

1939: CBS: Gertrude Lawrence and Orson Welles

1969: BBC: Moira Lister and Edward de Souza

1983: BBC: Patricia Routledge and Paul Scofield

Scenes from the play have frequently been broadcast and televised in extract and several are used in the revue *Noël and Gertie* (1989).

US PRODUCTIONS

PRESENTED by Charles B. Cochran at the Times Square Theatre, New York on 27 January 1931 (256 performances).

CHARACTERS	**Times Square, 1931**
SIBYL CHASE	Jill Esmond
ELYOT CHASE	Noël Coward
VICTOR PRYNNE	Laurence Olivier
AMANDA PRYNNE	Gertrude Lawrence
LOUISE	Thérèse Quadri

After three months, Noël and Gertie were replaced by Otto Kruger and Madge Kennedy.

The *New York Sun*: "Noël Coward, irrepressible in his universal facility, bubbled up last evening with a play in one hand and a comic performance in the other and writing jokes with his eyebrows. *Private Lives* is as irresistible a comedy as ever turned old situations into new fun."

The *New York Evening World*: "A rare blessing of the theatre, a merry, witty, smart light comedy with the airy grace of a feather brushing an idea as sentiment. Mr Coward gave an adroit, engaging performance as Elyot in his most intimate and irresistibly funny comedy."

The *New York World*: "An admirable piece of fluff acted as brilliantly, uproariously and happily, with as much resourceful neatness and variety as I have ever seen. Mr Coward's skill brings the freshness of surprise to things we have all seen before."

Noël recalled in *Present Indicative*: "The New York critics resented the thinness of the play less than the London critics, and enjoyed the lightness of it more; in fact, many of them came to see it several times. I think we retained, on the whole, the shine that we had started with; at all events, we strained every nerve to justify the almost overwhelming praise that was most generously lavished upon us."

Major US revivals of *Private Lives* since 1931 include:

Plymouth Theatre, New York, 1948 (248 performances following a national tour) with Tallulah Bankhead and Donald Cook:

The *New York Times*: "After 17 years, Noël Coward's *Private Lives* is still outrageously amusing. Since virtually the same thing is true of Tallulah Bankhead, the revival at the Plymouth is the funniest item in the season so far."

New York Daily News: "A tour de force which had sophisticates chattering when Mr Coward and Gertrude Lawrence first played it here. It was, one said, slight and brittle and in other than expert hands it wouldn't be much. The same can be said today – but the swivel-necked Mr Cook and the hag-voiced Miss Bankhead struck me as experts."

Billy Rose Theatre, New York, 4 December 1969 (204 performances), with Tammy Grimes and Brian Bedford. Transferred to the Broadhurst Theatre on 27 April 1970. Produced by David Merrick and the APA and directed by Stephen Porter:

The *New York Times*: "Gorgeous – that would be one word for Stephen Porter's re-staging of *Private Lives*. Delicate might be another word, dazzling if you want a third. *Private Lives* is, of course, a great test of style for both director and actors. Tammy Grimes is outrageously appealing. She plays every cheap trick in the histrionic book with supreme aplomb and adorable confidence. Everything came together to make me at last realise that *Private Lives* is not a revival but a classic."

The *New York Daily News*: "The sharp and catty dialogue, which once seemed so brilliant and which also was enjoyable when Tallulah Bankhead and Donald Cook battled it back and forth in 1948, now strikes me as quite dated. Bedford seems to have Coward style, but Miss Grimes doesn't."

Tammy Grimes won that year's Tony Award for Best Actress.

46th Street Theatre, New York, 6 February 1975 (92 performances), with Maggie Smith and John Standing (transferred from London). Produced by Arthur Cantor and directed by John Gielgud:

The *New York Times*: "Not only so very durable but remarkable. The fact that it is screamingly funny had also probably never hindered it. How perfect the play is. It is satisfyingly obvious and satisfyingly complete. The curtain falls on each act with a happy plop of fulfillment. A gorgeous, enchanting play."

The *New York Daily News*: "I've come to the no doubt rash conclusion that *Private Lives*, which is a mere 45-years-old, is an immaculate comedy."

Lunt-Fontanne Theatre, New York, 8 May 1963 (63 performances), with Elizabeth Taylor and Richard Burton. Produced by the Elizabeth Theatre Group (Zev Bufman and Elizabeth Taylor). Directed by Milton Katselas:

The *New York Times*: "A wise and painful statement about both the necessity and the impossibility of love. In this version... there's no attempt to mine the gold beneath the text – or to make the most of the on-the-surface dross. Instead we get an intermittent effort by the stars to create the fantasy that their own offstage private lives dovetail neatly with Coward's story. But life doesn't imitate art in this *Private Lives* – it obliterates it."

The *News*: "*Private Lives* is more spectacle than a theatrical performance. It's LIZ AND DICK TOGETHER AGAIN!"

FILM VERSION

The film version of *Private Lives* was made in America by Metro-Goldwyn-Mayer, 1931. It was directed by Sidney Franklin. Adapted for the screen by Hans Kraly, Richard Schayer and Claudine West.

CHARACTERS	Metro-Goldwyn-Mayer, 1931
SYBIL CHASE	Una Merkel
ELYOT CHASE	Robert Montgomery
VICTOR PRYNNE	Reginald Denny
AMANDA PRYNNE	Norma Shearer
OSCAR	Jean Hersholt
PAGE	George Davis

The film was first shown in London at the Empire, Leicester Square, 4 February 1932.

A French version of the play with the title, *Les Amants Terribles*, was produced in 1936, with Gaby Morlay and André Luguet. It was directed by Marc Allegret.

22
POST-MORTEM
A PLAY IN EIGHT SCENES
Written in 1930

FIRST PRESENTED at The King's Head Theatre, London, 6 October 1992.

CHARACTERS	The King's Head, 1992
JOHN CAVAN	Harry Burton
LADY CAVAN	Sylvia Syms
SIR JAMES CAVAN	Roy Sampson
ROBERT TILLEY	Max Gold
SHAW	Ian Mitchie
BABE ROBINS	Neil Roberts

PERRY LOMAS	Steven Pacey
MONICA CHELLERTON	Susannah Morley
BERTIE CHELLERTON	Max Gold
KITTY HARRIS	Carol Holt
EGGIE BRACE	Ian Mitchie
DRAKE (a butler)	Neil Roberts
ALFRED BORROW	Will Knightley
MISS BEAVER	Carol Holt
LARY STAGG-MORTIMER	Avril Angers
THE BISHOP OF KETCHWORTH	Walter Hall
Director	*Richard Stirling*
Designer	*Mark Friend*

SCENE 1:   A Company Headquarters in the front line (spring, 1917).

SCENE 2:   Sir James Cavan's house in Kent. A spring evening, about 9 p.m., in 1930.

SCENE 3:   The Chellertons' house in Mount Street. Monica's sitting-room.

SCENE 4:   Perry Lomas' sitting-room.

SCENE 5:   Sir James Cavan's private office in the *Daily Mercury* building, London.

SCENE 6:   A dining-room.

SCENE 7:   Lady Cavan's sitting-room.

SCENE 8:   The dug-out. Exactly as in Scene 1.

Author's Note: The action of this play should he continuous and the changes of scene managed as quickly as possible, during which the auditorium should remain in darkness.

SYNOPSIS

Scene 1: At Company Headquarters in a quiet section of the line in 1917 – a sandbagged shelter backed by a high trench wall – Tilley, Shaw, Babe Robins and John Cavan have just finished dinner. Babe is 19; the others are between 26 and 30. Tilley is the Company Commander: he has returned from leave, during which John has been acting as his deputy. Incited by the humorist, Shaw, the elder men are laughing over flamboyantly patriotic articles in the *Mercury*, owned by John's father, Sir James Cavan; but Robins is upset because his close friend, Armitage, has been badly wounded. He goes out to write to Armitage's parents, and Shaw also leaves on an inspection round.

Perry Lomas comes in, having heard at the dressing-station (where he has been treated for a slight wound in the hand) that Armitage is dead. Seeing the *Mercury*, he launches into a diatribe against newspaper magnates who gull the public with spurious heroics, keeping them ignorant of the real truth about war. John warns him that by giving his imagination rein (in civil life he is a poet) he is heading for a smash. John himself has an idea that, in an infinitesimal moment before death, we may be able to see the whole purpose of life – the past and future as a circle of time.

At this point Babe Robins comes back and hears that Armitage has died. He is so shaken that John offers to take his place on the wiring party that is just going out. The party is attacked and John is brought back mortally wounded. He opens his eyes and smiles at Perry, whispering: "I'm right. I tell you, I'm right – I'll know – I'll know..."

Scene 2: John's mother, Lady Cavan, is playing patience in the drawing-room of her house in Kent. It is a spring evening in 1930, and dusk is falling as John walks quietly into the room, still in khaki and looking unchanged. She is neither surprised nor alarmed, but merely holds out her arms to him and asks why he did not come sooner. "I wasn't hit until a few minutes ago," exclaims John. "Thirteen years ago," replies his mother.

She gives him news of his family and friends: his father is well and prosperous, and still has a roving eye for actresses; his sister Harriet is married and has become a Christian Scientist; Monica, whom he loved, has been married for ten years. (John comments rather bitterly that he is glad she waited for a while.) He picks up a book, *Post-Mortem*, by Perry Lomas, and his mother tells him it has been a great sensation. It is a violent and bitter commentary on the war, which has been attacked by the press as blasphemous and seditious, and will very likely be publicly burned.

Despite his mother's efforts to retain him, John goes to see for himself what they have all made of their lives and whether the suffering of the war has been worth while; but he promises to come back to her before his final departure.

Scene 3: In her smartly-furnished sitting-room in Mount Street, Monica Chellerton, clad in brilliant pyjamas, is lying on the sofa reading *Vogue*, with a panatrope blaring incessantly in the background. She is at first terrified to see John, but after a while accepts his presence as a vivid dream, offers him a drink and a cigarette, and at his request turns off the gramophone.

He finds that she is leading an empty and frivolous life. She is childless and glad of it, though she likes other people's children "in small doses". Their talk is interrupted by two of her friends, Kitty Harris and Eggie Brace, who have come to take her to a party. Monica introduces John, whom they accept without surprise, suggesting that he can come along too and talk about the war (qualified by Eggie, who fancies himself as a wit, as "the bore war"). But Monica chooses to stay behind with John.

After the visitors have gone, she begins to make love to him, and they are embracing when her husband unexpectedly arrives. Chellerton carries off the situation gracefully, leaving after a few minutes with the whispered comment: "For God's sake lock the door next time. That was damned awkward."

John says a final and somewhat wistful goodbye to Monica, whom he leaves in a disturbed and self-exculpatory mood, reflecting that it would be "funny to have an affair with a ghost".

Scene 4: Perry Lomas, with a revolver beside him, is writing a farewell letter when he looks up and sees John. Thinking it an hallucination, he raises the weapon to his temple and is surprised that John is sufficiently tangible to grab his arm and stop him. He consents to put the revolver down and talk, but can give no definite reason for suicide, beyond "a sort of hopelessness which isn't quite despair... A formless, deserted boredom." It is not, he insists, on account of the bad reception given to his book, but merely from a sense of futility.

John diagnoses this as the mental crash that he prophesied 13 years previously, and suggests that Perry had better go away for a holiday. This reminds his friend of their talk on the night when Armitage died. He asks whether John still believes that anything good has come out of the war. If he does, he should go back to the grave and come again later – he has picked a bad moment.

"Why so bad?" asks John. "What's happening?" Nothing is happening, Perry assures him: people are just the same as before, "individually pleasant and collectively idiotic... There's still poverty, unemployment, pain, greed, cruelty, passion and crime. There's still meanness, jealousy, money and disease." Preparations for the next war go forward "fully realised by everyone except the public that will be involved... The only difference in post-war conditions is that there are so many men maimed for life, and so many women whose heartache will never heal." The war has become merely a pleasantly harrowing film – even some of the men who took part in it remember it as vaguely glamorous. John's ideals will do nothing amid all this bunk (Perry savagely repeats the word several times); so he had better go back and be sweet to his mother.

John retorts that Perry is a far greater idealist than he – for his own ideals are individualistic, whereas Perry's catch at life itself. He picks up the revolver, hands it to Perry, and embraces him. As the lights fade, Perry again raises the weapon to his forehead.

The shot rings out in the dark, and as the curtain falls the voices of Robins, Tilley, Shaw and Perry are heard, talking in their shelter over the unconscious John.

Scene 5: Sir James Cavan is in his elaborately furnished private office with his secretary, Miss Beaver, and his colleague Alfred Borrow. The room is arranged for a conference.

When John comes in his father rises and embraces him theatrically: "John! My son! My boy!" He introduces him to Borrow, who assures the young man that England made him and he must "tell England everything". To the accompaniment of John's quietly disgusted comments, the correspondent then outlines a sentimental interview with the returned hero.

A phone call from Cavan's kept actress, Viola Blake, evokes some every plain speaking from Miss Beaver, who (unrebuked by Sir James) describes her as a "silly, drunken harlot".

Soon the members of the conference arrive: Lady Stagg-Mortimer, famous for her war work, the Bishop of Ketchworth, and Sir Harry Merstham, the Censor. They have been convened to discuss the immorality of post-war literature, with special reference to Perry's book, *Post-Mortem*.

Lady Stagg-Mortimer confesses that it makes her feel "humiliated and ashamed". ("Good for you!" interjects John.) Sir Harry considers it "a disgrace"; while the Bishop, who has not read it, contentedly signs a letter of protest drafted in his name, and goes to sleep. Anticipating that the book will be banned and thereby become valuable, Borrow has bought 20 copies.

A letter to the press, written for Lady Stagg-Mortimer to sign, is read by Borrow: it calls upon the women of England to demand that the "slandering scoundrels" who represent our gallant men in the trenches as ordinary whisky-drinking, bawdy men shall be taken out and shot. Here John violently interrupts, declaring that the men who died were the lucky ones, being released from the sad obligation of life in a Christian world which has not even proved itself worthy of death.

The scene takes on a nightmare-like quality, as far-away guns are heard, and everyone begins to chant softly "God and Country" as an accompaniment to John's closing speech. He tells them to listen to the guns "blasting your Christianity to pieces", and declares that the sons and husbands and lovers that they gave in their silly pride were being set free: "Free from your hates and loves and small, pitiful prayers, for eternity... They've escaped – escaped. You'll never find them again, either in your pantomime hell or your tinsel heaven. Long live war! Long live death and destruction, and despair. Through all that there may be a hope, a million-to-one chance for us somewhere, a promise of something cleaner and sweeter than anything your bloody gods have ever offered. Long live war..."

The sound of gunfire and the steady chanting grows louder as the light fades. Then in pitch darkness there is suddenly dead silence, and Perry's voice saying quietly: "I think he opened his eyes."

Scene 6: The light is focused upon a dinner table, where Tilley, Shaw, Babe Robins and John are finishing their meal with coffee and liqueurs. Tilley is now 43, iron-grey and wearing pince-nez. Shaw, at 39, is corpulent and pink; Robins, aged 32, looks like an average young man in the motor business. They drink the toast, proposed by John: "To contentment, peace and plenty." John tries to find out what each has made of his life: Tilley, still a disciplinarian, lives in Hampstead. He is married, with two sons, and, though he has only bitter memories of the last war, would not prevent them from joining up if there were another. Shaw, once so jolly, has stiffened into a hide-bound public school type who would bring up his sons (if he had any) "to believe in God, and the necessity of standing by their country in time of need, and to play the game according to the rules", and would shoot them if they failed.

Babe Robins, reminded of his love for Armitage and his indebtedness to John, breaks down in tears. From out of the shadows comes his 19-year-old self to stand behind his chair. Then, to the sound of guns, the gay young Shaw comes to contrast with the pompous middle-aged one; their older selves both beg John to go away, and Tilley says coldly that he hates him for stirring up trouble: he wants to forget this dream and remember John only as "a damn good soldier, a nice, un-complicated boy without overtones". He himself has accepted life and peace as he once accepted death and war; consequently, John cannot play upon his intellect as he has done on the sentimental emotions of the other two: he orders him to go back quickly and not keep them all hanging about.

Once more the lights fade and we hear the young men talking in their trench shelter.

Scene 7: A spotlight shows Lady Cavan again playing patience. John embraces her and says he is going back for ever. Not even her love can hold him in a world where there is no place for him. Perhaps there is one chance in a million that they will meet again in eternity. They kiss each other a last goodbye.

Scene 8: The lights come up on the dug-out, exactly as it was in Scene I. John opens his eyes. "You were right, Perry," he says. "A poor joke." Then he falls back, and Tilley gently lifts him on to the stretcher.

❖

PUBLICATIONS

Post Mortem was first published by Heinemann (London, 1931). It is dedicated to William Bolitho. Also published in *Noël Coward Collected Plays: Two*, Methuen World Classics (London, 1999).

❖

NOTES

While on his holiday in the East, after writing *Private Lives*, Coward appeared with J. Grant Anderson's repertory company, The Quaints, at the Victoria Theatre, Singapore, 4 April 1930, as Stanhope in *Journey's End* for three performances. His co-star was the young John Mills. He returned home from Ceylon by boat to Marseilles. He says:

"During that voyage I wrote an angry little vilification of war called *Post-Mortem*; my mind was strongly affected by *Journey's End*, and I had read several current war novels one after the other. I wrote *Post-Mortem* with the utmost sincerity; this, I think, must be fairly obvious to anyone who reads it. In fact, I tore my emotions to shreds over it. The result was similar to my performance as Stanhope: confused, under-rehearsed, and hysterical. Unlike my performance as Stanhope, however, it had some every fine moments. There is, I believe, some of the best writing I have ever done in it, also some of the worst. I have no deep regrets over it, as I know my intentions to have been of the purest. I passionately believed in the truth of what I was writing; too passionately. The truths I snarled out in that hot, uncomfortable little cabin were all too true and mostly too shallow. Through lack of detachment and lack of real experience of my subject, I muddled the issues of the play. I might have done better had I given more time to it and less vehemence. However, it helped to purge my system of certain accumulated acids."

Coward says in his introduction to *Play Parade, Volume I*:

"*Post-Mortem* was not actually written for the theatre. But, as I felt at the time, perhaps erroneously, that I had a lot to say, I put it into play form, for the simple reason that I felt more at home in that than in any other.

"It has not yet been produced, although one day perhaps it will be. I think it might probably be quite effective, provided that it is expertly directed and acted."

Post-Mortem, though performed in boys' schools and at a prisoner-of-war camp in Germany in World War II, has only had one major professional staging. It was also televised by the BBC in 1968.

23
SOME OTHER PRIVATE LIVES
PLAYLET, ONE ACT

Written in 1930

A parody of *Private Lives*

FIRST PRESENTED at a Gala Matinée in aid of Denville Hall at the London Hippodrome, 8 December 1930.

FIRST PUBLIC PRODUCTION by the Noël Coward Company at the Festival Theatre, Malvern, 1 September 1932.

CHARACTERS	Hippodrome, 1930
ELSIE	Adrianne Allen
FRED	Noël Coward
ALF	Laurence Olivier
FLOSSIE	Gertrude Lawrence
Director	*Noël Coward*

CHARACTERS	Malvern, 1932
FRED	Keith Sheperd
FLOSSIE	Joyce Wodeman
Director	*Under supervision of Noël Coward*

SCENE: Flossie's room in London.
In the published version the scene is a furnished sitting-room in a lower middle-class lodging-house.

SYNOPSIS (of printed version)

Fred and Floss are in a sitting-room furnished with a broken-down sofa and a deal table on which are bread, cheese, pickles, bottled beer, etc. They have been staying in for several evenings and feel inclined to remarry, as they have hit it off quite well together – in fact, they have hardly needed to use the warning phrase, "Solomon Isaacs" ("Sollocks" for short), which checks their quarrels. They wonder how their ex-partners, Alf and Daisy, are getting on.

After dancing to the gramophone for a while Floss breaks off – her conscience is troubling her about Daisy. When she begins to reminisce about Alf, a quarrel blows up and has to be stopped with "Sollocks". A singing interlude follows. Talk about another admirer of Floss, Ted Rawlins, leads to fresh bickering. She turns on the gramophone, but Fred orders her to stop it. They fight over the record, screaming "Sollocks" at each other, and end up with an undignified struggle on the floor.

PUBLICATIONS

The published version is shorter than that produced, and for two characters only (Fred and Floss). As originally acted, the other two characters (Elsie and Alf) appeared at the end of the quarrel as in the original play. (In the published text "Elsie" is referred to as "Daisy".) It is included in *Collected Sketches and Lyrics* (Hutchinson, 1931) with the title *Parody of Private Lives* and in *Collected Revue Sketches and Parodies* (Methuen, 1999).

NOTES

In his introduction to the playlet, Coward says:
"This is a parody of the second act of *Private Lives*. The circumstances are the same as those in the play, except that the characters are drawn from the poorer and less-educated class of society."

The matinée at the London Hippodrome, for which this playlet was especially written, was in aid of the funds of Denville Hall, a home for aged actors founded by Alfred Denville. The production of *Private Lives* at the Phoenix Theatre was nearing the end of its run when the parody was produced. It was introduced by Charles B. Cochran at the matinée.

The parody in its printed version was included in the repertoire of the Noël Coward Company on tour, 1932, and played as an after-piece to their

production of *Private Lives*, in which Amanda and Elyot were played by
Agatha Carroll and Wilson Barrett and Sybil and Victor by Marjorie Taylor
and James Mason.

This sketch has never subsequently been staged or broadcast.

24
CAVALCADE
A PLAY IN THREE PARTS
Written in 1930 and 1931

FIRST PRESENTED by Charles B. Cochran at the Theatre Royal, Drury Lane,
London, 13 October 1931 (405 performances).

CHARACTERS	Drury Lane, 1931
JANE MARRYOT	Mary Clare
ROBERT MARRYOT	Edward Sinclair
ELLEN BRIDGES	Una O'Connor
ALFRED BRIDGES	Fred Groves
MARGARET HARRIS	Irene Browne
EDITH HARRIS	Alison Leggatt
EDWARD MARRYOT	Arthur Macrae
JOE MARRYOT	John Mills
FANNY BRIDGES	Binnie Barnes
EDITH (as a child)	Veronica Vanderlyn
EDWARD (as a child)	Peter Vokes
JOE (as a child)	Leslie Flack
FANNY (as a child)	Dorothy Keefe

CHARACTERS in *Mirabelle* (Part 1, Scene 4)

LAURA MARSDEN (Mirabelle)	Stella Wilson
HENRY CHARTERIS (Lt Edgar)	Eric Purveur
ROSE DARLING (Ada)	Maidie Andrews
MICKY BANKS (Tom Jolly)	Billy Fry
COOK	Laura Smithson
ANNIE	Merle Tottenham
MRS SNAPPER	Edie Martin
FLO GRAINGER	Dorothy Monkman

GEORGE GRAINGER	Bobby Blythe
DAISY DEVON	Moya Nugent
MARION CHRISTIE	Betty Hare
NETTA LAKE	Phyllis Harding
CONNIE CRAWSHAY	Betty Shale
TIM BATEMAN	Philip Clarke
DOUGLAS FINN	John Beerbohm
LORD MARTLETT (Chubby)	Anthony Pélissier

TROUPE, "Uncle George And His Merry Men"

UNCLE HARRY	Aly Ford
UNCLE GEORGE	Charles Wingrove
UNCLE DICK	Walter Rayland
UNCLE JACK	Tod Squires
UNCLE BOB	Tom Carlisle
UNCLE JIM	William McGuigan

FREDA WEDDELL	Lena Brand
OLIVE FROST	Marcelle Turner
GLADYS (parlourmaid)	Dorothy Drover
A COMMUNIST	Anthony Blair
A RELIGIOUS FANATIC	Enid Clinton-Baddeley
A WIRELESS ANNOUNCER	W. A. H. Harrison
PIANIST AT NIGHT CLUB	Jack London
TRUMPETER AT NIGHTCLUB	Leslie Thompson

CROWDS, SOLDIERS, SAILORS, GUESTS, etc.

Director	*Noël Coward*
Designer	*G.E. Calthrop*

❖

SCENE: The play is in 22 scenes, and the action takes place between Sunday, 31 December 1899 and 1930. There will be an interval of ten minutes after Scene 8 (14 May 1903) and after Scene 19 (11 November 1918). The period of each scene is indicated by illuminated signs on the proscenium.

PART I: Scene 1: Sunday, 31 December 1899, the drawing-room of a London house.

Scene 2: Saturday, 27 January 1900. A dockside.

Scene 3: Friday, 18 May 1900. The drawing-room of a London house.

Scene 4: Friday, 18 May 1900. A theatre.

Scene 5: Monday, 21 January 1901. The kitchen of a London house.

Scene 6: Sunday. 27 January 1901. Kensington Gardens.

Scene 7: Saturday, 2 February 1901. The drawing-room (as Scene 1).

Scene 8: Thursday, 14 May 1903. The grand staircase of a London house.

PART II: Scene 1: Saturday, 16 June 1906. The bar parlour of a London public house.

Scene 2: Saturday, 16 June 1906. A London street (exterior of the public house).

Scene 3: Wednesday, 10 March 1909. The private room of a London restaurant.

Scene 4: Monday, 25 July 1910. The beach of a popular seaside resort.

Scene 5: Sunday, 14 April 1912. The deck of an Atlantic liner.

Scene 6: Tuesday, 4 August 1914. The drawing-room (as Part I, Scene 1).

Scene 7: 1914–1915–1916–1917–1918. Marching.

Scene 8: Tuesday, 22 October 1918. A restaurant.

Scene 9: Tuesday, 22 October 1918. A railway station.

Scene 10: Monday, 11 November 1918. The drawing-room (as Scene 6).

Scene 11: Monday, 11 November 1918. Trafalgar Square.

PART III: Scene 1: Tuesday, 31 December 1929. The drawing-room (as Part I, Scene 1).

Scene 2: Evening, 1930. A night club.

Scene 3: Chaos.

Music and lyrics of *Mirabelle* ("Lover Of My Dreams"), Scene 4, and "Twentieth Century Blues", Scene 21, by Noël Coward. Orchestra under the direction of Reginald Burston.

SYNOPSIS

PART I, Scene 1: It is nearly midnight on 31 December 1899, and Robert and Jane Marryot are celebrating the new century quietly together in their London house. Their happiness is somewhat clouded by the Boer War:

Jane's brother is besieged in Mafeking, and Robert himself will shortly be going to South Africa. The butler, Bridges, and his wife Ellen – who have decked the supper-table with flowers as a surprise gift – are invited in to share. Bells, shouting, and sirens outside usher in the New Year, and Robert proposes a toast: "1900!" Hearing her two boys stir upstairs, Jane runs up to see to them, and her husband calls to her to bring them down: "How very impolite of the twentieth century to waken the children," he comments, smiling.

Scene 2: One month later, a contingent of volunteers is leaving for the war. On the dockside Ellen is seeing off Bridges, and Jane is also taking leave of her husband. As the men go aboard, Jane comforts Ellen, who is crying. A band strikes up "Soldiers Of The Queen", while the volunteers wave their farewells to the cheering crowd.

Scene 3: The Marryot boys, Edward (aged 12) and Joe (aged 8), are playing soldiers with a little friend, Edith Harris. When she objects to being continually cast as "the Boers", they begin to quarrel, and the noise brings in their mothers. Joe throws a toy cannon at Edith, which hurts her knee. He is sharply slapped by Jane, whose nerves are on edge with anxiety about her brother and her husband.

Seeing this, Margaret Harris sends the children upstairs, and then gets rid of a barrel-organ which is playing "Soldiers Of The Queen" under the window. She tells Jane firmly to put on her best dress and come with her to dine out and see the popular musical comedy, *Mirabelle*. Then she leaves, promising to come back in time to fetch her. When another barrel-organ starts up the same tune, Jane's self-control snaps. She shouts at the man from the window, and then collapses on the sofa in hysterics.

Scene 4: Jane and Margaret are in a stage-box, watching *Mirabelle*. A sextet in uniform are singing: "Girls Of The C.I.V."; then Mirabelle herself (a princess disguised as a village maiden) sings with her suitor, Lieutenant Edgar Tyrell, R.N., the Mirabelle Waltz, "Lover Of My Dreams". Next come a comedy pair – Ada, the dairymaid (really, the Princess's lady-in-waiting) and Tom, the sailor, who sing, "Fun On The Farm". Mirabelle overhears Ada saying that the Lieutenant knows quite well who she is, and is marrying her for her money. Distracted, she launches into a finale with the chorus – but it is never finished, for the stage manager comes in and announces: "Ladies and Gentlemen, Mafeking has been relieved." Pandemonium breaks out; amid the clapping and cheering some of the audience begin to sing "Auld Lang Syne".

Scene 5: It is 21 January 1901. In the Marryot's kitchen the cook, the parlourmaid, Annie, and Ellen's mother, Mrs Snapper, are preparing a special tea in anticipation of Bridges' return from the war. He comes in with Ellen, looking very hale and hearty, and kisses his baby, Fanny, who is in her pram. Then he tells them his news: he has bought a public house from a friend in the forces, so that he and Ellen can be independent. Their gaiety is dampened when Annie brings in a newspaper which reports that Queen Victoria is dying.

Scene 6: This scene is entirely in mime. On Sunday, 27 January, Robert and Jane are walking in Kensington Gardens with their children when they meet Margaret and Edith Harris. They, and all the passers-by – even the children – are in black. Everyone is depressed and silent.

Scene 7: On the Marryots' drawing-room balcony Jane and Margaret, with their children and the servants, are watching Queen Victoria's funeral procession. Robert, who has won the V.C., is walking in the procession, and the children's excitement at seeing him is with difficulty checked by Jane, who makes them stand to attention as the coffin passes. "She must have been a very little lady," is Joe's comment as the lights fade.

Scene 8: Another scene in mime. Jane and Robert are attending a splendid ball given by the Duchess of Churt. The Major-domo announces: "Sir Robert and Lady Marryot."

PART II, Scene 1: Jane has brought her son Edward (now 18) to see Ellen in the living-quarters of the public house. They have just finished high tea, and seven-year-old Fanny has been dancing to entertain them. Some rather vulgar relatives of the Bridges – Flo and George – are also present; but Bridges himself is not there. Ellen explains rather unconvincingly that he is laid up after a cycling accident.

Just as the visitors are leaving, however, he staggers in – unkempt, unshaven, and obviously drunk. Jane's evident though politely veiled dismay angers him, and when she has gone he turns on his family. A noisy scene culminates in his throwing the doll which Jane has given to Fanny into the fire. After a general scuffle, George and Flo push him out of the room, leaving Ellen in tears.

Scene 2: A few hours have passed. It is now 10 p.m. and little Fanny is dancing in the street outside her home, where a German band, some coster youths with mouth-organs, and a Salvation Army band are all playing against one another. Bridges comes out of the pub and tries to grab hold of Fanny, but is prevented by the crowd. He goes on up the street, and suddenly there is a commotion – he has been run over and killed. Flo runs out, hears the news, and rushes back to Ellen.

Scene 3: On March 10, 1909, Edward Marryot is holding his twenty-first birthday party in a London restaurant. Several smart young men and their actress friends have been invited, and the party is very gay. Joe, aged 17, is the youngest person present, and has obviously had too much to drink. He is on affectionate terms with a fat blonde called Connie Crawshay. Rose Darling (who played Ada in *Mirabelle* nine years previously) rises to propose Edward's health, which is drunk enthusiastically by everyone, and is seconded in rambling fashion by Joe. After a good deal of banter and laughter, Rose consents to sing the "Mirabelle Waltz" – telling the company that the original Mirabelle, Laura Marsden, is now dead (of drink, she hints). The party concludes with a selection of popular tunes of the day, ending with the "Merry Widow Waltz".

Scene 4: It is 25 July 1910. A concert party of six "uncles", headed by Uncle George, is performing in a bandstand on the beach of a popular seaside resort. They present a prize to little Fanny Bridges for a song and dance competition. The child is there with Ellen, Mrs Snapper, Flo and George, and to their mutual surprise they meet Margaret Harris, Jane Marryot and Joe. Ellen tells them that she has kept on the business since her husband's death. Fanny is now at a dancing-school and very keen to go on the stage. Some bystanders pass, talking about the Crippen case, and there is great excitement at the approach of an aeroplane; then a thunderstorm clears the beach.

Scene 5: The date is 14 April 1912, and the scene is the deck of an Atlantic liner. Edward has married Edith Harris, and they are on their honeymoon. In idle content, they speculate about death, wondering how long their first rapture of love will last. As they walk away, she lifts her cloak from over the ship rail, revealing the name S.S. *Titanic* on a lifeboat. The lights fade into complete darkness, while the orchestra plays softly and tragically "Nearer, My God, To Thee".

Scene 6: On 4 August 1914, Jane and Margaret have just returned hurriedly from an interrupted holiday, after an uncomfortable journey. Robert fetches two bottles of hock from the wine-cellar in which to drink to the downfall of Germany. Both he and his son are eager to join the army; but Robert is a trifle anxious for Joe – since Edward has drowned, he is all that his parents have left.

A newsboy is heard shouting that war has been declared. Robert buys a paper. Outside, the crowd is laughing, cheering, and singing "Rule, Britannia". Jane, who is considerably upset, refuses to drink with the others. "Drink like the Germans are drinking, to victory and defeat, and stupid, tragic sorrow," she exclaims bitterly, "but leave me out of it."

Scene 7: Soldiers are seen endlessly marching uphill, "out of darkness into darkness", while the years 1914, 1915, 1916, 1917, 1918 are shown in lights over the proscenium, and the orchestra plays songs of the First World War.

Scene 8: On 22 October 1918, Joe and Fanny – now a charming young actress – are dining in a West End restaurant. Joe, in officer's uniform, has been on leave and is just going back to the Front. The girl gives him a locket with her portrait inside. They discuss marriage, but she, foreseeing opposition from his family, tells him to wait until he is back at home.

Scene 9: Later the same evening, Jane is seeing Joe off at the railway station. When he praises her self-control, she comments that her husband said the same thing when she saw him off to the Boer War. As Joe rushes through the barrier to the already moving train, the soldiers aboard it are singing; their womenfolk begin to cry; stretcher bearers carry wounded from an incoming train. With trembling hands, Jane lights a cigarette and turns away.

Scene 10: On the morning of 11 November 1918, Ellen calls upon Jane, having found out that Joe has been having an affair with her daughter. To Jane's disgust, she admits that she has been reading Fanny's private letters. Hearing that the girl is not "in trouble", Jane says rather coldly that they had better wait and let the young people settle it for themselves when Joe comes home. Under the impression that Jane does not consider Fanny a fit match for her son, Ellen becomes rather aggressive, and Jane realises that their long-standing pleasant relations are at an end.

Just as Ellen is leaving, the maid, Gladys, brings in a telegram and calls their attention to the maroons that are heralding the Armistice. Jane opens the telegram and says in a dead voice: "You needn't worry about Fanny and Joe any more, Ellen. He won't be able to come back at all, because he's dead."

Scene 11 : Amid the wild revelry of Armistice Night, Jane is threading her way like a sleep-walker through Trafalgar Square. With the tears streaming down her face, she is cheering wildly and brandishing a rattle, while the band loudly plays "Land Of Hope And Glory".

PART III, Scene 1: On the last day of 1929, Margaret and Jane, both old women, are sitting by the fire. Jane has aged gracefully, but Margaret, with dyed hair, heavy make-up, and bright clothes, still tries to look young. She goes off to her club, after wishing a happy New Year to Jane and Robert, who has come in to drink a New Year toast with his wife.

Jane first drinks to him, "loyal and loving always"; then she proposes the future of England: "The hope that one day this country of ours, which we love so much, will find dignity and greatness, and peace again."

Scene 2: Robert, Jane, Margaret, Ellen and the full company are in a night club on an evening in 1930. At the piano, Fanny is singing "Twentieth Century Blues", and after the song everyone begins to dance – "the dull dancing of habit".

Scene 3: The lights fade, and one vision after another is spotlighted in quick succession on a darkened stage: six "incurables" in hospital blue sitting making baskets; Fanny at the piano; Jane and Robert holding champagne glasses aloft; Ellen sitting in front of a radio loudspeaker; Margaret dancing with a young man. "The visions are repeated quicker and quicker, while across the darkness runs a Riley light sign spelling out news. Noise grows louder and louder. Steam rivets, loudspeakers, jazz bands, aeroplane propellers, etc., until the general effect is complete chaos. Suddenly it all fades into darkness and silence and away at the back a Union Jack glows through the darkness." The scene ends with the lights coming up on the massed company singing "God Save The King".

Alan Parsons in the *Daily Mail*, 1 November 1931:

"When the curtain fell last night at Drury Lane on Mr Noël Coward's *Cavalcade*, there was an ovation such as I have not heard in very many years' playgoing.

"Mr Coward, after returning thanks to all concerned, said: 'After all, it is a pretty exciting thing in these days to be English.' And therein lies the whole secret of *Cavalcade* – it is a magnificent play in which the note of national pride pervading every scene and every sentence must make each one of us face the future with courage and high hopes. The play tells in a series of short scenes the story of an Englishwoman during the last 30 years. To the middle-aged, like myself, the opening act was horribly poignant. We see a troopship leaving amid the cheers and tears of the people for the South African War, and we are given a glimpse of the funeral of Queen Victoria. I was then at a private school, but can still remember the curious sense of desolation which we all felt, as if the bottom had suddenly dropped out of our existence. The whole country wore black; I can just remember that myself – for some strange reason last night's audience laughed hilariously at that – while a ten-year-old boy spoke her epitaph: 'She must have been a very little woman, Mummy.' The second act takes us from 1906 to 1918. Glimpses of the early flying machines and strains of the Merry Widow bring us to the outbreak of war in 1914; with a strangely moving little interlude of two lovers in the ill-fated *Titanic*. '1914-1915-1916-1917-1918' runs the programme for one of these scenes, and what a tragic, touching picture of those years a short, five-minute scene gives us. In front we see music-hall singers carolling their idiotic songs, "We Don't Want To Lose You", and all the rest of it, while in the background the heroic B.E.F. marches in a continual, never-ending line, chanting "Tipperary" and "Pack Up Your Troubles".

"A little bitter, perhaps, but horribly real and affecting, as is the scene at Victoria Station, with the leave trains arriving and departing. Armistice Day comes with its rejoicings in Trafalgar Square, in the forefront the woman who lost her eldest son in the *Titanic*, and her other son at the moment that the maroons announced the peace. "In the last act, amid the chaos of 1930, we see the woman and her husband honouring the toast, 'Let's drink to the hope that one day this country of ours, which we love so much, will find dignity, greatness and peace again.' And when those words were spoken, I doubt if there were many dry eyes in that vast and fashionable Drury Lane audience. I have so often praised Mr Coward the playwright that I want to devote myself tonight to Mr Coward the producer. These huge, unruly crowd scenes were superbly handled. Hundreds and hundreds of people thronged the stage, and yet the story lives throughout. Miss Mary Clare is magnificent as the woman, splendid in her pride and unconquerable courage. Other excellent performances were by Mr Fred Groves, Miss Irene Browne and Miss Una O'Connor. Drury Lane has come into its own again – our national theatre has a theme worthy of itself."

PUBLICATIONS

Cavalcade was first published in book form by Heinemann (London, 1932). It is dedicated to G. B. Stern. (It was serialised in the *Daily Mail*, 10 December to 23 December, 1931). Also published in *Noël Coward Collected Plays: Three*, Methuen World Classics (London, 1999).

NOTES

It was during the London run of *Private Lives* (September to December 1930) that Coward discussed with Cochran the idea of a big spectacular production at the Coliseum. He says: "I felt an urge to test my producing powers on a large scale." Coward says in his introduction to *Play Parade, Volume I*:

"I toyed for a while with the thought of a French Revolution epic, a pageant of the Second Empire, and various other ideas which might give me enough scope for intimate characterisations against a background of crowd scenes. One day I happened to see in a back number of the *Illustrated London News* a photograph of a troopship leaving for the Boer War. Very soon after this the whole scheme of the play fell into my mind, and, after relating it to C. B. Cochran and asking him to get me the Coliseum at all costs, I left for New York to play *Private Lives*. A few months later I received a cable from him saying that the Coliseum was unobtainable, but that I could have Drury Lane provided that I would guarantee an approximate opening date. This was slightly agitating, but I cabled back that the play would be ready for production by the end of September. "When I returned to London in May, I carefully examined the facilities of the Drury Lane stage in company with G. E. Calthrop, who constructed the whole show with me in addition to designing all the scenery and dresses, and we retired to the country, after a series of conferences, to build the play according to blueprints, time-changes, electrical installations and hydraulic lifts. I had not one moment to waste on patriotic fervour.

"After a slight delay, owing to two extra hydraulic lifts which we had to install, *Cavalcade* was finally launched in October, and with it came the Deluge. A very gratifying Deluge. Letters of congratulation. Crowds in the streets. Superlatives in the press. I was told, on all sides, that I had done 'a big thing' and that a peerage was the least I could expect from a grateful monarch. I was also congratulated upon my uncanny shrewdness in slapping on a strong patriotic play two weeks before a General Election, which was bound to result in a sweeping Conservative majority. (Here I must regretfully admit that during rehearsals I was so very much occupied in the theatre and, as usual, so bleakly uninterested in politics that I had not the remotest idea, until a few days before production, that there was going to be an election at all! However, there was, and its effect on the box office was considerable.) "The excitement continued for the two weeks that I remained in London after the play had opened, and I left for South America flushed with heroism and extremely tired. I could relax on the boat and reflect that, although it was undoubtedly very pleasant to read in the press that my country was proud of me, I had escaped the grave danger of taking the idea seriously. True, there had been a few uneasy highbrows who had deplored my fall from sophisticated wit into the bathos of jingoism, and had even gone so far as to suggest that the whole thing was a wily commercial trick, conceived, written and produced in a spirit of cynical mockery, with my tongue fairly wedged in my cheek, but these shrill, small voices were drowned out by the general trumpetings of praise. The only thing that escaped notice in the uproar was the fact that *Cavalcade*, apart from its appeal as a spectacle, actually possessed two or three really well-written scenes, notably the funeral of Queen Victoria and the outbreak of the war in 1914. These two scenes had both dignity and brevity.

"Now that the whole thing is done, and has become an 'epic', and 'The Play of the Century', and 'The Picture of the Generation', I can meditate blissfully upon the good fortune that prompted me to pick up just that particular number of the *Illustrated London News*, instead of one of a later date depicting the storming of the Winter Palace at St Petersburg." On 28 October 1931, King George V and Queen Mary, with the Prince of Wales, the then Duke and Duchess of York, the Duke of Kent and other members of the Royal Family saw the play amid scenes of patriotic fervour and loyal enthusiasm. The 'Mirabelle musical comedy' (Part I, Scene 4) was revived with an all-star cast and chorus at the "... Merely Players" performance, London Coliseum, 20 November 1949. At a similar performance, 20 March 1952, at Drury Lane, the deck scene was revived with Margaret Lockwood and Michael Wilding."

Cavalcade was revived in 1 May 1985 (at Chichester) with Joanna McCallum and Lewis Fiander. It was directed by David Gilmore. For this production, the ending was altered and two hundred people sang "Jerusalem" at the close of the original scene in the 1929 nightclub.

The *Observer*: "The biggest surprise about Coward's *Cavalcade* is that it should prove so pitifully thin. Feeble and repetitive little domestic scenes alternate with mob appearances by a large part of Chichester's population, with their sisters and their cousins and their aunts. *Cavalcade* is solemn and meretricious crap."

Sheridan Morley in *Punch*: "This is an epic devoted to the much wider concept of duty that runs through most of (Coward's) work and somewhere in *Cavalcade* you can find almost everything that mattered about Coward as a dramatist and as a man: the strong sense of the immediate past, the concept of duty and decent behaviour as above all else, the brisk edginess of a love scene on the *Titanic* and overall a cascading sense of sheer theatre."

There have also been revivals at the Shaw Festival in Canada (1985) and the Redgrave Theatre in Farnham in 1981 (directed by David Horlock). In 1995 Dan Crawford directed a road tour which played briefly at Sadlers Wells on 8 April and 7 October. A new production opened at the Citizens Theatre, Glasgow on 25 November 1999.

The first BBC Radio production was in 1936 with Joyce Barbour and Jack Clayton; there was also an American (CBS) radio production in that year, starring Herbert Marshall, Madeleine Carroll and David Niven.

❖

FILM VERSION

A film version of *Cavalcade* was made in America in 1932 by the Fox Film Company. It was directed by Frank Lloyd. Adapted for the screen by Reginald Berkeley.

CHARACTERS	Fox Film Company, 1932
JANE MARRYOT	Diana Wynyard
ROBERT MARRYOT	Clive Brook
ALFRED BRIDGES	Herbert Mundin
ELLEN BRIDGES	Una O'Connor
JOEY MARRYOT	Frank Lawton
EDWARD MARRYOT	John Warbourton
FANNY BRIDGES	Ursula Jeans
MARGARET HARRIS	Irene Browne
EDITH HARRIS	Margaret Lindsay
ANNIE GRAINGER	Merle Tottenham
GEORGE GRAINGER	Billy Bevan
THE COOK	Beryl Mercer
MRS SNAPPER	Tempe Piggot
EDWARD MARRYOT (as a child)	Dick Henderson, Jnr.
JOEY MARRYOT (as a child)	Douglas Scott
EDITH HARRIS (as a child)	Sheila MacGill
FANNY BRIDGES (as a child)	Bonita Granville

The film was shown in London at the Tivoli in February 1933, and a Command Performance of the film was given at Windsor Castle on 2 May 1933. The stage production at Drury Lane was filmed during its run as a guide for the Hollywood producers.

In 1955 a 44-minute filmed version was made for television showing in America by Twentieth Century Fox. It was directed by Lewis Allen, and adapted for film by Peter Packer.

CHARACTERS	Twentieth Century Fox, 1955
ROBERT MARRYOT	Michael Wilding
JANE MARROYT	Merle Oberon
EDITH HARRIS	Marcia Henderson
FANNY BRIDGES	Caroline Jones

ALFRED BRIDGES	Noel Drayton
ELLEN BRIDGES	Nora O'Mahoney
MRS SNAPPER	Doris Lloyd
MARGARET HARRIS	Victoria Warde
JOEY MARRYOT	Richard Lupino
EDWARD MARRYOT	John Irving

This "Featurette" was generally released to cinemas in the UK in 1956, with the title *Heart of a Woman* and was shown on BBC Television on 20 June 1961.

25
WORDS AND MUSIC
REVUE
Written in 1932

FIRST PRESENTED by Charles B. Cochran at the Opera House, Manchester, 25 August 1932 (ran till 10 September).

SUBSEQUENTLY PRESENTED at the Adelphi Theatre, London, 16 September 1932 (164 performances).

Book, lyrics and music by Noël Coward. Produced by Noël Coward. Costumes and décor by G. E. Calthrop. Dances arranged by Buddy Bradley. Orchestra under the direction of Hyam Greenbaum. Orchestrations by Spike Hughes.

PART I

1. Opening Chorus

MAGGIE	Ivy St Helier
MR COCHRAN'S YOUNG LADIES	Margaret Braithwaite, Babs Blythe, Susan Brown, Peggy Duncan, Jean Gillie, Rita Grant, Larry Hodgson, Gladys Lincoln, Eve Lister, Jackie Marcon, Sheila Marlyn, Evelyn Murphy, Betty Scorer, Betty Wedgwood, Eily Wilson, Peggy Willoughby, Enid Wild, Verena Shaon

THE DANCING BOYS	George Bowler, Cyril Butcher, Jack Beaumont, Kenneth Carten, Jimmy Carney, Peter Crawford, Tony Hulley, Eddie Latimer, Tom Rees, Leslie Roberts, Clifford Seagrave, Cyril Wells, Jack Spurgeon, Bobbie Lindsay, James Seacombe, Warren Dalmayne, Frank Evans, Edward Britten

2. Debutantes

Phyllis Harding, Betty Hare, Moya Nugent

3. Children's Hour

FIRST MAMA	Ann Codrington
SECOND MAMA	Naomi Waters
LILLI	Steffi Duna
JANE	Doris Hare
BOBBY	John Mills

"Let's Live Dangerously"

4. Children Of The Ritz

Joyce Barbour and Thea Camacho, Eileen Clifton, Elizabeth Corcoran, Dorothy Cooper, Elizabeth Jenns, Eileen Moore, Naomi Waters, Betty Wedgwood

5. Mad Dogs And Englishmen

NATIVE POLICEMAN	Clifford Seagrave
FIRST ENGLISHMAN	Edward Underdown
SECOND ENGLISHMAN	Kenneth Carten
PLANTERS' WIVES	Ann Codrington, Naomi Waters, Doris Hare, Norah Howard, Effie Atherton, Millie Sim
SIR RONALD MULLENTY	Gerald Nodin
LADY MULLENTY	Ivy St Helier
THE REVEREND INIGO BANKS	Romney Brent
THE NATIVES, BANK CLERKS, etc.	Mr Cochran's Young Ladies and the Dancing Boys

6. Debutantes

Phyllis Harding, Betty Hare, Moya Nugent

7. Let's Say Goodbye

GINA	Rita Lyle
PAUL	Edward Underdown

8. The Hall Of Fame

ANNOUNCER	Joyce Barbour
CELEBRITIES	Gerald Nodin, Ivy St Helier, Romney Brent, Effie Atherton, John Mills, Naomi Waters

9. Mad About The Boy

THE LADY	Joyce Barbour
HER FRIEND	Millie Sim
THE STREET-WALKER	Steffi Duna
THE SCHOOLGIRL	Norah Howard
THE SISTER	Joy Spring
THE SERVANT	Doris Hare
THE FRIEND	Jack Spurgeon
THE STREET-SINGER	Graham Payn (added after first night)
THE BOX-OFFICE GIRL	Gladys Lincoln
THE BOY	Edward Underdown
THE TYPIST	Ann Codrington
THE MANICURIST	Elizabeth Jenns
HIS SECRETARY	Cyril Butcher
THE CROWD	Mr Cochran's Young Ladies and the Dancing Boys

10. Journey's End

(with acknowledgements to Erik Charell and apologies to R. C. Sherriff)

ANNOUNCER	Ivy St Helier
MARIE FRANÇOISE	Rita Lyle
STANHOPE	Romney Brent
TROTTER	Kenneth Ware
RALEIGH	Steffi Duna
FROU FROU	Joyce Barbour

HARRY HAPPY	John Mills
THE GENERAL	Gerald Nodin
THE EMPEROR	Bill Ham
PEASANTS	Moya Nugent, Phyllis Harding, Betty Hare, Effie Atherton, Eileen Moore, Eileen Clifton
TYPISTS	Doris Hare, Ann Codrington, Verena Shaxon, Nora Howard, Millie Sim, Joy Spring
STAFF OFFICERS	Leslie Roberts, Cyril Butcher, Tony Hulley, Jack Beaumont, Tom Rees, Edward Underdown, James Seacombe, Frank Evans
SEÑORITAS	Elizabeth Corcoran, Thea Camacho, Naomi Waters, Elizabeth Jenns, Betty Wedgwood, Dorothy Cooper
GERMAN PRISONERS	Clifford Seagrave, Cyril Wells, Peter Crawford, Jimmy Carney, Kenneth Carten, Eddie Latimer, Edward Britten, Warren Dalmayne
NUNS	Eileen Clifton, Phyllis Harding, Betty Hare, Moya Nugent

PART II

11. Housemaids Knees

Effie Atherton and Mr Cochran's Young Ladies

12. Fairy Whispers

(a) *A Suburban Villa*

JEAN	Doris Hare
MRS HARRISON	Ann Codrington
MR HARRISON	Gerald Nodin
MOLLY	Joy Spring
CUTHBERT	Tommy Hayes

(b) *The Gramophone Studios*

THE NARRATOR	Joyce Barbour
BETTY	Ivy St Helier
ROGER	John Mills

DOTSIE	Norah Howard
JANE	Elizabeth Corcoran
FAIRY QUEEN	Millie Sim

13. Three White Feathers

HE	Edward Underdown
SHE	Doris Hare

14. Children Of The Ritz

Joyce Barbour and Thea Camacho, Eileen Clifton, Elizabeth Corcoran, Dorothy Cooper, Elizabeth Jenns, Eileen Moore, Naomi Waters, Betty Wedgwood

15. Ballets

ANNOUNCER	Moya Nugent

(a) The Club

CARD PLAYERS	Peter Crawford, Eddie Latimer, Tony Hulley, John Beaumont
MEMBERS	Cyril Wells, Jimmy Carney, Leslie Roberts, Cyril Butcher, Jack Spurgeon
ELDERLY COLONELS	Clifford Seagrave, Tom Rees
DOORMAN	Kenneth Carten
PAGE BOY	Tommy Hayes

(b) A Boarding House At Ilfracombe

PROPRIETRESS	Sheila Marlyn
OLD LADY	Ivy St Helier
INVALID	Elizabeth Corcoran
A CLERGYMAN	Bobbie Lindsay
HIS WIFE	Doris Hare
A TENNIS GIRL	Betty Wedgwood
A BANK CLERK	John Mills
A SPINSTER	Betty Scorer
A SKIVVY	Joy Spring
THE SINGER	Rita Lyle

(c) A Crèche

THE MATRON	Steffi Duna
THE DOCTOR	Romney Brent
NURSES	Mr Cochran's Young Ladies

(Ballets arranged by the author)

16. Something To Do With Spring

Joyce Barbour, John Mills, and Mr Cochran's Young Ladies and the Dancing Boys

17. The Wife Of An Acrobat

Ivy St Helier

18. The Younger Generation

THE MOTHER	Rita Lyle
HER DAUGHTERS	Phyllis Harding, Betty Hare, Moya Nugent
MARIE (her maid)	Joy Spring

19. Midnight Matinée

(a) *The Committee Meeting*

(b) *The Midnight Matinée*

MRS ROWNTREE (organiser)	Ivy St. Helier
VISCOUNTESS HOGAN (Diane de Poitiers)	Millie Sim
LADY MILLICENT HEADLEY (Cleopatra)	Rita Lyle
THE MARCHIONESS OF LEMWORTH (Nell Gwynne)	Moya Nugent
THE HON. MRS DOUGLAS DRAYCOTT (Salome)	Joyce Barbour
MISS ESMÉ POINTING (Marie Antoinette)	Ann Codrington
MISS SPENCE (Joan of Arc)	Norah Howard
THE LADY WESTMORSHAM (Lady Blessington)	Naomi Waters
MRS F. N. J. WILSON (Lady Godiva)	Elizabeth Corcoran
MR STUART INGLEBY (announcer)	Romney Brent
GRECIAN CHORUS	Mr Cochran's Young Ladies
LADY ELEANOR SHERRELL (Court Lady)	Joy Spring
MISS REBECCA MOSENTHORPE (Court Lady)	Eileen Moore
LADY PATRICIA GAINTON (page)	Joan O'Neil
THE HON. JULIAN FOBRAGE (page)	Graham Payn

20.Prelude to Finale

DEBUTANTES	Phyllis Harding, Betty Hare, Moya Nugent

21. Finale: The Party's Over Now

A POLICEMAN	Gerald Nodin
FIRST STREET-CLEANER	Kenneth Ware
SECOND STREET-CLEANER	Bill Ham
A YOUNG MAN	John Mills
A YOUNG GIRL	Doris Hare
HOSTESS	Joyce Barbour
LEONORA	Steffi Duna
LORD SKEFFINGTON	Romney Brent
LADY SKEFFINGTON	Ivy St Helier
FINALE	Entire Company

Phyllis Dare replaced Rita Lyle, during the run. She made a surprise appearance at the matinée and evening performances on Saturday 23 November before officially taking over on Monday 25 November 1932.

Only very slight changes were made between the Manchester try-out and the London production.

In Manchester there was a fourth "Debutante" (Nancy Brown) and in the scene 'Mad About The Boy' there was a Street-singer (Graham Payn). This part, though, was introduced again later in the London run, after the first night.

Also, in Manchester, the item 'Children Of The Ritz' appeared only once, in the first half; in London it was divided into two parts, one in each half.

Noël Coward conducted the orchestra on the second night (with the assistance of Spike Hughes), and continued to do so during the Manchester try-out in place of Reginald Burston, who had conducted on the first night.

J.T. Grein in the *Sketch*, 28 September 1932:

"Thanks to Mr Noël Coward, the revue as a form of dramatic art is rehabilitated. He does not call it a revue, but merely *Words and Music*, without further qualification; but it is the real article, not the spurious degenerate of so many variety shows. It surveys and satirises actualities with pungent humour and playful music. As the production of one man's brain, who conceived and vitalised the show from A to Z, it is of its kind a model and a masterpiece, and one that is so vastly amusing that we are only too willing to overlook the arid patches in a field so rich. To the valiant sapper, which is Mr Noël Coward, nothing is sacred, and so he goes hell for leather for all manner of modern crazes, with side-blows at the elder and wiser, who are as dense as the young generation are 'bright' in the maniacal sense of modernity. It is a joy to behold these painless yet tickling bastinados of the stage gigolos, who are here made to work in the sweat of their brows; of the film fans of all ages pining for 'the boy'; of the mad dogs and Englishmen who perambulate in the sunshine while the native seeks the shade, because they do it in London; of the children of the Ritz – the *désoeuvrées* of the period; of the ladies, titled or nouveaux riches, who combine charity with vanity and revel in pageantry of historical dames whose names they cannot even place. It is not only joy but wonderment to behold Mr Noël Coward, at the end of the first half, jumbling Charell and Sherriff in a delightful stew of *Journey's End*, White Horse Inn, and *Casanova*, culminating in a swarm of balloons and magnified confetti all over the house. Here is the one great spectacular effect combining Venice and Tirolia as seen in a distorted mirror, Italians and yodellers pell-mell included, and it is as picturesque as it is absurd.

"While the verbal part of the performance is almost uniformly witty, the music often seems a little all too elementary and thin; the melodious notes of *Bitter Sweet* seem to be missing, yet it serves its purpose, and at least one number, the parody of Russian Ballet, is as apt and corrosive as an acid. Avowedly, there are no flamboyant stars in this revue, yet Miss Ivy St Helier – excellent in nearly a dozen changes and most pathetic in the song of the acrobat's wife – is more versatile and impressive by personality than many a would-be hall-marked leading lady; while Miss Joyce Barbour fascinates by her eerie appearance, and the deep notes of her voice had a charm of their own. Among a crowd of incidental thumb-nails, Miss Steffi Duna made a little mark in her feeling impersonation of a 'street-walker'; Mr Romney Brent was a capital compère and general handy-man; and, of course, Mr Cochran's bewitching Young Ladies, beautifully gowned and disrobed, were the cynosure of all eyes. The whole merry affair was a feast of wit, wisdom, and mockery, charmingly assembled in a picturesque frame. It will enjoy a long life and add to the laurels of Mr Noël Coward's genius and Mr C. B. Cochran's repute as the master showman of the day."

PUBLICATIONS

Words and Music is published in *Play Parade, Volume II*, Heinemann (London, 1939), and the full vocal score was published by William Chappell, 1932. The score is dedicated:

"To Dan O'Neil, whose loyalty, sense of humour, and uncanny skill in stage management have been of inestimable value to me throughout so many productions, these words and this music are affectionately and gratefully dedicated."

The lyric of "Mad Dogs And Englishmen" (written, 1930) is included in *Collected Sketches and Lyrics* (Hutchinson, 1931); and "Mad About The Boy", "Mad Dogs And Englishmen", and "The Party's Over Now" in *The Noël Coward Song Book* (Michael Joseph, 1953).

NOTES

After the production of *Cavalcade*, Coward left England for another long holiday – this time to South America – at the end of October 1931. At this point in his career his first autobiography, *Present Indicative* ends; his second volume, *Future Indefinite*, does not pick up the story again until 1939, and covers the years to 1945. Information on the birth and writing of the plays between the years 1932 and 1939 cannot be told, except by the prefaces which he wrote for *Play Parade* – the volumes of his collected plays (published by Heinemann and now out of print).

In his introduction to *Play Parade, Volume II*, he says:

"When I read *Words and Music*, I remember the terrible night when I had to conduct the orchestra unexpectedly, never having done so before." (This was on the second night of the preliminary run at Manchester.) "The breathless agony on the faces of Joyce Barbour and John Mills when I took the tempo of "Something To Do With Spring" so fast that they couldn't fit their very complicated dance to it and finally staggered off the stage cursing and exhausted."

The song "Mad Dogs And Englishmen" was first performed in *The Third Little Show*, New York, June 1931. It was sung by Beatrice Lillie (see Part III, page 570). The introductory sketch was written for *Words and Music*. The main items from *Words and Music* were used to form the revue *Set to Music*, produced in America in 1938 (see page 339).

The song and sketch "Mad About The Boy" was revived with an all-star cast for *Midnight Cavalcade*, the performance in aid of the Actors' Orphanage, etc., at the London Palladium on 18 March 1954. It was produced by John Gielgud.

At the 1999 Edinburgh Festival, Rex Berry produced a revised version of *Words and Music* with all the songs but none of the sketches.

26
DESIGN FOR LIVING
A COMEDY
Written in 1932

FIRST PRESENTED by Max Gordon at the Hanna Theatre, Cleveland, Ohio, USA, 2 January 1933; subsequently at the Ethel Barrymore Theatre, New York, 24 January 1933 (135 performances).

FIRST PRESENTED IN ENGLAND at the Theatre Royal, Brighton, 16 January 1939; subsequently at the Haymarket Theatre, London, on 25 January 1939. Transferred to the Savoy Theatre, London, 13 June 1939 (203 performances). The run was broken by the outbreak of war in September; the company toured, and the play returned to the Savoy Theatre, 23 December 1939 (33 performances).

REVIVED by H.M. Tennent Ltd at the Theatre Royal, Brighton, 30 October 1973.

CHARACTERS	Cleveland and Ethel Barrymore, US, 1933
GILDA	Lynn Fontanne
ERNEST FRIEDMAN	Campbell Gullan
OTTO	Alfred Lunt
LEO	Noël Coward
MISS HODGE	Gladys Henson
PHOTOGRAPHER	Ward Bishop (part cut for the London production)
MR BIRBECK	Philip Tonge
GRACE TORRANCE	Ethel Borden
HELEN CARVER	Phyllis Connard
HENRY CARVER	Alan Campbell
MATTHEW	Macleary Stennett
Director	*Noël Coward*
Designer	*G. E. Calthrop*

CHARACTERS	**Brighton and Haymarket, 1939**
GILDA	Diana Wynyard
ERNEST FRIEDMAN	Alan Webb
OTTO	Anton Walbrook
LEO	Rex Harrison
MISS HODGE	Dorothy Hamilton
PHOTOGRAPHER	(Cut in London)
MR BIRBECK	Cyril Wheeler
GRACE TORRANCE	Everley Gregg
HELEN CARVER	Cathleen Cordel
HENRY CARVER	Ross Landon
MATTHEW	James McIntyre
Director	*Harold French*
Designer	*Roger K. Furse*

CHARACTERS	**Savoy, 1939**
GILDA	Diana Wynyard
ERNEST FRIEDMAN	Alan Webb
OTTO	Anton Walbrook
LEO	Rex Harrison
MISS HODGE	Ella Miln
MR BIRBECK	Cyril Wheeler
GRACE TORRANCE	Dorothy Lane
HELEN CARVER	Kay Lewis
HENRY CARVER	Ross Landon
MATTHEW	Charles Peters
Director	*Harold French*
Designer	*Roger K. Furse*

❖

ACT I: Otto's studio in Paris.

ACT II: Scene 1 : Leo's flat in London. Eighteen months later.
          Scene 2: The same. A few days later.
          Scene 3: The same. The next morning.

ACT III: Scene 1: Ernest's apartment in New York. Two years later.
          Scene 2: The same. The next morning.

❖

SYNOPSIS

ACT I: A middle-aged picture-dealer, Ernest Friedman, calls at the Paris studio of his friend, Otto Sylvus, to ask his opinion of a Matisse that he has just bought. Gilda, an attractive woman of 30 who lives with Otto and works as an interior decorator, says he is asleep after a bout of neuralgia; but Ernest notices that the breakfast table is laid for two. Having greatly admired Gilda's mother, he feels "vaguely paternal" towards her, and, sensing that she is in a dissatisfied mood, asks why she does not marry Otto. "There's a very real reason," replies Gilda. "I love him." Women marry, she says, because they want children, a home, social status or to be provided for. She herself wants none of these things and is financially independent. Though she respects Otto as a person and as an artist, to be legally tied to him would be repellent to them both.

Somewhat bewildered, Ernest changes the subject by telling her that their mutual friend, Leo Mercuré, has returned from America and is staying at the Georges V hotel. The idea of a rich and successful Leo sends Gilda into peals of laughter.

Ernest, however, wonders what Otto will think. She assures him that Otto could not possibly be jealous of his old friend's success, but confesses that soon she may need help in "a full-blooded emotional crisis".

The practical Ernest suggests that she had better calm herself down with some coffee, and she is drinking it when Otto, in travelling clothes, bursts into the room. He has been away in Bordeaux, finishing a commissioned portrait, which the sitter refused to buy because she thought it unflattering. He has brought the picture back with him and is in high spirits, but he feels, from the constrained greeting of Ernest and Gilda, that something is wrong. However, he lets himself be sent off with Ernest to the Georges V.

Scarcely have they gone when Leo comes out of the inner room. "What now?" he asks, and they discuss the situation: they love each other – but they both love Otto, and he them. Conscience is troubling them, and Leo admits that he has always been subconsciously jealous of Otto, because of Gilda's preference for him. He starts to tell her a funny story about a quarrel, during which he held Otto down in a bath and poured water over him, and they are laughing helplessly over it when Otto himself comes back. He quickly sizes up the situation, and they confess that his suspicions are correct. Leo explains that he arrived unexpectedly, took Gilda out to dinner and... stayed the night. Otto remarks that they might at least have waited for his return and told him how they felt. He works himself up into a fury and slams out of the room with the parting shot: "I wish you were dead and in hell."

ACT II, Scene 1: Gilda is now sharing Leo's flat in London. He has just had a play produced and they are reading the flattering press notices, interrupted by telephone calls from social lion-hunters and journalists.

Leo suggests that they might celebrate his success by getting married, but Gilda refuses, on the ground that "Otto would hate it." Though they have not seen him since their quarrel: in Paris, she still feels that their three lives are linked together. She wonders why she is not feeling happier – something is missing and she does not know what it is. "I know perfectly well what's missing," says Leo, but before he can explain himself the telephone rings again.

It is a society hostess, inviting them both to a weekend party in the country. Gilda accepts for Leo, but refuses for herself, explaining to him afterwards that she is no good at house-parties and doesn't like "second-hand people". Their discussion is again interrupted by the telephone – a newspaper-man is below, wanting to see Leo. Exasperated, Gilda goes to her room.

Leo works off his temperament upon the reporter, Mr Birbeck, returning flippant answers to his stock questions, and at last turns upon him, declaring that he is tired and will talk to him another day. He consents, however, to being photographed, since Mr Birbeck has brought a photographer along with him. While the pose is being settled, Gilda comes back, dressed for the street, puts her arms round Leo's neck and says, "Sorry, darling," before she goes out. Leo smiles for the camera as the curtain falls.

Scene 2: The daily help, Miss Hodge, is just leaving when Gilda unexpectedly asks her: "Do you think it would be a good idea if Mr Mercuré and I got married?" The discovery that they are not is a shock to Miss Hodge's sense of propriety – though she herself has no great opinion of matrimony, having shed two husbands and reverted to her maiden name.

Gilda has settled down to read when suddenly she sees Otto (admitted by Miss Hodge, who found him on the doorstep as she left). After a little uncertainty, she flies into his arms. Now she knows what Leo meant when he said something was missing – of course, it was Otto! He shares her cold supper and recounts his adventures since their parting. In desperation, he had embarked on a long voyage in a Norwegian freighter, where he learned a philosophy of life. He knows now what is wrong with Gilda – she is the concentrated essence of "Love among the Artists". "Your critical faculty is first-rate... but you're liable to get side-tracked if you're not careful. Life is for living first and foremost."

Gilda realises that he has matured: no longer does he need her love more than Leo, as being the weaker of the two; but he still wants her physically. Conscience tells her that to renew their affair would be degrading; but he counters this by asserting that they are not creatures of convention: ordinary standards do not apply to them: "A gay, ironic chance threw the three of us together and tied our lives into a tight knot at the outset... The only thing left is to enjoy it thoroughly." Leaping over the sofa behind which Gilda has taken refuge, he clasps her in his arms.

Scene 3: Ernest has called to see Gilda. Announcing him, Miss Hodge looks into the bedroom, and returns with every symptom of disapproval. A moment later Gilda comes out, fully dressed for the street. Asking after Leo, Ernest is told – as in the first act with Otto – that he is asleep after a bad night. He says he has come to say goodbye before settling permanently in New York. Gilda asks if he wants a house keeper. "Yes; badly," he replies. "Will you come?" "Perhaps," she says, laughing.

It strikes Ernest that her gaiety is forced and that she is in a very strange mood. When she calls him a "safety-valve", he accepts a glass of sherry and prepares for confidences. Taking a letter addressed to Leo out of her bag, Gilda says she is going away – she wants to live her own life. After deliberating on this theme for some time, she fetches her packed dressing-case and goes out with Ernest, returning momentarily to leave a second note – this one addressed to Otto.

Hardly has she gone when Otto appears, in Leo's dressing-gown and pyjamas. He finds Miss Hodge, who expresses virtuous indignation at the "goings-on", and flounces out in a fury after he has told her to mind her own business. He is lying on the sofa smoking when Leo, bored by his house-party, unexpectedly returns. Their encounter in the Paris studio repeats itself in reverse, with Otto – who had previously been the victim – now giving Leo good advice: "We've made our own circumstances, you and Gilda and me, and we've bloody well got to put up with them."

A telephone bell interrupts their discussion, and Leo, going to lift the receiver, finds Gilda's two notes. To each man she has written: "Goodbye, my clever little dear... Thank you for the keys of the city."

Realising that she has escaped them, the two men settle down to get drunk. When the brandy runs out, they toast their freedom in sherry, and finally, realising their loneliness, burst into tears on each other's shoulders.

ACT III, Scene 1: Nearly two years have passed, and Gilda, "poised and mature" is now Mrs Friedman. In her luxurious New York apartment she is receiving guests – a young married couple, Henry and Helen Carver, and an older woman, Grace Torrence. It is about 11.30 on a summer night, and all are in evening dress.

When Grace admires the furnishing of the sitting-room, Gilda offers to show her the rest of the apartment, and in their absence Henry warns his wife that the Friedmans make their living by selling furniture and pictures at exorbitant prices to unwary guests.

There is a ring at the bell and Henry admits Otto and Leo, in faultless evening dress. They introduce themselves, help themselves to drinks, and set out to scandalise the Carvers by their extravagant conversation.

Coming downstairs with Grace, Gilda catches sight of them. After a slight start, she keeps her self-control, admirably, introduces them as old friends, and warns the others not to take their nonsense seriously. However, the conversation continues to be more or less unintelligible to the three Americans and soon, baffled and slightly offended, they take their leave.

Grace offers the visitors a lift in her car and, while farewells are being said, Gilda, who has insisted that Leo and Otto should leave with the rest, contrives to slip them her latchkey and tells them to come back in ten minutes. They both kiss her lightly on the lips and go out. In sudden panic, Gilda snatches up her cloak and handbag, turns off the lights, and runs out through the door leading to the fire-escape.

Scene 2: Next morning, the servant Matthew welcomes his master back and brings in several canvases bought during his journey. Ernest is pouring out his breakfast coffee when Otto and Leo come downstairs wearing his pyjamas (which are too small for them). Taken aback, he asks where Gilda is. "We don't know," replies Otto. "She's disappeared." The whole situation puzzles and annoys Ernest. However, he summons Matthew and orders coffee for the guests. He asks what they want, and they reply frankly that they want Gilda. When Ernest becomes proprietary about her, they tell him not be silly. "She could never be contented without us, because she belongs to us just as much as we belong to her." "She ran away from you," points out Ernest. "She'll come back," is Leo's reply – and in fact she does, still wearing her evening dress and carrying her cloak in a parcel. She explains that she slept at the Ritz and borrowed a coat and hat from the telephone operator.

Composedly sipping coffee out of Ernest's cup, she informs him that she is leaving him. For two years she has been a good wife, helping him with his buying and selling, entertaining his friends; but all the time she has missed Otto and Leo. Now that they have come back she is mad with relief – she cannot possibly live without them. This is too much for Ernest, who protests that he has tried to make her happy and contented, "quietly, without fuss". Gradually he works himself up into a frenzy of exasperation, declaring that he never wants to set eyes on any one of them again as long as he lives. Stamping out of the room, he trips over the parcel of canvases and falls headlong.

Gilda, Otto and Leo break down and roar with laughter. They are still laughing as the curtain falls.

❖

Brooks Atkinson in the *New York Times*, 25 January 1933, on the American production:

"Mr Coward, who has a way of his own with musical romances and historical pageantry, has a way of his own with the familiar triangle. *Design for Living*, which came to the Ethel Barrymore Theatre last evening, is the proof. It is a decadent way if you feel obliged to pull a long, moral face over his breezy fandango. It is an audacious and hilarious way if you relish the attack and retreat of artificial comedy that bristles with wit. Occasionally Mr Coward appears to be asking you to look upon the volatile emotions of his characters as real, and that – if it is true – would be a pity. For he is the master of impudence and tart whimsy, of plain words that leap out of the dialogue like shafts of laughter. At least, they do so on the lips of his three chief actors. As Leo, he is the sharpest corner of his own triangle. As Otto and Gilda, Alfred Lunt and Lynn Fontanne complete this design for frivolous living. They are an incomparable trio of high comedians. And they give *Design for Living* the sententious acting that transmutes artificial comedy into delight.

"What with friends, acquaintances and servants, there are more than three characters in this triangle. Mr Coward needs a few dull persons to victimise. But what he really enjoys is the bizarre nonsense of his three characters. One is a playwright. One is an artist. The third is a woman who is also an artist. Otto and Leo, who are close friends of very long standing, both love her very much, and she loves them. To save herself from the complications of this singular situation, she escapes from both and marries a sober art merchant who takes her to New York. But after a voyage around the world on a freighter the two wild oats turn up like Tweedledum and Tweedledee at her penthouse apartment. Their impudent gaiety disarms her. After a storm session with her husband, who knows the code of a gentleman, she returns to the exuberant disorder of her kind.

"Unfortunately for the uses of artificial comedy, establishing this triangular situation involves considerable sobriety. All through the first act Mr Coward writes as earnestly as a psychologist. Through a long stretch of the third act he surrenders to the patter of ordinary folk and, incidentally, to ordinary actors who can make little of the wrangling impertinence of their lines. When *Design for Living* sounds serious, you wish impatiently that Mr Coward would cut the cackle and come to the main business, which is his brand of satire comedy. He touches that off with remarkable dexterity: Otto and Leo drinking themselves into silly merriment after Gilda has left them. Otto and Leo striding pompously around Gilda's penthouse in the last act. The fluff of worldly success and the vaudeville of telephone conversations suit Mr Coward's skimming pen exactly. When he is in an impish mood, which is most of the time, he is enormously funny.

"But the acting supplies the final brilliance. *Design for Living* is written for actors – in fact, for the three actors who are now most conspicuous in it. They are extraordinarily well balanced. Miss Fontanne, with her slow, languorous deliberation, Mr Lunt with his boyish enthusiasm, Mr Coward with his nervous, biting charity create more variety in the acting than Mr Coward has got into the parts. They enjoy this comedy as much as the audience does. Being under no solemn delusions about it, they make *Design for Living* an actors' lark.

"It is one of the paradoxes of the theatre that the most trifling things are often the most priceless. Skill, art, clairvoyance about the stage, even erudition of a sort, have gone into this gay bit of drollery. It is highly diverting for the evening thereof."

The Times, 26 January 1939, on the London production:

"Mr Coward is always at his best when he is fooling, though it seemed long ago, in the old days of *The Vortex*, that he might become a master of satire. Here is the mixture of satire with fooling that is his special talent and his particular confusion. Sometimes, while telling of a woman who loved two men and was loved by both, he says openly, through them, what he believes to be true; sometimes he mocks at what he believes to be a lie; and the play, in these moments, is a serious play and deeply interesting. Some times, when the two men, abandoned by the girl, drink together in one of the most brilliant drunken scenes in the theatre, or when the same pair turn up in New York like a couple of music-hall comedians, Mr Coward's dialogue dips and swings and glitters as though he were writing a dazzling farce. Both moods, the serious and the flippant, are good, each in its kind, but they are dangerously joined.

"Suddenly Mr Coward, when discussing a theme that is after all related to the theme of Goethe's *Elective Affinities*, catches the eye of his fashionable audience, is embarrassed, and with a little shriek of surrender turns on the tap of flippancy. It is not a question only of mixing conventions; it is almost a question of running away. There is an instance in the final curtain, much debated in the past and explained by Mr Coward in his preface. All the people concerned go off into a howl of laughter and the play ends. They are laughing at themselves. Very well: a dramatist may choose his own period of action; he is not required to solve all problems, to untie all knots; but he must not put up smoke-screens to cover his retreat from thought that he himself has challenged. The theme is not faced; the subject is not worked out.

"For these reasons, the play is disappointing. It remains, in the aggregate of its parts, good entertainment, though with a bitter taste and sometimes with a callow 'daring'. Miss Wynyard and Mr Anton Walbrook are not perfectly cast. She has a lovely grace and a tenderness that goes far to vindicate Mr Coward's serious passages, and she is gloriously gay when Gilda is not bitter; but she has not the dragging sharpness – like the drag of a slate pencil on a slate – which Gilda's harsher flippancies require. Mr Walbrook is amusing with Mr Harrison, but too heavy on Mr Coward's difficult passages of sentiment. Mr Harrison is nearest to what seems to have been the author's intention – dry in tone, light-hearted in manner, not altogether without feeling – and there is a performance of precise and flawless judgement by Mr Alan Webb."

PUBLICATIONS

Design for Living was first published in America by Doubleday, Doran, New York (January 1933) and in England by Heinemann, London (April 1933). It is dedicated to Alexander Woollcott. Also published in *Noël Coward Collected Plays: Three* by Methuen World Classics (London, 1999).

NOTES

Coward says in his introduction to *Play Parade, Volume I*:

"*Design for Living* as a project rather than as a play sat patiently at the back of my mind for 11 years. It had to wait until Lynn Fontanne, Alfred Lunt, and I had arrived, by different roads, at the exact moment in our careers when we felt that we could all three play together with a more or less equal degree of success.

"We had met, discussed, argued and parted again many times, knowing that it was something that we wanted to do very much indeed, and searching wildly through our minds for suitable characters. At one moment we were to be three foreigners: Lynn, Eurasian; Alfred, German; and I, Chinese. At another we were to be three acrobats, tapping out 'Allez Ooops' and flicking handkerchiefs at one another. A further plan was that the entire play should be played in a gigantic bed, dealing with life and love in the Schnitzler manner. This, however, was hilariously discarded, after Alfred had suggested a few stage directions which, if followed faithfully, would undoubtedly have landed all three of us in gaol.

"Finally, when the whole idea seemed to have sunk out of sight for ever, I got a cable from them in the Argentine, where I happened to be at the moment, saying: 'Contract with the Guild up in June – we shall be free – what about it?'

"From that moment onwards my travelling lacked that sense of detachment which up to then had been its principal charm. Patagonia, Chile, Peru and Colombia presented themselves, in turn, less as strange thrilling countries brimming with historical interest than as painted theatrical backgrounds, against which three attractive, witty characters changed their minds and their colours with the rapidity of chameleons, but failed, unlike chameleons, to achieve even the meagre satisfaction of being alive.

"It was not until several months later, when I was on a small Norwegian freight boat travelling from Panama to Los Angeles, that the play suddenly emerged, and, with a superb disregard for the mountains and jungles and plains I had traversed in search of it and without even a salute to the flamboyant Mexican coastline on the starboard horizon, placed its own *mise en scène* firmly in Paris, London and New York.

"Since then, *Design for Living* has been produced, published and reviewed. It has been liked and disliked, and hated and admired, but never, I think, sufficiently loved by any but its three leading actors. This, perhaps, was only to be expected, as its central theme, from the point of view of the average, must appear to be definitely anti-social. People were certainly interested and entertained and occasionally even moved by it, but it seemed, to many of them, 'unpleasant'. This sense of 'unpleasantness' might have been mitigated for them a little if they had realised that the title was ironic rather than dogmatic. I never intended for a moment that the design for living suggested in the play should apply to anyone outside its three principal characters, Gilda, Otto and Leo. These glib, over-articulate and amoral creatures force their lives into fantastic shapes and problems because they cannot help themselves. Impelled chiefly by the impact of their personalities each upon the other, they are like moths in a pool of light, unable to tolerate the lonely outer darkness, and equally unable to share the light without colliding constantly and bruising one another's wings.

"The end of the play is equivocal. The three of them, after various partings and reunions and partings again, after torturing and loving and hating one another, are left together as the curtain falls, laughing. Different minds found different meanings in this laughter. Some considered it to be directed against Ernest, Gilda's husband and the time-honoured friend of all three.

If so, it was certainly cruel, and in the worst possible taste. Some saw in it a lascivious anticipation of a sort of triangular carnal frolic. Others, with less ribald imaginations, regarded it as a meaningless and slightly inept excuse to bring the curtain down. I as the author, however, prefer to think that Gilda and Otto and Leo were laughing at themselves."

Major UK revivals of *Design for Living* since 1939 have included:

21 November 1973 (Phoenix, London) with Vanessa Redgrave, Jeremy Brett and John Stride, directed by Michael Blakemore; 4 August 1983 (Globe, London) with Maria Aitken, Ian Ogilvy and Gary Bond; directed by Alan Strachan.

6 September 1994 at the Donmar Theatre with Clive Owen, Paul Rhys and Rachel Weisz, transferring on 20 February 1995 to the Gielgud Theatre, with Rachel Weisz, Rupert Graves and Marcus d'Amico; directed by Sean Mathias.

Broadcasts have included Granada TV in *A Choice of Coward*, 1964, and BBC Television with Rula Lenska in 1979.

US PRODUCTIONS

Design for Living was revived at the Circle in the Square, New York, in 1984 with Jill Clayburgh, Frank Langella and Raul Julia; directed by George C. Scott.

The New York Post on the Circle in the Square revival: "With a glance of wit, a dazzle of merriment and a finesse of style, Noël Coward's *Design for Living* finally returned to Broadway... As ever, where Coward shows the staying power of greatness is in his ability to invest the most ordinary phrase with, in its own context, a gurgling humour."

The New York Daily News: "The revival is neither ideally cast nor directed. But then, how could it be? For this utterly scandalous, yet strangely sexless comedy was created by the author expressly as a vehicle for himself and the Lunts. And who could ever possibly top, or even come close to that combination?"

The play was first heard on CBS Radio in New York in November 1993 with Gary Cooper.

FILM VERSION

A film version of *Design for Living* was made in America by Paramount in 1933. It was directed by Ernest Lubitsch. Adapted for the screen by Ben Hecht.

CHARACTERS	Paramount, 1933
TOM CHAMBERS	Fredric March
GEORGE CURTIS	Gary Cooper
GILDA	Miriam Hopkins
MAX PLUNKETT	Edward Everett Horton
MR DOUGLAS	Franklin Pangborn
LISPING STENOGRAPHER	Isabel Jewell
MR EGELBAUCER	Harry Dunkinson
MRS EGELBAUCER	Helena Phillips
FAT MAN	James Donlin
FIRST MANAGER	Vernon Steele
SECOND MANAGER	Thomas Braidon
HOUSEKEEPER	Jane Darwell
MR BURTON	Armand Kaliz
PROPRIETRESS OF CAFÉ	Adrienne d'Ambricourt
MAX'S BUTLER	Wyndham Standing
CONDUCTOR	Emile Chautard
TOM'S SECRETARY	Nora Cecil

The film was first shown in London at the Plaza, January 1934.

27
CONVERSATION PIECE
A ROMANTIC COMEDY WITH MUSIC
Written in 1933

FIRST PRESENTED by Charles B. Cochran at His Majesty's Theatre, 16 February 1934 (177 performances).

CHARACTERS	His Majesty's, 1934
SOPHIE OTFORD	Heather Thatcher
MARTHA JAMES	Moya Nugent
MRS DRAGON	Betty Shale
PAUL, DUC DE CHAUCIGNY-VARENNES	Noël Coward
MELANIE	Yvonne Printemps
ROSE (her maid)	Maidie Andrews
THE MARQUIS OF SHEERE	Louis Hayward

REGENCY RAKES

THE EARL OF HARRINGFORD	George Sanders
LORD DOYNING	Pat Worsley
LORD BRACEWORTH	Antony Brian
MR HAILSHAM	Sydney Grammar
THE DUCHESS OF BENEDEN	Winifred Davis
THE DUKE OF BENEDEN	Athole Stewart
LADY JULIA CHARTERIS	Irene Browne
HANNAH (her maid)	Elizabeth Corcoran
A TIGER	Tommy Hayes
MISS GOSLETT	Everley Gregg
MISS MENTION	Molly Lumley
LORD KENYON	Penryn Bannerman
LORD ST MARYS	Kim Peacock
FISHERMEN	Reginald Thurgood, William McGuigan, Evan Jones, Roy Hall
COUNTESS OF HARRINGFORD	Sheila Pattrick
LADY BRACEWORTH	Betty Elburn
MRS HAILSHAM	Winifred Campbell
HON. JULIAN KANE	St John Lauri
MR AMOS	Alex Robertson
BUTLER	Claude Farrow
MR JONES	Leonard Michel
COURTESAN	Jean Barnes
SOLDIERS, GUEST, ETC.	Albert Dudley, Ronald Pope, Geoffrey Brighton, Esmond Wilding
MILLINERS, LADIES OF THE TOWN, VISITORS, ETC.	Maidie Andrews, Jean Beckworth, Dorothy Drover, Grace Gorrod, Valerie Hobson, Vivienne Maurice, Beryl Norman, Enid Settle, June Spencer-Dyke, Marcelle Turner, Winifred Talbot
CHILDREN	John Jaques, Henry Bryce, Ryall Corderey, Lydia Craddock, Constance Bowdler, Betty Parker, Celia White
Director	*Noël Coward*
Designer	*G. E. Calthrop*

❖

The action of the play takes place in Brighton, 1811.

ACT I:	Scene 1: (Prologue): Painted curtains, which depict Regency Brighton.
	Scene 2: Part of the parade. About 11 a.m. on a sunny spring morning.
	Scene 3: The living-room of Melanie's House.
	Scene 4: The same as Scene 2.
	Scene 5: The same as Scene 3. About 3 p.m.
	Scene 6: The painted curtains again.
	Scene 7: The public gardens. Evening.
ACT II:	Scene 1: The painted curtains again.
	Scene 2: Melanie's room (as Act I, Scene 3). Early afternoon.
	Scene 3: Before the curtains again.
	Scene 4: A large room on the ground floor of Melanie's house.
ACT III:	Scene 1: The Steyne. About noon.
	Scene 2: Melanie's room.
	Scene 3: The public gardens. Evening.
	Scene 4: Melanie's room. Night.

MUSICAL NUMBERS (The orchestra under the direction of Reginald Burston.)

ACT I

1. The Parade	
2. "I'll Follow My Secret Heart"	Melanie
3. Quartet: "Regency Rakes"	Mr Hailsham, Lord Doyning, Earl of Harringford, Lord Braceworth
4. Quartet: "Charming, Charming"	Melanie, Rose, Sophie Otford, Martha James
5. Quartet: "Dear Little Soldiers"	Melanie, Rose, Sophie Otford, Martha James
6. Duet: "There's Always Something Fishy About The French"	Sophie Otford and Martha James

ACT II

7. Quartet: "Regency Rakes"	Mr Hailsham, Lord Doyning, Earl of Harringford, Lord Braceworth
8. "English Lesson"	Melanie
9. Reprise: "I'll Follow My Secret Heart"	Melanie

| 10. Quartet: "There Was Once A Little Village By The Sea" | The Fishermen |
| 11. Finale | Melanie and Ensemble |

ACT III

| 12. "Nevermore" | Melanie |
| *Orchestration* | *Charles Prentice* |

On 23 April 1934, Pierre Fresnay took over the part of Paul from Noël Coward. He played until Coward returned to the cast on 2 July. On 12 July, Coward was taken ill with appendicitis, and his part was played by Pierre Fresnay again till the run finished on 21 July.

SYNOPSIS

ACT I, Scene 1 (Prologue): The prologue, spoken in rhyming couplets by Sophie and Martha, who with Mrs Dragon set the scene in Regency Brighton.

Scene 2: This mimed scene represents the parade at Brighton, with two fishermen leaning against the railing, while soldiers, girls, children with their nursemaids, etc., pass across the set. Then Sophie Otford and Martha James appear – two pretty young women of the superior courtesan class – chatting with artificial vivacity. Finally we see Paul, the Duc de Chaucigny-Varennes, "a superbly dressed, neat little man of about forty-five, who appears to exude an aroma of perfection". He raps briskly at Melanie's door.

Scene 3: Paul walks into Melanie's living-room with an air of complete authority, ordering the chocolate which the maid, Rose, has already prepared for him. He questions her about Melanie, showing vexation when he hears that they have been talking French together.

Melanie comes in with her cheek bulged out by a humbug ("oomboog", she calls it). She offers one to Paul, who brusquely declines it, insisting that she shall always talk English. She asks him not to be angry, for it is her birthday. "Again?" says Paul. When Melanie explains she just means she feels happy, he retorts that she is a creature "entirely without balance". "I was an acrobat once," she reminds him, striking a pose. This still further annoys Paul. He insists that she must entirely forget Le Petit Girondin – the café where he found her; and remember only the aristocratic background that he has provided for her – a childhood passed in a tranquil château with parents who later died in the revolution. Everyone in England accepts her as the daughter of his old friend, the Marquis de Tramont. "It doesn't feel like my birthday any more," says the girl pathetically. But a gleam of sunshine cheers her up and she breaks into a song (the theme song of the play) "I'll Follow My Secret Heart", with the refrain:

> No matter what price is paid,
> What stars may fade
> Above,
> I'll follow my secret heart
> Till I find – love.

At the end she goes into her bedroom to dress in preparation for the visit of Edward, the Marquis of Sheere, who is paying court to her.

When the young man is announced he seems somewhat disconcerted to find the Duc (whom he has not met) instead of Melanie. But Paul introduces himself, explaining that Melanie is his ward, and pretends to take for granted that Edward is paying a formal call to ask for her hand. Although his intentions were not strictly matrimonial, Edward has no chance of evading the net. He is terrified when Paul proposes to call on his parents.

However, when Melanie appears, very beautifully dressed, he does what is expected of him and proposes to her, though he lets her see that he is not deceived by their elaborate story. She gives him no definite answer, telling him to go away – but to come back again. They take leave of each other formally, and Melanie, at the window, remains softly singing:

"I'll follow my secret heart…"

Scene 4: Back again on the parade, the Earl of Harringford, Lord Braceworth, Lord Doyning and Mr Hailsham, sing the quartet, "Regency Rakes". The Duke and Duchess of Beneden arrive at Melanie's door.

Scene 5: Sophie and Martha, with the ample, black-clad Mrs Dragon, are paying an afternoon visit to Melanie. They are ushered in by Rose, whom they cross-question about Melanie's relations with the Duc – obviously not believing that he is her "guardian". Martha recognises Rose from her previous situation (which, as Paul elsewhere remarks, "she would do well to forget"), and both girls are disconcerted when, nettled by their questions, Rose reveals what she knows of their affairs.

When Melanie enters, her limited English makes conversation difficult; but the ice is broken when Rose brings in a number of dress and hat boxes. Trying on the garments with exclamations of delight, they all join in a quartet: "Charming! Charming." When they catch sight of soldiers passing the window, they break into another number: "Dear Little Soldiers."

Towards the end of this there is a knock at the front door, and Rose admits the Duke and Duchess of Beneden, Edward's parents. They are elderly, haughty and grim, and their disapproval is heightened by the sight of Melanie's visitors. At a strong hint from the Duchess, the three take their leave, and then she comes direct to the point, requesting Melanie to discontinue her acquaintance with Edward. The girl suggests with dignity that the proper person to discuss this matter is her guardian, and the well-bred Duke agrees. But the Duchess offers Melanie money, raising the sum to £1,000, if she will give up Edward. At her indignant refusal they both walk out, leaving her helpless with laughter.

Paul then enters and she tells him about the scene, complaining that the Duchess has treated her like a prostitute. He remarks acidly that he hopes her behaviour gave the Duchess no cause for the mistake.

Unexpectedly, they hear the Duke returning – alone. Melanie sends Paul into the next room, saying she will call him back, at the right moment, with the words: "The sea is so pretty."

Beneden now makes Melanie a proposal: instead of his son, who will be disinherited if he marries her, why should she not accept his own protection? He can offer her a little house in town, a coach and an allowance of up to £300 a month. She demurs prettily, but takes no umbrage, and the Duke has his arms round her when she calls Paul in by the prearranged signal.

Acting the insulted uncle and guardian, Paul sends Melanie to her room and has the Duke shown out. Then he and Melanie, shaking with laughter, watch from the window as he retreats.

Scene 6: Before the curtains again, Martha and Sophie sing: "There's Always Something Fishy About The French."

Scene 7: It is evening in the public gardens, and the Pavilion windows are lighted. A mixed collection of people – residents, visitors, soldiers, etc. – with their backs to the audience are watching the Prince Regent pass by. Two elderly ladies, Miss Goslett and Miss Mention, who have been standing on a seat to see better, climb down and have a chat. They move away as the Duke of Beneden and his son appear, deep in talk about Melanie. Next, in turn, we see Sophie with her beau, Lord Kenyon and Martha with Lord St Marys, who is angling for an introduction to Melanie. All four pass out of sight as Beneden and Edward reappear and meet Lady Julia Charteris, an old flame of the Duke's. She says she has already met six "ghosts" out of her past that day, and there must surely be seven – her lucky number.

The seventh turns out to be Paul, whom she has not seen for many years. They greet each other with glad surprise, each having thought the other dead. In the midst of their reminiscences, Melanie joins them and is introduced as "Melanie de Tramont" – to Julia's bewilderment, as she knew that the late Marquis de Tramont was unmarried.

They are interrupted by Lord St Marys, who brings a supper invitation from the Prince Regent for Melanie. On her behalf, Paul refuses it, sending back the message that "I will be honoured to present my ward to him myself, on a more formal occasion."

ACT II, Scene 1: Again, as in the prologue, Sophie and Martha appear before the curtains, with a commentary in verse picturing the delights of Brighton under the Regency; the people, as in Act I, Scene 2, pass across the stage and there is a reprise of "Regency Rakes."

Scene 2: Melanie, wearing horn-spectacles, is in her room, laboriously learning English. She sings a bilingual song entitled "English Lesson", at the end of which she is nearly in tears with boredom. Rose announces Lady Julia, who sweeps into the room before Melanie can put her off. She questions the girl about her supposed father and her childhood in the château, telling her frankly that the whole story is idiotic, and that Paul should have rehearsed her better. Her remark that she came "to see what sort of mistress Paul had picked out for himself" puts Melanie in a rage. After a flaming tirade, she threatens to slap her visitor's face "and pull out your dead hair by the roots". "Obviously a guttersnipe," remarks Julia calmly – and this is the moment Paul chooses for his entry.

To Melanie's request to send her away, Paul replies that Lady Julia is an old friend of his and he will not have her spoken to in that tone. Melanie flounces into her bedroom, threatening to go back to France, even if she has to swim there.

After apologising to Julia, Paul explains the situation. Since the revolution he has been living from hand to mouth, in one ill-paid job after another. Now, on the proceeds of two valuable paintings from his old house, he has brought Melanie to England, with the idea that she is to make a rich marriage, on which he will take a commission. A good joke, in very bad taste, comments Julia: if it is money he wants, he had better marry her – she has plenty.

Melanie is then called back and, rather ungraciously, submits to being reconciled with Lady Julia. In a business-like way she enumerates her three suitors. First, the Prince, whose affection may not last long enough to be profitable. Next, the Duke of Beneden, with his offer of a little house, a coach and £300 a month. "Hard work," comments Julia, "but a little more lasting than the other." Thirdly, Lord Sheere, who really loves her but will be impoverished if he marries her. That, opines Lady Julia, might be avoided if Melanie's social position were improved: she herself will launch her into society, giving a party to which the best people shall be invited.

Scene 3: Before the curtains, a quartet of fishermen lament in song the metamorphosis of their quiet village into a fashionable watering-place:

> We're richer than ever before,
> But Brighton is Brighton no more.

Scene 4: A large circular room on the ground floor of Melanie's house has been arranged for the party, with a buffet, etc. Music from behind the closed double doors forms a background to the scene. Standing in the centre, Paul and Lady Julia receive their titled guests, who include the Duke and Duchess of Beneden. In her charming gown, Melanie makes an excellent impression.

But all is ruined by the entrance of Mrs Dragon, with Sophie Otford and Martha James – invited by Melanie. As a result, all the ladies in the party withdraw, making flimsy excuses. Sophie and Martha reproach Melanie for having brought them to meet "the wives of our gentlemen". When only they and the men are left, with Paul and Lady Julia, Melanie begins to sing.

With gentle malice she addresses herself to Beneden, refusing his protection; to Lord St Marys she sings smilingly and with a certain mocking deference, that –

> Handsome though your Prince may be,
> He is far too broad in the beam for me.

To Edward, with very genuine sweetness, she declares:

> Though we may be lovers never,
> We're friends for ever – for evermore.

Lastly she turns to Paul and, singing in French with her whole heart in her voice, tells him that it is he whom she really loves. At the end she swoons, and in the ensuing confusion everyone goes out, leaving her alone with Paul.

In a cold rage he accuses her of making him publicly ridiculous, of having ruined his entire plan and having broken their contract. She, for her part, says he is the cleverest man she has met – and at the same time the stupidest: he has taught her to falsify life, but life is something true – something more important than his peace of mind or his prudent cynicism. Repeating that she loves him, she asserts that, try as he may, he will never escape her. He goes out and leaves her sobbing.

ACT III. Scene 1: It is about noon on the Steyne, and fashionable Brighton is promenading. Miss Goslett and Miss Mention are discussing a recipe; Lady Braceworth and the Duchess of Beneden are joined by Mrs Hailsham and

Lady Harringford. They talk at length about their dogs and briefly about their husbands; and then about Julia's party, deciding that they will never forgive her.

The French Duke, says Lady Harringford, seemed polite but peculiar. They agree that "There's Always Something Fishy About The French", and this line leads them into a quartet, "Mothers And Wives", at the end of which they go out. (This part of the scene, including the quartet, is in the printed text but was omitted from the production. The quartet is not in the score.)

Paul and Julia enter together, talking over the events of the previous night. She tells him that she has been in love with him for years; and he, yielding to her offer of money, love and comradeship, kisses her hand.

Scene 2: Melanie and Edward, with the connivance of Rose, are rehearsing for Paul to discover them embracing. Each time the doorbell rings they rush into each other's arms, twice they are disappointed, and meanwhile Melanie sings a sad little song, "Nevermore", regretting that they, who have so much love to give, cannot gain their freedom of choice upon whom to bestow it.

At last Paul does arrive, to find Edward kissing Melanie. She tells him that they are engaged, and he retaliates by saying he is going to marry Lady Julia – news which she takes with apparent calm. Hearing that he means to leave next day for London, she asks him to bring Lady Julia to a farewell supper with herself and Edward.

Scene 3: A mimed scene in which Paul, walking in the gardens, is tormented by the sight of strolling lovers and haunted by the sound of Melanie's voice. "The whole scene slides almost imperceptibly into a form of ballet." Finally, he breaks away and runs distractedly off the stage.

Scene 4: Melanie's room has been dismantled. The floor is covered with straw and shavings, the windows are open, and moonlight floods the candle-lit room, around which are ranged boxes, trunks and packing-cases.

Edward enters, and is told by Rose that Melanie has gone on the evening boat to Dieppe. Then Lady Julia sweeps in and Edward passes on the news. When she remarks that they had better break it to Paul, Rose says that he also has sailed for France. With dignity, she asks Edward to escort her home, and they leave together.

Then Paul bursts in, white and trembling. Rose gives him a farewell note from Melanie, which he reads with every sign of despair; then she clatters out. In a moment or two her footsteps are heard returning; but this time it is Melanie who, imitating Rose's heavy tread, comes out of the bedroom dressed for travelling, with a paper bag of sweets in her hand. Paul takes no notice as she fastens down the trunks. Then she comes quietly up to him and sinks down beside him, kissing his hand. "*Mon cher amour*," she murmurs, proffering the paper bag, "would you like a 'oomboog'?"

❖

W.A. Darlington in the *Daily Telegraph*, 17 February 1934:

"Last night at His Majesty's was a great occasion. Even before we set out for the theatre we knew that Noël Coward's *Conversation Piece* – a successor to *Bitter Sweet* – was to have a first night in the grand style.

"People had paid higher prices for the reserved seats, or waited longer hours for the unreserved than ever before. The crowds of watchers outside the theatre as the audience went in formed a densely packed mass; and inside the theatre the air was electric with expectation.

"It was a big occasion, then, before ever the curtain rose. It became a great one as soon as Yvonne Printemps appeared.

"Mlle Printemps is no stranger to London audiences. Hitherto, however, she has been seen only in French plays, which necessarily have only a restricted appeal. Never before have she and the great London public met one another; and it was plain to be seen, as the evening went on, that both had great joy of the meeting.

"When the end came, and she took a call alone, the warmth and volume of applause moved her visibly to the verge of tears.

"She is, indeed, an exquisite actress, with a bewitching personality. She sings, too, with the unfettered ease of a bird. It was from the moment when she first sang the romantic theme song, "I'll Follow My Secret Heart" (of which we shall hear more anon from all the gramophones in the world), that she had her audience in thrall last night.

"Mr Coward shares her triumph. Or, rather, since he is author, composer, producer and chief male actor in this brilliant show, he enjoys a separate triumph all to himself.

"The play has in a high degree most of the qualities which we have come to look for in his work.

"It is a tale of Brighton in Regency days, slight in texture and artificial in manner. Yet the texture is so delicately woven, and the artifice handled witch such complete certainty of touch, that its sheer skill makes it moving.

"Mr Coward plays a French Duke, exiled during the revolution and now turned adventurer. Mlle Printemps is his ward, a young singer whom he has picked out of the Paris gutter and is now trying to foist on a sceptical Brighton as his ward, so that she shall make a rich marriage and he pouch the proceeds.

"Of course, the Duke and the singer fall in love and end in one another's arms. Equally, of course, this is the oldest and most sentimental story in the world. But, told with such grace, there is room for it to be told again. If you cannot afford a ticket for this show any other way, sell your wife's jewellery or your children's school books. You will never regret the sacrifice.

"Mr Cochran has staged the piece with his usual lavishness, and Mrs Calthrop has excelled herself as designer. The result, combined with Mr Coward's own sure pictorial sense as producer, is a continual delight to the eye. And the cunning devices by which Mr Coward continually insists, without ever intruding himself, that his play is a piece of deliberate artifice will be an added joy to the more sophisticated play goers.

"Cunning, also, is the way in which he has provided Mlle Printemps with opportunities to be fluent in French as well as captivating in her limited English. Also, this seems the appropriate place in which to congratulate him on the fluency of his own French.

"For the rest of the company, they are really to be praised as a team rather than as individuals, for none of them has a great deal to do. Irene Browne is an exception, and plays with a very firm touch; and others who are outstanding are Louis Hayward and Heather Thatcher."

PUBLICATIONS

Conversation Piece was published by Heinemann (London, 1934). It is dedicated to G. E. Calthrop. The vocal score was published by William Chappell and is dedicated:

"A ma chère Yvonne, pour qui a été composée cette musique, et par qui elle est si délicieusement chantée."

Separate sheet music of the following songs was published by William Chappell:
"There's Always Something Fishy About The French"
"I'll Follow My Secret Heart"
"Nevermore"
"Regency Rakes"
"I'll Follow My Secret Heart" "Nevermore", and "Regency Rakes" are also included in *The Noël Coward Song Book* (Michael Joseph, 1953).

Also published in *Noël Coward Collected Plays: Three* by Methuen World Classics (London, 1999).

NOTES

Coward says in his introduction to *Play Parade, Volume II*:

"*Conversation Piece* was conceived, written, and composed as a vehicle for Yvonne Printemps, and as such I must proudly say it was a success.

She, being a fine actress in addition to having one of the loveliest voices it has ever been my privilege to hear, endowed the play with a special magic and, in spite of the fact that her English began and ended with 'Good Morning', 'Yes', and 'No' she contrived to enchant the public, the critics, the supporting cast, the orchestra and even the stage hands. It is also an undoubted tribute to her that, by the end of the London and New York runs, most of the company spoke French fluently.

"The play itself has, I think, a certain amount of charm in its own right. The lyrics are good and the music excellent. The original production was tremendously enhanced by the exquisite settings and dresses of G. E. Calthrop. Upon re-reading it, I find that the story rambles a bit here and there and that there are also two startling anachronisms of which, at the time of writing it, I was blissfully unaware. It is never explained for instance why, in the last scene, Melanie has completely dismantled a rented house in Brighton, the furniture of which obviously doesn't belong to her! Also, the sentimental emphasis on the gleaming lights of the packet-boat sailing to France is unfortunate considering that in 1811, the year in which the action of the play passes, England and France were at war! However, apart from these minor defects it is a pleasant entertainment, and I hope that one day, if we can ever find an artiste half as good as Yvonne Printemps, it may be revived."

Conversation Piece was revived, in 1957, but only for eight off-Broadway performances, starring Louise Troy, and Arthur Miller's sister Joan Copeland. The musical director was John Kander and the orchestrator, Peter Matz. There has only been one major radio broadcast: 1936 (CBS, New York) with Lily Pons, Adophe Menjou and George Sanders.

In New York, 1956, *Conversation Piece* was recorded as a box set of LPs featuring Noël himself, Lily Pons and Richard Burton.

28
POINT VALAINE
A PLAY IN THREE ACTS
Written in 1934

FIRST PRESENTED by John C. Wilson at the Colonial Theatre, Boston, U.S.A., 25 December 1934. Subsequently at the Ethel Barrymore Theatre, New York, 16 January 1935 (55 performances).

FIRST PRESENTED IN THE UK by the Old Vic Company at the Playhouse, Liverpool, 18 October 1944 (37 performances).

FIRST PRESENTED IN LONDON by Envoy Productions at the Embassy Theatre, Swiss Cottage, 3 September 1947 (37 performances).

CHARACTERS	Boston and Ethel Barrymore, US, 1934–5
MRS TILLETT	Grayce Hampton
MAJOR TILLETT	Fred Leslie
MRS BIRLING	Lilian Tonge
ELISE BIRLING	Phyllis Connard
MORTIMER QUINN	Osgood Perkins
STEFAN	Alfred Lunt
LOLA	Ruth Boyd
MAY	Alberta Perkins
GEORGE FOX	Broderick Crawford
TED BURCHELL	Philip Tonge
LINDA VALAINE	Lynn Fontanne
MRS HALL-FENTON	Gladys Henson
GLADYS (her daughter)	Phyllis Harding
PHYLLIS (her daughter)	Margaret Curtis
SYLVIA (her daughter)	Valerie Cossart
HILDA JAMES	Everley Gregg
MARTIN WELFORD	Louis Hayward
Director	*Noël Coward*
Designer	*G. E. Calthrop*

CHARACTERS	Liverpool, 1944
MRS TILLETT	Marjorie Hellier
MAJOR TILLETT	William Monk
MRS BIRLING	Doris Rogers
ELISE BIRLING	Audrey Fildes
MORTIMER QUINN	Noel Willman
STEFAN	Frederick Valk
LOLA	Eleanor Wayland
MAY	Vera Jennings
GEORGE FOX	Paul Erickson
TED BURCHELL	Olaf Pooley
LINDA VALAINE	Mary Ellis

MRS HALL-FENTON	Phyllis Relph
GLADYS (her daughter)	Felicity Andreae
PHYLLIS (her daughter)	Julien Orde
SYLVIA (her daughter)	June Beswick
HILDA JAMES	June Daunt
MARTIN WELFORD	Julian Dallas
Director	*Peter Glenville*
Designer	*Tanya Moiseiwitsch*

CHARACTERS	**Embassy, 1947**
MRS TILLETT	Marjorie Hellier
MAJOR TILLETT	Charles Cameron
MRS BIRLING	Doris Rogers
ELISE BIRLING	Audrey Fildes
MORTIMER QUINN	Anthony Ireland
STEFAN	Ben-Astar
LOLA	Pauline Henriques
MAY	Loise Toummavoh
GEORGE FOX	Basil Appleby
TED BURCHELL	Neville Mapp
LINDA VALAINE	Mary Ellis
MRS HALL-FENTON	Isobel Ohmead
GLADYS (her daughter)	Pat Smylie
PHYLLIS (her daughter)	Prudence Hyman
SYLVIA (her daughter)	Alexis Milne
HILDA JAMES	Ambrosine Phillpotts
MARTIN WELFORD	Allan Cuthbertson
Director	*Peter Glenville*
Designer	*Tanya Moiseiwitsch*

❖

SCENE: The action of the play takes place on Point Valaine, a small island situated a mile or so south of one of the larger British West Indies.

ACT I: Scene 1: The veranda of the Point Valaine hotel. Morning.
Scene 2: Linda's sitting-room. Afternoon.
Scene 3: The veranda. Late afternoon.

ACT II: Scene 1: Linda's sitting-room. The afternoon, four days later.
Scene 2: The veranda. The evening of the next day.

> (During Act II, Scene 2, the curtain is lowered to denote the
> lapse of a few hours.)

ACT III: Scene 1: Linda's sitting-room. Night.
          Scene 2: The veranda. The next morning.

❖

SYNOPSIS

ACT I, Scene 1: On the veranda of the hotel owned by Linda Valaine on a small island in the West Indies, a group of guests is breakfasting. Two waitresses serve them, helped by the Russian steward, Stefan, a striking looking man with a strong Russian-American accent and a quiet manner that conveys a suggestion of controlled force.

Major and Mrs Tillett who are leaving for England in a few hours' time, chat to Mrs Birling and her daughter, Elise, an anaemic young woman in her middle twenties who is recuperating after a disappointment in love. Looking on with cynical detachment is the polished, middle-aged writer, Mortimer Quinn.

Two young sugar-planters, the American George Fox and the Englishman Ted Burchell, come running up the steps in their bathing trunks. They mention that they have found a jellyfish in the pool and have scooped it out.

It begins to rain, which Mortimer hails dryly as a dispensation of Providence to make him work instead of going fishing. "God is very domineering," he comments. Then Linda Valaine comes in. She is a handsome, red-haired woman, somewhere between thirty-five and forty-five, dressed casually in a cotton frock, with bare legs and sand-shoes. When Mrs Birling complains about the jellyfish, she says it is Stefan's duty to supervise the condition of the net, which is inspected every few days.

The party say goodbye to the Tilletts, who are being taken to their ship in a launch. Stefan brings down their luggage, and Linda tells him to see about the bathing-pool net, gives him the names of new guests who are arriving later in the day, and orders him to bring some up-to-date magazines on his next trip to the mainland.

Scene 2: Mortimer Quinn chats with Linda in her private sitting-room. As an author, he is interested in other people. He comments on the defection of Elise's fiancé, that he "sees his point" and wishes him luck of his escape; his only wonder is how even the tropical moonlight could have made her sufficiently attractive for anyone to propose to her. Linda says rather hotly that she pities Elise, not because she lost a romantic, moonlight lover, but because she lost a house and a maid and a position of her own.

Subtly, Quinn draws out her life-story. She was a missionary's daughter, she tells him; her early recollections are of rowing backwards and forwards between the island and the mainland with "boatloads of little snivelling half-caste children singing hymns, interminable whining hymns to the Lord". To escape it all she married a Frenchman whom she did not love, and went to live in Lyons. After his death in the 1914-18 War, she sent her widowed mother home to England and returned to the island, changing its original name of Shark Point to Point Valaine, and reopening the mission station as an hotel.

When he questions her about Stefan, who has been there for seven years, Linda tries to change the subject, and then suggests that Mortimer had better get his life-story direct from him. Quinn says he has already done so, but it is far too melodramatic to use in a book: stormy voyages in oil tankers, revolutions, escapes from prison – "magazine stuff".

Before he goes, Linda asks him to be pleasant to a girl journalist, Hilda James, who is coming to the island to interview him. After he has gone, she stands for a while listening to the rain. Then Stefan climbs silently on to the veranda, takes her in his arms and presses his lips on hers.

Scene 3: It is about six o'clock on the same day. The rain has stopped and the scene is bathed in sunlight. George and Ted, just back from fishing, are chatting over their drinks. Ted comments to Mortimer Quinn that he dislikes Russians and that Stefan gives him the creeps. Mrs Birling comes in with Elise, who has been bathing. When Linda enters, looking cool and fresh in a semi-evening dress, they complain to her about a splinter in the chute.

The new guests arrive: Mrs Hall-Fenton with her three daughters, Gladys Phyllis and Sylvia ("Shrill virgins", as Quinn later describes them), and the journalist Hilda James. With them is a young airman, Martin Welford, who is on sick leave after a terrible experience of being lost in the jungle. Quinn befriends him, inviting him to share his own table at dinner and preventing the others from cross-questioning him about his adventure. The girls greet Elise, who is an old friend, and go to get ready for a swim.

For a while Martin is left alone, except for Stefan, who scrutinises him covertly as he collects the glasses. Then Linda returns, speaks sympathetically to him, and shows him to his room.

ACT II, Scene 1: Four days later, Linda, in her private sitting-room, is checking over with her maid, Lola, the list of purchases Stefan is to make on the mainland. Martin Welford comes to thank her for her kindness during the bout of fever that attacked him immediately after his arrival. This leads them to talk of his jungle ordeal.

He tells her how, running short of petrol while flying in the Matto Grosso, he pancaked among the trees. He and his mechanic climbed out unhurt, but after five days' wandering the mechanic went mad and hanged himself. Martin struggled on alone, suffering from hunger, thirst and blood-poisoning from infected scratches. At last he collapsed on reaching the river, and a passing Indian took him in his canoe to the nearest mission station. The experience has affected his heart and eyesight, so that he will not be able to fly for a year – and flying has been his one passion since the age of 18.

They hear Stefan in his quarters playing the accordion; and Linda, as usual, reacts with some annoyance when Martin begins to talk about him.

Suddenly the young man, still weak from fever, drops in a faint. Linda drags him to the chaise longue, settles him among the cushions, and pets him while she gives him brandy. When he is sufficiently revived she helps him up to his room.

Meanwhile Stefan comes in, sniffs about the room like an animal, noticing the empty glass of brandy and the rumpled cushions; then he throws himself face downwards on the chaise-longue. Hearing Linda's door bang, he leaps up and disappears over the veranda.

Scene 2: It is about nine o'clock on the following evening, and the rain is still falling. The guests are all gathered on the veranda after dinner, some of them dancing to a gramophone record.

Mrs Hall-Fenton and her daughters are leaving by launch that evening. They sign the visitors' book and promise to come back in ten days' time. When they have gone the two young planters settle down to play cards with Hilda and Elise, while Quinn and Martin have a quiet chat. Over his drink the novelist wishes the young man "*Salud y amor y pesetas*" ("Health, love, and wealth"). Martin remarks bitterly that at the moment he has none of the three.

Breaking away from the card-players, Hilda comes to interview Mortimer Quinn; but he cleverly turns the conversation to make her talk about herself. She tells him all about a play she has written, and remains quite convinced that she has interviewed him.

Linda brings bad news: the launch that should have brought Stefan back from his shopping expedition has broken down and he will have to sleep in the boathouse, as the wind is too strong for him to row across. (Their second boat, the *Maria*, is under repair on the mainland, but they do not expect it to be ready for some time.) After Burchell and Welford have tinkered with the launch for a while, they give it up: Linda signals across the channel to Stefan with a flashlight and receives his reply.

When the others have gone to bed, Martin detains Linda for a chat. In reply to her questions, he tells her that he has been in love once, but the engagement was broken off because his fiancée resented his enthusiasm for flying.

"Were you ever her lover?" asks Linda. Once, he admits – adding that he felt "rather beastly" about it, but the girl did not seem to mind.

Linda gives him a gentle goodnight kiss. When he says that he loves her she tells him it is too late – she is too old, and he too young; but he replies that he is willing to take the risk: "Even if it's only for a little while, why shouldn't we be happy?" He takes her in his arms and kisses her, gently at first, then with increasing passion. The downpour on the roof reaches a crescendo as the lights fade.

When they come up again, a few hours have passed, and the rain has stopped. Mortimer Quinn comes down in his dressing-gown to smoke a cigarette in the moonlight. Suddenly he hears something, picks up the binoculars and scans the sea, then looks sharply at Linda's room. He hesitates awhile, then goes quietly and swiftly upstairs. Gradually, above the noise of insects and frogs, the chug-chug of a motor launch is heard.

ACT III, Scene 1: It is Linda's sitting-room, and the time is about 4 a.m. Stefan, with his accordion slung across his shoulder, comes stealthily through the bead curtains. He stands gazing at Linda's bedroom; then, "savagely and wildly", he begins to play. Linda comes out in her dressing-gown. "Have you gone mad?" she asks.

He continues to play for a while; when she orders him to go away, he spits in her face. "I will stay," he declares. Raising her voice to reach the bedroom, Linda takes the tone of a mistress rebuking a drunken servant. Then, dragging her down on to the chaise-longue and pressing his mouth on hers, he tells her to go back to her baby lover – "with my kisses on your lips and my spittle on your face".

Martin comes out of the bedroom in shirt and trousers, carrying his coat. Like a sleepwalker, he passes through without looking either at Linda or Stefan. The bead curtains jangle into place behind him.

Wearily, Linda goes towards the bedroom, saying she wishes Stefan were dead. He catches at her hand and begs for forgiveness. They have been together for seven years, he says, and they belong to each other. Linda, who knows that Martin will never speak to her again, replies that she has never loved Stefan and will never forgive him. "Go away and die!" are her last words as she locks her door on him.

Stefan climbs over the balustrade and is seen for a moment silhouetted against the sea. Then he jumps, and disappears from sight.

Scene 2: Mortimer Quinn is at breakfast next morning when Ted and George come in from their bathe, exclaiming in surprise that the *Maria* is back at her moorings. They speculate about this and comment that they have heard noises in the night.

As they run upstairs to dress, Martin comes down, suitcases in hand, looking so upset that Quinn makes him sit down at his own table and drink some coffee. The young man wants to leave at once, but Quinn points out that there will be no launch for some hours. He offers to accompany Martin to the mainland and stay there with him overnight, until the next boat leaves. Tactfully, he hints that he realises what has happened, and tells him that he has known for a long while about Linda and Stefan. To Martin's grateful remark that he is very considerate, he rejoins: "When you are as fundamentally selfish as I am, you have room to be considerate." One day, he says, when Martin is older, he will be able to look back upon the incident with detachment and will feel sorry for Linda; then, if he is wise, he will forget her.

By the time Mrs Birling and Elise come down, Martin is sufficiently recovered to greet them normally. The next to come is Hilda, who tells Quinn that she is reconstructing her play in accordance with his advice. Finally, George and Ted sit down to breakfast. They wonder whether Stefan is back.

There comes a sudden shriek from the direction of the landing stage, and May, the servant, rushes in screaming. The others run out to find what has happened, while Quinn and Martin stare at each other. Then Linda comes in. Quinn advises her to stay where she is until he has investigated. She is left alone with Martin, but he will not look up or speak to her.

Soon Quinn returns, saying quietly that she had better go back to her room – Stefan has been drowned. She thanks him and turns away: then, in a harsh, cold voice, she speaks Stefan's epitaph: "I must see about engaging a new head waiter."

Brooks Atkinson in the *New York Times*, 17 January 1935, on the American production:
"If there is any Coward manner discernible among all his talents, Mr Coward has departed from it in *Point Valaine*, which was acted at the Ethel Barrymore Theatre last evening. He has written the drama of a lurid episode of lust in

the semi-tropics, and Lynn Fontanne, Alfred Lunt, and Osgood Perkins appear in it. Although it contains only a trace of the darting banter and neurotic theatricalism that have been the hall marks of the Coward drama, it is unmistakably the work of a master of the stage. For Mr Coward's story, even when it seems aimless during half the play, has a sense of impending horror. And no one knows better than he does how monstrous Mr Lunt can be as a bestial Russian head waiter, and how much sultry deliberation Miss Fontanne can summon to the part of a middle-aged sensualist. *Point Valaine* is no great shakes for theme, and no masterpiece of craftsmanship. But the currents of sensuality that run through it are deep and dark in the best tradition of tropical passion. The news this morning is that Mr Coward knows how to drain ugliness and violence out of the tropical atmosphere.

"In fact, the atmosphere is essential to the tale. Down somewhere in the neighbourhood of Trinidad is the Point Valaine hotel on a secluded island. It is the personal enterprise of Linda Valaine, who keeps a genteel inn for the foot-loose men and the chattering women who loiter, half-bored, half-hopeful, in such places. Among her guests is a celebrated novelist who likes inquiring craftily into private lives and a gallant young aviator who is resting up after a ghastly accident. The head waiter is a primordial creature whose silent efficiency is almost frightening as he pads about the tables.

"As for the story, it is brief and cataclysmic. The romantic young aviator falls in love with the middle-aged hotel proprietor. She surrenders to him in spite of her maternal feeling of reluctance. But all these years her horrible secret has been that the Russian head waiter is her lover. The scene he makes when he discovers her disloyalty is hideous. In a moment of animal anguish, he slashes his wrist and hurls himself into the sea. Although that may not seem in print like anything of uncommon significance, it comes in the theatre as the climax of a vague, mounting fever in the detached life of *Point Valaine* and Mr Coward is ingenious enough to capture the fullness of the evil in his staging of the play.

"Against G. E. Calthrop's heat-laden settings and to the accompaniment of savage tropical showers the acting is brilliant. The chatter of tourists, the secretive routine of the hotel, the sputter of the launches, the indolent gossip of established guests, the night and the day have all been caught up skilfully into the web of the play. As the young aviator, Louis Hayward gives an attractive, touching performance. As the novelist, Mr Perkins is crisp and sardonic and a devil's chorus to the whole drama. Miss Fontanne endows Linda Valaine with the genius she has for perfect speaking and with that restlessness and reserve that throw character up into high significance. Although the artistic stakes are modest, here Miss Fontanne plays with the integrity of a fine actress.

"But the impact of *Point Valaine* depends upon Mr Lunt's acting as the head waiter. In any part Mr Lunt has extraordinary power. This is a macabre part; Stefan of *Point Valaine* is monster and fiend. Mr Lunt has thrown himself into the role with so much energy and garish detail that you can almost feel the play rock when his big scene finally appears. When he looms up in the narrative, *Point Valaine* is barbarous and inhuman and a mettlesome play.

"Mr Coward has written it for a pair of exhilarating actors, and they carry it beyond all reasonable expectations of so tawdry a theme. Although *Point Valaine* is a minor play of humid passion, Mr Lunt acts it with ferocity."

PUBLICATIONS

Point Valaine was first published in America by Doubleday, Doran (New York, January 1935) and in the UK by Heinemann (London, October 1935). It is dedicated to William Somerset Maugham. Also published in *Noël Coward Collected Plays: Six* by Methuen World Classics (London, 1999).

NOTES

Looking back on the play in 1944, when he saw the Liverpool production, Coward says in *Future Indefinite*:

"Mary Ellis and Frederick Valk played very well the parts created in America by Lynn Fontanne and Alfred Lunt, and the production was good; in spite of which, I saw more clearly than ever the fundamental weakness of the play was its basic theme. It was neither big enough for tragedy nor light enough for comedy; the characters were well drawn, but not one of them was either interesting or kind. The young man, the only one with any claim to sympathy from the audience, although played well in both productions, struck me on closer analysis as silly, over-idealistic, and a prig. The play had opened originally in Boston on Christmas night, 1934, with an excellent cast: Osgood Perkins, a subtle and fine actor, and Louis Hayward, whom I had imported from England to play the young man, in addition to Lynn and Alfred. Somehow everything seemed to go wrong from the beginning. Alfred and Lynn and I were irritable with each other, which we had never been before and seldom have since; Gladys Calthrop's sets were too heavy for the quick changes and had to be cut down at the last minute. There was a disastrous rain machine which flooded the whole stage at the dress rehearsal and had to be scrapped. We all pressed on with 'old trouper' determination, but none of us was happy, and none of us quite knew why until some time afterwards, and the revelation burst on us that what was really wrong was the play. The New York critics gleefully encouraged us in this belief after one of those doomed opening nights that occur, I think, more in New York than anywhere else. The first-nighters were soggy and comatose, if not actually hostile. Lynn and Alfred received only a spatter of applause when they came on, and Gladys, Jack Wilson, and I sat at the back of the theatre and watched the play march with unfaltering tread down the drain. It was not surprising that, seeing it again, however well done, should give me a few pangs of rather embittered nostalgia."

In his introduction to the play in *Play Parade, Volume VI* (1962), Coward wrote:

"The fact that it was the least successful of the four plays in this volume was nobody's fault but mine. In fairness to myself however I must say that in conceiving and writing it I was honestly attempting to break, for me, new ground by creating a group of characters and establishing an atmosphere as far removed as possible from anything I had done before. In this, at least, I succeeded. The play and the setting and the characters were different from anything I had done before but this achievement, although valid in its intention, was not quite good enough.

"On re-reading the play more than a quarter of a century later, I can see clearly where I went wrong. It is neither big enough for tragedy nor light enough for comedy. The characters are well drawn but not one of them is either truly interesting or kind. The young man, the only one with any claim to sympathy from the audience, although well played in both the American and English productions, strikes me on closer analysis as being both priggish and over idealistic. The heroine, or perhaps it would be better to describe her as the leading female character, is curiously disagreeable and, what is worse, indefinite. The situation in which she finds herself should arouse, if not sympathy, at least compassion. But this it fails to do. 'Stefan', the sinister Russian waiter who is her secret lover, should also, particularly in the last act, strike a chord of pity, but he too fails, again, I think, because of lack of definition. 'Mortimer Quinn', the novelist, is a stock character; the good old Greek Chorus-commentator-outside-observer type who has been a boon and a blessing to playwrights for centuries. I should have done better with him too.

"On the credit side however there are some effective theatrical scenes and there is a sense of mounting horror in the play which culminates in Act Three, Scene 1: 'Stefan', betrayed, humiliated and inarticulate, throws himself to the sharks."

The only major postwar revival of *Point Valaine* was at the Minerva Theatre in Chichester 30 May 1991, in a production by Tim Luscombe starring Edward Petherbridge, Sara Kestleman and Jack Klaff which, although well reviewed, did not transfer to London.

29
TONIGHT AT 8.30
THREE PROGRAMMES OF ONE-ACT PLAYS
Written in 1935 and 1936

The group consists of ten one-act plays combined in various orders to make three programmes, each of three plays.

THE FIRST PROGRAMME PRESENTED by John C. Wilson as *Tonight at 7.30* at the Opera Rouse, Manchester, 15 October 1935 (*We Were Dancing, The Astonished Heart, Red Peppers*).

THE SECOND PROGRAMME PRESENTED 18 October (*Hands Across the Sea, Fumed Oak, Shadow Play*). (9 weeks' tour: the company remained in Manchester for a second week, followed by Leeds, Glasgow, 2 weeks; Edinburgh, Liverpool, Newcastle and Birmingham.) At some of the towns the matinées of the plays were called *Today at 2.30*. At the Theatre Royal, Birmingham, on 9 December, *Family Album* was given its first production, replacing *We Were Dancing* in the first programme.

THE FIRST PROGRAMME PRESENTED IN LONDON at the Phoenix Theatre, 9 January 1936, as *Tonight at 8.30* (*Family Album, The Astonished Heart* and *Red Peppers*).

THE SECOND PROGRAMME PRESENTED, 13 January (*Hands Across the Sea, Fumed Oak* and *Shadow Play*).

On 29 January (matinée) *We Were Dancing* replaced *Family Album* in the first programme. The programmes remained in this order, alternating until 21 March, when *Star Chamber* was substituted for *Hands Across the Sea* for one performance only. The programmes then returned to their previous arrangement.

On 4 April Alison Leggatt was taken ill after the performance, and on 6 April Gertrude Lawrence was also taken ill after the performance. The theatre was then closed from 7 April until its reopening on 28 April. Joyce Carey then replaced Alison Leggatt for the remainder of the run.

On 5 May *Ways and Means* was added to the repertoire, and on 18 May *Still Life* was given its first production. All the plays (with the exception of *Star Chamber*) were now combined in three groups, alternating until the end of the run on 20 June (the production ran for 157 performances).

All the plays were produced by Noël Coward, with settings and costumes by G. E. Calthrop. Orchestra under the direction of Clifford Greenwood.

The plays are listed in order of production:

(a)   *We Were Dancing*
(b)   *The Astonished Heart*
(c)   *Red Peppers*
(d)   *Hands Across the Sea*
(e)   *Fumed Oak*
(f)   *Shadow Play*
(g)   *Family Album*
(h)   *Star Chamber*
(i)   *Ways and Means*
(j)   *Still Life*

GENERAL NOTES

About the one-act plays produced and published under this title, Coward says in his introduction to *Play Parade, Volume IV*:

"In the year 1935, upheld by my stubborn faith in the 'star system', I wrote the *Tonight at 8.30* plays as acting, singing and dancing vehicles for Gertrude Lawrence and myself. The success we had had with *Private Lives* both in London and New York encouraged me to believe that the public liked to see us playing together, and this belief, happily for us both and the managements concerned, turned out to be fully justified."

The order of the plays – and that in which they were published and noted in the prefaces – is not the order in which they were produced.

When the plays were produced in New York, November 1936, they were given in the following three groups:

First Programme: *We Were Dancing, The Astonished Heart* and *Red Peppers*.
Second Programme: *Hands Across the Sea, Fumed Oak* and *Shadow Play*.
Third Programme: *Ways and Means, Still Life* and *Family Album*.

This was the last occasion on which Gertrude Lawrence and Noël Coward worked together in London. When she died in 1952, Coward wrote the following tribute for *The Times*:

"This is a brief personal tribute to the memory of Gertrude Lawrence, my loving and beloved friend both in the theatre and out of it for 40 years. We first worked together as child actors in the Playhouse Theatre, Liverpool, in 1912; since then, whether we have been acting together or not, we have been integrally part of each other's lives. The last time I saw her was in April. We lunched together at her house in New York, and I promised to write a play for her to play in England next year. Almost the last words she said to me were: 'I want to come home.' I wish so very deeply that she had come home and that I could have seen her just once more playing in a play of mine, for no one I have ever known, however brilliant and however gifted, has contributed quite what she contributed to my work. Her quality was, to me, unique and her magic imperishable. Having acted with her so much and known her so well, there is no trick, mannerism, intonation, or turn of the head that I don't know by heart, and yet, watching her, as I have so often watched her, saying words that have not been written by me in scenes that I have not directed or even seen rehearsed, she has enslaved me as completely as if I were an enthusiastic layman seeing her for the first time.

"An analysis of her talent, however, would require a more detached pen than mine. I could never be really detached about Gertie if I tried to the end of my days. We have grown up in the theatre together, and now she is suddenly dead and I am left with a thousand memories of her, not one of which will ever fade. I have loved her always, as herself and as an artist."

The following note by Noël Coward was printed in the programme at the Phoenix Theatre:

"Ladies and Gentlemen, the idea of presenting three short plays in an evening instead of one long one is far from original. In fact, if one looks back over the years, one finds that the 'triple bill' formula has been used, with varying degrees of success, since the earliest days of the theatre. Latterly, however – that is, during the last quarter of a century – it has fallen from favour. Occasionally still a curtain-raiser appears in the provinces, but wearing a sadly hang-dog expression, because it knows only too well, poor thing, that it would not be there at all were the main attraction of the evening long enough.

"Its spirit is further humiliated by the fact that the leading actors treat it with the utmost disdain, seldom leaving their star dressing-rooms to glance at it, let alone play it. Therefore it has to get along as well as it can in the hands of small-part actors and understudies who, although frequently far more talented and charming than their principals, have neither the name, authority nor experience to triumph over rustling programmes, banging seats and a general atmosphere of bored impatience.

"A short play, having a great advantage over a long one in that it can sustain a mood without technical creaking or overpadding, deserves a better fate, and if by careful writing, acting, and producing I can do a little towards reinstating it in its rightful pride, I shall have achieved one of my more sentimental ambitions.

"From our point of view behind the footlights, the experiment will obviously be interesting. The monotony of repetition will be reduced considerably, and it is to be hoped that the stimulus Miss Lawrence, the company, and I will undoubtedly derive from playing several roles during a week instead of only one will communicate itself to the audience, thereby ensuring that a good time be had by all.

"All of the plays included in the programmes have been written specially. There has been no unworthy scuffling in cupboards and bureau drawers in search of forgotten manuscripts, and no hurried refurbishing of old, discarded ideas.

"The primary object of the scheme is to provide a full and varied evening's entertainment for theatre-goers who, we hope, will try their best to overcome any latent prejudice they may have against short plays and, at least, do us the honour of coming to judge for themselves."

PLAYS AND MUSIC

A special matinée in aid of the Actors' Orphanage was given at the Globe theatre, London, on 5 July 1940. It included *Fumed Oak* and *Hands Across the Sea* (for casts, see under entries for these plays). The programme also included *Swan-song*, by Chekov (John Gielgud and George Howe), and solos by Beatrice Lillie and Ivy St Helier.

On the strength of the success of this matinée, H. M. Tennent Ltd. presented a programme, under the title of *Plays and Music*, for a tour of the E.N.S.A. Garnson Theatres and some provincial dates (July to September 1940). The company included Beatrice Lillie, Ivy St Helier, Martita Hunt, Joyce Carey, John Gielgud and George Howe. Besides the two Coward plays, a scene from Gordon Daviot's play, *Queen of Scots*, and Shaw's *Dark Lady of the Sonnets* were added to the repertoire. Beatrice Lillie, besides her own numbers, played Noël Coward's sketch, 'Weary Of It All' (from *Set to Music*, USA, and *All Clear, London*).

A second edition of *Plays and Music* commenced a provincial tour in October 1940, with Beatrice Lillie and Vic Oliver heading a company which included Joyce Carey, Joan Swinstead, and Alan Webb. The plays performed were *Hands Across the Sea, Fumed Oak* and *Red Peppers*, with solos by Vic Oliver and Beatrice Lillie. The following year Sarah Churchill replaced Beatrice Lillie and *We Were Dancing* was substituted for *Red Peppers*. The plays were produced by Irene Hentschel.

PUBLICATIONS

Star Chamber was not included in the three volumes of *Tonight at 8.30* first published by Heinemann (London, 1936). *Volume I* (*We Were Dancing, The Astonished Heart* and *Red Peppers*) is dedicated to Rebecca West; *Volume II* (*Hands Across the Sea, Fumed Oak* and *Shadow Play*) to Gertrude Lawrence, and *Volume III* (*Ways and Means, Still Life* and *Family Album*) to Seymour Hicks.

Hands Across the Sea, Still Life and *Fumed Oak* are also published in *Noël Coward Collected Plays: Three*; *Ways and Means, The Astonished Heart* and *Red Peppers* in *Noël Coward Collected Plays: Four*; *We Were Dancing, Shadow Play, Family Album* and *Star Chamber* in *Noël Coward Collected Plays: Seven* (Methuen World Classics, London, 1999).

Separate sheet music was published by William Chappell of "Men About Town" and "Has Anybody Seen Our Ship?" (*Red Peppers*). "Play, Orchestra, Play", "You Were There" and "Then" (*Shadow Play*). "We Were Dancing" (*We Were Dancing*).

William Chappell also published a vocal score for *Family Album*. The lyrics were not included in the published play.

"You Were There" (*Shadow Play*) is also included in *The Noël Coward Song Book* (Michael Joseph, 1953).

FILM VERSIONS

A film version of *Red Peppers, Fumed Oak* and *Ways and Means* was made in the UK by Anthony Havelock-Allan Productions, 1952, under the title of *Meet Me Tonight*. It was directed by Anthony Pélissier. It was adapted for the screen by Noël Coward. (For casts, see under each separate play.)

A film version of *We Were Dancing* was made in America by Metro-Goldwyn-Mayer in 1942. (For cast, etc., see under play.)

A film version of *Still Life* was made in the UK by Cineguild, 1945, under the title of *Brief Encounter*. (For cast, etc., see under play.)

A film version of *The Astonished Heart* was made in the UK by Gainsborough Pictures, 1950. (For cast, etc., see under play.)

Three plays were televised in New York – *Red Peppers, Still Life* and *Shadow Play* (see Notes on page 325).

❖

(a) WE WERE DANCING
A COMEDY IN TWO SCENES

FIRST PRESENTED at the Opera House, Manchester, 15 October 1935.

FIRST PRESENTED IN LONDON at the Phoenix Theatre, 29 January 1936.

CHARACTERS	Manchester, 1935 and Phoenix, 1936
IPPAGA	Kenneth Carten
GEORGE DAVIES	Edward Underdown
EVA BLAKE	Moya Nugent
LOUISE CHARTERIS	Gertrude Lawrence
KARL SANDYS	Noël Coward
CLARA BETHEL	Alison Leggatt
HUBERT CHARTERIS	Alan Webb
MAJOR BLAKE	Anthony Pélissier

GUESTS AND MEMBERS OF THE COUNTRY CLUB ETC.

❖

Scene 1: Veranda of the country club at Samolo. Evening.
Scene 2: The same. Early morning.

Song, "We Were Dancing".

❖

SYNOPSIS

Scene 1: A dance is being held in the country club at Samolo. From the veranda a full moon can be seen shining over the sea, and, above the music of the dance band, from time to time there comes a wailing of music from the streets below.

A rather nondescript young man and woman, George Davies and Eva Blake, come out of the dance-room. They have arranged to slip away together in George's car and spend a few hours together on a lonely beach.

As they go off, Louise Charteris and Karl Sandys come in, dancing together "as though they had never been apart". They waltz three times round, finishing with a prolonged kiss. So entranced are they that they do not even notice when Louise's husband, Hubert Charteris and his sister, Clara Bethel, come out and discover them.

Louise, her social sense coming to her rescue, tries to make introductions, but realises that she does not know her partner's name: he introduces himself as Karl Sandys. With admirable self-control, her husband suggests that they had better leave. She refuses, gently but firmly.

The tension is eased by Karl's suggestion that they may as well sit down and have drinks. Hubert is still restrained and polite, checking his sister's angry expostulations when Karl and Louise explain that they really are deeply in love.

Major Blake comes in, looking for his wife, Eva, and Clara tells him that she has left the dance "with the Baileys". He goes back to the bar and the discussion continues. Karl makes Hubert admit that after 13 years of marriage he is no longer in love with his wife, though still very fond of her. His own feeling, he says, was like forked lightning – an earthquake, a tidal wave, a cataclysm.

When Hubert asks for some practical information, Karl explains that his father is Admiral Sandys, that he too has been in the navy, but, after being "axed" in 1924, has gone into the shipping business. He represents the Imperial Malayan China Line and is travelling to visit the various agents of the firm; on the following Wednesday he is due to sail.

Louise is disillusioned when he admits that he has been married, though he is now divorced. Nor does she like the idea of sailing to Australia on the *Euripides*, as some of her friends will be on board. "Do you really mean to go with him?" asks Hubert, and when she assents, says: "What has happened exactly? How do you know so surely, so soon?"

The reply takes the form of a song, "We Were Dancing":

> We were dancing,
> And the music and lights were enhancing
> Our desire.
> When the world caught on fire,
> We were dancing...

Louise then tries to explain the situation in prose, but emotion overcomes her and she faints in Karl's arms. As they try to revive her they hear the

Part II, Scene 4. The Beach of a Popular Seaside Resort

Part II, Scene 5. The Deck of an Atlantic Liner. Edward Marryot (Arthur Macrae) and Edith (Alison Leggat)

Part II, Scene 9. A Railway Station. Joe Marryot (John Mills) and Jane Marryot (Mary Clare), centre

Part II, Scene 11. Trafalgar Square, Armistice Night

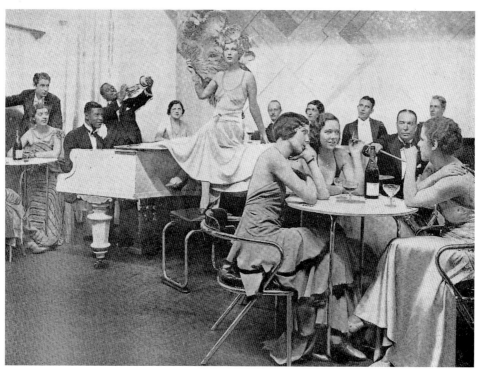

Part III, Scene 2. A Night Club "Twentieth Century Blues" Fanny Bridges (Binnie Barnes) on piano

Part III, Scene 3. Chaos.

"Children Of The Ritz" Joyce Barbour and Chorus

"Mad About The Boy" Opening Scene

"Journey's End" Stanhope (Romney Brent) and Dancers

"Mad Dogs And Englishmen" Lady Mullenty (Ivy St Helier), Sir Ronald Mullenty (Gerald Nodin) and the Reverend Inigo Banks (Romney Brent)

"Children's Hour" Lilli (Steffi Duna), Jane (Doris Hare) and Bobby (John Mills)

"Three White Feathers" She (Doris Hare), He (Edward Underdown)

"Midnight Matinée" Mr Stuart Ingleby (Romney Brent) and Mrs Rowntree (Ivy St Helier), left centre

Act 1. Gilda (Lynn Fontanne), Otto (Alfred Lunt) and Leo (Noël Coward)

Act II, Scene 1. Leo (Noël Coward) and Gilda (Lynn Fontanne)

Act III, Scene 2. Leo (Noël Coward), Otto (Alfred Lunt) and Gilda (Lynn Fontanne)

Haymarket Theatre, 1939

Act I. Gilda (Diana Wynyard), Otto (Anton Walbrook) and Leo (Rex Harrison)

Act II, Scene 1. Gilda (Diana Wynyard) and Leo (Rex Harrison)

Act III, Scene 1. Grace Torrence (Everley Gregg), Leo (Rex Harrison), Otto (Anton Walbrook) and Gilda (Diana Wynyard)

Act III, Scene 2. Ernest Friedman (Alan Webb), Gilda (Diana Wynyard), Leo (Rex Harrison) and Otto (Anton Walbrook)

Act I, Scene 4. Martha James (Moya Nugent), Mrs Dragon (Betty Shale), Sophie Otford (Heather Thatcher), Courtesan (Jean Barnes), Lord Doyning (Anthony Brian), Mr Hailsham (Sydney Grammer), The Earl of Harringford (George Saunders) and Lord Braceworth (Pat Worsley)

Act I, Scene 7. Melanie (Yvonne Printemps), Rose (Maidie Andrews), Paul (Noël Coward), Lady Julia Charteris (Irene Browne), Lord St Marys (Kim Peacock), Martha James (Moya Nugent) and Mrs Dragon (Betty Shale)

Act II. Scene 4. The Marquis of Sheere (Louis Hayward), Melanie (Yvonne Printemps), Paul (Noël Coward) and Lady Julia Charteris (Irene Brown)

Act III, Scene 2. Paul (Noël Coward), the Marquis of Sheere (Louis Hayward) and Melanie (Yvonne Printemps)

Act III, Scene 4. Paul (Noël Coward) and Melanie (Yvonne Printemps)

Act I, Scene 1. Ted Burchell (Philip Tonge), George Fox (Broderick Crawford), Mrs Birling (Lilian Tonge), Major Tillett (Fred Leslie), Mrs Tillett (Grayce Hampton), Linda Valaine (Lynn Fontanne), Elise Birling (Phyllis Connard) and Stefan (Alfred Lunt)

Act I, Scene 1. Stefan (Alfred Lunt) and Linda Valaine (Lynn Fontanne)

Act III, Scene 1. Stefan (Alfred Lunt) and Linda Valaine (Lynn Fontanne)

Act II, Scene 2. Sylvia (June Beswick), Mortimer Quinn (Noel Willman), Linda Valaine (Mary Ellis), Hilda James (June Daunt), George Fox (Paul Erickson), Mrs Birling (Doris Rogers), Elise Birling (Audrey Fildes), Ted Burchell (Olaf Pooley), Mrs Hall-Fenton (Phyllis Relph), Gladys (Felicity Andreae), Phyllis (Julien Orde) and Martin Welford (Julian Dallas)

Act II, Scene 1. Martin Welford (Julian Dallas) and Linda Valaine (Mary Ellis)

Act III, Scene 1. Linda Valaine (Mary Ellis) and Stefan (Frederick Valk)

We Were Dancing

Scene 1. Louise Charteris (Gertrude Lawrence) and Karl Sandys (Noël Coward)

The Astonished Heart

Scene 3. Christian Faber (Noël Coward) and Leonora Vail (Gertrude Lawrence)

Red Peppers

"Has Anybody Seen Our Ship?" George Pepper (Noël Coward) and Lily Pepper (Gertrude Lawrence)

Hands Across the Sea

Lady Maureen Gilpin (Gertrude Lawrence) and the Hon. Clare Wedderburn (Everley Gregg)

Fumed Oak

Scene 2. Doris (Gertrude Lawrence), Mrs Rockett (Alison Leggatt), Henry Gow (Noël Coward) and Elsie (Moya Nugent)

Family Album

"Here's A Toast" Jane (Gertrude Lawrence), Richard Featherways (Edward Underdown), Harriet Winter (Everley Gregg), Charles Winter (Anthony Pélissier), Lavinia Featherways (Alison Leggatt), Emily Valance (Moya Nugent), Edward Valance (Kenneth Carten) and Jasper Featherways (Noël Coward)

TONIGHT AT 8.30, Phoenix Theatre, 1936

Still Life

Scene 5. Dolly Messiter (Everley Gregg), Alec Harvey (Noël Coward)
and Laura Jesson (Gertrude Lawrence)

Shadow Play

Ways and Means

Lena (Moya Nugent), Martha Cunningham
(Everley Gregg), Victoria Gayforth (Gertrude
Lawrence) and Simon Gayforth (Noël Coward)

Scene 3. Toby Cartwright (Noël Coward),
Stevens (Edward Underdown) and Stella
Cartwright (Gertrude Lawrence)

dance band playing the National Anthem. She staggers up and stands to attention with the others.

Scene 2: The four have been talking all night, drinking whisky and eating sandwiches, and they are all exhausted.

Louise and Karl are arguing fitfully about the practical details of their journey. She does not want to go to Australia, and suggests that he should visit his South African agents instead. He points out that she cannot expect him to change the whole course of his career, and eventually she capitulates. Hubert then takes his sister away and says goodbye, asking Karl to try to make Louise happy. Clara's parting shot is to regret that her husband is not alive to horsewhip him.

Left alone, Karl and Louise look at each other critically in the cold light of dawn: the magic has vanished, and even when they dance with each other it does not come back. They no longer even want to be lovers. Louise asks the name of his agents in Sydney. "Give them my love," she says; then she pats his face gently and goes away.

As Karl stands staring out into the morning, Eva Blake and George Davies come furtively back, under the impression that their escapade has passed unnoticed. "Is your name Eva?" asks Karl, remembering the husband's inquiries. When she assents, he remarks sardonically: "I congratulate you."

NOTES

Coward says in his introduction to *Play Parade, Volume IV*:

"*We Were Dancing* is a light episode, little more than a curtain-raiser. It was never intended to be anything more than this and, unlike its author, it fulfilled its promise admirably."

FILM VERSION

A film version of *We Were Dancing* was made in America by Metro-Goldwyn-Mayer, 1942. It was directed by Robert Z. Leonard. Adapted for the screen by Claudine West, Hans Rameau and George Froeschel.

CHARACTERS	METRO-GOLDWYN-MAYER, 1942
VICKI WILOMIRSKA	Norma Shearer
NICKI PRAX	Melvyn Douglas

LINDA WAYNE	Gail Patrick
HUBERT TYLER	Lee Bowman
JUDGE SIDNEY HAWKES	Marjorie Main
MAJOR TYLER-BLANE	Reginald Owen
GRAND DUKE BASIL	Alan Mowbray
MRS VANDERLIP	Florence Bates
MRS TYLER-BLANE	Heather Thatcher
OLIVE RANSOME	Connie Gilchrist
MRS BENTLEY	Nella Walker
MRS CHARTERIS	Florence Shirley
MR BRYCE-CAREW	Russell Hicks
MRS BRYCE-CAREW	Norma Varden

The film bore little resemblance to the original play, as will be seen from the published synopsis. It also had a new musical score by Bronislau Kaper.

SYNOPSIS

When she falls in love at first sight with impecunious but irresistible Nicki Prax, Vicki Wilomirska breaks off her engagement to wealthy Hubert Tyler, even though she knows that Nicki, like herself, is a professional house-guest and they will have to live on their charm. Accordingly, they conceal their marriage and meet in secret until Linda Wayne, a fashionable decorator and one of Nicki's old flames, reveals their secret. They are finally reduced to being guests of the newly-rich. Nicki determines to look for a job and put their marriage on a respectable basis.

A particularly attractive invitation, however, proves his undoing, for when they decide to make this one last house-party stay, Vicki finds Linda pursuing her husband. She broken-heartedly sues for a divorce, and although Nicki defends himself ably and passionately, Hubert, acting as Vicki's lawyer, wins her the divorce. Again Vicki becomes engaged to Hubert, and they plan the decorating of a home Hubert has built for his intended bride.

But Nicki appears on the scene again. With the now-repentant Linda's help, he has arranged to get a job with the firm decorating the new house. At first behaving impersonally, he finally breaks down and confesses that he loves no one but Vicki. Vicki says it is too late. At the betrothal party Nicki comes to say farewell. The musicians strike up a tune. It is a waltz to which they danced when they first eloped; they waltz again, they kiss once more – and they elope!

The film was first shown in London at the Empire, Leicester Square, May 1942.

❖

(b) THE ASTONISHED HEART
A PLAY IN SIX SCENES

FIRST PRESENTED at the Opera House, Manchester, 15 October 1935.

FIRST PRESENTED IN LONDON at the Phoenix Theatre, 9 January 1936.

CHARACTERS	Manchester, 1935 and Phoenix, 1936
BARBARA FABER	Alison Leggatt
SUSAN BIRCH	Everley Gregg
TIM VERNEY	Anthony Pélissier
ERNEST	Edward Underdown
SIR REGINALD FRENCH	Alan Webb
LEONORA VAIL	Gertrude Lawrence
CHRISTIAN FABER	Noël Coward

❖

SCENE: The action of the entire play takes place in the
drawing-room of the Fabers' flat in London.
Scene 1: Late afternoon, November 1935.
Scene 2: Late afternoon, November 1934.
Scene 3: Midnight, January 1935.
Scene 4: Dawn, April 1935.
Scene 5: Evening, November 1935.
Scene 6: Late afternoon, November 1935.

❖

SYNOPSIS

Scene 1: On a November afternoon in the drawing-room of the psychiatrist Christian Faber's flat in London, his wife Barbara, his secretary Susan Birch, and his assistant Tim Verney, are waiting in keen and unhappy suspense for the arrival of Leonora Vail. Ringing for the butler Ernest, Barbara orders cocktails. Susan has just said that she hates Leonora Vail when the surgeon, Sir Reginald French, enters, asking if she has come yet. "There isn't much time, is there?" asks Barbara. "No. I'm afraid not," replies the surgeon, adding that "he" is asking for her in brief moments of consciousness.

Ernest has just brought the cocktails when the door-bell rings. Something suddenly occurs to Barbara: "It's the same – exactly the same as a year ago... the first time she ever came into this room." As Ernest announces Mrs Vail, the lights fade and come up again on –

Scene 2: Barbara, Tim, Susan and Ernest are all in the same positions, but with slight changes of costume. Ernest announces Mrs Vail – an old friend whom Barbara has not seen since her schooldays. They exchange reminiscences over a cocktail. When the others have gone out, Barbara talks about her husband, Chris. Leonora pretends not to know the difference between a psychiatrist, a chiropodist and a chiropractor, but her shrewd hostess realises that she is merely affecting ignorance.

When Chris looks in for a few moments, his manner to Leonora is so vague as to be almost rude. She tells Barbara afterwards that she doesn't like him half as well as Tim, and has given up her original plan of falling madly in love with him and having a lovely "old friends together" scene, "with everyone behaving beautifully all round". Barbara laughs at this, and accepts a dinner invitation for herself and Tim with the casual rider, "and bring your old chiropodist too if he'll come".

After Leonora's departure, Tim comes in, looking for a Bible... Chris wants a quotation for his next lecture on psychopathology. They borrow the cook's Bible and find the passage he wants: "The Lord shall smite thee with madness, and blindness, and astonishment of the heart."

Scene 3: About two months have passed. It is after midnight and Chris and Leonora, in evening dress, are kissing each other by the hearth. Troubled by conscience, Leonora confesses that she has deliberately tried to make him fall in love, to punish him for snubbing her at their first meeting. He takes her scruples lightly, telling her that she is foolish to get on her romantic high horse. Then he in turn admits that he was purposely rude to her at first because "You irritated me, you were so conscious of how beautiful you looked."

They discuss Barbara's probable reactions to their affair. Chris says it would probably upset her a good deal, but she would be even more upset if she thought they were denying themselves on her account: "Barbara's that sort of woman." He adds that he loves his wife "deeply and truly and for ever".

Leonora tries to leave, but gives way to his pleading and slips into his arms again as the lights fade.

Scene 4: It is early morning, three months later. Barbara has been sitting up all night, waiting for her husband to come home. She greets him quite calmly. There will be no scene, she says, but they must have a straight talk about Leonora. She is worried because his work is going to pieces. How can he help twisted, nerve-strained people if he is in the same state himself? The only solution, she thinks, is for him to go away with Leonora for two or three months, leaving Tim to carry on his practice. She asks how long he thinks this affair will last. "I'm submerged now – I can't tell," replies Chris. His wife tells him to relax, to go away and get on with it; then she sends him up to sleep.

Scene 5: Seven months have passed. It is midnight on the night before the first scene of the play. Chris and Leonora are in the midst of a violent quarrel. This time, she says, she is through with him – she is going away for good. She does not love him any more – he has strangled her love himself with his insane jealousies and cruelties, his insistence on probing her mind about her dead loves, and his refusal to leave them in peace. "Long live the dead!" sneers Chris, and she retorts bitterly:

"You are one of them now." They both realise that something irremediable has been said. When she comes to kiss him goodbye, he crushes her in his arms, kisses her violently and throws her from him with such force that she staggers and falls.

As she lies there, he sums up the course of their love as "an act of God, like fire and wind and pestilence... the triumphant, inevitable defeat of mind by matter". He had a life to live, and work to do, and people to love: now he has lost them all – the people who love him are trying to help him, but he is out of reach. "Get up and go!" he ends savagely.

When he is alone he nerves himself with two glasses of whisky, goes to the window and drops out.

Scene 6: This is a continuation of the first scene. Ernest announces: "Mrs Vail." Barbara gives her a quick drink and sends her straight into the inner room. The others wait, talking with great self-control, until she comes back. "Is it all over?" asks Barbara. "Is he – ?"

"Yes," replies Leonora, and adds that Chris did not know her. "He thought I was you. He said, 'Baba, I'm not submerged any more' – and then he said 'Baba' again – and then – then he died."

NOTES

Coward says in his introduction to *Play Parade, Volume IV*:

"*The Astonished Heart* is more ambitious in intent [than *We Were Dancing*], but I thought then and still think that its theme, the decay of a psychiatrist's mind through a personal sexual obsession, was too esoteric to appeal to a large public. It gave us, however, good opportunities for dramatic acting and provided a strong contrast to *We Were Dancing*, which preceded it, and *Red Peppers*, which followed it." (See General Notes, page 283.)

FILM VERSION

A film version of *The Astonished Heart* was made in the UK by Gainsborough Pictures, 1949–50. It was directed by Terence Fisher and Anthony Damborough. Adapted for the screen by Noël Coward, who also wrote the incidental music.

CHARACTERS	**Gainsborough Pictures, 1949–50**
CHRISTIAN FABER	Noël Coward
BARBARA FABER	Celia Johnson
LEONORA VAIL	Margaret Leighton
SUSAN BIRCH	Joyce Carey
TIM VERNEY	Graham Payn
ALICE SMITH	Amy Veness
PHILIP LUCAS	Ralph Michael
ERNEST	Michael Hordern
HELEN	Patricia Glyn
SIR REGINALD	Alan Webb
MISS HARPER	Everley Gregg
SOAMES	John Salew
WAITER	Gerald Anderson
BARMAN	John Warren

Mary Ellis made a short anonymous appearance as a patient of Faber's.

The film was first shown in London at the Odeon, Leicester Square, March 1950. A symphonic suite from the incidental music by Noël Coward was published by William Chappell, 1950.

(c) RED PEPPERS
AN INTERLUDE WITH MUSIC

FIRST PRESENTED at the Opera House, Manchester, 15 October 1935.

FIRST PRESENTED IN LONDON at the Phoenix Theatre, 9 January 1936.

CHARACTERS	**Manchester, 1935 and Phoenix, 1936**
LILY PEPPER	Gertrude Lawrence
GEORGE PEPPER	Noël Coward
ALF	Kenneth Carten
BERT BENTLEY	Anthony Pélissier
MR EDWARDS	Alan Webb
MABEL GRACE	Alison Leggatt

❖

SCENE: The action of the play takes place on the stage and in a dressing-room of the Palace of Varieties in one of the smaller English provincial towns. The time is Saturday night, present day.

MUSICAL NUMBERS

"Has Anybody Seen Our Ship?"
"Men About Town."

Dances arranged by Ralph Reader.

❖

SYNOPSIS

The *Red Peppers* are a husband-and-wife vaudeville team – George and Lily Pepper. The curtain rises in their first number, "Has Anybody Seen Our Ship?", which they perform in a nautical rig-out and curly red wigs. It relates the mishaps of two tars after a spree:

> We've lost our way
> And we've lost our pay,
> And, to make the thing complete,
> We've been and gone and lost the blooming fleet.

Their neat walk-off is spoiled by Lily dropping her telescope and going back to fetch it.

After a blackout they are seen quarrelling briskly as they change in their dressing-room. George accuses Lily of having ruined their number, while she blames the musical director, Bert Bentley, for taking the exit too fast.

During a "straight" number (which, we are told, is a dramatic sketch by an ex-West End actress, Mabel Grace) Bentley drops in and asks them to speed up their exit. Lily becomes aggressive, and her husband, at first inclined to agree with Bentley, stands up for her after the conductor has called them "a cheap little comedy act". A violent row, during which Lily accuses Bentley of drinking, is interrupted by Alf, the call-boy, bringing in the Peppers' supper and warning Bentley that he is due back. Husband and wife settle down to eat and the lights fade out.

When they come up again, the Peppers are making-up for their second number, "Men About Town", and putting on their dress shirts and tails. There is a knock at the door and the house manager, Mr Edwards, enters in a grim mood. He complains about the dropped telescope and George now comes hotly to his wife's defence. Mr Edwards who has obviously been sent by Bentley, says that the accusation of drinking during the show is slander. All three are shouting – the artistes disparaging the theatre and the Manager retorting that their act is a flop – when Mabel Grace comes to complain of the noise. The row has become pandemonium when Alf calls "Three minutes!" Then the visitors are pushed out while Lily and George put on smooth red wigs, powder their make-up and take up their hats and canes.

The curtain falls, and rises again on their "dude" number:

> As we stroll down Picc-Piccadilly
> In the bright morning air
> All the girls turn and stare,
> We're so nonchalant and frightfully debonair.

They end with a tap-dance, during which Bert Bentley vengefully speeds up the music until they cannot keep pace with it. Finally, George slips and falls, whereupon Lily flings her hat at Bentley, screaming: "You great drunken fool!" The curtain falls "amid discord".

NOTES

In his introduction to *Play Parade, Volume IV*, Coward says:

"*Red Peppers* is a vaudeville sketch sandwiched in between two parodies of music-hall songs. We always enjoyed playing it and the public always enjoyed watching us play it, which, of course, was highly satisfactory."

FILM VERSION

Red Peppers was the first of the three plays in *Meet Me Tonight*, made in the UK by Anthony Havelock-Allan Productions, 1952. It was directed by Anthony Pélissier. Adapted for the screen by Noël Coward.

CHARACTERS	**Anthony Havelock-Allan Productions, 1952**
LILY PEPPER	Kay Walsh
GEORGE PEPPER	Ted Ray
ALF	Ian Wilson
BERT BENTLEY	Bill Fraser
MR EDWARDS	Frank Pettingell
MABEL GRACE	Martita Hunt
STAGE MANAGER	Toke Townley
PERFORMING DOG ACT	Frank's Fox Terriers
CHINESE JUGGLERS	The Young China Troupe

The film was first shown in London at the Odeon, Leicester Square, September 1952.

(d) HANDS ACROSS THE SEA
A LIGHT COMEDY IN ONE SCENE

FIRST PRESENTED at the Opera House, Manchester, 18 October 1935.

FIRST PRESENTED IN LONDON at the Phoenix Theatre, 13 January 1936.

REVIVED for a special matinée in aid of the Actors' Orphanage at the Globe Theatre, London, 5 July 1940 (see Plays and Music, page 285).

CHARACTERS	**Manchester, 1935 and Phoenix, 1936**
WALTERS	Moya Nugent
LADY MAUREEN GILFIN (Piggie)	Gertrude Lawrence
COMMANDER PETER GILPIN, R.N. (her husband)	Noël Coward
LIEUT. COMMANDER ALASTAIR CORBETT, R.N.	Edward Underdown
MRS WADHURST	Alison Leggatt

MR WADHURST	Alan Webb
MR BURNHAM	Kenneth Carten
THE HON. CLARE WEDDERBURN	Everley Gregg
MAJOR GOSLING (Bogey)	Anthony Pélissier

CHARACTERS	**Globe, 1940**
WALTERS	Moya Nugent
LADY MAUREEN GILPIN (Piggie)	Beatrice Lillie
COMMANDER PETER GILPIN, R.N. (her husband)	John Gielgud
LIEUT. COMMANDER ALASTAIR CORBETT, R.N.	Hal Burton
MRS WADHURST	Joyce Carey
MR WADHURST	George Howe
MR BURNHAM	George Unwin
THE HON. CLARE WEDDERBURN	Ivy St Helier
MAJOR GOSLING (Bogey)	Felix Irwin

SCENE: The action of the play takes place in the drawing-room of the Gilpins' flat in London.

SYNOPSIS

Lady Maureen Gilpin (known to her friends as Piggie), with her husband, Commander Peter Gilpin, R.N., comes into her London flat to find a telephone message that a Mr and Mrs Rawlingson are in town. In a panic she telephones to various friends to come and help her out with them, explaining meanwhile to her husband that these people have put her up during a Far East tour: "Father and mother and daughter – pretty girl with bad legs." Now she feels bound to return their hospitality.

Lieutenant-Commander Alastair Corbett finds them still agitatedly discussing the situation, and is asked by Peter to take the visitors over the Dockyard and "give them a thrill", as he himself will be going to sea.

The two men go to look at plans of a speedboat, and Piggie goes up to dress. Then a pleasant, middle-aged couple, slightly diffident, are ushered in – Mr and Mrs Wadhurst. The man is doubtful whether they are expected, but his wife assures him that she has telephoned to Lady Maureen a few days previously: "She was perfectly charming and said that we were to come without fail and that it would be divine."

The parlourmaid, Walters, shows in Mr Burnham – a nondescript young man carrying a long cardboard roll – and the three sit talking rather awkwardly. Mrs Wadhurst explains that Lady Maureen has stayed with them on their rubber plantation in Malaya. They are wondering whether to answer the ringing telephone when two other visitors enter – Clare Wedderburn and "Bogey" Gosling, a Major in the marines – who are evidently quite at home. Clare takes the call while Bogey mixes drinks for everyone. A second message comes through for Bogey, and he is still on the line when Piggie rushes in, greeting the Wadhursts with the news that she has arranged for them to be shown over the Dockyard at Portsmouth.

Their conversation takes place simultaneously with the phone call, and during the rest of the scene Piggie's efforts to entertain them are continually interrupted by the telephone. One of the calls is from the real Mrs Rawlingson, and Piggie then grasps that she has mistaken the identity of her visitors.

Her husband and friends, guessing her predicament, try every means of finding out where the Wadhursts live, but all in vain until they are just leaving. Then Mrs Wadhurst says they are going to the theatre: "That's the one thing we do miss dreadfully in Pendarla." The name clarifies Piggie's recollections. She and Peter bid the Wadhursts a charming farewell; then she collapses on the sofa, saying it was the most awful half-hour she has ever spent. Peter remarks that next time she travels, she had better keep a diary.

The party breaks up, until only Clare is left. Catching sight of Mr Burnham, she exclaims in surprise: "I thought you'd left with your mother and father." The unfortunate young man explains that they were not his parents. He has been sent by his firm with designs of a speedboat for Commander Gilpin, but has had no chance to give them to him.

Piggie comes back with the necessary equipment for painting her toenails and begins to do it as Mr Burnham, leaving his designs on the table, creeps out of the room. Still convinced that he is connected with the Wadhursts, Piggie calls a cheerful goodbye after him: "It's been absolutely lovely. You're the sweetest family I've ever met in my life."

NOTES

Coward says in his introduction to *Play Parade, Volume IV*:

"*Hands Across the Sea* is a satire on the confusions of a London society woman suddenly faced with the unexpected arrival of two colonials with whom she once stayed while travelling in the Far East. It is a gay, unpretentious little play, and it was acted by Gertie with incomparable brilliance. I cannot think of it without remembering the infinite variety of her inflexions, her absurd, scatterbrained conversations on the telephone, her frantic desire to be hospitable and charming, and her expression of blank dismay when she suddenly realised that her visitors were not who she thought they were at all. It was a superb performance in the finest traditions of high comedy, already now over and done with for ever, but, as far as I am concerned, never to be forgotten."

In 1936, Sybil Thorndike and her company toured *Hands Across the Sea*, in which she played Lady Maureen Gilpin, and *Fumed Oak*, in which she played Doris Gow, with Lewis Casson as Henry Gow. The third item in the programme was *Village Wooing* by Bernard Shaw. The three plays were produced by Lewis Casson.

(e) FUMED OAK

AN UNPLEASANT COMEDY IN TWO SCENES

FIRST PRESENTED at the Opera House, Manchester, 18 October 1935.

FIRST PRESENTED IN LONDON at the Phoenix Theatre, 13 January 1936.

REVIVED for a special matinée in aid of the Actors' Orphanage at the Globe Theatre, London, 5 July 1940 (see Plays and Music, page 285).

REVIVED by Lance Hamilton and Charles Russell and Peter Daubeny Productions at the Shakespeare Memorial Theatre, Stratford-upon-Avon, 14 November 1949, and subsequently presented at the Ambassadors Theatre, London, 29 November 1949 (as a curtain-raiser to the revival of *Fallen Angels* for part of its run only).

CHARACTERS	Manchester, 1935 and Phoenix, 1936
HENRY GOW	Noël Coward
DORIS (his wife)	Gertrude Lawrence
ELSIE (his daughter)	Moya Nugent
MRS ROCKETT (his mother-in-law)	Alison Leggatt
Director	*Willard Stoker*
Designer	*Anthony Holland*

CHARACTERS	**Globe, 1940**
HENRY GOW	John Gielgud
DORIS (his wife)	Joyce Carey
ELSIE (his daughter)	Moya Nugent
MRS ROCKETT (his mother-in-law)	Ivy St Helier
Director	*Willard Stoker*
Designer	*Anthony Holland*

CHARACTERS	**Stratford and Ambassadors, 1949**
HENRY GOW	Maurice Denham
DORIS (his wife)	Hermione Baddeley
ELSIE (his daughter)	Diana Lincoln
MRS ROCKETT (his mother-in-law)	Hermione Gingold
Director	*Willard Stoker*
Designer	*Anthony Holland*

SCENE: The action of the play passes in the sitting-room of the Gows' house in South London.
Scene 1: Morning.
Scene 2: Evening.

SYNOPSIS

Scene 1: At breakfast on a wet morning in their suburban sitting-room, furnished in fumed oak, are Henry Gow and his wife Doris, their daughter, Elsie – a whining schoolgirl with a chronic cold – and Doris's stout mother, Mrs Rockett. The meal passes in a continual bickering, to which Henry listens in silence. Elsie, forbidden by her mother to put her hair up or cut it, rebuked for sniffling and refused a second piece of toast, is comforted by her grandmother, who gives her twopence to buy a sponge-cake. Mrs Rockett complains that she has been kept awake all night by the next-door baby crying. Reminded by Doris that if she is dissatisfied she can go elsewhere, she points out that she is paying for her accommodation.

Elsie, after a hunt for a piece of music which her grandmother eventually finds in her satchel, is at last got off to school, and Henry, hounded by his wife, gets up, leaving his breakfast unfinished. While he is putting on his outdoor things his mother-in-law remarks that he came in very late the previous night and had probably been drinking. They question him when he comes back for his newspaper, but he refuses to account for his movements, beyond saying that he was dining in town. As he goes out, the child next door begins to wail again. Mrs Rockett opines that it is probably hungry, and Doris says nastily that she had better give it twopence to buy a sponge-cake.

Scene 2: It is 7.30 in the evening of the same day. A cold supper has been laid for Henry on the half-cleared table, because Doris, with Elsie and Mrs Rockett, is going to the pictures. When Henry comes in, however, they sense something unusual in his manner. His mother-in-law accuses him of being drunk, and he admits cheerfully that he has had two whiskies and sodas and intends to have a third. He tells Doris that he is celebrating their "anniversary" – not, he stresses, their wedding, but the night, several weeks earlier, that preceded it, after which she had insisted that it was necessary for him to marry her... though it was over three years later that Elsie was born. During these revelations Doris tries to send the child upstairs, but her husband will not let her. He reproaches her with her bad temper and neglect of his comforts, and throws the cold supper all over the carpet. When Doris tries to leave the room, he locks the door and takes the key.

Mrs Rockett then opens the window and shouts for help, but Henry drags her away, slaps her face and fastens the window. Having quelled them both, he explains calmly that for years past he has been saving money from his wages: he now has £572, out of which he intends to leave Doris £50. With the rest he is going overseas, to see the world and start a new life. Doris, he says, is still young and strong enough to get a job; in a year or two Elsie will be able to work – and his advice to her is to spend her first earnings on having her adenoids out. He says goodbye and goes out jauntily, slamming the door behind him.

NOTES

Coward says in his introduction to *Play Parade, Volume IV*:

"*Fumed Oak* is a comedy based on the good old 'worm will turn' theme. I loved Henry Gow from the moment I started writing him, and I loved playing him more, I think, than anything else in the repertoire. A memorable performance was given in this by Moya Nugent as Elsie, the snivelling schoolgirl."

See also the note on *Hands Across the Sea* for the Thorndike-Casson tour.

The revival at the Ambassadors Theatre in 1949, when it preceded *Fallen Angels*, was not played for the entire run.

FILM VERSION

Fumed Oak was the second of the three plays in *Meet Me Tonight*, made in the UK by Anthony Havelock-Allan Productions, 1952. It was directed by Anthony Pélissier. Adapted for the screen by Noël Coward.

CHARACTERS	**Anthony Havelock-Allan Productions, 1952**
HENRY GOW	Stanley Holloway
DORIS	Betty Ann Davies
ELSIE	Dorothy Gordon
MRS ROCKETT	Mary Merrall

The film was first shown in London at the Odeon, Leicester Square, September 1952.

(f) SHADOW PLAY
A PLAY WITH MUSIC

FIRST PRESENTED at the Opera House, Manchester, 18 October 1935.

FIRST PRESENTED IN LONDON at the Phoenix Theatre, 13 January 1936.

CHARACTERS	**Manchester, 1935 and Phoenix, 1936**
LENA	Moya Nugent
VICTORIA GAYFORTH	Gertrude Lawrence
MARTHA CUNNINGHAM	Everley Gregg
SIMON GAYFORTH	Noël Coward
HODGE (dresser)	Kenneth Carten
A YOUNG MAN	Anthony Pélissier
GEORGE CUNNINGHAM	Alan Webb
SYBIL HESTON	Alison Leggatt
MICHAEL DOYLE	Edward Underdown

SCENE: The action of the play begins and ends in the Gayforths' house in Mayfair.

MUSICAL NUMBERS

"Then"

"Play, Orchestra, Play"

"You Were There"

Choreography   *Ralph Reader*

SYNOPSIS

It is about midnight when Victoria (Vicky) Gayforth comes into her bedroom with her friend, Martha Cunningham. She is in a bad temper and firmly refuses to go with Martha to a party: her husband, she knows, will be there with Sybil Heston, to whom he is paying attentions, and she intends to let them get on with it, while she herself takes three amytal tablets and goes to sleep. Both Martha and Lena, Vicky's maid, are somewhat uneasy at the strength of the dose, but Vicky insists.

She has just swallowed the tablets when her flirt, Michael Doyle, rings up – only to be told curtly to call back the next day, as she is worn out. To Martha she confides that she is upset by the play they have just seen, because "everybody seemed to be having such a good time".

Simon Gayforth comes to tell Martha that George, her husband, is waiting impatiently for her: he also has decided not to go to the party, and the Cunninghams must make excuses for them. He then starts a serious conversation with his wife, asking her to divorce him. "An amicable divorce – everything below board?" asks Vicky, and he assents.

"When did things begin to go wrong?" she wants to know. The sleeping tablets are making her head swim. She is very sad about the breakdown of their marriage, for "it was so lovely in the beginning".

From this point the scene takes on an unreal, dreamlike quality, with musical accompaniment, blackouts, and fade-outs and spotlights picking out the various characters.

Simon and Vicky sing a duet, "Then":

> Then, we knew the best of it,
> Then, our hearts stood the test of it.
> Now, the magic has flown
> We face the unknown
> Apart and alone.

This is followed by another song, "Play, Orchestra, Play" ("We Must Have Music"). After a blackout, Sybil Heston appears in a pool of light, remarking to Simon that they must tell Vicky the truth; they are joined by Michael, who asks them to give her his love. The lights fade on a reprise of "Play, Orchestra, Play".

We then see the first meeting of Vicky and Simon at a country ball. They sing a duet, "You Were There," finishing in each other's arms in a spotlight. Another spot picks up Lena, with sleeping tablets and a glass of water, singing "Then".

The lights come up on the interior of a limousine, where Martha and George Cunningham are discussing the Gayforths' matrimonial discords. Vicky, in a separate spotlight, runs on and accuses them of "spoiling it all".

Another spot shows all four of them meeting for the first time in an imaginary railway compartment on the Gayforths' honeymoon journey to Venice. Then Simon and Vicky climb into the car, which represents the taxi taking them to their hotel. They discuss their wedding and have a brief love-scene. Vicky goes to change her dress, while Simon sings "You Were There".

In the next scene, the honeymoon couple are dining at a little table. They talk of the future and Simon declares that, even if other people get between them, they will always come back to each other in the end, as English people return from abroad "to the white cliffs of Dover".

Then a band starts up, and Sybil Heston and Michael Doyle dance on together in a brilliant spotlight. Michael remarks, "We're a bit early, aren't we? They're still on their honeymoon," and Sybil replies: "The curtain will be lowered... to denote a lapse of four years." Another spotlight picks up Vicky and Simon, and the two couples dance on, sometimes changing partners, faster and faster to a rhythm of voices chanting the names of night-clubs, "The Florida, The Coconut Grove, The Four Hundred, The Blue Train." The noise rises to a crescendo and then stops suddenly with a blackout...

Lena is seen telephoning Martha asking her to come back because Mrs Gayforth is suffering from an overdose of sleeping tablets and her husband is alarmed about her. The next scene shows Simon, Lena and Martha clustered round Vicky, giving her black coffee. Simon tells her, when she asks for explanations, that, under the influence of the drug, she has "gone mad" and has been dancing about the room and raving. Deciding that she is now safe, the others leave her alone with her husband.

When she asks him about the divorce, he declares that he wants nothing of the sort; everything is all right again between them. He lifts her on to the bed, covers her over, and lies down on the sofa at her feet.

NOTES

Coward says in his introduction to *Play Parade, Volume IV*:

"*Shadow Play*, with which we finished the second bill, is a musical fantasy. It is a pleasant theatrical device which gave Gertie and me a chance to sing as romantically as we could, dance in the moonlight and, we hoped, convince the audience that we were very fascinating indeed. It always went extremely well, so I must presume that we succeeded."

(g) FAMILY ALBUM
A VICTORIAN COMEDY WITH MUSIC

FIRST PRESENTED at the Theatre Royal, Birmingham, 9 December 1935.

FIRST PRESENTED IN LONDON at the Phoenix Theatre, 9 January 1936.

CHARACTERS	Phoenix, 1936
JASPER FEATHERWAYS	Noël Coward
JANE (his wife)	Gertrude Lawrence
LAVINIA FEATHERWAYS	Alison Leggatt
RICHARD FEATHERWAYS	Edward Underdown
HARRIET WINTER	Everley Gregg
CHARLES WINTER	Anthony Pélissier
EMILY VALANCE	Moya Nugent
EDWARD VALANCE	Kenneth Carten
BURROWS	Alan Webb

SCENE: The action of the play passes in the drawing-room of the Featherways' house in Kent on an autumn evening in 1860.

MUSICAL NUMBERS

"Here's A Toast"
"Princes And Princesses"
"Let's Play A Tune On The Music Box"
"Hearts And Flowers"

SYNOPSIS

On an autumn evening in the year 1860 the Featherways family are assembled in the drawing-room of their house in Kent. They are all in mourning, having just returned from their father's funeral. The group consists of Jasper Featherways and his wife, Jane; his young brother, Richard; his unmarried sister, Lavinia; and his two married sisters, Harriet and Emily; with their respective husbands, Charles Winter and Edward Valance.

Burrows, the deaf old butler, brings in a tray with glasses and a decanter containing madeira. They agree that his depressed manner, like the heavy rain that has fallen during the funeral, is in keeping with the occasion.

Charles and Richard pour out wine for the ladies. Lavinia only accepts a glass under protest: she is scandalised when Jane proposes to drink a toast, and even more so when she starts talking cheerfully about the money they inherit, and their plans for spending it. Soon all but Lavinia are smiling as they drink. Eventually Jasper sings a short toast to each of them. Their merriment is interrupted by the clock striking ten: it is "Papa's eight-day clock", which no one but himself was allowed to wind, and they discuss who is to do it now.

Jasper rings for Burrows, with the request to bring in a box containing his father's papers. When Lavinia says it seems callous to pry upon poor Papa's secrets, Jane remarks caustically that she saw one of his more open secrets – a certain Mrs Wynant – in the church that morning. "Poor Mrs Wynant!" comments Emily, who thinks it rather hard lines that the lady should have been left out of Mr Featherways' will.

When they open the box, they find it is the wrong one. It is a "dressing-up box" which they used as children to play a game called "Princes and Princesses" . Reminiscently, they sing the little tune and go through the motions of the game, which includes crowning Lavinia with a paper crown. Suddenly she tears it off and sinks down on the sofa in tears, vowing that she will never forgive herself. Her brothers comfort her with another glass of wine, and the others also help themselves. By this time the drink is running short. They are wondering whether to send for more when Burrows discreetly enters with another decanter. They drink a toast to Burrows, "our first friend", whom they all remember from their childhood. Emily by this time is showing signs of intoxication, and Jane confesses to feeling "very curious".

In the chest Emily discovers a little musical-box. They wind it up and sing the well-remembered tunes it begins to play, to one of which Jasper and Jane dance together.

Lavinia starts to cry again. "Poor dear Papa!" says Emily. "To hell with Papa!" is Lavinia's unexpected reply. To her scandalised family she declares that they all hated Papa. "He was cruel to Mama, he was unkind to us, he was profligate and pompous, and, worse still, he was mean."

She reveals that the will they have just read was made ten years previously. A few days before his death he had made another, witnessed by Burrows and herself, which disinherited his family, leaving the bulk of his fortune to various mistresses, and the rest to a fund for the erection of a church containing a memorial to himself in black marble. Immediately after his death, she and Burrows had burnt the will.

Aghast at these revelations, they ring for Burrows and ask him if he did witness a will; but he staunchly maintains that his deafness is increasing, and "I shall never be able to hear that particular question."

They give him a drink. He winds up the musical-box, and they all dance round him as the curtain falls.

NOTES

Coward says in his introduction to *Play Parade, Volume IV*:

"*Family Album*, the last of the series (see General Notes, page 283), is a sly satire on Victorian hypocrisy, adorned with an unobtrusive but agreeable musical score. It was stylised both in its décor and its performance, was a joy to play, and provided the whole talented company with good parts."

(h) STAR CHAMBER
A LIGHT COMEDY IN ONE ACT

FIRST PRESENTED at the Phoenix Theatre, London, 21 March 1936 (1 performance only).

CHARACTERS	Phoenix, 1936
JIMMIE HORLICK	Kenneth Carten
J.M. FARMER	Anthony Pélissier
HESTER MORE	Moya Nugent
JOHNNY BOLTON	Noël Coward
JULIAN BREED	Alan Webb
VIOLET VIBART	Betty Hare

MAURICE SEARLE	Edward Underdown
DAME ROSE MAITLAND	Everley Gregg
ELISE BRODIE	Lumena Edwardes
XENIA JAMES	Gertrude Lawrence
PRESS PHOTOGRAPHER	Charles Peters

SCENE: The action of the play passes on the stage of a West End theatre.

SYNOPSIS

The time is about noon. On the dim and bare stage of a West End theatre the stage manager, Jimmie Horlick, is arranging chairs round a large table in preparation for a meeting of the Garrick Haven Fund.

First to arrive is Mr J. M. Farmer, Secretary of the Fund, who complains of the darkness and makes Jimmie switch on more lights. It is raining outside, and Hester More, a vague young woman in tweeds, arrives with a brown-paper parcel containing a pair of damp shoes, and hands her wet hat over to Jimmie's charge. She is followed by Johnny Bolton, "a star comedian of middle age but perennial youthfulness". Violet Vibart, an elderly actress of considerable reputation, arrives with the leading young actor of London, Julian Breed. They apologise for being late, but it appears that several others, including the President, Xenia James, have still not come.

Johnny fills in the gap with a lengthy anecdote, interrupted by the appearance of Maurice Searle, who has grown his hair to shoulder length for an historical film and feels self-conscious about it. Imperturbably Johnny goes on, though no one is listening, and they are all relieved when Dame Rose Maitland sails majestically on to the stage, followed by Elise Brodie, who, though quite a successful actress, is primarily preoccupied with her house and children. After greeting everyone affectionately, Dame Rose takes charge, telling them where to sit, and declaring that in Xenia's absence she herself will take the chair.

Just as she has declared the meeting open, however, Xenia James at last arrives, pulled in by her great dane, Atherton, to whom much of her conversation is addressed. After kissing the women and chattering inconsequentially to the men, she in turn opens the meeting, proposes a vote of thanks to Mr Farmer, and asks him to speak.

Amid interpolations, he explains that the Garrick Haven Fund was established in 1902 to provide a home for destitute actresses. The inmates originally numbered 11 and the total capital was under £1,700. By 1935, however, the assets had risen to £38,000, largely raised by an annual Fun Fayre.

This sets his listeners discussing last year's fair. Each of them suggests a re-organisation that will give better scope to their own individual side-show. All are talking at once, when Xenia calls them to order and asks Mr Farmer to speak.

He explains that the committee's permission must be obtained for any structural alterations to the house. At this point Atherton misbehaves and is gingerly removed by a nervous Jimmie to the property room. Dame Rose remarks acidly that it was a mistake to bring him to a committee meeting.

Proceeding with the business, Mr Farmer reads a letter from the inmates in which they ask for an extra bathroom and indoor lavatory. He has obtained an estimate for an entire new wing, comprising an entrance hall, recreation-room with platform stage, with bedrooms, bathrooms, lavatories, etc., on the floor above – the whole costing over £3,000. This estimate is passed unanimously. Julian and Johnny make the further suggestions that they will enliven the interior by sending some old playbills and posters.

Xenia goes to see if Atherton is all right, and reports that he is fast asleep. Meanwhile, Mr Farmer painstakingly reads a further estimate, totalling over £2,000, to which no one is listening. Xenia and Julian both have lunch appointments and are anxious to get away. However, they settle down again when a press photographer arrives; and Mr Farmer continues his estimate while they pose a group. As soon as it has been taken, Julian and Maurice dash out, followed by the photographer. Then Xenia makes a little speech appealing for gifts to the fund and promising to lead off with £100. Without formally winding up the meeting, she too rushes off, having quite forgotten her dog. The others in turn disperse – Johnny talking them off the stage with one of his endless anecdotes. Then Jimmie switches off the extra lights and goes off, while the deserted Atherton howls dismally in the property room.

❖

NOTES

The play was tried out at a Saturday matinée on 21 March 1936 and given one performance only.

❖

(i) WAYS AND MEANS
A COMEDY IN THREE SCENES

FIRST PRESENTED at the Phoenix Theatre, London, 5 May 1936.

CHARACTERS	Phoenix, 1936
STELLA CARTWRIGHT	Gertrude Lawrence
TOBY CARTWRIGHT	Noël Coward
GASTON	Kenneth Carten
LORD CHAPWORTH	Alan Webb
OLIVE LLOYD-RANSOME	Joyce Carey
PRINCESS ELENA KRASSILOFF	Moya Nugent
MURDOCH	Anthony Pélissier
NANNIE	Everley Gregg
STEVENS	Edward Underdown

SCENE: The action of the play takes place in a bedroom of the
           Lloyd-Ransomes' House, Villa Zéphyre, on the Côte d'Azur.
           Scene 1: 11.30 a.m. on an April morning.
           Scene 2: 1.30 a.m. the following morning.
           Scene 3: Two hours later.

SYNOPSIS

Scene 1: Stella and Toby Cartwright are breakfasting in bed at the Villa
Zéphyre on the Côte d'Azur, which belongs to their rich friend Olive
Lloyd-Ransome. Over the breakfast tray they discuss their critical financial
position. In an attempt to get money to pay their debts, Toby has lost £50 in
the casino overnight. Between them, they have an overdraft of £1,300 and
owe another £5,000, including about 2,400 francs lost at bridge, which
must be paid before they leave the house. Stella feels that they have over-
stayed their welcome and will soon be asked to go. The only saving feature
in the situation is that "Chaps" (Lord Chapworth) lost 7,000 francs to Stella
at backgammon. They are looking forward to getting this, so it is a blow
when Chaps drops in to say goodbye to them and asks Stella if she minds

waiting for the money, as he was cleaned out at the tables the night before. She says politely that it will be "quite all right".

They are joined by Olive Lloyd-Ransome and Princess Elena Krassiloff, a vague but predatory Russian who during the ensuing conversation (which includes references to a scandal about the chauffeur of a mutual friend) nibbles sugar from the bowl on the tray and sprays herself with the last of Stella's expensive perfume.

Olive tells an involved story about other guests arriving, which the Cartwrights rightly take for an excuse to get rid of themselves. Her butler, Murdoch, comes to say that he has booked their tickets and sleeper through to Venice – arrangements made, they realise, the previous evening before consulting them.

In desperation, the couple ask Stella's old nanny (whom she has brought with her as a maid) to pawn the last of their jewellery in Cannes.

Scene 2: The time is about 1.30 a.m. Stella is at the dressing-table and Toby, in dressing-gown and pyjamas, is lying on the bed. He is frantic because he has lost his last 2,000 francs at the tables, while Pearl Brandt, an elderly American woman who is a fellow-guest at the Villa, won 170,000 francs during the short time that she occupied his seat.

After a brief, pointless quarrel about Flora Macdonald, Toby goes to the bathroom and gives a yell of pain – he has cracked his forehead on a projecting cupboard edge. Stella puts iodine on the bruise and they go to sleep, deciding that their only course is to confess their difficulties to Olive in the morning.

Scene 3: Husband and wife are fast asleep when an intruder steals into the room. Toby wakes and switches on the light, whereupon the man covers him with a revolver and demands their jewellery. Toby says it is in pawn at Cannes. With a pillow he knocks the gun out of the burglar's hand and gets possession of it himself.

Stella unties the scarf which masks him, and they recognise him as Stevens, the chauffeur dismissed for philandering with his employer's wife. He is astounded to see the Cartwrights, whom he knows and likes, and he explains that, as Mr Bainbridge has thrown him out with no money and no reference, he has taken to burglary in desperation.

They agree not to call the police, and he is just going when Stella has a brilliant idea: why should he not burgle Mrs Brandt's room, take her 170,000 francs of winnings, then come back and share the swag with them? The bruise on Toby's forehead will be convincing evidence that he has attacked them, and he can leave them gagged and bound.

After some demur he agrees. Eventually he comes back with the notes and some jewellery. He insists upon their accepting the money, keeping only the jewellery and a few notes for travelling expenses himself. He then most politely ties them up and loosely gags them, making sure that they are quite comfortable; after which he bows and goes out of the window, leaving them convulsed with laughter. Stella loosens her gag enough to remark: "If I'd been May Bainbridge, I'd have married him!"

NOTES

Coward says in his introduction to *Play Parade, Volume IV*:

"The third bill started with *Ways and Means* (see General Note, page 283), a 'twentyish' little farce set in the then fashionable south of France. I never cared for it much, but as an 'opener' it served its purpose."

FILM VERSION

Ways and Means was the third of the three plays in *Meet Me Tonight*, made in the UK by Anthony Havelock-Allan Productions, 1952. It was directed by Anthony Pélissier. Adapted for the screen by Noël Coward.

CHARACTERS	Anthony Havelock-Allan Productions, 1952
STELLA CARTWRIGHT	Valerie Hobson
TOBY CARTWRIGHT	Nigel Patrick
LORD CHAPWORTH	Michael Trubshawe
OLIVE LLOYD-RANSOME	Jessie Royce Landis
PRINCESS ELENA KRASSILOFF	Yvonne Ferneau
MURDOCH	Jack Warner
NANNIE	Mary Jerrold
THE FENCE	Jacques Cey

The film was shown in London at the Odeon, Leicester Square, September 1952.

(j) STILL LIFE
A PLAY IN FIVE SCENES

FIRST PRESENTED at the Phoenix Theatre, London, 18 May 1936.

CHARACTERS	**Phoenix, 1936**
LAURA JESSON	Gertrude Lawrence
MYRTLE BAGOT	Joyce Carey
BERYL WATERS	Moya Nugent
YOUNG MAN	Charles Peters
STANLEY	Kenneth Carten
ALBERT GODBY	Alan Webb
ALEC HARVEY	Noël Coward
BILL	Edward Underdown
JOHNNIE	Anthony Pélissier
MILDRED	Betty Hare
DOLLY MESSITER	Everley Gregg

SCENE: The action of the play takes place in the refreshment-room
of Milford Junction Station.
Scene 1: April.
Scene 2: July.
Scene 3: October.
Scene 4: December.
Scene 5: March.

SYNOPSIS

Scene 1: In the refreshment-room of Milford Junction Station the waitress, Myrtle Bagot, is serving behind the counter, helped by young Beryl Waters. One of the customers is Laura Jesson, an attractive, simply-dressed woman in her thirties. As she sips her tea she is reading a library book. She has been shopping and several parcels are on the chair beside her.

Stanley, a youth with a food-tray, comes to the counter to get fresh supplies and have a chat with Myrtle. So does the ticket-inspector, Albert Godby, who is snubbed when he tries to flirt with her. Then Alec Harvey, a man of about thirty-five carrying a doctor's bag, comes in and orders a cup of tea.

Laura collects her parcels and goes out on to the platform, but almost immediately she comes back – a piece of coal-dust from a passing train has blown into her eye. Myrtle gives her a glass of water to bathe it and they all proffer helpful suggestions, but in vain. Then Alec, explaining that he is a doctor, quietly and efficiently removes the piece of grit. Laura thanks him and goes to catch her train.

Scene 2: Nearly three months have passed and now it is summer. Alec and Laura come into the refreshment room together and order tea. Since their first meeting, we gather, they have seen each other several times, have lunched together and been to the cinema. Laura, who is a married woman with three children, is feeling a trifle guilty. He reassures her: he too is married, with children and responsibilities. He tells her about his favourite line of research in preventive medicine, which is a study of pneumoconiosis. Laura does not understand much about it, but she finds his enthusiasm enjoyable. They agree to meet again on the following Thursday.

Scene 3: It is now October. Albert Godby is in high spirits and tries to kiss Myrtle. They scuffle and upset the cakes, which Stanley is helping them to pick up when Alec and Laura come in to tea.

A quiet, tense discussion ensues. Alec has suggested a meeting that evening in a flat belonging to one of his friends, who will be out. Laura finds the idea "cheap" and "furtive". She feels it would be better for them both if they were to part, for she is becoming obsessed with him to the point where she feels a stranger in her own house. Alec, too, admits that his unsatisfied love for her is coming between him and his work.

Two soldiers come in and try to persuade Myrtle to give them drinks out of hours. She sends Beryl to fetch Albert, who turns the men out.

Meanwhile, Alec's train comes into the station. He makes his decision to go on loving Laura, but without breaking up her home or his own. "Let's enclose this love of ours with real strength, and let that strength be that no one is hurt by it except ourselves." He lets the train go, gives her the address of the flat, and says he will be waiting there for her.

Laura sits smoking until her train is heard; then she makes a move towards the door, but turns back, takes up the paper with the address and goes out quietly.

Scene 4: It is about 9.45 on a December evening and nearly closing-time. Beryl is covering up the food for the night and Stanley is waiting to walk home with her; so she is not pleased when Laura comes in, looking pale and upset, and asks first for a glass of brandy and then for paper and an envelope. However, Beryl serves her and fetches the notepaper, with the reminder that the room closes in five minutes.

Laura sits down and begins to write, then buries her face in her hands. Alec comes in, equally agitated, and, finding her still there, exclaims in relief: "Thank God!" She tells him to go away.

It transpires that Alec's friend Stephen has come back unexpectedly while they were in his flat, and she has had to slip away furtively "like a prostitute". Feeling utterly miserable and degraded, she wants to end the affair. Alec apologises: he loves her and always will, but he too feels that this is the beginning of the end.

They are interrupted by Beryl, who comes to lock up. Slipping her a ten-shilling note, Alec asks her to let them stay a while longer. She agrees, on condition that the lights are turned out so that the room looks as if it were shut. Then she goes out and the conversation continues in semi-darkness by the light of the platform lamp.

Alec makes Laura promise to meet him the following Thursday at a café for a drive into the country. He breaks the news that he has been offered a good job in Johannesburg, and has been deliberating for three weeks whether to accept it. Now he has decided in his own mind, though he will still turn down the offer if Laura asks him. She bursts into tears and they beg each other's forgiveness. Then she leaves hurriedly to catch her train, and Beryl returns to lock up the room.

Scene 5: It is an afternoon in March, and Albert is flirting with Myrtle when Alec and Laura (now dubbed "Romeo and Juliet" by the restaurant staff) come in and order tea. The bookstall clerk, Mildred, comes to fetch Beryl, whose mother is seriously ill, and the two girls go off together. This upsets Albert, who has arranged to take Myrtle to the pictures that evening, for she will now have to stay at work.

In the meantime Alec and Laura have been looking unhappily at each other. This is their last meeting, for he is on the point of leaving to take up his post abroad. He says the memory of her will stay with him all his life. She declares that she wants to die. "If you died, you'd forget me," replies Alec. "I want to be remembered."

They have still a few precious moments together – but suddenly one of Laura's friends, Dolly Messiter, bursts in and catches sight of her. She sits down, is briefly introduced to "Dr Harvey", and swamps them with a flood of chatter about her shopping and her servant troubles.

Alec's train comes in, and he has to say a polite goodbye to Laura in front of her friend. Laura sits quite still, listening for the train to start, while Dolly gossips on. Suddenly she gets up, goes out on the platform and comes back, very white and shaky. Dolly persuades Myrtle to let her have a nip of brandy. Then they hear their train coming and prepare to leave.

❖

NOTES

Coward says in his introduction to *Play Parade, Volume IV*:

"*Still Life*… was the most mature play of the whole series (with the exception of *Hands Across the Sea*, which was equally mature but in a different idiom). Later it was made into an excellent film and retitled *Brief Encounter*. I am fond of both the play and the film with, as usual, a slight bias in favour of the former. It is well written, economical and well-constructed: the characters, I think, are true and I can say now, reading it with detachment after so many years, that I am proud to have written it."

FILM VERSION

A film version of *Still Life* was made in the UK by Cineguild, 1945, under the title of *Brief Encounter*. It was directed by David Lean. The screen adaptation was made by Noël Coward, who was also the producer.

CHARACTERS	**Cineguild, 1945**
LAURA JESSON	Celia Johnson
ALEC HARVEY	Trevor Howard
ALBERT GODBY	Stanley Holloway
MYRTLE BAGOT	Joyce Carey
FRED JESSON	Cyril Raymond
DOLLY MESSITER	Everley Gregg
BERYL WATERS	Margaret Barton
STANLEY	Dennis Harkin
STEPHEN LYNN	Valentine Dyall
MARY NORTON	Marjorie Mars
MRS ROLANDSON	Nuna Davey
WOMAN ORGANIST	Irene Handl
BILL	Edward Hodge
JOHNNIE	Sydney Bromley
POLICEMAN	Wilfred Babbage
WAITRESS	Avis Scott
MARGARET	Henrietta Vincent
BOBBIE	Richard Thomas
CLERGYMAN	George V. Sheldon
DOCTOR	Wally Bosco
BOATMAN	Jack May

The play was considerably expanded, as the synopsis of the film shows.

SYNOPSIS

Brief Encounter is the story of a chance meeting. The brief encounter which alters all our lives is an experience which most of us have had. To Laura Jesson, on her weekly shopping expedition to Milford Junction, the young doctor who takes a piece of coal-dust from her eye in the prosaic L.M.S. refreshment-room is merely another traveller. This brief encounter of two people who travel weekly to Milford Junction, the one to shop and break the monotony of domestic life, the other on his way to duty at the local hospital, is for them of great import.

Laura, contented, married, and fixed in her quiet, domestic round, is disturbed to find that she is looking forward to seeing Dr Alec Harvey again, and when they meet by accident the next Thursday it is to make a definite appointment for the following week. Laura's weekly trip to Milford Junction is no longer to change her library books, visit the cinema and shop; it becomes the focal point of her life. She is essentially conventional. She loves her two children and is very fond of Fred, her husband, and the realisation that Alec means so much to her is an appalling one. Neither she nor Alec are strong enough to cease seeing each other, and eventually Alec – who is also married, but now deeply in love with Laura – persuades her to meet him in the borrowed flat of a friend of his, Stephen Lynn, whom he believes to be away. The unexpected return of the friend prevents anything more than a humiliating flight for Laura and an unpleasant misunderstanding between Alec and Stephen Lynn.

This is a story in which the happenings are like life and not the conventional film script. Laura is hurt and unhappy, and it is with difficulty that Alec persuades her to see him the following week. He tells her that he has had a post offered to him in South Africa, which he will accept in order not to break up both their homes, but that he must see her once more to say goodbye.

When the final meeting takes place in the refreshment-room, where the ticket-collector Albert Godby is enjoying an illicit stolen few minutes with the barmaid, Myrtle Bagot – just as he was when they first met – and against a background of ham sandwiches and buns and the skirmishes of Beryl Waters, Mrs Bagot's assistant, with the chocolate-seller, Stanley, Laura and Alec know that they must part.

As they sit at a table waiting for his last train, their farewell is interrupted by the entry of a garrulous friend of Laura's, Dolly Messiter, a housewife on her way home to Laura's village, and through the barrage of small-town gossip rattled off by her unperceptive friend, Laura and Alec hear his train come in, he says a brief word of parting, and she hears his train pull out of the station – and out of her life.

NOTES

The film was first shown in London at the New Gallery, 26 November 1945.

In 1974 NBC TV made a second version. Directed by Alan Bridge, it starred Sophia Loren and Richard Burton. It received limited UK distribution.

A radio version by Maurice Horspool was produced on 4 May 1955, with Wendy Hiller and James McKechnie.

Brief Encounter formed, with *Fumed Oak*, a short-lived musical called *Mr and Mrs* at the Palace Theatre in the late 1970s, starring John Neville and Honor Blackman. In 1998 Hayley Mills toured a stage version of *Brief Encounter* alone.

CRITICISMS

Family Album, The Astonished Heart, Red Peppers

Ivor Brown in the *Observer*, 12 January 1936:

"Mr Coward describes the reinstatement of the short play on the professional stage as one of his more sentimental ambitions. It is also, on his part, a generous exercise; the man who used to write very slight, long plays (e.g. *Home Chat*) has now composed very full, brief ones, which really means that as actor, author, composer and producer he has to put in three times as much work as before. There has been no scamping; and if anybody regards the short play as short measure and a casual offering, he is mistaken here. When Mr Coward brings his three little pigs to market he is his own exhibitor – diligent, alert, and giving them every chance to be approved. They turn out to be considerable animals.

"The first piece, *Family Album*, is described as a comedy of manners with music (period 1860). It would, I think, be more accurately called a fantasy of mannerism.

"When the curtain rises we see an 1860 bourgeois family being as eighteen-sixtyish as Mr Coward's own whiskers and Mrs Calthrop's decoration can make them. They are all in solemn black, for Papa has been taken from them. Mr Noël Coward and Miss Gertrude Lawrence (Jasper and Jane) preside over remembrances of the dear departed, remembrances slightly warmed by the funeral madeira, and support with wine and wisdom the more tearful Lavvy (Miss Alison Leggatt). What is all this to prove? That mourning may become Noël and Gertrude as well as Eugene and Electra?

In the modes of 1860 it certainly does. The programme has announced music. Is it to be a lament for an eminent Victorian? When we wonder what is to come next, Mr Coward proceeds to cultivate nostalgic tenderness. The family produce an old trunk, old toys, the old music-box. 'Songs that I heard at mother's knee. They still appeal to me' – and to any audience. The toy swords clash again; the music tinkles once more, and the wine passes. Suddenly Lavvy, in whom the grape is working, lays aside her woe and denounces Papa as an old seducer, bully, humbug and general pest. Applause and relief are general. Now the skeleton is out of the cupboard and an uninhibited family can have recourse to wine and waltz.

"Naturally, this curious saraband for a dead parent is uneasy matter. The funeral plumes are nodding just off-stage. The dance moves embarrassingly between sarcasm and sentiment, between a real study of period manners and a pastiche of Victorian oddities. It is sometimes nearly vulgar, sometimes nearly mawkish, and sometimes modernly smart; but, thanks to Mr Coward's uncannily tactful direction, the gear-changes are not harsh. The piece, continuously decorative and brilliantly handled, has its own grace. But let nobody else attempt to perform it. As a member of the League of Audiences, in the interest of long-suffering cousins and aunts, I implore the dramatist to be jealous of his amateur rights. That Mrs Worthington, whose daughter Mr Coward has so tunefully deflected from the stage, will have her eye on those 1860 dresses and her ear on the tinkle of the musical box. Per-lease, Mr Coward, on my knees, Mr Coward, don't let *Family Album* be the rage, at least not Mrs Worthington's.

"Next *The Astonished Heart*. If no Bible be available, send for the cook's and consult Deut. xxviii. 28, where it is announced that, as penalty of disobedience, 'the Lord shall smite thee with madness and blindness and with astonishment of heart'. Dr Christian Faber, psychiatrist, busy, prosperous and comfortably married, falls into a mad infatuation for the inconstant Leonora Vail, and is, in the biblical sense, smitten, blinded and astonished even unto self-destruction. The story is told in six taut, short episodes, and it is much commended to our sympathy by the beautiful performance of Miss Alison Leggatt as the wife. Mr Coward and Miss Lawrence play the desperate lovers in the tight-lipped, back-to-the-audience, self-suppressive, word-swallowing style of emotional acting which is fashionable today. Of this style they offer a first-rate example, but it is not a good style of acting for a play the paramount interest of which lies in violence of erotic passion and in the virtuosity with which this demonic possession is portrayed. I should define *The Astonished Heart* as a piece for 'ham' actors presented by vegetarians of the first lustre.

"*Red Peppers* – an Interlude with Music. In other words, a music-hall performance about music-hall performers. Mr Coward and Miss Lawrence appear as a duo in a dude and nautical act. Fifteen years of married life, and the act is as good as when it belonged to mum and dad! But there are strains. Miss Lawrence, having dropped her telescope in her exit, is 'told off' in the dressing-room, and provides a gorgeous line in back answers. The writing and playing, the singing and dancing of this act are faultless. The conductor of the orchestra is accused of a faulty tempo, and he, too, can snap back. The manager, an almost-a-gentleman type, tries to be as spiky as his own moustaches, and gets some mud in his eye for his pains. It is a pretty brawl and full of exquisite burlesque on the public tricks and private lives of the vaudeville profession. In addition to Miss Leggart, Mr Alan Webb and Mr Anthony Pélissier are excellent supporters throughout. This, the least ambitious feature of the triple bill, is certainly the most successful. But the variety of the programme is a tribute to Mr Coward's interest in experiment. The presentation of it is a real piece of work."

Fumed Oak, Hands Across the Sea, Shadow Play

Ivor Brown in the *Observer*, 19 January 1936:

"Mr Coward's second programme maintains a better level than his first. There may be nothing so overwhelmingly amusing as *Red Peppers*, but *Fumed Oak* is a brisk and bitter entertainment about one of those domestic revolts which are now, as a rule, masculine. When Mr Maugham's 'The Breadwinner' walked away disgusted from the house and family which had enslaved him, he did so in a stockbroker's top-hat. Mr Coward translates the rebellion to Clapham, where the rebellious brain stirs beneath a shopwalker's bowler. He assumes, a little rashly, that a middle-aged salesman who has saved £500 is both free to cut all ties and able to find a new, adventurous career outside of England. Anyhow, Mr Coward's Mr Gow, first chilled by the melancholy and meagre spectacle of his cold supper and then ignited by a couple of unwonted whiskies, ups and does it, tells his wife, his mother-in-law, and his horrible, adenoidal daughter where they get off while he gets out, and generally takes the chair for all bread winners who find themselves with little but crusts and crotchets as the reward of long and faithful labour. Mr Coward as a pale and hairy specimen of suburban revolt, throws his supper, like a gauntlet, to the floor, and behaves more like Petruchio and looks more like an advertisement for liver pills or an iron tonic (before treatment) than one could possibly imagine. He somehow contrives to make this sad and sour story immensely diverting, in which he is considerably assisted by Miss Gertrude Lawrence and Miss Alison Leggatt as dowdy shrew and shrew's Mamma. Miss Moya Nugent, as the dreadful daughter, bravely mutilates her appearance in order to look every inch an adenoid.

"I had long thought that *Hands Across the Sea* was a slogan of Protectionist politicians to which the Free Trader replied, 'And into one another's pockets'. To Mr Coward *Hands Across the Sea* suggests the sequel to one of those reckless invitations issued in return for hospitality overseas. 'Come up and see us.' Of course they will not. But they may. And here they are, Mr and Mrs Wadhurst of Malaya, bravely butting in on Commander Peter and Lady Maureen (Piggie) Gilpin, in the kind of smart house where the telephone never stops, and there is a continuous scream representing a conversation which has never begun and will certainly never end. The pith of this piece is in the production, and Mr Coward has created a wonderful rattle of smart idiocy into which the Anglo-Malayans poke curious, solid and astonished heads. Miss Lawrence as first rattle, and Miss Everley Gregg as second, are nicely contrasted with the brilliant blankness and wonderment of Miss Leggatt and Mr Alan Webb.

"In *Shadow Play*, Mr Coward once more demonstrates, with music, that nobody can put a brisker, fresher look than he does on the surface of a simple and threadbare theme. A jaded and jealous wife takes drugs to mitigate her chagrin, and finds herself dreamily drifting back to the days of love's young actuality. A neat production coupled with one first-rate song, 'You Were There', whose tune is one of the best in the tender line that Mr Coward has ever given us, carries this fantasy with a dancing motion past the banalities on which it might easily stumble. Though the lyrical words are less gracious than the music and the spectacle, Miss Lawrence and Mr Coward make the affair so elegant and easy that, with senses charmed, we need not stop to inquire whether Mr Coward will end up as the pet poet of the English Association. He probably will not; but to be pet entertainer of an enormous public is harder as well as more profitable work. In that office he has once more confirmed himself."

Still Life, Ways and Means

George W. Bishop in the *Sunday Times*, 24 May 1936:
"The cycle of nine plays in *Tonight at 8.30* is now complete, and on Friday night there was an opportunity to see the latest additions Mr Coward has made to his programme. In *Still Life* he is almost at his best. The scene is a railway refreshment-room, and against the commonplace comedy of station sandwiches, a 'refaned' bar attendant, and little odds-and-ends of life there is a poignant tragedy told in five graphic episodes. A man and woman meet and fall in love. They are both married, and realise that they cannot evade their responsibilities. A few hours of happiness are snatched before the

realisation that they must part. The last scene is brilliant, for by a cruel stroke of fate they are not allowed even to say goodbye to each other.

"The play is a tiny masterpiece of economical writing, and is beautifully acted by Mr Coward and Miss Gertrude Lawrence. Miss Joyce Carey's sketch of the bar maid and the quick studies of familiar types by Miss Moya Nugent, Mr Alan Webb and the other members of the cast are first-rate.

"The author is less happy in the characteristic trifle, *Ways and Means*, which is set in a bedroom on the Riviera. Here Mr Coward and Miss Lawrence appear as a silly young couple who have lost all their money at the Casino. They chatter in the hard, glittering manner of the author's earlier plays, and the piece ends in an entirely arbitrary way."

US PRODUCTIONS

PRESENTED by John C. Wilson at the Colonial Theatre, Boston on 26 October 1936 and subsequently at the National Theatre, New York on 24 November 1936 (118 performances). The same nine plays were performed and the cast remained unchanged.

The *New York Times*: "The point of *Tonight at 8.30* is that Mr Coward and Miss Lawrence are in fine fettle. Give them the wisp of an idea and they can trip-clip-clop it into good theatre festivity, making the most of the gaudy world of make-believe."

The same paper a few days later: "No student of drama will ever grind out his doctor's thesis on Mr Coward's contribution to thought on the basis of the current one-act panels. Nor will anyone, save Mr Coward and Miss Lawrence, give them much vibrancy on the stage. For they are personal vehicles."

During the London run Gertie suffered from nervous exhaustion. The strain of playing nine varied roles also took its toll on Noël, who had his second nervous breakdown, causing the New York engagement to be terminated a month early.

PRESENTED by Homer Curran in association with Russell Lewis and Howard Young in 1947, in Baltimore, Boston, Philadelphia, San Francisco and Los Angeles and subsequently at the National Theatre, New York on 20 February 1948 (26 performances). Directed by Noël Coward. The cast included: Gertrude Lawrence, Graham Payn, Norah Howard, Valerie Cossart, Philip Tonge, Sarah Burton, Booth Colman, William Roerick, Rhoderick Walker.

The plays presented were *Ways and Means*, *Family Album*, *Red Peppers*, *Hands Across the Sea*, *Fumed Oak* and *Shadow Play*.

The *New York Times*: "Under Mr Coward's adroit direction, the plays are produced with taste. The cast is a good one. Everything crackles except entertainment. Miss Lawrence still looks as mischievous and sinful as Eve, casts lustre around her everywhere, sings in an enchantingly round and coquettish style, wears costumes magnificently and chops the wit cleanly out of the dialogue. We miss the brisk clicking of Mr Coward's sharp style, the lines rattling out like machine-gun fire. There is not much point in reviving these trifles without Mr Coward in the battery."

Three of the plays were also revived at the Anta Theatre, New York on 3 May 1967 (16 performances): *Ways and Means*, directed by Nina Foch; *Still Life*, directed by Jack Sydow and *Fumed Oak*, directed by G. Wood. Cast: Joan Bassie, John Church, Les Barkdull, Jeanne Hepple, Patricia Guinan, John Straub, Joan Force, Herbert Foster, G. Wood, Denholm Elliot, Priscilla Morrill, Geoff Garland, Geddeth Smith, Joan Force and Sloan Shelton.

Noël was always apprehensive about the 1940s American revival. Gertie and her lawyer, Fanny Holzman approached him in September 1947 with the idea, and he advised against it. A little later, though, when it was suggested that Graham Payn might play his old parts, he felt "it might be a good idea". By October the show was on tour. "Gertie is enchanting at moments but inclined to be piss-elegant."

In his diary for 24 January 1948, San Francisco, Coward says: "Went down to see Graham. He felt weak and so we decided he had better lay off the matinée and only play tonight. Suddenly decided to play the matinée myself: *Shadow Play* and *Hands Across the Sea*. I flew down to the theatre, started rehearsing at 1.20 and was on at 2.30. I was proud of the fact that I didn't dry up once. The performance was not bad. The company and audience were thrilled but it was all rather exhausting."

He did the same thing on two other occasions. It was to be the last time he acted with Gertrude Lawrence.

US television productions have included:

1951: CBS: *Red Peppers* with Rex Harrison and Beatrice Lillie.
1954: NBC: *Red Peppers, Still Life, Shadow Play* with Ginger Rogers, Trevor Howard, Gig Young, and Martyn Green; directed by Otto Preminger.
1960: CBS: *Red Peppers* with Art Carney and Elaine Stritch.
1961: NBC: *Brief Encounter* with Dinah Shore and Ralph Bellamy.

US radio broadcasts have included (in one or more of the plays)

1936: NBC, with Noël Coward and Gertrude Lawrence.
1937: CBS, with Robert Montgomery and Binnie Barnes.

1945:   CBS, with Alfred Drake and Helen Hayes.

1947:   ABC, with Sam Wanamaker and Ingrid Bergman.

       CBS, with Herbert Marshall and Lilli Palmer.

1948:   CBS, with Van Heflin, Greer Garson.

       ABC, with David Niven and Helen Hayes.

1951:   CBS, with Richard Basehart and Olivia de Havilland.

UK PRODUCTIONS

Certain selections from the *Tonight at 8.30* sequence have been revived in the UK as follows:

1968:   Palace Theatre, London: *Mr and Mrs*, a musical by John Taylor based on *Fumed Oak* and *Still Life*, starring John Neville and Honor Blackman and directed by Ross Taylor.

1970:   Hampstead Theatre: *We Were Dancing, Red Peppers, Family Album* with Gary Bond and Millicent Martin, and directed by Gillian Lynne.

1981:   Lyric Theatre: *Shadow Play, Hands Across the Sea, Red Peppers*, with John Standing and Estelle Kohler, directed by Jonathan Lynn.

1996:   Thorndike Theatre, Leatherhead and UK tour: *Brief Encounter* adapted by Andrew Taylor from *Still Life* and the screenplay of the film with Hayley Mills.

UK television productions have included:

1969:   BBC: *Red Peppers* with Bruce Forsyth and Dora Bryan.

1991:   BBC: eight of the plays, with Joan Collins, Siân Phillips, Anthony Newley, Edward Duke, Simon Williams and Jane Asher.

UK radio broadcasts have included:

1955:   BBC: a selection of the plays, with James McKechnie and Wendy Hiller.

1999:   BBC: six plays adapted by Malcolm McKee.

Extracts from three plays from the *Tonight at 8.30* sequence are also included in the revue *Noël and Gertie* (with Simon Cadell, Patricia Hodge, London 1989–91 and Twiggy, US 1998–9).

30
OPERETTE
A MUSICAL PLAY
Written in 1937

FIRST PRESENTED by John C. Wilson at the Opera House, Manchester, 17 February 1938 (season to 12 March).

SUBSEQUENTLY PRESENTED at His Majesty's Theatre, London, 16 March 1938 (133 performances).

CHARACTERS	Manchester and His Majesty's, 1938
MAISIE WELBEY (PANSY BROWN in *The Model Maid*)	Phyllis Monkman
PHILLIP JOHNS (MONSIEUR FELIX in *The Model Maid*)	John Laurie
EDDIE GOSLING (MONSIEUR POM-POM in *The Model Maid*)	Edward Cooper
SEXTET in *The Model Maid*	
GRACE MENTEITH	Pamela Randell
VIOLET TRAVERS	Linda Gray
ROZANNE GRAY	Peggy Wood
LALA MONTAGUE	Lisa d'Esterre
ELEANOR WEST	Hedli Anderson
DOREEN	Jean Barnes
LIESL HAREN (COUNTESS MITZI in *The Model Maid*)	Fritzi Massary
DUGGIE (a call-boy)	Tommy Hayes
DECIMA DRURY (DUCHESS OF TRENTON in *The Model Maid*)	Winifred Davis
EDGAR FAWCETT (DUKE OF TRENTON in *The Model Maid*)	Gerald Nodin
PAUL TREVOR (MARQUIS OF FAIRFIELD in *The Model Maid*)	Max Oldaker
ALBERT (Paul Trevor's dresser)	Duncan Rider
ELSIE JEWELL (MARY DALE in *The Model Maid*)	Muriel Barron
DORA (Elsie Jewell's dresser)	Gladys Henson
TRUDI (Liesl Haren's maid)	Violet Oldak

LILY (a dresser)	Molly Lumley
CHARLES (Liesl Haren's butler)	Charles Peters
NIGEL VAYNHAM	Griffith Jones
THE HON. DAVID MESSITER (his brother)	Peter Vokes
LORD ELDERLEY	Hugh French
LORD CAMP	Kenneth Carten
LORD SICKERT	John Gatrell
LORD BORROWMERE	Ross Landon
THE HON. HUMPHREY GORDON	Denis Carew
JENNER (stage door-keeper of the Jubilee Theatre)	J. Grant Anderson
MABEL (a gallery girl)	Marcelle Turner
DORIS (a gallery girl)	Rosemary Lomax
GEORGE (a waiter)	Leonard Morris
JOHNNIE KNOWLES (stage manager, Jubilee Theatre)	Richard Haydn
BLANCHE WALLACE	Moya Nugent
CHARLES HOBSON	George Butler
THE COUNTESS OF MESSITER	Irene Vanbrugh
GENTLEMEN OF THE SEXTET	Anthony Nicholls, Gordon Brand, Dunstan Hart, Peter Gibson, Donald Gordon, Angus Menzies,
LADIES OF THE CHORUS	Judy Bennett, Edna Brough, Winifred Comatock, Daphne Day, Janet Dunn, June Spencer-Dyke, Phyllis Edmundsen, Jacqueline Le Geyt, Peggy Hale, Doris Ingham, Maria Luth, Dorothy Moyne, Diana Nash, Ida Nicklin, Dorothy O'Shann, Dilys Rees, Jessica Roland, Adele Sliviere, Nina Terry, Iris White
GENTLEMEN OF THE CHORUS	Denis Carew, Raymond Clifford, Peter Evans, John Laurie, Peter Luxton, Hugh Moor, Ronald Pope, Farleigh Price, Richard Richards, Richard Stovold, R. J. Thurgood, Brian Vogel, (Terry Delaney – Manchester only)
Director	*Noël Coward*
Designer	*G. E. Calthrop*

Scenery, The Model Maid	*Edward and Joseph Hawkins*
Musical director, The Model Maid	*Herman Linz*
Orchestral direction	*Frank Collinson (Manchester)*
	Benjamin Frankel (His Majesty's)

SCENE: The action of the play takes place in London in 1906.

ACT I: Prologue: A row of hansom cabs.

Scene 1: The stage of the Jubilee Theatre.
(Act 1, *The Model Maid* – Trouville.)

Scene 2: The green-room. A few minutes later.

Scene 3: The stage of the Jubilee Theatre. A few minutes later.

Scene 4: The drawing-room of Liesl Haren's house in Hill Street. Late the same evening.

Scene 5: A series of six hansom cabs. Later still the same evening.

Scene 6: Before the curtain.

Scene 7: Outside the stage door of the Jubilee Theatre. 11.30 p.m., five weeks later.

Scene 8: A private room at Romano's. A few minutes later.

Scene 9: The green-room. Two weeks later.

Scene 10: The stage of the Jubilee Theatre. The same evening. (Finale, Act III, of *The Model Maid* – the Pré Catalan.)

ACT II: Prologue: A row of hansom cabs.

Scene 1: Rozanne's dressing-room at the Jubilee Theatre. 10 p.m., an evening in April.

Scene 2: The stage of the Jubilee Theatre. A minute later. (Finale, Act II, *The Model Maid* – the Opera Ball.)

Scene 3: The drawing-room of Liesl's house. 4.30 p.m., a few days later.

Scene 4: Before the curtain.

Scene 5: A private room at Romano's.

Scene 6: Rozanne's dressing-room. The same evening.

Scene 7: The stage of the Jubilee Theatre. The same evening. (Finale, Act III, *The Model Maid* – the Pré Catalan.)

(The scenes are given as in the programme, in the printed text they are re-numbered.)

A 'Programme' for *The Model Maid*, the musical comedy within *Operette*, was produced with the programme both in Manchester and London.

MUSICAL NUMBERS

ACT I

1. Prologue	Pamela Randell, Linda Gray, Peggy Wood, Lisa d'Esterre, Hedli Anderson, Jean Barnes, Anthony Nicolls, Gordon Brand, Peter Gibson, Donald Gordon, Dunstan Hart, Angus Menzies
2. Opening Chorus "Trouville"	Chorus
3. "Countess Mitzi"	Fritzi Massary and Chorus
4. "Dearest Love"	Muriel Barron and Max Oldaker
5. "Foolish Virgins"	Pamela Randell, Linda Gray, Peggy Wood, Lisa d'Esterre, Hedli Anderson, Jean Barnes, Anthony Nicholls, Gordon Brand, Peter Gibson, Donald Gordon, Dunstan Hart, Angus Menzies
6. "Dearest Love" (Reprise)	Peggy Wood
7. "The Stately Homes Of England"	Hugh French, Ross Landon, John Gatrell, Kenneth Carten
8. "Where Are The Songs We Sung?"	Peggy Wood
9. "The Island Of Bollamazoo"	Edward Cooper and Chorus
10. "Dearest Love" (Reprise)	Peggy Wood, Max Oldaker, and Chorus

ACT II

1. Prologue	Pamela Randell, Linda Gray, Moya Nugent, Lisa d'Esterre, Hedli Anderson, Jean Barnes, Anthony Nicholls, Gordon Brand, Peter Gibson, Donald Gordon, Dunstan Hart, Angus Menzies
2. "Sing For Joy"	Peggy Wood and Chorus
3. "Operette"	Fritzi Moya, Jean Massary, with Pamela Randell, Linda Gray, Moya Nugent, Lisa d'Esterre, Hedli Anderson, Jean Barnes
4. "The Stately Homes Of England"	Hugh French, Ross Landon, John Gatrell, Kenneth Carten
5. Finale	Entire Company
Orchestration	*Charles Prentice*

A song, "Gipsy Melody", was sung at Manchester by Fritzi Massary and Chorus. This was cut during the try-out, and "The Stately Homes Of England" was sung in the second act only. Also, in consequence of a dispute with Frank Collinson, the musical director, Noël Coward himself conducted several performances.

SYNOPSIS

(The scenes are numbered as in the production – in the printed text they are renumbered, making the prologues to each Act, Scene 1.)

ACT I, Prologue: A chorus of six ladies and six gentlemen, seated in pairs in a row of hansom cabs, sing of the delights of the Edwardian era.

Scene 1: The principal characters are on the stage of the Jubilee Theatre, playing the first act of *The Model Maid*, a musical comedy of 1905. Elsie Jewell is the soprano, Maisie Welbey a light soubrette and dancer, Paul Trevor the tenor, and Eddie Gosling the comedian. A famous Viennese star, Liesl Haren, has been imported to play the lead. Among the singing sextet of show-girls is Rozanne Gray, an actress of 30 who is still waiting for her chance of fame.

The opening scene of the comedy shows the dress-designer, Monsieur Pom-Pom (Eddie Gosling) arriving at Trouville with his six lovely models, to find all the accommodation taken by Countess Mitzi (Liesl Haren), who introduces herself in song.

Scene 2: Next we see the green-room, where various members of the company are waiting to go on the stage. Edgar Fawcett and Decima Drury, the "character woman", are dressed, respectively, as the Duke and Duchess of Trenton. Paul Trevor, as the Marquis of Fairfield, is having his throat sprayed and testing his voice, when Elsie Jewell comes in and works up a quarrel with him about the singing methods of a certain Madame Lavani. (The company recognise this as one of three recurrent topics of dispute between Elsie and Paul.) As they sweep out, Liesl enters from the stage, followed by Eddie and Maisie. She is complaining about the tempo of the conductor, and she scolds her maid Trudi for not having her lemon-juice ready.

The six show-girls then enter, handing their motor-coats and hats to the dresser, Lily. Having just been appointed Elsie's understudy, Rozanne exasperates the others by continually repeating her lines. Duggie, the call-boy, rushes in to say that Elsie is fainting and she is needed on the stage – but this is only his idea of a joke.

Another show-girl, Grace Menteith, shows Liesl an emerald ring sent her in a bouquet by an admirer, "Stubby" Vivian. She intimates that her other suitor, David Messiter, is inclined to jealousy.

The sextet are given their parasols for the next scene; then the lights fade and come up again upon –

Scene 3: The Trouville set of *The Model Maid*, where Paul Trevor and Elsie Jewell (as John, Lord Fairfield, and Mary Dale, hero and heroine of the musical comedy) are singing a love-song, "Dearest Love", which is also the theme-song of the main play.

The comedy continues with the Duke and Duchess of Trenton interrogating Countess Mitzi about the antecedents of Mary Dale, her ward. The latter then sings a reprise of "Countess Mitzi", followed by a double sextet of six men and six girls singing "Foolish Virgins". The lights fade on a dance.

Scene 4: It is about 1 a.m. and Liesl is giving a party at her house in Hill Street, when Nigel (Lord Vaynham) comes to fetch his brother David away. He sermonises the young man, who has promised his father to break with Grace Menteith; and he tells him about the expensive ring which "Stubby" Vivian has bought her. The brothers are arguing hotly when Liesl enters. Sizing up the situation, she sends David back to the supper-room and asks Nigel for explanations. He says his parents are worried because David is spending far too much money upon Grace, who does not really care for him. Liesl (who does not like the girl much) agrees to help him on two conditions; that he stops to have a glass of wine with her; and that he comes to see her again after he has been through his first real love-affair and has recovered from it. He agrees, and she calls in the rest of her guests, who include the sextet girls and an equivalent number of titled young men.

Liesl humorously introduces Nigel as an old friend and they all drink champagne. Among the girls is Rozanne, who hands her script to Nigel, asking him to read her cues. He, having fallen in love with her at first sight, obeys with dexterity; the orchestra strikes up "Dearest Love", with Rozanne singing and Nigel reading the words. At the end they remain gazing at each other while the lights fade.

Scene 5: A series of six vignettes, each in one of the hansom cabs in which the girls and their escorts are returning from Liesl's party: Violet Travers and Lord Sickert. Eleanor West and Lord Elderley; Doreen Manners and Lord Camp. The first two girls, while allowing a little discreet petting, tell the men that relatives are waiting up for them; Doreen, however, makes no such pretence.

Lala Montague patiently endures a big-game yarn from Lord Borrowmere. Grace Menteith is in tears, for David has made a scene about the ring. She tells her escort, Humphrey Gordon, that Liesl must have given her away – and eventually she cheers up sufficiently to invite him in for "a little cocoa".

In the last cab are Nigel and Rozanne. He is furious with his brother for getting drunk and making a scene in public. Rozanne points out that people often behave badly when they are in love; but Nigel maintains that David does not know the meaning of real love, and that good behaviour is important under any stress. The girl warns him that she is very ambitious and, if she is to achieve fame, has no time to waste: she wants to be a star, not a duchess. Nigel declares that his own life is bound up with his regiment; however, he accepts her invitation to come upstairs.

Scene 6: A quartet – Lord Elderley, Lord Borrowmere, Lord Sickert and Lord Camp sing "The Stately Homes Of England" and go out.

Scene 7: At the stage door of the Jubilee Theatre, a few weeks later, a few hangers-on appear out of the darkness, hailing the various members of the company as they leave the theatre. At last Elsie Jewell appears, carrying a bouquet from which she hands flowers to her "fans". Then Nigel arrives with a large bunch of violets – in time to receive a rose from Liesl Haren. At last he sees Rozanne, gives her the violets and takes her off to supper at Romano's.

Scene 8: Nigel and Rozanne – who by this time are lovers – are having supper together in a private room. She tells him of her early days and her first love-affair, and sings a romantic number:

> Where are the songs we sung,
> When love in our hearts was young?

But, though she loves him deeply, she does not want to marry him: it would make trouble with his parents and would ruin her own career just as she has reached the West End. At last Nigel's pleading overcomes her resistance and she consents to become his wife.

Scene 9: In the green-room of the Jubilee Theatre, Paul and Elsie have a violent quarrel. She has been drinking and is in an aggressive mood. Neither Liesl Haren's intervention nor the Stage Manager's protest that she can be heard all over the theatre suffices to quieten her. She screams at Paul that he is a conceited amateur, slaps his face, and storms out, vowing never to return.

The first call comes through just as the sextet girls arrive. Elsie's first entrance is due in three minutes, and Johnny Knowles, the Stage Manager, tells Rozanne to take over, just as she is, and he will have her understudy dresses ready for her next change. Paul gives her her first line and promises to help her through as they hear Johnny announcing that "owing to Miss

Elsie Jewell's sudden indisposition, the part of Mary Dale will be played by Miss Rozanne Gray". Liesl kisses her and wishes her luck.

The lights fade, and in the darkness Duggie's voice can be heard calling the entrances for the various acts.

Scene 10: Towards the end of "The Model Maid", Monsieur Pom-Pom (Eddie Gosling) and the chorus are finishing a topical song, "The Island Of Bollamazoo". After Countess Mitzi has reconciled Mary Dale (Rozanne) with her repentant suitor, Lord Fairfield, there is an ensemble of "Dearest Love", and the curtain falls and rises several times to enthusiastic applause. As Rozanne takes a solo call, a large bunch of violets falls from one of the boxes. Holding it close, she looks up and smiles.

ACT II, Prologue: This is again sung by the double sextet of men and girls, paired in hansom cabs.

Scene 1: Several weeks have passed, and Rozanne is now established as the star of "The Model Maid". Waiting in her dressing-room till she comes off stage, Nigel has a chat with Liesl Haren, telling her that his brother has now forsaken Grace Menteith for another charmer, Maude Lovell at Daly's Theatre. Liesl remarks that one of her own former admirers, Prince Lichtenstein, is eager to meet Rozanne, and she intends to introduce them that evening. There is no need to be jealous, she reminds him, for soon he will have Rozanne all to himself.

At last Rozanne comes in. Her mind is on her work, and she shows no enthusiasm when Nigel reminds her that it will soon be a thing of the past. The "Governor", Charles Hobson, comes to speak to her, and Nigel takes his hint to depart. When the run ends, says Hobson, there will be a new part specially written for her, as a beautiful geisha in a Japanese play. It is a magnificent score, he adds. Rozanne turns down the offer, saying that she is retiring from the stage after her marriage; but he advises her to think it over and let him know her decision later.

Scene 2: The finale of the second act of *The Model Maid* is in progress. Mary Dale, who is planning an elopement with her aristocratic suitor, has a song with the full chorus, "Sing For Joy". But the Duke and Duchess of Trenton bring a letter from their son, saying that he has reconsidered the plan, and Mary sings broken heartedly:

> What have I done that you should treat me so?
> What bitter Fate should wish to cheat me so?

She tells the Duchess spiritedly that she never wishes to see her or her son again, tears the letter up, and throws it at her feet. Then, wildly, she exclaims: "Play something gay! I want to dance – to dance..." She whirls around to a gay waltz, and then falls, swooning.

Scene 3: A few days later Liesl is giving a tea-party to the sextet girls (a new one, Rhoda Wallace, has replaced Rozanne). When they ask her about her early career she answers them in a song, "Operette".

At the end of this, Nigel's mother Lady Messiter is announced. She seems disconcerted at finding so many people, but smiles graciously when Liesl introduces the girls and speaks a few words of recognition to Grace Menteith. In due course the guests take their leave and Lady Messiter settles down to talk to Liesl about Nigel's engagement to Rozanne. Liesl says that the girl really loves him and is sacrificing a great deal to marry him.

At this point Rozanne herself appears, and Liesl, after introducing her to Lady Messiter, makes an excuse to leave them alone. Lady Messiter says she does not want to behave like the ill-mannered Duchess in "The Model Maid", but she must point out that if Nigel marries an actress he will have to send in his papers and give up the army career, which has been his whole life. Touched by Rozanne's evident sincerity and devotion to Nigel, she leaves her with the request to "do what you think best – for him".

Scene 4: The same quartet as before sing more verses of "The Stately Homes Of England".

Scene 5: Nigel and Rozanne are having a farewell dinner at Romano's before the show. Next day he is rejoining his regiment, which has been posted to India. In tears, Rozanne tells him that his mother has invited her to stay, but the prospect of seeing his world, without him, is too much for her. Consolingly, he reminds her that he will be back in five years' time. Rozanne, however, is clearer-sighted: she knows that by then they will have changed and circumstances will be different; so the goodbye she says to him is final. When she has gone, Nigel repeats the final couplet from the song:

> Where in the shadows that we have to pass among
> Lie those songs that once we sung?

Scene 6: In her dressing-room, Rozanne is mechanically completing her make-up when the stage manager comes to warn her that Grace Menteith is not playing: she has just married Lord Borrowmere and has decided not to act again.

When Liesl brings her a glass of champagne, Rozanne breaks down and cries, saying she cannot go on with the performance. Liesl insists that she must – whatever her private troubles, the theatre comes first: "Go on and act – act better than you have ever acted in your life!"

Asking her maid, Dora, to put Nigel's violets out of sight, Rozanne goes on stage. As before, we hear Duggie calling successive acts of *The Model Maid*.

Scene 7: The curtain goes up on the last act of *The Model Maid*, but this time it is seen from back-stage. The actors are performing to an imaginary audience, with their backs to the real one.

As before, Monsieur Pom-Pom is finishing his comic song, "Bollamazoo". The chorus, as they make their exit, are seen hanging about in the wings. Waiting for their entrance, Liesl and Rozanne whisper together. The end of the play proceeds as before, but now it is seen in reverse. At last the curtain drops (between the company and the imaginary audience) and they take their calls. When Rozanne steps forward, a bouquet of Parma violets falls at her feet. She takes it up and moves slowly away, singing very softly "Dearest Love":

> Tho' we have to part,
> Thank you for your loving heart
> My only love-goodbye.

As she goes, the stage hands begin to strike the scenery.

Ivor Brown in the *Sketch*, 30 March 1938:

"It is odd to think nowadays that Mr Noël Coward was once regarded as the spirit of flaming and audacious youth. His new piece is modishly nostalgic, gently romantic, and shows a definite dislike, except in one song, for smartness and brilliance. *Operette*, at His Majesty's, is not a work of scholarship, except in so far as it deals (most amusingly) with the architectural, atmospheric, and sanitary details of the 'Stately Homes Of England'. But for the rest it can be accepted with calm at the Athenaeum Club, whither I am told Mr Coward has gone to join the eminents of College, Church, and State. Mr Coward now tells a tender tale of the officer and the actress, who, at the risk of breaking her heart, refused to ruin his career and to embarrass his family by uxoriously implanting herself, as he demanded, in the full glory of a nobleman's seat.

"This fable is attached to the year 1906, a year disastrous to the Conservative party, but not to a conservative way of life. As Mr Coward reminds us, the hansoms went clippety-clop, carrying gilded cargo from the Jubilee Theatre to Romano's, and the ladies of the chorus had fine matrimonial chances. Back-stage and up-stage were the same as ever. I once asked a Scottish gardener about the house with which I happened to have a family link. It was hidden behind trees. He said: 'It's in the style of the period – massive.' So did the ladies of 1906 attire themselves in the style of the period, massively. Sleeve and headdress were formidable as the dowagers below them. Mr Coward may begin by laughing gently at 1906 and its Jubilee Theatre; but he ends by liking it, even loving it, because he has begun to like, even to love, the star-crossed couple whom Miss Peggy Wood and Mr Griffith Jones sincerely and movingly impersonate.

"Miss Fritzi Massary plays the familiar but always effective part of the gay consultant, the actress who has seen a deal of life and can sympathetically give the old the air of perpetual youth and the young the air of elderly experience. She and Miss Irene Van brugh, as an estimable countess who knows the real secret of life, which is to make other people suggest your ideas and then act on them gladly, believing them to be their own, contribute two very fine performances to the production. This has been devised by the author and decorated by G. E. Calthrop with their usual knowledge of how to make a small and ordinary object or story seem large and delightful, which is, after all, the main business of the theatre. The music is sweet and soothing, and wholly suitable. It contributes to an entertainment as far removed as possible from the world of jazz and jitters."

PUBLICATIONS

Operette was published by Heinemann (London, 1938), and is dedicated to Fritzi Massary.

The vocal score was published by William Chappell, who also published separate sheet music of:

"Dearest Love"
"The Stately Homes Of England"
"Where Are The Songs We Sung?"
"Operette"

"Dearest Love", "The Stately Homes Of England", and "Where Are The Songs We Sung?" are included in *The Noël Coward Song Book* (Michael Joseph, 1953).

NOTES

Coward says in his introduction to *Play Parade, Volume II*:

"*Operette*, from my point of view, is the least successful musical play I have ever done. The reason for this is that it is over-written and under-composed. The story of an imaginary 'Gaiety Girl' of the early 1900s who achieves overnight stardom and then has to sacrifice her love-life to her career, while not fiercely original, is an agreeable enough background for gay music and lyrics and beguiling 'period' costumes. Unfortunately, however, the plot, which should have been the background, became the foreground, and the music, which should have dominated the action, established the atmosphere, and whirled the play into a lilting success, was meagre and only at moments adequate. The principal waltz song, 'Dearest Love', wasn't bad, but it was not nearly as good as 'I'll See You Again' or 'I Follow My Secret Heart'. 'Where Are The Songs We Sung?' was melodic, but depressing, and the only real lyric success of the entertainment was 'The Stately Homes Of England', which had very little connection with the story.

"The four principal players were Peggy Wood, Fritzi Massary, Irene Vanbrugh and Griffith Jones. Fritzi Massary, one of the greatest stars of middle Europe, emerged from her retirement and studied English for months in order to play Liesl Haren. Her performance was exquisite and her behaviour magnificent. She knew as well as I knew, during the try-out in Manchester, that neither her part nor the songs she had to sing were worthy of her, but never, at the time or since, has she ever uttered a word of reproach. I hasten to add that she made an enormous personal success, but I am forced to admit, with the utmost regret, that it was more her fault than mine. Peggy Wood, as usual, sang and acted with consummate taste and charm. Irene Vanbrugh played her one boring scene with unassailable dignity. Poor Griffith Jones, uneasily aware that he couldn't sing a note, acted well on the rare occasions that he had an opportunity to do so, and for the rest of the time stood or sat about attentively while other people sang at him. Another aspect of *Operette* was the triumphant confusion it established in the minds of the audience. This was cunningly achieved by the switching of the action back and forth between the stage play and the real play. I remember peering from my box in the Opera House, Manchester, and watching bewildered playgoers rustling their programmes and furtively striking matches in a frantic effort to discover where they were and what was going on. By that time, however, it was too late to do anything about it, beyond cutting and simplifying whenever possible. In order really to save the situation then, it would have been necessary to rewrite and reconstruct the entire play; re-rehearse the company and scrap and rebuild the scenery. It would also have helped if I had sat down and dashed off half a dozen entrancing new musical numbers. Unfortunately, however, we were due to open at His Majesty's in two weeks and, even if the management had agreed to treble the production costs which such drastic alterations would inevitably have entailed, there was no time.

"In the last analysis, it was not the dead failure I feared it would be, but it was far from being the success I had hoped it would be when I first conceived and wrote it. If the reader of this volume is interested in how not to write a musical play, in how to overload a light, insignificant story with long stretches of accurate but uninspired dialogue, and in how to reduce an audience of average intelligence to a state of frustrated confusion, he will probably enjoy it immensely."

After the London run the production toured until the end of the year with most of the London company. Ivy St Helier replaced Fritzi Massary and Margaret Damer replaced Irene Vanbrugh.

During the run of *Operette*, Irene Vanbrugh celebrated her stage jubilee. The occasion was marked by a matinée at His Majesty's Theatre on 20 June 1938, at which a prologue by Alfred Noyes was spoken by Noël Coward.

On 6 November 1950 (after the death of Irene Vanbrugh in 1949), an all-star matinée was given at the Theatre Royal, Drury Lane, titled *Yesterday and Today*. This was in aid of the Irene Vanbrugh Memorial Fund to rebuild the Vanbrugh Theatre at the Royal Academy of Dramatic Art. The epilogue to this performance was written and spoken by Noël Coward. He said:

> Your Majesty, ladies and gentlemen.
> A little while ago a lady died,
> A lady who, for many of us here
> Epitomised the dignity and pride
> Of our profession. Over fifty years
> Have passed since young Miss Vanbrugh's quality
> Was stamped indelibly upon the hearts
> Of Londoners. During those changing years
> We were most privileged, not only us,
> Her colleagues who so loved and honoured her,
> But you as well, you on the other side.
> Perhaps you took for granted (as you should)
> The lightness of her touch in comedy;
> The note of hidden laughter in her voice;
> The way she used her hands to illustrate
> Some subtle implication. She could charge
> Any ordinary line with so much wit
> That even critics thought the play was good;
> They too took her for granted (as they should).
> Then on the other hand, the other mask,
> The mask of tragedy; she could wear that
> With such authority that even we,

Her fellow actors, plainly could perceive
Through her most accurate and sure technique
Her truth, which was her talent, shining clear.
Your Majesty, ladies and gentlemen,
A little while ago this lady died
Apparently, only apparently,
For even though the art that she adorned
Must in its essence be ephemeral,
Players of her integrity and grace
Can never die. Although we shall not hear
That lyrical, gay voice again, nor see
That personal, inimitable smile
That she bestowed on us at curtain calls
The theatre that she loved will still go on
Enriched immeasurably by the years
She gave to it. This epilogue is but
A prelude to the future she endowed
With so much legend, so much memory
For all the young beginners who will learn
Their intricate and fascinating trade
And owe, perhaps, some measure of their fame
To the undying magic of her name.

There have been no revivals of *Operette* since the Second World War.

31
SET TO MUSIC
REVUE
Written in 1938

FIRST PRESENTED by John C. Wilson at the Shubert Theatre, Boston, 26 December 1938; subsequently at the Music Box Theatre, New York, 18 January 1939 (129 performances).

ACT I

1. A Fragonard Impression

SINGER	Eva Ortega
LISETTE	Mary Ann Carr

TIGER PLON PLON	Leonard Gibson
LA MARQUISE DESAURIOLE (MAMAN)	Maidie Andrews
MONSIEUR L'ABBÉ	Sanders Draper
BLANCHE	Penelope Dudley Ward
GERMAINE	Moya Nugent
EUGÉNIE	Rosemary Lomax
MARGUERITE	Sarah Burton
GISELLE	Beatrice Lillie

2. Three Little Débutantes

Anna Jackson, Laura Duncan, Ruby Green

3. Mad About The Boy

(a) Outside a London Cinema

(b) A SOCIETY WOMAN	Penelope Dudley Ward
HER FRIEND	Rosemary Lomax
(c) A HOUSEMAID	Gladys Henson
(d) A GIRL OF THE TOWN	Laura Duncan
(e) A SCHOOLGIRL	Beatrice Lillie
HER YOUNGER SISTER	Moya Nugent

4. The Stately Homes Of England

SINGERS	Hugh French, Angus Menzies, Kenneth Carten, Anthony Pélissier

5. Weary Of It All

LORD BITCHETTE	Ray Dennis
DAISY (a dresser)	Gladys Henson
ELMER VON ROBESPIERRE	Robert Shackleton
HENRY BEARDWORTH	Anthony Pélissier
MARION DAY	Beatrice Lillie

6. Children Of The Ritz

SINGER	Eva Ortega

Toni Sorel, Helen Bennett, Helene Hudson, Verna Long, Ann Eden, Tilda Getze, Sylvia Dale, Anne Graham, Hilda Knight, Laurie Douglas

7. *Madame Dines Alone*

MRS JOHN ILLSWORTH-POINDEXTER	Beatrice Lillie
WITHERS	Richard Haydn

8. *Never Again*

SINGERS	Eva Ortega and Hugh French
DANCERS	Robert Shackleton, Kenneth Carten, Victor Cutrer

9. *Midnight Matinée*

(a)
VISCOUNTESS HOGAN	Florence Britton
LADY MILLICENT HEADLEY	Sarah Burton
THE MARCHIONESS OF LEMWORTH	Maidie Andrews
THE HON. MRS DOUGLAS DRAYCOTT	Moya Nugent
MISS ESME PONTING	Rosemary Lomax
MISS SPENCE	Gladys Henson
THE LADY WESTMORSHAM	Penelope Dudley Ward
MRS F. N. J. WILSON	Tilda Getze

(b)
GREEK CHORUS	Toni Sorel, Helen Bennett, Helene Hudson, Ann Eden, Sylvia Dale, Verna Long, Anne Graham, Hilda Knight

(c)
MR STUART-INGLEBY (announcer)	Richard Haydn
MRS ROWNTREE (organiser)	Beatrice Lillie
VISCOUNTESS HOGAN (as Diane de Poitiers)	Florence Britton
LADY MILLICENT HEADLEY (as Cleopatra)	Sarah Burton
THE MARCHIONESS OF LEMWORTH (as Nell Gwynn)	Maidie Andrews
THE HON. MRS DOUGLAS DRAYCOTT (as Salome)	Moya Nugent
MISS ESME PONTING (as Marie Antoinette)	Rosemary Lomax
MISS ELEANOR SHERRELL (as a court lady)	Anne Graham
MISS REBECCA MOSENTHORPE (as a court lady)	Laurie Douglas
LADY PATRICIA GAINTON (as a page)	Carol Louise Wanderman
THE HON. JULIAN FORRAGE (as a page)	John Mathews

MISS SPENCE (as Joan of Arc)	Gladys Henson
THE LADY WESTMORSHAM (as Lady Blessington)	Penelope Dudley Ward
MRS F. N. J. WILSON (as Lady Godiva)	Tilda Getze
ANGELS	Mary Anne Carr, Toni Sorel
LORD ACKLE	Sanders Draper

ACT II

10. Children Of The Ritz

SINGER	Eva Ortega
	Toni Sorel, Helen Bennett, Helene Hudson, Verna Long, Ann Eden, Tilda Getze, Sylvia Dale, Anne Graham, Hilda Knight, Laurie Douglas

11. Three White Feathers

SHE	Beatrice Lillie
HE	Hugh French

12. Fish Mimicry (Richard Haydn)

EDWIN CARP	Richard Haydn

13. Three Little Débutantes

	Anna Jackson, Laura Duncan, Ruby Green

14. Marvellous Party

SINGER	Beatrice Lillie

15. The Stately Homes Of England

SINGERS	Hugh French, Angus Menzies, Kenneth Carten, Anthony Pélissier

16. Secret Service

THE COUNTESS	Beatrice Lillie
MADAME MOULE	Gladys Henson
LIZI	Moya Nugent
LEOPOLD ROSEN	Angus Menzies

FIRST OFFICER	Richard Haydn
SECOND OFFICER	Hugh French
MAURICE	Victor Cutrer
JITTONO	Kenneth Carten
FRITZ	Ray Dennis
SERGE	Sanders Draper
IVAN	Gilbert Wilson
A SPANISH LADY	Eva Ortega
MASHA	Florence Britton
LUBA	Sarah Burton
SASHA	Robert Shackleton
LORETTE	Mary Anne Carr

17. Three Little Débutantes

Anna Jackson, Laura Duncan, Ruby Green

18. The Party's Over Now

SINGERS	Penelope Dudley Ward, Hugh French
DANCER	Bronson Dudley

19. Finale	Entire Company

Director, book, lyrics and music	*Noël Coward*
Décor and costumes	*G. E. Calthrop*
Orchestra direction	*John McManus*
Orchestrations	*Hans Spialek*

Brooks Atkinson in the *New York Times*, 19 January 1939:

"Whether Noël Coward is Beatrice Lillie's best friend or whether the honours are the other way round is an academic question at best. For the simple fact is that *Set to Music*, which was set to the Music Box last evening, represents both of them at their best. With his familiar prodigality of talents, Mr Coward has written it and staged it, sketches and songs alike, some of it having been retrieved from a revue he wrote for London last season. On the spur of the moment, it seems like the best show he has written. Although Miss Lillie has been synonymous with perfection in comedy for quite a long time, an old admirer may be forgiven for believing that she also is more incandescently witty now than before. For light amusement, written and acted with impeccable taste, this London revue is off the top of the pack.

"Yet 'London revue' is not the most accurate description. 'Lillie revue' comes closer to the mark. After making her entrance on a white horse early in the evening, it is distinctly her show. Whenever they are not changing the scenery, the radiant lady turns up in a whole bag of tricks, from schoolgirl admiration of a movie star to the ironic abandon of a secret service burlesque in a railroad station. She is the world-weary actress disdainfully clutching at the treasures her admirers bring. She is the condescending manager of a charity ball, and the mistress of society revels in an English colony in Europe. And whatever she is, she is always the miracle woman of mockery – keeping high comedy just a bit on the vulgar side and rescuing low comedy from common excesses. For that incandescent intelligence that has long since put her at the top of her profession discovers the weakness in every pretension she assumes, gives it a gleaming nudge and translates it into hilarity.

"Mr Coward also has that sort of genius. He has composed any number of withering melodies and laments for felicity with lyrics that represent perfection in their diction. Among the marvels of modern music satire 'The Stately Homes Of England' stands in the front rank. It has been available for some time on the records, with his croaking voice performing the word and music gymnastics. Although the four young men who sing it here are not that expert, they give it an admirable hearing. This is not a full-bodied revue; it is not weighted down with material. It is the refinement of mannered gaiety, and it includes two satiric sketches of remarkable skill. Mr Coward ridiculing the pompous gaucheries of a charity ball and the mumbo-jumbo of international spying are in his best style of adroit fooling.

"Once Miss Lillie and Mr Coward stand aside while someone else takes charge of the evening. They are well advised. For Richard Haydn, visible elsewhere on the programme, has a turn of his own composing that must now be enshrined in every theatregoer's memory book. In a make-up that the Moscow Art Theatre would approve, he appears as Edwin Carp, the phenomenal fish mimic in some demented vaudeville programme. It was something to think of that act; it is something to have written the long introduction that caricatures the hackneyed literary effusions of dull people, and it is great to be able to master the accent and style of Mr Haydn's delivery. Any fish would feel thoroughly at home in Mr Haydn's presence; his astonished humility is completely fishified.

"Now there is no time left to distribute appreciative compliments to the other people who have helped bring this revue up to the footlights: Gladys Henson for her slow-witted clowning; Bronson Dudley for his bizarre tap-dancing; Eva Ortega for her vibrant singing; and G. E. Calthrop for her stunning décor and costumes. They have all helped to create a revue that represents the quintessence of style and skill, with Noël Coward and Beatrice Lillie as the presiding geniuses."

PUBLICATIONS

The songs "I Went To A Marvellous Party" and "Never Again" are included in *The Noël Coward Song Book* (Michael Joseph, 1953). "Weary Of It All" and "Secret Service" are included in *Collected Revue Sketches and Parodies* (Methuen, 1999).

The items from *Words and Music* are published in the book of the revue in *Play Parade, Volume II* (Heinemann, 1939), and in the vocal score (William Chappell, 1932).

NOTES

This revue is more or less an American edition of *Words and Music* (London, 1932), with some new and additional material, which included:

"The Stately Homes Of England" (from *Operette*, unproduced in America)
"A Fragonard Impression" (unproduced in London)
"Madame Dines Alone" (unproduced in London)

Three items were later produced in *All Clear*, London, 1939, "I'm So Weary Of It All", "I Went To A Marvellous Party" and "Secret Service". Also "Never Again" was introduced into *Sigh No More*, London, 1945.

Many of the songs here, though none of the sketches, were included in the revues *Cowardy Custard* (page 530), *Oh, Coward!* (page 534) and in *Noël and Gertie* (page 537).

32
PRESENT LAUGHTER

(Originally called *Sweet Sorrow*)

A PLAY IN THREE ACTS

Written in 1939

FIRST PRESENTED by H. M. Tennent Ltd. and John C. Wilson at the Grand Theatre, Blackpool, 20 September 1942 (25 weeks' tour: Leeds, Bristol, Nottingham, Manchester [2 weeks], Liverpool, Sheffield, Hull, Newcastle,

Edinburgh, Glasgow [2 weeks], Aberdeen [2 weeks], Inverness, Carlisle, Cardiff, Northampton, Oxford, Leicester, Southsea, Coventry, Exeter and Bournemouth) with *This Happy Breed* and *Blithe Spirit*. Under the title of *Play Parade*, the three plays were played alternately.

SUBSEQUENTLY FIRST PRESENTED IN LONDON at the Haymarket Theatre, 29 April 1943 (38 performances). The play was produced alternately with *This Happy Breed* during the season.

REVIVED by H. M. Tennent Ltd. and John C. Wilson at the Royal Court Theatre, Liverpool, 7 April 1947. Subsequently at the Haymarket Theatre, London, 16 April 1947 (528 performances).

CHARACTERS	**Blackpool, 1942 and Haymarket, 1943**
DAPHNE STILLINGTON	Jennifer Gray
MISS ERIKSON	Molly Johnson
FRED	Billy Thatcher
MONICA REED	Beryl Measor
GARRY ESSENDINE	Noël Coward
LIZ ESSENDINE	Joyce Carey
ROLAND MAULE	James Donald
HENRY LYPPIATT	Gerald Case
MORRIS DIXON	Dennis Price
JOANNA LYPPIATT	Judy Campbell
LADY SALTBURN	Gwen Floyd
Director	*Noël Coward*
Designer	*G. E. Calthrop*

CHARACTERS	**Liverpool and Haymarket, 1947**
DAPHNE STILLINGTON	Avis Scott
MISS ERIKSON	Daphne Newton
FRED	Billy Thatcher
MONICA REED	Joan Swinstead
GARRY ESSENDINE	Noël Coward, succeeded by Hugh Sinclair (14 July 1947)
LIZ ESSENDINE	Joyce Carey
ROLAND MAULE	Robert Eddison
HENRY LYPPIATT	Gerald Case
MORRIS DIXON	Peter Gray
JOANNA LYPPIATT	Moira Lister
LADY SALTBURN	Gwen Floyd

Director	*Noël Coward*
Designer	*G. E. Calthrop*

SCENE: The action of the play passes in Garry Essendine's studio
in London.

ACT I: Morning.

ACT II: Scene 1: Evening. Three days later.
Scene 2: The next morning.

ACT III: Evening. A week later.

❖

SYNOPSIS

ACT I: The scene throughout is the studio of the popular actor, Garry Essendine, from which doors open into the spare room and the office, and a staircase leads to Garry's bedroom on the floor above. It is 10.30 a.m. and an attractive girl, Daphne Stillington, comes quietly out of the spare room, wearing Garry's dressing-gown and pyjamas, and telephones a girl friend, asking her to provide her with an alibi if necessary.

To the Swedish housekeeper, Miss Erikson, Daphne explains that she has stayed the night because she had lost her own latch key. The housekeeper goes to get her some breakfast, and Monica Reed, Garry's secretary, comes in bringing the morning's mail. After questioning her rather soulfully about Garry, Daphne says she hopes Monica doesn't think... The secretary retorts crisply that she has been with Garry for 17 years, and: "I gave up that sort of thinking in the spring of 1922."

When the valet Fred brings in a tray, Monica suggests that Daphne had better breakfast in her room as the studio will soon get busy. She sends Fred to ask Mrs Erikson to prepare the girl a bath.

Unexpectedly, Garry appears at the top of the stairs in his pyjamas, furious at having been awakened by all the talking. He has forgotten Daphne, but when Monica recalls her to his mind he declares that he is "mad about her"... However, he thinks she should have been told to dress quietly and go home.

Hearing his voice, Daphne comes out and he greets her with charm. His secretary tactfully withdraws, after reminding him of various engagements that morning, whereupon Daphne flings herself into his arms. He adroitly disengages himself and plays a graceful "renunciation" scene, quoting Shelley and assuring her that he is too old for her and that his life is not his own: "I belong to the public and my work." In a fortnight he is going on a theatrical tour to Africa. He kisses her *au revoir*, and she returns to the bedroom in tears.

Fred brings in his breakfast and Monica returns with the opened mail. They discuss the letters as he eats, with interruptions from the telephone; then he goes to have his bath.

An early caller is Liz Essendine, just back from abroad with presents for Monica and Garry. She and Garry live apart, but (as she explains later to Daphne) never "quite got around" to being divorced. It is a great shock to Daphne to find that Garry is still married, but she accepts Liz's kind offer to send her home in her own car.

Discussing the episode, Liz and Monica decide that it is really time Garry began to settle down. They plan a concerted attack, to be backed up by his manager, Morris Dixon and his best friend, Henry Lyppiatt, though Monica remarks that their reliability has been lessened by Henry's marriage.

When Garry comes downstairs, Liz produces the bright dressing-gown she has brought him, and he puts it on with great delight. She then starts her sermon: at the age of 40, she declares, his "casual scampering around" with girls is undignified. Garry runs through the gamut of emotions – indignation, sweet reasonableness, sarcasm and pathos. At the end of the scene Liz asks him to concentrate: she wants to talk about Morris, who is behaving very oddly and is reputed to be in love with Henry's wife, Joanna. Could Garry not take him to Africa, out of her way?

A doorbell warns them of the arrival of Roland Maule, a young playwright who has an appointment. They arrange a telephone code: if Garry rings her and says, "Sorry. It's a wrong number," she will know that he has settled the trouble about Morris; but if he says, "I'm so terribly sorry. It's a wrong number," Liz will come to his help.

Roland is an earnest and intense young man in glasses. When Garry tells him tactfully that his play is not very good, he talks loftily about the "play of ideas" as opposed to the "commercial theatre" in which Garry is prostituting his talent every night. Then Garry lets fly, describing the play as "a meaningless jumble of adolescent pseudo-intellectual poppycock". He advises Roland to get a job as a butler in a repertory company and learn play-construction from the ground up; then to write 20 plays in succession. "And if you can get the twenty-first produced for a Sunday night performance you'll be damned lucky."

The young man is entranced: now, he says, he knows what Garry is really like and will be able to sublimate him. With relief, Garry sees him out and gives orders to Monica not to admit him again.

Henry and Morris find him thoroughly out of temper, and he is still further upset when they tell him that his proposed character-woman for the African tour has broken her leg and will have to be replaced. The last straw is when he learns that they have been unable to secure the Mayfair Theatre for his next London season, so he will have to take the Forum instead – a theatre which he particularly dislikes.

Henry leaves to catch a plane for Brussels, after asking Morris to look after his wife in his absence. This is Garry's cue to tax Morris with his attentions to Joanna. He says that the five of them – Morris, Henry, Liz, Monica and himself – share a mutual respect and trust which is too valuable to risk breaking. Joanna doesn't really "belong", and she is a potential danger; so he had better be careful.

Morris takes the lecture meekly, and Garry rings Liz with his prearranged "O.K." signal: "Sorry. It's a wrong number."

ACT II, Scene 1: It is midnight, three days later. Garry, with a dressing-gown over his evening clothes, is playing the piano. He says good night to his valet, who, very smartly dressed, is off to meet his girlfriend in a night club. Then he rings Liz at her flat, telling her that he and Morris have just seen Joanna home.

Hardly has he rung off, however, when Joanna herself comes to the front door, explaining that she has lost her latchkey and has been unable to contact Liz. Garry quizzically offers her a drink and a cigarette and looks on while, after reproaching him for his hostile attitude and asking him to be kind to her, she pretends to telephone for a taxi. Then he takes the receiver out of her hand: "You win!" he says.

Joanna opens up with provocative skirmishing, asking him to stop his eternal performance and be friendly and genuine for a while. He retorts that she is "as predatory as hell" and tells her to go away; whereupon she confesses that she has been in love with him for seven years, and only married Henry to get into his orbit. She adds that Henry has been "lightly unfaithful" to her for years. Under Garry's suspicious questioning, she persists that Morris means nothing to her and has never been her lover. She gets her way in the end and the curtain falls as they embrace.

Scene 2: Once more it is 10.30 in the morning, and this time it is Joanna who emerges in Garry's dressing-gown and asks Miss Erikson for breakfast. Again Monica comes in with the mail and hears the familiar story of a lost latchkey. Her attitude is so disapproving that they are on the verge of a quarrel when Liz appears. Told about the latchkey and her own unanswered telephone, she answers sweetly that she was in from ten o'clock onwards.

Fred, highly intrigued, brings in coffee; then Liz tries to send Joanna back to the spare room, but she declines to move. Liz then takes a strong line, threatening that if Joanna does not stay away until Garry has left for Africa she will reveal all to Garry, Morris and Henry. At first Joanna refuses indignantly, but she is frightened into acquiescence when the doorbell rings and Liz tells her it is Morris. She goes hurriedly into the spare room.

The caller, however, is Roland Maule, who asserts that he has an appointment, and Monica sends him into the office to wait for Garry. Expecting trouble with Morris, Liz checks with Monica that the telephone in the spare room is on a separate line, and goes in there.

Garry, fully dressed, comes downstairs just as Morris appears in a state of agitation. He insists upon seeing the occupant of the spare room and is taken aback when Liz calmly comes out of it. Saying he hasn't slept for three nights, he blurts out a confession of his love for Joanna, whose disappearance has completely unbalanced him. Liz explains that Joanna, having lost her latchkey, spent the night with her, and she dials the number Monica has given her, pretending that it is her own flat; then she hands the receiver to Morris. ("How did you get her out?" whispers Garry "I didn't. She's in there!" replies Liz.) She dissuades Morris from rushing round to the flat, saying he had better wait until he has calmed down.

Monica is breaking the news of Roland Maule's arrival when the young man himself bursts out of the office. They all try to send him away, but he insists upon staying, because: "I get smoother and smoother and smoother: my whole rhythm improves tremendously."

Meanwhile, Henry, who has returned unexpectedly and found Joanna missing, comes along to see if they know what has happened. Again Liz tries the telephone trick, and this time Joanna hangs up, remarking that she feels as if she were in a French farce and is sick of it.

The next visitor is Lady Saltburn, who has brought her niece for an audition. She is too generous a contributor to theatrical charities to be put off, so Garry reluctantly consents to see them. The niece is Daphne Stillington. She recites the passage from Shelley which Garry had previously quoted to her. During the last verse, Joanna, in evening dress and cloak, comes out of the spare room in a furious rage.

Telling Garry that she is going away for a month and will not see him again before he sails, she makes some very unpleasant remarks about his "circus of satellites" and goes out. Daphne falls in a faint.

ACT III: It is Garry's last evening in England. He has said good night to Fred, who is off to say goodbye to his girlfriend, and is going through arrears of mail with Monica, tearing up most of the letters. Before leaving, she warns him to be careful of the telephone, as Roland Maule keeps ringing. Miss Erikson also says good night, on her way to a spiritualist meeting, so Garry is alone in the house when the doorbell rings. It is Daphne, in travelling clothes and carrying a dressing-case. To his horror, she declares that she knows he needs her, so she is coming to Africa with him. He tells her furiously to go straight back to her aunt, but she is resolved to stay. When another caller rings, Garry hurriedly puts her into the office.

This time it is Roland, also determined to come on the voyage. When Garry threatens him with the police, he runs into the spare room and locks himself in, just as there is a third ring.

The new visitor is Joanna, also wanting to go to Africa, and the situation has got beyond Garry's control. He telephones an urgent SOS to Liz: "I'm so terribly, terribly, terribly sorry. It's a wrong number."

Joanna says that, since both of them no longer need or desire the pangs of love, but are perfectly willing to settle for the fun of love, they meet on the same terms. They need each other, and she is not only coming on the voyage, but has written a note to Henry, telling him that they are lovers. Before Garry can reply, Liz arrives and takes charge. She says brightly that she is coming too, so that from the social and publicity angle Joanna will be there as a friend of hers.

Henry and Morris then call in a state of fury, demanding to know whether Joanna's assertion is true. By this time Garry is exasperated. Recklessly, he tells Henry about Joanna's affair with Morris, and reveals to Joanna that Henry himself has been carrying on a furtive intrigue for months. An all-round shouting scene is terminated by Joanna calling him an unmitigated cad, slapping his face, and walking out.

Garry hardly notices her exit: far more important to him is Henry's statement that he and Morris have just signed a contract for the Forum Theatre. He protests that he will not play in an auditorium that looks like a Gothic edition of Wembley Stadium, and is calmed down with difficulty by Liz, who points out that it is being redecorated and that the designs are good. In a final burst of melodrama – which drives Henry to remark, "It's a pity they're pulling down the Lyceum!" – Garry sends them away.

Then he has a tranquil drink with Liz, who declares that she is coming back to him for good. Suddenly he remembers his unwelcome visitors and has an inspiration:

"You're not coming back to me, dear," he says. "I'm coming back to you." And they tiptoe out together as the curtain falls.

❖

W. A. Darlington in the *Daily Telegraph*, 30 April 1943:

"It is a commonplace in the theatre that almost any phrase from Shakespeare makes an effective play title. What more attractive label could there be for a light comedy than *Present Laughter*, which Noël Coward has used for the first of his two new plays at the Haymarket?

"True, it has nothing whatever to do with the action of the play. But we can excuse that, seeing how accurately it describes the reaction of the audience.

"Mr Coward has laughed at the absurdities of his own world of the theatre before. This time his view is more detached than of old. His chief characters are all members of a highly successful theatrical firm, with Mr Coward himself playing Garry Essendine, the romantic actor who is the firm's chief asset.

"The members of the firm, men and women, fall in and out of love with each other, marry and get divorced from each other, and make a tremendous fuss about their amorous permutations and combinations.

"But the joke is that, in spite of the fuss, when it comes to the point these affairs are less important than, and take second place to, the interests of the firm.

"Let us be clear about it. There is no edification in this play, but there is any amount of fun.

"A mad little world with a topsy-turvy code of its own needs to be shown to us through a pair of sane eyes if we are to appreciate its full absurdity. Mr Coward supplies such a pair of eyes in the head of Garry's calm and capable secretary.

"This is a beautifully written part, without which half the satirical effect of the play would be lost. It is perfectly played by Beryl Measor.

"Another brilliant piece of concerted work between actor and author is James Donald's playing of a young cub of an incipient dramatist. Every time Mr Donald opened his mouth last night I rocked in my seat with laughter.

"A very accomplished piece of acting by Joyce Carey, some effective vamping by Judy Campbell, and Mr Coward's own burlesque of his hero's constant self-dramatisation – these are the other major attractions in a production gleaming with polish like a lacquer cabinet."

PUBLICATIONS

Present Laughter was first published by Heinemann (London, 1943). It is dedicated to Clemence Dane.

NOTES

Coward went to America for the production of *Set to Music*. He says in *Future Indefinite:*

"In February 1939, I went to Honolulu with the express purpose of writing a play for myself, but wrote some short stories instead. These were later published under the title of *To Step Aside*. In March, feeling that another crisis was imminent, I returned to England. During April and May I stayed in my house in the country and wrote two plays: *Present Laughter* and *This Happy Breed*. I planned to appear in both of these myself in the autumn, acting them on alternate nights with the same company. They both turned out well, in spite of the fact that while I was writing them I was aware that they would in all probability never be produced, at least not at the time that I intended them to be. This dismal clairvoyance was ultimately justified."

The plays were cast and ready for rehearsal. In the six weeks before these were due to start Coward went on a trip to Europe. He returned for rehearsals of the tour due to commence at Manchester on 11 September. The productions went as far as the dress rehearsals on 30 and 31 August, but war broke out on 3 September, and the whole project was abandoned.

Coward commenced his war work immediately, and it was not till 1942 that the plays were finally staged.

In the meantime, two other plays had been written (*Time Remembered*, 1941, and *Blithe Spirit*, 1941), and the film *In Which We Serve* written and made. Coward decided to return to the stage in the two long-delayed plays which, with *Blithe Spirit*, were to make up a tour of three plays, entitled *Play Parade*. (*Blithe Spirit* was by then launched on its record-breaking run in London.)

When the year finished, the two new plays (*Present Laughter* and *This Happy Breed*) were presented at the Haymarket Theatre for a season, being performed alternately.

In his preface to *Play Parade, Volume IV*, Coward says:

"*Present Laughter* is a very light comedy, and was written with the sensible object of providing me with a bravura part. It was an enormous success. I received excellent notices and, to my bewilderment and considerable dismay, the play also was reasonably acclaimed. This so unnerved me that I can say no more."

In 1948 *Present Laughter* was translated into French by André Roussin and Pierre Gay as *Joyeux Chagrins*. Coward went to Paris and produced the play, again playing Garry (in this version named Max Aramont) at the Théâtre Edouard VII on 17 November. Coward's plays have been popular in France since *Hay Fever* (titled *Weekend*) was produced in Paris in 1928. Others include *Les Amants Terribles* (*Private Lives*), *Sérénade à Trois* (*Design for Living*), *Le Printemps de Saint-Martin* (*Fallen Angels*), and *Jeux d'Esprits* (*Blithe Spirit*).

Major UK revivals of *Present Laughter* since 1947 include: 21 April 1965, Queen's Theatre, with Nigel Patrick; 1974, Forum, Billingham and UK tour, with Peter Wyngarde; 31 March 1977, Manchester Royal Exchange, with Albert Finney; 17 March 1981, Vaudeville, with Donald Sinden; 23 June 1993, Globe Theatre, with Tom Conti; 21 February 1996, Aldwych, with Peter Bowles; 10 December 1998, West Yorkshire Playhouse, with Ian McKellen.

In September 1996 a French version entitled *Bagatelle* opened at the Théâtre de Paris with Michel Sardon.

Television productions of *Present Laughter* include: 1964, Granada, with Peter Wyngarde; 1967, ITV, with Peter O'Toole; 1981, BBC, with Donald Sinden.

US PRODUCTIONS

PRODUCED and directed by John C. Wilson. Presented at the Playhouse, Wilmington, Delaware on 26 September 1946 and subsequently at the Plymouth Theatre, New York on 29 October 1946 (158 performances).

CHARACTERS	Plymouth, 1946
DAPHNE STILLINGTON	Jan Sterling
MISS ERIKSON	Grace Mills
FRED	Aidan Turner
MONICA KEED	Evelyn Varden
GARRY ESSENDINE	Clifton Webb
LIZ ESSENDINE	Doris Dalton
ROLAND MAULE	Chris Alexander
HUGO	Gordon Mills
JOANNA LYPPIATT	Marta Linden
LADY SALTBURN	Leonore Harris

The *New York Sun*: "*Present Laughter* is far from being Noël Coward's best comedy. It is not continuously or devastatingly funny, but it offers a measure of entertainment and a precise, sharp and well-sustained performance from Clifton Webb. *Present Laughter* is second best Noël Coward but it still has enough waggish moments to afford a generally entertaining evening."

The *New York Times*: "For, good or hackneyed, Mr Coward can give casual lines hilarious inflections, and his whole point of view towards ordinary affairs is suitably crack-brained. At the moment he is writing a narrative of inferior quality – conventional, unimaginative and generally commonplace;

and although Clifton Webb acts the chief part brilliantly, the pace of the performance would be slow even for burial."

Although concerned by the reviews, Noël was not able to see the production until the following February. He found his fears were justified: "A gruesome evening. Clifton was excellent, lacking in fire and virility but compensating by comedy technique. The production of the play was lamentable. The cast was tatty and fifth rate... [Jack] has let me down by presenting and directing one of my best properties with lack of taste and imagination... I came home weary and depressed."

New York's reception of *Nude with Violin* at the end of 1957 – even with Noël playing the part of Sebastien – was disappointing.

In his diary for 5 January 1958 he wrote: "I have decided with some misgivings and perhaps misguided optimism to finish here as planned... and then play four weeks in San Francisco and two in Hollywood. I have also decided to play *Present Laughter* alternately with *Nude* and use the same set with a few slight alterations... I couldn't bear to fizzle out here drearily with *Nude*. *Present Laughter* will cheer me up and there are good parts for all the company."

ALSO PRESENTED by the The Playwrights' Company and Lance Hamilton and Charles Russell at the Belasco Theatre, New York on 31 January 1958 (6 performances). The two productions were then taken to the Curran Theatre, San Francisco (11 February 1958 for four weeks) and the Huntington Hartford Theatre, Hollywood (11 March for two weeks), where they alternated.

CHARACTERS	San Francisco and Hollywood, 1958
DAPHNE STILLINGTON	Angela Thornton
MISS ERIKSON	Avril Gentles
FRED	Robert Thurston
MONICA REED	Mona Washbourne
GARRY ESSENDINE	Noël Coward
LIZ ESSENDINE	Joyce Carey
ROLAND MAULE	William Traylor
HENRY LYPPIATT	Winston Ross
MORRIS DIXON	John Ainsworth
JOANNA LYPPIATT	Eve Gabor
CONTESSE DE VRIAC	Thérèse Quadri

In his diary Noël recorded: "It was a triumphant success and the [New York] audience cheered the roof off. The performance was excellent on the whole,

Eva enchanting and everyone else fine. I gave a good performance and, fortunately, looked about twenty years younger than I should have looked on account of a wonderful front piece, some superb dressing gowns, two very good new suits... and my own regained slim figure. It is a great part for me and I am obviously good in it... It has grown over the years, and little tricks and bits of business have miraculously reappeared without being consciously summoned."

The *Los Angeles Examiner*: "The advent of Noël Coward in the Los Angeles theatre last night made us regret all the years we have spent without him. He brought with him the glitter of mock wickedness, the tingle of the choicely framed epigram, the atmosphere of delightfully impossible wit and divertingly malicious banter."

Subsequent revivals have included:
John F. Kennedy Center for the Performing Arts. Directed by Stephen Porter. Presented at the Kennedy Center, Washington on 29 March 1975. The cast included Douglas Fairbanks, Jr. (Garry), Jane Alexander (Liz) and Ilka Chase (Monica).

Ed Mirvish's Royal Alexandra Theatre Company. Directed by Roderick Cook. Presented at the Kennedy Center, Washington, November 1978. The cast included Peter O'Toole (Garry). O'Toole also did a British television production of the play (15 March 1967 – shown in the US on ABC, 28 February 1968).

Circle in the Square (Theodore Mann and Paul Libin). Directed by George C. Scott. Presented at the Circle in the Square Theatre, New York on 15 July 1982 (175 performances). The cast included George C. Scott (Garry), Elizabeth Hubbard (Liz) and Dana Ivey (Monica).

The *New York Post* on the New York production: "This is a most civilised play. Coward used the English language with a deftness that had not been heard since Oscar Wilde. He can dazzle with the commonplace. He can make strange English place names, such as Uckfield or Stoke Poges, extravagantly funny. With climactic timing he can bring the house down with a line like 'What a day for Cunard!' Genius."

The *New York Daily News*: "George C. Scott has taken this very fragile comedy and pointed it in the direction of knockabout farce while still trying to retain some semblance of Cowardian style. And fragile though it is, the play is somehow resilient enough to sustain such treatment and provide enormously funny entertainment."

David Richenthal and Anita Waxman in association with Jujamcyn Theatres. Directed by Scott Elliott. Opened at the Walter Kerr Theatre on 18 November

1996 (175 performances). Cast included Frank Langella (Garry), Alison Janney (Liz), Lisa Emery (Monica), and Steve Ross who doubled as pianist and Fred.

The *New Yorker*: "A rogue revival... one of Coward's enduring comedies of bad manners. As commercial vehicles go, it's as time-tested, as surefire, and, in its way, as elegant as a vintage Aston Martin. And, as with one of those old masterpieces of engineering, everything still works, but you have to know how to handle it. Frank Langella does. He has a big voice and a big sense of himself (and) keeps the core of the comedy alive with a vivacious, full-tilt assault on Essendine's outrageousness. Langella is a ham, but he moves quickly and gracefully on stage, and takes a lot of oxygen out of the air during his temperamental tirades... The real wonder is why the director, Scott Elliot, seems to think that by turning *Present Laughter* into a bi-sexual romp he's liberating Coward. On the night... the audience stood for Langella. But if Elliott had done his job properly it would have stood for the play."

33
THIS HAPPY BREED
A PLAY IN THREE ACTS
Written in 1939

FIRST PRESENTED by H. M. Tennent Ltd. and John C. Wilson at the Grand Theatre, Blackpool, 21 September 1942 (25 weeks' tour with *Present Laughter* and *Blithe Spirit* under the title of *Play Parade*. The three plays were played alternately).

SUBSEQUENTLY FIRST PRESENTED IN LONDON at the Haymarket Theatre, 30 April 1943 (38 performances). The play was produced alternately with *Present Laughter* during the season.

CHARACTERS	Blackpool, 1942 and Haymarket, 1943
MRS FLINT (Frank's mother-in-law)	Gwen Floyd
ETHEL (his wife)	Judy Campbell
SYLVIA (his sister)	Joyce Carey
FRANK GIBBONS	Noël Coward
BOB MITCHELL	Gerald Case
REG (Frank's son)	Billy Thatcher
QUEENIE (Frank's daughter)	Jennifer Gray

VI (Frank's daughter)	Molly Johnson
SAM LEADBITTER	Dennis Price
PHYLLIS BLAKE	Meg Titheradge
EDIE (a maid)	Beryl Messor
BILLY	James Donald
Director	*Noël Coward*
Designer	*G. E. Calthrop*

❖

SCENE: The action of the play passes in the dining-room of the
               Gibbons' house, No.17, Sycamore Road, Clapham Common.

ACT I: Scene 1: June 1919.
               Scene 2: December 1925.
               Scene 3: May 1926.

ACT II: Scene 1: October 1931.
               Scene 2: November 1931.
               Scene 3: May 1932.

ACT III: Scene 1: December 1936.
               Scene 2: September 1938.
               Scene 3: June 1939.

❖

SYNOPSIS

ACT I, Scene 1: It is June 1919 and the Gibbons family are moving into a new house in Clapham Common. Mrs Gibbons (Ethel) is bustling about while her mother, Mrs Flint, sits in a chair and complains. Her delicate sister-in-law Sylvia is also peevish when she returns from buying groceries, but Frank Gibbons, who has been hanging curtains upstairs, is sympathetic with his wife's fatigue, and full of pleasure at having a home at last, after four years at the war.

A neighbour, Bob Mitchell, calls in to offer help, and is recognised by Frank as an old friend from the trenches. They exchange reminiscences, and Bob invites them to come and meet his wife and his son, Billy, who is nearly fifteen. Frank says that his own children – Vi, Queenie and Reg – are staying with an aunt until the move is over. Having no other drink handy, they toast "Happy days!" with Sylvia's Wincarnis.

Scene 2: Over six years have passed and the children are now grown up. They have just finished their Christmas lunch and are pulling crackers. The older folks have gone into the parlour, leaving the three young Gibbons with their friends, Phyllis Blake and Sam Leadbitter – a young Communist whom Reg is inclined to hero-worship. A speech by him, referring to his hosts as the "bourgeoisie" and reproaching their indifference to the sufferings of "the starving millions", is interrupted by facetious remarks from pretty, flashy Queenie. The only person impressed is Reg, who takes Sam off to his room for a surreptitious smoke, while the girls, helped by the maid-of-all-work, Edie, clear the table.

Billy Mitchell, now 21 and a sailor, drops in to say goodbye before rejoining his ship. He asks to speak to Queenie alone and proposes to her, but she tells him frankly that she wants a husband with money who can take her out of her petty suburban surroundings. She runs upstairs crying just as her father enters. He is sympathetic with Billy but tells him that the girl is head-strong and will certainly please herself.

When Sylvia begins to sing, Ethel slips out of the parlour and has a quiet chat with her husband in the dusk. She is worried about Sam's influence on Reg, fearing that their "Bolshie" views will get them into trouble; but Frank replies that their only mistake is trying to get things done too quickly: ideas, he says, are like plants in a garden – they have to grow quietly, in their own time.

Scene 3: The General Strike of May 1926, has just come to an end. The women of the family are at supper, with old Mrs Flint snapping at Sylvia from her armchair by the fire. For once, Ethel is out of temper; she is worried about Reg, who has been away for three days and is known to be with Sam. Eventually, Vi takes her grandmother up to bed, and the weeping Sylvia also goes up, after being consoled with a cup of tea. Queenie and her mother agree that Sylvia is a great trial, but, as she is not strong enough to earn her own living, they must continue to put up with her.

They are startled by the doorbell: it is only Phyllis, however, come for news of Reg. Then Frank Gibbons and Bert Mitchell, who have been out together as driver and conductor of a bus, come back, slightly intoxicated and in high spirits.

Shortly afterwards Reg, with his head bandaged, is brought in by Sam, who explains that he was hit by a stone in the Whitechapel Road. Ethel asks her husband not to "go for" the boy, as he looks worn out; to which Frank retorts that he is not "going for" anybody – he wants his supper. He sits down and eats, while Vi calls Sam "a great silly show-off" who is leading her brother into trouble, and orders him to leave the house and not to come courting her any more. Then she bursts into tears and runs out into the garden.

When the others have dispersed, Frank, gives his son a drink and talks to him, man to man. He has a right to his own opinions, says Frank, but let them be his own, and not second-hand ideas picked up from Sam and his friends. They are not even new ideas, but as old as the hills.

The root cause of inequality and injustice, he opines, lies not in systems and governments, but in human nature. His advice is to remember that England is tired after the war. "But the old girl's got stamina, and don't you make any mistake about it, and it's up to us ordinary people to keep things steady." He sends the boy up to bed, telling him not to forget to say goodnight to his mother.

ACT II, Scene 1: Another five and a half years have passed, and Frank is beginning to age. He sits chatting to Edie as she clears the breakfast table. In the background the family are heard scurrying about: it is the morning of Reg's wedding to Phyllis, and the house is in turmoil.

Bob Mitchell comes in for a chat, during which we learn that his wife is now an invalid and that Sam has given up his "Bombshell Bookshop", married Vi and settled down. Later Frank has an intimate talk with his son, advising him to remember that women are sensitive, and to keep his "bits of fun" tactfully hidden, so that Phyllis is not hurt by them – anything liable to break up his home is just not worthwhile.

Frank goes upstairs just as Billy Mitchell – now a petty officer – arrives. Coming down in her bridesmaid's dress, Queenie is slightly embarrassed to see Billy, whose offer of marriage she has just turned down. After his seven years' courtship he is rather bitter about this, and eventually makes her admit that she is in love with a married man whom she met while working as a manicurist. He warns her that she is laying up trouble for herself and everyone else; then he goes up to join Reg. Ethel and Frank come down in their wedding finery, and Queenie – on edge after her scene with Billy – tells them she is sick of their petty suburban life and wants to get away from it all. Her father tells her sharply that "there are worse things than being ordinary and respectable", and that while she stops at home he expects her to behave herself. She runs upstairs in a temper.

The wedding car drives up and Reg, palpably nervous, starts for the church with his best man, Billy. Waiting for the car to return, the others are joined by Sylvia and Mrs Flint who, as usual, are sparring with each other. Then Sam comes in with Vi in a pink dress that she has made herself. The family compliment her on it, but Queenie says it is "awful".

Ethel begins to worry that the car will be late, and Sylvia, nagged by Mrs Flint, makes a scene and bursts into tears; but when the car does come they all troop out, their grievances forgotten.

Scene 2: It is about midnight, a month after the wedding. Queenie creeps downstairs, carrying a suitcase, puts a letter on the mantelpiece, and stealthily lets herself out.

Frank and Bob Mitchell have been to an "Old Comrades" dinner, and they come back together slightly drunk, deciding to have a final nightcap before going to bed. They discuss their children and Frank admits he is worried about Queenie and he wishes she could settle down and marry Billy. Then they talk about the war, wondering when the next one will be, and what troubles the "old men at the top" are storing up for the nation.

One final drink gets them into mischief – they drop the bottle with a crash and wake Ethel, who is indignant at having her dining-room turned into a "bar-parlour". Bob leaves hurriedly, and Ethel is on the point of sending her husband upstairs in disgrace when she catches sight of Queenie's letter. It says that she has eloped with a married man. Frank's first impulse is to trace the man and bring her back but Ethel is adamant. Queenie has disgraced them, she declares; she will never forgive her or take her back again.

Scene 3: It is a fine afternoon in May 1932. Mrs Flint is sitting in her chair by the hearth and Sylvia is doing a crossword puzzle. Now she has taken up with Christian Science, she has a steady job at the library and is no longer preoccupied with her ailments; but her affected ways still irritate the family.

Coming in from the garden, Fred is upset to see a bunch of may on the mantel piece. He takes it out with him, reminding Sylvia sharply that it is unlucky. Mrs Flint comments that he has been a changed man since Queenie left, and this leads Sylvia to remark that she has noticed a letter from the girl to her father with a French stamp. They are discussing it when Ethel comes down and reprimands them, saying that she will not have Queenie's name mentioned.

Over tea she apologises for her outburst, saying she has been upset by a bad dream. She takes a cup of tea to Fred in the garden.

Suddenly Vi appears, pale and trembling, with the news that Reg and Phyllis have been killed in a motor accident. While she goes to tell her parents, Sylvia, crying, helps Mrs Flint upstairs. Then Fred and Ethel come in alone and sit quietly, hand in hand.

ACT III, Scene 1: It is the night of the Abdication – 10 December 1936. King Edward's speech has just ended and the family are gathered unhappily round the radio. Sam and Vi, who have come in to hear the news, take their leave after an argument with Sylvia about Christian Science. Later, Fred and Ethel talk about Queenie, who is still unforgiven by her mother.

They are surprised to see Billy Mitchell, now promoted to warrant officer, who brings them news of their daughter. She was abandoned in Brussels by her lover, he tells them, and has since been keeping herself in various jobs. At the time when he met her, she was helping to run an English tea-room in Mentone. "Is she there now?" asks Ethel. "No," replies Billy. "She's here – next door with Dad." And he adds that he married her a few days previously in Plymouth.

Frank rushes out and soon returns with Queenie. After the years of estrangement, her mother welcomes her with an embrace.

Scene 2: On the evening of 30 September 1938, Vi and Sylvia are discussing the Munich Agreement. Mr Chamberlain must be a Christian Scientist at heart, thinks Sylvia. "Well, let's hope that Hitler and Mussolini are too," is Vi's retort.

By this time old Mrs Flint has, in Sylvia's jargon, "passed on", and Mrs Mitchell has, according to Ethel, "been taken". Frank insists with some heat that both of them have died. He is out of temper, having just come in from streets where the cheering crowds are "yelling themselves hoarse without the faintest idea what they're yelling about"; and he expresses the hope that the country will never again be in the position of having to appease anybody. Calling him a war-monger, Sylvia runs out in tears.

Frank and his wife talk about Queenie's baby son, who will be left in their care when she goes to join her husband at Singapore. Soon afterwards Bob Mitchell, who is leaving his house next day, comes in for a "farewell binge".

They talk over all that has happened during the years that they have been neighbours, and Frank, who is himself contemplating a move, wonders what happens to houses that have been inhabited for a long time – whether the new people will "feel any bits of us left about the place". With mutual promises to visit one another, they once more drink the toast, "Happy days!"

Scene 3: It is June 1939, just 20 years since the Gibbons took their house. They are moving out and most of the furniture has already gone. Vi, who has been looking after Queenie's baby, wheels him in and says good night.

After the tiring day, Ethel is depressed and peevish, but Frank comforts her by talking about their fine new flat, and assures her that he doesn't mind where they go or what they do, so long as he has got her.

While Ethel is making the supper, Frank rocks the pram of his grandson and namesake, and sums up for his benefit his own philosophy of life: "You've got to have trouble of some kind or another, whoever you are. But if you don't let it get you down, however bad it is, you won't go far wrong." Little Frank, he says, is part of something that no one can break, though many are trying to do it – jealous foreigners and British pacifists alike. The trouble with the world is that there are too many ideals and too little horse sense. For human beings do not really like universal peace and goodwill: they like eating and drinking, loving and hating, "fighting for their rights and bossing everybody who will give 'em half a chance". England has been the boss for years because she has behaved decently and treated people right. Lately she has been let down by her politicians, but the people themselves know what they belong to, where they come from, and where they are going. For hundreds of years they have struggled to get decency and justice and freedom, and they will fight 50 wars if need be to keep them. Ethel finds him talking and fetches him in to supper.

W. A. Darlington in the *Daily Telegraph*, 1 May 1943:

"*This Happy Breed*, the second of Noël Coward's two plays now running in alternation at the Haymarket, is as different as possible from its satirical and uproarious companion. It is Mr Coward's tribute to John Citizen, the ordinary Englishman.

"In shape it is the simple chronicle of what happened to the Gibbons family in the years 1919-39, when they lived at No. 17, Sycamore Road, Clapham Common.

"Although the son of the house is killed in a motor accident and one of the daughters runs away with a married man, the actual story is unsensational. The manner of its telling, also, is gentle.

"Flashes of wit and happy turns of phrase are not absent, but the author is here using them only incidentally.

"Not a typical Coward play, you perceive. Yet it represents a most important development in the author's quality and power.

"Here, for the first time in his brilliant career, we have him writing with sympathy, understanding and admiration of the common man. And as the play was written in May 1938, Mr Coward owes this quickening and deepening of the imagination, not to the war, but to his own spiritual growth.

"The same company appears in this play as in the other, and it is fascinating to watch how the players tackle their widely contrasted parts.

"Judy Campbell, destroying every trace of glamour, does an extraordinarily honest piece of acting as the harassed mother of a family. Joyce Carey loses her poise and becomes a fussy, disgruntled old maid. James Donald, fresh from his triumph as a self-centred young highbrow, becomes a steady and solid sailor.

"As for Mr Coward himself, he has never acted better than in this part, as the ex-soldier who is so sound of heart and so quietly proud of his English heritage."

PUBLICATIONS

This Happy Breed was first published by Heinemann (London, 1943). It is dedicated to Hugh Beaumont. Also published in *Noël Coward Collected Plays: Four* by Methuen World Classics (London, 1999).

❖

NOTES

For the writing and production of this play, see Notes section of *Present Laughter*, page 345.

Coward says in his introduction to *Play Parade, Volume IV*:

"*This Happy Breed* is a suburban middle-class family comedy covering the period between the Armistice in 1918 to the humiliating year of 1938, when the late Neville Chamberlain spent so much time in the air. Many of the critics detected in this play an attitude on my part of amused patronage and condescension toward the habits and manners of suburban London. They implied that in setting the play in a milieu so far removed from the cocktail and caviare stratum where I so obviously belonged, I was over-reaching myself and writing about people far removed from my superficial comprehension. In this, as usual, they were quite wrong. Having been born in Teddington and having lived respectively at Sutton, Battersea Park and Clapham Common during all my formative years, I can confidently assert that I know a great deal more about the hearts and minds of ordinary south Londoners than they gave me credit for. My metamorphosis into a 'Mayfair playboy' many years later was entirely a journalistic conception. Since I achieved my first real theatrical success with *The Vortex* in 1924, I have moved observantly and eagerly through many different cliques and classes of society. Being a natural writer with a constant eye on human behaviour, I have also moved, without undue imaginative strain, through Regency and Victorian society as well. I have also a sound working knowledge of the navy, the army and the air force. To ascribe preconceived social limitations to a creative writer is a common error of the critical mind; it is also a critical revelation of the common mind.

"I wrote *This Happy Breed* in the spring of 1939. My personal criticism of it as a play is that the character of Frank Gibbons is a fraction more than life-size. His views are too clearly expressed to be quite true to life. I have no doubt whatever that he would hold such views, but, to my mind, his articulateness throughout the play concedes too much to theatrical effectiveness. Had he been a character in a novel, this error could have been eliminated; the author could have explained his feelings and reactions without imposing upon him the burden of speaking them aloud. However, *This Happy Breed* was a play written for the theatre and must stand or fall within the theatre's necessary limitations. The other characters are well drawn, and I am particularly attached to Aunt Sylvia and Granny. They were none of them written with the faintest patronage or condescension, but with sincerity, affection and the inherent understanding that is the result of personal experience."

Though there has been no West End revival since the Second World War, *This Happy Breed* toured extensively in 1980, with Richard Todd and Lana Morris, and has been frequently broadcast. Television productions include: 1969, BBC2, with Frank Finlay and Dandy Nichols.

On 5 May 1956, Coward directed a live television production of the play for CBS from New York (sponsored by the "Ford Star Jubilee").

CHARACTERS	CBS, 1956
MRS FLINT	Norah Howard
ETHEL	Edna Best
SYLVIA	Beulah Garrick
FRANK GIBBONS	Noël Coward
BOB MITCHELL	Guy S. Paull
REG	Robert Chapman
QUEENIE	Patricia Cutts
VI	Joyce Ash
SAM LEADBITTER	Rhoderick Walker
PHYLLIS BLAKE	Sally Pierce
EDIE	Vera Marshall
BILLY	Roger Moore

FILM VERSION

A film version of *This Happy Breed* was made in the UK in 1943 by Cineguild for Two Cities. It was directed by David Lean and produced by Coward, with Anthony Havelock-Allan.

CHARACTERS	Cineguild, 1943
MRS FLINT	Amy Veness
ETHEL	Celia Johnson
SYLVIA	Alison Leggatt

FRANK GIBBONS	Robert Newton
BOB MITCHELL	Stanley Holloway
REG	John Blythe
QUEENIE	Kay Walsh
VI	Eileen Erskine
SAM LEADBITTER	Guy Verney
PHYLLIS BLAKE	Betty Fleetwood
EDIE	Merle Tottenham
BILLY	John Mills

The film was first shown in London at the Gaumont, Haymarket, and at the Marble Arch Pavilion simultaneously, 29 May 1944.

34
BLITHE SPIRIT
AN IMPROBABLE FARCE IN THREE ACTS
Written in 1941

FIRST PRESENTED by H. M. Tennent Ltd. and John C. Wilson at the Opera House, Manchester, on 16 June 1941. (The following week the company played at Leeds.)

SUBSEQUENTLY PRESENTED at the Piccadilly Theatre, London, on 2 July 1941. Transferred to the St James's Theatre, 23 March 1942. Transferred to the Duchess Theatre, 6 October 1942 (1,997 performances).

CHARACTERS	**Manchester and Piccadilly, 1941**
EDITH (a maid)	Ruth Reeves
RUTH	Fay Compton
CHARLES	Cecil Parker
DR BRADMAN	Martin Lewis
MRS BRADMAN	Moya Nugent
MADAME ARCATI	Margaret Rutherford
ELVIRA	Kay Hammond
Director	*Noël Coward*
Designer	*G. E. Calthrop*

❖

SCENE: The action of the play passes in the living-room of Charles Condomine's house in Kent.

ACT I: Scene 1: Before dinner on a summer evening.
    Scene 2: After dinner.

ACT II: Scene 1: The next morning.
    Scene 2: Late the following afternoon.
    Scene 3: Early evening. A few days later.

ACT III: Scene 1: After dinner. A few days later.
    Scene 2: Several hours later.

At the St James's Theatre on 20 August 1942, Noël Coward took over the part of Charles for two weeks. Cecil Parker then returned to the cast.

In October 1942, Irene Browne took over the part of Ruth (from Fay Compton).

At the Duchess Theatre in December 1942, Agnes Lauchlan took over the part of Madame Arcati (from Margaret Rutherford). In January 1943, Ronald Squire played Charles for a few weeks. Cecil Parker then returned to the cast. In July 1943, Judy Campbell took over the part of Elvira (from Kay Hammond). In August 1943, Beryl Measor took over the part of Madame Arcati (from Agnes Lauchlan). Dennis Price played Charles for a time from August 1943, while Cecil Parker was on holiday. Joyce Carey and Nicholas Phipps, who had toured the parts in 1943 played them at the Duchess in November 1943, while Irene Browne and Cecil Parker had a holiday, at this time also Madame Arcati was played by Ella Miln. In December 1943, Betty Ann Davies replaced Judy Campbell for some six weeks. On 1 June 1944, Penelope Dudley Ward took over the part of Elvira (from Judy Campbell), Joyce Carey took over the part of Ruth (from Irene Browne), and Nicholas Phipps took over the part of Charles (from Cecil Parker). In April 1945, Irene Browne returned to the cast, this time to play Madame Arcati (succeeding Beryl Measor), and in September 1945, she was succeeded in the part by Joyce Barbour, who played till the end of the run in March 1946. In November 1945, Alan Webb succeeded Nicholas Phipps as Charles. Edith was later played by Julia Lang, who replaced Ruth Reeves during the run.

The remaining members of the cast, Moya Nugent and Martin Lewis, played for the entire run.

SYNOPSIS

ACT I, Scene 1: In the living-room of her pleasant house in Kent, Ruth Condomine is instructing her new maid, Edith, how to wait at table that evening. Her husband, the writer Charles Condomine, has planned a séance with the medium Madame Arcati, in order to get copy for his next book.

Before the guests arrive, Charles talks to Ruth about his dead wife, Elvira, whom he remembers as "fascinating and maddening". Ruth shows jealousy when he stresses Elvira's physical attractiveness. However, she is a sensible woman who has been married before, and she feels that she thoroughly understands her husband.

The first to arrive are Dr and Mrs Bradman, who mention that they have overtaken Madame Arcati on her bicycle. All are sceptical about the séance – particularly Charles, who as a boy used to make fun of an aunt addicted to spiritualism.

Madame Arcati is a striking, middle-aged woman, dressed in somewhat barbaric style. Her manner is hearty and she cheerfully drinks two dry martinis in succession while she talks about the biography she is writing of a certain Princess Palliatani, with whose spirit she claims to be in communication.

Edith announces dinner, and they all move into the dining-room.

Scene 2: Over coffee Madame Arcati tells her hostess and Mrs Bradman about her child "control", Daphne. Ruth gives her maid instructions that they are not to be disturbed. Then the two men join them and they settle down at a small, square table. Madame Arcati puts on the gramophone record "Always" and switches off the lights. She then sits down between Charles and Ruth, and the table begins to move. Talking (by means of raps) to Daphne, the medium announces that someone wishes to speak to Mr Condomine. "Tell them to leave a message," remarks Charles flippantly. His wife apologises for him, and they all make helpful suggestions as to the identity of the caller – which the table emphatically negatives.

The medium then goes into a trance: with a scream she falls to the floor, while the table becomes uncontrollable and overturns. The sitters are discussing whether to right it when a charming voice – heard only by Charles – says, "Leave it where it is." "Who are you?" asks Charles, and the voice replies: "Elvira, of course. Don't be silly." In great agitation, Charles turns up the lights, pretending that he had invented the voice as a joke. The doctor revives Madame Arcati, who goes off happily on her bicycle, after declaring that she feels a "presence" in the room. The Bradmans are preparing to follow, when Elvira comes through the closed French windows. She is charmingly dressed, but everything about her is grey – hair, skin, dress, hands: "so we must accept that she is not quite of this world". No one sees her.

When Charles returns after saying goodbye to the Bradmans, Ruth mixes him a drink. Suddenly he catches sight of Elvira and drops his glass, exclaiming: "My God!" His wife still sees nothing. She is not sure whether Charles is drunk, joking, or merely, as an author, inventing a situation to test her reactions.

Matters are made worse by Elvira's flippant interjections and Charles' attempts to shut her up, which Ruth takes as being addressed to herself. After he has called Elvira "a guttersnipe", Ruth goes upstairs in a temper, leaving the two of them alone.

The ghost is disappointed that she has not been more warmly welcomed. She says she didn't want to come, but that awful child, Daphne, "paged" her while she was playing backgammon with Genghis Khan – and she doesn't know how to go back. Soon she and Charles are sitting comfortably together on the sofa (though he is unable to touch her). "Poor Ruth," says Charles drowsily – to which Elvira replies, gently and sweetly: "To hell with Ruth!"

ACT II, Scene 1: At breakfast next morning Ruth is still annoyed with Charles, fully convinced that he had been very rude to her the previous evening while under the influence of drink. But when Elvira enters with a bunch of roses and he begins to talk to her, Ruth can stand it no longer and bursts into tears. She now thinks her husband is out of his mind and wants him to go to bed until Dr Bradman has seen him.

She starts to humour him: but when he asks Elvira to demonstrate her presence by carrying a bowl of flowers to the mantelpiece and back again she is furious – sure that this is a trick. Elvira's final gesture of smashing a vase into the grate, however, really frightens her, and she goes into violent hysterics.

Scene 2: Ruth has appealed to Madame Arcati, who comes over to tea and is told of the mysterious happenings. The medium is overjoyed at what she regards as a professional success. She produces a notebook to report the case to the Psychical Research Society. But when Ruth asks her to exorcise Elvira, she has to admit that she does not know how – the old "bell and book" methods that worked in the days of simple faith are now no longer effective. At this Ruth loses her temper and accuses the medium of amateur muddling, which sends her away in a huff.

Charles comes in with Elvira and a three-cornered conversation takes place, with Ruth addressing herself directly to the (to her) invisible and inaudible spirit, and Charles transmitting a polite paraphrase of Elvira's caustic rejoinders.

Elvira, though angry that they should have wanted to send her away, is gleeful when she learns that Madame Arcati cannot do it; but Ruth, with the threat to consult the Psychical Research Society and, if necessary, the Archbishop of Canterbury, sweeps out of the room. After gently scolding Elvira for upsetting her, Charles goes upstairs to calm her down; and the little ghost, left alone, puts the record "Always" on the gramophone and begins to dance.

Coming in to fetch the tea tray, Edith sees the gramophone apparently playing by itself, turns it off and puts the record away. Elvira takes it out and starts it again, and Edith with a shriek drops the tray and rushes out of the room, while Elvira continues to waltz gaily.

Scene 3: Mrs Bradman is sympathising with Ruth on the accidents that have happened recently in her house – Edith has fallen downstairs and sustained concussion, and Charles has hurt his arm through a ladder breaking. Dr Bradman, who has been examining him, comes down and reports that the arm is only strained; but the patient ought to go away for a holiday, as he is in a nervous condition and his conversation shows "marked irrelevancies". (Ruth, surmising that Elvira is the cause, hurriedly says that her husband often behaves strangely when he is writing a book.)

Charles then comes down with his arm in a sling. Unseen by the others, Elvira follows him. He proposes to drive into Folkestone and the doctor rather unwillingly gives him permission. The Bradmans leave and Elvira, after throwing a rose at Ruth, goes out into the garden.

Ruth talks seriously to her husband, saying she is sure that Elvira means to kill him, so that she can have him to herself on the astral plane: the maid's accident was due to grease on the stairs, and the ladder had been sawn almost through. The idea strikes Charles as absurd, but Ruth says she is going to drive over to Madame Arcati and beg for her help. She goes out on this errand soon after Elvira comes back.

The latter insists that Charles shall drive her to the cinema at Folkestone. He demurs that it is a wet evening and he wants a drink first. In any case, he says, there is no hurry – they must wait until Ruth brings the car back. At this Elvira becomes so frantic that Charles guesses she has tampered with the car. While he is trying to find out what she has done there is a telephone call – Ruth has crashed and been killed.

Suddenly the door bursts open. Elvira retreats before an invisible presence, shielding her head with her hands and crying, "Ow! Stop it, Ruth. Let go!" The door, which she has closed behind her, opens and shuts again while Charles looks on aghast.

ACT III, Scene 1: A few days later Madame Arcati has come to call on Charles after dinner. Her conscience is troubling her – she feels that if she had not walked out in a huff the tragedy might not have happened. By this time she has found a formula for dematerialising spirits, and she offers to use it.

At this moment Elvira comes into the room and is introduced by Charles (still the only person who can see her) to Madame Arcati, who gushes over her. After several days of Ruth's company, she is very much upset and wants to be sent back at once. She asks to speak to Charles alone, and the medium is sent into the other room while husband and ex-wife have a long and acrimonious discussion.

He says the whole situation is her fault: she declares that Ruth's influence was ruining his books. He points out that she herself never helped him with his writing at all – her only thought was to enjoy herself. "Why shouldn't I have fun?" retorts Elvira "I died young, didn't I?"

Charles says that she need not have died if she hadn't gone out on the river with Guy Henderson and got soaked to the skin. This leads to an exchange of accusations about various people of whom one or other of them was jealous. At last Elvira bursts into tears, declaring that she wants to go home.

Madame Arcati is brought back and proceeds to the exorcism – consisting of a rhyme accompanied by the sprinkling of salt and pepper. After talking to Daphne by means of table-rapping, the medium falls into a trance. Meanwhile Elvira, enjoying the spectacle hugely, remains unaffected. Suddenly the window curtains part and Ruth comes in, dressed as she was in the previous scene, but now, like Elvira, entirely in grey. She goes straight to her husband and demands: "Once and for all, Charles, what does this mean?"

Scene 2: Several hours have passed and it is nearly dawn. The room has been decked with crossed birch-boughs, and on the table are playing cards, a crystal and a ouija board. Madame Arcati is asleep on a sofa. Ruth and Elvira are talking to Charles. All are exhausted. The two spirit-wives find their situation intolerable and have only one desire – to get away. But one séance after another has failed to shift them. They tell Charles to wake the medium and try again.

Refreshed by her sleep, Madame Arcati is full of energy and schoolgirl jollity: she attacks the sandwiches with appetite. It is clear to her that someone in the house must have summoned Elvira in the first place, but she is at last obliged to accept Charles' assurance that it was not he. He cannot think of anyone else, except the Bradmans, who were in the house during the first séance.

Gazing into her crystal, Madame Arcati sees "a white bandage". She utters an invocation which brings down the maid, Edith, her head still bandaged after her accident. Though the girl denies that she can see the ghosts, it is obvious that she is lying, as she follows them with her eyes. Madame Arcati realises that Edith is the medium through whom they have materialised. She sends her into a trance and turns off the lights. For a while Elvira and Ruth are heard talking, but gradually their voices fade into silence. When Charles opens the curtains, letting in the morning sunlight, they have disappeared.

Madame Arcati then rouses Edith, who awakes completely bewildered at finding herself downstairs, and she is sent back to bed with a £1 tip from Charles.

After advising him to go away for a voyage, Madame Arcati collects her paraphernalia and leaves. Charles then addresses his invisible wives, telling them that he is going away to get out of their reach, and adding some home truths about both of them. Their reaction to this is an outbreak of poltergeist activity – vases and pictures are hurled about, a sofa cushion is thrown at Charles, and the gramophone starts playing "Always". He goes out of the room just as the overmantel crashes to the floor and the curtain pole comes tumbling down.

Philip Page in the *Daily Mail*, 3 July 1941:

"Probably sincere spiritualists will be annoyed, or even exasperated, by Noël Coward's *Blithe Spirit* at the Piccadilly Theatre. And any man whose first wife is dead and whose companion in the stalls, or elsewhere, is his second wife, will be embarrassed to the point of a hasty departure.

"None the less, this is riotously witty stuff. Not having occasion for either annoyance or embarrassment, I laughed and laughed and laughed at an impudent yarn about a writer whose first wife was conjured from the grave to squabble cattily with her successor, and at the humour of Miss Margaret Rutherford's platitudinous hocus-pocus.

"If there are suggestions of bad taste, they are swamped by the delicious fun of it all, by the immaculate production, and by the fine performances of Mr Cecil Parker, Miss Fay Compton, and Miss Kay Hammond, with her pouting drawl even in the eerie guise of a visitor from the other side.

"Some opposition which greeted the author's speech seemed to be purely personal. Of future performances of this fantastic fun, it will, I think, be safe to say:

> Hail to thee, Blithe Spirit,
> Bird thou'll never get."

❖

PUBLICATIONS

The play was first published in America by Doubleday, Doran (New York, 1941) and in the UK by Heinemann (London, 1942). It is dedicated to Joyce Carey. Also published in *Noël Coward Collected Plays: Four* by Methuen World Classics (London, 1999).

❖

NOTES

On the outbreak of war Coward commenced his war work, which took him to Paris from September 1939 to April 1940. From France he went to America until June, when he returned to London via Lisbon. He left again for New York in July and remained in America until October. During this period he wrote a play called *Time Remembered*, which has not been produced. He then went to Australia and New Zealand, where he worked until March 1941, returning to London via New York. He says in *Future Indefinite*:

"On Friday, May the 2nd, Joyce Carey and I caught a morning train from Paddington, bound for Port Meirion in North Wales. For some time past an idea for a light comedy had been rattling at the door of my mind, and I thought the time had come to let it in and show it a little courtesy. Joyce was engaged in writing a play about Keats, so here we were, 'Hurrah for the holidays', without buckets and spades, but with typewriters, paper, carbons, bathing-suits, sun-tan oil and bezique cards. We arrived on a golden evening, sighed with pleasure at the mountains and the sea in the late sunlight, and settled ourselves into a pink guest-house. The next morning we sat on the beach with our backs against the sea-wall and discussed my idea exclusively for several hours. Keats, I regret to say, was not referred to. By lunch-time the title had emerged together with the names of the characters, and a rough – very rough – outline of the plot. At 7.30 the next morning I sat, with the usual nervous palpitations, at my typewriter. Joyce was upstairs in her room wrestling with Fanny Brawne. There was a pile of virgin paper on my left and a box of carbons on my right. The table wobbled and I had to put a wedge under one of its legs. I smoked several cigarettes in rapid succession, staring gloomily out of the window at the tide running out. I fixed the paper into the machine and started: *Blithe Spirit. A Light Comedy in Three Acts.*

"For six days I worked from eight to one each morning and from two to seven each afternoon. On Friday evening, May the 9th, the play was finished and, disdaining archness and false modesty, I will admit that I knew it was witty, I knew it was well constructed, and I also knew that it would be a success. My gift for comedy dialogue, which I feared might have atrophied from disuse, had obviously profited from its period of inactivity. Beyond a few typographical errors, I made no corrections, and only two lines of the original script were ultimately cut. I take pride in these assertions, but it is a detached pride, natural enough in the circumstances and not to be confused with boastfulness. I was not attempting to break any records, to prove how quickly I could write and how clever I was. I was fully prepared to revise and re-write the whole play had I thought it necessary, but I did not think it necessary. I knew from the first morning's work that I was on the right track and that it would be difficult, with that situation and those characters, to go far wrong. I can see no particular virtue in writing quickly; on the contrary, I am well aware that too great a facility is often dangerous, and should be curbed when it shows signs of getting the bit too freely between its teeth. No reputable writer should permit his talent to bolt with him. I am also aware though, from past experience, that when the right note is struck and the structure of a play is carefully built in advance, it is both wise and profitable to start at the beginning and write through to the end in as short a time as possible."

The play was immediately put into rehearsal and produced. Its run of 1,997 performances was the record for a straight play until it was overtaken by *The Mousetrap*. A touring company went out with the play in February 1942. The cast included Ronald Squire (Charles) Irene Browne (Ruth), Ursula Jeans (Elvira), and Agnes Lauchlan (Madame Arcati). Another tour went out in 1943.

The play was also toured with *Present Laughter* and *This Happy Breed*, as *Play Parade*, from September 1942 for 25 weeks. Noël Coward played Charles; Joyce Carey, Ruth; Judy Campbell, Elvira; and Beryl Measor, Madame Arcati. Most of these principals eventually and at various times appeared in the London production.

From February 1944, an E.N.S.A. company toured the Middle East and the continent with *Blithe Spirit*. Emlyn Williams played Charles; Jessie Evans (and Elliot Mason), Madame Arcati; Adrianne Allen, Ruth; and Leueen MacGrath, Elvira.

From October 1945 to February 1946, another E.N.S.A. company played *Blithe Spirit* and *Hamlet* in India and Burma for the Forces. John Gielgud played Charles; Irene Browne, Madame Arcati; Marian Spencer, Ruth; and Hazel Terry, Elvira.

In the revue *Sigh No More*, Coward included a ballet version of *Blithe Spirit*.

Since 1946 major UK stage revivals of *Blithe Spirit* have included: 23 July 1970, Globe, with Patrick Cargill, Phyllis Calvert and Beryl Reid; 24 June 1976, National Theatre, with Richard Johnson, Maria Aitken and Elizabeth Spriggs, directed by Harold Pinter; 30 January 1986, Vaudeville, with Simon Cadell, Joanna Lumley and Jane Asher; 12 June 1989, Lyric Hammersmith, with Neil Stacy, Peggy Mount and Rula Lenska; 11 June 1997, Chichester Festival, with Belinda Lang, Twiggy, Dora Bryan and Neil Stacy, directed by Tim Luscombe. Extracts from *Blithe Spirit* are also included in *Noël and Gertie* (1989).

UK television productions include:

1948: BBC, with Ronald Squire, Beryl Measor and Marian Spencer.

1964: Granada, with Griffith Jones, Hattie Jacques and Helen Cherry.

US PRODUCTIONS

PRESENTED by John C. Wilson at the Morosco Theatre, New York on 4 November 1941 (657 performances).

CHARACTERS	Morosco, 1941
EDITH (a maid)	Doreen Long
RUTH	Peggy Wood
CHARLES	Clifton Webb
DR BRADMAN	Philip Tonge
MRS BRADMAN	Valerie Cossart
MADAME ARCATI	Mildred Natwick
ELVIRA	Leonora Corbett
Director	*John C. Wilson*

The *New York Post*: "Deliberately impudent. One of his most ingenious plots."

The *New York Journal American*: "Hilariously funny, brilliantly clever and about as cockeyed as a play can be and still stay on the stage."

The play won that year's award for Best Play from the Drama Critics' Circle.

ALSO PRODUCED by Karl Allison, Douglas Urbanski and Sandra Moss in association with Jerome Minskoff and Duncan C. Weldon. Presented at the Neil Simon Theatre, New York on 31 March 1987 (103 performances).

CHARACTERS	**Neil Simon, 1987**
EDITH (a maid)	Norah Cavendish
RUTH	Judith Ivey
CHARLES	Richard Chamberlain
DR BRADMAN	William LeMessena
MRS BRADMAN	Patricia Connolly
MADAME ARCATI	Geraldine Page
ELVIRA	Blythe Danner
Director	*Brian Murray*

The *New York Daily News*: "Though full of fizz, (the production) has been mounted cold by people who think you have to shake the bottle. There are laughs, but it's Cold Duck, not Mumms."

The *New York Times*: "Four first-rate actors, all except Blythe Danner miscast, none in top form, struggle for three acts to find the light touch that might make this lark, written in less than a week in 1941, take flight."

Newsweek: "Coward's beautiful bitcheries are enough in evidence to remind us that he was the precursor of playwrights like Harold Pinter and Joe Orton."

In 1964 there was a musical version of *Blithe Spirit* with music and lyrics by Hugh Martin and Timothy Gray. Originally called *Faster than Sound*, when it opened at the Shubert Theatre, New Haven on 1 February, it was retitled *High Spirits* (*An Improbable Musical*). Directed by Coward – and later by Gower Champion – it moved to the Alvin Theatre, New York on 4 April 1964 where it ran for 375 performances, starring Beatrice Lillie (Madame Arcati), Tammy Grimes (Elvira), Louise Troy (Ruth) and Edward Woodward (Charles). The British version, starring Cicely Courtneidge, Dennis Quilley and Marti Stevens ran at the Savoy Theatre from 3 November 1964 (94 performances).

NOTE: While there were no Coward songs in the show during either the Broadway or London runs, there is archival evidence that he did write lyrical variants on the show's hit song – "Home Sweet Heaven" – some of which appeared in his own recording of it. He also wrote one complete song – "Something Has Happened To Charles" – which was tried out for one performance in New Haven, then dropped as being "too English".

In 1982 *Blithe Spirit* was revived at Stratford, Ontario, with Brian Bedford, Carole Shelley and Tammy Grimes.

US television productions include:

1946:   NBC, with Philip Tonge, Estelle Winwood and Leonore Corbett.

On 14 January 1956, Coward also directed a live colour television production of the play for CBS from Hollywood, USA (sponsored by the "Ford Star Jubilee").

CHARACTERS	CBS, 1956
EDITH (a maid)	Marion Ross
RUTH	Claudette Colbert
CHARLES	Noël Coward
MADAME ARCATI	Mildred Natwick
MRS BRADMAN	Brenda Forbes
DR BRADMAN	Philip Tonge
ELVIRA	Lauren Bacall

US radio productions include:

1944:   NBC, with Ronald Colman, Loretta Young and Edna Best.

1947:   ABC, with Clifton Webb, Leonora Corbett and Mildred Natwick.

1952:   NBC, with John Loder and Mildred Natwick.

1956:   NBC, with Noël Coward and Margaret Leighton in scenes from *Blithe Spirit*, *Brief Encounter* and *Present Laughter*.

FILM VERSION

A film version of *Blithe Spirit* was made in the UK by Cineguild for Two Cities in 1944–5. It was directed by David Lean. Incidental music was composed by Richard Addinsell.

CHARACTERS	Cineguild, 1945
EDITH (a maid)	Jacqueline Clark
RUTH	Constance Cummings
CHARLES	Rex Harrison
DR BRADMAN	Hugh Wakefield
MRS BRADMAN	Joyce Carey
MADAME ARCATI	Margaret Rutherford
ELVIRA	Kay Hammond

The film was shown in London at the Odeon, Leicester Square, April 1945.

35
SIGH NO MORE
REVUE
Written in 1945

FIRST PRESENTED by John C. Wilson and H. M. Tennent Ltd. at the Opera House, Manchester, 11 July 1945 (to 4 August). The company played the following week at Liverpool.

SUBSEQUENTLY PRESENTED at the Piccadilly Theatre, London, 22 August 1945 (213 performances).

Written, composed and directed by Noël Coward. Décor by G. E. Calthrop. Choreography by George Carden, Sheila Nicholson, and Wendy Toye. Orchestra under the direction of Mantovani.

PART I

1. Sigh No More

HARLEQUIN	Graham Payn
SINGING SYLPHIDES	Renee Stocker, Ann Martin, Daphne Anderson, Ann Sullivan, Joy O'Neill, Irlin Hall, Marion Gordon, Gretta Grayson, Mavis Ray, Nancy McNaught, Barbara Jdanova, Silvia Ashmole, Enid Meredith, Barbara Barrie, Vivien Merchant, Betty Matthews, Sheila Calder, Jean Allison, Zoe Jack

2. Du Maurier

SOCIETY LADY	Joyce Grenfell
Music	*Richard Addinsell*
Lyrics	*Joyce Grenfell*

3. Parting Of The Ways

LEONORA	Madge Elliott
MICHAEL	Cyril Ritchard

4. Language – French – Troops, For The Use Of

Cliff Gordon

5. Mother And Daughter

THE MOTHER   Gwen Bateman
THE DAUGHTER   Joy O'Neill

6. Indian Army Officer

Cyril Ritchard

Song, "I Wonder What Happened To Him"

7. Music Hath Charms

MISS LAWSON   Madge Elliott
MISS FREEMAN   Ann Martin
MR ELPHINSTONE   Alan Clive
TWO GIRLS   Daphne Anderson, Irlin Hall
A BOY   Grant Tyler
A GIRL   Gail Kendal

Music and lyrics   *Norman Hackforth*

8. Never Again

THE SINGER   Graham Payn
EXTRAS   Zoe Jack, Mavis Ray, Barbara Jdanova,
        Silvia Ashmole, Barbara Barrie

9. This Is The End Of The News

Joyce Grenfell

10. Loch Lomond

Gail Kendal

Arrangement   *Norman Hackforth*

11. Pageant

COUNTESS OF FAIRFIELD Madge Elliott
HERALD   Gail Kendal
HOUSEMAIDS   Daphne Anderson, Betty Matthews
VIKING   Lance Hamilton
SPIRIT OF MASQUE   Cyril Ritchard
LADY MAUD HAILSBURY Ann Martin
MISTRESS JOAN   Joy O'Neill
MISTRESS ALICE   Renee Stocker

SIR GUY DE BELCHAMP	John Hugo
VILLAGE GIRLS	Zoe Jack, Mavis Ray, Irlin Hall, Vivien Merchant, Jean Allison, Sheila Calder
CARDINAL WOLSEY	Alan Clive
QUEEN ELIZABETH	Josephine Wray
LORD BELCHAMP	Howard Gilbert
CHARLES II'S PAGES	Silvia Ashmole, Gretta Grayson
LADY PRIMROSE FAIRFIELD	Joyce Grenfell
NURSE (to Lady Primrose)	Fedora Bernard
CHARLES II	Graham Payn
NELSON	Cliff Gordon
LORD FAIRFIELD	Frank O'Connor
LADY FAIRFIELD	Daphne Anderson
LADY HAMILTON	Marion Gordon
TOWN CRIER	Alan Clive
NELSONIAN VILLAGERS	Silvia Ashmole, Gretta Grayson, Barbara Jdanova, Gwen Bateman, Joy O'Neill, Ann Sullivan, Betty Matthews, Enid Meredith, Renee Stocker
NELSONIAN SAILORS	Charles Russell, Grant Tyler, Leslie Baker, Howard Gilbert
BRITANNIA	Madge Elliott
NEPTUNE	Tom Linden

PART II

12. Mantovani And His Orchestra

13. Willy

WILLY	Tom Linden
GOOD ANGEL	Madge Elliot
BAD ANGEL	Cyril Ritchard

14. Wait A Bit, Joe

Graham Payn

15. Travelling Broadens The Mind

Joyce Grenfell

16. Nina

GIGOLO	Tom Linden

NINA	Gail Kendal
SINGER	Cyril Ritchard
Choreography	*Wendy Toye*

17. The Merry Wives Of Windsor

MRS MACADOO	Madge Elliott
LADIES	Marion Gordon, Renee Stocker, Ann Martin, Irlin Hall, Daphne Anderson
PRIVATE NIVEN	Cyril Ritchard

18. Matelot

Graham Payn

19. Blithe Spirit Ballet

CHARLES	Tom Linden
MADAME ARCATI	Daphne Anderson
EDITH	Betty Matthews
RUTHS	Barbara Barrie, Enid Meredith, Irlin Hall, Mavis Ray, Sheila Calder, Jean Allison
ELVIRAS	Nancy McNaught, Barbara Jdanova, Zoe Jack, Silvia Ashmole, Gretta Grayson, Vivien Merchant
Choreography	*Wendy Toye*

The music to the ballet was composed by Richard Addinsell, adapted from Noël Coward's film, *Blithe Spirit.*

20. The Burchells Of Battersea Rise

Cyril Ritchard, Madge Elliott, Joyce Grenfell, Graham Payn

21. Finale. Sigh No More

Entire Company

At Manchester a sketch 'Japanese Spies' (Madge Elliott and Cyril Ritchard) was included. This was omitted in London. There were rearrangements in the running order in London, some minor changes of cast, and two non-Coward items played at Manchester were cut and replaced by 'Wait A Bit, Joe' and 'The Merry Wives Of Windsor'.

Noël Coward himself appeared in this revue on the evenings of 5 and 6 September 1945, in place of Cyril Ritchard, who had laryngitis (the understudy played the matinée of 5 September).

The song "Never Again" was first used in *Set to Music* in New York in 1939.

The Times, 23 August 1945:

"A light, easy, amusing entertainment, disconcertingly without the impress of a definite style – disconcertingly, because it has been 'written, composed, and directed' by Mr Noël Coward.

"Mr Coward's touch throughout is of the lightest. In one or two songs it is instantly recognisable and the stage is suddenly alive with acid wit. The Argentine lady who is bored with dancing the famous Argentine dance and curses the memory of the man who taught her the thing lodges herself affectionately in the memory, as does the Indian Army officer who, oblivious to the 'shrieking desolation' of the Indian scene, is insatiably curious to hear what has happened to this fellow and that who did this or that here or there. But the revue chiefly takes its colour and its character from Mr Cyril Ritchard, Miss Madge Elliott, and, above all, Miss Joyce Grenfell.

"Mr Ritchard is as lightly various as ever, putting across the best of Mr Coward's songs with that stare of glittering gaiety which is all his own. Miss Madge Elliott is usually his partner, sometimes in the glamorously Merry Widow vein, sometimes the languishingly loquacious lady president of the local pageant and then toothlessly plaintive as one of the Burchells of Battersea Rise resentful of that author who referred to them Shakespearianly as "this happy breed". Miss Grenfell is in her best form, doing quite perfectly the kind of thing she has often done before, but securing for it once again that effect of surprise which perfection never loses. She is the insanely cheerful schoolgirl greeting every fresh family misfortune with an ecstatic grin, for is she not the sworn foe of alarm and despondency? And in 'Travelling Broadens The Mind' she proves once again that a ninny may circle the globe and be a ninny still, and incidentally succeeds in establishing a character which few of us have had the good fortune not to meet. Practically the whole company is enrolled in the local pageant; and as laughter rolls cumulatively through the house who cares that it is the easiest of all easy targets?"

PUBLICATIONS

The book of *Sigh No More* is unpublished. The sketch "Pageant" is published in *Collected Revue Sketches and Parodies* (Methuen, 1999).

The following revue items are included in *The Noël Coward Song Book* (Michael Joseph, 1953):

"I Wonder What Happened To Him"
"Matelot"
"Never Again" (from *Set to Music*, New York, 1939)
"Nina"
"Sigh No More"
"That Is The End Of The News" (first and only publication)

NOTES

After writing *Blithe Spirit*, Coward started work on his first film script, *In Which We Serve*, in which he appeared as well as directed. Work commenced on the film in February 1942. This was followed by his tour of *Play Parade* and his London appearance in *Present Laughter* and *This Happy Breed*. After the season finished (in July 1943), Coward began a series of visits to entertain the troops in Gibraltar and the Middle East, which occupied him until October 1943. In December he set off again on his travels, once more going to America, thence to Jamaica and to South Africa, where he arrived in February for a three months' stay. A visit to Ceylon, India and Burma followed.

On his return to London he adapted *Still Life* (*Tonight at 8.30*) into the film, *Brief Encounter*. Other E.N.S.A. conceits followed in Paris and London. In the New Year of 1945 he produced a new revue, *Sigh No More*. The title, he says, "turned out to be the best part".

While working on the film *In Which We Serve*, Coward proposed the toast of Esmond Knight at the close of the Esmond Knight Matinée, given under the auspices of the Green Room Club in association with St Dunstan's, at the London Palladium on 18 January 1942. Coward was also the President and Chairman of the Matinée, which was occasioned by Esmond Knight's partial loss of eyesight in the action between H.M.S. *Prince of Wales* and H.M.S. *Hood* and the *Bismarck* during hostilities. At the end of the performance Coward said:

"Dear Esmond Knight, on behalf of all the members of your profession in England in wartime I am about to propose a toast to you. You must forgive us for making such a fuss and try not to be too embarrassed. You as an actor know well how all actors love to show off, and that is why we are here today. To show off by proving definitely that we know you, and by strutting for a little in your reflected glory.

"God bless you for the incalculable sacrifice you have made for your country and for all of us. Thank you now and for ever for the pride you have given us in the honour and dignity of our profession.

"We know that in the years ahead your courage will not fail, but we do so very much want you to know that our proud affection for you will never fail either.

"Ladies and Gentlemen, I give you – Sub-Lieutenant Esmond Knight, R.N.V.R."

36
PACIFIC 1860
A MUSICAL ROMANCE
Written in 1946

FIRST PRESENTED by Prince Littler on behalf of the Board of the Theatre Royal, Drury Lane, Ltd., at the Theatre Royal, Drury Lane, London, 19 December 1946 (129 performances).

CHARACTERS	Drury Lane, 1946
ELENA SALVADOR	Mary Martin
ROSA CARIATANZA (her duenna)	Sylvia Cecil
SOLANGE (her maid)	Maria Perilli
TRUDI (her cook)	Winefride Ingham
MRS STIRLING	Maidie Andrews
LOUISE (her daughter)	Ann Martin
CAROLINE (her daughter)	Irlin Hall
HENRIETTA (her daughter)	Peggy Thompson
AGNES (her daughter)	Joy O'Neill
SARAH (her daughter)	Daphne Peretz
GEORGINA (her daughter)	Ann Sullivan
MRS CAWTHORNE	Rose Hignell
PENELOPE (her daughter)	Daphne Anderson
MRS PELHAM	Gwen Bateman
MELITA (her daughter)	Celia Lamb
LADY GRAYSHOTT	Helen Horsey
MISS SCOBIE	Moya Nugent
MISS TERESA SCOBIE	Betty Hare
PRIMROSE LARCH	Jacqueline Jones

Act I, Prologue. A Row of Hansom Cabs

Act I, Scene I. "Countess Mitzi" Liesl Haren (Fritzi Massary) and Company

Act I, Scene 4. Liesl Haren (Fritzi Massary) and Nigel Vaynham (Griffith Jones), centre;
Rozanne Gray (Peggy Wood), extreme left

Act I, Scene 5. "The Stately Homes Of England" Lord Camp (Kenneth Carten), Lord Borrowmere
(Ross Landon), Lord Sickert (John Gatrell) and Lord Elderley (Hugh French)

Act I, Scene 8. Rozanne Gray (Peggy Wood)
and Nigel Vaynham (Griffith Jones)

Act II, Scene 3. Rozanne Gray (Peggy Wood) and the Countess of Messiter (Irene Vanbrugh)

"Weary Of It All" Lord Bitchette (Ray Dennis), Marion Day (Beatrice Lillie), Henry Beardworth (Anthony Pélissier), Elmer von Robespierre (Robert Shackleton) and Daisy (Gladys Henson)

"Secret Service" The Countess (Beatrice Lillie) and First Officer (Richard Haydn)

"Marvellous Party" Beatrice Lillie

Act II, Scene 2. Garry Essendine (Noël Coward), Joanna Lyppiatt (Judy Campbell), Lady Saltburn (Gwen Floyd), Liz Essendine (Joyce Carey), Daphne Stillington (Jennifer Gray), Roland Maule (James Donald) and Monica Reed (Beryl Measor)

Act I. Garry Essendine (Noël Coward) and Roland Maule (James Donald)

Act III. Liz Essendine (Joyce Carey), Henry Lyppiatt (Gerald Case), Garry Essendine (Noël Coward), Joanna Lyppiatt (Judy Campbell) and Morris Dixon (Dennis Price)

Act I, Scene 1. Bob Mitchell (Gerald Case), Ethel (Judy Campbell) and Frank Gibbons (Noël Coward)

Act I, Scene 2. Reg (Billy Thatcher), Vi (Molly Johnson), Mrs Flint (Gwen Floyd, Ethel (Judy Campbell), Sam Leadbitter (Dennis Price), Phyllis Blake (Meg Titheradge), Edie (Beryl Measor), Queenie (Jennifer Gray), Frank Gibbons (Noël Coward) and Sylvia (Joyce Carey)

Act II, Scene 1. Frank Gibbons (Noël Coward) and Ethel (Judy Campbell)

Act III, Scene 3. Frank Gibbons (Noël Coward)

Act I, Scene 2. Charles (Cecil Parker), Ruth (Fay
Compton), Mrs Bradman (Moya Nugent),
Madame Arcati (Margaret Rutherford) and
Dr. Bradman (Martin Lewis)

Act III, Scene 1. Madame Arcati (Margaret
Rutherford), Elvira (Kay Hammond)
and Ruth (Fay Compton)

Act III, Scene 2. Charles (Cecil Parker), Madame Arcati (Margaret Rutherford), Edith (Ruth Reeves),
Ruth (Fay Compton) and Elvira (Kay Hammond)

"Sigh No More" Harlequin (Graham Payn)

"Matelot" Graham Payn

"Parting Of The Ways" Leonora (Madge Elliott) and Michael (Cyril Ritchard)

Act II, Scene 1. Elena Salvador (Mary Martin) and Kerry Stirling (Graham Payn), on staircase

Act II, Scene 3. The Harbour

Act III, Scene 1. Elena Salvador (Mary Martin) and Rosa Cariatanza (Sylvia Cecil)

Act III, Scene 2. The Garden of the Stirling Plantation

Act II, Scene 1. Archie Jenkins (John Molecey), Mr Grainger (Trevor Ward), Alfie Blake (Brian Carey), Janet Braid (Elspeth March), Mrs Grainger (Sybil Wise), Alma Boughton (Helen Horsey), Mr Lawrence (George Lane), Nora Shattock (Beatrice Varley), Fred Shattock (Bernard Lee) and Doris Shattock (Maureen Pryor)

Act II, Scene 2. George Bourne (Kenneth More), Fred Shattock (Bernard Lee), Lyia Vivian (Hazel Terry), Lily Blake (Dandy Nichols), German Soldier (Charles Russell), Gladys Mott (Daphne Maddox), Nora Shattock (Beatrice Varley), First SS Guard (Douglas Vine), Doris Shattock (Maureen Pryor), Albrecht Richter (Ralph Michael), Mrs Grainger (Sybil Wise), Mr Grainger (Trevor Ward), Second SS Guard (Peter Drury), Mrs Massiter (Janet Barrow). (Photo taken during preliminary week at Brighton)

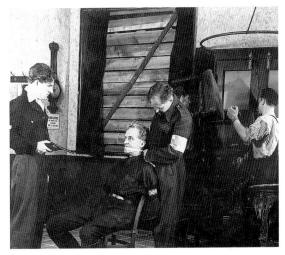

Act II, Scene 4. George Bourne (Kenneth More), Albrecht Richter (Ralph Michael), Dr. Venning (Michael Kent), Ben Capper (Manfred Priestly) and Stevie (Alan Badel)

Act I. The Hon. Maud Witterby (Edith Meiser), Lady Alexandra Shotter (Claudette Colbert) and the Earl of Sharpenhoe (Chester Stratton)

Act II, Scene 2. Lady Alexandra Shotter (Claudette Colbert) and Hali Alani (Leon Janney)

Act II, Scene 1. Sanyamo (William Peacock), Edward Honey (John Moore), Admiral Turling (Nicholas Grimshaw), Mrs Turling (Daphne Newton), Robert Frome (Eric Phillips), Sir George Shotter (Ian Hunter), Lady Alexandra Shotter (Vivien Leigh), Hali Alani (Ronald Lewis), Captain Christopher Mortlock (Peter Barkworth), Cuckoo Honey (Joyce Carey) and John Blair Kennedy (Arthur Macrae)

Act II, Scene 2. Hali Alani (Ronald Lewis) and Lady Alexandra Shotter (Vivien Leigh)

Act III. Robert Frome (Eric Phillips), Lady Alexandra Shotter (Vivien Leigh), Sir George Shotter (Ian Hunter) and John Blair Kennedy (Arthur Macrae)

Act I, Scene 1. The Club

Act I, Scene 3. Harry Hornby (Graham Payn),
Pinkie Leroy (Pat Kirkwood), Joseph Snyder
(Elwyn Brook-Jones), Clarice (Eileen Tatler)
and Benny Lucas (Raymond Young)

Act I, Scene 8. "Josephine"
Pinkie Leroy (Pat Kirkwood)

Act II, Scene 1. Felicity (Gladys Cooper), The Hon. Peter Ingleton (Simon Lack), Crestwell (Richard Leech), Lady Hayling (Dorothy Batley), Admiral Sir John Hayling (Charles Cullum), Mrs Moxton (Angela Baddeley), the Earl of Marshwood (Ralph Michael) and Miranda Frayle (Judy Campbell)

Act I, Scene 2. Mrs Moxton (Angela Baddeley) and Felicity (Gladys Cooper)

Act III. Crestwell (Richard Leech) and Mrs Moxton (Angela Baddley)

Act I, Scene 2. Serena (Lynn Fontanne), Lady
Harriet Ripley (Joyce Carey), Axel Diensen (Alfred
Lunt) and Catchpole (Gordon Phillott)

Act II, Scene 2. Hubert (Griffith Jones), Charlotte
(Marian Spencer), Axel Diensen (Alfred Lunt) and
Serena (Lynn Fontanne)

Act III, Scene 1. Lady Harriet Ripley
(Joyce Carey), Serena (Lynn Fontanne)
and Hubert (Griffith Jones)

Act II, Scene 2. Serena (Lynn Fontanne), Axel
Diensen (Alfred Lunt), Travellers (Derek Prouse
and Allegra Nicole), Gwendolyn (Pamela Grant)
and Courier (Timothy Forbes Adam)

SAMOLAN MAIDS (at the Stirling Plantation)

KARA	Carol Graye
MALIANE	Elizabeth Todd
TELEETE	Lucy Peters
LAIELA	Jacqueline Browning

KERRY STIRLING	Graham Payn
ROLLO (his elder brother)	Pat McGnath
MR STIRLING (his father)	Tudor Evans
FELIX KAMNER (Elena's manager)	Carl Jaffe
HIS EXCELLENCY	Cyril Butcher
SIR LEWIS GRAYSHOTT	
ADEN GRAYSHOTT (his son)	Denis Martin
D'ARCY GRAYSHOTT (his son)	John Warwick
CAPTAIN EDWARD HARMBY	Peter Evans
(Comptroller at Government House)	
LORD WILLIAM RAVENSCAR (A.D.C.)	Angus Menzies
JAMES CULEOSS (A.D.C.)	David Carey
THE HON. EVAN ST. MAWES (A.D.C.)	Peter Mosley
ROBIN PELHAM (Melita's brother)	Grant Tyler
CANON BANKS	Jack Martin
HUBERT CAWTHORNE	Harry Weste
(Penelope's father)	
MR MARRYOT	Emlyn Weeks
AYANO (Samolan butler at the Stirling Plantation)	Gustav Sacher

SAMOLAN HOUSE-BOYS

ELISHA	Howard Gilbert
SAUL	Ronald Evans
PAENO	Anthony Kay
NIAHU	Lionel Baker

GUESTS, MISSIONARIES, NATIVES, etc.

Director	*Noël Coward*
Designer	*G.E. Calthrop*

❖

SCENE: The action of the play takes place on the island of Samolo in the Southern Pacific.
The time is somewhere in the 1860s.

385

ACT I: The garden of the Stirling plantation. Morning.

ACT II: Scene 1: The main room of the Stirling house. Evening, a few
           days later.

           Scene 2: Interior of Elena's house. Night, a week later.

           Scene 3: The harbour. A few hours later, just before dawn.

ACT III: Scene 1: Elena's boudoir. A year later, afternoon.

           Scene 2: The same as Act I. Late that evening.

Orchestra direction   *Mantovani*

MUSICAL NUMBERS

ACT I

1. "Family Grace"	Mr Stirling
2. "If I Were A Man"	Louise, Henrietta, Caroline, Sarah, Agnes and Georgina
3. "Dear Madame Salvador" (Letter Song)	Kerry
4. "My Horse Has Cast A Shoe"	Elena and Kerry
5. "I Wish I Wasn't Quite Such A Big Girl"	Penelope and Girls
6. "Ka Tahua"	Ayano and Servants
7. "Bright Was The Day"	Elena and Kerry

ACT II, SCENE 1

8. "Invitation To The Waltz"	Louisa, Henrietta, Caroline, Sarah, Agnes, Georgina, Edward, William, James, Evan, D'Arcy and Aden
9. "His Excellency Regrets"	Louise, Henrietta, Caroline, Sarah, Agnes, Georgina, Edward, William, James, Evan, D'Arcy and Aden
10. "Dear Friends, Forgive Me, Pray"	Mr Stirling
11. "Make Way For Their Excellencies"	Entire Company
12. "Fumfumbolo"	Kerry and Servants
13. "One, Two, Three"	Elena

ACT II, SCENE 2

14. "This Is A Night For Lovers"	Rosa, Solange and Trudi
15. "I Never Knew"	Elena and Kerry
16. "This Is A Changing World"	Rosa

ACT II, SCENE 3

17. Finale: Entire Company
    "Come Back To The Island"

ACT III, SCENE 1

18. "Poor Lady In The   Rosa, Solange and Trudi
    Throes Of Love"
19. Reprise:
    "My Horse Has Cast A Shoe"   Elena and Rosa
    "This Is A Changing World"   Elena

ACT III, SCENE 2

20. Opening Chorus   Entire Company
    "This Is The Night"
21. "Mother's Lament"   Mrs Stirling, Mrs Pelham, and
                                    Mrs Cawthorne
22. "Pretty Little Bridesmaids"   Louise, Henrietta, Caroline, Sarah,
                                    Agnes, and Georgina
23. "I Saw No Shadow"   Elena
24. "Wedding Chorus"   Entire Company
25. Finale, Reprise   Elena and Kerry
    "Bright Was The Day"

Orchestrations   *Ronald Binge and Mantovani*
Musical assistant to Noël Coward   *Robb Stewart*

ADDITIONAL NUMBERS

Extra numbers were added to the production after the first night. These
include:

"Uncle Harry"   Kerry, Rollo, Henrietta, Louise,
                                    Caroline, Georgina, Agnes, and Sarah
                                    (This came between Nos. 2 and 3)

"The Party's Going   Kerry, Penelope, Rollo, and Melita
    With A Swing"   (This came between Nos. 9 and 10)
"Gipsy Melody"   Rosa, with Solange and Trudi
                                    (This replaced No. 18)

"Gipsy Melody" was cut from *Operette* after its opening in Manchester.

All these numbers are included in the vocal score.

The original script included a song "Alice Is At It Again" for Elena, on her entrance in Act II, Scene 1, but this was not used. Coward himself used it extensively in cabaret.

"Uncle Harry" was in the original script, but placed in Act II, Scene 1; it was removed before production, but replaced later.

SYNOPSIS

ACT I: The Stirling family and their guests, Mrs Pelham, her young son, Robin, and her daughter, Melita (engaged to Mr Stirling's younger son, Kerry), are breakfasting in the garden of their house on the tropical island of Samolo. Mr Stirling, an imposing Victorian *paterfamilias*, concludes the meal by singing grace, and the party breaks up. The Pelhams are driving home, though the young people plead that Robin and Melita may come with them on the picnic they have planned, but Mr Stirling upholds their mother's authority. He and his wife accompany the guests indoors, leaving the Stirling girls with their brothers, Rollo and Kerry.

Rollo, the eldest, is 29, solid and responsible; but Kerry is slim and dark "and possesses more romantic imagination than is good for him". The girls – Louise, Caroline, Henrietta, the twins Agnes and Sarah, and Georgina – range from 26 to 18. They all hold differing views on life, which each in turn expresses in the song, "If I Were A Man". The pious Henrietta wants domestic bliss, a nice house and a large family; Caroline, to be a millionaire. Louise primly declares that she would not shoot birds, fish, get drunk or wheedle money from her parents (a hit against Rollo) – in short, she would not be her brother. On the contrary, Georgina – who adores Kerry – would like his talent for wandering in solitary places and writing poetry, and would –

> ... Search the world over
> To find my true lover,
> And give her my passionate heart.

The twins, who sing (as they usually speak) together, opt for a gay life and a gallant death.

At this point Melita and Robin come back, and they all talk about the twins coming birthday party. The Stirlings are wondering whether to invite Madame Salvador, an opera-singer, convalescing in Samolo after an illness. They feel sure that their father would object, as Kerry dryly remarks, "(a) because she is a singer, (b) because she hasn't been to Government House, and (c) because she has been seen wearing riding breeches". The elder people hear the end of this discussion, and Mr Stirling emphatically says that Madame Salvador must not be invited.

Everyone then goes to see the Pelhams off, Kerry and Melita lingering for a few words together – both are angry at Mr Stirling's dictatorial attitude and would like to call on the singer.

A guest for the picnic, Penelope Cawthorn – a jolly, rather plump girl – then appears and is welcomed by the returning family. The girls take her indoors, while their brothers continue the topic of Madame Salvador. Sarcastically, Rollo suggests writing her a letter of apology: Kerry takes this seriously, composes a little note in rhyme and sings it.

Meanwhile, Elena Salvador comes in quietly: she is a lovely woman in her early thirties, exquisitely dressed. At the end of the song she speaks to the startled Kerry, thanking him for taking her part and telling him that he is a romantic. She explains that she is in difficulties because the horse which she was driving has cast a shoe. Kerry offers to drive her home and they sing a duet, "My Horse Has Cast A Shoe".

The young man orders Ayano, the servant, to bring them drinks, and while they are waiting Elena tells him about her early life: she was married very young to a Spanish operatic tenor, who left her a wealthy widow at 20; then she took up singing, became famous, and after a breakdown due to overwork came to Samolo to convalesce. She admires the beautiful garden, and Kerry suggests showing her round it. After a short duet they move off together, just as Ayano brings the drinks and is interrupted by Louise. The other girls come out in a bevy, chattering about the picnic. Only Penelope is worried at the probable effect on her figure of the rich cakes and cream. With the others as a chorus, she sings, "I Wish I Wasn't Quite Such A Big Girl."

The girls go off and the four Samolan maids and four house-boys come on to the veranda, singing as they draw down the sunblinds. Elena and Kerry return, chatting happily. He invites her to the party, and they sing a duet:

Bright was the day when you came to me.

In the background, the natives take up the melody.

ACT II, Scene 1: The birthday party is in full swing. A double sextet, consisting of the six Stirling girls and their partners, Captain Edward Harmby, Comptroller at Government House, Lord William Ravenscar, two A.D.C.s, James Culross, and the Hon. Evan St Mawes; and the Governor's two sons, D'Arcy and Aden Grayshott, sing an "Invitation To The Waltz". Then they join with the other guests in dancing.

The girls talk to the young men about their duties at Government House, which leads to another double sextet, "His Excellency Regrets". At the end they all dance off, while Mrs Stirling comes in with two elderly Scots, Miss Scobie and Miss Teresa Scobie. They go into the dining-room, while Rollo and Penelope come on, evidently enjoying each other's company, and are joined shortly by Kerry and Melita.

They dance off after a quartet, "The Party's Going With A Swing", and several of the older people appear – Mr and Mrs Cawthorne, Mrs Pelham, Mr and Mrs Stirling and the Misses Scobie. Discussing Madame Salvador rather acrimoniously, they agree that it would have been impossible to invite her to meet the Governor and his lady.

Mr Stirling welcomes the guests in song, and proposes a toast to his twin daughters. Just as it has been drunk, Ayano announces Madame Salvador, with her companion, Rosa Cariatanza, and her impresario, Felix Kammer. In the dead silence that follows, Kerry introduces Elena to his parents, who receive her frigidly and almost immediately leave the room, as do all the older people. The Stirling girls, however – except Henrietta and Louise – welcome her warmly, as does Melita. Though angry at the situation, Elena treats it lightly and gets Kerry to take her to the supper-room.

Meanwhile, there is consternation among the older people, and Rollo is sent to intercept Their Excellencies and tell them the news.

In the supper-room Elena has fascinated all the young men and they come back with her, laughing and talking.

There is a general stir as the Governor, Sir Lewis Grayshott, and Lady Grayshott are announced. They walk down the lines of assembled guests, with a few pleasant words to each, until Lady Grayshott catches sight of Elena. She kisses her warmly, saying how delighted she is now that she has recovered, and explains to the Stirlings that they are old friends. After this, Elena is *persona grata* with her hosts, who apologise for their rudeness.

An orchestra is called in, while Kerry sings a Samolan song which is a traditional feature of the Stirlings' annual party. Elena then sings a polka song, "One, Two, Three", at the end of which all the young people try this daring new dance. One after another the girls are dragged from their partners by their scandalised parents, until only Kerry and Elena are left dancing. When the music stops Elena leans forward and kisses him on the mouth. In the shocked silence that follows, she curtsies to the Governor and, with Rosa and Felix, leaves the ball.

Scene 2: It is about midnight a week later. In the living-room of Elena's house, waiting for her return, Rosa, Trudi (the cook) and Solange (the lady's maid) sing a trio:

> This is a night for lovers,
> This is a night for love.

Rosa follows this with a solo, "All My Life Ago", after which Felix enters, saying that he has heard Elena's carriage returning. He sends the maids off and asks Rosa to let him know when he can speak to Elena alone. Then he goes out.

Elena and Kerry come in laughing – so happy that Rosa's patent disapproval does not affect them. She says a curt good night to Kerry and goes, leaving the lovers alone. After a song from Elena –

> I never knew
> That love could be so sweet before

Kerry leaves and Rosa comes back. She talks seriously to Elena, pointing out that they are all homesick for Europe, and that this love affair with a man so young is most unwise and must not be allowed to jeopardise her career. Rosa herself might have been a prima donna if she had not sacrificed everything for a man who left her. She advises Elena in a song to take love lightly:

> This is a changing world, my dear;
> New songs are sung – new stars appear.
> Though we grow older year by year,
> Our hearts can still be gay.

Then she goes, and Felix comes to remind Elena that she has contracts in Europe in the spring and that time is running short. A boat is leaving Samolo next day and, without consulting her, he has made all arrangements for them to travel by it.

Elena resists desperately, but as he is in control of her business arrangements and her money, she cannot stand out against him. She writes a farewell letter to Kerry, stipulating that it shall reach him in time for him to come to the ship and say goodbye.

Scene 3: The scene is the harbour. The ship is being seen off in Samolan fashion, with music and song and the casting of leis of coloured flowers into the water. Pushing his way frantically through the crowd, Kerry arrives just as the ship is moving out of sight. He cries, "Elena! Elena!" then turns on the crowd, shouting, "Stop singing, damn you!" Then he bursts into tears and staggers away.

ACT III, Scene 1: A year has passed and Elena has just returned to Samolo. Rosa and the two maids, though still feeling seasick, are singing as they unpack her trunks.

Elena comes in, radiant at the prospect of seeing Kerry again. But her rejoicings are cut short when Felix brings the news that the town is *en fête* for the marriage of "A Young Master Stirling". Terribly shaken, she tells her staff not to go on unpacking, as they will leave in a couple of days on the same boat in which they came.

She apologises to Felix for having dragged him across the world for nothing and rushes out of the room, laughing hysterically.

Scene 2: It is evening, and the Stirlings' garden is festooned with coloured lights. There is an air of tremendous festivity, as servants move around with refreshments and the assembled guests sing about the joys of matrimony. The older people praise the decorations and lament the passing of the years; then the six Stirling girls in their wedding finery sing a sextet:

> We're sick to death of being pretty little bridesmaids,
> Instead of being pretty little brides.

They all troop into the house and the stage remains deserted until Elena, in a dark cloak, comes quietly on with Felix. Against his advice, she is determined to see the last of Kerry. Felix leaves her, while she sits under the tree and sings.

Everyone comes out to see the bridal couple depart – they are not Kerry and Melita, but Rollo and Penelope. As best man, Kerry – who is obviously very much upset – proposes a musical toast to them. Then Penelope takes Rollo's arm; they come down the steps, followed by their bridesmaids, and all go out of the gate. Kerry and Melita are left alone, with Elena watching in the background. The girl gives Kerry back his engagement ring, saying that she understands and will always be ready to help him. Then she kisses him lightly and runs off.

As he turns to go, Elena begins to sing softly, "Bright Was The Day". He comes down the steps towards her. "Oh, my love – my dear, dear love!" he exclaims, and she draws him into her arms.

The Times, 20 December 1946:

"With a perversity which has by this time become a settled characteristic, Drury Lane, for all its dignity in the eyes of the world, insists that it was born to be gay. And as to the manner born, the grand old place reopens after the war with musical romance. It is, of course, musical romance with a difference completely certain of its effects, whether musical or scenic, beautifully dressed, and demonstrating that stage pictures and groupings may be works of art, and almost startlingly small in scale and quiet in its romanticism.

"Mr Coward no doubt judges the public mood shrewdly when he sets his daisy-chain story in a beautiful, little-known island of the Samolan Archipelago in 1860. The programme, somewhat oddly, endeavours to establish the authenticity of the island, and the guide-book extract which describes the climate seems fairly to describe the play. Samolo, it explains, has an equable temperature, abundant sunshine, and very few tropical storms. This mild romance with its abundance of easy theatrical sentiment so gracefully expressed has precisely the same climate, and there are moments, as one pretty song succeeds another, when we rather hanker after a tropical storm. The nearest approach to it is the glittering social triumph won by a singer of doubtful reputation at a colonial birthday party. She is ostracised until the arrival of the Governor and his wife, who are old friends of hers. Then in the midst of a polka (that scandalous Parisian importation) she bestows a public kiss on the son of the house. Thereafter, she is called upon to choose between love and a career, but the choice is made and reconsidered to music which is amusing, tuneful and equable.

"Miss Mary Martin sings the heroine with much assurance and charm and Mr Graham Payn is fully equal to the demands made upon her 'opposite number'. To Miss Daphne Anderson falls perhaps the best of the songs, 'I Wish I Wasn't Quite Such A Big Girl', and Miss Sylvia Cecil has one almost as good in 'This Is A Changing World'. The singing reaches a high standard throughout, and always there is Mr Coward's sure handling of the stage to make it clear that this effect or the other, however simple, is precisely what he intends it to be."

PUBLICATIONS

Pacific 1860 was published in *Play Parade: Volume V* (1958).

The vocal score was published by William Chappell, 1947. They also published separate sheet music of "Bright Was The Day", "This Is A Changing World", "One, Two, Three" and "I Saw No Shadow".

"Bright Was The Day", "This Is A Changing World", and "His Excellency Regrets" are included in *The Noël Coward Song Book* (Michael Joseph, 1953).

NOTES

The programme contains the following "note" on Samolo:

"Samolo is the principal island of the Samolan Archipelago in the south-western Pacific. Latitude, 18 degrees north. Longitude, 75 degrees west.

"The Samolan group, consisting of 34 islands (seven of which are inhabited and a few privately owned), was discovered in 1786 by Captain Evangelous Cobb.

"The first English missionaries appeared there in 1815.

"Christianity was adopted by the Samolans in 1815 during the reign of King Kefumalani.

"The islands became officially a British possession in 1855 during the reign of King Kefumalani II, who wrote personally to Queen Victoria begging her to allow his land to have the privilege of belonging to the British Empire.

"The first British Governor-General of Samolo was Sir Douglas Markham, K.C.B.E., 1855.

"In the 1860s the British population of the islands numbered approximately 1,400. Sir Lewis Grayshott had succeeded to Douglas Markham as Governor-General.

"The island of Samolo is of volcanic origin and is 108 miles long and 70 miles wide.

"The climate is chiefly determined by the prevailing north-east trade winds, the result being an equable temperature, abundant sunshine and, except in the months of June and July, very few tropical storms. In these months – June and July – southerly gales are liable to occur, in rare instances reaching almost hurricane velocity.

"The southern coast from Paiana Head to Bakhua Point is remarkable for its beauty. Beaches of the finest white coral sand abound, together with limpid lagoons, secluded coves, palm-fringed inlets, and all the tropical charm with which writers of adventure stories have tantalised us since time immemorial.

"The immense coral reef which semi-encircles the island is closest to the land at Bakhua Point, being only two and a half miles distant from the shore. It is farthest away from the land off Pendarla and Narouchi, and at one point is actually five miles away. This makes possible the splendid surf for which Narouchi beach is so justly famous. The reef comes to an end at the northernmost end of Paiana Bay and the northernmost end of the Tola Swamps. Thus the northern coast – approximately from the mouth of the Yekki-Bolo River to the mouth of the Belo-Bolo River, is entirely unprotected and Bero Head, the northern part of the island, receives the full force of all the north winds and seas. The headland is rough and barren with black rocks and a profusion of sea-birds, including albatrosses, which 'indulge much in curious dances two by two' (see *Encyclopaedia Britannica*).

"(Extract from *A Guide to Samolo*, published by Ross, Wishart and Sons, 1906.)"

Coward originally "created" this island for *We Were Dancing* (*Tonight at 8.30*).

In his introduction to *Play Parade, Volume V* (1958), Coward wrote that "*Pacific 1860* [was] a flop. Not, let it be said, a resounding flop, not one of those immediate disasters in which the management is forced to cut its losses and close within a few days or weeks. *Pacific 1860* ran about six months although the last three of these were less a run than a convulsive stagger... Generally, the play is the basic cause of failure, but in the case of *Pacific 1860* this actually did not apply. The story was light, romantic and without any startling originality but it was pleasant and convincing enough to provide a peg on which to hand the score and the lyrics which, after all, was all that it was intended to be in the first place. In Operetta, as in Grand Opera although to a slightly lesser degree, it is the musical score that counts far and away above everything else. The fabulous success of the Gilbert and Sullivan operas could hardly have been achieved on the strength of their plots, construction and dialogue; it was the continued genius of the lyrics and music that spread them so triumphantly across the civilised world. That is a fact that our present-day critics, among so many other things, overlook. I am convinced that the slow decay of English musical comedy is largely attributable to this complete ignorance of light music. Why should an ambitious young composer spend months conceiving and evolving a full musical score when he knows at the outset that the highest praise he can hope to get for it will be the adjectives 'Tuneful' or 'Pleasantly reminiscent'.

"In America, on the other hand, when a new musical is produced out of town for its try-out, the first question put to those who have attended the opening is invariably "How was the score?" Light music is important in America, is treated with proper respect and criticised accordingly. Here, it is treated with no respect and criticised, if at all, with contemptuous ignorance."

A special gala performance of *Pacific 1860* was given on 23 January 1947, in aid of King George's Fund for Sailors, in the presence of the Royal Family.

There have been no major revivals of *Pacific 1860* since 1947; nor has it ever been seen in the US.

37
PEACE IN OUR TIME
A PLAY IN TWO ACTS AND EIGHT SCENES
Written in 1946

FIRST PRESENTED by H. M. Tennent Ltd. and John C. Wilson at the Theatre Royal, Brighton, 15 July 1947.

SUBSEQUENTLY PRESENTED at the Lyric Theatre, London, 22 July 1947. Transferred to the Aldwych Theatre on 29 September 1947 (167 performances).

CHARACTERS	Brighton and Lyric, 1947
ALMA BOUGHTON	Helen Horsey
FRED SHATTOCK	Bernard Lee
JANET BRAID	Elspeth March
DORIS SHATTOCK	Maureen Pryor
MR GRAINGER	Trevor Ward
MRS GRAINGER	Sybil Wise
NORA SHATTOCK	Beatrice Varley
LYIA VIVIAN	Hazel Terry
GEORGE BOURNE	Kenneth More
A MAN	Walter Plinge (Brighton)
	Douglas Vine (Lyric)
A WOMAN	Stella Chapman
CHORLEY BANNISTER	Olaf Pooley
BOBBY PAXTON	Derek Aylward
ALBRECHT RICHTER	Ralph Michael
PHYLLIS MERE	Dora Bryan
MR LAWRENCE	George Lane
MAUDIE	Irene Relph
GLADYS MOTT	Daphne Maddox
ALFIE BLAKE	Brian Carey
GERMAN SOLDIER	Charles Russell
HERR HUBERMAN	Richard Scott
FRAU HUBERMAN	Betty Woolfe
FIRST S.S. GUARD	Douglas Vine (Brighton)
	Anthony Peek (Lyric)
SECOND S.S. GUARD	Peter Drury (Brighton)
	William Murray (Lyric)
BILLY GRAINGER	Philip Guard
DR VENNING	Michael Kent
BEN CAPPER	Manfred Priestley
LILY BLAKE	Dandy Nichols
MR WILLIAMS	William Murray
STEVIE	Alan Badel
ARCHIE JENKINS	John Molecey
KURT FORSTER	Michael Anthony

MRS MASSITER	Janet Barrow
YOUNG GERMAN SOLDIER	Anthony Peek
THIRD S.S. GUARD	Peter Drury (Lyric only)
FOURTH S.S. GUARD	Douglas Vine (Lyric only)
Director	*Alan Webb, supervised by Noël Coward*
Designer	*G.E. Calthrop*

SCENE: The entire action of the play takes place in the saloon bar of a public house called "The Shy Gazelle" situated somewhere between Knightsbridge and Sloane Square.

ACT I: Scene 1: November 1940. About 8.30 in the evening.
Scene 2: June 1941. About 2.30 in the afternoon.
Scene 3: January 1942. Between 9.30 and 10 in the evening.
Scene 4: February 1942. About 9.30 in the evening.

ACT II: Scene 1: January 1945. Nine o'clock in the evening.
Scene 2: February 1945. Between 5.30 and 6 in the evening.
Scene 3: Three days later. Early afternoon.
Scene 4: May 1945. Early afternoon.

❖

SYNOPSIS

ACT I, Scene 1: The scene is the saloon bar of "The Shy Gazelle", a public house in the Knightsbridge district, on a November evening in 1940. The manager, Fred Shattock, his wife Nora and their daughter Doris, a pretty, quick-witted girl of 21, are all serving behind the bar. Among the customers are the cabaret artist, Lyia Vivian, with her lover, George Bourne; Janet Braid, a novelist of 40 whose son has been killed in the Battle of Britain; Chorley Bannister, an intellectual who edits a highbrow magazine called *Progress*; and a commonplace couple, Mr and Mrs Grainger.

Alma Boughton comes in and greets Janet. She orders a glass of whisky to warm herself after a long, cold train journey. Mr Grainger, at the bar, tells Nora Shattock that he has just had a postcard – "one of those printed ones" – from his son in the Isle of Wight.

Bannister has a passage of arms with Janet and Lyia, who object to the opinions expressed in his paper. He retaliates by calling Lyia an "amateur" – which so infuriates George Bourne that the two men nearly come to blows, but are calmed down by the Shattocks.

When a good-looking, well-dressed German, Albrecht Richter, comes into the saloon there is a general silence... Ordering a whisky and soda he looks around smiling; but, as nobody speaks to him, he finishes his drink says good night and goes out.

A general discussion follows, in which Bannister pleads that "a little toleration" is only common sense, and is told by Janet that timid expediency is *not* common sense.

Nora turns on the nine o'clock news. It announces a military parade for the reopening of parliament: "In the first open landau will be seated the Führer. The carriages following will contain Air Chief Marshal Goering, Dr Goebbels, and high-ranking army, navy and air force officers...

Scene 2: It is about 2.30 on an afternoon in June 1941. A new barmaid, Phyllis Mere, has replaced Doris Shattock, who now works as a receptionist at the Savoy during the daytime. After a chat with an unseen customer, Mr Lawrence, in the public bar, Phyllis gleefully announces that, the previous night, this man and a friend had attacked an insolent German officer and knocked him down. Fred warns her to keep quiet about it.

Mr Grainger shows him a newspaper with a portrait of the royal family and the information that they intend to stay on at Windsor. He has not heard recently from his son Billy. The Graingers go out just as Alma Boughton enters, asking for brandy. She drinks two glasses in quick succession, explaining that she is upset because she has just heard that a Jewish tailor whom she knows fairly well has been taken away by the S.S. Guards.

Fred says cautiously that there have not been many similar cases "yet"; but he advises Alma to be less uncompromising. After all, life has to go on – they have been conquered and must accept that it was their own fault, for their stupidity and complacency before 1939. Unexpectedly, Alma rejoins that it was better that England did lose the Battle of Britain, because if they had won they would have grown lazy and vainglorious again: "As it is, in defeat, we still have a chance... We can be united now – we shall have to be – until we have driven them away, until we're clean again." She drinks a third brandy and asks after Nora. Fred replies that the shooting of Winston Churchill has upset her terribly, and Alma utters the earnest warning not to be taken in by the Germans' "good behaviour" policy: "They're our enemies, now and for ever."

Nora comes down from the luncheon-room, reporting that Miss Vivian and Mr Bourne are at one table and Albrecht Richter and Mr Bannister at another. Soon afterwards Lyia and George come downstairs, and Alma, who is slightly drunk, tries to quarrel with Lyia, suggesting that she is a collaborationist, but is side-tracked by the appearance of Bannister and Richter. After icily refusing the latter's offer of cigarettes, she goes out.

Bannister, Bourne and Lyia let the German stand them a brandy, but the Shattocks decline to be included in the round. Some banter about Epps' Cocoa and the Secret Service bewilders Richter: he assumes, however, that it is only the peculiar English sense of humour. When he raises his glass with the toast "Heil, Hitler!" there is a dead silence. George Bourne politely tells him he has made a psychological error – defeat is an attitude of mind and the English have not yet acquired it. Though obviously annoyed, Richter controls his temper and offers to honour any toast they care to propose. George says lightly, "Epp's Cocoa!" and they drink to this as the lights fade.

Scene 3: It is now January 1942, just before closing time. All three Shattocks are serving. Alma is there; so is Bannister, who is drinking with a sleek young man, Bobby Paxton. There are also several newcomers: Gladys Mott ("obviously a tart"), with a German soldier; a civil service couple, Herr and Frau Hubermann; and a sporting type, Alfred Blake.

Gladys is laughing loudly when Janet joins Alma at the bar. Drinks are by this time in short supply, and she rather unwillingly accepts rum. Commenting on Glady's high spirits, Fred says that her mood is due to a generous gift of silk stockings and perfume, brought over from Germany by her "steady" boyfriend.

Bannister introduces Bobby Paxton to Janet, asking her to use her influence to get him a part in a play with which a certain Grant Madison is reopening His Majesty's Theatre. She firmly refuses, disapproving of Grant Madison's policy of keeping on good terms with the enemy, which signifies acceptance of defeat. And she adds that she disapproves of Bannister himself, for the same reasons. She goes out with Alma as George Bourne and Lyia enter. George amiably agrees to give Bobby the required introduction, and Bannister orders drinks for all four.

Just then Richter comes in with two uniformed Gestapo men, demanding the identity cards of all present. There is a moment's alarm when Alfred Blake mislays his card, but it is soon found. Offered a drink by George, Richter asks for gin, but is told by Fred that there is only rum. His offer to supply the bar with gin is politely but firmly turned down. This makes him ask Fred how soon he and his kind – the ordinary hard-working people of England – will be reconciled to the inevitable.

He points out that America is fully occupied with wars in the Atlantic and the Pacific, "both of which she will eventually lose"; that the Dominions are indifferent to Britain's fate, and India is in chaos. How long will it be, he repeats, before Fred and his kind accept the situation? "Never!" is Fred's reply. "Nor our children after us, nor their children's children."

"Admirable!" says Richter, adding that the Führer has based his plans on his knowledge of the indomitable British spirit: when once the country is convinced that the German aim is not domination, but co-operation, British common sense will assert itself, and the two countries together will proceed to liquidate the Jews and convert the communists.

Fred brusquely says that it is closing time and Richter leaves. All the customers except Lyia and George have also gone; and Fred, bringing a secret bottle of gin from under the counter, is preparing to stand these two a drink when the door bursts open and Billy Grainger staggers in. His head is bandaged, his clothing torn and he is obviously exhausted.

Explaining that he has escaped from the prison camp, he asks where to find his parents and then faints. Hurriedly, they lock the doors and curtain the windows; while Fred revives him with rum, Doris goes to fetch a doctor, and Nora to make tea for him.

When Dr Venning arrives, Billy is able to tell how he escaped: he swam to the mainland with a companion who was drowned on the way; and various people have helped him to reach London. When, after protests on his part, the doctor removes the bandage, they see the letters "K.G." (*Kriegsgefangener*) on his forehead – he has been branded after a previous effort to escape.

After exchanging some remarks with Dr Venning about Dunkirk – a code-word by which fellow members of the Resistance recognise one another – George leaves with Lyia by the back door. The doctor re-bandages Billy's head and takes him home for the night, promising to smuggle him into a clinic where a skin-grafting operation will remove the brand. He warns the Shattocks not to tell the news to Billy's parents. When he has taken the young man away, Nora bursts into tears, saying she is glad now that her own son, Stevie, was killed, instead of being imprisoned and tortured like Billy.

Scene 4: Another month has passed, and again it is nearly closing time. The Shattocks are serving, and the customers include the Graingers and Alfred Blake's wife, Lily.

Dr Venning enters and passes the message that his young friend, John Fawcett, "who was burned in the garage fire", is now out of hospital and driving a truck, and that he would like Mr and Mrs Grainger to know that he is alright. After Ben Capper, the son of a neighbour, has handed him a note, he goes out, leaving a message for Bourne to telephone him.

Alfie Blake then enters with a business friend, Mr Williams. They fetch Lily and all leave together. The Graingers are now alone in the saloon, and when Mr Grainger comes to pay for his drinks Doris very quietly tells him that Billy (from whom they have heard nothing since the report of his escape) is safe and well. She warns him not to tell his wife until they are back home. They go out, and the Shattocks close the house.

Nora hears their dog Nipper barking wildly in the yard, and sends Doris to let him in. Meanwhile, they discuss Dr Venning and the organisation to which he must obviously belong, since he has been able to organise Billy's rescue so efficiently. Nora would like to help her country in this way, but Fred preaches caution.

Suddenly Doris comes back, white and trembling, telling her mother to prepare for a shock. She tries to break the news gently, then blurts out: "Stevie wasn't killed after all. He's here." Nora says quietly that she knew it – for some time she had had a presentiment, and when she heard the dog barking she was sure. When Stephen comes in and takes her in his arms, however, she breaks down and sobs. An emotional situation is resolved by the young man's suggestion that Doris had better go and make tea for them all.

When he hears that Doris is working at the Savoy – which is requisitioned for German V.I.P.s – he guesses that she belongs to the Resistance movement, and her use of the word "Dunkirk" confirms it. From the cryptic remarks of the brother and sister, their parents learn for the first time what Doris is doing. They are hurt that she did not trust them with the secret, but she explains that it was for their own sakes – she did not want them to run the danger of knowledge.

Stephen – who now has false identity papers – dare not stay the night, and he asks them to burn his photographs, in case they are recognised. Before leaving, he gives them a rapid sketch of his adventures: shot down near Boulogne, he escaped in March 1941, from a prison camp at Lyons and was smuggled to Gibraltar, where he has been trained in wireless work, in preparation for a counter-invasion. He was landed from a submarine in the Western Isles and has worked his way southwards, sent from one Resistance agent to another. It may be a year or two, he says, before the invasion actually takes place, but it is beginning: "The Beginning for us – the beginning of the end for them!"

ACT II, Scene 1: Three years have passed. It is January 1945, and there are various changes in the saloon and its customers: the windows are covered with blackout material; Fred and Nora have aged considerably and Doris looks white and strained; everyone is shabby, and many people are wearing wooden-soled shoes. Very little liquor is obtainable, so most of them drink a poisonous mixture called "Stubbs' Special".

They are listening to the official nine o'clock news bulletin, which recounts a series of Allied disasters, and ends with a warning that the penalty for listening to unauthorised stations is death.

The Resistance broadcast is just due, however, and Doris fetches in two customers from the public bar – Mr Lawrence and his friend Archie Jenkins

– to listen. The Blakes, the Graingers and Alma Boughton are all there, and Janet, just evacuated from Cornwall, joins them unexpectedly. They gather closely round the hardly audible set, while Nora keeps watch at the window. The radio voice declares that Marseilles and Toulon have been liberated, the Allied armies are advancing through France, and the Germans have been defeated at sea.

At an urgent warning from Nora, Doris switches on to the Home Station, which is blaring out Wagner as Chorley Bannister comes in with a young Austrian, whom he introduces as Kurt Forster, a designer at Covent Garden Opera. Ordering ginger ale, Bannister produces a bottle of Canadian whisky. He offers a drink to Alma and Janet, but only Janet accepts. She is sarcastically amiable to Forster, who talks patronisingly about the superiority of German opera. When he toasts "Heil, Hitler!" Alma jogs his elbow and spills the drink. Considerably annoyed, Bannister takes him off to sponge down his suit.

Meanwhile, the others concoct a practical joke: Fred pours off half the whisky and refills the bottle with Stubbs.

Billy (now unscarred and passing as Johnny Fawcett) comes in and makes a telephone call. On his way out again he catches his parents' eye, but no sign of recognition passes. Pouring fresh drinks, Bannister is puzzled by the unpleasant taste of the liquor, but drinks it all the same.

Forster leaves, and Bannister, reproaching the two women for their behaviour, is told that his German friends are not wanted in this exclusive pub. Asked what she gains by her belligerent attitude, Janet replies firmly: "Self-respect!" Bannister's defence of the Nazi ideology leads her to quote Shakespeare's line: "This blessed plot, this earth, this realm, this England..." After some very plain speaking, she slaps his face and walks out, followed by Alma. Bannister consoles himself with more of the doctored whisky.

It is now closing time and the Shattocks are tidying up. The Blakes go out and Bannister starts to follow. But the doctored whisky has made him sick and he hurries to the lavatory.

Thinking everyone has gone, Doris locks the street door and calls in her brother and Ben Capper. Nora is a trifle worried, lest Janet's outburst may lead to serious trouble. They are waiting for George and Lyia and Dr Venning, who come in through the back door. The cellar has now been organised as a Resistance centre and, after a brief chat, they switch off the lights and go down there.

The passage door opens slowly and Bannister tiptoes out. Nora comes back and puts on the light just in time to see him, but he wrenches the door open and escapes. In panic, she calls Fred and Stephen.

Scene 2: Another month has passed. It is early evening and Doris has not yet returned but Phyllis is eager to get to the cinema. Fred lets her go, after a sermon on her empty-headed frivolity at a time of crisis.

There is a ring at the back door and Nora admits Lyia, with her arm in a sling – she has faked the injury so as to call on Dr Venning and reach the pub through his premises, evading the sentinels who have been posted in the mews since, at Bannister's instigation, the place was raided. She gives an urgent message for Doris – that her report has reached Headquarters, and that she is being followed home. Then she leaves by the back way.

The Shattocks are very anxious about their daughter. When she does come in she brings important news: Himmler is arriving to round up all Resistance groups throughout the country. She has learned this through a decoded telegram – and this is the report she has forwarded, through Billy, to Headquarters. It signifies in her opinion, that the counter-invasion is imminent.

The first customers that evening are the Graingers, who bring a beautiful Staffordshire jug as a present, in token of their gratitude. Then Alma Boughton arrives with her mother, Mrs Massiter, a gallant old warhorse up from the country, who electrifies everyone by openly announcing that she is head of her local Resistance group, and by giving the toast: "Down with Hitler!"

The Blakes come in, joyously reporting a practical joke played on the Germans at a cinema. They are followed by Gladys Mott with a young German soldier, and by George and Lyia.

Suddenly Albrecht Richter appears with two S.S. Guards, and identity cards are checked as before. His manner is urbane, but he has obviously come to cross-question Doris, who has left work early, under the pretext of feeling unwell, to pass her report to Billy in the park. She tries to turn it off lightly as a lovers' assignation. However, he persists and, despite a protest from George Bourne, takes her away for questioning. Doris goes bravely, telling her parents not to worry.

Scene 3: Three days have passed. It is near closing time on a Saturday afternoon, and Alfie Blake, with the aid of beer-mugs and ashtrays, is explaining Allied strategy to his carping wife and the barmaid, Phyllis. Billy comes in and is upset to learn that the Gestapo have seized Doris.

Fred, looking "leaden and hopeless", comes back from a fruitless attempt to see Doris. All Richter would tell him was that they would send her back when she had answered their questions satisfactorily.

They hear a car drawing up outside. Two S.S. Guards walk in, carrying between them the inert body of Doris, which they fling at her mother's feet.

She has been tortured, and is only able to gasp "I didn't say anything!" before she dies. As the curtain falls, Nora begins to scream.

Scene 4: It is early afternoon in May 1945. Fred and Phyllis behind the bar, and their customers, Alma, Mrs Massiter, the Blakes and Mr Lawrence, are listening intently to the sound of distant firing. The Resistance men have risen, though the relieving troops are still two or three days' march away.

Gladys Mott, breathless and frightened, runs in and asks for a drink, but Fred flatly refuses. He flings her money on the floor, telling her never to come in again.

Back again from the country, Janet Braid is introduced to Alma's mother, and Fred, as an advance celebration of victory, brings out a bottle of champagne, hidden since 1939. They all drink to him "with affection and gratitude", and he goes to find Nora, who has been ill since the shock of Doris's death. When the other customers have gone, however, she comes down for a few words with Janet before she, too, leaves.

Husband and wife are alone when Billy rushes in through the back door, with orders from "the Boss", Mr Bourne, to take them away immediately. They refuse to go, and are still arguing when George himself comes in, followed by Ben and Dr Venning, who are dragging the half-conscious Richter. They gag him, tie him to a chair, and tell him that he is to be "liquidated" for his murder of Doris Shattock.

At this point Stephen, bloodstained and dishevelled, runs in to warn them that the Germans are on their way to rescue Richter. Quickly they barricade the door, place their captive in the direct line of fire, and hurriedly disguise him with a Resistance armband and a cap over his face. Then they all escape through the back entrance, leaving him there.

The radio voice is heard announcing that liberation is near, and "God Save the King" rings out as the Germans begin to batter at the door. There is a spatter of machine-gun bullets, and Richter, in his death-struggle, topples to the ground.

W. A. Darlington in the *Daily Telegraph*, 21 July 1947:
"Is there any one of us who lived in these islands during the war who has not at some time tried to imagine what would have happened here if the Battle of Britain has been lost and a successful German invasion made?

"If so, he will perhaps not be interested in *Peace in Our Time*, Noël Coward's new play at the Lyric, which sets out to show us what occupied Britain would have been like. For the rest of us, the play is one long thrill.

"Mr Coward's account rings true. So, and not otherwise, we feel, would the clientéle of a London 'local', with its mixture of highbrows and cockney types, have reacted to the arrival of the Germans. So, and not otherwise, would it have progressed from a campaign of individual pinpricks to an organised and efficient resistance movement.

"So, too, would these people have kept their gaiety and their irreverence in the presence of humourless authoritarianism; and thus they would have faced torture and death.

"The saloon bar of 'The Shy Gazelle' is the perfect setting for this play, and no less than Mr Coward's sincerity one admires his theatrical skill, which enables him to build up to a finish at once plausible and telling when the Gestapo agent dies with the sound of the secret radio in his ears announcing the arrival at Dover of the liberation army.

"This play cannot possibly fail. It is too moving, too exciting, too deft – and too timely. We need to be reminded, just now, that we are people of spirit.

"The acting of an enormous cast, under the direction of Alan Webb, and in a superbly realistic setting by G. E. Calthrop, is without flaw.

"If I single out Bernard Lee, Beatrice Varley, Maureen Pryor, Helen Horsey and Kenneth More among the patriots, it is because they have the largest parts; if Elspeth March, it is because she is given two tremendous tirades to deliver and delivers them with great force.

"Ralph Michael deals thoroughly with the Gestapo man.

"Apart from all that, however, memory dwells gratefully on a dozen small bits of acting by people whom I cannot even identify for certain in the programme."

PUBLICATIONS

Peace in Our Time was first published by Heinemann (London, 1947) and is dedicated to Ingram Fraser, with the following appreciation:

"I am dedicating *Peace in Our Time* to you as a very small gesture of gratitude for all the invaluable help and technical advice you gave me when I was constructing and writing it. The infinite pains you took to plan and map 'Operation Bulldog' – the imagined reinvasion of occupied England by the Free British, the American, the Free French and the Dominion Forces, made it possible for me to visualise the end of the play clearly. Also, without your knowledge of 'Resistance' activities and your quick and precise eye for detail, much of the dialogue might have been muddled and obscure. As it is, thanks to you, I think that within its imagined limits it is fairly accurate. At any rate the operative phrase in all this is: 'Thanks to you.'" The play is also included in *Play Parade, Volume V* (1958), where the title is given in quotes, presumably to underline its origin in Neville Chamberlain's victorious speech.

Also published in *Noël Coward Collected Plays: Seven* by Methuen World Classics (London, 1999).

❖

NOTES

Some changes were made between the try-out at Brighton and the production in London. A report at the time said:

"One of the central characters of the play was a British quisling, played by Olaf Pooley, who was finally trapped by the British Resistance Movement and in a dramatic climax shot by the German S.S.

"But somehow the character of the British quisling didn't seem to get across to the audience. Something stronger was needed. So, two nights before the London opening, Noël sat down and re-wrote the best part of the last two acts, replacing the British quisling with a Gestapo official (Albrecht Richter). For a character that has existed in reality and who can be identified with known behaviour is stronger than a creature of the imagination whose behaviour can only be guessed at. And who doesn't know about Gestapo officials?"

It is interesting to see the traditional *nom du théâtre* for a double, Walter Plinge, make a reappearance on a programme (at the Brighton try-out). London did not witness the performance of Walter Plinge in *Peace in Our Time*. The tradition of using the name Walter Plinge to cover an actor playing two parts (professionally known as doubling) dates back to the Benson Company. There was a real Walter Plinge, the proprietor of a public house near the stage door of the Lyceum Theatre. It is said that Benson, short of an actor at the last moment, to say a few lines in *Hamlet* in 1900, asked Walter to step into the breach. From that time, whenever a fictitious name was needed on the programme of the Benson Company, Walter Plinge's was used. Many afterwards famous actors in this company appeared under this name. The custom spread into other companies up and down the country, particularly those Bensonians who went into management. Matheson Lang used a series of Mr Plinges into the 1930s. Noël Coward is to be congratulated for bringing this grand old actor back to the legitimate stage and giving him a week's sea air at the Theatre Royal, Brighton. The versatility of Walter was proved by his regular appearance for some years with the International Ballet Company.

In the introduction to *Play Parade, Volume V* (1958), Coward wrote: "The idea of *Peace in our Time* was conceived in Paris shortly after the Liberation.

Readers of the second volume of my autobiography *Future Indefinite* may remember that I spent the first eight months of the war in Paris, in course of which I came into contact with more varieties of French people than I ever had before. I also grew to understand them and appreciate them more than I ever had before. The Fall of France therefore had more personal implications for me than it had for many others. I had countless friends to wonder about and worry about and my imagination was plagued with visions of Nazis swaggering along under the arcades of the Rue de Rivoli and Gestapo officials letting themselves in and out of my flat in the Place Vendome (which incidentally they occupied for the duration).

"When I returned soon after the Germans had been driven away, the city itself seemed to be unchanged, physically at least untouched by the horror of enemy occupation. It didn't take me long, however, to realise that behind the façade a great deal had changed, the sense of immediate relief and exaltation had faded and there was an atmosphere of subtle disintegration, lassitude and, above all, suspicion."

Peace in Our Time was revived at the Jeannetta Cochrane Theatre on 3 May 1989 by the Arts Educational School's acting company directed by David Harris. This production transferred to the King's Head, Islington, on 24 May 1989. On 28 February 1995, a touring production directed by Wyn Jones opened at the New Victoria, Woking. Despite good reviews, it did not reach the West End.

38
ISLAND FLING (US)
SOUTH SEA BUBBLE (UK)

(Originally called *Home and Colonial*)

A NEW LIGHT COMEDY

Written in 1949

FIRST PRESENTED by Lawrence Langner, Armina Marshall, and John C. Wilson at the Country Playhouse, Westport, Conn., 22 July 1951 (8 performances). Played the following week at the Cape Playhouse, Dennis, Mass.; then returned to Westport for a further 8 performances.

FIRST PRESENTED IN ENGLAND at the Opera House, Manchester, 19 March 1956, by H. M. Tennent Ltd. (5 weeks' tour: Liverpool, Edinburgh, Glasgow and Newcastle).

SUBSEQUENTLY PRESENTED at the Lyric Theatre, London, 25 April 1956 (276 performances).

CHARACTERS	Westport, US, 1951
THE EARL OF SHARPENHOE (Boffin) (America)	Arthur Macrae
THE HON. MAUD WITTERBY (America only)	Edith Meiser
CAPTAIN CHRISTOPHER MORTLOCK, A.D.C.	Gordon Mills
SIR GEORGE SHOTTER (Governor of the Samolan Islands)	Berry
LADY ALEXANDRA SHOTTER (his wife)	Claudette Colbert
PUNALO ALANI (Father of Hali Alani)	Reginald Mason
SANYAMO (a butler)	Don Glenn
NAEENA (America only)	Judy Fineman
EDWARD HONEY (the colonial secretary)	Peter Boyne
CUCKOO HONEY (his wife)	Cherry Hardy
ADMIRAL TURLING (in America "Commander")	A. J. Herbert
MRS TURLING (his wife)	Esther Mitchell
ROBERT FROME (the Chief of Police)	Roy Johnson
HALI ALANI	Leon Janney
Director	*John C. Wilson*
Designer	*Eldon Elder*

CHARACTERS	Manchester and Lyric, 1956
JOHN BLAIR KENNEDY (Boffin) (England)	Arthur Macrae
CAPTAIN CHRISTOPHER MORTLOCK, A.D.C.	Clifford Elkin (Manchester) Peter Barkworth (Lyric)
SIR GEORGE SHOTTER (Governor of the Samolan Islands)	Ian Hunter
LADY ALEXANDRA SHOTTER (his wife)	Vivien Leigh (succeeded by Elizabeth Sellars, 13 August)

PUNALO ALANI (father of Hali Alani)	Alan Webb
SANYAMO (a butler)	William Peacock
EDWARD HONEY (the colonial secretary)	John Moore
CUCKOO HONEY (his wife)	Joyce Carey (succeeded by Daphne Newton, 25 September)
ADMIRAL TURLING	Nicholas Grimshaw
MRS TURLING (his wife)	Daphne Newton (succeeded by Betty Woolfe, 21 September)
ROBERT FROME (the Chief of Police)	Eric Phillips
HALI ALANI	Ronald Lewis
Director	*William Chappell*
Designer	*Peter Snow*

SCENE: The action of the play passes on the island of Samolo, a British
           possession in the Pacific Ocean.
ACT I: Scene 1: The veranda of Government house. Evening.
           Scene 2: The same. A few minutes later.
ACT II: Scene 1: The same. A few hours later.
           Scene 2: Hali Alani's beach house. Later the same night.
ACT III: Scene 1: The veranda. The next morning.
           Scene 2: The same. A few hours later.

In Manchester, Act I was divided into two scenes as written but in London
the two scenes were played continually as one act.

❖

SYNOPSIS

ACT I, Scene 1: The witty and famous novelist, John Blair Kennedy (Boffin to his
   friends), has arrived at Government House, Pendarla, on the British-owned
   Pacific island of Samolo. The Governor's A.D.C., Captain Christopher
   Mortlock, receives him, offers him a drink and chats until his host, Sir George
   Shotter, appears. Sir George is a self-made man, whose left-wing politics
   have not endeared him to the locals. On edge after a trying flight and a bad

landing, Boffin is not soothed when the Governor intimates that he is expected to give a couple of lectures and to open a new wing of the University library. At first he flatly refuses, but when Lady Alexandra Shotter (Sandra), rushing in breathless from a meeting which has detained her, adds her persuasions, he compromises, agreeing to open the library provided they excuse him from the lectures.

Sandra has planned a dinner party for him, to which she has invited some leading English residents and Hali Alani, head of the People's Imperial Party – one of the two main political groups in the island. Sir George considers it "damned retrogressive". His own sympathies are with the Samolan Socialist Nationals, who demand self-government for the native population and Dominion status. Sandra thinks the native population is much better left in its happy ignorance; however, she agrees to her husband's suggestion that she should use her fascination upon Hali Alani (whom she describes as "frightfully good-looking in rather a bogus sort of way") in order to make him politically more progressive.

The A.D.C. announces that Hali's father, Punalo Alani, wishes to see Sir George, who grants him an interview while the others are dressing for dinner. Punalo, a dignified old man, has come to protest against the Socialist Nationals' proposed bill to make all lavatories in the island entirely free. He points out that the institution of a single tourist class in the inter-island boat service has sent it into liquidation, since the wealthier families have refused to travel herded up with the livestock brought by the lower classes. This new proposal will be an insult to those who can afford to spend a penny and a grave menace to public health. Sir George, however, faithful to his democratic principles, declines to veto the bill. His visitor, who has been at Eton and is perfectly conversant with conditions in England, points out that Samolo is not an industrial country: it is quite contented with the "cosy imperialism" which has guided it for so long, and has no wish to endure the discomforts of state-controlled democracy that are racking the Western nations. "Well, I'll be damned!" is Sir George's comment as Punalo walks out.

Scene 2: While Christopher and the butler, Sanyamo, attend to cigarettes and drinks, guests begin to arrive. The Colonial Secretary, Edward Honey, is an earnest and painstaking man who suffers from hay fever; his wife, Cuckoo, is "pure Kensington with an Anglo-Indian background". They talk to Christopher about Blair Kennedy's novels, which Cuckoo considers too flippant. She hints that Kennedy was in love with Sandra before her marriage, and criticises the parties at Government House, to which she thinks too many natives are invited. Christopher, who finds her ill-natured gossip annoying, is relieved when the arrival of Admiral and Mrs Turling creates a diversion. Boffin comes in and is introduced to the other guests; then Sir George enters.

Next comes the Chief of Police, Robert Frome, who apologises for being late – he has been investigating a car robbery, of which there has recently been an epidemic.

As usual, Sandra is rather late and slightly breathless. She asks Mrs Turling's advice about a local girl who is "in trouble". This leads to a discussion on the morals of the Samolans and the growing problem of miscegenation – a topic which is hastily dropped when Hali Alani arrives. He is tall, handsome and picturesque in a white dinner jacket worn over a brilliant sarong. In place of his father's faultless English, he speaks an engaging mixture of flowery but inaccurate idiom and up-to-date slang. At first he refuses a cocktail, on the ground that he has a bad head for liquor; but, overpersuaded by Sandra, he drinks a toast to her: "Because of your great kindness and understanding of my people... because you always laugh at serious things and make the little, swift jokes to ease away the difficulty of living, and above all, Lady Alexandra... because you do not miss a bloody trick."

"How am I doing, darling?" whispers Sandra to her husband as they go in to dinner.

ACT II, Scene 1: The dinner-party is over and the guests are ready to go. Hali is out in the garden with Sandra, and Boffin has been cornered by Cuckoo Honey, who dryly amuses him by disparaging his novels. Christopher comes in after seeing off the Turlings. He is going on to a party given by a certain Mitzi Radlett, whose gay mixed gatherings are a feature of the island. When he has left, Cuckoo expresses strong disapproval, and goes on to make Boffin really angry by criticising Sandra for her preoccupation with her native guest. His sarcastic reception of her remarks drives her away in a huff, just before Sandra and Hali come in from the garden.

At a hint from his hostess, Boffin goes into the next room and begins to play the piano, while she continues to fascinate the young man. Hali asks her suspiciously whether His Excellency suggested this talk in the garden, but she lightly evades the question. He leads the conversation round to the burning topic of public conveniences, and she assures him that her husband did not wish her to influence him on that subject. Gravely he warns her that no beautiful woman – "even you, Lady Sandra, in the moonlight and under the bright stars" – could alter his political views.

When Boffin begins to play dance music, Hali persuades her to dance with him. They are discovered by Cuckoo, who has come back for her handbag, and who is patently shocked. When Hali has gone to move his car, she tackles Sandra upon her indiscretion. The return of Boffin and Sir George stops a conversation that is becoming acrimonious.

The Governor raises some objections when his wife tells him that Hali is driving her to Mitzi's party: he thinks it too late to "go cavorting round the island", and flatly refuses to accompany her. Sandra goes off with Hali, after a parting shot aimed at Cuckoo.

Scene 2: Instead of driving Sandra home after the party, Hali has brought her to his beach house on the shore of Paiana Bay, which is incongruously furnished with a couple of native war-drums and an up-to-date cocktail cabinet. It is after midnight and Sandra is too tired, and too dazed by the breakneck speed of the journey, to be angry, though at first she refuses a drink and asks to be taken back to Government House at once. Hali eventually persuades her to try a kala-kala and drinks several himself.

Then he suggests playing to her on the war-drums given to his ancestor by King Kefumalani. As he plays he works himself up into a state of atavistic excitement and Sandra grows nervous. Unable to stop him any other way, she pushes one of the drums over. Hali, hovering between rage and passion, seizes her and kisses her violently. She slaps his face and runs to the other side of the room.

Still angry at her cavalier treatment of his revered heirloom, Hali consoles himself with another drink. Sandra tries to control the situation by asking him quietly for his car key: she says she will drive herself home and send someone over with the car next day. By this time Hali is very drunk and Sandra, to keep him in a good humour, accepts two successive glasses of the powerful liquor. They at first give her hiccups, then make her feel gay and reckless. She quotes Pope and Wordsworth and sings the Roedean hockey song; then once more she asks Hali for the key of his car, which he again refuses. She suggests that he should play to her again, and dances round in a circle to his music. As she does so she picks up a bottle from the drink cabinet and cracks him on the back of the head with it. Then she takes the key from his pocket, snatches up her cloak and bag and runs out.

ACT III, Scene 1: It is breakfast time at Government House next morning. Sir George is annoyed with his A.D.C. for letting Sandra leave the party with Hali Alani instead of driving her home himself. Christopher explains that he was preoccupied with his girlfriend, but the excuse does not go down well. Arriving in excellent spirits after a good night, Boffin senses tension when Sir George curtly dismisses Christopher, telling him to go and do some work.

The Governor is obviously worried at the effect that his wife's double drive with Hali, as retailed by Cuckoo, will have on the English colony. But Sandra herself, though suffering from a hangover, turns up in a gaily unrepentant mood. To her husband's reproaches she merely replies that he is being unreasonable, since it was he who asked her to fascinate Hali in the first place.

Christopher comes back, saying that the Chief of Police wants to see Sir George urgently. The shock revives Sandra's hiccups, but they are checked by her still greater alarm when Robert Frome brings the news that Hali is in hospital with concussion, having apparently been attacked in his beach house after a drunken orgy. He asks Sandra what time she got home, and, on the basis of her reply that they drove straight back after the end of the party, works out that it must have been about 12.45 a.m. Frome says that Hali's attacker must have stolen his car, which has been found smashed up about a mile from Government House.

When Christopher has taken Frome off to telephone, the others speculate as to what has happened. Sandra makes the bright suggestion that Hali probably had a woman with him – a half-caste, "very sinuous, and clattering with cheap jewellery", who "fetched him a nice wallop" with the bottle after a row, took his car, and drove home.

By this time Boffin has a shrewd idea of what really happened, and Sir George is highly suspicious. He cross-examines Sandra about the time she came home – which can be checked by the sentry at the gate. She says the man was asleep and, when pressed further, turns defence into attack, accusing her husband of being out of temper because his liver is upset by his unwise feeding. Not to be side-tracked, Sir George asks her outright: "Did you or did you not go with Hali Alani to his beach house last night and bash him over the head with a bottle?" "Certainly I did," retorts Sandra in exasperation. "And if you don't stop bellowing at me I'll do the same to you. Come, Boffin!" And she sweeps out of the room.

Scene 2: Punalo Alani has come to see the Governor. While waiting, he has an illuminating conversation with Sanyamo, from whom he learns that Hali had a long tête-à-tête with Sandra in the garden and was given a white flower, that they left together in Hali's car, and that she returned on foot through the hedge at 25 past four in the morning (according to the sentry, who, being devoted to her, pretended not to see her).

With this information in his possession, Punalo proceeds in gentlemanly fashion to blackmail Sir George. He explains that a jewelled clip belonging to Lady Alexandra has been found in the beach house and is now in his possession. Briefly, his proposition is that he will refrain from giving the whole story to the press provided Sir George promises to veto the Public Conveniences Bill and withdraw his allegiance to the Samolan Socialist National Party. In this case, he can find a "professional scapegoat", who, for a consideration, will confess to the attack upon Hali, allow himself to be sentenced and imprisoned and shortly afterwards will be enabled to escape to another island.

The Governor indignantly refuses, and the two men are on the brink of an explosion when Sandra sails into the room. Ignoring her husband's attempts to get her out of the way, she greets Punalo with great charm and invites him to lunch. The situation becomes distinctly easier when Sanyamo brings in a tray of drinks. Meanwhile, Christopher brings a message that Hali Alani wishes to see Lady Alexandra privately "on a matter of great importance". She promptly extends her invitation to include Hali, remarking that, if he wants to talk to her privately, he must wait till after lunch.

Hali comes in with his head bandaged, looking far from well, but he is now sober and repentant. Father and son have a brief altercation in Samolan, which Sandra breaks up by telling them that they sound like a Yugoslavian drama festival. Then Hali returns the jewelled clip, saying that it was found on the floor of his car. Significantly, he tells his father that the man who attacked him has now confessed. "Which on the list?" asks Punalo drily. "Number Two or Number Three?" "Number Three," says Hali, unabashed. His father then decides to accept defeat with a good grace. Hali tells Sandra that he has brought one of his drums as a present for her, in the hope that she will forgive him. All are on the best of terms with one another when they go in to lunch.

George Freedley in the *New York Telegraph*, 20 August 1951, on the American production:

"We made one of our infrequent visits this summer to the silo circuit the other night. If there is anything less like the traditional summer barn than the Country Playhouse at Westport, the most chi-chi of the midsummer theatres, it simply doesn't come to mind. Like everyone else, I was curious to catch a glimpse of the new Noël Coward comedy, *Island Fling*, and to find out for myself whether my memory of the lovely Claudette Colbert was a true one. When I say that I had one of the pleasantest playgoing evenings in a long time, it is an understatement. There has been much talk of the slightness of the comedy, which seems beside the point. Mr Coward is no profound writer, but he is a deft comedian and he has certainly written a funnier and better play than his *Present Laughter*, which ran a season on Broadway.

"Back in my salad days I stage-managed Eugene O'Neill's tragic *Dynamo* for the Theatre Guild. The dynamic ingenue was none other than Claudette Colbert. I thought her a brilliant young actress then, and now, just as beautiful as ever, she is an even better technician, as her forte was always comedy. The last time I saw her on stage was in *See Naples and Die*, and she doesn't look a day older, nor has she lost her talent for acting on the stage. She projects as delightfully now as then. Her handling of the drunken scene was deft and delicious, taking the sting out of it, but never losing character. The hundreds of theatregoers who saw her in Westport and Dennis will certainly deplore the fact that she is returning to Hollywood, and Broadway apparently isn't to have a chance to see how really good Miss Colbert is.

"Certainly, Edith Meiser should not be accused of deliberately stealing the show, but Mr Coward gave her the best lines, and John C. Wilson, as director, gave her the funniest business. Miss Meiser is one of our best comediennes, and it seems a pity that we can't see her more often. As the weary sophisticate, the Honourable Maud Witterby, Miss Meiser uses her considerable length and slenderness to excellent advantage. When she is describing the lack of imperturbability of Chinese children, I howled along with the rest of the audience. As she languidly presses her highball against her forehead to indicate the extreme heat and humidity of this South Sea British possession, you chuckled at the knowingness of the gesture. Whether this was pure Meiser or there were Wilson directorial touches is unknown to me. However, as one who attends the theatre, I want Meiser.

"Berry Kroeger gives a splendidly bumptious performance as the North of England Labour politician who has become Sir George and the Governor of the island. He is particularly good in his scenes with Miss Colbert. They establish a genuine rapport as man and wife. Cherry Hardy is superb as Cuckoo Honey, the local Mrs Grundy. She is so exasperating, she is wonderful. Chester Stratton plays the Earl of Sharpenhoe, who is the inevitable impersonation of Mr Coward himself, who must appear in all his comedies. He is splendidly amusing.

"Leon Janney gives the best performance I have seen him give as Hali Alani, the local political leader who conceives an overpowering yen for Lady Alexandra (Miss Colbert). Gordon Mills is effective as a Government House aide, and could do nicely with a romantic lead in a different kind of play."

Harold Hobson in the *Sunday Times*, 29 April 1956, of the London production:

"Mr Noël Coward, at over fifty, still retains that power to surprise, scandalise and amuse which made him the adored, as well as the abused, *enfant terrible* of the 1920s. You never know whether he will be stormy petrel, petard, pianist, Puritan, or even, very occasionally, puerile; though you can be certain he will never be peasant, poet, pedant or Pecksniff. In the first instalment of his autobiography he told gleefully of his lack of enthusiasm for the military life; in the second he emerged as the thoughtful elder statesman, mindful of the responsibilities of Empire.

"One might say that in this Mr Coward follows a normal line of development; it is frequent for rebellion to pass into reconciliation. But with Mr Coward things are not so simple. In *Cavalcade*, a work of his middle period, he was imbued with a sense of the glories of British imperialism. But in his latest play he makes the loss of India the subject of a joke that is only a little wry, and finds it stimulating that the wife of a governor of a British colony should spend a gay night banging drums and drinking strong liquor in a secluded beach hut with one of its aborigines. It is true that her husband, the governor, holds socialist views, and comes from Huddersfield rather than Harrow. Neither of these facts seems to commend him to Mr Coward. Even so, the heroine of *Cavalcade* would have been as shocked by Lady Alexandra Shotter's behaviour as were some of Wednesday night's audience. But it is, of course, precisely in this provocative unexpectedness of his attitude, and the calculated but apparently casual wit with which he expresses it, that Mr Coward's entertainment lies.

"*South Sea Bubble* is an almost perfect example of co-operation between author, company and director. When it comes to the roaring megaphones of contemporary violence, the West End stage cuts a poor figure by the side of Broadway; neither has it the intellectual vitality of Paris; but in presentation of the glittering, slippery surfaces of what used to be called 'high life' it is unrivalled.

"The first scene of the play, set on a veranda ablaze with sunlight and looking on to a glimmering sea, somewhere off the coast of China, introduces us to the most exalted personages of that shining area: the progressive, stodgy Governor, Sir George Shotter; Edward Honey, the Colonial Secretary, and his plain-spoken wife; an Admiral, an A.D.C., the Chief of Police; a wealthy, classically educated native and his son, Hali Alani; and a distinguished visitor, John Blair Kennedy, an author than whom Mr Coward himself could not be more blasé, witty, or, on occasion, quietly and deliberately insolent; and, of course, more important than all, Lady Alexandra herself, an amusing rattle, surpassingly pretty, and ready at a moment's notice to turn any man's head. The best part of this act is a dialogue on political differences between the wealthy and Conservative subject, played brilliantly by Mr Alan Webb, and Mr Ian Hunter's serviceable Governor; and it is typical of Mr Coward's provocativeness that he should make the political issue depend on the question of public conveniences, with a side-kick at British Railways.

"The director, Mr William Chappell, has caused his players to take this act at what must be the fastest speed ever heard on the West End stage; it is almost incredible that the players, speaking as rapidly as they do, should remain both human and audible. Not till the pace is dropped in the second act for an excellent scene in which Mr Arthur Macrae, as Kennedy, by a series of insulting monosyllables, reduces to silence Miss Joyce Carey's excellently irritating Mrs Honey does one begin to suspect that the speed of the opening is designed to disguise its thinness. In this it succeeds; the dialogue seems to flash and sparkle; rarely, if I am right, has the fear of players worn a gayer air.

"The drunken scene – I am not fond of drunken scenes – has an agreeably unforeseen conclusion; and Lady Alexandra's spirited defence of herself before her indignant husband a genuinely witty excitement; but it would have been better for the play had Lady Alexandra extricated herself from her difficulties by her own resource, instead of through the magnanimity of Hali Alani, which is tame and out of character. All the same, *South Sea Bubble* is the best play Mr Coward has written for a long time.

"I have already suggested the quality of the acting and the direction. Mr Ronald Lewis plays Hali Alani with a sing-song voice and a fascinating smile. But, naturally, Miss Vivien Leigh as Lady Alexandra is the splendour of the production. Her performance shines like the stars, and is as troubling as the inconstant moon."

PUBLICATIONS

Island Fling/South Sea Bubble was first published by Heinemann (London, 1956); it is undedicated. It is also included in *Play Parade, Volume VI* (1962), and in *Noël Coward Collected Plays: Six*, Methuen World Classics (London, 1999).

NOTES

Between writing *Peace in Our Time* (1946) and *Home and Colonial* (1949), Coward adapted in 1947 one of his own short stories, *What Mad Pursuit?* from *To Step Aside* (1939) into a play called *Long Island Sound*. This has not been produced. *Home and Colonial* was revised and retitled *Island Fling* for its try-out at Westport, one of America's principal summer theatres.

Once again Coward uses, as a setting for his play, the mythical Pacific island of Samolo, which he created for *We Were Dancing* (*Tonight at 8.30*) and for which he wrote a "guide" in the programme of *Pacific 1860* when he used it again.

In 1955 it was again retitled and revised, and produced in England as *South Sea Bubble* in 1956.

The revision included the omission of two characters, some minor changes of names, and the division of Act I into two scenes, which was abandoned after the Manchester try-out.

In his introduction in *Play Parade*, Coward wrote: "While I am quite prepared to admit that *South Sea Bubble* does not rank among my best comedies such as *Hay Fever, Private Lives, Design for Living, Present Laughter* and *Blithe Spirit*, it still has, to my prejudiced eye, a good deal to recommend it. I find Sandra a gay and enchanting character, so much so that I have re-introduced her in my recent novel *Pomp and Circumstance*. Hali Alani, George Shotter and Cuckoo Honey have also achieved this literary distinction, although in a minor degree.

"To be honest, I consider the first act to be rather verbose and lacking in action, but from then on the play gathers momentum and I have found it highly entertaining both to write and read. The fact that my inner vision of it has never been distracted by seeing it performed may have a lot to do with my pleasure in it. In fact I still envisage it being played by Gertrude Lawrence and, with all loving respect to Vivien and courteous bows to Claudette Colbert, Elizabeth Sellars, and whoever else decides to have a bash at Sandra, I still know that no one in the world, however gifted and charming, could endow her with the unique quality that was Gertie's own special enchantment."

A charity preview of the London production was given at the Lyric Theatre, London, on 24 April in aid of the Central School of Speech and Drama.

Act II, Scenes 1 and 2 were televised by the BBC from the theatre before an invited audience on 14 September 1956.

South Sea Bubble was revived on 4 September 1985 at the Connaught Theatre, Worthing, with Barbara Murray and Glyn Houston and directed by Allan Davis.

418

39
ACE OF CLUBS
A NEW MUSICAL PLAY
Written in 1949

FIRST PRESENTED by Tom Arnold at the Palace Theatre, Manchester, 16 May 1950. (The company remained in Manchester for 3 weeks, then visited Liverpool for 2 weeks and Birmingham for 2 weeks.)

SUBSEQUENTLY PRESENTED at the Cambridge Theatre, London, 7 July 1950 (211 performances).

CHARACTERS	Manchester and Cambridge, 1950
ELAINE	Bubbly Rogers
RITA MARBURY	Sylvia Cecil
BENNY LUCAS	Raymond Young
SAMMY BLAKE	Robb Stewart
FELIX FULTON	Myles Eason
ACE OF CLUBS GIRLS	
DAWN O'HARA	Sylvia Verney
DOREEN HARVEY	Margaret Miles
SUNNY CLAIRE	June Whitfield
RUBY FOWLER	Erica Yorke
GRETA HUGHES	Pamela Devis
BETTY CLEMENTS	Lorna Drewes
MIMI JOSHUA	Vivien Merchant
JUNE APRIL	Lisbeth Kearns
BABY BELGRAVE	Jean Carson
HERCULES BROTHERS	Victor Harman, Ronald Francis, Stanley Howlett
JOSEPH SNYDER	Elwyn Brook-Jones
GUS	Patrick Westwood
PINKIE LEROY	Pat Kirkwood
HARRY HORNBY	Graham Payn
CLARICE	Eileen Tatler
EVA	Renee Hill
YVONNE HALL	Jean Inglis
MAVIS DEAN	Gail Kendall

DETECTIVE-INSPECTOR WARRILOVE	Jack Lambert
POLICEMAN	Michael Darbyshire
MR PRICE	Philip Rose
MRS PRICE	Stella White
JUVENILE DELINQUENTS	Peter Tuddenham, Colin Kemball, Norman Warwick
FIRST PLAIN-CLOTHES MAN	Manfred Priestley
SECOND PLAIN-CLOTHES MAN	Christopher Calthrop
DRUMMER	Don Fitz Stanford
WAITERS	George Selfe, Richard Gill, Jacques Gautier
NIGHT CLUB HABITUÉS AND VISITORS	Nina Alvis, Irene Derek, Hilda Fayre, Julia Hand, Diana Houlston, Lorna Kilner, Melanie Paul, Claire Pollock, Barbara Dalby Smith, Susan Swinford, Dorothy Thomas, Madge White, Stella White, Peter Armsten, Charles Belchier, Peter Fairaine, George Humphries, Tony Hilton, Vernon Kelso, Carl Lacey, Herbert Lister, Michael Mellinger, Arthur Norman, Stuart Pearce, John Raymonde, Philip Rose, Frank Singuineau, Bernard Verrey
Director	*Noël Coward*
Designer	*G. E. Calthrop*

❖

SCENE: The action of the play takes place in the Ace of Clubs,
         a night-club in Soho, and in Soho Square, London.

ACT I: Scene 1: The Club. 1 a.m.
         Scene 2: The Office. A few minutes later.
         Scene 3: The Club. A few minutes later.
         Scene 4: Soho Square. A minute later.
         Scene 5: The Club. A few minutes later.
         Scene 6: The Club. 5.30 the next afternoon.
         Scene 7: Soho Square. 10.30 a.m.
         Scene 8: The Club. Midnight.

Scene 9: The Office. About 1 a.m.

Scene 10: The Club. A few minutes later.

ACT II: Scene 1: The Club. About two minutes later.

Scene 2: Soho Square. The same time.

Scene 3: The Office. A few minutes later.

Scene 4: The Club. The next afternoon.

Scene 5: Soho Square. About 7 p.m.

Scene 6: The Office. Just after midnight.

Scene 7: The Club. A little later.

Scene 8: The Office. A little later.

Scene 9: The Club. A little later.

Orchestra direction	*Mantovani*
Orchestration	*Ronald Binge and Mantovani*

MUSICAL NUMBERS

ACT I

"Top Of The Morning"	Baby and Ace of Clubs' Girls
"My Kind Of Man"	Pinkie
"This Could Be True"	Pinkie and Harry
"Nothing Can Last For Ever"	Rita
"Something About A Sailor"	Harry
(*Dance arranged by Freddie Carpenter*)	
"I'd Never, Never Know"	Pinkie
"Three Juvenile Delinquents"	Juvenile Delinquents
"Sail Away"	Harry
"Josephine"	Pinkie
Reprise: "My Kind Of Man"	Pinkie
"Would You Like To Stick A Pin In My Balloon?"	Ace of Clubs' Girls

ACT II

"In A Boat On A Lake With My Darling"	Sextet
"I Like America"	Harry and Ace of Clubs' Girls
(*Dance arranged by Freddie Carpenter*)	
"Why Does Love Get In The Way?"	Pinkie
"Three Juvenile Delinquents"	Juvenile Delinquents
"Evening In Summer"	Rita

Reprise: "Sail Away"	Harry
"Time For Baby's Bottle"	Baby, Yvonne, Mavis
"Chase Me, Charlie"	Pinkie
Reprise: "Nothing Can Last For Ever"	Rita
Reprise: "My Kind Of Man"	Pinkie

SYNOPSIS

ACT I, Scene 1: The Ace of Clubs is a Soho night-club, owned by Rita Marbury and run by the sleek and shady Benny Lucas. The star of its floor show, "London Frolic", is Pinkie Leroy. It is about 1 a.m. and the dance floor is crowded. The compère, Felix Fulton, announces "London Frolic", which begins with a coster number. The Ace of Clubs' Girls, in "pearly" brassières and trunks and large, feathered hats, form a background to Baby Belgrave, the soubrette, who, as a Covent Garden porter, sings "Top Of The Morning", The lights fade as the next number – an acrobatic turn by the Hercules Brothers – is announced.

Scene 2: In the office a few minutes later, Benny Lucas is receiving instructions from the dangerous racketeer, Smiling Snyder. A mackintosh with a parcel in its pocket will be checked in at the cloakroom and the ticket given to Benny, who must then collect it, take the parcel out and put it in the safe, for delivery to Snyder after the show. At closing time the mackintosh will be collected by Gus, Snyder's attendant thug.

Scene 3: The Hercules Brothers have just finished. It is time for Pinkie's song, "My Kind Of Man". Singing, she moves among the tables. As she passes near Snyder, he grabs her and forcibly kisses her. A young sailor who has given Pinkie a bunch of roses comes to her help and knocks him down. The gangster draws a gun and fires it. In the ensuing confusion, Pinkie seizes her champion by the hand and drags him out through the gentlemen's cloakroom.

Scene 4: Pinkie and the sailor come running out into Soho Square. Over her glittering evening dress the girl has thrown a mackintosh which she snatched as they passed through the cloakroom.

They sit down on a seat to recover their breath. Pinkie thanks the young man, but warns him that he will get into serious trouble if he fights gangsters in night clubs. He introduces himself as Harry Hornby, on leave from his ship, and assures her that his intentions towards her are strictly honourable. She says she must go back to the club, but he had better not accompany her.

Investigating the contents of the mackintosh pockets, she finds the parcel; as she puts the things back, it drops out unobserved.

When Harry asks if he can see her again, she at first demurs; but then the music starts up and they sing a duet, "This Could Be True", at the end of which they embrace. She agrees to see him next day at the rehearsal, warning him not to come to the night show, when Snyder and his gang will be on the look-out. After Pinkie has gone, Harry sings a reprise of the song; then, catching sight of the packet, he picks it up and saunters away.

Scene 5: In the now empty club Benny is cross-questioning Eva, the cloakroom girl, about the mackintosh. Tearfully, she says someone must have taken it when she ran out in a panic after the shots were fired. On her return she found it missing, with the torn-off ticket lying on the floor. Benny sacks her and she stamps out indignantly. Then Gus tells Benny that "the Boss" will be furious at his failure to carry through their scheme.

Still wearing the mackintosh, Pinkie steals in and overhears enough to realise that the package is valuable. Searching her pockets, she finds that it is gone. Benny catches sight of her, tears the mackintosh from her shoulders, and runs through the pockets.

Meantime, the proprietress, Rita, comes out to investigate the cause of the shots. She gathers that Gus has some underhand plan, and tells him firmly to "get out". Then she tries to find out more from Benny. She realises that he is in trouble with the Snyder gang, but her questioning is unsuccessful. Losing his temper, he declares that he is sick of being bossed by her. He accuses her of running the club like a church social, and of keeping him short of money. Rita quietly says he had better go – they can talk it over next day, if he is not in gaol.

When Benny and Pinkie have gone, Rita, obviously upset, pulls herself together and sings "Nothing Can Last For Ever."

Scene 6: It is 5.30 next afternoon, and Felix is rehearsing the eight dancing girls in a new routine. Three other artistes, Baby Belgrave, Yvonne Hall and Mavis Dean, are present, but not in practice dress, and their badinage does not improve the temper of Felix, who is exasperated by the mistakes made by one of the girls, June April.

During a break Harry Hornby comes on, carrying a bunch of roses. Pinkie is at the dressmaker's, but the others invite him to come with them for a cup of coffee. They go off together, after he has sung "Something About A Sailor".

Rita and Benny then enter with Detective-Inspector Warrilove, who is investigating the shooting incident. He suspects that the gunman was Snyder, though they deny it, and before leaving he warns them that the gangster was involved in the Sunningdale jewel robbery, and that if they do not keep clear of him the club may have to be closed down.

Pinkie finds Benny in a very bad temper. He advises her to keep her sailor away from the club, as he has caused enough trouble already. The girl replies with spirit that she is not paid to let herself be mauled by Benny's dirty gangster friends. Uncertain how much she knows, the Manager becomes conciliatory. He points out Harry's roses and draws a graphic picture of the life that Pinkie may expect as a sailor's wife in a small house at Chatham, with "a child in her arms, two more at her knee – and another at borstal". With a final warning not to forget her career, he leaves her, and Pinkie, sitting with the roses in her lap, sings "I'll Never, Never Know".

Scene 7: In Soho Square Pinkie and Harry are sitting locked in each other's arms. Talking about Benny's warning, the girl remembers that Harry still has the parcel, and they discuss whether to take it to the police, but decide that Harry shall bring it to the rehearsal next day, to be returned unopened to Benny. Though Pinkie feels that it is unsafe for Harry to visit the club after dark, he insists on coming to the show. After she has hurried away to dress for it, he stays behind and sings "Sail Away".

Scene 8: In the floor show, Baby Belgrave, Yvonne Hall and Mavis Dean, dressed as little girls, are taking a call after their turn. Then Felix announces Pinkie as the Empress Josephine. Supported by eight Ace of Clubs' Girls dressed as Directoire belles and gallants, she descends the steps in a white dress, a long blue velvet cloak, and a glittering crown, singing "Josephine".

Scene 9: In the office, Snyder, with bandaged head, is conspiring with Gus to kidnap Harry, who is at his usual table. They have got Rita out of the way by a faked telephone call, so that the coast will be clear for them.

Scene 10: The floor show continues. Moving among the tables, Pinkie sings "My Kind Of Man". Harry makes a movement to give her the roses he has brought, but she signs to him to wait. Passing on, she continues her song at another table on the opposite side and does not hear a slight scuffle. When she returns Harry's table is empty. Seeing his overturned chair, she guesses that something drastic has happened, hurriedly finishes her number and runs off. Felix, realising that something is wrong, calls on the girls for the next number. They run on, waving coloured balloons and singing "Would You Like To Stick A Pin In My Balloon?"

ACT II, Scene 1: The girls are finishing their balloon number as the curtain rises. Then Felix and Baby in summer clothes, reclining in a canvas boat against a backdrop painted as a lake, sing a duet, "In A Boat On A Lake With My Darling".

Scene 2: After knocking Harry on the head, Gus and Snyder have dragged him out into Soho Square. To a passing policeman they explain that he is a young sailor friend of theirs who has been overcome by drink and they are trying to revive him in the open air. During this conversation Harry revives, and when Gus goes to fetch a car to carry him off he attacks Snyder and escapes.

Scene 3: Rita has returned to the club with Detective-Inspector Warrilove. Both are mystified by the faked telephone call. They realise that it was made to get her out of the way, but everything in the club appears normal. The detective tells Rita that an emerald necklace, missing after the Sunningdale jewel robbery, has been traced to the club, and that Benny may be mixed up with its disappearance. In return, Rita admits to him that Snyder was, in fact, responsible for the shooting incident of the previous night.

They go out together and Harry cautiously slips in, hiding behind the desk as he hears someone approaching. He sees Pinkie come in with Benny. The girl has been crying, but is now grimly determined, insisting that she will not go on with the show unless he promises to find out immediately what has happened to Harry. She threatens to tell the police about the parcel in the mackintosh pocket, but agrees to keep silent and return it to Benny if he lets her know about Harry within 20 minutes. When he has gone out she bursts into tears. Harry puts his arms round her and says reassuringly: "It's all right. The navy's here."

Scene 4: Felix is rehearsing the girls in a new number, "Time For Baby's Bottle", in which they represent luxury brands of perfume. As usual, June is out of step, and Felix, exasperated, calls her a "flat-chested dumb-cluck". She retaliates and there is a violent row, which leads to his dismissing the rehearsal and stamping out.

The girls sit down to rest and June reminds them (not for the first time) that the next day is her birthday. After they have passed some caustic remarks about her elderly lover, Mr Lazarus, she goes off to her dressing-room.

Baby, Yvonne and Mavis come back from a shopping expedition. Irritated by June's continual hints for a birthday present, they have bought her a pair of false bosoms. They put a card in the parcel and tie it up again, deciding to give it to her at midnight between the shows.

Meanwhile Harry comes in, bringing roses and the parcel from the mackintosh, which he puts down on the table. He gives the girls a graphic account of his adventure with Snyder, which they think he is inventing for a joke. In response to their request for details of his travels, he sings "I Like America", at the end of which the girls dance off. Baby snatches up the package with her own hat and handbag, and the parcel with June's birthday present is left on the table.

Pinkie comes in and Harry gives her the flowers. She is about to take the parcel to Benny when Harry suggests that they ought to give it to the police.

He is jealous of Benny, and the argument works up to a quarrel. Throwing the parcel at Pinkie's feet, he stamps out.

Benny then appears and Pinkie, thoroughly upset, tells him she is sick of the club and everything to do with it. She in turn throws the parcel at him, and he, muttering "Thank God!" grabs it and returns to his office. Disconsolately, Pinkie sings "Why Does Love Get In The Way?"

Scene 5: While taking a breath of air in Soho Square, Rita has a friendly chat with a policeman and then sings "Evening In Summer", after which she strolls off. In a gloomy mood, Harry sits on the seat, where he is found by June April. Her well-meant comments on Pinkie's popularity with everyone – including Benny – do little to cheer him up. After she has left him he sings a reprise of "Sail Away".

Scene 6: It is just before midnight, and the girls are waiting in the office for their salary. Suddenly June bursts in, radiant, and thanks them effusively for their birthday present: "Of course, I know they're only props, but they look absolutely genuine. I'm thrilled." She promises to wear them for the perfume number. Coming on hurriedly with Snyder and Gus, Benny sends the girls away. He says he will pay them later. Now he has important business to discuss. He unlocks the safe and gives the parcel to Snyder, receiving in exchange an envelope full of banknotes. Surprised by the amount of money, he asks: "What's in the package, anyway – the Koh-i-noor diamond?"

Rita comes in and orders the two men to leave. She has heard from Warrilove that an emerald necklace, missing from the Sunningdale robbery, has been traced to the club, and she warns Benny that he has done for himself this time.

Scene 7: The floor show is again in full swing. Felix introduces Yvonne, Mavis and Baby, who sing "Time For Baby's Bottle", supported by the eight girls dressed in cellophane crinolines, their headgear shaped like bottle-stoppers, each one representing a luxury perfume. The last of them is June April as "Shocking", wearing a dazzling necklace and earrings of pearls and emeralds. Seeing this, Detective-Inspector Warrilove in the audience half rises from his chair. When the song is finished he goes out, accompanied by his two plain-clothes men, and follows June backstage.

The scene closes with Pinkie, dressed as a small girl and carrying a toy black cat, singing "Chase Me, Charlie".

Scene 8: Benny, in his office, is checking over the salary list when Snyder and Gus come in, livid with rage. To Benny's bewilderment, they fling the false bosoms on the desk. "What have you done with the necklace and earrings?" shouts Snyder seizing Benny and shaking him. Gus also grabs him and twists his arms – Benny still protesting that he has no idea what they mean.

Suddenly Warrilove emerges from behind the curtain with a gun in one hand and the necklace in the other. "Is this what you were looking for, Snyder?" he asks.

The two plain-clothes men handcuff Snyder and Gus. When Rita comes in, the Inspector lets her know that he does not intend to charge Benny, though he gives him a stiff warning that he will not escape next time.

After Gus and Snyder have been removed, Rita puts her hand on Benny's shoulder and softly sings a reprise of her waltz song, "Nothing Can Last For Ever".

Scene 9: The finale of the floor show is in progress, and the company are massing for an ensemble. As Pinkie sings "My Kind Of Man", she catches sight of Harry sitting at his usual table with a bunch of roses. He rises and hands them to her. Everyone applauds as he takes her in his arms and they sing together:

> On the wings of the morning
> With your own true love,
> Sail away – sail away – sail away.

Alan Dent in the *News Chronicle*, 2 July 1950:

"It is not the ace of trumps. But it will serve to take a trick.

"Mr Coward has had the courage of his affections, and has set his new 'musical' in dear old London – or, at least, dear old Soho – and in the present day.

"Such a daring choice raises two immediate problems for the author-composer to solve and overcome: (1) He must reconcile us to the operetta convention among scenes so familiar to most of us. (2) He must devise a plot exciting enough to compensate us for the romance of other times and distant places.

"Does Mr Coward remove these two big snags? Well, he is at least well aware of them, and he does all that ingenuity, wit, a kind of bitter-sweet tunefulness, a crafty hand with sentiment, and a dash of genius can do to make us pretend they don't exist.

"He sets us bang in the middle of a Soho night-club, and never takes us any further away from it than a bench in Soho Square. His heroine is a night-club singer (Pat Kirkwood) who 'falls for' an infatuated sailor on leave (Graham Payn).

"The course of this sudden but true love affair runs far from smoothly on account of crooks and spivs and a little parcel containing an emerald necklace.

"Yes, it is that kind of story – necklace and all. And the lovers have a misunderstanding and a quarrel – and they make it up again. And there is an ageing but dignified lady – a night-club queen, if you please – who cannot be left alone without breaking into nostalgic songs with titles like "Nothing Can Last For Ever".

"Such is Mr Coward's skill that we can accept even this, the spectacle of a handsome harridan who has spent her life conniving at crime with one eye, beaming at the police with the other, and who is now lamenting inexorable autumn in sugary sweet strains and Sylvia Cecil's true soprano voice.

"In the case of Miss Kirkwood and Mr Payn, the convention is far more easily accepted and acceptable.

"Our heroine sings most of her songs in the course of her job. And our hero sings most of his to entertain the chorus-girls (and us) while waiting for his sweetie to change her dress.

"Their duets? Well, these have to take place in Soho Square. The musical comedy law allows it, and the court apparently does not condemn it.

"Besides, Miss Kirkwood and Mr Payn, whether apart or together, sing, act, behave and dance so delightfully that only a churl – or an exceptionally officious bobby! – could question the concatenation of such a time, such a place, and such loved ones.

"Early on these two have a shy little duet with a shy little dance – 'This Could Be True' – which is, to my way of thinking and responding, the most charming item in a score quite reasonably full of charming items.

"The wittiest is a trio for 'Three Juvenile Delinquents' – which, in its punch and incisiveness, takes us away back twelve years to that quartet in Mr Coward's *Operette*, which had an even jollier tune.

"This is a brilliantly nasty trio of cunning young animals; each one is a cosh personified; and they liken themselves to Faith and Hope and Charitee!

"For the rest, the show is lively and well ordered, and has many happy little pieces of observation and invention which add up to the impression of a night-club that is only too like the real thing.

"It is a show to make the visitor to London think that Soho is the heart of London, and it will make even the Londoner think that Soho has a heart. This is quite a feat on Mr Coward's part.

"He put out his witty tongue three or four times, but for the rest he keeps it in either cheek, alternately. It is all as though he had set out to satirise the conventional musical play, become seriously and tenderly interested, and concluded by achieving a little masterpiece of convention, banality, piquancy, freshness, cuteness, impudence and characteristic self-expression."

❖

PUBLICATIONS

Ace of Clubs was published in *Play Parade, Volume VI* (1962).

The following songs are included in *The Noël Coward Song Book* (Michael Joseph, 1953): "Chase Me, Charlie", "Josephine", "Sail Away", "Why Does Love Get In The Way?", "I Like America", and "Three Juvenile Delinquents".

NOTES

In his introduction to *Play Parade, Volume VI*, Coward wrote: "*Ace of Clubs* was another attempt to break away from a tradition I had established for myself. With the exception of revues my only musicals to date had been in period – *Bitter Sweet* Victorian, *Conversation Piece* Regency, *Operette* Edwardian and *Pacific 1860* Victorian colonial. I considered that the time had come to write a musical play in a modern setting with contemporary songs. Most of the contemporary songs were good but the book was uninspired and was not helped by either the setting or the production. The leading parts were played with willing gusto by Pat Kirkwood, Sylvia Cecil and Graham Payn; and three young men, Peter Tuddenham, Colin Kemball and Norman Warwick, stopped the show nightly with a trio 'Three Juvenile Delinquents'. There is not much more to be said about it really. The situation is not entirely without merit and the whole show had a certain breeziness, but something went wrong somewhere along the line and the finished product fell far short of what I hoped it would be. At least it anticipated the present rash of Soho-Gangster British musicals by some years, so I can always comfort myself with the reflection that it was 'Before its Time'."

In the final typescript of the play a song "Three Theatrical Dames" was included for Baby, Yvonne and Mavis. This was to be sung as the first item in the Cabaret Scene, Act II, Scene 7, but was omitted in production. It was produced eventually as an item in The *Night of 100 Stars* at the London Palladium on 28 June 1956 (a Midnight Matinée in aid of the Actors' Orphanage), and the song was sung, with some introductory dialogue, by Peter Ustinov (Dame Rosie), Laurence Harvey (Dame Margaret), and Paul Scofield (Dame Laura). It was produced by Henry Kendall.

At a similar performance in 1953, "Three Juvenile Delinquents" was sung by Laurence Olivier, John Gielgud and John Mills. It was repeated in 1955, Danny Kaye replacing John Gielgud.

These were no professional stage revivals of *Ace of Clubs* at home or abroad after 1950 until 7 January 1999 when, to celebrate the centenary of Coward's birth, the Attic Theatre Company staged a small-scale revival at the Wimbledon Studio Theatre, directed by Jenny Lee.

Ace of Clubs was the final form of a show that not only changed its title – it was variously called *Over the Garden Wall* and *Hoi Polloi* – but also its storyline. As *Hoi Polloi* it told the story of the same sailor, Harry Hornby, on a one-day leave in London. He meets Pinky, who in this version is a nice cockney girl with a family in Stepney. After sharing the day together – outside Buckingham Palace, in the park and at a society party – they part but with an understanding to go on meeting. The story reads in many ways like a post-war continuation of *This Happy Breed*. Several of the songs in that fully realised book were taken into *Ace of Clubs*.

40
RELATIVE VALUES

(Originally called *Moxie*)

A LIGHT COMEDY

Written in 1951

FIRST PRESENTED by H. M. Tennent Ltd. and John C. Wilson at the Theatre Royal, Newcastle, 15 October 1951 (6 weeks' tour: Glasgow, Oxford, Brighton, Bournemouth and Leeds).

SUBSEQUENTLY PRESENTED at the Savoy Theatre, London, 28 November 1951 (477 performances).

CHARACTERS	Newcastle and Savoy, 1951
CRESTWELL	Richard Leech
ALICE	Renee Hill
MRS MOXTON (Moxie)	Angela Baddeley
FELICITY, COUNTESS OF MARSHWOOD	Gladys Cooper
LADY HAYLING	Dorothy Batley
THE HON. PETER INGLETON	Simon Lack
ADMIRAL SIR JOHN HAYLING	Charles Cullum
MIRANDA FRAYLE	Judy Campbell
THE EARL OF MARSHWOOD (Nigel)	Ralph Michael
DON LUCAS	Hugh McDermott
Director	*Noël Coward*
Designer	*Michael Relph*

❖

SCENE: The action of the play takes place in Marshwood House, East Kent.

TIME: Early July.

ACT I: Scene I: Saturday afternoon. After lunch.

               Scene 2: A few hours later.

ACT II: Scene 1: Before dinner.

               Scene 2: After dinner.

ACT III: The next morning.

SYNOPSIS

ACT I, Scene 1: Alice, a young housemaid at Marshwood House, is chattering to the butler, Crestwell, as she helps him tidy cocktail glasses from the living-room (known as "the library"). While the Countess of Marshwood is at lunch. The son of the house has just become engaged to a film star, Miranda Frayle, and Alice is thrilled at the prospect of seeing her screen heroine in the flesh; but Crestwell makes dryly humorous comments on the situation.

When the lady's maid, Mrs Moxton (Moxie), joins them and sends Alice about her business, she is obviously very much upset. She tells Crestwell that when Miranda walks into the house she herself will walk out – a point of view which strikes the sardonically tolerant butler as extremely arbitrary.

The Countess of Marshwood (Felicity) then enters with her luncheon guests, Admiral Sir John Hayling, Lady Hayling and the Hon. Peter Ingleton. She was obviously a beauty in her day: "indeed, a vestige of the foolish, maligned twenties still clings to her". Asking Moxie for the church fête list and a plan of the ground, she tries in scatter-brained fashion to rearrange the side-shows. It occurs to her that Moxie looks ill, and, sending her to lie down, she asks Crestwell what is the matter. The butler tactfully hints that she is distressed at the Earl of Marshwood's forthcoming marriage. When he has gone out, Felicity comments that he is invaluable, and she will miss him when she leaves the house, as she is determined to do when her son Nigel is married. She found his first wife sufficiently trying – in fact, she felt on the verge of strangling her when the marriage disintegrated. However, she is used to Nigel's habit of falling in love with impossible women, and – in contrast to the Haylings' indignation – she takes the situation calmly, deciding that "masterly inaction" is her best policy. When they have gone, she confesses to her quizzical and sympathetic nephew, Peter, that she is really unhappy about his choice – she would have liked someone of his own class to run Marshwood and be a stepmother to Jeremy, the son of his first wife.

A long-distance call comes from Nigel, saying that he and Miranda are on their way and will arrive at Marshwood about six in the evening. Moxie, who has been waiting impatiently to speak to her employer, comes with an improbable story about a sick aunt as an excuse for leaving at once. Felicity points out that Moxie has been with her for 20 years and surely cannot desert her in this crisis. The suspicion crosses her mind that the housekeeper may at one time have been Nigel's mistress. Repudiating the suggestion with horror, Moxie blurts out her real reason: "Miss Miranda Frayle happens to be my young sister!"

Scene 2: Over tea, Felicity discusses the situation with Peter. By now she has heard Miranda's history: her real name was Freda Birch, daughter of a Brixton greengrocer. A flighty girl who "kept on almost having babies, but not quite", she had left home 20 years previously, after a violent scene, going to America with her theatrical agent. Soon afterwards her mother died, the shop failed, and the elder sister, Dora (Moxie), came to Marshwood as a housemaid.

Peter has the brilliant idea that things would be less awkward if Moxie were described as Felicity's secretary-companion instead of her personal maid. Rather dubiously, Felicity calls Crestwell and puts the suggestion to him, asking how this arrangement would affect the other servants. The butler points out the difficulty of meals – Moxie could no longer eat in the kitchen; she would have to have a tray upstairs. When his employer, in strict confidence, tells him the reason for all this, he replies imperturbably that it is "a coincidence in the best traditions of English high comedy".

However, Moxie flatly refuses to pose as something she is not, merely to save her sister from embarrassment. Crestwell then has an idea. Why not pretend that Moxie has inherited money and, being attached to Marshwood, is staying on as a friend of the family? She would then meet her sister on equal terms, not as one of the staff. Reluctantly, Moxie consents, and they have just reached this decision when they hear the visitors arriving.

ACT II, Scene 1: Felicity and Nigel, dressed for dinner, are discussing the metamorphosis of Moxie, which the young man finds highly unsuitable and embarrassing. His mother makes him promise to say nothing to Miranda, and assures him that she and Moxie will both be leaving Marshwood after his marriage.

Nigel tells her about his lightning romance with Miranda, whom he first met on a bathing-raft at the Cap d'Antibes. He retells her own version of her life-story: how she has been married to a man called Greenberg who was "foul" to her, and how her rumoured love affair with her leading man, Don Lucas, was "three-quarters studio publicity". Of her early days he knows merely that after her mother's death she went to America as a dancer, and that she had one elder sister who went to the bad and is now dead.

Crestwell and Alice, bringing in cocktail equipment, report that there are some Girl Guides in the shrubbery, wanting Miranda's autograph. Felicity sends Alice to collect their albums and tell them to call for them in the morning. To Nigel's annoyance, Crestwell says that the local newspaper reporter wants to interview Miranda next day, and Felicity insists that the young man – who writes up her church bazaar each year – must be seen.

While the cocktails are being made, Miranda comes down, dressed discreetly for a country house and carrying a work-bag. Evidently determined to be meek and dutiful, she refuses drinks and sits sipping lemonade. She does not recognise her sister, who looks very smart in an evening gown and jewellery lent by her employer. Putting on her glasses, Miranda settles to needlework, telling meanwhile – to Moxie's rising indignation – a picturesque story of her neglected childhood in a slum: how, when her mother sent her to fetch beer from a pub, she used to dance in the streets to a barrel organ. She adds that her elder sister Dora took to drink and died in squalor.

In answer to Peter, she declares she is definitely giving up her career when she marries: "The Countess of Marshwood shall be the longest and greatest part I have ever played." Felicity expresses the hope that she will not find it too much of a strain.

There is a moment's awkwardness when Admiral and Lady Hayling arrive. The latter – surprised to find Moxie so smartly dressed – casually asks her to do a small sewing job which she forgot to ask her own maid, and is outraged when Moxie replies lightly: "Really, Cynthia, you'll be forgetting your head next!" Hastily, Felicity takes the Haylings off to explain the situation.

When dinner is announced, everyone goes in except Moxie, who remains behind for a few moments with Crestwell, telling him she is so angry at Miranda's lies about their mother ("Who never touched a drop in her life") that she cannot go through with her part. The butler gives her a martini and tells her to "get cracking".

Scene 2: The family are still at dinner when there is an unexpected caller – Don Lucas, Miranda's handsome American screen *vis-à-vis*. Obviously upset and also slightly drunk, he demands to see her. Crestwell, with tact, dry humour and the offer of Scotch whisky, wins his confidence and hears that he has flown over from Hollywood immediately upon hearing of the engagement. He fetches Miranda from the dining-room on the pretext that Don is a reporter from the famous *Life Magazine*.

Furious at the trick, Miranda calls Don a snake, adding that she has cut him out of her life like a withered limb and never wants to see him again. He retaliates by catching her in his arms and kissing her violently.

They have a rapid argument about their respective careers, which culminates in Don saying that she is only marrying her titled guy because she is "on the skids" since her last picture. She tells him repeatedly to go away, and he has just pressed a fervent farewell kiss on her lips when Felicity enters.

Making the best of the situation, Miranda introduces Don as an old friend who has dropped in to see her on his way up to London. Felicity extends a pressing invitation to him to stay the night, which, to Miranda's embarrassment, he accepts. His hostess rings for Crestwell to prepare a room for him. Don is then introduced to the others, and they make polite conversation over the coffee-cups. Emotion soon overcomes him, however. He goes out on to the terrace, and Nigel immediately protests to his mother about her inconsiderateness in inviting him to stay. Obviously he suspects a plot, and his reaction is to declare that he will drive Miranda up to London on Monday morning and marry her immediately.

At this, Moxie rises with the startling statement: "You are not going to marry her on Monday, nor on any other day of the week. You are not going to marry her at all." Miranda is horrified when she realises that Moxie is her not-so-dead sister, Dora, and has to listen while her tissue of romantic lies about herself is demolished. She collapses in tears, and Moxie firmly declares her intention of leaving the house for good next morning.

ACT III: It is 9.30 on Sunday morning, and Peter – the only member of the house-party who has come down to breakfast – is reading the newspaper when Don Lucas appears, suffering from a gloomy hangover. While Crestwell goes to mix him a "horse's neck", he confides his troubles to Peter and grasps his hand in token of friendship. Arriving just at this moment, Felicity sends Peter out and tells Don in confidence that she realises her son's projected marriage is a ghastly mistake, for Miranda obviously loves Don – all he need do is to keep up his courage and wait.

When Nigel returns, ill-humoured, from an early ride, his mother sends Peter and Don for a walk. She reminds her son that the local reporter has been waiting over an hour for an interview. Nigel is worried that she will spread the tales about Miranda's early life, and Felicity cleverly points out how impossible it is to have the future Lady Marshwood telling lies about herself. Moxie is leaving for Bexhill, she says, where she herself intends to join her soon. Suddenly Nigel blurts out:

"How can I marry Miranda in these circumstances?" His mother suggests he had better take the girl out for a picnic lunch and talk things over.

Don and Peter return, having come back on seeing a crowd of autograph-hunters at the gates; then they and Nigel go off separately. Crestwell brings in a pile of albums, and Felicity asks him to have Don Lucas's car brought round, as it may be needed.

Miranda then comes down, looking pale and unhappy. When Felicity asks her, as a favour, to give the reporter an interview, she refuses, saying she is going away – she cannot stay so long as her sister is there. Sweetly, Felicity remarks that "of course" she and Moxie will stay on at Marshwood after Nigel's marriage – a prospect that horrifies Miranda, who realises that the whole situation has been planned to make her look foolish in front of Nigel. Felicity goes to dress for church, and Nigel comes in to find Miranda in a fury. When she declares that she will not share a house with his mother, he takes a firm line, saying that she will live where he lives, and do what he asks her to do. He makes a dignified exit, leaving her in tears.

Don arrives in time to comfort her, and she is again discovered in his arms by Felicity, Nigel and Peter. She says she is driving up to town with Don and sweeps out, leaving Nigel and his mother to confess their mutual relief.

Coming to say goodbye, Moxie is told that Miranda has gone and everything is alright. The family go off to church, leaving Crestwell to cheer Moxie up with a drink. He toasts : "The final inglorious disintegration of the most unlikely dream that ever troubled the foolish heart of man – Social Equality."

J.C. Trewin in *John o'London's Weekly*, 14 December 1951:
"On the first night of an American farce at the Strand Theatre, the players bundled and scrambled their way through the third act, loyally speaking the lines and prepared obviously for the worst. If ever a play appeared with the mark of doom on its forehead, this was it. I remembered Shaw at another affair in the nineties: 'The actor who played Geoffrey Tempest fulfilled his obligations scrupulously, but with the air of a man who is resolved to shoot himself the moment the curtain is down.'

"So it was at the farce called *Mary had a Little...*, one of the four most painfully inept pieces I can recall. When the rush and clatter had ended, and the cast had scrupulously fulfilled all but one of its obligations, the curtain began to descend and booing broke out in a cannonade. The curtain rose – once only – the company remembered its last obligation (that of bowing to the boos) and the night was over; one of the West End's disastrous 'flops'.

"Next night, at about the same time, in the Savoy Theatre, the curtain fell to a sustained clamour of cheering. Six, eight times the company bowed. The author, Noël Coward, in the stage-box, waved his hand to the house and disappeared. The lights went up and the premiere was over; one of the

West End's shouting triumphs. There could hardly have been a sharper contrast. As someone said coming out, Coward, with complicated ingenuity, might almost have persuaded the three authors of the American play to write it so that its failure – inevitable from the first five minutes – would heighten the success of *Relative Values*.

"When I got back from *Relative Values*, I opened one of Coward's earliest comedies, *The Young Idea*, written 30 years ago and first presented at the same theatre, the Savoy. And in it I found such lines as these:

"'Wouldn't it have been awful if she'd got all impulsive and wept a little and said she wanted us to be all girls together? Thank heaven, she really is an unpleasant woman.

"'I loved it all – the floral decorations and the nice jolly girls in pinks and blues and the heat and everyone treading on everyone else – such a merry prank!'

"'Sholto, you forget! Mrs Peasemarsh was burnt to death last Tuesday week.'

"Coward's sense of humour has not changed radically through the years. He has still his special epithets (Lady Marshwood, in *Relative Values*, talks of a lot of 'brisk Waafs'); his cheerful cynicism; and his love of nonsense-talk for its own sake, with the quick improvisation, the line-shooting, the rattle of repartee that cannot be fixed in cold print, but in the theatre keeps a responsive audience in steady mirth, each laugh kindled from the sparks of the last.

"It is this very theatricality that, I feel, will harm Coward's comedies in years ahead. They will act well as period pieces – given a company in key and an appreciative producer. But they will be extremely difficult to read – since so much depends on tone and timing – and, acted flatly, they will be dire. Coward is an enviable technician, but he must have other technicians to interpret him. That is why amateur performances of his work can embarrass.

"*Relative Values*, his first straight comedy for some years, has all the proper marks, and I imagine we shall hear all the usual things about it. Thus people less than rapturous will observe with glee that the main idea is familiar, that many of the characters are grabbed from stock, and that the dialogue is a shallow trickle. Others will overpraise the glitter of the dialogue, call the business a masterpiece of comedy, and spend the evening hugging themselves. Both types will go to the Savoy in battalions and regiments, for *Relative Values* has success stamped on every link.

"I would say simply that it is a very agreeable evening in the theatre if, as I do, you like Coward's brand of nonsense at its least self-conscious; and if, too, you like to glance backward now and again to the roaring 1920s. (No; this is not 'nostalgia', that exasperating vogue-word which, let it be said very firmly, means 'home sickness as a disease'.) Coward, as a young writer and the fashionable heart of the mid-twenties, was able to tap off the swift irrelevance, the near-witticism, with a deftness that none of his imitators managed. In effect, *Relative Values* is – in its dialogue – a return journey to the best days of the younger Coward, the period that produced, within five years or so, *Hay Fever* and *Private Lives*.

"There is a touch of *The Admirable Crichton* in the theme, the mingling of drawing-room and servants' hall; but we need not worry about Coward on the social revolution. His plot, very briefly, is about the woe of the Dowager Countess's faithful lady's maid who learns that her younger, detested, and almost forgotten sister, a Hollywood film actress, is hoping to become the new Countess of Marshwood. We have at one moment (not a moment of truth) an admirable situation in which the lady's maid, disguised heavily as a family friend, hears the sister telling a romantic and quite false tale of her upbringing as a cockney 'gutter-child', a waif who danced to barrel-organs, and who had a drunken mother. Not in the least a reasonable view of the tradesman's daughter, Freda Birch (now Miranda Frayle), who was born at Sidcup and lived respectably in Brixton.

"Once the comedy has fairly begun – it takes 20 minutes to get going – Coward is away, flicking out the lines as in the vanished years:

"'One of the worst aspects of modern English life is that so many of one's friends have to work, and they are so bad at it.'

"'It's unwise to believe what you read in the newspapers.'

"'I know it is, but somehow one does.'

"'She used to walk across a ballroom as if she were trudging through deep snow.'

"'The aristocracy, what's left of it, owes a lot to the theatrical profession.'

"And so on, if I can trust my programme scrawls. Shallow, unimportant, cynical: yes, yes, agreed. The point is that you have to hear Coward's lines flicked out on the stage: you need the time, the place and the swift one all together. The piece is not intended for one second to be a serious contribution to British drama. It is quick, scratch-flare, scratch-flare stuff, like a succession of lighted matches. And it does hold the theatre. I know, because the playgoer in front of me, who spent the first quarter of an hour striking his own matches in a state of frenzied fidgets, barely moved afterwards except to laugh. And an evening that can stifle both the match-king and the man-with-the-lighter is something to welcome.

"Coward, remembering the *Cavalcade* toast, ends amusingly with another toast – this time against social equality. And he has spiked critical guns by making his butler (a variation on a very old type) observe that the main situation is fit for a high comedy by Maugham: 'Our later playwrights would miss the subtler nuances. They are all too brittle.'

"What can one do except dodge the brittle dramatist (after thrusting at him a few sprigs of laurel) and run on hastily to the cast? We are in Marshwood House, East Kent, a Michael Relph set that manages to put into the crowded shelves a few plausibly readable books, beside the usual editions of encyclopaedias. (It is a long time since I have seen a more plausible stage bookcase.) Assembled in the house in the evening are ten people, of whom four are there to fill the cracks. The evening depends on the other half-dozen, headed by Gladys Cooper as Felicity, Countess of Marshwood.

"And how right the choice of her Christian name! This is a most felicitous piece of comedy. Gladys Cooper can give the exact weight to any line, with the accurate touch of a golfer holing a long putt. Throughout she governs the stage. Her poise is perfect; and many, I think, will remember her as she sits on the sofa in the second act, draped in tangerine and gallantly knitting.

"Angela Baddeley is armed at all points as the lovable Moxie, on and off her best behaviour; Hugh McDermott, with his sleepwalker's strut, enjoys guying the film actor who arrives in time to save the Marshwood's name; and Judy Campbell is the husky violet, Miranda Frayle (Freda Birch at home). Richard Leech, the dictionary-swallowing butler, rolls out the syllables as though the part were entirely new: indeed, he and Coward between them make us believe that it is.

"If you gather that I enjoyed the evening, you are right. It is a happy return journey to an earlier Coward. But (I warn you) do not go expecting that you will recall the piece for longer than a few weeks. Once you are outside in the Strand, *Relative Values* begins to fade. What matters is that it is all right on the night. Coward remains a Man of the Theatre."

PUBLICATIONS

Relative Values was first published by Heinemann (London, 1952). It is dedicated to Joyce (Carey) and Cole (Lesley). It also appears in *Play Parade, Volume V* (1958), and in *Noël Coward Collected Plays:Five* by Methuen World Classics (London, 1999).

NOTES

In his introduction to *Play Parade, Volume V*, Coward wrote: "*Relative Values* ran for over a year at the Savoy Theatre and was beautifully played by an excellent cast including Angela Baddeley, Judy Campbell, Richard Leech, Ralph Michael, Hugh Macdermott and Simon Lack. Gladys Cooper as 'Felicity' gave one of the most incisive, witty and altogether enchanting comedy performances that it has ever been my pleasure to see. But then Gladys Cooper learned her job in her young days from four of the most brilliant actor-manager-directors who ever graced our theatre – Seymour Hicks, Charles Hawtrey, Dennis Eadie and Gerald du Maurier. To watch the precision with which she timed her lines (not, I hasten to add, until she had learned them, which took quite a while) was to me an exquisite pleasure. She also continued, obviously because she made no effort to do so, to look as lovely as she had ever looked, even in the old days when her picture postcards could be bought by the bushel, twopence glacé and coloured but never penny plain. From the above eulogy the perceptive reader may gather that I am very fond of Gladys Cooper."

The end of Act I and both scenes of Act II, in a condensed version, were televised from the theatre by the BBC before an invited audience on 11 December 1956.

Relative Values has, since the original staging, been professionally revived in the UK twice: by Henry Sherwood Productions, 6 September 1973, at the Westminster Theatre, with the following cast:

CHARACTERS	**Westminster, 1973**
CRESTWELL	John Stone
ALICE	Heather Bell
MRS MOXTON	Gwen Cherrell
FELICITY	Margaret Lockwood
LADY HAYLING	Margaret Gibson
THE HON. PETER INGLETON	Bryan Stanion
ADMIRAL SIR JOHN HAYLING	Derek Ensor
MIRANDA FRAYLE	Joyce Blair
THE EARL OF MARSHWOOD (Nigel)	Kenneth Fortescue
DON LUCAS	Drewe Henley
Director	*Charles Hickman*
Designers	*Set: Geoffrey Scott*
	Costumes: Anthony Holland

and on 19 May 1993, at the Chichester Festival Theatre, with Susan Hampshire and Sarah Brightman. On 8 November it transferred to the Savoy Theatre with Sara Crowe replacing Sarah Brightman for the initial part of the run.

In the summer of 1999, shooting started in Britain for the first film version of *Relative Values*, with a cast headed by Julie Andrews, Colin Firth, Sophie Thompson, Stephen Fry, Jeanne Tripplehorn and William Baldwin, directed by Eric Styles.

41
QUADRILLE
A ROMANTIC COMEDY
Written in 1951–2

FIRST PRESENTED by H. M. Tennent Ltd. and John C. Wilson at the Opera House, Manchester, 15 July 1952 (8 weeks' tour: stay of 2 weeks in Manchester, Edinburgh, Glasgow, and Liverpool).

SUBSEQUENTLY PRESENTED at the Phoenix Theatre, London, 12 September 1952 (329 performances).

CHARACTERS	Manchester and Phoenix, 1952
THE REV. EDGAR SPEVIN	John Gill
SARAH (his wife)	Moya Nugent
GWENDOLYN (his daughter)	Pamela Grant
WAITER	Michael Allinson
COURIER	Timothy Forbes Adam
THE MARQUESS OF HERONDEN (Hubert)	Griffith Jones
MRS AXEL DIENSEN (Charlotte)	Marian Spencer
CATCHPOLE (a butler)	Gordon Phillott
THE MARCHIONESS OF HERONDEN (Serena)	Lynn Fontanne
LADY HARRIET RIPLEY	Joyce Carey
FOSTER (a maid)	Sybil Wise
FOOTMAN	Rhoderick Walker
AXEL DIENSEN	Alfred Lunt
OCTAVIA, COUNTESS OF BONNINGTON	Sylvia Coleridge
WAITER	Charles Rennison
TRAVELLERS, ETC	Allegra Nicole, Derek Prouse, Betty Hare, Gillian Raine, Richard Scott, Dorothy Blythe
Director	*Noël Coward "with grateful acknowledgement to Miss Fontanne and Mr Lunt"*
Designer	*Cecil Beaton*
Incidental music	*Noël Coward*

❖

ACT I: Scene 1: The Buffet de la Gare, Boulogne. Early morning,
              May 1873.
            Scene 2: Serena's sitting-room in Heronden house, Belgrave
            Square. Some hours later.
ACT II: Scene 1: The Villa Zodiaque, St Guillaume des Fleurs, France.
              Two days later.
            Scene 2: The same. The next morning.
            Scene 3: The same. Some hours later.
ACT III: Scene 1: Serena's sitting-room in Heronden House, Belgrave
            Square, June, 1874. Afternoon.
            Scene 2: The Buffet de la Gare, Boulogne. Early the next
            morning.

SYNOPSIS

ACT I, Scene 1: It is early morning at the Buffet de la Gare, Boulogne, in the year
    1873. Among the travellers from the English Channel boat who are drowsily
    sipping coffee are the Rev. Edgar Spevin, his wife Sarah, and his 14-year-old
    daughter, Gwendolyn. The latter, sick from the crossing, makes a hurried
    exit with her mother to the lavatory.

        A uniformed courier ushers in the Marquess of Heronden (Hubert) and
    Mrs Axel Diensen (Charlotte), who are eloping together. The waiter,
    knowing Hubert by sight, greets him as "Milor", but is warned that he is
    travelling incognito as Mr Baxter-Ellis. Charlotte appears depressed, so
    Hubert tries to cheer her with pictures of the idyllic life they will lead in his
    Mediterranean villa. She, however, is convinced that his wife Serena and
    her own husband, an American railway engineer, who are both forceful
    characters, will follow them. Her nervousness makes her impatient with
    Hubert's eloquence, and they are on the verge of a quarrel when Mr Spevin
    comes over to their table.

        He introduces himself to Hubert, whom he recognises, explaining that
    he has just been appointed vicar of the English church at Nice, and would
    be grateful for his patronage. Hubert replies suavely that he can make no
    promises, as he is recuperating after a nervous breakdown. He undertakes
    to give Mr Spevin a subscription, stressing that his incognito as Mr Baxter-Ellis
    is to be preserved.

        Politely dismissing the clergyman, Hubert continues his squabble with
    Charlotte, who is apprehensive about the English community at Nice.

He assures her that all will be forgiven them when, after their respective divorces, she becomes Lady Heronden; but Charlotte fears that Serena will never consent to a divorce. At last Hubert's charm dissipates her uneasiness, and they sit staring into each other's eyes until a bell on the platform warns them to take their seats in the train.

Mrs Spevin comes charging back with Gwendolyn and is told by her husband that he has spoken to "the Marquess and Marchioness". "That woman's not the Marchioness," she retorts as they go out towards the train.

Scene 2: Lady Heronden (Serena) enters her Belgrave Square sitting-room at five o'clock in the afternoon of the same day, having returned with her friend Lady Harriet Ripley from an overnight stay in Richmond. She asks Catchpole, the butler, if her husband has left for Heronden as arranged. Catchpole replies that he has, and that he has left a note for her on the bureau.

Over tea, Harriet reveals that she has seen Hubert at the zoo with a veiled woman. Serena pretends to take this lightly, assuring her that it was only a young country cousin, veiled to hide the disfigurement caused by a hunting accident. She cleverly evades Harriet's efforts to force her confidence about her relations with her husband; then, to soothe her hurt feelings, offers to read her Hubert's note. Its contents are obviously a shock, and Harriet does not quite believe her when she reads aloud an apology for selling some family portraits without consulting her.

Catchpole announces an unexpected visitor, Mr Axel Diensen, and after a formal introduction Harriet goes out, leaving Diensen to explain his call. He obviously finds this difficult. After striding around the room talking about a "crisis" and exclaiming, "Hell and damnation" he at last blurts out: "Your husband has left you!" "Yes. I know he has," says Serena quietly, now realising that Diensen's wife must be Hubert's companion.

At first she turns down his proposal that they should both follow up the couple (whom he knows to be at the Villa Zodiaque on the French Riviera). The idea strikes her as humiliating and vulgar; but eventually he talks her round, and they agree to take the night train for the continent. When he has gone, Serena tears Hubert's letter into tiny pieces and drops them into the waste-paper basket, echoing Diensen's favourite phrase: "Hell and damnation!"

ACT II, Scene 1: Breakfasting at the Villa Zodiaque two days later, Hubert and Charlotte feel that the first rapture has worn off their romance. Charlotte in particular is nervous and upset, and finds Hubert's high-flown speeches irritating. He takes her in his arms and is soothing her with kisses when Serena and Axel Diensen catch them unawares.

The latter dryly presents Charlotte with the necklace (sent for repair in the name of Mrs Baxter-Ellis) through which he has traced her. Serena firmly announces her intention of staying to lunch – in fact, she and Axel mean to stay indefinitely, and Hubert's discouragement is of no avail.

The two men are on the point of coming to blows when they are side-tracked by the visit of Mr Spevin. With calmness and presence of mind, Serena introduces herself, explaining that he had not seen her at Boulogne because, feeling unwell after the crossing, she had asked Mr Diensen to escort her to the train while their respective partners had breakfast. To Hubert's annoyance, she accepts, for herself and him, the clergyman's invitation to attend his church jumble sale and give the prizes.

When Mr Spevin has gone, Hubert takes Charlotte out on to the terrace. Serena asks Axel if he is not afraid to leave them together under the sky.

"They'll be back soon," he affirms. "It is beginning to rain." They look at each other with a smile.

Scene 2: Next morning Axel and Serena are still at the villa. He congratulates her on her masterly handling of the situation, comparing her with Abraham Lincoln. Rather bitterly, she rejoins that Lincoln abolished slavery: she herself is fighting to re-establish it, and their success will resolve itself into "each of us leading home in triumph a whimpering hostage".

Suspecting that her resolution is on the wane, he tries to restore it, but in such a proprietary fashion that Serena is indignant. She calls him sharply to order, and he stamps out in a rage just as Charlotte comes to look for him.

Serena detains her for a serious talk. "Do you really love my husband?" she asks, but Charlotte will give no direct answer. Hubert has been madly in love several times before, remarks Serena: the condition is impermanent. She points out that Charlotte is demanding a great deal of Hubert, who will require a substantial dividend later on; whereas she, after a double divorce, will at least be recompensed by becoming Lady Heronden.

At this point Hubert enters, and Charlotte, in tears, begs him to send Serena away. Axel comes in a moment later, and suggests that she had better lie down before the jumble sale.

Charlotte confesses herself defeated. She tells Hubert that Serena has asked whether she really loved him, and now that she has seen him in his true colours, the answer is "No": she is ready to return to London with her husband. She makes a dignified exit, while Hubert again stamps out in a rage, leaving Serena and Axel to discuss their victory, which has left them weary and dejected.

They are interrupted by Octavia, Countess of Bonnington, an eccentric elderly neighbour whose affections are lavished on her pug-dog (which has just died) and her parrots. Under the pseudonym, Lucien Snow, she writes passionate love stories. Having heard that a pair of illicit lovers are at the villa, she assumes they are Serena and Axel, and proceeds to congratulate them, ignoring all Serena's attempts to explain the situation. Finally, she dashes out with an invitation to visit her at her Villa la Joie. Axel, who has taken a liking to her, raises his glass and drinks to "her frantic imagery, to her wild fervent inner voices, to her dead pug-dog and to her kindly, lonely heart". Serena thinks that he too must be mad.

Scene 3: The two couples, in their travelling clothes, are drinking coffee. They have just returned from the church jumble sale, and the atmosphere is a trifle strained as they wait for the carriage that will take them to the station. After they have made conversation for a while, Hubert suddenly bursts out, reproaching Serena with the abuse of her position as conqueror. Axel takes exception to his tone, and Hubert once more goes off in a rage. Charlotte goes to pack, leaving Serena and Axel together. In a long, intimate talk, he describes his early days: how he started work at 13 as a "news-butcher" – selling magazines, peanuts and chewing tobacco on the American trains; and how, after working in various jobs on the railways for years, he inherited the money which was the basis of his fortune.

He asks Serena to come to America some day, and lyrically describes the delights of watching the scenery from the caboose of a freight train. Then he kisses her hand.

Hubert comes back in his overcoat, announcing that the carriage is waiting, and they all prepare to leave.

ACT III, Scene 1: A year has passed, and Serena is in her sitting-room, writing what is obviously an important letter. She is sealing it up when Hubert enters and, with a slight start, she slips it into her reticule.

In an irascible mood, Hubert objects to the hurdy-gurdy playing in the square; which strikes his wife, on the contrary, as gay and charming. He is expecting her to leave for Heronden that evening, and he now says he has planned to go hunting big game in Africa – a decision which astonishes Serena, who knows his aversion to discomfort. To his relief, however, she takes the news very calmly. He explains that he is accompanying a new friend, Mallory.

Just before tea is served, Lady Harriet arrives, and she too expresses surprise at Hubert's project. When he leaves them, Serena kisses him goodbye, rather solemnly assuring him that she wishes him well, "neither pityingly nor patronisingly, but with all my heart".

The two women settle down to gossip. Through her manicurist Harriet has heard of Charlotte Diensen's escapade – that she had eloped with "a Mr

Baxter-Ellis" and had been brought back by her husband after "the most appalling scenes". She adds that Charlotte has gone back to her family in Boston while her divorce is being arranged. Meanwhile, she says, Diensen has been seen in Kew Gardens with a heavily veiled lady.

She also remarks that Hubert has a new "friend", a Mrs Mallory. At the name, Serena realises the purport of Hubert's big-game expedition. "Poor Hubert!" she comments.

Harriet notices Serena's mood of gaiety and excitement, and is surprised by the fervour of her goodbye, which is accompanied by the gift of an heirloom brooch: "To remember me by."

When she has gone, Serena rings for Catchpole, takes the letter from her bag, and instructs him to give it to her husband as soon as he returns: "I shall be gone, and it is rather urgent."

Scene 2: Again it is early morning in the buffet at Boulogne, and the Spevin family are breakfasting there. This time they are going in the reverse direction, to England. Mrs Spevin is fussing about a mislaid pilgrim basket, and Gwendolyn – as usual when travelling – feels sick. In exasperation, Mr Spevin gives them their tickets to go on board, and finishes his meal alone.

He is reading a French newspaper when the Courier ushers in Axel Diensen and Serena. He addresses the latter as "Milady", and is told that she is travelling as Mrs Baxter-Ellis. The couple order coffee and croissants, Axel showing some embarrassment at his ignorance of French. He fancies that his lack of education may come to irritate Serena; but she assures him that she has faced up to this possibility:

"When one elopes with an uncivilised ruffian, one must be prepared for anything." He swears that he will love her "until the end of time", and is reminded lightly that he has already said the same thing in Kew Gardens.

Mr Spevin now recognises them and comes over to their table. He takes for granted that Hubert is travelling with them, and Serena does not undeceive him. They tell him they are returning to the Villa Zodiaque, and he explains that Gwendolyn has been unwell, so he is taking her to an aunt in Wales for a change of air. After he has gone out, the platform bell rings. Axel and Serena remain talking, conscious only of each other. She looks back on the long year since they met, and forward to visiting his "brave New World", which he assures her is "young in heart" and will be glad to welcome her.

Serena sighs that she wishes they themselves were younger and had more time. "There is time enough, my dear love," replies Axel, "Time and to spare. Come." And they go out into a flood of sunshine.

❖

Geoffrey Tarran in the *Morning Advertiser*, 13 September 1952:

"Noël Coward's glittering record of successes has become a handicap to him. His comedies and musical plays are now expected to have cutting wit and gentle wisdom – and the slightest lapse is apt to provoke severe censure. His latest play, *Quadrille*, at the Phoenix Theatre, does not reach his high standard.

"Nevertheless, it has a number of merits. He has gained lasting gratitude by writing excellent parts for two of the greatest players of our time, Alfred Lunt and Lynn Fontanne.

"To see them once is to be drawn into the huge and ever-growing circle of their lifelong admirers.

"They have added substantially to the stock of cherished recollections left for me by their contributions to *Reunion* in Vienna, *Amphitryon 38* and *Love in Idleness*.

"In writing this comedy for them, Mr Coward has taken things a little too easily.

"He has not bothered to introduce much originality into the plot, and his supply of wit is less generous than usual.

"A variant of *Private Lives* has been richly decked with Victorian elaborations.

"Developments take an obvious course, and with less expert treatment this material would wear dangerously thin in places.

"Yet there is no looseness about the knitting of the threads, and the play has satisfying symmetry and a high polish.

"Mr Coward's gift of writing happily-turned repartee and phrases precisely communicating an atmosphere and a mood is in no way impaired, and his touch with sentiment is as sure and firm as ever.

"He has always favoured railway stations for romantic encounters and this particular design begins and ends in the 'Buffet de la Gare, Boulogne'.

"All the agitation engendered by cross-Channel prospects is skilfully suggested, and there are many authentic signs of Continental manners and modes.

"The Marquess of Heronden and the wife of an American railway magnate pause at the station during their elopement to his French villa and later, in a sitting-room of Heronden House in Belgrave Square, the deserted wife and husband plan a pursuit.

"Surprising the lovers at the villa, their astute diplomacy shatters romantic illusions, and the respective marriages are perfunctorily resumed for another year.

"Then the inevitable happens and the Marchioness and the American pass through Boulogne on the way to start a new life together.

"Mr Coward is concerned with nothing more than this marital reassortment, but Miss Fontanne and Mr Lunt transform it into as brilliant a piece of theatrical contrivance as Londoners have seen for some years.

"The art of acting is given a spell-binding and unforgettable demonstration and, through their magic, ordinary sentences carry the wittiest implications.

"Miss Fontanne endows the Marchioness with beguiling glamour, infectious gaiety, effortless grace and impressive dignity.

"Her exquisite voice most appealingly rises and falls, and she can turn in an instant from sparkling merriment to subtle mockery, from cold sarcasm to warm tenderness.

"Miss Fontanne and Mr Lunt make remarkable use of their hands in the stressing of their feelings, and the immense significance which he can give to a shrug of the shoulders and an unforeseen movement of his body has been an important factor in the building up of his reputation.

"He is refreshingly natural in the indication of the American's acute appreciation of realities and abundant common sense.

"When he declares his belief in the value of railroads in the fostering of American unity and prosperity and describes the scenic beauties surrounding the tracks, he strikingly proves how lyrical a man can be over tasks to which he is devoted.

"Convincing testimony of the 'exuberant romanticism' of the Marquess is submitted by Griffith Jones, and as the pretty but insipid wife from Boston, Marian Spencer adds to knowledge of her temperament with every tearful outburst.

"Joyce Carey engagingly flaunts social affectations as the scandal-loving friend of the Marchioness.

"In the settings, Cecil Beaton has included singularly taking reminders of decorative ideas of the period, and Mr Coward's incidental music is exactly attuned to the matters in hand.

"But it is on the outstanding achievement of the Lunts that the mind dwells. Comments about people of the New World, in the closing moments of the play, apply equally to them: 'We are young in heart... eager to enchant our visitors.'

"The enchantment is strong and it never fails."

❖

PUBLICATIONS

Quadrille was first published by Heinemann (London, 1952). It is dedicated to Lynn (Fontanne) and Alfred (Lunt). Also included in *Play Parade, Volume V* (1958), and in *Noël Coward Collected Plays: Seven* by Methuen World Classics (London, 1999).

NOTES

In his introduction in *Play Parade, Volume I*, Coward wrote: "*Quadrille*, which I wrote specifically for Lynn Fontanne and Alfred Lunt, is a romantic Victorian comedy which the critics detested and the public liked enough to fill the Phoenix Theatre for a year. It has, to my biased mind, a great deal to recommend it. To enlarge on the Lunts' performance of it would be redundant. They brought to it, as they bring to every play they appear in, the full measure of their own particular richness and all the loving care and thought and meticulous attention to detail which has established them over the years as a living legend. In addition to their ineffable contribution, the decor and the dresses were designed with exquisite colour and taste by Cecil Beaton. In addition even to these matchless attributes it had in it some evocative and well written scenes, notably the 'Railway' speech spoken by Alfred Lunt as 'Axel' in act three, scene three.

"Later on I saw an excellent performance of *Quadrille* at the Connaught Theatre, Worthing, without the Lunts or the Beaton decor and believe it or not the much abused little piece stood up remarkably well."

The play was given three Charity Previews in London. The first, on 9 September 1952, was in aid of the United Nations Association.

Quadrille was revived at the Forum Theatre, Billingham, on 28 March 1977, with Margaret Lockwood and John Stone, and toured without coming to the West End.

US PRODUCTIONS

PRESENTED by John C. Wilson and H. M. Tennent, Ltd at the Coronet Theatre, New York on 3 November 1954 (159 performances).

CHARACTERS	**Coronet, 1954**
THE REV. EDGAR SPEVIN	Jerome Kilty
SARAH (his wife)	Phyllis Connard

GWENDOLYN (his daughter)	Nina Reader
COURIER	Bruce Webster
THE MARQUESS OF HERONDEN (Hubert)	Brian Aherne
MRS AXEL DIENSEN (Charlotte)	Edna Best
CATCHPOLE (a butler)	Harold Crane
THE MARCHIONESS OF HERONDEN (Serena)	Lynn Fontanne
LADY HARRIET RIPLEY	Brenda Forbes
FOSTER (a maid)	Mildred Clinton
FOOTMAN	Rhoderick Walker
AXEL DIENSEN	Alfred Lunt
OCTAVIA, COUNTESS OF BONNINGTON	Dorothy Sand
EXTRAS	Madeleine Clive, Byron Mitchell, Patricia Quinn O'Hara, Michael Lewis.

Director	*Alfred Lunt*
Costumes (as London)	*Cecil Beaton*

The *New York Times*: "It lacks the hard, ricocheting wit of Mr Coward's characteristic works and it looks suspiciously like the libretto for a Viennese operetta. But this theatre-goer is not throwing any stones at it this morning. For there is some excellent writing in *Quadrille*, especially a rhapsody about railroading in America. There is also a respect for the two chief characters, who are people of mind and valour, and free of piety. *Quadrille* is an acting piece for the Lunts, and the Lunts are, as always, superbly accomplished."

New York Daily Mirror: "Coward wrote this romantic comedy to display the virtuosity of his friends and partners. It is a disarming work – not robustly amusing, never very moving, but freighted with some of the master's more incisive and urbane lines. There is little plot and not too much action, but the characters are quite wonderful."

New York Post: "If it by no means reveals Mr Coward in one of his wittiest or most urbane moods, it does show him writing what he correctly calls a 'romantic comedy' with considerable grace and style."

This was to be the last production under the auspices of Transatlantic Productions, Inc., the company set up by Coward and the Lunts with Jack Wilson back in 1934 to produce *Point Valaine*.

42
AFTER THE BALL
A MUSICAL PLAY

Written in 1953

Based on Oscar Wilde's *Lady Windermere's Fan*

FIRST PRESENTED by Tennent Productions Ltd. at the Royal Court Theatre, Liverpool, 1 March 1954 (12 weeks' tour: Cardiff, Bournemouth, Birmingham, Bristol, Manchester, Leeds, Newcastle, Edinburgh, Glasgow, Brighton and Southsea).

SUBSEQUENTLY PRESENTED at the Globe Theatre, London, June in 1954 (188 performances).

CHARACTERS	Liverpool and Globe, 1954
LADY JEDBURGH	Betty Felstead
LADY PAISLEY	Anna Halinka
MRS COWPER-COWPER	Ailsa Gamley
LADY PLYMDALE	Lois Green
LADY STUTFIELD	Pam Marmont
MR DUMBY	Dennis Bowen
LORD PAISLEY (part not in original version at Liverpool)	John Morley
MR CECIL GRAHAM	Tom Gill
LADY WINDERMERE	Vanessa Lee
LORD WINDERMERE	Peter Graves
MR HOPPER	Graham Payn
LORD DARLINGTON	Shamus Locke
THE DUCHESS OF BERWICK	Irene Browne
LADY AGATHA CARLISLE	Patricia Cree
PARKER	Leslie Pearson
LORD AUGUSTUS LORTON	Donald Scott
MRS ERLYNNE	Mary Ellis
MR GUY BERKELEY	Raymond Savigear
MR RUFFORD	Bill Horsley
LADY RUCKINGE	Silvia Beamish
MISS GRAHAM	Maureen Quinney
MRS HURST-GREEN	Marion Grimaldi
MRS ARTHUR BOWDEN	Margaret Gibson

FOOTMAN TO LORD DARLINGTON	Bill Horsley
FOOTMAN TO DUCHESS OF BERWICK	Andrew Sachs (Liverpool only)

Director	*Robert Helpmann*
Designer	*Doris Zinkeisen*

❖

ACT I: Hyde Park. Afternoon, July 1892.
ACT II: Scene 1: The Ball, Carlton House terrace. The same night.
        Scene 2: Lord Darlington's rooms. Later that night.
ACT III: Scene 1: Morning-room in Lord Windermere's house.
             The following morning.
         Scene 2: The garden of Berwick house. The same night.

Orchestra direction	*Philip Martell*

MUSICAL NUMBERS

ACT I

"Oh, What A Century It's Been"	Lady Jedburgh, Lady Paisley, Mrs Cowper-Cowper, Lady Plymdale, Lady Stutfield, Mr Dumby, Mr Cecil Graham, Lord Paisley, Mr Berkeley, Mr Rufford, Miss Graham, Mrs Hurst-Green and Mrs Arthur Bowden
"I Knew That You Would Be My Love"	Lord and Lady Windermere
"Mr Hopper's Chanty"	Mr Hopper, Mr Dumby and Mr Cecil Graham
"Sweet Day"	Lady Windermere
"Stay On The Side Of The Angels"	Lord Darlington
"Oh, What A Century" (quartet)	Lady Plymdale, Lady Stutfield, Mr Dumby and Lord Paisley
Reprise: "Sweet Lady"	Lady Windermere

ACT II

"Crème De La Crème"	Lady Plymdale, Lady Stutfield, Lady Ruckinge, Mrs Hurst-Green, Mrs Bowden, Miss Graham, Mr Dumby,

	Mr Cecil Graham, Mr Rufford, and Mr Berkeley
"Light Is The Heart"	Mrs Erlynne
"May I Have The Pleasure?"	Duchess of Berwick, Lady Agatha and Mr Hopper
"I Offer You My Heart"	Lady Windermere and Lord Darlington
Reprise: "Sweet Day"	Lady Windermere
"Why Is It The Woman Who Pays?"	Lady Stutfield, Lady Plymdale, and Mrs Hurst-Green
"Aria"	Lady Windermere
"Go, I Beg You, Go"	Mrs Erlynne and Lady Windermere
"London At Night"	Lord Augustus, Mr Dumby, Mr Cecil Graham, Mr Hopper, Lord Windermere and Lord Darlington

ACT III

"Clear, Bright Morning"	Lady Windermere
"All My Life Ago"	Mrs Erlynne
Reprise: " London At Night"	Lord Augustus, Mr Dumby, Mr Hopper and Mr Cecil Graham
"Oh, What A Season This Has Been"	Lady Stutfield, Lady Plymdale, Lady Jedburgh, Lady Paisley, Mrs Hurst-Green, Mrs Bowden, Miss Graham, Mrs Cowper-Cowper and Lady Ruckinge
"Farewell Song"	Lord Augustus
'Something On A Tray"	Duchess of Berwick, Lady Jedburgh, Lady Paisley and Mrs Cowper-Cowper
"Faraway Land"	Mr Hopper
Reprise: "May I Have The Pleasure?"	Lady Agatha and Mr Hopper
Reprise: "I Knew That You Would Be My Love"	Lord Windermere
Reprise: "Sweet Day"	Lady Windermere
Reprise: "Light Is The Heart"	Mrs Erlynne
Orchestration	*Philip Green*

At Liverpool the play (then called an operetta) was divided into two acts. (Act I, Scene 2, was omitted in London.)

The character of Lord Paisley was also introduced later. Originally his part in the quartet was allotted to the character of Cecil Graham.

The orchestra at Liverpool was under the direction of Norman Hackforth and the orchestrations were by J. Marr Mackie. Before the London production it was re-orchestrated and the order of certain numbers was changed. Two numbers, "Good Evening, Lady Windermere" and "What Can It Mean?", both sung by Mrs Erlynne, and a "Letter Song" sung by Lord Darlington,* were omitted. A new number "Clear, Bright Morning", was added for Lady Windermere.

* This song is included in the book of lyrics.

SYNOPSIS

ACT I, Scene 1: On a sunny afternoon in July 1892, a number of elegant ladies and gentlemen are strolling in Hyde Park. They sing an opening chorus, "Oh, What A Century It's Been", followed by a quartet on the same theme, sung by Lady Plymdale, Lady Stutfield, Lord Paisley and Mr Dumby.

They all go off as Lord and Lady Windermere appear, talking about the ball they are giving to celebrate her twenty-first birthday. After two years of marriage, they are still in love, as they explain in a duet, "I Knew That You Would Be My Love." They continue their promenade as the Australian, Mr Hopper, comes in, followed by Mr Dumby and Mr Cecil Graham, who chaff him about his admiration for Lady Agatha Carlisle, youngest daughter of the Duchess of Berwick. Their inquiry about his family and his native country leads them into a trio, "Mr Hopper's Chanty", beginning:

> My grandpa landed from a convict ship
> On the beach of Botany Bay.

As they go out, the Windermeres come back. Lord Windermere tells his wife that he has a surprise for her, but cannot yet tell her what it is. Saying that she wants to enjoy every moment of her birthday, she sings "Sweet Day", after the first refrain of which Lord Windermere takes leave of her. She continues singing until Lord Darlington approaches. Reproving him for having paid her extravagant compliments, she warns him that she has been brought up very strictly and has something of the puritan in her nature – she allows no compromise between right and wrong. If, therefore, they are to remain friends, he must be more discreet.

Darlington puts the hypothetical case to her: if a husband, only two years married, becomes the intimate friend of a woman of doubtful character, should his wife not console herself? "Because the husband is vile, should the wife be vile also?" replies Lady Windermere sententiously – adding that she enjoys listening to his advice, though she would never dream of taking it. This inspires Lord Darlington to sing:

> Stay on the side of the angels,
> Serene and remote and apart,
> But Lady Windermere, dear Lady Windermere,
> Keep a compassionate heart.

They go out, and the same quartet sings a reprise of "Oh, What A Century", and passes on as Lady Windermere and Lord Darlington come back, together with Mr Rufford and some ladies. Soon afterwards they meet the Duchess of Berwick and Lady Agatha Carlisle, to whom the Duchess introduces Lord Darlington, with the warning that she must not believe a word he says. After some badinage, he again sings the last verse of "Stay On The Side Of The Angels" and goes out.

Sending Lady Agatha out of hearing, the Duchess warns Lady Windermere that her husband is paying attentions to a mysterious widow, Mrs Erlynne, and apparently also financing her, since she came to London with very little money and now has a charming house in Mayfair and drives her own ponies in the Park. Now Lady Windermere sees the point of Lord Darlington's hypothesis. She is very much upset, but the Duchess advises her not to take it too much to heart, but to wait patiently until her husband comes back to her.

When Lord Windermere comes back with his "surprise" in the shape of a beautiful fan, he realises from his wife's manner that something is wrong, but she attributes her depression to a headache. However, at his request that she should invite Mrs Erlynne to their ball, she bursts out with all that she has heard. Windermere assures her that he has never loved anyone in the world but her, but he will not give any explanation. On her flat refusal to send the invitation, he says he will do it himself. Lady Windermere then threatens that, if Mrs Erlynne does come, she will strike her across the face with her fan. "You will ruin us!" exclaims her husband, adding that he has a particular reason for wishing her to receive Mrs Erlynne. He goes out considerably annoyed, leaving Lady Windermere to sing a melancholy reprise of "Sweet Day".

ACT II, Prologue (before a front-cloth): The society ladies and gentlemen proclaim their own virtues in a song, "Crème De La Crème".

Scene 1: The ball is in full swing. Most of the guests are already assembled, and the manservant Parker announces the others as they arrive. Lord Augustus Lorton (the Duchess' brother) questions Lord Windermere about Mrs Erlynne, to whom he himself is strongly attracted. He is surprised and relieved to hear that she has been invited; this, in his opinion, establishes her as "alright".

The Duchess and Lady Agatha are then announced. Lord Windermere makes an opportunity to talk quietly to his wife, begging her not to implement her threat, but she persists that she intends to do as she said. She reclaims the fan, which she had asked Lord Darlington to hold, remarking: "A useful thing, a fan, isn't it?" And she tells Lord Darlington: "I need a friend tonight."

Lord Windermere is on the point of telling his wife the reason of his action when Mrs Erlynne herself is announced. The fan falls from Lady Windermere's hand, and she goes out on the terrace with Lord Darlington.

After greeting Lord Augustus with flirtatious charm, Mrs Erlynne, with support from the chorus, sings "Light Is The Heart". The Duchess of Berwick, finding that the beautiful stranger is the dubious Mrs Erlynne, asks her brother whether he was responsible for her presence: she is astonished to hear that it was Lady Windermere who invited her. Lord Windermere then introduces Mrs Erlynne to the Duchess, whose icy hauteur is almost melted by the newcomer's charm before she calls her daughter and walks away. Next Mrs Erlynne obtains an introduction to Lady Jedburgh and wins her over so successfully that she obtains an invitation to lunch. With a few words to Mr Dumby (which involve him in awkward explanations to Lady Plymdale), she leaves the room.

The Duchess returns with Lady Agatha, whom she has instructed to reserve five dances for Mr Hopper, the first of which he claims in a duet, "May I Have The Pleasure?" They dance the polka together.

Telling Lord Darlington how her husband insisted on inviting Mrs Erlynne, Lady Windermere asks for his friendship. He replies: "Between men and women there is no friendship possible. There is passion, enmity, worship, love, but no friendship. I love you." This theme he expands in a song, "I Offer You My Heart", in which Lady Windermere joins, beseeching him: "I Beg You Go Away."

The Duchess returns, quite won over to Mrs Erlynne's side after a further talk with her. She says good night to Lady Windermere and leaves with Lady Agatha. Other guests also depart, mingling praise of Mrs Erlynne with their thanks to their hostess.

Herself unseen, Lady Windermere overhears a conversation between her husband and Mrs Erlynne, who says that she intends to marry Lord

Augustus and asks for a financial settlement. They go out on the terrace, and Lady Windermere, in her distress, determines to join Lord Darlington. She goes out after singing a reprise of "I Knew That You Would Be My Love".

Some of the menfolk then arrange to go to their club for brandy and a game of cards, but Lord Augustus, having promised Mrs Erlynne not to drink or gamble, will not accompany them.

Parker, carrying a letter on a tray, is intercepted by Mrs Erlynne. He tells her that Lady Windermere has just gone out. Offering to give the letter to Lord Windermere herself, Mrs Erlynne takes it and reads it. "The same words that I wrote to her father 20 years ago!" she exclaims. She suppresses the letter. Her only idea now is to find her daughter, Lady Windermere, and save her.

To Lord Augustus' surprise, she now asks him to take Lord Windermere to his club and keep him there, if possible, all night; then she hurries out to find Lady Windermere and bring her back.

Interlude (before a front-cloth): A trio, "Why Is It The Woman Who Pays?" sung by Lady Plymdale, Lady Stutfield and Mrs Hurst-Green.

Scene 2: In Lord Darlington's room, Lady Windermere sings an aria, the theme of which is:

> I feel so terribly alone,
> Lost and alone.

"Thank heaven I am in time!" exclaims Mrs Erlynne as she enters. "You must go back to your husband immediately."

To Lady Windermere's growing indignation, she explains that she has intercepted her letter and beseeches her in song: "Go, I beg you, go!"

She defends herself warmly against Lady Windermere's accusation that she is a vile woman who comes between husband and wife: "I may have wrecked my own life, but I will not allow you to wreck yours." Her appeal to Lady Windermere not to abandon her child is successful; after another short duet, the young mother decides to return.

They are just leaving when they hear steps and voices outside. Lord Darlington and his friends, including Lord Windermere and Lord Augustus ("Then it is I who am lost!" exclaims Mrs Erlynne on seeing him) are back from their club. Mrs Erlynne hides Lady Windermere behind the curtains, telling her to slip out at the first opportunity, and then retreats to the inner room.

The young men sing a sextet "London At Night". Then they begin to talk about women, chaffing Lord Augustus for his devotion to Mrs Erlynne. Darlington confesses that he is going abroad because of his unrequited love for a married woman.

Suddenly Cecil Graham sees Lady Windermere's fan on the sofa. All are highly amused to think that the melancholy romantic, Darlington, has a woman hidden in his rooms; but Lord Windermere recognises the fan and threatens to search for his wife.

The situation is saved by Mrs Erlynne, who comes out and confronts them, saying that she took Lady Windermere's fan by mistake for her own. While their attention is fixed upon her, Lady Windermere makes her escape unobserved. In silence, Lord Windermere hands the fan to Mrs Erlynne and she leaves the room.

ACT III, Scene 1: In her morning-room next day, Lady Windermere reflects on the past night and sings of the "Clear, Bright Morning" which has shown her the folly of her jealous despair.

Her husband, seeing how pale she is, suggests that they should go down to the country. He is now thoroughly disgusted with Mrs Erlynne and forbids his wife to receive her again. But when the fan is brought up by Parker, with a note from Mrs Erlynne asking to see her, Lady Windermere insists that she must do it.

Apologising for having taken the fan, Mrs Erlynne announces that she is going abroad almost immediately. When, at her request, Lady Windermere has gone to fetch a photograph, Mrs Erlynne has a straight talk with Lord Windermere, who says she has been publicly disgraced and must not see his wife again. "My daughter, you mean," retorts Mrs Erlynne, once more affirming that she is going abroad, out of their lives.

Lady Windermere returns with a photograph of herself and her child, which Mrs Erlynne gratefully accepts, and then sings a musical farewell, "All My Life Ago".

Interlude (before a front-cloth): A reprise of "London At Night", sung by Lord Augustus, Mr Dumby, Mr Hopper and Mr Graham.

Scene 2: In the garden of Berwick House nine society ladies sing "Oh, What A Season This Has Been".

Then Lord Augustus enters with Cecil Graham, to whom he confides that Mrs Erlynne has satisfactorily explained her presence in Lord Darlington's room, and that he still wants to marry her. When the lady enters, Graham tactfully leaves them together, but Mrs Erlynne politely and firmly refuses the proposal of marriage. Lord Augustus sings a "Farewell Song", and they go out together.

The Duchess of Berwick comes in with Lady Agatha and various friends. Having sent her daughter to look for Mr Hopper, she sings a song expressing her relief that, now the season is over, she can relax and –

Enjoy a little something on a tray.

Lady Agatha comes back with Mr Hopper, who talks to her about Australia and praises its beauties in a song, "Faraway Land". He then proposes and is accepted. The Duchess is delighted to hear the news, though somewhat taken aback when she learns that they intend to live in Australia: she thinks Grosvenor Square would be far better.

Mrs Erlynne congratulates the engaged couple before singing "May I Have The Pleasure?", they dance away together, and she is at last able to have a private talk to Lady Windermere. The latter wants to tell her husband the whole truth, but this is strenuously opposed by Mrs Erlynne, who says the best way she can repay her debt is by silence. "Don't spoil the one good thing I have done in my life by telling anyone about it," she pleads, reinforcing the request with an appeal to Lady Windermere's devotion to her supposedly dead mother.

Lady Windermere says she would like to give Mrs Erlynne her fan as a souvenir, but it has her own name on it. "Margaret is my name too," is Mrs Erlynne's reply as she accepts the gift.

The Duchess takes Mrs Erlynne away while Lord Windermere reconciles himself with his wife and they sing a reprise of "I Knew That You Would Be My Love", followed by "Sweet Day".

Finally, Mrs Erlynne returns and tells them that she has refused Lord Augustus and is going to live abroad. They say farewell and leave her to sing a reprise of "Light Is The Heart".

Eric Keown in *Punch*, 16 June 1954:

"One of Noël Coward's difficulties in turning *Lady Windermere's Fan* into a musical comedy is that, not unnaturally, he finds the Victorian period funny, so that, although he uses some of Wilde's epigrams in addition to his own, he cannot escape a spoiling note of burlesque. The song 'Why Is It The Woman Who Pays?' is in his best vein, but its sentiments are very far from Wilde. And a graver obstacle is the basic melodrama of the original. This involves him at moments of crisis in operatic ding-dong which is heavily undramatic and slows up the second act badly, as well as forcing on Mrs Erlynne a long explanatory monologue sounding like a plot synopsis at the top of a serial.

"In other words, the tincture of Wilde is a very uncertain asset, but if one can forget it there is still a good deal in *After the Ball* to be enjoyed simply as musical comedy. Mr Coward has written pleasing music and a number of extremely nimble lyrics. Robert Helpmann, having good voices at his disposal, has seen to it that they are sung with maximum effect, and Doris Zinkeisen, although I found her sets a little dull, has dressed the production charmingly. The cast is by no means uniform in style – Shamus Locke's Lord Darlington, for instance, is the wrong kind of Irishman – but Mary Ellis and Vanessa Lee are impressive as Mrs Erlynne and Lady Windermere, Irene Browne scores as the outrageous Duchess, and Mr Hopper and Mr Dumby are particularly happy with Graham Payn and Dennis Bowen. The ecstatic little ballet in which Mr Hopper and Lady Agatha (Patricia Cree) celebrate their engagement must have given Mr Helpmann as much pleasure as it does us."

PUBLICATIONS

After the Ball is unpublished, as also is the vocal score. The book of lyrics and separate sheet music of the following songs was published by William Chappell:

"Faraway Land"
"I Knew That You Would Be My Love"
"Light Is The Heart"
"Sweet Day"

NOTES

The first US production was staged at St John Terrell's Music Circus, Lambertville, N.J., on 2 August 1955, and was "in the round" (an Arena production).

After the Ball has never had a major revival, although on 27 May 1999 the Peacock Theatre presented a concert production of Coward's original version for the Covent Garden Festival, adapted by Barry Day, and this was subsequently broadcast on Radio 3. It was a genuine premiere, since it included Mrs Erlynne's "Good Evening, Lady Windermere" and "What Can It Mean?" which were cut from the original West End production because of certain vocal limitations in the cast, as well as Mr Darlington's "Letter Song".

The production was subsequently staged on 13 November at the Chicago Humanities Festival at the Auditorium Theatre, with many of the same cast.

43
NUDE WITH VIOLIN
A LIGHT COMEDY IN THREE ACTS
Written in 1954

FIRST PRESENTED by H. M. Tennent Ltd. at the Olympia, Dublin,
24 September 1956 (2 weeks). Followed by 4 weeks' tour: Liverpool,
Manchester, Newcastle, Edinburgh.

SUBSEQUENTLY PRESENTED at the Globe Theatre, London, 7 November 1956.

CHARACTERS	**Dublin and Globe, 1956**
SEBASTIEN	John Gielgud *[1]
MARIE-CELESTE	Gillian Webb
CLINTON PREMINGER, JUNIOR	Peter Sallis (Dublin)
	John Sterland (tour and Globe)
ISOBEL SORODIN	Joyce Carey *[2]
JANE (her daughter)	Ann Castle
COLIN (her son)	Basil Henson
PAMELA (Colin's wife)	Patricia Raine
JACOB FRIEDLAND	David Horne *[3]
ANYA PAVLIKOV	Patience Collier
CHERRY-MAY WATERTON	Kathleen Harrison
FABRICE	Douglas Robinson
OBADIAH LLEWELLYN	Thomas Baptiste
GEORGE (a press photographer)	John Sterland (Dublin)
	Keith Green (tour and Globe)
LAUDERDALE	Nicky Edmett
Director	*John Gielgud and Noël Coward*
Designer	*Paul Anstee*

*[1] Succeeded by Michael Wilding, 24 June 1957 and Robert Helpmann,
    23 November 1957
*[2] Succeeded by Zena Dare, 23 September 1957
*[3] Succeeded by Geoffrey Dunn, 23 September 1957

SCENE: The action of the play takes place in Paul Sorodin's studio
         in Paris.
ACT I: Afternoon.
ACT II: Scene 1: A few hours later.
         Scene 2: The following afternoon.
ACT III: Scene 1: A few hours later.
         Scene 2: The following morning.

The play was directed in London by John Gielgud, prior to the Dublin opening. Noël Coward who was in America arrived in Dublin in time for the second night. During his stay there the play was cut and revised under his direction. When Helpmann took over in London, the alterations made when Noël played the role in New York were incorporated.

The painting "Nude with Violin" (by Graham Payn) used on the first night caused a mild sensation and was later replaced by another for London. The final Tableau Curtain as written and produced in Dublin proved an anti-climax and was cut after a few performances.

In Dublin also the play was presented, as written in three acts (one scene in act one, two scenes in act two and two scenes in act three). The play was re-grouped for London into two acts (act one, two scenes, and act two, three scenes). It was published as originally written.

SYNOPSIS

ACT I: The famous but eccentric painter, Paul Sorodin, has died. In his studio, Sebastien Lacreole, his polyglot valet with a chequered past, and the maid, Marie-Celeste, are awaiting the family's return from his funeral. A young American reporter, Clinton Preminger, Jr., forces his way in, insisting upon an interview with Mme Sorodin for the magazine *Life*. This intrusion upon her grief, says Sebastien, is quite unwarrantable; but Preminger points out that as she has not lived with her husband since 1926, her sorrow can hardly be overwhelming. Finally, he persuades Sebastien to let him stay.

Sorodin's widow, Isobel, is an Englishwoman. She enters with her son Colin, a Major in the army, her daughter-in-law Pamela, a typical Major's wife, and her daughter Jane, who has inherited from Sorodin a sense of humour and a sympathetic outlook. With them is Jacob Friedland, an art dealer who has handled Sorodin's pictures and financial matters for many years. He too tries to get rid of Preminger, and after several pointed hints from Sebastien the young man finally leaves.

Being tired and thirsty, all are glad when Sebastien suggests drinking champagne. He himself proposes a toast to his former employer – "a man who… contrived to enjoy life to the full, and at the same time remain a hero to his own valet". After which he smashes the glass in continental fashion, and goes quickly from the room.

Jane, who does not remember her father, is inclined to idealise him, and asks Jacob about his work. The dealer explains that this may be classified into four periods: the Farouche, dating from 1927 into the early thirties; the Circular, from 1933 to 1939; the post-war or Jamaican; and, finally, the Neo-Infantilism, lasting until his death.

Distressed at the hypocrisy of their attendance at the funeral (which her mother and brother take as a matter of course), the girl insists that, since the painter died intestate and Isobel will consequently inherit his considerable fortune, proper provision should be made for the faithful Sebastien. Isobel would have dismissed him with a month's wages, but Jacob agrees with Jane that this is quite inadequate. Eventually they call in Sebastien (who has been listening outside) and ask him whether he would prefer a small pension or a sum in cash. He politely declines both. Then he springs a bombshell upon the company in the form of a letter from the artist, declaring that he has never painted a picture in his life.

ACT II, Scene 1: A few hours have elapsed. The Sorodins and Jacob are discussing the situation as they dejectedly toy with their supper. They feel that the essential is to trace the "ghost" artist and buy his silence. Jane, however, feels that this person ought ultimately to be given recognition, and Jacob supports this view. The others are anxious to get possession of Sebastien's letter and destroy it. The original, he assures them, has been deposited with the keys of Sorodin's studio at St Cloud, in the bank. In this studio there is one final masterpiece, "Nude with Violin".

Just after this new revelation, the bell rings and Clinton Preminger bursts in. A cable from America has told him about this picture and announced that Elmore P. Riskin, Director of the Manhattan Museum of Modern Art, is flying over to buy it. Preminger urges them to show it to him. Sebastien pretends that it is being varnished and, after Jane has promised to telephone him next day if it is ready, he leaves.

The next visitor is a Russian princess, Anya Pavlikov. Sebastien says significantly that they had better see her, for she knew Sorodin intimately at the start of his career.

Anya, a stylish woman of 50, claims to have painted the Farouche pictures between 1925 and 1929, when Sorodin was her lover. Originally she had been a sculptress, but he had persuaded her to give it up and take to painting instead until, tiring of the smell of turpentine, she had eloped with a motor mechanic named Egmont. Jacob reads out to the family a typed copy of Sorodin's letter promising her an annuity of 300,000 francs, on condition that she renounced all claims on her paintings and swore never to reveal the transaction. Anya hints that it would make a good joke for the press if she were to publish this letter, and Jacob eventually agrees to continue and increase her annuity if she surrenders the original.

She is just leaving when Sebastien enters and takes charge of proceedings. He has recognised her lover, Egmont, as an ex-criminal, and, by some adroit blackmail in Russian and English, contrives to get the better of her. She leaves in a fury.

Scene 2: About five o'clock the next afternoon Sebastien telephones Jacob Friedland, telling him that Egmont and the Princess have gone to Brussels by air and will return with Sorodin's letter.

Jane is distressed to learn that her father was a fake, but Sebastien comforts her with the assurance the Sorodin was in fact an idealist with a burning hatred of dishonesty, a crusader who loved good painting and loathed the cant, intellectual snobbism and commercialism of art critics and dealers. He regarded Jacob Friedland in particular as "a pompous, plausible, double-crossing old weasel".

These psychological explanations are interrupted by Cherry-May Waterton, a blowsy, cheerful, middle-aged blonde, who enters accompanied by her elegant but powerfully-built gigolo, Fabrice. Cherry-May – an ex-Jackson-girl from the Casino de Paris – was, it appears, the painter of Sorodin's Circular style pictures. Finding that she could only paint under the influence of drink, he had plied her with alcohol in Shanghai until she developed jaundice and sailed for home. She too has brought a copy of a document setting out his obligations to her, and hints that her claims may be settled by the provision of a chicken farm for Fabrice. When Colin becomes truculent, Cherry-May slaps his face and Fabrice knocks him down.

The ensuing brawl is abruptly checked by Marie-Celeste's announcement of Mr Obadiah Llewellyn, a respectably dressed black man, holding a document in his hand. "My God!" exclaims Sebastien. "The Jamaican period!"

ACT III, Scene 1: Once more the Sorodins are picking at a desultory supper. Colin alone, despite the sticking-plaster on his forehead, has a hearty appetite. Friedlander is closeted in the library with the new arrival, and they are awaiting the outcome of this discussion.

Jane tells her brother frankly that his misadventure was entirely due to his tactless bullying of Miss Waterton, which has resulted in her going away without leaving an address.

When Jacob returns he reports that Obadiah Llewellyn is not bribable: he is a Seventh Day Adventist and has developed religious scruples about his deception, feeling that to save Sorodin's soul, the truth must be published. The ingenious Sebastien suggests that, if all else fails, some of his underworld friends will abstract the document from Llewellyn's pocket.

Unexpectedly, Cherry-May returns, with the silent and sullen Fabrice, to apologise for losing her temper. The two men rather grudgingly shake hands and their reconciliation is sealed with a drink. Jacob agrees to supply the funds for her chicken farm and sends her off to fly to Biarritz for the original document. The visitors are somewhat startled to hear Llewellyn loudly singing a negro spiritual in the adjoining room, but Sebastien explains that he is a West Indian friend practising for a concert. When they have gone, Sebastien sends the almost hysterical Jacob home to bed, and summons his shady acquaintances by telephone.

Scene 2: Next morning, Clinton Preminger has called with a press photographer to take a picture of "Nude with a Violin". He is ecstatic, but the photographer George is obviously unimpressed, and the family, when they appear, giggle helplessly at the massive and shapeless female form with its green and mauve-tinted flesh and small scarlet violin. Jacob is highly shocked at this levity, but Sebastien cheers him with the news that Obadiah Llewellyn is on his way back to Jamaica. No pilfering has been necessary – the underworld gang staged a revivalist meeting and persuaded him to destroy the document as an act of faith. As compensation, Obadiah has been fully satisfied with £50 for a stained-glass window in his chapel.

Now that three of Sorodin's artistic periods have been satisfactorily accounted for, Jane presses Sebastien to tell her about the fourth. Did he himself paint the monstrous "Nude with Violin"? He firmly denies it.

At that moment his son Lauderdale, a boy of about fourteen, bursts into the room. He is in a towering rage because his picture has been put on show unfinished. Sebastien explains that Lauderdale (who has been brought up in Cheltenham and, like his father, is bilingual) has painted since he was seven years old, and has won prizes in exhibitions of children's art. (He hastily reassures Jacob that these early efforts were water-colours and bear no suspicious resemblance to the Sorodin masterpiece.) Lauderdale, who is sobbing with fury, is only pacified and persuaded to leave the room by his father's promise that he shall be allowed to finish the picture later, when he comes back from school.

Sebastien adds smoothly that he has about thirty of his son's canvases, signed by Sorodin, which he can unload on the market at collector's prices. Jacob, aghast, threatens to expose the swindle, but realises that, after paying off the other three "ghosts", he cannot afford to fall out with Sebastien. The family ultimately agree to leave matters as they are, and the curtain falls as Sebastien is about to usher in Mr Elmore P. Riskin and his English counterpart, Sir Alaric Craigie. It rises again to show Lauderdale at work in the empty studio, industriously adding the final touches to "Nude with Violin".

W.A. Darlington in the *Daily Telegraph*, 8 November 1956:

"Over the years I have seen three plays on the theme of the artist (or poet) who didn't paint (or write) his own pictures (or poems). These are Arnold Bennett's *The Great Adventure* (from the novel *Buried Alive*), A. A. Milne's *The Truth about Blayds* and – last night at the Globe – Noël Coward's *Nude with Violin*.

"All these have had the same shape – a brilliant opening, followed by a gradual tailing off to an unsatisfactory finish.

"I am led to the logical conclusion that this plot, which has attracted three fine craftsmen and eluded them all, must have something inherently wrong with it, and I can suggest what that something is.

"Inevitably the climax comes at the end of the first act, when the imposture is revealed. After that the dramatist is left with nothing to relate but other people's reactions to it. And somehow, that doesn't make an exciting story.

"Mr Coward's artist has perpetrated his fraud deliberately because he hated humanity in general and artistic pretenders in particular. The pictures he had foisted on the world were daubs done by anyone handy – his mistresses, a Jamaican missionary, a small boy – and were solemnly hailed as his different periods.

"When the truth comes out after Paul Sorodin's death his deserted English family are shocked, but they hardly care. Only one person really minds, the elderly art-dealer who has made Sorodin's reputation. Now his own reputation is threatened.

"Mr Coward bases his development of the story on the distracted dealer's efforts to hush up the truth; and the play's chief weakness is that this character is conventionally drawn and defies David Horne's frantic efforts to force it to come to life.

"John Gielgud has the leading character, that of the artist's best friend and man servant, a rather shady but likeable character, who begins by giving Sir John plenty of opportunity and then becomes monotonous.

"Of the family group, Joyce Carey is starved of chances as the widow, but takes admirably what she is given. A daughter, the only figure with life of its own, is pleasantly played by Ann Castle.

"It is, however, to Kathleen Harrison, as one of the ex-mistresses, a blatant, good-hearted cockney, that we have to look for the most amusing passages in the later scenes. She wears disreputability with a delightful ease, though I don't remember ever having seen her as a fallen woman before."

PUBLICATIONS

Nude with Violin was first published in two instalments in the December 1956 and January 1957 issues of *Plays and Players*, and in book form by Heinemann (London, 1957). It is dedicated: For John Gielgud, in admiration and affection. Also published in *Play Parade, Volume VI* (1962), and in *Noël Coward Collected Plays: Six*, Methuen World Classics (London, 1999).

NOTES

Coward wrote in his introduction to *Play Parade, Volume VI*:

"*Nude with Violin* is a satirical light comedy which received almost unanimous abuse from the critics and ran to capacity for 18 months. It was finely placed by John Gielgud, Joyce Carey, Kathleen Harrison, Patience Collier and an expert company. After playing it for nine months John Gielgud left the cast and was replaced by Michael Wilding who brought to it even larger audiences, immense personal charm and startling inaudibility. After six months he in turn was replaced by Robert Helpmann. I unfortunately was unable to see his performance but from all accounts he was extremely funny and enjoyed it almost as much as the audience.

"In the autumn of 1957 I played *Nude with Violin* myself for a limited season of three months in New York and later for a season in San Francisco and Los Angeles, when I alternated it with a revival of *Present Laughter*. The play received tepid critical acclaim in New York but ran comfortably enough for the three months it was intended to run. My personal opinion of it is that although it achieved its original purpose, which was to entertain the public and at the same time satirise certain aspects of modern art appreciation, it did not completely succeed because the situation of the play as established at the end of the first act becomes a trifle threadbare by the end of the last. I was acutely aware of this structural defect when I was playing the part of Sebastien myself, much more so than when I wrote it. The critics pounced on this failing with ill-concealed satisfaction and of course they were quite right to do so. They were not quite right however to dismiss the play as a whole with such withering contempt. It has in it some excellent character drawing and some fine comedy scenes. The proof of this lies in the enthusiastic audience reaction it receives whenever and wherever it is played."

The end of Act I and both scenes of Act II, in a condensed version, were televised by the BBC before an invited audience on 11 December 1956, and the complete play was also seen on BBC Television in 1959.

Nude with Violin was revived to celebrate Coward's centenary, 28 June 1999, at the Royal Exchange, Manchester, with a cast headed by Derek Griffiths and Marcia Warren.

US PRODUCTIONS

In his diary for 12 May 1957 Noël writes: "The time has come to stir my stumps... and, being temperamentally restless, I am now sniffing the sawdust again... I think seriously of playing *Nude* myself for a limited season on Broadway. With me in it it would be practically sure-fire and also make an attractive television and movie proposition."

In due course the play opened in Wilmington on 22 October for one week, followed by two in Philadelphia before its New York opening on 14 November at the Belasco Theatre. In his diary entry for 17 November he acknowledges that his optimism was premature: "Both Brooks Atkinson (*New York Times*) and Walter Kerr were contemptuous of the play, although they praise me as a comedian... There is obviously a quality in *Nude* which irritates the critical mind. Perhaps because the whole play is a blistering satire on the critical mind? At all events, in London it didn't receive one even civil notice and has played to capacity for over a year... I fear, even with me in it, that it will not do that here. In England the audience can identify with the family and its dilemmas. Here there is no line of identification with what, to us, is the ordinary, well-behaved middle class. Such a class really doesn't exist in America."

PRESENTED by The Playwright's Company with Lance Hamilton and Charles Russell. Eighty performances at the Belasco Theatre, New York on 14 November 1957 after one week in Wilmington (14 October) and two weeks in Philadelphia (2 October).

CHARACTERS	Belasco, 1957
SEBASTIEN	Noël Coward
MARIE-CELESTE	Thérèse Quadri
CLINTON PREMINGER, JUNIOR	William Traylor
ISOBEL SORODIN	Joyce Carey
JANE (her daughter)	Angela Thornton
COLIN (her son)	John Ainsworth
PAMELA (Colin's wife)	Iola Lynn
JACOB FRIEDLAND	Morris Carnovsky
ANYA PAVLIKOV	Luba Malina
CHERRY-MAY WATERTON	Mona Washbourne
FABRICE	Robert Thurston
OBADIAH LLEWELLYN	Cory Devlin
GEORGE (a press photographer)	Robert Wark
LAUDERDALE	Bobby Alford
Director	*Noël Coward*
Designer	*Oliver Smith*

The *New York Mirror*: "Coward is quite amusing as the resourceful gentleman's gentleman. *Nude with Violin* spells hilarity as slick as a seal's overcoat."

The *New York Times*: "He [Coward] plays the part of the valet. But even here the clipped phrase seems a little slovenly. The cackling vocal style of 20 years ago, the meticulous design of the spoken sentence and the acid emphasis has succumbed to maturity and good nature. With the sting gone there is not much exhilaration left,"

The *New York Herald Tribune*: "It is delightful to have Mr Coward back in the theatre. It would be even more delightful to have him back in a play."

It was this critical reaction that determined Coward to revive *Present Laughter* and play the two productions in tandem.

In February 1956 it was announced that Coward had given up residence in this country and would in future spend his time chiefly in Bermuda and Jamaica. His country house, Goldenhurst, and his London home were sold. During 1956 he adapted, produced and acted in television versions of *Blithe Spirit* and *This Happy Breed* in America (see under each play), and visited Dublin for the production of his latest play, *Nude with Violin*.

During the winter of 1956-7 Coward was at Spithead Lodge in Bermuda and Blue Harbour, his home in Jamaica, where he was joined by Lorn Loraine at the time of the minor earthquake. In March 1957, in the space of two and a half weeks, he wrote a new play, *Volcano*. It is set on the island of Samolo, which he had invented for "We Were Dancing" (*Tonight at 8.30*), in 1935 and used again as the setting for *Pacific 1860* in 1946 and *Island Fling* (*South Sea Bubble*) in 1949.

The play was turned down by Tennent's originally and later in June 1959 announced in the *Stage* for production the following month at the Connaught Theatre, Worthing, by the resident repertory company but was then withdrawn by the author. The play has since remained among Coward's unproduced and unpublished works.

At the same time as *Volcano* he commenced work on a full-length novel, also set in Samolo and including some of the characters from *South Sea Bubble*. This was eventually published as *Pomp and Circumstance* in 1960.

44
LOOK AFTER LULU!
A FARCE
Written in 1958

Adapted from *Occupe-toi d'Amélie* by Georges Feydeau

FIRST PRESENTED in America by Roger Stevens at the Shubert Theatre, New Haven on 19 January 1959 and subsequently at the Henry Miller Theatre, New York on 3 March 1959 (39 performances).

FIRST PRESENTED in the UK by H.M. Tennent Ltd., and L.O.P. Ltd, in association with the English Stage Company at the Theatre Royal, Newcastle-upon-Tyne, 20 July 1959 (45 performances) and at the Royal Court on 29 July 1959 (45 performances). Transferred to the New Theatre, 8 September 1959 (110 performances).

CHARACTERS	Henry Miller, US, 1959
LULU	Tammy Grimes
BOMBA	Rory Harrity
VALERY	Craig Huebling
EMILE	Bill Berger

469

GABY	Barbara Loden
YVONNE	Sasha von Scherlet
PAULETTE	Grace Gaynor
PHILIPPE DE CROZE	George Baker
ADONIS	Paul Smith
GIGOT	Eric Christmas
CLAIR	Polly Rowles
MARCEL BLANCHARD	Roddy McDowall
GENERAL KOSCHNADIEFF	Ellis Rabb
HERR VAN PUTZEBOUM	Jack Gilford
FLORIST'S BOYS	David Faulkner, David Thurman
PRINCE OF SALESTRIA	Kurt Kasznar
ROSE	Reva Rose
OUDATTE	Earl Montgomery
CORNETTE	John Alderman
MAYOR	Arthur Malet
PHOTOGRAPHER	William Griffis
AUNT GABRIELLE	Philippa Bevans
LITTLE GIRL	Ina Cummings
INSPECTOR OF POLICE	David Hurst
Director	*Cyril Ritchard and Noël Coward*
Designer	*Cecil Beaton*

CHARACTERS	**Royal Court and New, 1959**
LULU	Vivien Leigh
BOMBA	Peter Stephens
VALERY	John Gatre
EMILE	Cecil Brock
GABY	Jeanne Watts
YVONNE	Shirley Cameron
PAULETTE	Fanny Carby
PHILIPPE DE CROZE	Robert Stephens
ADONIS	Sean Kelly
GIGOT	Peter Sallis
CLAIR	Meriel Forbes
MARCEL BLANCHARD	Anthony Quayle
GENERAL KOSCHNADIEFF	Lawrence Davidson
HERR VAN PUTZEBOUM	George Devine

FLORIST'S BOYS	David Ryder, Arnold Yarrow (Florist's boys omitted at the New Theatre)
PRINCE OF SALESTRIA	Max Adrian
ROSE	Anne Bishop
OUDATTE	Arnold Yarrow
CORNETTE	Peter Wyatt
MAYOR	Richard Goolden
PHOTOGRAPHER	David Ryder
AUNT GABRIELLE	Barbara Hicks
LITTLE GIRL	Elaine Millar
INSPECTOR OF POLICE	Michael Bates
Director	*Tony Richardson*
Designer	*Roger Furse*

ACT I: Lulu's apartment in Paris. 1908.
ACT II: Mariel's bedroom. Some days later.
ACT III: Scene 1: The registrar's office in the town hall. A few days later.
           Scene 2: Lulu's apartment. Later that day.

❖

SYNOPSIS

ACT I: Lulu is entertaining a number of her friends. Her lover Philippe arrives. He has to go off on his annual two weeks of military service and is nervous about leaving Lulu to the overtures of other men.

An unexpected visitor is announced: Claire, the Duchess of Clausonnes. She is married, madly in love with Philippe's best friend, Marcel, and now convinced that Marcel and Lulu are having an affair and intend to marry. She has seen a letter from Marcel saying as much. As they try and convince her she is mistaken, Marcel arrives. He explains that the letter was to his rich godfather. He is broke and the only way to restore his fortunes is to marry – or appear to marry. When he does this, his godfather will make him a generous settlement. In desperation he has told his godfather of his 'engagement', enclosing the nearest picture he had to hand – one of Lulu.

The godfather, Herr van Putzeboum, is due at any moment, and Marcel asks Lulu to help him, in return for ten per cent of the fortune. She agrees to do so. Another visitor is announced – General Koschnadieff, the emissary

471

of Prince Nicholas of Palestria. The Prince once saw Lulu from a distance and is now hopelessly besotted with her. The General is here to arrange an assignation.

At this moment Marcel rushes in, distraught. His godfather is arriving. Koschnadieff departs, vowing to return within the hour for Lulu's answer. Putzeboum enters and is enchanted with the "little snowdrop" (Lulu). Seeing that his flowers haven't been delivered, he goes out to hurry them up. Philippe reluctantly agrees to the charade of the pretended marriage between Marcel and Lulu but confides his concerns to Marcel. He asks him to look after Lulu while he is away.

Van Putzboum returns with the flowers at precisely the moment when the Prince also arrives and assumes the flowers are to greet his arrival.

ACT II: Marcel wakes up with a hangover to find to his horror that the bump in the bed next to him, that he assumed was his dog Roger is, in fact, Lulu. The situation is distinctly compromising. Lulu's main concern is how she will be able to walk home through the Paris streets wearing an evening dress.

She solves the problem by writing a note to her father asking him to come round with her clothes. While Lulu is doing this, Marcel receives a letter from his godfather, announcing his imminent arrival. He is giving a surprise dinner party for the engaged couple. This is disconcerting news for Lulu, since she had planned her delayed assignation with the Prince. She now writes to the Prince. Naturally, in putting the two letters in their envelopes, they get switched.

Now Claire arrives to see her "demon lover". Lulu hides under the bed, where she pretends to be a mouse until Claire finally flees. Relieved, the exhausted Lulu climbs back into the bed – just as Herr van Putzeboum enters to discover what he thinks is the engaged couple anticipating marital bliss. He announces that he will now be staying in Paris until after the wedding, at which time he will hand over Marcel's inheritance.

Lulu's father arrives to announce that Philippe has returned early from his military service and will be arriving at any moment. Before they have time to register this added complication, the Prince arrives, having received the note asking him to bring Lulu's clothes. Van Putzeboum and Philippe arrive in quick succession, each new arrival causing the assembled company to hide in the bathroom.

Philippe concludes that Marcel has deceived him and determines to be avenged on the pair of them. He pretends to know an actor who would be willing to impersonate the Mayor and conduct the marriage service between Lulu and Marcel.

The Prince appears from the bathroom and demands to know what is going on. Lulu explains:

LULU: A great deal, Your Royal Highness, but it's all perfectly simple. Marcel and I are going to pretend to be married at the Town Hall by Toto Bardac who sometimes appears in *Les Cloches de Corneville* for the Stock Exchange Dramatic Society, because, if we don't, Herr van Putzeboum won't go back to the Hook and won't give Marcel his twelve hundred thousand francs of which I am to receive ten per cent. Philippe de Croze's regiment has got mumps and so he has returned unexpectedly, and the Duchess of Clausonnes has just fainted because she had a presentiment on the Left Bank, in addition to which there's a small revolution in Salestria.

PRINCE: This is becoming farcical!

ACT III, Scene 1: Everyone is gathered at the Registrar's Office in the Town Hall. All of Lulu's friends are present. The Mayor enters and those who are in on the deception remark on Toto's uncanny resemblance to the real Mayor. The ceremony over, Lulu is anxious to leave for her assignation with the Prince, who must return home. Philippe is grimly triumphant as he accepts Marcel's thanks. Only he knows that the 'Mayor' was the Mayor and the couple is now really married! When Claire discovers this from the Mayor himself, she faints – not for the first time.

Scene 2. The impatient Prince is waiting for Lulu in her bedroom. As she steps out of her dress and into his anxious embrace, Marcel arrives to break the news. Lulu is a little annoyed that he is so upset to be married to her, when everyone else she knows wants to be. Then, realising that she is now married, she puts her clothes back on. Marcel, even more upset, throws the Prince's clothes out of the bedroom window, locks the two of them in and rushes to the police station opposite, bringing back an inspector to provide evidence of adultery that will annul the marriage.

However, when the inspector arrives, he refuses to take action against royalty travelling incognito, since it comes roughly under the heading of Diplomatic Immunity. As he leaves, Philippe enters and Marcel tries once more. Since the Prince is still trouserless, Marcel produces a revolver and makes Philippe take off his trousers and give them to the Prince, who then leaves. As he does so, the inspector returns with a gift of flowers for Lulu. Seeing a man *déshabillé* who is clearly not royalty travelling incognito, he is perfectly happy to act as a witness.

473

As Lulu and Philippe happily resign themselves to their fate, Marcel has one final word to say to his old friend: "Look after Lulu!"

The *New York Herald Tribune*, on the US production:
"Mr Coward has not neglected the stout old maxim that a true-blue farce should roll, *Look After Lulu!* rolls. The only trouble is that it keeps rolling backward."

The *New York Daily News*: "There were excellent moments of gay and truly farcical humour, but they were followed by moments of desperation in which people seemed to be trying to keep things going while the stagehands changed the grand sets or the girls changed their wonderful robes and hats or the men took off their pants."

The *New York Daily Mirror*: "A swanky first-night audience relished Noël's caper. The white-tie-and-chinchilla set shook the Miller with howls of delight."

The *Mirror*: "As for your aisle-sitter, he won't have to visit a doctor this morning to have his ribs taped up. And he cannot recommend that you Look After Lulu".

The *Times*, 30 July 1959, on the UK (Royal Court) production:
"[Coward] has been writing like this for so long, without developing, gaining in seriousness, or putting his gifts to the strain of any earnest endeavour, that one is inclined to forget the elegance and ease with which he does it. *Look After Lulu!* is considerably more mechanical than Mr Coward's work when he is not indebted to an original, but the machine he has taken over is highly powered, smooth running, and graceful in design.

"The evening is Miss Vivien Leigh's. Beautiful, delectably cool and matter of fact, she is mistress of every situation, and situations occur with the terrifying rapidity of stations to a traveller on a runaway train on the Underground. She is adept at explanation, reducing lunatic coincidences to normality, inventive at extricating herself, physically and verbally from their tentacles. Nothing can embarrass her, nothing shocks her; she drives complications four-in-hand to the destination she has chosen."

PUBLICATIONS
Look After Lulu! was first published in a solo edition by Heinemann (London, 1959). It was dedicated: "For Vivien, with my love as always."

Also published in *Noël Coward Collected Plays: Five* by Methuen World Classics (London, 1999).

❖

NOTES

Look After Lulu! belongs to a period in Coward's career (whilst a tax exile in Bermuda) when he concentrated on acting, cabaret and writing short stories.

After the London visits by the Barrault-Renaud Company and the *Comédie Française* in the 1950s, Georges Feydeau (1862–1921) had been "discovered". Though his farces had been pilfered and adapted by English authors since the 1890s, his name had not impressed itself on the English play-going public. His farce *Occupe-toi d'Amélie* was first produced at the Théatre Nouveautés, Paris, on 19 March 1908, with Armande Cassive, Marcel Simon and Suzanne Carlix in the leading parts. It was suggested by Jean-Louis Barrault that Vivien Leigh and Laurence Olivier should ask Coward to make an adaptation; the play had not previously been translated into English.

Noël found the adaptation heavy going. In his diaries he records that, "The trouble is that none of it, apart from visual action, is very funny". He found Feydeau "a very untidy playwright. He leaves characters about all over the place and disposes of them without explanation".

Coward became more optimistic, however, and by early November of 1958, he had completed *Look After Lulu!* A production was planned for both sides of the Atlantic. Coward originally hoped for a casting of Shirley MacLaine and Roddy McDowall but Maclaine's film commitments proved a problem. Carol Channing turned the part down, saying that she didn't want to play a prostitute. Finally, after seeing her in cabaret, Coward persuaded Tammy Grimes to star in the US production. Vivien Leigh was to open in London.

At the end of the US run he says: "Poor *Lulu* finally closed last night (4 April) after staggering along to decreasing business for six weeks. The general consensus of opinion is that Cyril (Ritchard) over-directed it, that Tammy didn't quite come up to expectations and that Roddy, although an excellent actor, is not intrinsically a comedian. All of this, I think, is quite true but it doesn't really explain the failure. The reasons for that are deeper. The Broadway theatre for some years has been in the doldrums owing to the racket of theatre parties, which destroy audience participation, and the sheep-like attitude of the public to the two leading critics, Brooks Atkinson and Walter Kerr... Also the American public is not attuned to stylised farce, neither are the American actors. Personally, I have few regrets. I saw the play rapturously received in New Haven by audiences who had not been told much about it one way or the other. I found it, in spite of the above-mentioned defects, very enjoyable. It was a bit common and lacked coherent style."

During the London rehearsals for Lulu, John Osborne is said to have wandered into the Royal Court, seen Vivien Leigh rehearsing on the stage with Anthony Quayle and Max Adrian, and assumed that in some nightmarish way he had been suddenly transported from Sloane Square to the heart of Shaftesbury Avenue. The idea had been for the Court to conquer the West End; instead it seemed that the reverse had happened.

The morning after *Lulu* opened at the Royal Court, to bad notices and a certain amount of journalistic shrieking about the betrayal of the avant-garde values in Sloane Square, Coward flew to Athens for a fortnight's cruising around the Greek Islands aboard an Onassis family yacht. Rested, he returned to London to find that *Look After Lulu!* had survived its notices and that business at the Court had in fact been good enough to justify a transfer to the West End on 8 September; there *Lulu* played to adequate business at the New Theatre, just one more in a long line of Coward comedies which nobody liked except the public.

UK PRODUCTIONS

Look After Lulu! was revived at the 1978 Chichester Festival Theatre season (directed by Patrick Garland) and transferred to the Theatre Royal, Haymarket (with some changes in the minor roles) on 9 October (56 performances).

CHARACTERS	Chichester, 1978
LULU	Geraldine McEwan
BOMBA	Martin Milman
VALERY	Rom Karol
EMILE	Michael Hughes
YVONNE	Kate Percival
PAULETTE	Shelley Borkhum
PHILIPPE DE CROZE	Gary Raymond
ADONIS	Martin Chamberlain
GIGOT	George Howe
CLAIR	Fenella Fielding
MARCEL BLANCHARD	Clive Francis
GENERAL KOSCHNADIEFF	Paul Hardwick

HERR VAN PUTZEBOUM	Nigel Stock
FLORIST'S BOYS	Michael Hughes, John Haden
THE PRINCE OF SALESTRIA	Peter Bowles
ROSE	Yvette Byrne
OUDATTE	Martin Milman
CORNETTE	Tom Karol
MAYOR	Robert Perceval
PHOTOGRAPHER	Michael Hughes
INSPECTOR OF POLICE	Nigel Stock

45
VOLCANO
A PLAY IN TWO ACTS
Written in 1957

Never fully staged in the UK or US, but given a single rehearsed reading on 26 June 1989 at The Mill at Sonning. This was the first in a series of Coward play readings, with the overall title of *The Coward Collection*.

CHARACTERS	**The Mill at Sonning, 1989**
ELLEN DANBURY	Sally Hughes
ADELA SHELLEY	Judi Dench
GRIZELDA CRAIGIE	Jennifer Hilary
ROBIN CRAIGIE	Adam Faith
(Grizelda's husband)	
GUY LITTLETON	Michael Williams
MELISSA LITTLETON (Guy's wife)	Polly Adams
MAMMY ALEENA	Cleo Sylvestre
(the guest house caretaker)	
MR IMALAKI	Osei Bentil
(a newspaper reporter)	
KEITH DANBURY (Ellen's husband)	Benedick Blythe
Director	*Stuart Wood*
Producer	*Martin Tickner*

❖

SCENE: The action of the play takes place on the islands of Samolo
          (the mythic island of Coward's *South Sea Bubble* and *Pacific
          1860*) and Nooneo in the Samolan archipelago. The year is 1956.
ACT I: Scene 1: The verandah of Adela Shelley's house on the lower
          slopes of the Lailanu mountains, Samolo. Evening.
          Scene 2: The living-room of the Fumfumbolo guest-house on
          Nooneo. A week later, Evening.
ACT II: Scene 1: The guest-house. Around noon the following day.
          Scene 2: The verandah of Adela's house. The following
          morning.
          Scene 3: The same. Ten days later. Evening.

SYNOPSIS

Adela Shelley, an attractive widow, runs a guest house on Samolo. In a rash moment a year or so before the play opens she had a brief affair with Guy Littleton, a younger married man and the island's resident roué. Guy's unpleasant wife Melissa, described by Coward as "assured but with an underlying note of neuroticism", arrives to assess her rival.

Adela's other house-guest is Ellen Danbury, a young woman whose own marriage is having problems. Making up the party are neighbours, Grizelda and Robin Craigie. Grizelda is the narrator/heroine of *Pomp and Circumstance*. The group makes an expedition up the slopes of the island's still active volcano Fumfumbolo and, during their overnight stay at the guest house, tensions mount. Guy takes off on a side trip with Ellen, leaving the others stranded, and the volcano, which has been behaving threateningly and symbolically, begins to erupt. Although they all escape safely, certain personal decisions have been made.

Melissa departs, having finally decided, it seems, to divorce Guy. Ellen is apparently reconciled with her husband Keith. Adela and Melissa have reached an understanding from which Guy is most definitely excluded.

With the guests gone, Guy returns to Adela attempting to make up with her, bearing a handful of seashells as a gift. To his surprise, she rejects him dismissively: "You wreak too much havoc, swaggering through people's lives touting your illusion that physical love is 'the one irreplacable ecstasy'. Shakespeare described your creed more accurately, 'An expense of spirit in a waste of shame'. I'm tired of the noise you make with your shrill, boastful trumpeting. Please go away and leave me alone." She then drops the seashells he has given her onto the ground.

❖

PUBLICATIONS

Volcano is unpublished.

❖

NOTES

On Sunday 10 March, 1957 Coward, then aged 57, was visiting the Cayman Islands from his Jamaican home. In his diaries he wrote: "I am half way, or nearly half way through a new play. The idea came to me quite suddenly and I discussed it with Lornie [Lorn Loraine, his manager]. She thought it very good indeed and in about twenty minutes the whole story had set itself into three acts and six scenes without any conscious effort from me. And then the title obligingly dropped into my mind, *Volcano*, and I started right away and wrote the first scene, then a day or two later, half of the second scene. It is a serious play, so far I think, very well written. The concentration on verse (he had recently written a series of verses) has, as I suspected, enriched my vocabulary and improved my style. The story is concerned with the emotional problems of six people, notably four of them, and is played against the background of a minor volcanic eruption. The second act takes place in a guest-house on the volcano itself, good old Fumfumbolo. I know that my psychology is sound and, for the first time for a long while, I am conscious of the real magic of my gift. It always surprises me each time it happens and I shall never cease to marvel at it. Why suddenly, after months of barrenness, should the right words flow out of me with so little effort beyond concentration. I am sure, by the way this is absorbing my mind, and by the pleasure it is giving me to write it, that it is intrinsically right. All of which, not unnaturally, makes me very happy. On Saturday I finished off the first act and today I begin the second."

A week later, in Jamaica: "Home again, with the second act of *Volcano* done. I am very pleased with it and there now only remains the last act. Only! Still, I have the shape of it fairly clear in my mind." And a week after that, "*Volcano* is finished completely and I have typed through the whole script and revised it. The last act is strong, even, I think, stronger than the second. I am really happy because it is well balanced and well written. I am sure the press will say that such people don't exist for the very good reason that they could never have had the remotest opportunity of meeting them. However, I know I've done a good piece of work and I am feeling immensely relieved and cheerful. The play has been sent off to Lornie in London to be mimeographed and I have written to Binkie [Hugh 'Binkie' Beaumont, head of the production company, H. M. Tennent Ltd.] warning him that it is on the way."

In the event, Beaumont did not share Coward's enthusiasm. On 5 May Coward wrote: "[I had] a letter from Binkie not liking *Volcano* and saying that I should have written it as a comedy and that such people (i.e: cultured and articulate, I presume) no longer exist or if they do are apparently not acceptable as serious characters. This is a blow and disappointing. I have no idea what to do. I've re-read the play myself and it's first rate and I fear Binkie's judgement is at fault. I've written to him calmly, disagreeing with him and we shall see whether or not he thinks it worth doing in spite of his personal feeling. I know that, according to the present trend, he is possibly right but I have no faith in the trend of squalour and dreariness lasting for much longer [John Osborne's *Look Back in Anger* which had started this 'trend' had opened at the Royal Court almost exactly a year before, on 6 May, 1956]. There are still many million middle-aged, middle-class English people who would, I think, appreciate the values of *Volcano*. However, perhaps I am more old fashioned than I realise."

Coward eventually rewrote a lot of *Volcano* but even the revised version was not to Hugh Beaumont's liking and the play has remained unproduced apart from as a rehearsed reading.

The imaginary Pacific island of Samolo was also used in *We Were Dancing*, *Pacific 1860*, *Island Fling* and in Coward's only published book, *Pomp and Circumstance* in 1960. Coward invented a language and history for the island (see pages 393 to 394).

The two versions of *Volcano* differ only in small but significant detail. In the original version, Adela, though in love with Guy, has not yet had a relationship with him due to her sense of loyalty to her dead husband. In the second version (performed at Sonning) they are established lovers from the beginning. In the original, Melissa seems reluctantly prepared to condone Guy's behaviour, whereas in the revised plot she declares her intent to divorce him.

Act I. Lord Darlington (Shamus Locke), Lady Agatha Carlisle (Patricia Cree), The Duchess of Berwick (Irene Browne) and Lady Windermere (Vanessa Lee)

Act I. "Mr Hopper's Chanty" Mr Hopper (Graham Payn), Mr Dumby (Dennis Bowen) and Mr Cecil Graham (Tom Gill)

Act II, Scene 1. Lord Darlington (Shamus Locke), Lady Windermere (Vanessa Lee), Mrs Erlynne (Mary Ellis), Lord Windermere (Peter Graves), Mr Dumby (Dennis Bowen) and Mr Cecil Graham (Tom Gill)

AFTER THE BALL, Globe Theatre, 1954

Act II, Scene 2. Lord Augustus Lorton (Donald Scott), Mrs Erlynne (Mary Ellis), Mr Dumby (Dennis Bowen), Lord Windermere (Peter Graves), Mr Hopper (Graham Payn), Mr Cecil Graham (Tom Gill), Lady Windermere (Vanessa Lee) and Lord Darlington (Shamus Locke)

NUDE WITH VIOLIN, Globe Theatre, 1956

Act I. Jacob Friedland (David Horne), Jane (Ann Castle), Pamela (Patricia Raine), Isobel Sorodin (Joyce Carey), Colin (Basil Henson) and Sebastien (John Gielgud)

Act II, Scene 2. Cherry-May Waterton (Kathleen Harrison), Jacob Friedland (David Horne),
Jane (Ann Castle), Isobel Sorodin (Joyce Carey), Marie-Celeste (Gillian Webb), Obadiah Llewellyn
(Thomas Baptiste), Fabrice (Douglas Robinson), Colin (Basil Henson), Pamela (Patricia Raine)
and Sebastien (John Gielgud)

Act III, Scene 2. Lauderdale (Nicky Edmett), Sebastien (John Gielgud) and Isobel Sorodin (Joyce Carey)

Claire, Duchess of Clausonnes (Meriel Forbes) and Lulu d'Arville (Vivien Leigh)

Lulu d'Arville (Vivien Leigh) and
the Prince of Salestria (Max Adrian)

Adonis (Sean Kelly), Gigot (Peter Sallis)
and Lulu d'Arville (Vivien Leigh)

Lulu d'Arville (Vivien Leigh), Herr von Putzeboum (George Divine)
and Marcel Blanchard (Anthony Quayle)

Act I, Scene 2. Lotta Bainbridge (Sybil Thorndike) and May Davenport (Marie Löhr)

Deirdre O'Malley (Maureen Delany), Lotta Bainbridge (Sybil Thorndike) and May Davenport (Marie Löhr)

May Davenport (Marie Löhr), Sarita Myrtle (Nora Nicholson), Lotta Bainbridge (Sybil Thorndike), Maud Melrose (Norah Blaney) and Estelle Craven (Edith Day)

Act III. The Christmas party at The Wings

Mimi Paragon (Elaine Stritch) and Johny van Mier (David Holliday)

Act II. Mimi Paragon (Elaine Stritch) and the "Little Ones' ABC"

Mimi Paragon (Elaine Stritch) and Company

"Come To Me" Mimi Paragon (Elaine Stritch)

Elaine Stritch and Noël Coward: a publicity still for the cover of *Playbill*

THE GIRL WHO CAME TO SUPPER, Broadway Theatre, 1963

Act II. "Coronation Chorale" in Westminster Abbey

Mary Morgan (Florence Henderson) and the Prince Regent (José Ferrer)

Act I. "Swing Song" Jessie Maynard (Marion Haraldson) in *The Coconut Girl*

The Prince Regent (José Ferrer), the Queen Mother (Irene Browne) and Mary (Florence Henderson)

Act I. The Seance. Ruth Condomine (Louise Troy), Dr. Bradman (Laurence Keith), Mrs Bradman (Margaret Hall), Charles Condomine (Edward Woodward) and Madame Arcati (Beatrice Lillie)

Act II. Scene 5. Madame Arcati (Beatrice Lillie)

Ruth Condomine (Marti Stevens) and Company

Elvira (Tammy Grimes) and Company

Act I. Dr. Bradman (Peter Vernon), Madame Arcati (Cicely Courtneidge), Charles Condomine (Denis Quilley), Elvira (Marti Stevens) and Ruth (Jan Waters)

Madame Arcati (Cicely Courtneidge) and her Inner Circle Club

SUITE IN THREE KEYS, Queens Theatre, 1966

A SONG AT TWILIGHT

Hugo Latymer (Noël Coward) and Carlotta Gray (Lilli Palmer)

COME INTO THE GARDEN, MAUD

Verner Conklin (Noël Coward) and Maud Caragnani (Lilli Palmer)

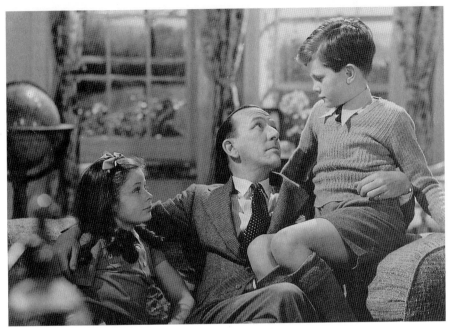

Capt.'D' (Noël Coward) at home with his children: Lavinia (Amy Stephens) and Bobby (Daniel Messey)

Capt.'D' (Noël Coward) says goodbye in Alexandria to the survivors of the *Torrin*

IN WHICH WE SERVE, Film, 1942

The shipwrecked crew round the float. Capt.'D' (Noël Coward), extreme right with John Mills (behind)

TOGETHER WITH MUSIC, Television, New York, 1955

"Together With Music" Mary Martin and Noël Coward

46
WAITING IN THE WINGS
A PLAY IN THREE ACTS
Written in 1959–60

FIRST PRESENTED by F.B.S. (Plays) Ltd., in association with Michael Redgrave Productions Ltd., at the Olympia Theatre, Dublin, Eire, 8 August 1960 (two weeks), followed by the Royal Court Theatre, Liverpool (one week), subsequently at the Duke of York's Theatre, London, 7 September 1960 (188 performances).

CHARACTERS	Duke of York's, 1960
MAY DAVENPORT	Marie Löhr
CORA CLARKE	Una Venning
BONITA BELGRAVE	Maidie Andrews
MAUD MELROSE	Norah Blaney
DEIRDRE O'MALLEY	Maureen Delany
ESTELLE CRAVEN	Edith Day
ALMINA CLARE	Mary Clare
PERRY LASCOE	Graham Payn
MISS ARCHIE	Margot Boyd
OSGOOD MEEKER	Lewis Casson
LETTA BAINBRIDGE	Sybil Thorndike
DORA	Berry Hare
DOREEN	Jean Conroy
SARITA MYRTLE	Nora Nicholson
ZELDA FENWICK	Jessica Dunning
DOCTOR JEVONS	William Hutt
TOPSY BASKERVILLE	Molly Lumley
	(succeeded by Ethel Gabriel)

Director	*Margaret Webster*
Set and costumes	*Motley*

SCENE: The action of the play passes in the lounge of The Wings, a charity home for retired actresses, in the Thames Valley, not far from Bourne End.

ACT I: Scene 1: A Sunday afternoon in June
            Scene 2: 3 a.m. on a Monday morning, a month later
ACT II: Scene 1: A Sunday afternoon in September
            Scene 2: Several hours later
ACT III: Scene 1: The evening of Christmas Day
            Scene 2: A Sunday afternoon in June
TIME: The present

MUSICAL NUMBERS
    "Waiting In The Wings"
    "Champagne"
    "Miss Mouse"
    "Over The Hill"
    "Come The Wild, Wild Weather"
    "Oh, Mister Kaiser"

SYNOPSIS

ACT I, Scene 1: Four residents are sitting in the pleasantly furnished lounge of The Wings. Bonita Belgrave, an ex-musical-comedy star, is playing cards with Cora Clarke, a dissatisfied woman with a caustic tongue. Maud Melrose is reading the theatre page of the *Sunday Times*, and May Davenport is working at an embroidery frame. Almina Clare and Estelle Craven are on the verandah.

There is some conversation about a forthcoming charity matinée in aid of The Wings, interrupted by Deirdre O'Malley, an aggressive Irish Catholic, who is indignant because the television has failed in the middle of her favourite programme. Bonita offers to fetch Archie (Miss Archibald, the superintendent) to fix it, but Deirdre decides to go upstairs for a nap.

Estelle and Almina come in, complaining of the cold; this leads them to talk about the possibility of glassing-in the verandah to make a solarium. Perry Lascoe, the young secretary, has been pressing the Committee to agree to this but it is a question of funds.

It transpires that they are expecting a new resident that afternoon: Lotta Bainbridge. The news has been known for some time, but has been carefully kept from May Davenport, as everyone knows that she and Lotta have not spoken to each other for 30 years. On finding out, May makes a dramatic exit, declaring that she will continue to ignore Lotta.

The sound of a motorbike heralds Perry Lascoe making his usual Sunday afternoon visit. He is a pleasant young man who makes much of the old ladies and is adored by them. They discuss the oldest resident, Martha Carrington, now 95, bedridden and only intermittently lucid. However, she still has an elderly admirer, Osgood Meeker, who comes every Sunday to bring her a bunch of violets. A few minutes later he arrives with his flowers and goes straight upstairs to see her.

Meanwhile, Perry is questioned about the solarium, and has to admit that the Committee has rejected the idea as too expensive. He promises, however, to get a reduced estimate and take it to the next meeting.

Lotta Bainbridge arrives with her devoted dresser, Dora, who is heartbroken at having to part from her. Lotta, perfectly composed, says a few pleasant words to each of the women that reveals an interest in their past successes. Warned of May's attitude, Lotta says she will try to make friends with her.

Lotta is left alone with Perry. She asks him why he gave up the theatre so young, to cope with "all these old shadows". He says he realised that he would never become a star and, having his mother to support, opted for a fixed salary; moreover, he loves "the old shadows".

Miss Archie enters and begins to explain the regulations of the house, but as Dora comes down from unpacking, Lotta asks to be left alone with her to say goodbye. It is a touching scene: Dora, who intends to marry a widower, is ready to give him up if Lotta can find another flat and let her stay on as before. Lotta refuses the offer and sends Dora away. Controlling her tears, she collects her belongings and goes upstairs.

Scene 2: The old ladies, as a treat, have been taken to rehearsal of the Midnight Matinée given to raise funds for The Wings. It is 3 a.m. and they are expected back any minute. The maid Doreen, supervised by Miss Archie, is preparing soup and sandwiches.

A resident, Sarita Myrtle (usually kept upstairs because she is unbalanced) appears and cannot be persuaded to return to her room. She believes she is in a theatre just after a performance.

The party comes back. They help themselves to sandwiches while Miss Archie induces Sarita to return upstairs. Lotta makes a determined attempt to break down May's hostility. She begs her, for the sake of all the others, to forget the past and "welcome our limited future with as much grace as possible." May replies bitterly: "I would be the last to deny your sentimental appeal to an audience. It was all you ever had." She exits and Lotta sighs: "I did my best. I shan't try anymore."

ACT II, Scene 1: Sunday afternoon three months later. Perry ushers in a young journalist, Zelda Fenwick. She has come to get a story about The Wings for her column. It is part of Perry's plan, that she will also make an appeal on her new television programme for the solarium. Warning her that the old ladies will be upset if they know she is a journalist, Perry proposes to introduce her as "Miss Starkey".

Miss Archie comes in and is introduced. Miss Archie guesses from her manner that 'Miss Starkey' is actually from the press and, as Zelda goes out to photograph the building, reminds Perry that press interviews are against Committee rules. Perry confesses that he has arranged this in the hope of raising funds for the solarium, and Miss Archie agrees not to intervene. They exit just before Zelda reappears. Sarita then steals downstairs and picks up a box of matches. Striking them one by one, she starts up an incoherent conversation with the bewildered Zelda. Deirdre then bursts in, scolds Sarita and sends her back upstairs; she confides to Zelda all her grievances against the Committee.

The others enter. Lotta instantly recognises Zelda as author of the 'People Are News' column in the *Sunday Clarion*. May, in particular, is indignant with Perry. Lotta asks Zelda to promise not to write about the home, because: "We'd like to be remembered as we were, not as we are." Zelda says she is professionally obliged to give her editor the story; but in compensation, she intends to make a television appeal for the solarium. Deirdre, however, attacks her in such violent terms that she is forced to leave.

They all go in to tea (except Miss Archie and Perry, who feel the need for a stronger drink). As soon as the lounge is empty, Sarita comes down and helps herself to two boxes of matches.

Scene 2: Everyone has gone to bed, but Bonita has been roused by the smell of smoke. She comes out on the landing, realises that Sarita's room is on fire and calls to Deirdre to warn the others, while she fetches the superintendent. Miss Archie seizes a fire extinguisher and goes straight in. One after another, the residents wake and come downstairs. Miss Archie reappears to set their minds at rest: it was only the curtains that were alight, and she has put them out. Lotta brings down Sarita, wrapped in a blanket.

While Doreen goes upstairs to help Miss Archie transfer Sarita's belongings into another room, Bonita suggests fetching a bottle of whisky. When Miss Archie comes back, Lotta expresses their gratitude for her presence of mind, and to everyone's amazement May endorses this with "Hear, Hear!" Lotta smiles at her and the two women exchange a glance. When the others have gone up to bed, Lotta and May stay together on the sofa. They talk about the man who caused their long feud. "Why did you take him from me?" asks May.

Lotta says that, in fact, she did not: in between leaving May and coming to Lotta, Charles was living with another woman. This further placates May, who asks Lotta about her first husband, Walter Bennet. After their divorce he went to Canada and died out there. Lotta says that her son, who took his father's part, is still in Canada and that she has not heard from him for 17 years. The two women make a toast to "Happy days!"

Scene 3: A week has passed, and Bonita is reading aloud the *Sunday Clarion* column, which is all that they had feared. Zelda has reported the Lotta-May story under the heading "Old foes still feuding in the twilight of their lives". She ends with an appeal to "remember how much we owe to these old, faithful servants of the public, wearily playing out the last of their lives – just waiting, waiting in The Wings." Their indignation changes to laughter as Bonita declares: "That would make a wonderful musical number!" With Maud accompanying her at the piano, she sings:

> Older than God,
> On we plod,
> Waiting in the wings

And they join in a bravura finish: "Waiting, waiting, waiting in the wings".

Amid the applause, Osgood enters with his flowers. He, too, has seen the *Sunday Clarion* and thinks it touching. He goes upstairs.

Hearing Perry's motorbike, the residents wonder what will happen to him: if he is sacked, they say, they will go on strike. Perry tells them that he had indeed had a bad time with the Committee. At one meeting they did dismiss him, but thanks to a telephone call from May (who has kept up a pretence of being most indignant with him) to an influential friend of hers, he has been reinstated.

Their satisfaction is dampened by the arrival of Dr Jevons to take Sarita to a mental hospital. Everyone is so upset that Lotta asks Maud to cover up by playing the piano. Sarita, coming downstairs, thinks she is leaving a hotel in order to stay with friends, and is quite happy.

ACT III, Scene 1: It is the evening of Christmas Day. Doreen is tidying up. Miss Archibald gives her some crackers and tells her to go home early. Zelda arrives. She has brought a case of champagne and a cheque from her boss, Lord Charkley, for £2000, for the solarium. Zelda leaves, sending her love to all the residents.

Coffee is brought in by Doreen, and the residents, accompanied by Perry and Osgood, troop in to drink it. Miss Archie tells them the good news. Perry goes to fetch some champagne, suggesting that they drink the health of Zelda Fenwich and Lord Charkley. Maud, at the piano, plays "For They Are Jolly Good Fellows" and all join in singing it. Perry waltzes with Miss Archie while Maud sings the song "Champagne", followed by the theme song, "Miss Mouse". Then Bonita sings one of her successes, "Over The Hill" and Perry, after some urging, launches into his own number, "Come The Wild, Wild Weather".

Maud plays an Irish jig, which Deirdre, aged 82, dances with Perry. Suddenly Deirdre stops dancing, and collapses. She is lifted onto a sofa and Lotta fetches brandy, but all is in vain.

Scene 2: Once again it is June; through the windows of the lounge the new solarium can be seen. Cora comes out of it, grumbling at the heat, and May remarks that she was always dissatisfied. When Lotta says that Cora probably hates The Wings more than anyone else, May declares that she, too, hates it.

Doreen announces a visitor, Lotta's son, Alan Bennet. Mother and son, embarrassed, keep up a desultory conversation about Alan's life in Winnipeg. At last Lotta asks why he has come. He replies that, months after its publication, he has seen the *Sunday Clarion* article and, for the first time, realised the straits to which she has been reduced. He gives her a letter from his wife, inviting her to come and live with them. Lotta thanks him but declines, saying she would rather live upon public than private charity. Relieved, Alan offers to take her out to lunch in the next couple of days. He leaves. May finds Lotta in tears on the sofa. She sympathises and the other ladies enter with Perry, who has brought a bottle of perfume for May's birthday. A new resident, Topsy Baskerville, is expected imminently and Maud plays one of Topsy's songs "Oh, Mr Kaiser". Lotta remembers that she was in despair when she arrived a year ago, feeling as though she were going to prison, but now feels free. Topsy Baskerville enters and recognises her song. The residents greet her warmly.

Financial Times, September 1960:
"There is a lot of old shop talked and a lot of old songs sung, and it gets more nauseating as the evening wears on."

Manchester Guardian, September 1960: "Probably the play will serve as a broad target for scorn in some quarters, and may justifiably be called shameless in its exploitation of the sentimentalities inherent in a tale of old actresses backbiting and sighing in a home for the aged of the profession. But as long as the mood is one of outraged grandeur, mild dottiness, theatrical slander, and the game of upstaging the last speaker, Mr Coward's touch remains what it has always been: and sometimes touches the level of inspired cattiness found in such pieces as the *Red Peppers*."

PUBLICATIONS

Waiting in the Wings was published by Heinemann (London 1960). It is dedicated "For Dame Sybil Thorndike with my love, admiration and gratitude". Also published in *Noël Coward Collected Plays: Five* by Methuen World Classics (London, 1999).

The words and music of "Come The Wild, Wild Weather" were published by Chappell & Co (1960) and all the six incidental songs were published as *Waiting in the Wings "A Folio of Songs"* by Chappell & Co (1962).

All the lyrics are included in *The Complete Lyrics* (Methuen/Overlook, 1998).

NOTES

In the published play Coward included the following preliminary note:

" The Wings is a small charity home for retired actresses. It differs from other organisations of its kind in that it provides only for those who have been stars or leading ladies and who, through age, lack of providence, misfortune etc., have been reduced to poverty.

"Some of these have been granted a pension of four pounds a week by the King George's Pension Fund; others have small, pitifully small incomes of their own.

"No actress under the age of 60 is eligible for admittance to the home.

"The Wings is subscribed to by public funds and was founded in 1925 by Sir Hilary Brooks, a leading actor-manager and producer of his day.

"The organisation is controlled from London by a committee of leading actors and actresses who attend meetings once a month and make decisions on policy, investments etc."

In his introduction in *Play Parade, Volume VI* (1962) Coward wrote:

"From the moment the curtain rose on the opening performance at the Duke of York's Theatre I knew instinctively that that particular audience was warm, well-disposed and eager to find the play good. Actually it was one of the most moving first nights I have ever attended. The cast, immediately conscious that the atmosphere was favourable, played the play, if possible, better than they had ever played it before. They handled the salvos of applause, the laughter and the cheering with the grace and dignity of experienced experts, which, after all, most of them were. Marie Löhr, a young woman of 70, who had fallen down and broken her right wrist that very afternoon, gave an assured and impeccable performance in spite of agonising pain which would have sent many a lesser actress moaning to the nearest hospital. Sybil Thorndike, to my mind one the few really great actresses of our time, played the part I had written with such unswerving truth, restraint, lack of sentimentality and sheer beauty that I saw much of it through a haze of grateful tears. In fact each member of that remarkable company gave to my play their shining best, and for me, together with the majority of the audience, it was a great night in the theatre.

"The next morning when I read the reviews I was, for the first time in many years, very angry indeed. Not especially because the critics hadn't liked the play, which I was fully prepared for, but because they had neither the wit nor the generosity to pay sufficient tribute to the acting. It was the so-called popular press which, not unnaturally, roused my ire, for they gave to their wide circulation of readers the wholly inaccurate impression that the play had been a failure from every point of view. This, apart from its inherent personal malice, was dishonest reporting and as such should have been severely reprimanded by the editors and owners of the newspapers concerned. However, in spite of it, *Waiting in the Wings* proceeded to play to absolute capacity for three months and actually, I believe, broke the record of the Duke of York's Theatre.

"I recommend this play, more than any I have written for many years, to the reader's most earnest attention."

Despite this recommendation the play did not fulfil Coward's expectations and led eventually to a series of articles in the *Sunday Times*, aimed at the critics and expressing his growing distaste for the modern playwrights and actors of the "Scratch and mumble school" which they encouraged. With that off his chest, he began working on a musical which he had started earlier as *Later than Spring* and was now retitled *Sail Away*. Apart from *The Girl Who Came to Supper*, an adaptation of Terence Rattigan's play *The Sleeping Prince* for which he wrote the music and lyrics only (produced in New York, 1963), he did not write again for the theatre until *Suite in Three Keys* in 1965.

The first American production of *Waiting in the Wings* is due to open on Broadway on Coward's hundredth birthday, 16 December 1999, after a short tour. It will be produced by Alexander Cohen and will star Lauren Bacall and Rosemary Harris.

47
SAIL AWAY
A NEW MUSICAL COMEDY
Written in 1959–61

FIRST PRESENTED by Bonard Productions in association with Charles Russell at the Colonial Theatre, Boston, 9 August 1961. The company moved to the Forrest Theatre, Philadelphia on 7 September.

SUBSEQUENTLY PRESENTED at the Broadhurst Theatre, New York on 3 October 1961 (167 performances).

CHARACTERS	Boston and Philadelphia, US, 1961
JOE COLERIDGE (the ship's purser)	Charles Braswell
SHUTTLEWORTH (Chief Steward)	Keith Prentice
RAWLINGS (a passenger who drinks)	James Pritchett
SIR GERARD NUTFIELD	C. Stafford Dickens
LADY NUTFIELD	Margaret Mower
BARNABY SLADE	Grover Dale
ELMER CANDIJACK	Henry Lawrence
MAIMIE CANDIJACK (his wife)	Betty Jane Watson
GLEN CANDIJACK (their son)	Alan Helms
SHIRLEY CANDIJACK (their daughter)	Patti Mariano
VERITY CRAIG	Jean Fenn
LAWFORD CRAIG (her husband)	William Hutt
MR SWEENEY	Jon Richards
MRS SWEENEY	Paula Bauersmith
ELINOR SPENCER-BOLLARD	Alice Pearce
NANCY FOYLE (her niece)	Patricia Harty
ALVIN LUSH	Paul O'Keefe
MRS LUSH (his mother)	Evelyn Russell
JOHN VAN MIER	James Hurst
MRS VAN MIER (his mother)	Margalo Gilmore
MIMI PARAGON	Elaine Stritch
CLARA BRASSEY (a stewardess)	Wish Mary Hunt
ALI (an Arab guide)	Charles Braswell

MAN (from American Express)	Richard Woods
PASSENGERS, STEWARDS, ARABS,	
ITALIANS, CHILDREN	Jere Admire, Bobby Allen, Gary Crabbe, David Evans, Pat Ferrier, Dorothy Frank, Ann Fraser, James Frasher, Gene Gavin, Curtis Hood, Wish Mary Hunt, Bridget Knapp, Nancy Lynch, Patti Mariano, Mary Ellen O'Keefe, Alan Peterson, Robby Reed, Dennis Scott, Alice Shanahan, Dan Siretta, Gloria Stevens
Director	*Noël Coward*
Designer	*Oliver Smith*

❖

SCENE: The action of the play takes place on various parts of the cruise ship, the S.S. *Carolonia*, and in Tangier, Taormina and at the Parthenon

ACT I: Scene 1: The main hall of the Cunard steam-ship, *Carolonia* (Noon).

Scene 2: Verity Craig's cabin. A few minutes later.

Scene 3: John Van Mier's cabin. A few minutes later.

Scene 4: The sun deck, New York harbour. A quarter of an hour later.

Scene 5: Elinor Spencer-Bollard's cabin. A few minutes later.

Scene 6: The sun deck. At sea several days later. Noon.

Scene 7: The promenade deck. A few days later. Late afternoon.

Scene 8: The sun deck. That evening.

Scene 9: Mimi Paragon's cabin. The following evening.

Scene 10: The promenade deck. At four in the morning.

Scene 11: The sun deck, Gibraltar. Midnight.

ACT II: Scene 1: Tangier.

Scene 2: The ship's nursery.

Scene 3: The sun deck. The Bay of Naples.

Scene 4: Taormina.

Scene 5: The Parthenon.

Scene 6: The sun deck. Villefranche.

Scene 7: The promenade deck.

Scene 8: The main hall.

Musical direction and	Peter Matz
dance arrangements	
Musical numbers and dances	Joe Layton

MUSICAL NUMBERS

ACT I

"Come To Me"	Mimi and the Stewards
"I Am No Good At Love"	Verity
"Sail Away"	Johnny
Reprise: "Come To Me"	Mimi
"Where Shall I Find Him?"	Nancy
"Beatnik Love Affair"	Barnaby and Nancy with the Passengers
"Later Than Spring"	Johnny
"The Passenger's Always Right"	Joe and the Stewards
Reprise: "Sail Away"	Johnny
"Where Shall I Find Her?"	Barnaby
"Useful Phrases"	Mimi
"This Is A Night For Lovers"	Verity and Johnny
"You're A Long, Long Way From America"	Mimi and the Company

ACT II

"The Customer's Always Right"	Ali and the Arabs
"Something Very Strange"	Verity
"The Little Ones' ABC"	Mimi and the Children
"This Is A Changing World"	Verity
"I Never Knew"	Verity
"Sicilian Interlude" (Ballet)	The Company
"When You Want Me"	Barnaby and Nancy
"Why Do The Wrong People Travel?"	Mimi
Reprise: "Later Than Spring"	Mimi
"Bronxville Darby and Joan"	Mr and Mrs Sweeney
"This Is A Changing World" (Reprise)	Verity
"When You Want Me" (Reprise)	Company
Finale	Company

❖

SYNOPSIS

ACT I, Scene 1: We are in the main hall of the S.S. *Carolonia* as the passengers arrive. They are greeted and dispatched to their cabins by Joe Coleridge, the Purser and Shuttleworth, the Chief Steward. We see the following:

Verity Craig, a beautiful elegant woman in her late thirties, and her husband, Lawford, some ten years older. They are clearly unhappy in each other's company. Nancy Foyle, a pretty young girl and her aunt, Elinor Spencer-Bollard, a famous American novelist and "the ideal of Women's Clubs from San Francisco to Portland, Maine"... Johnny Van Mier, a tall, good-looking young man in his twenties, accompanied by his mother, Mrs Van Mier, a "prominent Bostonian matron" with a steely eye... Barnaby Slade, a hyperactive young man, laden with cameras and books.

Interspersed with them are the supporting characters: Sir Gerald Nutfield, a retired Colonial Governor and his faded wife; Mrs Lush, an overly-indulgent mother and her son-from-hell, Alvin; Mr and Mrs Sweeny, an over-awed elderly couple on their once-in-a-lifetime cruise; the Candijack Family, "young middle-aged... noisy and slightly common"; Elmer and Maimie and their two teenage children, Glen and Shirley.

When they're all safely stowed, Joe and Shuttleworth realise that someone is still missing. At that moment Mimi Paragon rushes in. She is the Cruise Director and, as she anticipates yet another voyage, she runs through her duties in song ("Come To Me") accompanied by the crew, all of whom obviously adore her.

Scene 2: In Verity's cabin she and Lawford are saying their goodbyes. Their marriage, her second and his first, is breaking up. They run out of things to say and he leaves. Verity sings "I Am No Good At Love".

Scene 3: In Johnny's cabin he is being lectured by his mother about the unsuitable girl he is leaving behind. Determined to protect him from similar dangers, she is taking the cruise with him. As their conversation drifts into the usual row, she slams out of the cabin, leaving Johnny to express his own philosophy of life in "Sail Away".

Scene 4: There is the usual hullaballoo as the ship sails. As the passengers line the rails and wave their goodbyes, Mimi passes among them introducing herself and summing them up. There is no one and nothing she has not seen before. Amid the to-ing and fro-ing Johnny falls into conversation with Verity and they sense they have something in common, even if it is only that both of them are glad to be sailing away from their present lives.

Scene 5: In Mrs Spencer-Bollard's cabin Elinor is resting while Nancy unpacks. It becomes clear that on this trip she is to be her aunt's secretary, a prospect that she finds daunting. Although she is grateful for the chance to spread her wings, her real desire is to find the Perfect He. After Elinor leaves, she wonders "Where Shall I Find Him?"

Scene 6: It's now several days later and everyone has settled into some sort of shipboard routine. Elinor is seated in a deck chair dictating to Nancy; Verity is reading a book; the Candijacks are dominating the pool; Alvin Lush is making a nuisance of himself. Among them all Mimi buzzes around trying to organise various entertainments. Finally, the distractions become too much for Elinor and she decamps to her cabin for some peace. No sooner is Nancy left alone than Barnaby appears. He has clearly been waiting for his moment to declare his feelings for her ("Beatnik Love Affair"). His wooing turns into a dance that soon has other passengers joining in.

As Nancy and Barnaby leave, Johnny approaches Verity. He asks her if she will join him and his mother for a drink before lunch, and she accepts. He then tells her how much he enjoyed dancing with her the previous evening. Being perfectly well aware of what is in the wind, she warns him to be careful of his feelings since she is a married woman and a good deal older than him. He tells her that age is immaterial and that the feeling of now is what matters ("Later Than Spring").

As they leave Sir Gerald enters and complains to the Purser. Top of his list is that the ship is "crawling with Americans". Joe agrees with everything that he says and when Sir Gerald and his wife have gone, he and the stewards sing "The Passenger's Always Right".

Scene 7: Later on the promenade deck Verity is subjected to an inquisition by Mrs Van Mier. When Verity leaves, Johnny enters and his mother warns him about unsuitable women. She goes off to dress for dinner and Johnny manages to shake off his irritation. He sings the last few bars of "Sail Away":

> But when soon or late
> You recognise your fate
> That will be your great, great day.
> On the wings of the morning,
> With your own true love
> Sail Away – Sail Away – Sail Away.

Scene 8: The sun deck at night. Nancy and Barnaby enter dressed for dinner. He has just kissed her and she is pretending to be annoyed. When she leaves, Barnaby reprises her opening number, "How Shall I Find Her".

Scene 9: It is the following evening and Mimi is in her cabin, wrestling with her Italian phrasebook in preparation for their arrival in Italy. It is difficult as none of the words seem to have anything to do with real life ("Useless Useful Phrases").

Scene 10: The promenade deck at 4:00 a.m. Unable to sleep and very unhappy, Verity enters and stands looking out over the rail. Johnny joins her and begins to tell her that he has fallen in love with her. Knowing herself to be in a vulnerable state, Verity tries to talk him out of it but his sincerity undermines her resistance. He takes her in his arms and they sing "This Is A Night For Lovers".

Scene 11: Everyone is in festive mood on the sun deck. Some people are dancing, others are propping up the bar. Suddenly Mimi dashes in and announces that land has been sighted – Europe! There is great excitement. And as Mimi reminds them – "You're A Long, Long Way From America".

ACT II, Scene 1: A square in Tangier. Tourists are sitting at the café tables, while the locals are preparing their various ways of fleecing them. Ali, "a disreputable looking Arab dressed as a guide" enters and summons up a motley collection of characters who sing "The Customer's Always Right".

As they depart, Mimi enters the square with a party of passengers who have lots of questions for her. She answers these before taking them off to see the "great big gorgeous Kasbah".

Johnny and Verity are left behind. He tells her he has found a wonderful place for them to have lunch away from the crowds and insists she join him. As he leaves to arrange the transportation, Verity reflects ("Something Very Strange").

Scene 2: At sea again, in the ship's nursery. Mimi is trying to cope with a bunch of young thugs led by Alvin Lush. In an attempt to divert them she sings "The Little Ones' ABC".

Scene 3: A few days later the *Carolonia* is anchored in the Bay of Naples and a group of the passengers are relaxing on the sun deck, comparing notes about that day's visit to Vesuvius. Johnny and Verity are part of the crowd but in a world of their own. Left alone she sings "I Never Knew".

Scene 4: Taormina. The town is sleeping, when suddenly the tourists pour into the square. The natives rouse themselves and behave as the tourists expect. As dramatically as they arrived, the visitors depart and the town resumes its siesta slumbers.

Scene 5: The Parthenon. Nancy and Aunt Elinor are occupied as they usually are, with Elinor attempting to dictate. Today, however, Nancy doesn't even pretend to pay attention. She tells her aunt that she has fallen love.

Elinor Spencer-Bollard does not write love stories for nothing and the news is not entirely a surprise. Once she has departed, Barnaby emerges from his hiding place. He tells Nancy that she had better get used to it as he intends to be a perpetual popper-up ("When You Want Me").

Mimi now arrives with a collection of hardcore tourists. When she has successfully diverted them, she sits down exhausted and sings "Why Do The Wrong People Travel?"

The Parthenon by moonlight. Verity and Johnny are now lovers but Verity feels badly about the secretive nature of their relationship. She wonders if they shouldn't just remember their love at its best before reality spoils everything. Johnny can't understand and she explains that life isn't always simple ("This Is A Changing World").

As she finishes, Mrs Van Mier appears and orders Johnny to join her. She tells him that they are leaving the cruise. Turning to Verity, she demands that the relationship end. She explains that she has been following them all day and knows precisely what has happened. "You're too late," Verity replies, "It's already come to an end." Appalled by his mother's behaviour, Johnny doesn't want to leave but Verity makes him. When the Van Miers have gone she leans against the column where the two of them were sitting and bursts into tears.

Scene 6: The sun deck at night. Verity is standing at the rail. Nancy and Barnaby join her and can't wait to tell her their news – they are engaged. They go off and a very drunk Mr Rawlings appears and makes a clumsy pass at Verity. She rushes away.

The ship is at anchor in the bay of Villefranche. Only a few of the passengers are still on board. Verity's husband, Lawford Craig enters, accompanied by Joe the Purser. They are joined by Mimi who, it transpires, cabled Verity's husband some time earlier to fly over and meet the ship. Verity has taken an overdose of sleeping pills but is now out of danger. Mimi advises Lawford to be patient and supportive. When Lawford leaves to find his cabin, Mimi sings a reprise of "Later Than Spring".

She departs as the passengers begin to return. First among them are the Sweenys. Mr Sweeny has squandered their pocket money in the casino and it becomes clear that they are not the sweet old couple they first appeared to be as they sing "Bronxville Darby and Joan".

Scene 7: The promenade deck a few evenings later. Verity is sitting quietly with her book, when Lawford appears at her side. Until this moment she had not realised he was on the ship. Tentatively they explore their relationship. They conclude that it may be worth another try. Verity sings a quiet reprise of "This Is A Changing World".

Scene 8: We are back in the main hall and this time the passengers are getting ready to disembark. They disappear down the gangway, vowing to meet again ("When You Want Me" – reprise). Last to leave are Verity and Lawford. As they descend the stairs they meet Johnny at the bottom. He hands Verity a bouquet of roses. She is startled but accepts them with a smile. She and Lawford then exit, leaving Johnny alone. As the rush of new passengers surround him, he wanders off singing the last phrase of "Sail Away".

> When the wind and the weather
> Blow your dreams sky high
> Sail away – sail away – sail away!

On the Boston production:

The *Boston Herald*: "Coward's *Sail Away* has brilliant opening. The newest of the remarkable Mr Coward's solo achievements is a bright, funny, sassy and every now and then romantic musical comedy... the evening was Mr Coward's and for all of his functions he should take a low bow."

L. A. Gafney in the *Boston Daily Record*: "Glamour is the word as new Coward comedy thrills... It may not be as good as *Bitter Sweet* but each musical interval seems delightful to sing. More, the mating of the words to musical sound is as good as anything Mr Coward has ever done."

Cyrus Durgin in the *Boston Globe*: "*Sail Away* music good but show needs comedy... but fitfully entertaining... goes back to the musical-show-for-fun in the formula of vignette treatment that *Grand Hotel* started years ago."

The *Herald*: "Jean Fenn (as Verity) sings beautifully and looks exquisite in a role that seems oddly artificial and even cold, despite its emotional outlines."

On the New York production:

Howard Taubman in the *New York Times*: "A big, handsome, rakish musical."

Richard Colman in the *New York Daily Mirror*: "*Sail Away* docked at the Broadhurst last evening and we predict that it will be tied up at that amusement pier for many months to come. This is not masterpiece of song and dance, not off Coward's top comedy shelf, and doesn't have a song comparable to those pop classics he penned for *Bitter Sweet* but it has an invigorating vitality that we find irresistible."

The *New York Journal American*: "Coward Musical cruises to Nowhere."

Walter Kerr in the *New York Herald Tribune*: "There is one thing to be said for *Sail Away*. It's easy. And there is one thing to be said against it. It's too easy. The new Noël Coward musical looks like vanilla ice cream, slides about as smoothly as though it were melting on the palate, and has no particular flavour... Seeming to salute with both hands and both feet as she jig-steps a first-act finale, Miss Strich is the breeze that comes after a long day in port. She is good when she is simple (as in a fine Coward ballad called "Something Very Strange"). She is good when she is noisy (as in a summit meeting with a child called Alvin). And she is best of all when she is telling us the weary, blistering truth ("Why Do The Wrong People Travel?") with the steel in her eyes showing that "Oh, Pshaw" smile intervening to say she doesn't mean it, and her long legs tapping insistently beneath a striped canvas chair."

Norman Nadel in the *New York World Telegram*: "Noël Coward's *Sail Away* easily could have qualified as the musical of the year if it had opened in 1936, give or take a few seasons. A quarter-century ago everything about it would have tingled. The fox-trot familiarity is charming in its lack of pretense, tension and travail. The style is dated but the production is spirited. Life aboard the *Coronia*, much of the time, at least, is fun."

PUBLICATIONS

Sail Away is unpublished.

NOTES

The *Herald's* comment on Jean Fenn's performance underlined what Noël and his production team had felt increasingly. In his diary entry for 13 August, Coward wrote: "The notices, from the box office point of view, were excellent. Stritch was marvellous and deservedly got raves. Grover and Pat, to my joy, made a tremendous success. Jean and Jimmy came off less well. They sang beautifully but were far from convincing as actors, also the love story is not right and I have been busy revising and reconstructing it. They were, after all, engaged for their voices and I fear I have asked too much of them. It is madness to expect two singers to play subtle 'Noël Coward' love scenes with the right values and sing at the same time. However, all this will be worked on."

When the Philadelphia audiences gave the same reaction, it became clear that more than a little tinkering was required. Joe Layton made the radical suggestion that the whole romantic plot involving Verity and Johnny should be cut for the New York production. This was duly effected and Mimi's part was built up so that she became the romantic as well as comic female lead.

With the exception of the characters of Verity and Lawford Craig, the characters in the New York production were as the previous cast. Of the Passengers, Stewards, Arabs, Italians, Children... Don Atkinson, Paul Gross, Cheryl Kilgren and Christopher Votos were added. Robby Reed did not appear.

The songs "This Is A Night For Lovers" and "This Is A Changing World" (both recycled from *Pacific 1860*) were taken out, as well as "I Am No Good At Love". Only one of Verity's original songs ("Something Very Strange") was retained and given to Mimi. Johnny was given two new songs: "Go Slow, Johnny" and "Don't Turn Away From Love".

The S.S. *Carolonia* became the S.S. *Coronia* (not too far away from the real Cunard liner, the S.S. *Caronia*.)

The New York production opened with a box office advance of $1.4 million, but the ambiguous reviews and critical word of mouth soon began to erode that. The opening of Frank Loesser's *How to Succeed in Business* to uniformly glowing notices did not help. When it became obvious that *Sail Away* was not going to be the immediate hit he hoped it would be, Coward tried to analyse what was lacking. He wrote in his diaries "I know, with my deepest instinct, that there is something about *Sail Away* that doesn't satisfy me. I am proud of the music and the lyrics, I am not especially proud of the 'book', but it is adroitly constructed, does not drag, and fulfils its purpose, which is to carry the show through to its conclusion. The 'books' of musicals, with one or two notable exceptions, are always unsatisfactory. There is never enough time to develop characters, and the music and the dancing, which after all is what the public come for, take up the major portion of the time allotted. In this instance I have deliberately kept the 'book' down to the minimum, in the belief that the public would be relieved at not having to sit through acres of dialogue between numbers. In fact I have used a revue formula with a mere thread of story running through it. Presumably I was wrong. Most of the critics seemed to mourn the lack of 'strong' story without realising that a 'strong' story was never intended in the first place. I planned a light, musical entertainment with neither overtones or undertones of solemnity, and this, so help me, is exactly what I have achieved. It will have to succeed or fail on its own merits, there is nothing more to be done with it. It is, of course, disappointing that it didn't get raves and become an immediate smash, but I have had disappointments before and a great deal worse than this."

Two songs were used and rejected during rehearsals without appearing in either version of the show. They were "Bronxville Darby And Joan" ("Dear Old Couple") and "Somethin' You Gotta Find Out Yourself".

Sail Away evolved from an earlier show that Coward abandoned. *Later Than Spring* began life as an idea for a film starring Marlene Dietrich and himself. It then became the further adventures of Mrs Wentworth-Brewster (she of the Bar on the Piccola Marina). Polly Wentworth-Brewster, now an American widow, takes a cruise, meets a slightly questionable Prince on board and goes to Paris. Also on the cruise is a Monroe-type movie star and her admirer. Having got his cast as far as Paris, Coward tired of the enterprise and abandoned it.

Several of the songs were then incorporated into the next version – *Sail Away*. The songs included were "Later Than Spring", "The Passenger's Always Right", "Where Shall I Find Him?" and "Why Do The Wrong People Travel?"

UK PRODUCTIONS

Elaine Strich (Mimi) led the cast of the London premiere when it came to the Savoy Theatre, 21 June 1962, with David Holliday (Johnny Van Mier), Mavis Villiers (Mrs Van Mier) and Grover Dale (Barnaby Slade). Maggie FitzGibbon and Kevin Colson subsequently led the Australian production.

Financial Times, June 1962: "Basically, it's a good old-fashioned musical: colour scenes, and other comedy scenes, backdrops of Tangier and the Parthenon, travel jokes, American jokes, and smutty jokes, and a clutch of shipboard romances. But open the bright wrappings and what's inside? In the first half the answer if not very much – Mr Coward takes and unconscionable time in getting his American to Europe, and the bon-bons were few and far between.

"After the interval, the transformation. The drops of acid, so long awaited, suddenly appeared, so did one or two of those mercurial lyrics which seem to create their own music.

"If the old nostalgia looks a little shop-soiled in places and the romance is sometimes palely middle-aged, then one must be indulgent. The second act of *Sail Away* offers just about the most enjoyable hour to be found in the West End at the moment."

On 2 September 1998, *Sail Away* was revived by an amateur dramatic society in Woking. A drastically revised version (*Bon Voyage*) was produced at the Denver Performing Arts Centre in Colorado in 1994. A new version adapted by Barry Day and with additional Coward songs was staged at the amateur Tower Theatre in London on 17 July 1999.

In November 1999 Elaine Stritch once again played Mimi in two weeks of concert performances at Carnegie Hall's Weill Recital Hall, directed by Gerald Gutierrez.

48
THE GIRL WHO CAME TO SUPPER
A NEW MUSICAL COMEDY

Written in 1963

Based on Terence Rattigan's 1953 play, *The Sleeping Prince*

FIRST PRESENTED by Herman Levin at the Colonial Theatre, Boston, on 30 September 1963. The production then moved to the O'Keefe Centre, Toronto and the Shubert Theatre, Philadelphia.

SUBSEQUENTLY PRESENTED at the Broadway Theatre on 8 December 1963 (112 performances).

CHARACTERS	Boston and Broadway, US, 1963
JESSIE MAYNARD	Marian Haraldson
MARY MORGAN	Florence Henderson
TONY MORELLI	Jack Eddleman
MR GRIMES	Peter Pagan
VIOLETTA VINES	Maggie Worth
PETER NORTHBROOK	Roderick Cook
COLONEL HOFMAN	Chris Gampel
THE GRAND DUKE CHARLES, PRINCE REGENT OF CARPATHIA	José Ferrer
FIRST GIRL	Donna Monroe
SECOND GIRL	Ruth Shepard
MAJOR DOMO	Carey Nairnes
KING NICOLAS III OF CARPATHIA	Sean Scully
SIMKA	Murray Adler
QUEEN MOTHER	Irene Browne
ADA COCKLE	Tessie O'Shea
BARONESS BRUNHEIM	Lucie Lancaster
LADY SUNNINGDALE	Ilona Murai
DANCERS	Nancy Lynch, Julie Drake, Sheila Forbes, Jami Landi, Sandy Leeds,

SINGERS   Carmen Morales, Ilona Murai, Mari
Shelton, Gloria Smith, Mary Zahn, Ivan
Allen, Robert Fitch, José Gutierrez,
Peter Holmes, Scott Ray, Paul
Reid Roman, Dan Siretta, Mike Toles
Jeremy Brown, Kellie Brytt, Carol
Glade, Marian Haraldson, Elaine
Labour, Donna Monroe, Ruth
Shepard, Maggie Worth, Jack
Eddleman, John Felton, Dell Hanley,
Barney Johnston, Art Matthews, Bruce
Peyton, Jack Rains, Mitchell Taylor

The characters of Louisa, Princess of Kroll (Tracy Rogers) and the
Bodyguard (Robert Finch) were included in the Boston production but
were dropped for Broadway.

Music and lyrics	*Noël Coward*
Book	*Harry Kurnitz*
Musical direction	*Jay Blackton*
Director	*Joe Layton*
Designer	*Oliver Smith*

SCENE: London, just prior to and during the Coronation of
H.M. George V, June 21-22, 1911.

ACT I: Scene 1: The stage of the Majestic Theatre.
Scene 2: Backstage.
Scene 3: The same.
Scene 4: The Regent's apartment, Carpathian Embassy,
   Belgrave Square.
Scene 5: St Martin's Lane.
Scene 6: Trafalgar Square, London.
Scene 7: St Martin's Lane.
Scene 8: The Regent's apartment. The next morning.
Scene 9: The Great Hall of the Embassy.

ACT II: Scene 1: Westminster Abbey.
Scene 2: The Regent's apartment.
Scene 3: A drawing room, Carpathian Embassy.

Scene 4: The Foreign Office ball.
Scene 5: St Martin's Lane.
Scene 6: The Regent's apartment. After the ball.
Scene 7: The Regent's apartment. The next morning.

MUSICAL NUMBERS

ACT I

"Swing Song"	Jessie Maynard, Tony Morelli and Ensemble
Carpathian National Anthem: "Yasni Kozkolai"	Ensemble
"My Family Tree"	Prince Regent, Northbrook and Regent's Aides
"I've Been Invited To A Party"	Mary
"When Foreign Princes Come To Visit Us"	Major-Domo, Footmen
"Sir Or Ma'am"	Northbrook
"Soliloquies"	Prince Regent, Mary
"Lonely"	Prince Regent
"London Is A Little Bit Of All Right"	Ada Cockle, Ensemble
"What Ho, Mrs Brisket"	Ada Cockle, Ensemble
"Don't Take Our Charlie For The Army"	Ada Cockle, Ensemble
"Saturday Night At The Rose And Crown"	Ada Cockle, Nicolas, Ensemble
Reprise: "London Is A Little Bit Of All Right"	Ada Cockle
"Here And Now"	Mary
Reprise: "I've Been Invited To A Party"	Mary
Reprise: "Soliloquies"	Prince Regent, Mary

ACT II

"Coronation Chorale"	Mary, Prince Regent, Principals, Ensemble
"How Do You Do, Middle Age?"	Prince Regent
Reprise: "Here And Now"	Mary
Dance: "The Stingaree"	Prince Regent, Lady Sunningdale, Ensemble

| "Curt, Clear And Concise" | Prince Regent, Northbrook |
| Dance: "Tango" | Prince Regent, Mary, Dancing Ensemble |

THE COCONUT GIRL

"Welcome To Pootzie Van Doyle"	Mary
"The Coconut Girl"	Mary
"Paddy MacNeil And His Automobile"	Mary
"Swing Song"	Mary
"Six Lillies Of The Valley"	Mary
"The Walla Walla Boola"	Mary
"This Time It's True Love"	Mary
"This Time It's True Love"	Prince Regent
"I'll Remember Her"	Prince Regent

Several songs were rearranged or cut during rehearsal and the out-of-town try-outs.

The Prince Regent's opening number "Long Live The King (If He Can)" (Act I, Scene 1) – sung with Hofman and the Secret Policemen – was proving popular with audiences until 22 November, the day President Kennedy was shot. It was dropped immediately and replaced in Philadelphia by a solo, "My Family Tree", a song originally written for *Operette* as "Countess Mitzi".

Northbrook's "Sir Or Ma'am" was originally staged in the dressing room (Scene 2) but later transposed to the Regent's apartment (Scene 4).

In the same scene the chorus girls originally had a song in which they give Mary advice on dining with the Prince Regent. "Put Not Your Trust In Princes" was cut before the Boston opening.

In the Boston version there was a scene (between the New York Scenes 3 and 4) set in a drawing room in the Carpathian Embassy in which the Queen Mother, Nicolas and Princess Louisa sing a parody of English folk songs called "Hey, Nonny No". The scene, the song and the character of Princess Louisa were cut before New York. This necessitated the removal of a later (Act II) duet between Nicolas and Louisa ("Just People") and the plot's secondary love interest.

In rehearsal the Prince Regent's song, "Lonely" (Act I, Scene 4) was called "I'm A Lonely Man" and had different lyrics. "Lonely" was cut after the New York opening night.

In the same scene a duet between Mary and the Prince Regent in which she defends the American way of life against an attack from his 'old world' was also cut. It was called "If Only Mrs Applejohn Were Here", then, in a simpler version, "Free Speech". The number "When Foreign Princes Come To Visit Us" was originally "Footman's Sextet". "Coronation Chorale" was originally "Westminster Abbey".

In Boston Tessie O'Shea's "London" song sequence (Act I, Scene 6) included an additional number, "What's The Matter With A Nice Beef Stew?", which was dropped before New York.

In the Foreign Office Ball scene (Act II, Scene 4) the opening dance number, "One Step" in Boston became "The Stingaree" by New York.

"The Coconut Girl" sequence (Act II, Scene 5) originally featured two other songs: "Time Will Tell" and "Play The Game".

In Act II, Scene 6 (The Regent's Apartment) in Boston the Prince Regent and Mary reprise "Here And Now". In New York this was replaced by Mary's solo, "This Time It's True Love". Conversely, in Scene 7 (Boston) there was a duet for the Prince Regent and Mary, "Come Be My True Love", which had turned into a solo for the Prince Regent as he reprises "This Time It's True Love" (New York). Another of the Prince Regent's songs which did not survive rehearsal was "Life Without Love".

SYNOPSIS

ACT I, Scene 1: It is the night before King George V's Coronation. We are in London's Majestic Theatre, where the first act finale of a musical is under way. The leading lady, Jessie Maynard, is sitting on her garden swing, singing about her complicated love life ("Swing Song").

Scene 2: The curtain falls and the cast rush around backstage in anticipation of a visit from the Grand Duke Charles, Prince Regent of Carpathia. On his arrival, he compliments the cast on their performance. The ladies all curtsey gracefully, with the exception of the American Mary Morgan, who trips and falls into the accommodating arms of the Prince Regent. In honour of their royal visitor the cast then sing the Carpathian national anthem, "Yasni Kozkolai" and his bodyguards dance an impassioned czardas. This leads the Prince to attempt an explanation of his ancestry in "My Family Tree".

Scene 3: Mary, it transpires, has not only been caught by the Prince Regent but has also caught his eye. He sends Northbrook, the diplomat assigned to the royal party by the Foreign Office, to deliver an invitation to Mary to dine with him at the embassy after the show. Mary's head is immediately turned and in "I've Been Invited To A Party" she imagines that she will soon be the toast of international society.

Scene 4: Over at the Carpathian Embassy the state visits have disrupted the usual routine and Major-Domo and his footmen go about their business with long faces ("When Foreign Princes Come To Visit Us"), as they prepare the private apartment for an intimate supper. The Prince arrives, concerned by news of civil unrest back in Carpathia. He goes off to get ready and Northbrook arrives with Mary, nervous about the protocol for the evening: Milwaukee and the five-and-dime store where she worked are, she feels, little preparation for dining with royalty.

Mary sees the table set just for two and Northbrook quickly invokes the importance of maintaining diplomatic relations and hints darkly of threats to European peace, totally confusing her. Mary agrees to stay but only briefly.

Mary and the Prince Regent seem to be getting on well and express their private thoughts in their "Soliloquies". He insists she try vodka, a drink she is not used to, but his romantic plans are foiled by a series of interruptions. First, the Queen Mother enters, a vague woman who mistakes Mary for a variety of other people, including a close friend of Sarah Bernhardt. She begs the Prince to be less hard on his son, King Nicolas, who has been supporting the Carpathian rebels against his father's high-handed regime. To confuse the courtship even further, a phone call brings news of the arrest of the rebel leader; a tipsy Mary insists on reciting the American Bill of Rights; and then Nicolas himself arrives protesting about the treatment of his rebel friends. Northbrook also turns up, hoping to save Mary from what he fears is her fate. Finally alone with her, the Prince Regent tries to arouse Mary's sympathy for his plight ("Lonely") but to no avail: Mary has passed out.

Scene 7: Frustrated by recent developments and his father's unbending attitude, King Nicolas storms out of the embassy to walk the London streets. In St Martin's Lane he meets Ada Cockle, purveyor of fish and chips and homely philosophy. She belts out her repertoire of London ballads ("London Is A Little Bit Of All Right", "What Ho, Mrs Brisket", "Don't Take Our Charlie For The Army" and "Saturday Night At The Rose And Crown".)

Scene 8: In the morning Mary and the Prince Regent emerge from separate rooms. Mary, still befuddled from the night before, is under the impression that she has spent the night with the Prince. Consequently, she decides she must now be in love ("Here And Now"). However, the Prince's icy responses soon bring her back down to earth and when Northbrook arrives, she is anxious to leave. On her way out she runs into Nicolas and tells him she is on his side against his tyrannical father. Nicolas responds by saying that he likes her better than any of his father's other mistresses.

Scene 9: Before Mary can make a complete escape she encounters the Carpathian delegation in full regalia on their way to the Coronation. The Queen Mother's lady-in-waiting has been taken ill and she insists that Mary take on the role. But before she can do so, she has to be invested by the Prince Regent with Carpathia's Order of Perseverance, awarded for "personal service to the head of state".

ACT II, Scene 1: At Westminster Abbey the crowned heads and aristocracy of numerous nations wait. The assembled peers and gentry express their boredom in song with an enthralled Mary from Milwaukee the only dissenting voice ("Coronation Chorale").

Scene 2: Back at the embassy to return her borrowed clothes, Mary is persuaded by Nicolas to make a secret phone call to the German ambassador telling of his plight. The call, however, is intercepted by the Prince and the King is placed under house arrest. The Prince then rounds on Mary for her complicity. She stands up for herself vigorously before being dismissed. Left alone, the Prince contemplates how this unusual woman affects him. ("How Do You Do, Middle Age?")

Scene 3: The Prince, now persuaded by Mary of his duty to be a loving father, releases Nicolas from house arrest for the evening, and orders him to attend the Foreign Office Ball – and to enjoy himself. The Queen Mother commands Mary to accompany the King as his partner.

Scene 4: At the ball the guests throw themselves into a ragtime dance number ("The Stingaree"). The Prince Regent invites Lady Sunningdale to join him later for an intimate supper at the embassy. He is pleased to meet a woman who knows the rules, unlike Mary ("Curt, Clear And Concise"). Mary and the Prince then tango together.

Scene 5: On their way home, Mary and Nicolas are relaxed and happy. He urges her to tell him more about this strange world of fantasy she inhabits. She tries to tell him in song ("The Coconut Girl": "Welcome To Pootzie Van Doyle", "Paddy MacNeil And His Automobile", "Swing Song", "Six Lillies Of The Valley" and "The Walla Walla Boola").

Scene 6: Back again at the embassy to return her borrowed jewels, Mary sees the arrangements for supper and happily imagines that the Prince is hoping for a second engagement. The Prince, with some time to waste before Lady Sunningdale's arrival, decides to have his revenge and brings out the vodka. To his astonishment, Mary produces a proclamation she has written for Nicolas, which repudiates his alliance with the Germans and the rebels to overthrow his father. He expresses his admiration for this worthy adversary for whom he is now beginning to admit his true feelings ("This Time It's True Love").

Scene 7: Next morning, the Prince Regent is a new man. He has decided there will be free elections in Carpathia and has asked Mary to return there with him. The young King, delighted at this change of mood, insists that Mary must visit his country, and the Queen Mother agrees. All of this is too much for Mary Morgan, who knows that life doesn't happen like this. Regretfully the lovers part. However, the Prince Regent now realises that he cannot stand in the way of progress. As he leaves, he reflects on the experience ("I'll Remember Her").

As the servants cover the furniture, Mary looks around her, picks up a single rose as a souvenir and quietly steals away.

Kevin Kelly in the *Boston Globe*:

"Light and Lilting New Musical by Noël Coward... a rich Graustarkian dessert, a multi-layered confection frosted with filigree and rococo roses... it is also slightly top-heavy... and it has enough material for a show and a half. Trimmed of its padding, it should be a hit... Where the Rattigan play had a feeling for satire, Coward has developed it with the steady cocktail banter that is his wit-in-trade..." (actually the script was by Kurnitz not Coward).

Elinor Hughes in the *Boston Herald*: "Ferrer suggests a sardonic rather than romantic viewpoint and, to be honest, he hasn't much voice."

Morris Duff in the *Toronto Daily Star*: "Boston Loves It, Toronto Deplores It. This is a trite and inanimate enterprise... its debit list includes an apathetic script by Harry Kurnitz, shopworn music and waxwork lyrics by Noël Coward, generally lacklustre acting and direction by Joe Layton, which is as sleek as it is sterile – *Supper* musical mostly leftovers."

The *Philadelphia Enquirer*: "Coward show is a melodious hit."

Howard Taubman in the *New York Times*: "An earnest attempt to recover the gaiety and deviltry of a sentimental past. Somehow the heart of the old gallantry is missing; and the glamour and romance seem imposed, as if by an effort of will."

Time: "Even in his grave George S. Kaufman could think of funnier lines than Harry Kurnitz has been able to confect... and Noël Coward could have given *Supper* some Noël Coward songs instead of the badly toasted marshmelodies he provided."

Richard Watts of the *New York Post*: "A romantic delight... ALL of its music is in his [Coward's] best characteristic vein."

John McClain of the *New York Journal American*: "Not since *My Fair Lady* have I been so moved by a musical; it is the embodiment of what we do best... nice to be able to say *Girl* is here to stay."

Walter Kerr in the *New York Herald Tribune* on the lyrics: "What is wonderful to listen to in the theatre once more is an inventor who can sustain a long lyric line without crowding the syntax or running out of musical breath. All over the evening there are gliding, dipping, run-on verbal improvisations that may not be altogether hilarious when they stop for a deliberate wink but that are poised, supple, effortless and intelligently graceful. Tessie O'Shea is a name to be conjured with, a face to be cherished. You'll be mad for her."

PUBLICATIONS

The Girl Who Came to Supper is unpublished.

NOTES

Coward's diary, 15 April 1962: "Herman Levin has called me up from New York and asked me to do the score and lyrics for *The Sleeping Prince* which is being turned into a musical by Harry Kurnitz (a Hollywood screenwriter). I feel rather torn about this. At the moment I naturally feel that I don't want to have anything to do with an American musical ever in my life again (because of the problems with *Sail Away*) but this, of course, will pass and I have always loved *The Sleeping Prince*. Also it is period and a perfect period, what's more, for my music and lyrics. I have given an evasive answer."

However, in early July he flew to Paris to discuss the project with Levin and Kurnitz. He became convinced the show could be a hit and agreed to write the musical score.

He thought the first run-through "disastrous. Vastly over-directed. Too much movement, too many props and everybody overacting like mad and trying to be funny. So much of it is brilliant and the brilliance was obscured by Joe's choreographic passion for incorrect movement. Why do choreographers have no respect for words or lyrics? Anyway, I let fly, lost my temper and flounced off and the next day refused to go near the theatre."

The outburst apparently had the desired effect and Noël looked back on the Boston opening as "quite palpably a smash hit. The orchestra is excellent. The lighting – by now – improving. The whole show by now much better... Tessie O'Shea stopped the show cold... and has done so ever since. Florence is miraculous and I love her every minute. José Ferrer a bit inaudible and an ugly voice and appearance, but great charm, a fine comedian." Toronto was not nearly so successful: "Harry Kurnitz, who had been taking several bows in New York, went into deep shock. Personally I was delighted. Everyone concerned was far too complacent."

He was surprised at how positive the New York notices were, especially for his own contribution: "None of them has been really very good for the book. Poor Harry. He is such a dear, but he is a writer of lines and jokes rather than a writer of plays." At this stage Coward felt confident that the show was a hit but he still had reservations about the whole experience. "It has all been rather a gruelling and frustrating experience for me and I shall never again put myself into such a tricky position."

In March 1964 the notice to close went up and Noël conducted his personal post mortem in his diaries: "Three factors have contributed to this disaster. José Ferrer, the book and the Broadway Theatre, all three of which I have shrieked about from the beginning. Florence didn't really come off either. I think, however, she would have had a better chance with a physically attractive leading man. I tried to wishful-think myself into believing that José would be good, but I knew in my heart from the very beginning that he was miscast. Another factor – which I hate to have to admit – is that dear Joe Layton really directed it wrong from the very first. He staged it brilliantly but the actual direction was common and farcical, whereas it should have been witty and romantic. However, that is that and it's definitely spilt milk department."

What Noël did not choose to see was the show's resemblance to *My Fair Lady*. The story of an older, cynical man redeemed by a simpler girl reminded audiences of Higgins and Eliza, with the non-singing Ferrer standing in for the non-singing but more charming Rex Harrison and with Florence Henderson as a less interesting Julie Andrews.

Unfortunately, the similarities did not stop there. O'Shea and her cockney numbers parallelled Stanley Holloway's Alfred Dolittle, while Roderick Cook and Irene Browne replicated the characters played by Robert Coote and Cathleen Nesbitt in the original. There was even a second-half set piece in the Coronation scene to replicate *My Fair Lady's* Ascot, and the Embassy Ball was simply turned into the Foreign Office ball. A sense of *déjà-vu* loomed over the whole enterprise and when it had to compete with new arrivals like *Hello Dolly* and *Funny Girl*, it had to fail.

The Girl Who Came to Supper has never been produced in the UK, although there was a full-scale BBC radio production on 21 September 1979. Parts of the "London Song" sequence have been included in Coward compilations.

On 17 September 1999, the York Theatre Company in New York gave three concert performances of the show, starring Simon Jones (as Prince Regent).

49
HIGH SPIRITS

(Originally called *Faster than Sound*)

AN IMPROBABLE MUSICAL

Written in 1963 by Hugh Martin and Timothy Gray

Based on *Blithe Spirit*

FIRST PRESENTED by Lester Osterman, Robert Fletcher and Richard Horner at the Shubert Theatre, New Haven on 1 February 1964. The production then moved to the Colonial Theatre, Boston and the Shubert Theatre, Philadelphia.

Subsequently presented at the Alvin Theatre, New York on 4 April 1964 (375 performances).

CHARACTERS	New Haven, US, 1964
CHARLES CONDOMINE	Edward Woodward
EDITH	Carol Arthur
RUTH CONDOMINE	Louise Troy
MRS BRADMAN	Margaret Hall
DR BRADMAN	Lawrence Keith
MADAME ARCATI	Beatrice Lillie
ELVIRA	Tammy Grimes
BOB	Robert Lenn
BETH	Beth Howland
RUPERT	Gene Castle

In New Haven, Boston and Philadelphia the character of a 'Vicar' was played by Jack Kauflin; in New Haven there were additional characters: Mr Berkeley (Al Lanti), First Member (Joe McGrath), Second Member (Adrienne Angel), Third Member (Robert Lenn) and Eustace (Don Percassi). All of these were cut from the Broadway production.

Composers, Lyricists and Librettists	*Hugh Martin and Timothy Gray*
Director	*Noël Coward (subsequently Gower Champion)*

Norman Nadel in the *New York World Telegraph*:

"Beatrice Lillie's performance as Madame Arcati, the happy medium in *High Spirits*, reaffirms her place in the recorded history of the 20th century, along with the Battle of Jutland and Salk vaccine. When she is on stage, the musical achieves both the sublime and the uproariously ridiculous."

The *New Haven Register*: "Light and fantastic."

The *Boston Globe*: "A blithe new musical."

The *Philadelphia Enquirer*: "A gay and glossy poltergeist gem."

Walter Kerr in the *New York Herald Tribune*: "I will remember it as the musical comedy in which Beatrice Lillie killed me... in about two seconds I'd turned in my critical faculties to someone who was sitting near me and had surrendered."

John Chapman in the *New York News*: "It has elevated by several notches the tone of Broadway's current musical theatre simply by being beguiling."

PUBLICATIONS

High Spirits is unpublished.

NOTES

Early in February 1963 Noël received a visit in New York from composer Hugh Martin and lyricist Timothy Gray. They were to play the score for their musical adaptation of *Blithe Spirit*, initially called *Faster than Sound*. Coward recalls in his diaries: "I was all set to turn it down because it really has been going on far too long and I was sick of all the frigging about. Coley and I sat with our mouths open. It is quite brilliant. The music is melodic and delightful, the lyrics really witty, and they have done a complete book outline keeping to my original play and yet making it effective as a musical. I am not only relieved but delighted." As work continued, Noël continued to feel that "taken all round it is one of the best potential musicals I have ever seen... I intend to keep a firm eye on it from the word go." He agreed to direct and rehearsals started the following January.

Before the show reached Broadway, Lester Osterman and Richard Horner (two of the show's three producers) approached Noël with the idea of bringing Gower Champion in to pull the show together. Coward agreed, with the idea and with Champion's suggestions. This was effectively the end of his contribution to the production. He noted in his diary at this time: "I am really very tired indeed. I took on far too much. I am sick of *High Spirits* and everyone connected with it. I think, galvanized by Gower, it may be a success. At any rate, I have done all I can do." By the time the show had had its successful Broadway opening, he was more objective. His previous irritation with Bea Lillie, who seemed unable to memorise lines, fell away. She was, he wrote, "unquestionably a great star and has that indestructible capacity for making audiences love her... so far as the public is concerned, it doesn't matter how many lines she forgets and how many mistakes she makes. She is adored."

UK PRODUCTIONS

On 3 November 1964, *High Spirits* opened in London at the Savoy Theatre (94 performances). Although "supervised by Noël Coward", Noël was otherwise occupied with the National Theatre's production of *Hay Fever*, so it was directed by Graham Payn and Timothy Gray and produced by Geoffrey Russell for Linnit & Dunfee. The cast included Cicely Courtneidge, Denis Quilley, Fenella Fielding (replaced by Tammi Grimes), Jan Waters and Marti Stevens.

The *Sunday Telegraph*: "*High Spirits* emerges as an evening of low jinks."

After depressing previews, Noël was pleasantly suprised that the show opened "to a wildly enthusiastic audience... The show went wonderfully and the next morning, as I had anticipated, disaster. All the notices horrible... The main burden of the notices is that the beautiful play has been mucked about with".

50
SUITE IN THREE KEYS
A TRILOGY

A Song at Twilight, Shadows of the Evening, Come into the Garden, Maud

Written in 1965

FIRST PRESENTED at the Queen's Theatre on 14 April 1966 (*A Song at Twilight*) and on 25 April (*Shadows of the Evening, Come into the Garden, Maud*), then running in repertoire for a season until the end of July (64 performances of *A Song at Twilight* and 60 of the double-bill).

CHARACTERS	Queen's, 1966

A Song at Twilight

HILDE LATYMER	Irene Worth
FELIX (a waiter)	Sean Barrett
HUGO LATYMER	Noël Coward
CARLOTTA GRAY	Lilli Palmer

SCENE: Scene 1: Evening.
Scene 2: A few minutes later.

Shadows of the Evening

LINDA SAVIGNAC	Lilli Palmer
FELIX (a waiter)	Sean Barrett
ANNE HILGAY	Irene Worth
GEORGE HILGAY	Noël Coward

SCENE: Scene 1: Afternoon.
Scene 2: That evening.

Come into the Garden, Maud

ANNE-MARY CONKLIN	Irene Worth
FELIX (a waiter)	Sean Barrett
VERNER CONKLIN	Noël Coward
MAUD CARAGNANI	Lilli Palmer

SCENE   Scene 1: An evening in summer.
              Scene 2: Later that night.

Trilogy director   *Vivian Matalon*

The action of all three plays passes in a private suite in a luxurious hotel in Switzerland.

SYNOPSIS

Song at Twilight

Scene 1: The suite of a luxury hotel in Switzerland. The writer, Sir Hugo Latymer, occupies the same suite for three months each year; hence it contains some of his own furniture, pictures and personal belongings. His German wife, Hilde (his former secretary) is seated at his desk, talking to the waiter Felix, a handsome young man with much charm and acumen. She asks him to serve dinner at about 8.30 p.m., by which time Sir Hugo's guest will have arrived. As Felix leaves, she picks up the telephone and begins to discuss a film contract with Hugo's agent in London. Hugo, recently recovered from a nervous illness, enters in a peevish frame of mind. He declares that he won't sign the film contract as he is tired of having his works murdered by film directors.

Husband and wife bicker for a while until Hugo is interrupted by a telephone call from a friend, Mariette, whose invitation for the evening he declines on the grounds that he has "a rendezvous with the past". Hilde is nettled by his romantic tone, says he has been indiscreet as Mariette an incorrigible gossip. She adds that his invitation to Carlotta Gray, a failing actress with whom he was once involved, is a mistake: to see her again will only upset him and, in any case, she probably only wants to borrow money. Hugo accuses her of being jealous, not only of Carlotta but of all his friends. The quarrel intensifies to the point where he asks her if she wants to leave him. If she did, replies Hilde, she would have done so already but she's left it too late.

Hilde has arranged to spend the evening at the cinema with her friend Liesel. Hugo, suddenly alarmed at the prospect of seeing Carlotta alone, asks her to stay, but she refuses. Hilde rings for Felix to give Hugo a drink, remarking that she has ordered caviar and pink champagne for his supper-party. When Felix arrives, Hugo tells him to expect the guest in about half an hour, but a moment after this, a call from reception announces

Carlotta. Still in his dressing gown, Hugo hurries off to get ready, leaving his wife to receive the visitor.

Carlotta Gray is no longer young, but is attractive and smartly dressed. The two women take stock of each other. Hilde gives Carlotta a warning not to excite Hugo unduly, as he has been ill and has always been highly strung. This leads to a discussion of his brilliant career, and Carlotta, with typical frankness, says she has always imagined Hilde as "a dragon guarding the throne" but finds her "less grim, more vulnerable" than she had expected. By the time Hugo returns, in an emerald velvet smoking jacket, they are almost on friendly terms.

The supper-party with Hugo does not go so well for, as Carlotta says, his pomposity brings out the guttersnipe in her. She is, however, touched when she finds that the menu (chosen by Hilde) exactly reproduces one with which they have sentimental associations. During the meal she reproaches him with speaking unkindly of her in his autobiography.

She goes on to tell him her life story. She went to America with a play of Hugo's (which failed), and has remained out there. Her first husband was killed in a plane crash and she miscarried their baby; her second husband, by whom she had a son, died in the war; she is now separated from her third, a film agent.

Hugo asks her why she has come and Carlotta confesses that she has written an autobiography and already secured a publisher. Hugo, congratulating her, says: "I suppose you want me to write a preface." He is furious when he finds out that what she really wants is permission to publish his love-letters to her.

Felix brings in the soufflé and Carlotta chats pleasantly with him, praising the excellent meal and perfect service. As he leaves, Hugo says crossly, "I hate familiarity with servants" and this triggers off a discussion that ends in a flaming quarrel. Carlotta, on the point of leaving, refers again to the letters. She tells him he can have them as she has no further need for them, but warns him that she won't give him the others – his letters to Perry Sheldon, the only true love of his life. With this, she bids him goodnight.

Scene 2: Having thought it over for a few minutes, Hugo telephones Carlotta (who is staying in the same hotel) asking her to come back immediately. She does, telling him that she has asked Felix to bring another bottle of champagne. She remarks that when Perry died all the tragedy was drained out of the situation: "There's only comedy left now. Rather bitter comedy, I admit, but still not entirely unenjoyable."

She dismisses Hugo's accusation of blackmail as melodramatic. The letters, she explains, were given to her by Perry on his deathbed, with the request to keep them until they could be used by a biographer. Carlotta has now found a distinguished American writer, Justin Chandler, who is collecting material for a book on Hugo's life. She refuses to sell the letters back to Hugo and, on the verge of hysteria, he tells her to "publish and be damned!"

They continue rowing, and Carlotta accuses Hugo of having indirectly brought about Perry's death by driving him to drink. When the discussion moves to their own relationship, she attacks him for merely using her as a symbol of heterosexuality, (whereas she had truly loved him). The row ends with Hugo calling her "an unregenerate old bitch."

At this point Hilde comes quietly into the room. She has been drinking but is making a gallant effort to conceal it. After some backchat, Hugo crossly tells her to drink some black coffee and go to bed. Instead, she pours herself some brandy, quotes Goethe, and begins to speak German, which she knows annoys him. When she realises his bad temper, she asks if there is anything wrong between him and Carlotta. "Oh no," he replies ironically, "it has been delightful. Carlotta came here this evening either to blackmail me or to soften me. I have not discovered which."

Hilde doesn't understand and he tells her that if she had spent less time drinking with her friend Liesel her mind would be clearer. Hilde responds angrily and demands to know what happened in her absence.

Eventually Hugo confesses that he has refused Carlotta's request to publish his love-letters to her. Then, in roundabout terms, he approaches the subject of his own letters to Perry. To his surprise, Hilde has not only corresponded with Justin Chandler, whom she describes as a brilliant writer, but also knows all about Perry Sheldon, and has lodged Hugo's letters to him safely in the bank.

Though she has always seen through Hugo, Hilde remains entirely loyal to him. As she says to Carlotta, she has much more commonsense than either of them. She realises that Carlotta's desire is not to blackmail Hugo but to repair her own ego, damaged by a love affair long ago. Carlotta admits this but says she also wanted to prove to Hugo the value of compassion. She now realises that she has failed. Hilde explains that she could never have succeeded: she herself, being German, is a sentimentalist, so is Carlotta; Hugo is not.

Carlotta asks Hilde how she can be so loyal to Hugo, knowing this. Hilde explains that Hugo is all she has; that she came to him as a refugee, after the only man she ever loved had died in a concentration camp. She has accepted the façade of their marriage, and her reward has been that, with increasing age, Hugo is coming to rely on her and need her more and more. She also knows that Justin Chandler will not be able to publish Hugo's letters to Sheldon without his permission and adds that, in any case, Perry Sheldon was a wastrel, whose affair with Hugo was in no way important.

After thinking it over, Carlotta opens her handbag and gives the letters to Hugo, who in return promises her a written authorisation to publish his letters to herself. While Hilde is seeing Carlotta out, he begins to read the letters and is deeply moved. He looks up, to find Hilde again at his side.

SYNOPSIS

Shadows of the Evening

Scene 1: The scene is a private suite of a luxury hotel in Lausanne. It is early summer, and through the open French windows is a view of Lake Geneva and the French mountains opposite.

Linda Savignac is playing patience. She has just finished tea and Felix has taken away the trolley. From her nervous manner and frequent glances at her watch she is evidently expecting a visit. At last, a call from the reception desk announces Anne Hilgay. The two women, who have not met for seven years, greet each other unsmilingly and with some embarrassment. Linda says it was good of Anne to come so quickly. Anne replies that she gathered from Linda's somewhat incoherent message that something serious had happened to George, and asks if he has had an accident. Linda explains that a few weeks previously, George had had a minor operation (the removal of a small cyst) from which he apparently recovered in a few days. But now, during a check-up, the doctor has discovered that he has developed a melanoma from which he will die within a few months. George himself is completely unaware of this. Linda breaks down in tears.

After leaving a telephone message with Dr Pasquier to ring back, they decide that George should be told about his illness. The two women discuss which of them shall tell him. "What is relevant," says Linda, "is that you are still his wife. I am merely his mistress." Anne asks whether, if she had divorced George as both of them had wanted her to do, Linda would still have sent for her. They argue for a little while but, after a strong drink, things begin to go better.

They begin to exchange wartime reminiscences and recall their first meeting: Anne had come to Linda's help after her lorry had skidded in the Suez Canal. They are laughing over this episode when, unexpectedly, George returns from the clinic. He stares at them with amazement: his first idea is that one of his children must be ill but Anne reassures him, saying she has just "come on a little jaunt".

The call from the doctor comes through, but Linda stalls, saying she will ring again next morning. To George, she pretends that the call is from American Express about some air tickets.

As George sips his drink, Anne admits that Linda asked her to come, and Linda admits that this was after talking to Dr Pasquier. He asks both of them, "What had you decided? Which of you was to tell me?"

He then proceeds to tell them the exact situation, just as he compelled the doctor to tell it to him: he will die possibly within nine months, but more probably within three, and there will be no pain. On the whole, he has accepted it.

Linda breaks down at this point and goes to cry in her bedroom. Left alone, Anne and George discuss their failed marriage. He asks her whether she was in love with him at the time he left her. No, she replies, but she cared for him deeply and missed him sadly: "I still do. Perhaps I shall miss you less when you are dead."

George announces that he will soon be coming back home as he wants to get to know his children (now grown-up) and to see the garden again. They begin to reminisce; then suddenly George's nerve deserts him. He has never been afraid of the dark, he says: as a child he used to go downstairs at night, just to prove to himself that he wasn't frightened. "Now it's different. There'll be no familiar, friendly objects to touch –" "Maybe the eternal darkness will be lighter than you think," Anne says consolingly, but he won't accept this. The curtain falls on his plea to his wife: "Don't let go of my hand!"

Scene 2: That evening, the three have decided to take the nine o'clock boat to Evian and gamble at the casino. Felix has brought them a bottle of champagne. George and Linda are already in evening dress.

Linda doubts her ability to keep cheerful throughout the evening, and to steady her George suggests opening the champagne. Meanwhile, he outlines his immediate plans: a fortnight with Linda in Capri, then back to London to settle his business affairs; then home to Anne, to see his children and "look through some old trunks in the attic". Linda is upset at the idea of his leaving her for Anne, but tells her not to fret: he still loves her, though he has never stopped loving Anne. She tells him then that the last seven years, spent with him, have been the happiest of her life, and that she will always be grateful to him.

At this point Anne comes in and shares the champagne. They talk about the casino and make feeble jokes until George protests: "If we try to maintain an attitude of artificial casualness, the strain will become intolerable – I am definitely against a policy of evasion – I'm going to die alone, because everybody dies alone. That fact is hard enough to face, without your God-damned loving-kindness and pity and synthetic heroics."

Anne suggests that she return to England immediately but Linda begs her to stay: "The charade is over and everyone has guessed the word."

George, however, insists they have guessed wrongly: the word is not Death but Life: "While Death is the ultimate reality, it is also a negative one. Courage and honesty and humour, on the other hand, are positive, because they belong to life; and life, up until that last bewildering second, is all we have, and all we know. It is also our most important responsibility."

Anne breaks down in tears and Linda gives her a glass of brandy. The discussion continues a while longer, until it is interrupted by the siren of the Evian steamer. The three gather up their belongings and go out together.

SYNOPSIS

Come into the Garden, Maud

Scene 1: Once more we are in the Lausanne Hotel, but this time the view is from a window on the stage right. Anna-Mary Conklin, a wealthy American matron, is complaining to Felix about the level of service he and the chambermaid provide. Coward's stage direction reads, "Her expression is disagreeable because she happens to be talking to a member of the lower classes."

Felix accepts her remarks with unfailing courtesy. After he has left, she telephones her hairdresser to protest about the blue rinse on her hair and the way her nails have been manicured. She then calls a friend Mariette (a Countess) for advice on etiquette at a dinner-party she is giving, at which the guests of honour will be a prince and his wife.

Her husband, Verner Conklin, a tall, pleasant-looking man, comes into the room carrying a bag of golf clubs, which he flings on the sofa. Anna-Mary scolds him for being late and is furious when he says he has been unable to buy a special brand of cigars for the prince. He cuts her short by saying cheerfully that if the prince doesn't like them, he can smoke his own.

The bickering continues until it is interrupted by an announcement that Maud Carignani (the English widow of a Sicilian prince) is on her way up. Verner likes Maud, whom they met in Rome, but Anna-Mary does not. Anna-Mary says he only likes her because she threw herself at him, and they argue bitterly until she goes into her dressing room to get ready.

It is Verner, therefore, who opens the door to Maud. They greet each other with pleasure and are soon talking easily together. When, with reference to the dinner-party (which Maud won't be attending), he asks what the prince is like, Maud says frankly that he is a horror: "A great one for lavatory jokes and a bit of bottom-pinching on the side."

Felix comes in with a bucket of ice, and Maud chats gaily with him in Italian. While Verner is mixing the drinks Anna-Mary comes out and greets Maud effusively. Maud tells her that she has come to Lausanne because her son's wife has just had a baby, her first grandchild. Anna-Mary details all the titled or otherwise distinguished people who are coming to her party, ending with "Their Royal Highnesses", and is taken aback when Maud corrects her: "Not Royal, dear, just Serene!" She orders Verner to go downstairs and see if he can find the special cigars in the hotel bar, as she wants to have a private talk with Maud. When he has gone, she starts running him down, describing him as a "sort of frustrated Buffalo Bill, who's had his horse taken away from him".

The telephone rings: it is Bobo Larkin, one of the her dinner guests, telling her that he is ill and cannot come to the party. This is a disaster, as there will now be 13 at table. She presses Maud to come, but Maud firmly declines: she is dining with her son and cannot put off her journey to Rome. Desperately, Anna-Mary tries to contact Mariette, but is told she has gone out.

When Verner comes back, she tells him that he will have to eat his dinner upstairs. He takes this quite well and Anna-Mary goes into her room to dress. Verner offers Maud a drink and gives the toast "Here's to our next meeting". Maud asks him why he puts up with Anna-Mary's bullying and he cannot find an answer. She assures him that they will meet again and leaves.

Scene 2: Having dined in his room, Verner is lying on the sofa reading a novel. He has a friendly chat with Felix, who has come to take away the trolley, questioning him about Maud. Felix describes her as an enchanting lady of whom everyone is fond. Hearing that Felix has a fiancée, Verner gives him a 50 dollar tip to buy her a present. Overwhelmed by his generosity, Felix withdraws.

The telephone rings and Maud, from the hotel lobby, asks if she may come up. Leaping up with a beaming smile, Verner quickly spruces himself up. When Maud enters, he repeats what Felix has said about her, and this leads her to confess that she has been talking to her son about Verner. She proceeds to confide the story of her marriage to a Sicilian prince, his death in a car accident during the first year of their marriage, the birth of her son in Cornwall, her return to Sicily, quarrels with her mother-in-law and so forth.

When Verner asks why she has come back she replies that she thought he might be feeling lonely. For a while they discuss her motives, then he sums up: "The fact that you came back at all is good enough for me." He puts his arms round her and kisses her. They discuss what to do next. When Maud suggests that they could meet later in Rome, Verner declares: "I am coming with you this very night." Brushing aside her protests, he convinces her that he is in earnest, and that he intends to marry her. However, she resolutely declines the offer, saying that they must both be free to see how things turn out. She leaves him with a promise to pick him up at 12.30 in her Volkswagen.

Verner lies down again on the sofa. When Anna-Mary comes back, he is pretending to be asleep but she insists on rousing him to hear her grumbles about the party, from which she has returned in a fury because Mariette has monopolised the prince. To annoy her, Verner pretends to be drunk. Exasperated, Anna-Mary tells him that he has changed beyond recognition, and he agrees with her. She orders him to leave her alone. "Okay," says Verner, as he goes out, "that's exactly what I intend to do. Good night, sweetheart!"

The Times, April 1966:

"For all their determined glitter and the authentic disclaimers of any purpose beyond entertainment, Noël Coward's plays are among the most earnestly moral works to be found anywhere in modern drama; and in *A Song at Twilight* he slips off all comic disguise and returns to the vein of melodramatic indignation with which, in plays like *Fumed Oak* and *The Vortex*, he began his career – it seems, beyond question, to be based on the last years of Somerset Maugham, its central figure being a celebrated old writer who has managed to conceal his weaknesses from the world at the price of warping his talent and cutting off his human sympathies. The title refers to Goethe's warning against self-denial.

"The form is that of old-fashioned problem play in which an eminent public figure is visited by an old acquaintance who possesses scandalous information about the past. In this case, the visitor is an ex-mistress with whom Hugh Latymer had once attempted to acquire heterosexual taste: now she returns bearing love letters he had written to his male secretary which also show him in the act of cold-hearted betrayal. This formula permits Mr Coward to address a strong plea for homosexual tolerance to a popular West End audience; and to anatomise with painful accuracy the effect of emotional withdrawal on his hermit-crab hero."

PUBLICATIONS

Suite in Three Keys was first published by Heinemann (London, 1966).

Also published in *Noël Coward Collected Plays: Five* by Methuen World Classics (London, 1999).

NOTES

This trilogy was begun by Coward in 1965 as a personal vehicle for his farewell to the London stage, with Margaret Leighton and Irene Worth in support. Cole Lesley in *The Life of Noël Coward* says:

"For many years Noël had cherished a dream, rather vague at first, of appearing once more on the stage in the West End. It had to be in London, nowhere else, "where I first started more than fifty years ago, to sort of round off the dinner". The dream sometimes seemed unlikely to materialise; effective star parts for men in their mid-sixties do not grow on trees, and moreover both the part and the play would have to be certain of success. The idea of Noël appearing, possibly for the last time, in a failure was unthinkable. The idea was never far from his mind for long, and more and more it grew to be the one definite ambition left for him to achieve: "I must search for or write a play to do in London as a sort of Swan Song. I would like to act once more before I fold my bedraggled wings." In the end he decided that he would have to do what he had usually done and write the vehicle for himself and, as already related, he had the idea of the comedy about Max Beerbohm and Constance Collier. *A Song at Twilight* is not autobiographical – Noël himself noted, when halfway through writing, "My play is now more sinister, and there is Maugham in it as well as Max."

The finished plays were intended to be tried out on tour but illness struck Coward and their production which was scheduled for January 1966 had to be postponed. In the meantime Lilli Palmer had replaced Margaret Leighton, who was unavailable.

Coward wrote in his diaries: "Well, the most incredible thing has happened. Not only has *A Song at Twilight* opened triumphantly but the press notices have on the whole been extremely good. Most particularly the *Express* and *Evening Standard*! Fortunately, the *Sun* struck a sour note and said, "Coward's Return Very Tedious", which convinced me that I hadn't entirely slipped – the play is such a sell-out that we have had to engage extra people to cope with the ticket demand. On the opening night I gave an excellent, un-nervous, controlled performance, thank God – I am back again, like Dolly, where I belong and have always belonged." He added on 27 April: "After an exhausting week of two performances a day, a Sunday night and a Monday matinee, we opened *Shadows* and *Maud* on Monday night to a fantastic audience. *Shadows* I played well apparently, and the customers were attentive and controllable. *Maud* was an absolute riot from beginning to end and the ovation at the final curtain was quite, quite wonderful. I haven't experienced anything like it for many a long day and it made everything worthwhile. People came pouring on to the stage afterwards and it was altogether a heart-warming triumph."

Robert Flemyng played with Margaret Lockwood and Phyllis Calvert in a touring revival of *A Song at Twilight* in 1978, and there was another with Michael Denison and Dulcie Gray in 1983, neither of which came into London. The full-length *A Song at Twilight* was seen at Greenwich in 1994, with a cast headed by John Quentin.

A version of *A Song at Twilight* was also revived at The King's Head Theatre on 29 December 1998.

CHARACTERS	King's Head, 1998
HILDE LATYMER	Kika Markham
FELIX (a waiter)	Matthew Bose
HUGO LATYMER	Corin Redgrave
CARLOTTA GRAY	Nyree Dawn Porter
Director	*Sheridan Morley*
Designer	*Saul Radomsky*

The production ran until to 24 January 1999. A second version of this production, with Vanessa Redgrave replacing Nyree Dawn Porter, opened at the Gielgud Theatre, 20 October 1999.

The *Sunday Telegraph*: "By modern standards, the play takes a mere peep outside the closet. It belongs to the moment of time when homosexuality was becoming discussable on the West End stage, but only just. This gives it considerable historical interest; but it shows its age in other respects too. The small talk often seems tired. The construction and characterisation frequently display an old-fashioned staginess. Above all, Hugo is a distinguished writer as might have been conceived in a popular magazine story around 1927. It is hard to get very worked up about what might or might not have happened to his literary gift. Yet what we are left with in Sheridan Morley's excellent production turns out to be much more than a period-piece. There is real emotional drive in the writing, especially in the second half, when Hugo is forced to confront the fact that the two women are wiser (and more wised-up about him) than he had realised. It is pseudo-heterosexuality that is arraigned most sharply. The strain of his double life is plausibly linked to his dryness and arrogance, though at the same time, the play pulls in more than one direction, you can still respect his claim to privacy."

The *Guardian*: "Coward always claimed that Somerset Maugham was his main source. But the play is much richer if it is seen as a forensic autobiographical study in which Coward acts as counsel for both prosecution and defence. The play's virtues are old-fashioned ones: a strong first-act curtain and an ability to see both sides of the argument. Its main weakness is the suggestion that Latymer/Coward might have been a great writer if only he had come clean sexually."

The *Financial Times*: "*A Song at Twilight* disarms the audience by becoming something quite unlike any previous Coward play. It is about character, sexuality, honesty, understanding, and repression; and it unfolds like something by Ibsen, full of suspense as it discloses the surprising past of its protagonist and, more suprisingly, addresses the ethical and psychological implications of these disclosures. The King's Head revival holds the full attention. Everyone speaks their lines with unusual musicality, and the play booms accordingly. Theirs (Redgrave and Dawn Porter's) are not ideal performances: it is hard to see Redgrave as an ill, old writer who has been repressing his gay core, or Porter as a femme fatale. But it is very touching to see that she gives a subtle and complex performance. As does Redgrave; both of them spring many expressive surprises in their delivery. There should be greater tension between them at points, and yet Porter makes a virtue out of her very fragility, as does Redgrave from his blustery forcefulness."

US PRODUCTIONS

Suite in Three Keys, which only Noël's increasing illness prevented him opening on Broadway as originally planned, was never staged as a trio in a major American production, though two of them were later performed by Hume Cronyn and Jessica Tandy, when, a year after Noël's death, his last play was given its American premiere. *Suite in Three Keys* became *Noël Coward in Two Keys*, as the American producers felt that the third play, *Shadows of the Evening*, was too depressing.

FIRST PRESENTED by Richard Barr and Charles Woodward at the Ethel Barrymore Theatre, New York on 28 February 1974, after a ten week provincial tour (140 performances).

CHARACTERS

Ethel Barrymore, 1974

A Song at Twilight

HILDE LATYMER	Jessica Tandy
FELIX (a waiter)	Thom Christopher
HUGO LATYMER	Hume Cronyn
CARLOTTA GRAY	Anne Baxter

Come into the Garden, Maud

ANNA-MARY CONKLIN	Jessica Tandy
FELIX (a waiter)	Thom Christopher
VERNER CONKLIN	Hume Cronyn
MAUD CARAGNANI	Anne Baxter
Director	*Vivian Matalon*

Walter Kerr in the *New York Times Sunday*: "More's the Pity Coward's Gone. Let it be said that the performing is wonder enough. The very best Coward? No, not that... But we have the plays, and may still our quibbles in gratitude. Like the actors Mr Coward knew he was serving, they are marvellously accomplished."

Clive Barnes in a review for the same paper: "It was part of Sir Noël's genius always to be able to give you a soufflé and send you out feeling as though you have had a meal. The touch never deserted him. These two one-act plays, one boisterously funny in an oddly sad fashion, and the other teetering ironically on tragedy in an oddly waspish fashion, are knowingly entertaining and yet still substantial. Those soufflés of his have always contained more nourishment than might have been expected... Suppressed passion is what Coward was all about; it is what makes him so much more interesting than most of his contemporaries. He suffered like a hermit crab who had had his shell decorated, at no little cost, by Cecil Beaton." Barnes was particularly impressed by Hume Cronyn in the original Coward parts: "Hume Cronyn... as a questioning millionaire and hardcore bitch artist, dances through the performance of his life. Watch for the laughs that are too easy, and for the tears that will not come... This is a rare combination – a smooth but thoughtful evening."

The *New York Daily News*: "An exceedingly attractive way to finish a brilliant career... The late playwright would have been pleased with the evening, I feel sure, and you should be too. In it, the Cronyns, Hume and Jessica, seem like transfigured Lunts, and Miss Baxter makes an admirable companion."

The *New York Post*: "The two plays were wonderfully entertaining in themselves, but they have the important additional value of showing the scope of Sir Noël's talent as a dramatist. As we all know, he had a brilliantly civilised wit and could toss off sparkling dialogue with apparent ease. But *A Song at Twilight* shows he was equally skillful with serious drama. What a tragedy to the theatre the death of Noël Coward was!"

Suite in Three Keys has always been considered Coward's last dramatic work but with the publication of *The Noël Coward Diaries* in 1982 it was revealed that on 16 December 1966 (his 67th birthday) he began an adaptation for the stage of *Star Quality*, a short story written and published in 1951 from a collection of six short stories. He wrote: "I intend to start a new play today – just as a sort of private celebration. It is to be a light comedy based on *Star Quality*, so I shall have a good deal of the dialogue already done. It should, I think, be fun to do." On 22 January he added "I have finished the second act of *Star Quality*, I am pleased with it but only up to a point. The dialogue is good but it lacks something; perhaps the something it lacks is better construction. I will press on and finish it and then leave it lie for a bit and have another look at it. My voices tell me that a certain amount of rewriting will have to be done."

The Master died in Jamaica on 26 March 1973, and *Star Quality* remained unrevised. However, in November 1982, the world premiere of the play was granted by the Trustees of the Coward estate for a Gala Benefit to commemorate the restoration of the Theatre Royal, Bath.

51
MUSICAL REVUES AND GALA CONCERTS

(a) NOËL COWARD'S SWEET POTATO
(Originally called *And Now Noël Coward*)
A MUSICAL REVUE

FIRST PRESENTED by Robert L. Steele (in association with the Erani Corporation) at the Ethel Barrymore Theatre on 29 September 1968

(17 performances). Moved to the Booth Theatre on 1 November 1968 (36 performances).

CAST	George Grizzard, Dorothy Loudon, Carole Shelley, Arthur Mitchell, Tom Kneebone, Robert LuPone, Bonnie Schon, Ian Tucker, Stephen Reinhardt
Words and music	*Noël Coward*
Conception	*Roderick Cook*
Directed and choreographed	*Lee Theodore*

When the show moved to the Booth Theatre, Mary Louise Wilson replaced Dorothy Loudon.

MUSICAL NUMBERS

ACT I

"A Beginning"	The Company
"Useful Phrases"	George, Dorothy, Arthur and Bonnie
"Dance, Little Lady"	Bonnie and Boys
(*Music arrangement by Roland Hanna*)	
"Mad Dogs And Englishmen"	George, Dorothy, Carole and Tom
"World Weary"	Arthur, Bonnie and Boys
"A Bar On The Piccola Marina"	George
Literature	Dorothy and Tom
"Why Does Love Get In The Way?"	Carole
"Men About Town"	George, Dorothy and Tom
"Matelot"	Arthur, Carole and Bonnie
Eve	Tom
Consecutive Fifths	George
(*Music by Fred Werner and Roderick Cook*)	
"Mad About The Boy"	Dorothy, Carole, Bonnie and Boys
"I Wonder What Happened To Him?"	George and Tom
Karate	Bonnie
"A Room With A View"	Dorothy
Waltzes	George and Boys
"I Like America"	Company

ACT II

Sweet Potato	Carole and Boys
Party Chat (Amanda, Elyot and Friends)	Carole, George and Company
"If Love Were All"	Dorothy
Sex Talk	Tom
Sunset in Samolo (*Music by Fred Werner and Roderick Cook*)	Carole
"Teach Me To Dance Like Grandma"	Dorothy and Arthur
Boy Actor	George
"World Weary" (Reprise)	Company
An Ending	Company

Clive Barnes in the *New York Times*:

"Essentially a show for the middle-aged at heart. The material itself is thin and bland, and this is hardly the fault of Mr Coward. Revue writing is the stage's equivalent of journalism and not intended to last. To resurrect old sketches is almost an act of cruelty, and the old revue songs – even when revamped – more often than not seemed to have outstayed their welcome. A few numbers, such as 'Mad Dogs and Englishmen', which sounds disappointingly dated, incidentally, and needs Mr Coward's own mordant and mortuary voice, were given straight. But most of the material was defensively twisted. 'Mrs Worthington' is now for some obscure reason implored not to put her daughter on the stage by a swinging parson, and even the famous balcony scene from *Private Lives* has to be brightened by having Amanda and Elyot on roller skates!"

The *New York Daily News*: "At the Barrymore, Coward seems bright and new again."

(b) A TALENT TO AMUSE
GALA CONCERT

On 5 December 1969, to mark Noël Coward's seventieth birthday and on the eve of his knighthood, there was a one-night-only midnight staging at the Phoenix Theatre of *A Talent to Amuse*, a Gala Concert devised by Sheridan Morley from his Coward biography of the same title, produced by Martin Tickner and directed by Wendy Toye, Nigel Patrick and Douglas Squires.

Musical direction by Grant Hossack; hosted by Robert Morley and Richard Attenborough.

PART ONE

Overture	
"The Boy Actor"	John Gielgud
"This Is Not A Day Like Any Other Day"	Maggie Fitzgibbon
"Early Mourning"	Irene Worth
"I've Been To A Marvellous Party"	Danny La Rue
"What's Going To Happen To The Tots?"	Gretchen Franklin, Doris Hare, Alison Leggatt, Dandy Nichols, Elsie Randolph, Dorothy Reynolds, George Benson, Robert Coote, Jack Kruschen, John Merivale, Daphne Anderson, Amanda Barrie, Sheila Bernette, Joyce Blair, Josephine Gordon, Gay Soper, Billy Boyle, Neil Fitzwilliam, John Gower, Terence Knapp, Rod McLennan, Terry Mitchell
"A Room With A View"	Cheryl Kennedy, David Kernan
"Ladies Of The Town"	Faith Brook, Patricia Burke, Judy Campbell, Dulcie Gray, Marion Grimaldi, Gynis Johns, Vanessa Lee, Moira Lister, Dinah Sheridan, Eleanor Summerfield Assisted by Kim Grant, Lewis Fiander, Norman Warwick, Stephen Warwick
Private Lives (scene)	Susannah York, Richard Briers
"Green Carnation"	Patrick Allen, Ray Barrett, Michael Denison
"If Love Were All"	Joyce Grenfell
At the piano	William Blezard
"Any Little Fish"	Caryl Little, Sheila White, Jonathan Dennis, Graham James
"The Stately Homes Of England"	Tony Britton, Peter Graves, John Moffatt, John Standing
"I've Just Come Out From England"	Celia Johnson
"Sigh No More"	Anne Rogers

"Matelot"	Mark Wynter
"Thee Juvenile Delinquents"	Nicky Henson, Julian Holloway, Bunny May, Gary Bond, Anthony Roberts, Norman Warwick, Hubert Gregg, Gordon Jackson, David Knight, Bryan Forbes, Guy Hamilton, John Schlesinger
"There Are Bad Times Just Around The Corner"	Joan Heal, Ian Carmichael, Graham Payn Assisted by Terry Mitchell
"London Pride"	Stanley Holloway
"London"	Tessie O'Shea

PART TWO

Introduction	John Clements
"You Were There"	Susan Hampshire, Denis Quilley
"Chase Me, Charlie"	Pat Kirkwood
"Twentieth Century Blues"	Elisabeth Welch
"Why Do The Wrong People Travel?"	Maggie Fitzgibbon
"Mary Make Believe"	Jessie Matthews
"That Is The End Of The News"	Avril Angers, Hy Hazell, Stella Moray, June Whitfield
"I'll Follow My Secret Heart"	Patricia Routledge
"Nina"	Cyril Ritchard
"Parisian Pierrot"	Richard Rodney Bennett
"Time And Again"	Anne Rogers, Jeremy Brett
"Dance Little Lady"	Anna Neagle
"Melanie's Aria"	June Bronhill
"Beatnik Love Affair"	Una Stubbs, Cliff Richard
"Mad About The Boy"	Cleo Laine
Accompaniment	*John Dankworth*
Vocal accompaniment	*The Mike Sammes Singers*

(b) COWARDY CUSTARD
A MUSICAL REVUE

This first-ever major anthology of the songs of Noël Coward. First opened at the Mermaid Theatre in London, 10 July 1972.

Devised by Gerald Frow, Alan Strachan and Wendy Toye. Directed by Wendy Toye and the cast. Designed by Tim Goodchild, with orchestrations by Keith Amos, and John Burrows as musical director.

PART ONE

MEDLEY: "If Love Were All", "I'll See You Again", "Time And Again", "Has Anybody Seen Our Ship", "Try To Learn To Love", "Kiss Me", "Go Slow, Johnny", "Tokay", "Could You Please Oblige Us With A Bren Gun", "Come The Wild, Wild Weather", "Spinning Song", "Parisian Pierrot"

The Boy Actor	John Moffat
Shadow Play, from	
Tonight at 8.30 (scene)	Patricia Routledge, Peter Gale, Derek Waring
"Play, Orchestra, Play"	Company
"You Were There"	Patricia Routledge, Derek Waring

DUETS

Personal Reminiscence	John Moffatt
"Any Little Fish"	Anna Sharkey, Peter Gale
Teddington	Derek Waring
"In A Boat, On A Lake"	Jonathan Cecil, Olivia Breeze
Darewski	Patricia Routledge
"A Room With A View"	Laurel Ford, Geoffrey Burridge
New York Poverty	Tudor Davies
"When You Want Me"	Elaine Delmar, Derek Waring
"Specially For You"	Patricia Routledge, John Moffat
"Beatnik Love Affair"	Una Stubbs, Tudor Davies
Success	Derek Waring
"I'm Mad About You"	Company
"Poor Little Rich Girl"	Una Stubbs, Derek Waring
New York New Year; 1926	John Moffatt
"Louisa"	Olivia Breeze, Patricia Routledge, John Moffat

"Mad About The Boy"	
SOCIETY WOMAN	Patricia Routledge
SCHOOL GIRL	Una Stubbs
COCKNEY	Anna Sharkey
TART	Elaine Delmar
"The Stately Homes Of England"	Jonathan Cecil, Tudor Davies,

	John Moffatt, Derek Waring
1930 (from *Post-Mortem*)	Peter Gale
"Twentieth Century Blues"	Peter Gale, Elaine Delmar
Party Time	Company
"I've Been To A Marvellous Party"	Patricia Routledge
Magic Of An Empty Theatre	John Moffatt
Present Laughter (scene)	John Moffatt, Jonathan Cecil, Olivia Breeze
Auditions	Derek Waring
"The Coconut Girl" (from *The Girl Who Came to Supper*")	Anna Sharkey
"Mrs Worthington"	John Moffatt
Critics	Company
"Why Must The Show Go On?"	Company

PART TWO

1. *London Sequence*

"London Pride"	Company
"London Is A Bit Of All Right", "What Ho, Mrs Brisket", "Don't Take Our Charley For The Army", "Saturday Night At The Rose And Crown" (from *The Girl Who Came to Supper*)	Company
"London At Night"	Company
"London Finale"	Company
I've Just Come Out From England	Patricia Routledge
Return to London, 1941	Derek Waring
"There Are Bad Times Just Around The Corner"	Peter Gale, John Moffatt, Derek Waring
"Alice"	Una Stubbs, Tudor Davies

2. *Travel*

"The Passenger's Always Right"	Company
"Useless Useful Phrases"	Patricia Routledge
"The Passenger's Always Right" (Reprise)	Company
"Mad Dogs And Englishmen"	Elaine Delmar, Geoffrey Burridge, Peter Gale
"Why Do The Wrong People Travel?"	Company
St Peter's	Company
"Nina"	John Moffatt

The New World (from *Quadrille*)	Derek Waring
"I Like America"	Peter Gale
"Bronxville Darby And Joan"	Patricia Routledge, John Moffatt
Darjeeling	Company
"I Wonder What Happened To Him?"	Jonathan Cecil, John Moffatt, Derek Waring
Holiday Mermaid	Patricia Routledge
"Miss Mouse"	Una Stubbs
Philosophy	Derek Waring
Last Words (from *South Sea Bubble*)	Una Stubbs, John Moffatt
"Let's Do It" (*music by Cole Porter*)	Geoffrey Burridge, Tudor Davies, Jonathan Cecil, Peter Gale, John Moffatt, Derek Waring
The Boy Actor	John Moffatt

MEDLEY: "Touring Days"; "Nothing Can Last For Ever"; "Would You Like To Stick A Pin In My Balloon?"; "Mary Make-Believe"; "Dance, Little Lady"; "Men About Town"; "Forbidden Fruit"; "Sigh No More"; "Younger Generation"; "I'll Follow My Secret Heart"; "If Love Were All".

Harold Hobson in the *Sunday Times*:

"More than a little anthology. By setting the famous songs and gloriously impertinent retorts of his affectionate but combative nature against memories of his life, *Cowardy Custard* becomes a piece of creative criticism. The spoken words scoff; those unspoken are filled with pride and affection. Coward has always steadfastly maintained that the Theatre of Entertainment is itself high and noble, not to be ashamed of before the pretensions of other forms of drama."

Variety: "Sparkling proof of Coward's vast and eclectic talent."

This production, though it has never had a major London revival, has been seen in many regional UK theatres since 1972; the original run at the Mermaid lasted nearly two years, and there were several changes of cast.

NOTES

The title was Coward's own idea. An earlier suggestion was *Cream of Coward* but Noël thought it too risqué.

(d) OH COWARD!
A MUSICAL REVUE

FIRST PRESENTED by Wroderick Productions at the off-Broadway New Theatre, New York on 4 October 1972 (294 performances).

CAST	Barbara Carson, Roderick Cook, Jamie Ross
Words and music	*Noël Coward*
Director	*Roderick Cook*

SUBSEQUENTLY PRESENTED by Raymond J. Greenwald at the Helen Hayes Theatre, New York on 17 November 1986 (56 performances)

CAST	Roderick Cook, Catherine Cox, Patrick Quinn
Devised and directed	*Roderick Cook*

ACT I

Introduction

The Boy Actor	Catherine, Patrick, Roderick
Oh, Coward!	Catherine, Patrick, Roderick

"Something To Do With Spring", "Bright Young People", "Poor Little Rich Girl", "Zigeuner", "Let's Say Goodbye", "This Is A Changing World", "We Were Dancing", "Dance Little Lady", "Room With A View", "Sail Away"

England

"London Is A Little Bit Of All Right"	Patrick
"The End Of The News"	Catherine, Roderick
"The Stately Homes Of England"	Patrick, Roderick
"London Pride"	Catherine

Family Album

"Aunt Jessie"	Roderick
"Uncle Harry"	Catherine, Patrick

Music Hall

Introduction	Roderick

"Chase Me Charlie"	Catherine
"Saturday Night At The Rose And Crown"	Catherine, Patrick, Roderick
"Island Of Bolamazoo"	Patrick
"What Ho, Mrs Brisket!"	Roderick
"Has Anybody Seen Our Ship?"	Catherine, Patrick, Roderick
"Men About Town"	Patrick, Roderick
If Love Were All	Catherine

Travel

Too Early Or Too Late	Roderick
"Why Do The Wrong People Travel?"	Catherine, Patrick
"The Passenger's Always Right"	Catherine, Patrick, Roderick
Mrs Worthington	Catherine, Patrick, Roderick

ACT II

Mad Dogs And Englishmen	Catherine, Patrick, Roderick

A Marvellous Party

"The Party's Over Now"	Roderick

Design For Living

"Dance Little Lady"	Catherine, Patrick, Roderick
You Were There	Patrick

Theatre

"Three White Feathers"	Catherine, Roderick
"The Star"	Patrick
"The Critic"	Roderick
"The Elderly Actress"	Catherine

Love

"Gertie"	Roderick
"Loving"	Patrick
"I Am No Good At Love"	Roderick
"Sex Talk"	Patrick
"Mad About The Boy"	Catherine

Women

Introduction	Roderick
"Nina"	Patrick
"Mrs Wentworth-Brewster"	Roderick
World Weary	Catherine, Patrick, Roderick
Let's Do It (Music: Cole Porter)	Catherine, Patrick, Roderick

Finale

"Where Are The Songs We Sung?"	Patrick
"Someday I'll Find You"	Roderick
"I'll Follow My Secret Heart"	Catherine
"If Love Were All"	Catherine, Patrick, Roderick
"Play Orchestra Play"	Catherine, Patrick, Roderick
"I'll See You Again"	Catherine, Patrick, Roderick

The *New York Times* on the original off-Broadway production:

"A modest, thoroughly diverting evening in the company of a master wordsmith. This is a musical evening in which the words point the way. *Oh, Coward!* lets Sir Noël speak for himself."

Douglas Watt in the *New York News*: "An enchanting evening of song and patter... everything is in beautiful order."

The *New York*: "3 People. 50 Numbers. 3 Cheers."

John Simon in *New York Magazine*: "*Oh, Coward!* avoids the pitfalls into which similar tributes have tended to hurtle. It is all wit, polish, taste and style... [it] covers much the same ground as *Cowardy Custard*, but less elaborately. It is more intimate and perhaps a little less exciting."

Time: "Coward is a word wizard, but his subtlest gift is inflection, and he was master of the pause before Pinter was born. This sometimes defeats actors, but not the impeccably polished trio in this show. They sing and deliver their lines with sly, artful perfection. They help to make *Oh, Coward!* the most marvellous party in town."

Clive Barnes in *The Times*: "[Roderick] Cook looks like a cross between a moderately successful diplomat and a fabulously successful undertaker... [he] is effortlessly urbane."

❖

NOTES

Oh, Coward! – the title was a parody of the long-running and, at the time, shocking Kenneth Tynan revue, *Oh! Calcutta!* – kept Cook busy for the next fifteen years or so. He staged many revivals, often casting himself in one of the leading roles.

Oh, Coward! was the last show Noël ever saw. At New York's New Theatre on the evening of 14 January 1973, accompanied by Marlene Dietrich, Graham Payn and Cole Lesley, Coward attended a special gala performance. The *New York Times* noted that, "The occasion suggested three of his best known titles, for he has been a blithe spirit in this century and *Oh, Coward!* afforded him a brief encounter with his past, one that must certainly have seemed bittersweet." "During the performance," the *New York Daily News* noted, "Coward was completely absorbed by the three clever performers on stage, alternately applauding, nodding smiling approval and grinning happily."

Oh, Coward! was presented at the Criterion Theatre, London, with Geraldine McEwan, Roderick Cook and Jamie Ross on 5 June 1975.

It was also briefly revived in 1999 off-Broadway at the Irish Classical Theatre Company in New York. It starred William B. Hubert, Brendon Powers and Maggie Runfola and was directed by Augustine Towey.

(e) NOËL AND GERTIE
A PLAY WITH MUSIC

A play with music, devised by Sheridan Morley from his biographies of Noël Coward (*A Talent to Amuse*) and Gertrude Lawrence (*A Bright Particular Star*), with extracts from Noël's letters, diaries, plays, films and songs.

First performed at the Hong Kong Arts Festival of 1982, with a cast headed by Gary Bond and Maria Aitken, *Noël and Gertie* opened a few months later at the King's Head in Islington, in a production by Alan Strachan starring Simon Cadell and Joanna Lumley. Two years later, in 1984, it ran at the Donmar Warehouse in a production by David Horlock starring Lewis Fiander and Patricia Hodge. In 1986, Alan Strachan directed a production starring Simon Cadell and Patricia Hodge which opened at Guildford and came in to the Comedy Theatre, where it ran for nine months.

In 1987, Edward Petherbridge and Susan Hampshire led a major UK tour, which came in to the Duke of York's, directed by Sean Mathias.

Since then there have been 25 productions of *Noël and Gertie* at home and abroad; in 1997 Sheridan Morley directed it for the first time, with a cast headed by Peter Land and Elizabeth Counsell. This production opened at the Mill at Sonning, and subsequently ran at the Jermyn Street Theatre and the Theatre Royal, Windsor. In 1998, Leigh Lawson directed the first major American staging at Sag Harbor, with James Warwick and Twiggy. In 1999, Twiggy and Harry Groener opened this production, retitled *If Love Were All*, at the Lucille Lortel Theatre off-Broadway, and *Noël and Gertie* was also staged by Matthew Francis for Alan Ayckbourn's company in Scarborough in August 1999. A third production in 1999 starred Kate O'Mara and Ian Lavender on regional tour in Britain.

Australian and South African revivals are also planned, as is a BBC Radio production. The play text is published by Oberon Books.

(f) OTHER MUSICAL REVUES AND GALA CONCERTS

Let's Do It
A Celebration of the Words and Music of Noël Coward and Cole Porter
Staged at the Chichester Festival, 20 July to 1 October 1994.

This revue was devised by David Kernan and written by Robin Ray and Dick Vosburgh. It starred David Kernan, Liz Robertson, Peter Greenwell, Pat Kirkwood and Robin Ray.

Blithe Spirit
A two-hour BBC Radio 2 celebration in August 1999.

Devised and presented by Sheridan Morley with an all-star cast including Edward Fox, Christopher Lee, Judy Campbell, Hubert Gregg, Martin Jarvis, June Whitfield and Marion Montgomery.

Coward Centenary
In December 1999, a number of events were staged to celebrate the Coward centenary. These included Gala concerts at the Savoy Theatre, (produced by Hugh Wooldridge), *Mad about the Boy*, Carnegie Hall, New York (produced and directed by Don Smith); and *A Marvellous Party; Celebrating the Words and Music of Noël Coward*, at the Mark Taper Forum, Los Angeles. A new Coward revue, *MASTERpieces*, was also produced. It was devised by Christopher Luscombe and Malcolm McKee.

PART II

FILM, TELEVISION AND RADIO

IN WHICH WE SERVE

FILM SCRIPT

Written in 1941

Filmed by Two Cities at Denham Studios, England, 1942. Produced by Noël Coward and directed by Noël Coward and David Lean.

First shown in London at the Gaumont, Haymarket, and the Marble Arch Pavilion (simultaneously), 27 September 1942.

CHARACTERS	Two Cities, 1942
CAPTAIN 'D'	Noël Coward
SHORTY BLAKE	John Mills
WALTER HARDY	Bernard Miles
ALIX (Mrs Kinross)	Celia Johnson
MRS HARDY	Joyce Carey
FREDA LEWIS	Kay Walsh
'NUMBER ONE'	Derek Elphinstone
'FLAGS'	Michael Wilding
'GUNS'	Robert Sanson
'TORPS'	Philip Friend
DOCTOR	James Donald
ENGINEER COMMANDER	Ballard Berkeley
'SNOTTY'	Chimmo Branson
SUB-LIEUTENANT R. N. V. R.	Kenneth Carten
MR BLAKE	George Carney
MRS BLAKE	Kathleen Harrison
UNCLE FRED	Wally Patch
YOUNG STOKER	Richard Attenborough
MAUREEN FENWICK	Penelope Dudley Ward
PILOT	Hubert Gregg
EDGECOMBE	Frederick Piper
BRODIE	Caven Watson
COXSWAIN	Johnnie Schofield
A. B. JOEY MACKRIDGE	Geoffrey Hibbert
A. B. HOLLETT	John Boxer
PARKINSON	Leslie Dwyer
COLONEL LUMSDEN	Walter Fitzgerald
CAPTAIN JASPER FRY	Gerald Case

MRS LEMMON	Dora Gregory
REYNOLDS	Lionel Grose
MR SCATTERTHWAITE	Norman Pierce
LAVINIA	Ann Stephens
BOBBY	Daniel Massey
MAY BLAKE	Jill Stephens
MRS FARRELL	Eileen Peel
MRS MACADOO	Barbara Waring
BARMAID	Kay Young
FREDA'S BABY	Juliet Mills
Art director	*David Rawnsley*
Art supervisor	*G. E. Calthrop*
Music	*Noël Coward*

SYNOPSIS

An opening sequence shows the building of the destroyer *Torrin* from the moment the first section of the keel is swung into the blocks, through her christening and trials, till the White Ensign is broken at the mast.

The ship is then seen in action off Crete in May 1940. Captain Edward Kinross (Captain D), commanding No. 35 Destroyer Flotilla, is on the bridge directing firing operations. They sink a *caique* full of Germans, torpedo one transport ship, and hit another, but are then attacked by successive waves of dive-bombers. Two aircraft are shot down, but the destroyer receives damage from which she sinks.

Just in time, a Carley float is cut loose. The Captain, still clutching his compass, is thrown into the water. As he goes under, we see in flashback the thoughts passing through his mind: the comfortable cabin with a photograph of his wife, Alix, in her wedding dress; the 'taking-over ceremony' when he was installed as Captain; his home, with his wife, his children Lavinia and Bobby, and their spaniel, Trafalgar...

He comes to the surface and swims to the float, where he is joined by Shorty Blake, towing Chief Petty Officer Walter Hardy, who is unconscious. Already on the float are several officers – nicknamed respectively Number One, Torps, Guns, Flags – and eight seamen. The Captain helps Shorty to get Walter aboard.

While they try to revive Walter we see a flashback of his home life with his wife Kath, who does not believe that there will be a war, and his stout, slatternly mother-in-law, Mrs Lemmon.

We then hear the Captain's speech to his men on Commissioning Day, welcoming his former shipmates and saying that he wants a happy and efficient ship, and that, since war is imminent, they must be ready to sail in three days. Stores and ammunition are brought aboard, and we hear Mr Chamberlain announcing the outbreak of war.

From the float the Captain watches the upturned keel of the *Torrin*. This reminds him of Alix's voice as she christened the ship, and of the Christmas service and carols that he held aboard her. We see the various Christmas parties held in the homes of Shorty Blake and Walter Hardy, and for the officers and their wives in the wardroom of the *Torrin* – at all three of which the ship is toasted.

The float is shot up by the German aircraft and Shorty is wounded in the arm, which is tattooed with the name 'Freda'. While the wound is being dressed he faints and we see his dream-recollections of his romance. He first meets Freda in a railway carriage, when he protects her against the ill-natured ragging of a boisterous fellow-passenger. He finds out that his shipmate, Walter, is married to her aunt. They quickly fall in love with each other, marry and have a week's honeymoon (meeting the Captain and Alix on the journey); then Freda goes back to live with her Aunt Kath.

A long sequence shows the *Torrin* in action against four German destroyers, three of which she sinks. A young stoker employed in the ammunition hoist loses his nerve and deserts his post. The ship is hit by a torpedo which knocks out the gun-crew. Although suffering from concussion, Shorty struggles to his feet and goes on firing. The *Torrin*, partially disabled, is taken in tow by another destroyer.

After comforting the badly wounded and congratulating Shorty on his courage, the Captain reads the burial service over the dead and their bodies are lowered into the sea. Arriving at port, the Captain addresses his crew, saying that he is proud of them. With one exception, they have behaved splendidly. The one man who left his post has been let off with a caution – but this will not happen again. The young stoker, avoided by his comrades, goes to a public house and tries to get drunk.

The stoker is now seen on the float, asking another seaman, Joey, to play a tune on his mouth-organ. It is "Roll Out The Barrel" which reminds the half-conscious Walter of an evening spent at the Palace Theatre, Plymouth, with Kath, Shorty and Freda, and of their farewells next morning at the dockyard gates.

Another long flashback shows the *Torrin* rescuing men and officers from Dunkirk and bringing them into Dover. The ship then puts in at Plymouth, where her crew receive shore leave. We see Shorty and Freda on a seat in the park; Walter and Kath watching the war news at a cinema; the Captain and his family picnicking cheerfully while an aerial 'dog-fight' goes on overhead; Flags and his new wife Maureen, returning from their honeymoon.

After several more shots of life aboard the *Torrin*, the action switches to Kath's home on the night of the air-raid. She will not go to a shelter or leave London, as she feels responsible to Walter for looking after his house. When the raid intensifies, however, she puts Freda (who is expecting a baby) in a safe place under the stairs. The house is hit. Kath and Mrs Lemmon are killed, but Freda is rescued unhurt and taken to hospital, where her son is born. Shorty, aboard the *Torrin*, gets a letter from her and has to break the news to Walter, who is in the act of writing to his wife when he learns that she is dead.

The survivors on the Carley float watch the keel of their ship slide below the water, and give her three cheers as she goes down. They are attacked by German aircraft and the young stoker is hit; so is Number One, who drops overboard. Flags swims to him and holds him up but a fresh burst of machine-gun fire kills them both.

From the bridge of the sister destroyer, *Tomahawk*, the float is spotted, and the survivors are rescued and brought aboard. About ninety men from the *Torrin* have been picked up already, many of them badly hurt. The Captain visits the sick and dying, taking down messages for their families. He assures the young stoker that he will tell his people they can be proud of him. Telegrams are delivered to Freda Blake and Alix Kinross with the news that their respective husbands are safe.

The survivors are landed at Alexandria and, before they are dispersed to fill vacancies in other ships, the Captain makes a farewell speech, declaring that the spirit of the *Torrin* will go on inspiring them till victory is won.

Finally, we see the Captain in command of a new ship, with different officers around him, steaming out to a fresh battle.

Dilys Powell in the *Sunday Times*, 1 September 1942:

"*In Which We Serve*, written, produced and directed by Noël Coward, with David Lean as co-director, is the best film about the war yet made in this country or in America. The Americans, of course, have hardly begun to produce films about their own part in the war; they have made up for that by a series of pieces highly flattering to our national vanity and about as accurate in mood and manners as, let us say, Queen Victoria's notion of the home life of Cleopatra. A correspondent very sensibly complained to me the other day that we could hardly blame Hollywood for caricaturing our working people when we caricature them in our own cinema. Well, here is a film in which character scarcely ever slips into caricature. The tradition of English life has imposed on its ruling classes a veneer of good manners and imperturbability which brilliantly conceals surface as well as temperamental individuality; to look like a character thus becomes eccentric. The working and lower middle classes, however, have no such mask, and the temptation for the screen-writer to exaggerate natural individuality until it turns to farce is clear. The story of a destroyer, *In Which We Serve* makes a distinction between the superficial smoothness of officers and their wives and the more obvious individuality of petty officers and ordinary seamen, but without denying the first their character and the second their humanity."

NOTES

In July 1941, Coward was asked to make a film of which he would have complete control as director. The story of the sinking of H.M.S. *Kelly* off the island of Crete gave him the idea he needed and in the next few weeks *In Which We Serve* was conceived. The Royal Navy gave their co-operation and the script was written during the rest of the year and put into production at Denham Studios on 5 February 1942. The shooting took five months, and the film was shown the following September. A detailed account of the making of the film is given in *Future Indefinite*.

Coward also wrote the incidental background music for the film, and a piano suite (arranged by Elsie April) from this was published by William Chappell (London, 1942). The script of the film is unpublished.

The following note by Noël Coward was used in conjunction with the publicity for the film:

"This is the story of a destroyer of the Royal Navy and those who serve in her. In the Battle of Crete she is dive-bombed while steaming at 30 knots, and goes down fighting. Among those of her survivors who are able to reach a Carley float are Captain Edward Kinross, R. N. (Captain D, commanding the flotilla), Chief Petty Officer Walter Hardy, and Ordinary Seaman Shorty Blake. As they cling to the float exhausted, wounded and machine-gunned, we see, through the memories of these three characters, their families and their home lives interwoven and dominated by their ship. Through their minds we are shown the ordeals, the achievements, and the gallantry of H.M.S. *Torrin* from her commissioning as a unit of His Majesty's Fleet until she sinks in her last battle.

"The *Torrin* has gone, and so have most of her crew. But they, no less than the survivors, carry on the fight. For they are the spirit of the British Navy, past, present and future, which will guard our shores and keep our honour on all the oceans of the world.

"Here ends the story of a ship, but there will always be other ships, for we are an island race. Through all our centuries the sea has ruled our destiny. There will always be other ships and men to sail in them. It is these men, in peace or war, to whom we owe so much. Above all victories, beyond all loss, in spite of changing values in a changing world, they give, to us their countrymen, eternal and indomitable pride. God bless our ships and all who sail in them."

OTHER FILM SCRIPTS

Coward also wrote the scripts for the film versions of his own plays, *The Astonished Heart* (*Tonight at 8.30*), *Brief Encounter* (*Still Life, Tonight at 8.30*), and *Meet Me Tonight* (three plays from *Tonight at 8.30 – Red Peppers, Fumed Oak* and *Ways and Means*). For details, see under Film Version at end of each separate play.

THAT LAST RESOURCE
ONE-ACT SKETCH

Radio Broadcast
Written in 1926

A duologue specially written for radio. Heard in *My Programme*, by George Grossmith, from 2LO, London, 11 December 1926. It was performed by Heather Thatcher and Harry Hilliard. (The script of this is untraceable.)

NOTES

Many of Coward's plays have been broadcast on radio, and he himself faced the microphone on numerous occasions. On 26 October 1924, he gave as his first radio broadcast readings from "The Poems of Miss Hernia Whittlebot" (see *London Calling!*), later published as *Chelsea Buns* (1925).

On 5 August 1925, he sang some of his own songs at the piano from 2LO. He was a guest in Henry Hall's *Guest Night* on 27 October 1934.

His propaganda radio broadcasts during the Second World War in Australia in 1940 were published there in pamphlet form in aid of the Red Cross, and later in London as *Australia Visited* (Heinemann, 1941). When, in July 1943, he broadcast a new song, "Don't Let's Be Beastly To The Germans", he raised a storm of protest.

TOGETHER WITH MUSIC
A 90-MINUTE LIVE ENTERTAINMENT

In the Ford Star Jubilee Series on CBS-TV broadcast in colour from New York on 22 October 1955.

The programme was written and directed by Noël Coward for himself and Mary Martin and contained some specially written items. There were three segments, divided by commercial breaks, each of which began with a short duologue.

Director for television	*Jerome Shaw*
Designer	*Robert Markell*
Orchestration and orchestra	
director	*Tutti Camarata*

PART I

Duologue outside the dressing-room, with song, "Ninety Minutes Is A Long, Long Time"
Duet: "Together With Music"

Noël Coward solo items, introduced by Mary Martin:
"Uncle Harry" (*Pacific 1860*)
"Loch Lomond" (new version by Norman Hackforth)
"Nina" (*Sigh No More*)

Mary Martin solo items not by Coward, introduced by Noël Coward:
"I Only Have Eyes For You"
"I Get A Kick Out Of You"
"Les Filles De Cadiz"

PART II

Duologue with reprise of "Ninety Minutes Is A Long, Long Time"

Noël Coward with a medley of his songs:
"I'll See You Again" (*Bitter Sweet*)
"Dance, Little Lady" (*This Year of Grace!*)
"A Room With A View" (*This Year of Grace!*)
"Some Day I'll Find You" (*Private Lives*)
"I'll Follow My Secret Heart" (*Conversation Piece*)
"If Love Were All" (*Bitter Sweet*)
"Play, Orchestra, Play" (*Shadow Play: Tonight At 8:30*)

Song, "What's Going To Happen To The Tots?" (a revised version of
    "What Is To Become Of The Children?" (*Whitebirds*, 1927)
Mary Martin in a medley from *South Pacific* and "My Heart Belongs
    To Daddy" (not by Coward).

Noël Coward solos:
"World Weary" (*This Year of Grace!*)
"Mad Dogs And Englishmen" (*The Third Little Show* and
    Words and Music)

Mary Martin, burlesque, "One Fine Day" (*Madame Butterfly*)

PART III

Duologue outside the dressing-room, with reprise of "Ninety Minutes Is
A Long, Long Time" and third refrain of "Together With Music".

Mary Martin solo: "London Pride"

Noël Coward solo: "Deep In The Heart Of Texas" (swing version by
    Coward)

Duets:
"Get Out Those Old Records" (medley of songs, not by Coward)
"The Party's Over Now" (Words and Music)

The original plan was for Coward to sing a version of "Tit Willow" from
The Mikado but the item was dropped.

Ben Gross in the *Daily News*, 23 October 1955:
"A genius and a superb singer of musical comedy songs highlighted
television over the weekend. The genius is that amazingly versatile Britisher,

Noël Coward, and the one-in-a-million intoner of tuneful ditties, that pride of Texas, Mary Martin.

"It was Noël's TV debut, and he may write off the occasion as one of the triumphs of his career. During ninety minutes, less time out for commercials, the Britisher and Mary, alone and together, faced the inexorable cameras and presented the brightest, most intelligent, and most captivating musical revue I have ever seen on video. Telecast in colour and black and white, it was a knock-out of a show.

"It all came off smoothly, swiftly, and with impeccable taste. One couldn't find a jarring note during the entire hour and a half. Here was renewed proof that the most precious ingredient in entertainment is talent. Have that and you don't need elaborate spectaculars, dozens of chorus-girls, and supporting acts.

"It was Coward himself who staged and directed this production. Eliminating all that was extraneous, he and Mary offered only themselves. It was as if they had agreed, "The millions watching us tonight want only the best. Let's give it to them", and that they did, in full measure.

"Mary Martin is this column's ideal of a musical comedy star. But this being Noël Coward's television bow, the major interest centred on him. That is, it did after their revue, titled *Together with Music*, had entered its latter segments.

"During the early portions, to this viewer at least, Coward was a disappointment. He appeared to be stiff and ill at ease. At best, he is no great shakes as a singer and at times his mediocre voice is apt to go off pitch.

"So one was about ready to conclude that TV was not the medium for him. Subtle, suave, and sophisticated, yes; but he seemed to be lacking in the charm and the grace that have made him such a phenomenal hit in theatres, movies, swank night clubs, and even in the hard-boiled precincts of Las Vegas.

"Then a miraculous transformation took place. Noël came off stage to give us a medley of his famous songs: 'I'll See You Again', 'Some Day I'll Find You', and many others. Then he sang 'Mad Dogs And Englishmen', and, suddenly, he became a new personality, immensely likeable and of ingratiating warmth.

"These qualities were in fullest evidence when he and Mary joined in musical tributes to each other. She sang Noël's 'London Pride', and he responded with his Mayfairish version of 'Deep In The Heart Of Texas'. That bowled 'em over, pardner! You've never heard the likes of it.

"And the triumphant march of the Britisher led still further on to one of his recent numbers, which asked 'What's Going to Happen To The Children When There Aren't Any More Grown-ups?' – a perfect example of Cowardian cleverness. It came to a climax in his finale duet with Mary Martin, an entrancingly done medley of Kern, Gershwin and Porter favourites, plus another new tuneful ditty of his, 'Together With Music'.

"As for Mary Martin, an old video hand by now, she added the earthy buoyancy and the incandescent glow which were needed to set off the more brittle art of the Englishman. Her group of numbers from *South Pacific*, her 'My Heart Belongs To Daddy', and her *Madame Butterfly* take-off were delivered in that enchanting style which no other singer on the American musical comedy or operetta stage can approach.

"On TV she had already won acclaim in *Peter Pan* and *The Skin of Our Teeth*. And now, with this show among her trophies, she is entitled to be called the first singing lady of television.

"But this was Noël's night, topping a truly amazing career.

"Weren't there any defects? Yes. In addition to those already mentioned, some of the dialogue between Noël and Mary verged on obvious coyness. But these were minor matters one is willing to forget.

At the beginning of the programme, Noël and Mary sang 'Ninety Minutes Is A Long, Long Time'... but I'm sure it didn't seem that way to millions of viewers."

PUBLICATIONS

The song, "Together With Music" was published by William Chappell (New York, 1955).

SELECTED TELEVISION PRODUCTIONS OF COWARD PLAYS

Private Lives
Broadcast on 16 January 1959, ATV
With Maxine Audley and Peter Gray

Play of the Week: Hay Fever
Broadcast on 24 May 1960, ATV
Director: Casper Wrede
With Edith Evans, Pamela Brown, George Devine, Maggie Smith, Paul Eddington and Richard Wattis

A Choice of Coward: Present Laughter
Broadcast on 10 August 1964, Granada

Director: Joan Kemp Welch
With Peter Wyngarde and Barbara Murray

A Choice of Coward: Blithe Spirit
Broadcast on 17 August 1964, Granada
Director: Joan Kemp Welch
With Hattie Jacques and Helen Cherry

A Choice of Coward: The Vortex
Broadcast on 24 August 1964, Granada
Director: Joan Kemp Welch
With Margaret Johnston and Nicholas Pennell

A Choice of Coward: Design for Living
Broadcast on 31 August 1964, Granada
Director: Joan Kemp Welch
With Daniel Massey, Jill Bennett and John Wood

Playhouse: Star Quality
Broadcast on 5 August 1968, Thames
Director: Guy Verney
With Glynis Johns and Robert Hardy

The Jazz Age: Post-Mortem
Broadcast on 17 September 1968, BBC
Director: John MacKensie
With Keith Barron and Colin Jeavons

The Wednesday Play: The Vortex
Broadcast on 10 December 1969, BBC
With Margaret Leighton

This Happy Breed
Broadcast on 11 December 1969
With Dandy Nichols and Frank Findlay

Play of the Month: The Marquise
Broadcast on 14 December 1969
With Celia Johnson

Red Peppers
Broadcast on 15 December 1969, BBC
With Dora Bryan and Bruce Forsyth

Private Lives
Broadcast on 28 December 1976, BBC
With Penelope Keith and Alec McCowen

Play of the Month: Design for Living
Broadcast on 6 May 1979, BBC
Director: Philip Savile
With Rula Lenska

Present Laughter
Broadcast on 16 December 1981, BBC
With Donald Sinden, Dinah Sheridan and Gwen Watford

Playhouse: Come into the Garden, Maud
Broadcast on 9 July 1982, BBC
Director: Cedric Messina
With Paul Scofield and Geraldine McEwan

Playhouse: A Song at Twilight
Broadcast on 9 July 1982, BBC
Director: Cedric Messina
With Paul Scofield, Deborah Kerr

Tonight at 8.30: Hands Across the Sea
Broadcast on 14 April 1991, BBC
Director: Paul Annett
With Joan Collins

Tonight at 8.30: Red Peppers
Broadcast on 21 April 1991, BBC
Director: Bryan Izzard
With Joan Collins and Anthony Newley

Tonight at 8.30: Fumed Oak
Broadcast on 12 May 1991
Director: John Glenister
With Joan Collins and Anthony Newley

Tonight at 8.30: Ways and Means
Broadcast on 19 May 1991
Director: Paul Annett
With Joan Collins, John Standing and Siân Phillips

Tonight at 8.30: Still Life
Broadcast on 26 May 1991
Director: Sydney Lotterby
With Joan Collins, John Alderton and Jane Asher

Tonight at 8.30: Shadow Play
Broadcast on 2 June 1991, BBC

Director: John Glenister
With Joan Collins and Simon Williams

TELEVISION ADAPTATIONS OF COWARD SHORT STORIES

Armchair Theatre: Pretty Polly
Broadcast on 23 July 1966, ABC
With Lynn Redgrave, Donald Houston and Dandy Nicholls
(Based on *Pretty Polly Barlow*, see page 586)

Playhouse: The Kindness of Mrs Radcliffe
Broadcast on 23 January 1981, BBC
Directed by Chris Menaul. With Elizabeth Spriggs

Star Quality: Star Quality
Broadcast on 10 November 1985, BBC
Director: Alan Dossor
With Susannah York and Ian Richardson

Star Quality: Mrs Capper's Birthday
Broadcast on 17 November 1985, BBC
Director: Mike Ockrent
With Patricia Hayes, Max Wall, Avis Bunnage

Star Quality: What Mad Pursuit?
Broadcast on 24 November 1985, BBC
Director: Anthony Smith
With Carroll Baker, Paul Daneman

Star Quality: Me and the Girls
Broadcast on 1 December 1985, BBC
Director: Jack Gold
With Tom Courtenay, Nichola McAuliffe

Star Quality: Bon Voyage
Broadcast on 8 December 1985, BBC
Director: Mike Vardy
With Judy Parfitt, Nigel Havers

Star Quality: Mr and Mrs Edgehill
Broadcast on 15 December 1985, BBC
Director: Gavin Millar
With Ian Holm and Judi Dench

❖

TELEVISION PRODUCTIONS OF COWARD PLAYS – US

BLITHE SPIRIT

CBS (Colour)
Ford Star Jubilee .
Broadcast live from Hollywood on 14 January 1956.
Adapted and directed by Noël Coward.
Produced by Richard Levine and Lance Howard.
TV direction by Frederick de Cordova.
(For cast details, see page 377).

New York Daily News: "*Blithe Spirit* brings ghostly laughter to TV. Light as thistledown and merry as an epigram tossed off in a glittery drawing room. A frothy delight. Debonair and suave as ever, Coward made Charles a scintillating character."

Time: "Viewers last night were treated to the raciest and most profane language that has ever been heard on TV. The show itself was one of the highlights of a drama-studded week."

Cue Magazine: "It's patent that Mr Coward... takes his television work as seriously as he's taken all the other creative tasks to which he's affixed his name. It's a joy to have him around."

THIS HAPPY BREED

CBS (Colour)
Broadcast live from New York on 5 May 1956.
Adapted and directed by Noël Coward.
Produced by Richard Levine.
TV direction by Ralph Nelson.
(For cast details, see page 365).

New York Daily News: "Coward's production and direction were smooth and the cast was of a high quality. Noël seemed in some of his emotional moments a bit too casual but, on the whole he gave a lovable and solid portrayal of as un-Cowardian character as you can imagine."

Variety: "Rewarding viewing if only for Coward's performance. Divorcing himself completely from the white tie and tail identity, Coward was the sincere father and the perfect husband with all the middle-class virtues and standards indelibly portrayed. It was a capital performance."

HAY FEVER

NBC – RCA
Broadcast on 1 August 1939

JUDITH BLISS	Isobel Elsom
DAVID BLISS	Dennis Hoey
SIMON BLISS	Montgomery Clift
SOREL BLISS	Virginia Campbell
Producer/Director	*Edward Sobol*

With a running time of 80 minutes, this was the first play to be adapted at full length for television.

BLITHE SPIRIT

NBC
Broadcast on 12 May 1946

CHARLES CONDOMINE	Philip Tonge
ELVIRA	Leonore Corbett
RUTH	Carol Godner
MADAME ARCATI	Estelle Winwood
Producer/Director/Adapter	*Edward Sobol*

TONIGHT AT 8:30 – RED PEPPERS

NBC
Broadcast on 18 March 1951

GEORGE PEPPER	Rex Harrison
LILY PEPPER	Beatrice Lille

TONIGHT AT 8:30 – STILL LIFE

CBS Schlitz Playhouse of Stars
Broadcast on 26 October 1951

LAURA JESSON	Margaret Sullivan
ALEC HARVEY	Wendell Corey
Producer/Director	*Frank Telford*
Adapter	*Robert Anderson*

❖

TONIGHT AT 8:30

NBC Producer's Showcase
Broadcast on 18 October 1954

Red Peppers

LILY PEPPER	Ginger Rogers
GEORGE PEPPER	Martyn Green
MABEL GRACE	Estelle Winwood

Still Life

LAURA JESSON	Ginger Rogers
ALEX HARVEY	Trevor Howard
DOLLY MESSITER	Ilka Chase

Shadow Play

VICTORIA GAYFORTH	Ginger Rogers
SIMON GAYFORTH	Gig Young
SIBYL HESTON	Gloria Vanderbilt
Producer/Director	*Otto Preminger*
TV adaptation	*F. Hugh Herbert*

❖

TONIGHT AT 8:30 RED PEPPERS

Broadcast on 8 February 1960
Three In One (Art Carney Show)

LILY PEPPER	Elaine Stritch
GEORGE PEPPER	Art Carney
Producer	*David Susskind*
Director	*Marc Daniels*

❖

BRIEF ENCOUNTER

NBC Dinah Shore Show for Chevrolet
Broadcast on 26 March 1961
TV adaptation of film version

LAURA JESSON	Dinah Shore
ALEX HARVEY	Ralph Bellamy
Producer	*Bob Finkel*
Directors	*Dean Whitmore and Bob Finkel*
Adaptation	*Joseph Schrank*
Music: Brief Encounter *theme*	*W. Earl Brown*

❖

BLITHE SPIRIT

NBC HALLMARK HALL OF FAME
Broadcast on 7 December 1966
90 minute adaptation

CHARLES CONDOMINE	Dirk Bogarde
ELVIRA	Rosemary Harris
RUTH	Rachel Roberts
MADAME ARCATI	Ruth Gordon
Producer/Director	*George Shaefer*
Adaptation	*Robert Hartung*

PART III

MISCELLANEOUS SONGS AND SKETCHES
CONTRIBUTED TO REVUES IN LONDON
AND NEW YORK OF WHICH HE WAS
NOT THE COMPLETE AUTHOR

MISCELLANEOUS SONGS AND SKETCHES CONTRIBUTED TO REVUES

Songs and sketches written by Noël Coward for or included in revues, etc.

1   *Tails Up!*, London, 1918

2   *The Co-optimists*, London, 1922 and 1923

3   *Charlot's Revue*, New York, 1924-5. London, 1924-5

4   *Yoicks!*, London, 1924

5   *Whitebirds*, London, 1927

6   *Charles B. Cochran's 1931 Revue*, London

7   *The Third Little Show*, New York, 1931

8   *All Clear*, London, 1939

9   *Up And Doing*, London, 1940

10   *The Lyric Revue*, London, 1951

11   *The Globe Revue*, London, 1952

1
TAILS UP!

A MUSICAL ENTERTAINMENT IN TWO ACTS
BY JOHN HASTINGS TURNER

Music by Philip Braham

PRESENTED by André Charlot at the Comedy Theatre, London, 1 June, 1918.

Scene 2, "The Journalist's Tale Of The Deserted Park" contained a song, "Peter Pan", lyric by Noël Coward, music by Doris Joel.

AN OLD TICKET COLLECTOR	J. M. Campbell
PETER PAN	Phyllis Titmuss

On the first night programme the lyric is credited to "Noël Farque". (This is corrected in later issues.)

PUBLICATIONS

> The song was published as "The Story Of Peter Pan" by the Herman Darewski Music Publishing Co. It incorrectly credits the lyrics to Doris Joel as well as Noël Coward.

❖

NOTES

> This was Coward's first appearance on a London programme as a lyric-writer.

❖

2
THE CO-OPTIMISTS
A PIERROTIC ENTERTAINMENT

> FIRST PRODUCED at the Royalty Theatre, London, 24 June 1921 (transferred to the Palace Theatre, October 1921).

> Five seasons were given at the Prince of Wales Theatre (1922 and 1923), the Palace Theatre (1924), His Majesty's Theatre (1925 and 1926). The company was disbanded in 1927, but reformed in 1929 at the Vaudeville Theatre and the Hippodrome, 1930. A final season was given at the Palace Theatre in 1935, which only survived ten nights.

> The third programme of the original run (Palace Theatre, May, 1922) contained a Noël Coward item:

> "The Co-Communists"   Laddie Cliff, Davy Burnaby, Gilbert Childs, and Stanley Holloway

> "Down With The Whole D – Lot"

> Lyric by Noël Coward. Music by Melville Gideon. The song was published by Francis, Day and Hunter (as " Down With The Whole Darn Lot", a Democratic Quartet).

> The seventh programme (January 1924) during the third season, at the Prince of Wales Theatre, which commenced on 11 October 1923, contained:

> "There May Be Days" The Company (Introduction to Part II)

Words by Noël Coward; music by Melville Gideon. The song was
published by Francis, Day and Hunter.

3
CHARLOT'S REVUE
A REVUE

ANDRÉ CHARLOT'S LONDON REVUE OF 1924

This revue, mainly compiled from previous successes, was tried out at
Golders Green Hippodrome, 3 December 1923, prior to its production at
the Times Square Theatre, New York, 9 January 1924.

It contained the following Noël Coward items:

(a) "There's Life In The Old Girl Yet"
    (song from *London Calling!*)   Beatrice Lillie and Chorus
                                       (later sung by Effie Atherton)

(b) "Parisian Pierrot"
    (song from *London Calling!*)

PIERROT	Gertrude Lawrence
HARLEQUIN	Barbara Roberts
COLUMBINE	Jill Williams
THE DOLLS	The Chorus

(c) "Sentiment"
    (song from *London Calling!*)   Jack Buchanan

CHARLOT'S REVUE

Charlot's Revue was first presented in London at the Prince of Wales
Theatre, 23 September 1924. The revue was staged by Dion Titheradge
and Laddie Cliff. The costumes were by G. K. Benda and scenery by Marc
Henry. The orchestra was under the direction of Philip Braham. This
revue changed its cast and material many times during its long run of 518
performances. (The company which had played in New York came to the
Prince of Wales Theatre, 23 March 1925.)

The first programme (September 1924) contained the following Coward
items:

(a) "That'll Be Very Useful Later On" (song)
Phyllis Monkman

(b) "A Scotch Interlude" (monologue and song)
"Jessie Hooper" (song)   Morris Harvey

(c) *After-Dinner Music* (sketch with songs)
"Miss Fancy Robinson in Selections from Her Repertoire. At the piano Mr Edgar Stoope. N.B. Miss Robinson only sings the works of Mr Noël Coward."   Maisie Gay

(d) "Specially For You" (song)
Phyllis Monkman and Henry Kendall

(e) *Love, Life, And Laughter* (sketch with duet)

ROBETT SHUFFLEBOTHAM	Morris Harvey
HERBERT FRAMPTON	Hugh Sinclair
MADAME	Nellie Bowman
A WAITER	Leonard Henry
LA FLAMME	Maisie Gay

SCENE: The Cabaret "La Chatte Vierge", Paris, 1890.

The American edition, performed at the Prince of Wales, 23 March 1925, included the same material as used in America, but partly re-cast:

(a) "There's Life In The Old Girl Yet"
Beatrice Lillie

(b) "Parisian Pierrot"

PEIRROT	Gertrude Lawrence
HARLEQUIN	Theo Verdier
COLUMBINE	Elvira Henderson
THE DOLLS	The Chorus

(c) "Sentiment"   Peter Haddon

Later editions included:

July Issue

"Early Mourning" (sketch from *London Calling!*)

POPPY BAKER	Gertrude Lawrence
HER MAID	Sybil Chester

September Issue

"Carrie" (song from *London Calling!*)
Gertrude Lawrence

CHARLOT'S REVUE OF 1926

On 5 October 1925, another edition for America was tried out at the Golders Green Hippodrome. This opened in New York at the Selwyn Theatre, 10 November 1925, as *Charlot's Revue of 1926*.

It included the following Coward numbers, some of which were in the revue at Golders Green; the others were added in New York:

(a) "Russian Blues" (From *London Calling!*)
   (Golders Green and New York)   Gertrude Lawrence and Chorus

(b) "After-Dinner Music" (From *Charlot's Revue*)
   (New York only)   Beatrice Lillie
   (at the piano, Hugh Sinclair)

(c) "Poor Little Rich Girl" (From *On with the Dance*)
   (New York only)

DAISY	Gertrude Lawrence
POLICEMAN	George Pugh
GEORGE	Hugh Sinclair
ANNE	Constance Carpenter

(d) "Early Mourning" (From *London Calling!*)
   (Golders Green and New York)

MISTRESS	Gertrude Lawrence
MAID	Eve Wynne

(e) "Carrie"
   (Golders Green and New York)   Gertrude Lawrence

NOTES

Charlot's Revue was the cradle of many musical comedy stars. These include Jessie Matthews, who started in the chorus and became understudy to Gertrude Lawrence in New York and later in the London company (she sang "Parisian Pierrot" in the *June Issue*); Anna Neagle, who, under her own name of Marjorie Robertson, made her stage début in the *September Issue*;

Hugh Sinclair and Leonard Henry had small parts and understudied; Betty Stockfeld and Eileen Peel were in the chorus and also understudied in the original Prince of Wales' production.

The Saturday matinée, 16 May 1925, was titled:
Understudy Performance of Charlot's Revue – For the Benefit of the Charlot Chorus Club.

The Noël Coward items were performed by:

"Parisian Pierrot"

PIERROT	Jessie Matthews
HARLEQUIN	Marjorie Cogle
COLUMBINE	Rhoda Sewell

"There's Life In The Old Girl Yet" Hazel Wynne and Company

"Sentiment"   Hugh Sinclair

When the London run of *Charlot's Revue* ended in December 1925, Charlot toured *Charlot's Repertoire Revue* during 1926, a compilation of all the versions including more Coward numbers from *London Calling!* such as "When We Were Girls Together". The cast included Jessie Matthews, Heather Thatcher, Herbert Munden and Henry Lytton Jnr.

PUBLICATIONS

Besides the numbers from other revues already published, the song, "Specially For You", written for *Charlot's Revue*, was published by William Chappell.

"Love, Life, And Laughter" (written 1924) was included in *Collected Sketches and Lyrics* (Hutchinson, 1931), as well as *Collected Revue Sketches and Parodies* (Methuen, 1999).

After-Dinner Music
This sketch consists of three songs:

"A Little Slut Of Six"
"The Roses Have Made Me Remember"
"The Girls I Am Leaving In England Today"

They were sung to the accompaniment of a piano on the stage by Maisie Gay in London (*Charlot's Revue*) 1924 and by Beatrice Lillie in New York (*Charlot's Revue of 1926*).

Maisie Gay, in her autobiography, *Laughing Through Life* (1931), says:

"He [Noël Coward] has written three amusing ballads; one for a child, another for an 'adenoidy' amateur, and the last for a professional singer. He wanted me to sing these at the piano, playing my own accompaniment, but my technique was much too wobbly to do that. You can't carry conviction if you have to keep looking at the keyboard to see that you don't hit a white note instead of a black.

"For several days I thought about that group of songs, and didn't see how I was going to do anything with them. Then one night I woke up in a bath of perspiration as the result of a sudden brain-wave. I would have a male accompanist on the stage, a grand piano, a bunch of property flowers, and a gold chair, and I would work like a third-rate music-hall act.

"Then I happened to drop in at the Palladium one afternoon, where I saw that brilliant American artist, Nora Bayes. I loved her performance, and was fascinated by the way she used a chair on the stage, always making as if just about to sit down, yet never actually doing so. The clever way in which she manipulated a huge feather fan also gave me food for thought.

"I sang my first two songs in the way I had originally thought of, but in the last number I gave a slightly exaggerated impression of Nora Bayes.

"I appeared on the programme as 'Miss Fancy Robinson', and was told it was rather amusing to hear people, when they had looked at their programmes, say: 'Who is this woman? I don't think much of her.' Before I came to the Bayes number they were 'wise' to me."

The song "The Roses Have Made Me Remember" is not to be confused with another of the same title, words by Lilian Gray, music by Herman Darewski.

Beatrice Lillie made her music-hall début at the London Palladium, 17 September 1928, in this sketch (with Lloyd Williams at the piano). In 1930 she appeared in a film revue, *The Show of Shows*, for Warner Brothers. Her contribution included the song "Just A Ballad" ("The Roses Have Made Me Remember") from this sketch. When the film was released, her items were deleted, and later issued as a Vitaphone short. She fought an unsuccessful law action to restrain them from doing this in January 1931.

❖

4
YOICKS!
A REVUE

PRESENTED by Donald Calthrop at the Kingsway Theatre, London, 11 June 1924 (271 performances).

Produced by Donald Calthrop and John Hastings Turner. Costumes by Doris Zinkeisen.

This contained two items by Noël Coward:

"I'd Like To See You Try"　　　Mary Leigh and Richard Dolman
　　Arranged by Fred Astaire
(Later in the run it was sung by Sunday Wilshin, who replaced Mary Leigh.)

"It's The Peach"　　　Mary Leigh

PUBLICATIONS

The song "Every Little Peach", written in 1916, was Coward's first complete lyric and music. It is included in *The Noël Coward Song Book* with the title, "Forbidden Fruit". It was sung by Daniel Massey (playing Noël) in the 1968 film, *Star!*

5
WHITEBIRDS
A REVUE

PRESENTED by Mithayrion and produced by Lew Leslie at His Majesty's Theatre, London, 31 May 1927 (80 performances). Staged by Lew Leslie. Settings by John Bull.

This contained one number by Noël Coward, "What Is To Become Of The Children?" sung by Maisie Gay. The song was in the programme for part of the run only. It was later sung as "What's Going To Happen To The Tots?" by Betty Chester in *The Bow-Wows*, a musical show produced by Laddie Cliff and performed at the Prince of Wales Theatre, 12 October 1927 (124 performances).

The song was then substantially rewritten and sung by Coward in *Together with Music* in 1955, again as "What's Going To Happen To The Tots?"

6
CHARLES B. COCHRAN'S 1931 REVUE

FIRST PRESENTED at Palace Theatre, Manchester, 18 February 1931 (29 performances).

SUBSEQUENTLY PRESENTED in London at the London Pavilion, 19 March 1931 (27 performances).

Orchestra under the direction of Percival Mackey.

This revue, stated on the programme to have "Music by Noël Coward and others", had only the following items by Coward in London:

(a) Opening Chorus

(b) "City"   Bernardi
     Scene design   *G. E. Calthrop*

(c) "I Can't Do Anything At All But Just Love You"
     ("Any Little Fish")   Ada-May

(d) "Bright Young People"   Queenie Leonard, Edward Cooper,
                                                            and Effie Atherton

     Scene and costume design   *G. E. Calthrop*

(e) "Half-Caste Woman"

DAISY	Ada-May
A SEAMAN	Henry Mollison
HIS FRIEND	Edward Coventry
A CHINESE WOMAN	Betty Shale
A HALF-CASTE WAITER	John Mills
A FRUIT SELLER	Miles Arlen
LOLA	Sonia Watson
ZAZA	Molly Molloy
OTHER SEAMEN	Fred Leroy, William Tinkler, Anthony Pelissier
Scene and costume design	*Nicholas De Molas*

An extra number was used in Manchester, but not in London:

"Foolish Virgins"   Effie Atherton, Queenie Leonard,
                                          Jane Welsh
Scene and costume design   *Nicholas De Molas*

PUBLICATIONS

The following lyrics were published in *Collected Sketches and Lyrics* (Hutchinson, 1931):

"Bright Young People" (written, 1930)
"Any Little Fish" (written, 1930)
"Half-Caste Woman" (written, 1930)
"City" (written, 1930)

The sheet music for these was published by William Chappell.

"Half-Caste Woman" and "Any Little Fish" are also included in *The Noël Coward Song Book* (Michael Joseph, 1953).

NOTES

The song, "Half-Caste Woman", was sung by Helen Morgan in *The Ziegfeld Follies* of 1931 at the Ziegfeld Theatre, New York, 1 July 1931.

"Any Little Fish" was sung by Ernest Truex in *The Third Little Show* on tour in America in May 1931 (see following entry).

7
THE THIRD LITTLE SHOW

FIRST PRESENTED by Dwight Deer Wiman at the Shubert Theatre, New Haven, Conn., 4 May 1931.

SUBSEQUENTLY PRESENTED at the Music Box Theatre, New York, 1 June 1931.

Settings by Jo Mielziner, costumes by Raymond Sovey. Produced by Alexander Leftwich.

This revue contained the following Coward items:

"Mad Dogs And Englishmen"   Beatrice Lillie and Chorus

(Only the song was sung in this revue, when it was used in *Words and Music* in London, 1932; an introductory sketch was added. See under main entry.)

"Cat's Cradle"

MISS TASSELL	Beatrice Lillie
MR MAWDSLEY	Ernest Truex

This sketch as written is for two women. The New York production made it for a man and a woman. In London (*All Clear*) it was acted as published, with Miss Mawdsley played by a man.

On the preliminary tour, Ernest Truex sang "Any Little Fish" (*Charles B. Cochran's 1931 Revue*), but this was not included in the New York production.

PUBLICATIONS

"Cat's Cradle" and the lyric for "Mad Dogs And Englishmen" are included in *Collected Sketches and Lyrics* (Hutchinson, 1931). The music was published by William Chappell. "Cat's Cradle" is also included in *The Noël Coward Song Book* (Michael Joseph, 1953), as well as *Collected Revue Sketches and Parodies* (Methuen, 1999).

8
ALL CLEAR

FIRST PRESENTED by H. M. Tennent Ltd. at the Theatre Royal, Brighton, 4 December 1939 (1 week).

SUBSEQUENTLY PRESENTED at the Queen's Theatre, London, 20 December 1939 (162 performances).

Décor by G. E. Calthrop. Produced by Harold French. Orchestra under the direction of Dennis Van Thal.

This revue contained the following Coward items:

(a) "Cat's Cradle" (sketch from *The Third Little Show*)

MISS EVA TASSELL	Beatrice Lillie
MISS LILLIAN MAWDSLEY	Bobby Howes

SCENE: The back gardens of two suburban villas.

(b) "Secret Service" (sketch)

THE COUNTESS	Beatrice Lillie
MADAME MOULE	Gladys Henson
ZIZI	Moya Nugent
LEOPOLD ROSEN	John Stevens
FIRST OFFICER	Robert Eddison
SECOND OFFICER	Hugh French
FRITZ (a waiter)	Tony Hulley
FROU-FROU	Hilde Palmer
MIMI	Lois Green (tour) Mary Lynn (London)

SCENE: The buffet of a railway station between Oursk and Tourak.

(c) "Marvellous Party"

"I Went To A Marvellous Party" (song)
  Beatrice Lillie

(d) "Weary Of It All" (sketch and song)

DAISY (a presser)	Moya Nugent
HENRY BEARDSWORTH	Hugh French
LORD BITCHETTE	Tony Hulley
ELMER VON ROBESPIERRE	Robert Eddison
MARION DAY	Beatrice Lillie

SCENE: A cabaret star's dressing-room.

PUBLICATIONS

The songs, "I Went To A Marvellous Party", and "I'm So Weary Of It All" were published by William Chappell. "I Went To A Marvellous Party" is included in *The Noël Coward Song Book* (Michael Joseph, 1953).

NOTES

"Secret Service", "Marvellous Party", and "Weary Of It All" were written for *Set to Music*, New York, 18 January 1939.

9
UP AND DOING

FIRST PRESENTED in London by Firth Sheppard at the Saville Theatre, 17 April 1940 (171 performances). Run interrupted by the Blitz. Returned to London, 20 May 1941 (332 performances).

During the run, in the summer of 1941, Noël Coward's song, "London Pride", written in the spring of 1941, was introduced into the programme and sung by Binnie Hale.

PUBLICATIONS

The song was published by William Chappell, and is also included in *The Noël Coward Song Book* (Michael Joseph, 1953).

10
THE LYRIC REVUE

FIRST PRESENTED by Tennent Productions Ltd. at the Pavilion, Bournemouth, 7 May 1951. (The company played at Brighton the following week.)

SUBSEQUENTLY PRESENTED IN LONDON at the Lyric Theatre, Hammersmith, 24 May 1951 (141 performances).

TRANSFERRED to the Globe Theatre, London, 26 September 1951 (313 performances).

Produced by William Chappell. Décor by Loudon Sainthill.

The revue contained one quartet by Coward:

"Don't Make Fun Of The Fair"

MERRYMAKERS	Graham Payn, Dora Bryan, Roberta Huby, Ian Carmichael

PUBLICATIONS

The song was published by William Chappell, and is also included in *The Noël Coward Song Book* (Michael Joseph, 1953).

11
THE GLOBE REVUE

FIRST PRESENTED by Tennent Productions Ltd. at the Theatre Royal, Brighton, 30 June 1952.

SUBSEQUENTLY PRESENTED at the Globe Theatre, London, 10 July 1952 (234 performances).

Produced by William Chappell. Décor by Loudon Sainthill.

This revue contained two numbers by Coward:

"Kingston By-pass"

THE MECHANIC	Graham Payn

"Bad Times Are Just Around The Corner"

THE MORRIS DANCERS	Graham Payn, Dora Bryan, Joan Heal, Ian Carmichael

In 1953 a compilation of both revues toured as *The Lyric and Globe Revue*. Coward numbers included "Bad Times" and "Matelot". Myles Eason replaced Ian Carmichael.

PUBLICATIONS

The songs were published by William Chappell as "Love On The Kingston By-pass" and "There Are Bad Times Just Around The Corner".

PART IV

(a) PLAYS UNPRODUCED AND UNPUBLISHED

(b) INDIVIDUAL SONGS AND PUBLISHED BUT
UNPRODUCED SKETCHES AND LYRICS

(a) PLAYS UNPRODUCED AND UNPUBLISHED

1 *The Last Trick.* Written 1918
2 *The Impossible Wife.* Written 1918
3 *The Unattainable.* Written 1918
4 *Barriers Down.* Written 1920
5 *A Young Man's Fancy* (adaptation from the French). Written 1922
6 *Time Remembered.* Written 1941
7 *Long Island Sound* (founded on his own short story, *What Mad Pursuit?* in *To Step Aside*). Written 1947
8 *Volcano.** Written 1957
9 *Star Quality* (based on his own short story of that name). Written 1967

*Given a single 'rehearsed reading' at the Mill at Sonning on 26 June 1989, with a cast led by Judi Dench, Adam Faith, Jennifer Hillary and Sally Hughes.

(b) INDIVIDUAL SONGS AND PUBLISHED BUT UNPRODUCED SKETCHES AND LYRICS

Songs and sketches published in *Collected Sketches and Lyrics* (Hutchinson, 1931) and *The Noël Coward Song Book* (Michael Joseph, 1953).

The items listed here do not appear ever to have been included in revues or performed. (The date is the date of writing.) All of this material has since been published in either *Collected Revue Sketches and Parodies* (Methuen, 1999) or *Complete Lyrics* (Methuen/Overlook 1998).

1 *Collected Sketches and Lyrics*
"Customs House, Dover" (1923). Sketch and duet. "Touring Days", an abridged version of this song, was included in *Cowardy Custard* (1972).
*"The Touch Of A Woman's Hand" (1925). Song
"Shop Girls" (1928). Sketch
*"She Was A Good Girl Then" (1926). Song
*"Back To Nature" (1928). Trio
"Growing Pains" (1927). Sketch

*These songs were published separately by William Chappell.

2 *The Noël Coward Song Book*
   "I Travel Alone" (1934)
   "Mrs Worthington" (1935)
   "Could You Please Oblige Us With A Bren Gun?" (1941)
   "There Have Been Songs In England" (1941)
   *"Don't Let's Be Beastly To The Germans" (1943)

*This song was to have been sung by Douglas Byng in the revue *Flying Colours* at the Lyric Theatre, 26 August 1943. It was, in fact, on the first night programme and remained billed for a few nights, though it was decided to omit it after the dress rehearsal. Some of the contemporary press notices comment on the omission.

The above songs have mostly been sung by Coward himself in cabaret. They have also been recorded by him, and all have been published separately by William Chappell.

3 *Numbers recorded by Noël Coward, but not published in the two previous books – only as separate sheet music by William Chappell*
   "The Dream Is Over" (recorded, 1928; published, 1928)
      This song was sung by Anna Neagle in the film, *The Little Damozel* (British and Dominion, 1932) and recorded by her.
   "I Travel Alone" (Recorded, 1931; published, 1934)
   "Most Of Ev'ry Day" (Recorded, 1931; published 1934)
   "Imagine The Duchess's Feelings" (Recorded, 1941; published, 1941)
   "Time And Again" (Recorded, 1952; published, 1952)

4 *Songs recorded, but unpublished*
   "Alice" Recorded by Noël Coward, 1954 and 1955 (US).

This song, "Alice Is At It Again" was originally in the score of *Pacific 1860* (1946) to be sung by Elena in Act II, Scene 1, but was omitted before production.

"Spinning Song"
"The Irish Song"
"Piccolo Marina"
These three songs and "Weary Of It All" (*Set to Music*) are included, with other items, in the recording *An Evening with Beatrice Lillie.*
   This record, made in September 1955, has a short appreciation of Beatrice Lillie by Noël Coward printed on the sleeve.

An arrangement for two pianos of Coward's "Dance, Little Lady" is in the overture and "The Party's Over Now", played by her accompanists, Eadie and Rack, concludes the recording.

These three songs were sung by Coward himself in his Café de Paris season, 1954. "A Bar In The Piccolo Marina" was recorded by Coward himself in his Las Vegas record with a slightly different lyric.

5 *Songs published as sheet music* (not included under previous headings)
   "The Baseball Rag" Lyric by Noël Coward; music by Doris Doris (Joel).
      Published by Ascherberg, Hopwood, and Crew, 1919.
   "We Must All Be Very Kind To Auntie Jessie" (Written, *c.* 1924.)
      Published by William Chappell, 1938.
   "One Fine Day" by Noël Coward. (Written, 1924.) Published by Francis,
      Day, and Hunter, 1924.
   "He Never Did That To Me" by Noël Coward. (Written, 1924.) Published by
      William Chappell, 1938. (Lyric included in *Collected Sketches and Lyrics*.)

The last two songs were specially written for Nora Bayes, who sang them in a variety season at the New Oxford Theatre, London, in September 1924. In addition, Coward wrote many other songs that were previously both unpublished and unperformed. They are now published in *Noël Coward: The Complete Lyrics* (Methuen/Overlook, 1998).

APPENDICES

APPENDICES

1 The plays etc. in order of writing, with year of first production (British and American)
2 (a) Film versions of plays, etc.;
   (b) Film appearances of Noël Coward
3 Television appearances of Noël Coward (not including televised productions of his plays – see Part II)
4 Stage appearances of Noël Coward
5 The Noël Coward Company, 1932
6 Ballet versions of plays, etc.
7 Noël Coward in France

APPENDIX 1

THE PLAYS, ETC., IN ORDER OF WRITING, WITH YEAR OF FIRST PRODUCTION (BRITISH AND AMERICAN)

Title	Written	UK	US
1 *The Rat Trap*	1918	1926	–
2 *I'll Leave It to You*	1919	1920	1923
3 *The Young Idea*	1921	1922 (tour)	1932
		1923 (London)	–
4 *Sirocco*	1921	1927	–
5 *The Better Half*	1922	1922	–
6 *The Queen Was in the Parlour*	1922	1926	1929
7 *Mild Oats*	1922	–	–
8 *London Calling!*	1922-3	1923	–
9 *Weatherwise*	1923	1932	–
10 *Fallen Angels*	1923	1925	1927
11 *The Vortex*	1923	1924	1925
12 *Hay Fever*	1924	1925	1925
13 *Easy Virtue*	1924	1926	1925
14 *On with the Dance*	1924-5	1925	–
15 *Semi-Monde*	1926	1977	–
16 *This Was a Man*	1926	–	1926

17 *The Marquise*	1926	1927	1927
18 *Home Chat*	1927	1927	1932
19 *This Year of Grace!*	1927-8	1928	1928
20 *Bitter Sweet*	1928-9	1929	1929
21 *Private Lives*	1929	1930	1931
22 *Post-Mortem*	1930	–	–
23 *Some Other Private Lives*	1930	1930	–
24 *Cavalcade*	1930-1	1931	–
25 *Words and Music*	1932	1932	–
26 *Design for Living*	1932	1937	1933
27 *Conversation Piece*	1933	1934	1934
28 *Point Valaine*	1934	1944	1935
29 *Tonight at 8.30*	1935	1935-6	1936
30 *Operette*	1937	1938	–
31 *Set to Music*	1932-8	–	1938
32 *Present Laughter*	1939	1942	1946
33 *This Happy Breed*	1939	1942	1949
34 *Blithe Spirit*	1941	1941	1941
35 *Sigh No More*	1945	1945	–
36 *Pacific 1860*	1946	1946	–
37 *Peace in Our Time*	1946	1947	–
38 *Island Fling* (*South Sea Bubble*)	1949	1956	1951
39 *Ace of Clubs*	1949	1950	–
40 *Relative Values*	1951	1951	1954
41 *Quadrille*	1951-2	1952	1954
42 *After the Ball*	1953	1954	1955
43 *Nude with Violin*	1954	1956	–
44 *Volcano*	1957		

(unproduced, though given staged reading at the Mill at Sonning, 1989)

45 *Look After Lulu!*	1958	1959	1959
46 *Waiting in the Wings*	1959	1960	1999
47 *Sail Away*	1961	1962	1961
48 *The Girl Who Came to Supper* (words and music only)	1963	–	1963
49 *High Spirits* (direction only)	1963	1964	1964
50 *Suite in Three Keys*	1965	1966	1968
51a *Noël Coward's Sweet Potato*	1968	–	1968
51b *A Talent to Amuse*	1969	1969	–
51c *Cowardy Custard*	1972	1972	1981

51d *Oh, Coward!*	1972	1975	1972
51e *Noël and Gertie*	1988	1989	1998

❖

APPENDIX 2

(a) FILM VERSIONS OF THE PLAYS, ETC.

The following Noël Coward works have been filmed (for casts and particulars, see under each individual entry):

The Queen Was in the Parlour (two versions, second titled *Tonight is Ours*)
The Vortex
Easy Virtue
"After-dinner Music" (from *Charlot's Revue*)
Bitter Sweet (two versions)
Private Lives (two versions)
Cavalcade (two versions)
Design for Living
We Were Dancing (from *Tonight at 8.30*)
The Astonished Heart (from *Tonight at 8.30*)
Hands Across the Sea (from *Tonight at 8.30*)
Still Life (from *Tonight at 8.30*; retitled *Brief Encounter*)

From *Tonight at 8.30* three together as *Meet Me Tonight*:
    Red Peppers
    Fumed Oak
    Ways and Means

This Happy Breed
Blithe Spirit
Pretty Polly
Relative Values

(b) FILM APPEARANCES OF NOËL COWARD

Besides acting in the film versions of his own plays, *The Astonished Heart* (1950) and *In Which We Serve*, written for the screen (1941), Noël Coward made several other screen appearances.

His first was as an extra in D. W. Griffith's "Soul-stirring Spectacle", *Hearts of the World*, made in the UK in 1917. He says in *Present Indicative*: "I was paid, I think, a pound a day, for which I wheeled a wheelbarrow up and down a village street in Worcestershire with Lillian Gish." The film was shown in London at the Palace Theatre in 1918.

His first major film was *The Scoundrel*, made in the US by Paramount at the Long Island Studios in 1935. It was shown in New York in April 1935, and in London at the Plaza, 23 May 1935. It was originally called *Miracle on 49th Street*, and was written and directed by Ben Hecht and Charles McArthur.

Coward also made a short appearance in one other film; as Hesketh-Baggot in *Around the World in Eighty Days* (1955). The film was first shown at the Rivoli Theatre, New York, 17 October 1956.

Subsequent film appearances:

1959   Hawthorne in *Our Man in Havana*, directed by Carol Reed

1960   King Pavel in *Surprise Package*, directed by Stanley Donen

1964   Alexander Meyerheim, in *Paris When It Sizzles*, directed by Richard Quine

1965   Wilson in *Bunny Lake is Missing*, directed by Otto Preminger

1968   The Witch of Capri in *Boom*, directed by Joe Losey

1969   Mr Bridger in *The Italian Job*, directed by Peter Collinson

Coward's music was also used throughout *The Grass is Greener* (1960, directed by Stanley Donen) and he was played by his godson Daniel Massey in the film *Star!* (1968, directed by Robert Wise).

His short story *Pretty Polly Barlow* also became a feature film, *Pretty Polly*, retitled *A Matter of Innocence* in the US (1968, directed by Guy Green).

APPENDIX 3

TELEVISION APPEARANCES OF NOËL COWARD

Not including televised productions of his plays – see Part II

The Ed Sullivan Show (US)
Broadcast on 8 April 1956, CBS
Coward performs an abridged version of Saint-Saens *Carnival of Animals* and sings "Mad Dogs And Englishmen".

Person to Person (US)
Broadcast on 27 April 1956, CBS
Coward interviewed by Ed Murrow.

The Ed Sullivan Show (US)
Broadcast on 8 December 1957, CBS
Coward sings a medley of his hits and "What's Going To Happen To The Tots?"

Small World (US)
Broadcast on 22 March and 29 March, 1959, CBS
Coward appears on this Ed Murrow show with James Thurber and Siobhan McKenna.

Tonight Show with Jack Paar (US)
Broadcast on 28 February 1961, NBC
Coward appears as a guest on this late night talk show.

Today Show (US)
Broadcast on 3 October 1963 as a two-hour "Salute to Noël Coward", NBC
Guests include Beatrice Lillie, Sally Ann Howes and Skitch Henderson and his Orchestra.

Choice of Coward (UK)
Broadcast July 1964, Granada
Coward makes separate on-camera introductions to *The Vortex, Design for Living, Blithe Spirit* and *Present Laughter.*

Ninety Years On (UK)
Broadcast on 29 November 1964, BBC
A celebration by the world of entertainment on the eve of Winston Churchill's ninetieth birthday. Script by Terence Rattigan. Coward sings "Mad Dogs And Englishmen" and tells the story of how Churchill and Roosevelt argued about the lyrics during the Yalta Confererence of the Second World War.

Golden Drama (UK)
Broadcast on 31 January 1965
A series of excerpts from stage productions introduced by Coward, Robert Morley and Anthony Quayle.

Noël Coward on Acting (UK)
Broadcast on 12 March 1966, BBC
Interview with Michael MacOwan. The programme is illustrated with extracts from *In Which We Serve* and sound recordings from *Private Lives* and *The Apple Cart.*

Eamonn Andrews Show (UK)
Broadcast on 22 May 1966
Other guests on this chat show included Milt Kamen, Dudley Moore,

Lucille Ball and Muhammed Ali. At the time, Coward was appearing on stage for the first time in 13 years, in the trilogy *Suite in Three Keys* at the Queens Theatre, London.

Before the Fringe (UK)
Series one broadcast 30 Jan to 20 March 1967, BBC; Series two broadcast 18 September to 23 October 1967 (*More Before the Fringe*)
Sketch show including Coward material.

Androcles and the Lion (US)
Broadcast on 15 November 1967, NBC
A television musical, written by Richard Rogers and based on the play by George Bernard Shaw.
Coward starred as Caesar, and sang two songs: "The Emperor's Thumb" and "Don't Be Afraid Of An Animal" (a duet with Norman Wisdom).

Don't Count the Candles (UK)
Broadcast in 1968, BBC
Appearance in documentary film on ageing by Lord Snowdon.

Frost on Friday: Noël Coward (UK)
Broadcast on 27 December 1968
David Frost interviews Noël Coward. Frost's autobiography states the programme was recorded at the Mayfair Theatre, London. Coward's diaries give the recording date as around 16 September 1968.

The David Frost Show (US)
Broadcast on 16 September 1968, WNEW-NY

Omnibus: Noël Coward's Birthday Dinner (UK)
Broadcast on 16 December 1969, BBC
Coward's seventieth birthday celebrations, narrated by Sheridan Morley. With Laurence Olivier, Louis Mountbatten and Patrick Garland.

The Dick Cavett Show (US)
Broadcast on 10 February 1970
Coward appears with Alfred Lunt and Lynn Fontanne; Tammy Grimes and Brian Bedford (who were appearing in the Broadway production of *Private Lives*) sing a medley of Coward songs before joining the interview.

The David Frost Show (US)
Broadcast on 11 February 1970

Moviemen!: *David Lean* (UK)
Broadcast on 17 March 1970, Thames

A profile of David Lean, made while he was on location in Ireland shooting *Ryan's Daughter*. Includes comments from Coward.

A Man Called Intrepid (Canada)
CBC (Canada)
A profile of Second World War spymaster, William ('Little Bill') Stephenson. Coward was interviewed at the Savoy Hotel, London on his wartime activities in February 1973. The programme was broadcast later that year.

This is Noël Coward (UK)
Broadcast on 2 April 1973, Thames
First shown at Riviera television festivals March-April 1972
A profile of Coward, his life and work.

Noël Coward (UK)
Broadcast on 29 June 1978
Part of a series celebrating 80 years of British popular music. This episode looks at the music of Coward.

Beryl Reid (UK)
Broadcast on 18 December 1979, BBC
Sketch show including Coward material.

Noël Coward: A Private Life (UK)
Broadcast on 25 March 1983, BBC
Documentary which looks at the private face of Coward with the aid of his own home movies and rare footage from USA, with the personal reminiscences of Graham Payn, Harold Pinter, John Mills, Joyce Carey George C. Scott and Maggie Smith. Re-issued on video, 1999.

Let's Face the Music: Noël Coward (UK)
Broadcast on 16 July 1989
Profile of Coward's music.

The South Bank Show: Noël Coward (UK)
Broadcast on 1 March 1992, LWT
Profile of Coward and his work.

Arena (UK)
Broadcast in 1998, BBC
Three part documentary on Coward.
Subsequently broadcast in a two-hour version in the US on PBS.

❖

APPENDIX 4

STAGE APPEARANCES OF NOEL COWARD

(London unless otherwise stated)

1911: 27 January: Prince Mussel in *The Goldfish*. Little Theatre. Revived at the
    Royal Court Theatre, 17 April (1 week) and at the Crystal Palace
    Theatre, 16 May (2 matinées)
September: Cannard in *The Great Name*. Prince of Wales Theatre
December: William in *Where the Rainbow Ends*. Savoy Theatre

1912: 2 February: Produced *The Daisy Chain*, by Dot Temple. Savoy Theatre
    (special matinée)
25 June: A Mushroom in *An Autumn Idyll* (ballet), by Ruby Ginner.
    Savoy Theatre (1 performance)
October: The Boy in *A Little Fowl Play*, by Harold Owen. London Coliseum
December: William in *Where the Rainbow Ends*, by Clifford Mills and John
    Ramsey Garrick Theatre

1913: March: An Angel in *Hannele*, by Gerhart Hauptmann. Liverpool
    Repertory Theatre (produced also, Gaiety Theatre, Manchester)
June: Tommy in *War in the Air*, by Frank Duprée. London Palladium
September: Understudy for Reginald Sheffield as Buster in *Never Say Die*,
    by W. H. Post. Apollo Theatre
November: Charity matinée of *A Little Fowl Play* at the London Opera House.
December: Slightly in *Peter Pan*, by J. M. Barrie. Duke of York's Theatre

1914: February-March: Toured as Slightly in *Peter Pan*

1915: January: Slightly in *Peter Pan* (succeeded A. W. Bascomb).
    Duke of York's Theatre
December: The Slacker in *Where the Rainbow Ends*. Garrick Theatre

1916: February: Charles Wykeham in *Charley's Aunt*, by Brandon Thomas (tour)
September: Basil Pyecroft in *The Light Blues*, by Mark Ambient and Jack
    Hulbert. Music, Talbot and Fink. Shaftesbury Theatre. (And under
    study to Jack Hulbert)
October: Dances with Eileen Denis at the Elysée Restaurant
December: Jack Morrison in *The Happy Family*, by Cecil Aldin and
    Adrian Ross. Music, Cuthbert Clarke. Prince of Wales Theatre

1917: August: Leicester Boyd in *Wild Heather*, by Dorothy Brandon.
    Gaiety Theatre, Manchester
October: Ripley Guildford in *The Saving Grace*, by Haddon Chambers.
    Garrick Theatre

1918: December: Courtney Borner in *Scandal*, by Cosmo Hamilton.
    Strand Theatre

1919: August: Ralph in *The Knight of the Burning Pestle*, by Beaumont and
    Fletcher. Birmingham Repertory Theatre

1920: May: Bobbie Dermott in his own play, *I'll Leave It to You*. Gaiety Theatre,
    Manchester
    July: Appeared in the same part. New Theatre, London
    November: Ralph in *The Knight of the Burning Pestle*. Kingsway Theatre

1921: March: Clay Collins in *Polly with a Past*, by George Middleton and Guy
    Bolton. St James's Theatre

1922: September-November: Sholto Brent in his own play, *The Young Idea*.
    Prince's Theatre, Bristol, and tour

1923: February: Appeared in the same part. Savoy Theatre, London
    September: Appeared in *London Calling!* (of which he was part author).
    Duke of York's Theatre

1924: October or November: Appeared in a sketch of his own. 11 Carlton
    House Terrace (charity matinée)
    November: Nicky Lancaster in his own play, *The Vortex*. Everyman Theatre,
    Hampstead
    December: Appeared in the same part. Royalty Theatre, London
    (transferred to Comedy and Little theatres)

1925: September: Appeared in the same part. The Henry Miller Theatre, New York

1926: September: Lewis Dodd in *The Constant Nymph*, by Margaret Kennedy
    and Basil Dean. New Theatre

1928: January: Clark Storey in *The Second Man*, by S. N. Behrman.
    Playhouse Theatre
    October-November: Appeared in his own revue, *This Year of Grace!*,
    Baltimore. Subsequently produced at the Selwyn Theatre, New York

1930: April: Captain Stanhope in *Journey's End*, by R. C. Sherriff
    (3 performances). Victoria Theatre, Singapore
    August-September: Elyot Chase in *Private Lives*. King's Theatre,
    Edinburgh, and tour. Subsequently appeared in the same part at the
    Phoenix Theatre, London
    December: Fred in his own *Some Other Private Lives*. London Hippodrome
    (charity matinée)

1931: January: Elyot Chase in *Private Lives*. Times Square Theatre, New York

1933: January: Leo in his own play, *Design for Living*. Hanna Theatre, Cleveland, Ohio. Subsequently at the Ethel Barrymore Theatre, New York

1934: February: Paul, Duc de Chaucigny-Varennes, in his own operetta, *Conversation Piece*. His Majesty's Theatre

1935: October-November: Toured in his own one-act plays, *Tonight at 8.30*

1936: January: Appeared in ten plays in *Tonight at 8.30*. Phoenix Theatre
    November: Appeared in the same plays. National Theatre, New York
    (with the exception of *Star Chamber*)

1942: August Charles Condomine in his own play, *Blithe Spirit*. St James's Theatre
    September: Toured in the same part and his own plays, *Present Laughter* (Garry Essendine) and *This Happy Breed* (Frank Gibbons), under the title of *Play Parade*

1943: April: Appeared as Garry Essendine in *Present Laughter* and Frank Gibbons in *This Happy Breed* (his own plays). Haymarket Theatre

1945: September: Appeared for two performances in his own revue, *Sigh No More*. Piccadilly Theatre

1947: April: Appeared as Garry Essendine in his own play, *Present Laughter* (revival). Haymarket Theatre

1948: January: Appeared in place of Graham Payn in *Tonight at 8.30* (*Hands Across the Sea*, *Shadow Play* and *Fumed Oak*) for three performances during tour in San Francisco
    November: Appeared as Max Aramont in his own play, *Joyeux Chagrins* (*Present Laughter*) (in French). Théâtre Edouard VII, Paris

1951: October: Gave a concert of his songs at the Theatre Royal, Brighton, preparatory to his first Café de Paris season
    October: Appeared in cabaret at the Café de Paris, London

1952: January: Appeared in cabaret with Mary Martin. Café de Paris, London. Special performance in aid of the Actors' Orphanage
    June: Appeared in cabaret at the Café de Paris, London
    November: Appeared in cabaret with Mary Martin. Café de Paris, London. Special performance in aid of the Actors' Orphanage

1953: May: King Magnus in *The Apple Cart*, by George Bernard Shaw. Haymarket Theatre

May: Appeared in cabaret at the Café de Paris, London

May: Appeared in *Stars at Midnight*, London Palladium. Special
performance in aid of the Actors' Orphanage

1954: June: Introduced Marlene Dietrich's act at the Café de Paris, London.
Appeared in *Night of 100 Stars*, London Palladium. Special
performance in aid of the Actors' Orphanage
October: Appeared in cabaret at the Café de Paris, London
November: Appeared at the Royal Variety Performance.
London Palladium

1955: June: Appeared in cabaret at the Desert Inn, Las Vegas

1956: Conducted *Carnival of the Animals*, Carnegie Hall

1957: Sebastien in *Nude with Violin*. Tour and opened at the Belasco Theatre,
New York (14 November)

1958: January: Garry in *Present Laughter* at the Belasco Theatre (He then took
both productions to San Francisco for four weeks and Hollywood for
two weeks)
Sebastien in *Nude with Violin* (New York and US tour)
July: Appeared in *Night of 100 Stars* at London Palladium
August: Appeared in Gala Cabaret in Nice

1966: April: Hugo Latymer, George Hilgay and Verner Conklin in *Suite in Three
Keys* at the Queens Theatre, London (two nights)

Besides directing many of his own plays, etc., Coward also produced:

Biography, by S. N. Behrman. Globe Theatre, London, 25 April 1934

Theatre Royal, by Edna Ferber and George S. Kaufman. Lyric Theatre,
London, 23 October 1934

Mademoiselle, by Jacques Deval (adapted by Audrey and Waveney Carten).
Wyndham's Theatre, London, 15 September 1936

George and Margaret, by Gerald Savory. Morosco Theatre, New York,
September 1937

APPENDIX 5
THE NOËL COWARD COMPANY, 1932

In 1932 a touring repertory company was formed, with Gatenby Bell as
General Manager – under the title of The Noël Coward Company – to "present

the works of this brilliant author under his own personal supervision. The plays are staged to an absolutely West End standard. Mr Coward has himself approved of the cast of this company – he has himself supervised the production of the plays."

The settings were designed by Arthur Hambling. The company included Kate Cutler, Agatha Carroll, Janet Burnell, Marjorie Harwood, Joyce Wodeman, Marjorie Taylor, Wilson Barrett, James Mason, Keith Shepherd and Farries Moss.

They opened their first season at the Festival Theatre, Malvern, 1 September, 1932 (to 17 September).

The repertoire of the Malvern season included:

September 1, 2, and 3 (matinée and evening): *Private Lives*, followed by
  Parody of Private Lives (*Some Other Private Lives*)
September 5, 6 and 7 (matinée and evening): *Hay Fever*
September 8, 9 and 10: *Home Chat*, followed by *Weatherwise*
September 12, 13 and 14 (matinée and evening): *The Vortex*, followed by
  "Rain Before Seven"
September 15, 16 and 17 (matinée and evening): *Fallen Angels*

This appears to be the first occasion on which *Weatherwise*, a one-act play written in 1923, was performed. It was published in *Collected Sketches and Lyrics*. "Rain Before Seven" was a sketch from *London Calling!* (Duke of York's, 1923).

Following Malvern, the company visited Birmingham (Prince of Wales's), Liverpool (Royal Court), Exeter (Theatre Royal: 2 weeks), Eastbourne (Devonshire Park), Brighton (Theatre Royal), Oxford (New Theatre: 2 weeks), Bournemouth (Pavilion), and Eastbourne (Devonshire Park: return visit and last week of tour, 28 November 1932).

The Queen Was in the Parlour was added to the repertoire at Exeter on 3 October and "I'll Leave It to You" at Eastbourne, on 28 November.

Noël Coward wrote the following introduction for the Company: "The Noël Coward Company sounds strangely important and significant to me, not only because I happen to be Noël Coward, but because it is composed, with one or two exceptions, of as yet unknown actors and actresses who in the future may quite conceivably look back upon this enterprise as a notable milestone on their road to stardom.

"The repertory includes most of my work of the last 14 years, and when I remember all those rehearsals, and dress rehearsals, and first nights, and the cheers and boos, triumphs and failures, nostalgic tears dim my old eyes and a certain hoary tenderness wells up in my heart, not only for the plays themselves, but for the people who are going to act them. I do hope that they and the public will enjoy them as much as I did.

"The presence of Miss Kate Cutler invests this company with just so much extra glamour for me, as it was she who was holding my hand as we stood together on the stage of the Gaiety Theatre, Manchester, in 1920, and gave me a sharp little push forward to make my first author's speech; and my admiration for her as an artiste is only equalled by my affection for her as a friend.

"It is obviously to my interest to wish this company every success, but I do so with all sincerity, not only so far as my plays are concerned, but far beyond them."

APPENDIX 6
BALLET VERSIONS OF PLAYS ETC.,

BLITHE SPIRIT
> Written in 1958

The music for the ballet by Richard Addinsell in *Sigh No More* was adapted from the score for the film of *Blithe Spirit* (see *Sigh No More*, page 381).

LONDON MORNING
> Written in 1958

PRESENTED by London's Festival Ballet in association with Associated Redifusion TV Ltd., at the Royal Festival Hall, 14 July 1959.

It was given a Charity Preview on 13 July (7 performances in repertoire).

CHARACTERS	Festival Hall, 1959
THE SAILOR	John Gilpin
THE GENTLEMAN IN THE BATH CHAIR	Anton Dolin
THE AMERICAN GIRL WITH A CAMERA	Jeannette Minty
THE NURSE	Marilyn Burr
THE STREATHAM FAMILY	Anita Landa, Michael Hogan, Ronald Emblen
THE BUSINESS MAN	Louis Godfrey, Terry Gilbert, Peter Brownlee

THE LADIES OF THE TOWN	Janet Overton, Diuanne Richards, Janet Kedge
THE CHIEF GUARDSMAN	Vassilie Trunof
THE MODEL	Pamela Hart
HER ESCORT	Jean-Pierre Alban
THE SLOANE STREET LADIES	Mary Duchene and Deirdre O'Connaire
THE COMPANION	Dalton Davis
THE GIRL IN THE BLUE DRESS	Joan Potter
THE GIRL IN THE PINK DRESS	Anne Morrell
THE TYPIST	Gaye Fulton
THE DELINQUENTS	Pixie Bevan, Susan Foster, Sally Judd, Donald McAlpine, Max Natiez, Barry McGrath
THE INDIAN LADY	Valerie Duke
THE INDIAN GENTLEMAN	Len Martin
THE AMERICAN TOURIST	Geoffrey Davidson
THE CADET	Keith Beckett
THE POLICEMAN	Peter White
THE NUNS	Wendy Barry and Clare Duncan
THE SCHOOLGIRLS	Diane Westerman, Sheila Wright, Jennifer Alderton, Christina Katin, Mary Couson and Selena Wylie
THE SENTRIES	Kenneth Sudell and Peter Cazalet
THE GUARDSMEN	Jean-Pierre Alban, Kenneth Sudell, Geoffrey Davidson, Ivan Baptie, Peter Brownlee, Terry Gilbert, Donald McAlpine, Len Martin, Max Natiez, Desmond Kelly, Kenneth Mansfield, Peter Cazalet, Dalton Davis
THE MATRONS	Anne Rowse and Diane Elesmore
THE FLOWER SELLER	Susan Winterton
Choreography	*Jack Carter*
Décor	*William Constable*
Costumes	*Norman McDowell*
Orchestration	*Gordon Jacob*

Alternative casts, during the original performances, included Louis Godfrey (The Sailor), Anita Landa (The American Girl), Anne Rowse (The Streatham Lady), Ivan Baptie (The First Businessman), Andre Prokovsky (The Chief Guardsman).

❖

SCENE: Outside Buckingham Palace.

❖

Duncan Harrison in the *Evening News*:

"It would hardly be rash to predict that Noël Coward's ballet *London Morning* will be a winner for London's Festival Ballet.

"It will lightly sustain the weight of the new London season, which started last night with the ballet's premiere at the Royal Festival Hall.

"And it will be a wow if the company achieve another American tour.

"It will owe its success, I suggest, to the popular love of this Coward blend of nostalgia and sentimentality. Especially when the sentimentality is tempered – just a little – with astringency by the adroit Mr Coward.

"But with the great Coward vintage years in mind – *Bitter Sweet* (1929) and *Cavalcade* (1931) – this latest offering seems a little thin, charming enough but nevertheless a rather pale distillation of the maestro's art.

"The admixture of characters in this so-very-lighthearted ballet is in the true Coward manner; soldiers in red uniforms, smart young businessmen (with decorated bowler hats). Ladies of the town and the inevitable cockneys – but should the Streatham family have not shed their Edwardian mannerisms long ago?

"Mr Coward is fortunate in his chief collaborator, Jack Carter. His choreography does not call for virtuosity, only slickness.

"There are two *pas de deux* for the Sailor (John Gilpin) and the American Girl (Jeanette Minty) which are the highspots of the ballet. The first is more balletic and therefore better than the second revue-type arrangement.

"Gilpin was outstandingly good. There is no male dancer in England today who dances consistently better than this slightly built young man."

❖

PUBLICATIONS

A piano score of the ballet music was published by Warner Chappell & Co, 1959.

❖

NOTES

The ballet was a joint commission by Festival Ballet and Associated Re-Diffusion to mark the Ballet Company's tenth anniversary. It was televised on 3 August 1959. The original title was *London Glory*. It remained in the Company's repertoire on tour until 1962. It was last given in February at the Theatre Royal, Exeter, followed by performances during the Company's season at La Fenice, Venice. It has not been revived since.

In his *Diary* Coward wrote: "The ballet has been an enormous success with the public, for whom it was written, but not with the critics, for whom it was not written... It is no use pretending it is not irritating because it is: it's maddening to have a triumphant performance with everyone yelling and cheering and then read the next day that the wole thing is terrible."

In his biography of Coward, *A Talent to Amuse*, Sheridan Morley says, after the run of *Nude with Violin* in New York, and its subsequent tour, which lasted into March 1958:

"Then he (Coward) returned to Blue Harbour in Jamaica to start work in one of the few fields still entirely fresh to him: ballet. He had been commissioned by Anton Dolin to compose something new for the tenth anniversary season of the London Festival Ballet which was coming up in the following year. Dolin had left Coward with a wide and generous brief, asking only that the result should be fairly typical of England in general and of London in particular. Through the rest of the spring and early summer of 1958 Noël wrote the score for *London Morning*, a ballet set outside the gates of Buckingham Palace where, as the composer himself has said, remarkably little actually happens...

"The theme of the ballet, insofar as it had one, was that it was still exciting to go to London to see the Queen; but there were moments in *London Morning* when one might have been forgiven for thinking that the work had been commissioned by American Express rather than the Festival Ballet."

Coward went to Barcelona in May 1959 when the Festival Ballet was appearing, to meet the company and the choreographer, Jack Carter, and to explain his ideas and begin rehearsals. Julius Braunsweg in his reminiscences says:

"Coward charmed everyone and was on first-name terms with the dancers very quickly. His directions, however, were as detailed and precise as those for a play and Carter found it difficult to fit steps around the libretto. Quite unused to the mad world of ballet, the maestro began to have doubts whether the work would ever be ready in time for its premiere."

Coward was in London for the premiere and *Look After Lulu!* opened its pre-London tour a few days later.

TAORMINA BALLET
   Written in 1961

   Devised by Joe Layton (see *Sail Away,* page 489).

   The locals are sitting about lethargically when the ship's passengers
   come ashore. They leap into frenetic folkloric life for the visitors' benefit
   and sell them everything in sight. The passengers return to the ship and
   somnolence returns to Taormina.

THE GRAND TOUR

   FIRST PRESENTED by the Royal Ballet Company at the Theatre Royal,
   Norwich, 10 February 1971 and subsequently at Sadler's Wells Theatre,
   London, 27 May 1971 (seven performances in the season).

CHARACTERS	Theatre Royal and Sadler's Wells, 1971
AMERICAN LADY	Vyvyan Lorrayne
STEWARDS	Stephen Jeffries, David Gordon and Donald Kirpatrick
STOWAWAYS	Brenda Last and Wayne Sleep
GERTRUDE LAWRENCE	Deirdre O'Conaire
NOËL COWARD	Gary Sherwood
G. B. SHAW	David Drew
MARY PICKFORD	Doreen Wells
DOUGLAS FAIRBANKS	Paul Clarke (London)
	Hendirk Davel (Norwich)
GERTRUDE STEIN	Nicholas Johnson
ALICE B. TOKLAS	Jeanetta Laurence
THEDA BARA	Sheila Humphreys
Music	*Noël Coward*
Musical arrangement	*Hershy Kaye*
Choreography	*Joe Layton*
Scenery and costume design	*John Conklin*
Conductor	*David Taylor*

SYNOPSIS

From the ship's embarkation to the first port of call a 1930 holiday cruise provides the following activities on the promenade deck: exercise and sports, romance and the Captain's gala. On board are world famous celebrities, two lively stowaways, an American spinster on her first trip abroad and a friendly steward who tries to help her "belong".

The 30 minute ballet was commissioned for the junior section of the Royal Ballet and remained in its repertoire. It was last seen in London at the Wells in February 1974. Coward was present for the first London performance.

When asked by an interviewer if there was anything he could not do, Coward replied: "I could not dance in my own ballet."

❖

APPENDIX 7
NOËL COWARD IN FRANCE

1925: *Le Weekend* (*Hay Fever*). Translated by Antoine Bibesco and Andrée Mery.
 Petite Vertu (*Easy Virtue*). Translated as above
1927: *Ragots* (*Home Chat*)
1928: *Le Printemps de Saint-Martin* (*Fallen Angels*). Translated by Claude-André Puget and Virginia Vernon
1930: *Les Amants Terribles* (*Private Lives*). Translated by Claude-André Puget and Virginia Vernon
1933: *Serenade à Trois* (*Design for Living*). Translated by Jean Bommart
1936: *Brève Rencontre* (*Still Life*). Translated by Jenaine Delpeche
1941: *L'Espirit s'Amuse* (*Blithe Spirit*)
1948: *Joyeux Chagrins* (*Present Laughter*). Translated by André Roussin and Pierre Gay. This was the translation in which Noël himself played in Paris and Brussels after the war; see notes to *Present Laughter*
1951: *Félicité* (*Relative Values*). Translated by Pierre Sabatier
1956: *Nu avec Violin* (*Nude with Violin*)